NATIONS OF THE MODERN WORLD

ARGENTINA   H. S. Ferns

Professor of Political Science,
University of Birmingham

AUSTRALIA   O. H. K. Spate

Director, Research School of Pacific Studies,
Australian National University, Canberra

BELGIUM   Vernon Mallinson

Professor of Comparative Education
University of Reading

CEYLON   S. A. Pakeman

Formerly Professor of Modern History, Ceylon
University College; Appointed Member, House of
Representatives, Ceylon, 1947–52

CYPRUS   H. D. Purcell

Lecturer in English Literature,
Queen's University, Belfast

EAST
  GERMANY   David Childs

Lecturer in Politics, University of Nottingham

MODERN EGYPT   Tom Little

Managing Director and General Manager of
Regional News Services (Middle East), Ltd, London

ENGLAND   John Bowle

Professor of Political Theory, Collège d'Europe,
Bruges

FINLAND   W. R. Mead

Professor of Geography, University College, London;
Formerly Chairman, Anglo-Finnish Society

MODERN GREECE   John Campbell

Fellow of St. Antony's College, Oxford

Philip Sherrard

Assistant Director, British School of Archaeology,
Athens, 1958–62

MODERN INDIA	Sir Percival Griffiths *President of the India, Pakistan and Burma* *Associations*
MODERN IRAN	Peter Avery *Lecturer in Persian and Fellow of King's College,* *Cambridge*
ITALY	Muriel Grindrod *Formerly Editor of* International Affairs *and* The World Today *Assistant Editor of* The Annual Register
JAPAN	Sir Esler Dening *H.M. Ambassador to Japan, 1952–57*
KENYA	A. Marshall MacPhee *Formerly Managing Editor of* The East African Standard Group; *producer with British Broadcasting* *Corporation*
LIBYA	John Wright *Formerly of the* Sunday Ghibli, *Tripoli*
MALAYSIA	J. M. Gullick *Formerly of the Malayan Civil Service*
MOROCCO	Mark I. Cohen *Director of Taxation, American Express* Lorna Hahn *Professor of African Studies, American University*
NEW ZEALAND	James W. Rowe *Director of New Zealand Institute of Economic* *Research, Inc.* Margaret A. Rowe *Tutor in English, Victoria University, Wellington*
NIGERIA	Sir Rex Niven *Colonial Service, Nigeria, 1921–59; Member of* *Northern House of Assembly, 1947–59*
PAKISTAN	Ian Stephens *Formerly Editor of* The Statesman *Calcutta and* *Delhi, 1942–51; Fellow of King's College,* *Cambridge, 1952–58*

PERU	Sir Robert Marett *H.M. Ambassador in Lima, 1963–67*
SOUTH AFRICA	John Cope *Formerly Editor-in-Chief of* The Forum; *South African Correspondent of* The Guardian
SPAIN	George Hills *Formerly Spanish Programme Organizer, and Latin America Correspondent, British Broadcasting Corporation*
SUDAN REPUBLIC	K. D. D. Henderson *Formerly of the Sudan Political Service; Governor of Darfur Province, 1949–53*
TURKEY	Geoffrey Lewis *Senior Lecturer on Islamic Studies, Oxford*
THE UNITED STATES OF AMERICA	H. C. Allen *Commonwealth Fund Professor of American History, University College, London*
WEST GERMANY	Michael Balfour *Reader in European History, University of East Anglia*
YUGOSLAVIA	Muriel Heppell and F. B. Singleton

NATIONS OF THE MODERN WORLD

SPAIN

SPAIN

By
GEORGE HILLS

PRAEGER PUBLISHERS
NEW YORK · WASHINGTON

BOOKS THAT MATTER

Published in the United States of America in 1970
by Praeger Publishers, Inc., 111 Fourth Avenue,
New York, N.Y. 10003

© 1970 in London, England, by George Hills

Library of Congress Catalog Card Number: 70-100936

Printed in Great Britain

TO

MARIE

AND FOR

CATHERINE AND EDMUND

Preface

MUCH HAS BEEN WRITTEN of the land contained within the political unity Spain; of its physical features, a central plateau surrounded by a labyrinth of mountain ranges and spurs which divide and subdivide the country; of its wide regional differences of soil, of vegetation, and of climate; of the overall poverty of its natural resources. The details are readily available in a dozen and more books. I have referred to them in this book only in so far as they are relevant to the divisions and the history of the peoples of Spain and I have sought to unravel the tangled skein of their history only in so far as a study of modern Spain, or rather of Spaniards today, might require it. For the book is of men more than of arms : men whose modes of thought and action are conditioned no less by their Celtic, Roman, Visigothic, Arabic, and Jewish heritages than by their more recent borrowings from France, Germany, or Russia; and since towards an understanding of Spain today, as yesterday, some knowledge is essential of philosophies as well as politics and of religious beliefs as well as economics, philosophers figure no less than politicians and priests no less than economists.

I must acknowledge with gratitude the help given me by Don Carlos Robles Piquer and Don Joaquín Benítez Fumbreras of the Spanish Ministry of Information who provided me with all the statistics and the documents for which I asked, and more; the Organization for Economic Co-operation and Development which has allowed me to make use of several statistical tables; to the Research Department of the Bank of London and South America; to members too many to name of the Ministries of Education, Labour, and Agriculture who showed me both their successes and failures with total frankness; to members of the government and opponents, to professors and students, bishops and priests, workers and industrialists, journalists, diplomatists, and the general public with whom I have discussed current events and problems at frequent intervals over the past twenty years and more, in Spain and outside Spain.

London   G.A.M.H.
15 October 1969

Abbreviations

APE   *Asociaciones Profesionales de Estudiantes*
CEDA   *Confederación Española de Derechas Autonómas*
CNT   *Confederación Nacional del Trabajo*
ETA   *Euzkadi Ta Azkatasuna*
FAI   *Federación Anarquista Ibérica*
FET y de las JONS   *Falange Española Tradicionalista y de las Juntas de Ofensiva Nacional-Sindicalista*
FLP   *Frente de Liberación Popular*
HOAC   *Hermandades Obreras de Acción Católica*
INE   *Instituto Nacional de Estadística*
INI   *Instituto Nacional de Industria*
JAP   *Juventudes de Acción Popular*
JONS   *Juntas de Ofensiva Nacional-Sindicalista*
POUM   *Partido Obrero de Unificación Marxista*
SDEUB   *Sindicato Democrático de Estudiantes de la Universidad de Barcelona*
SDEUM   *Sindicato Democrático de Estudiantes de la Universidad de Madrid*
SEU   *Sindicato Español Universitario*
UGT   *Unión General de Trabajadores*

Contents

List of Illustrations

Map

Spain, Physical and Political   *facing page* 450

    With insets showing the typical effect of *Concentración* on the
environs of a village

Acknowledgements

ACKNOWLEDGEMENT for kind permission to reproduce illustrations is
made to the following, to whom the copyright of the illustrations
belongs:

    Informations Catholiques Internationales, Paris: 26
    Museo del Prado, Madrid: 1
    Museo Romantico, Madrid: 5
    Museu de Arte de São Paulo: 4
    Real Academia de Bellas Artes de San Fernando, Madrid: 2
    Servicio Oficial del Ministerio de Información y Turismo,
        Madrid: 6, 7, 8, 9, 10, 11, 12, 14, 18
    Spain Today, London: 13, 15, 16, 17, 19, 20, 21, 22, 23, 24, 25,
        27, 28
    Acknowledgement is also due to Mr. Ian Robertson who checked
    the proofs.

PART ONE

The Making of Spain

Chapter 1

The Relevance of History to Modern Spain

UPPERMOST IN THE CONSCIENCE of the greater number of Spaniards is the belief that life on earth is of secondary importance. They believe in a hereafter, a higher life in which there are no national or political divisions. Perhaps that is why in this life nationality and politics have been so important to them. Spain was among the first polities of modern Europe to become a nation-state, and there is no other European nation, unless it be the Irish, more conscious of its history. The people of the far south identify themselves both with the Turdetani, whom Livy classified as 'of all the Spaniards the least bellicose',[1] and the Tartessoi, whom Strabo credited with laws and customs 6,000 years old when he wrote about them.[2] At the other extreme, the Basques claim that their language is the oldest in Europe; they recall with pride that it took the Romans two centuries to conquer them, that the Muslims never did, and that for good measure they defeated the forces of Charlemagne. These events live in their minds as if they had happened only yesterday.

History is to all Spaniards a living thing, something to live with, and to live up to. It has no Dark Ages in the sense that the term is used of a period of English history. More of the work of Spanish than of English chroniclers of early mediaeval days has survived to modern times. There is an unending stream of historians – as opposed to chroniclers – from as early as 1470 onwards.

In the latter years of the nineteenth century when Spaniards, having lost an empire, were asking themselves – much as the British in the 1960s – what had gone wrong and what their role in the future of the world would be or ought to be, philosophers, poets, and novelists joined historians in looking to the past for answers. This preoccupation with history, however, was not limited to the writers and orators. At the turn of the century 60 per cent of the population was illiterate, yet the people knew their history, or at least the heroic deeds of their ancestors. In the early 1960s the middle-aged could recall how their parents would recite at length

[1] Liv., XXXIV. 17.
[2] Strabo, III 1. 6.

19

the epic poems or ballads that recounted them. Into the twentieth century there were also public readers who could count on a receptive audience, in particular for the short novels in which Galdós sought to give an account of the nineteenth century. In the rural and impoverished society in which most Spaniards lived into the second quarter of this century, the winter evenings were spent in the handing over of historical knowledge, poetry, and belief. The technical skills of the illiterate were minimal, but their intellectual powers were highly developed, in particular those of the memory. Illiterates were not necessarily and not normally unlearned.

Today illiterates number at most 2 per cent of the total population. A new generation is reaching adulthood which has had at least primary education to the age of fourteen. It is one with many practical skills. It is also one which even in remote country areas has had television to divert its mind with a nightly dose of wholly fictional and immemorable trivialities. Nevertheless, not enough time has elapsed for a deeply engrained tradition to be erased, and it is a generation which has seen many historical monuments restored. History therefore continues to be almost the present in the minds of the Spaniards : and the Spaniards cannot be understood without some knowledge of their long past.

It is a longer and more complex history than that of many other nations, certainly of the English-speaking nations. However, what is essential to any understanding by a foreigner of the Spaniard's thoughts, words, deeds, and omissions, is not an exhaustive knowledge, but an acquaintance with those events, however distant in time, which the mass of the people know about; with those which have had lasting effects, and lastly with the various opinions of Spaniards on those events.

Chapter 2

Spaniards at the Beginning of Their History

ABOUT 1100 B.C., and possibly earlier, the Phoenicians established a colony, Gadir, where Cadiz now stands. They came to terms with the local inhabitants.

Spain had been inhabited for centuries. Cave paintings in various parts of the peninsula are a witness to this. The inhabitants with whom the Phoenicians came to terms were possibly the Tartessoi of Strabo or the Turdetani of Livy. On a wide belt running north to south along the eastern coast there were numerous peoples to whom the generic term Iberian is given. Some time between 1000 and 500 B.C. Celts settled on the west and north-west of the peninsula and, as they moved inland and met the Iberians, who were spreading westwards, a new group came into existence to whom the name Celtiberian is given.

The Spanish Celtic civilization was similar to that of their Scottish or Irish cousins. The tribe was the political unit. The Iberian civilization was Mediterranean. Its unit was the walled city or town, each with its ruler and Senate of Elders. The cities had small temples. Town planning was fairly regular, the streets running east to west against the heat of the sun. Cereals were stored underground. The inhabitants were skilled in sculpture and metalworking. They were monogamous. Women were the equals of men in their duty to work in the fields and in rights of inheritance. The men alone formed expeditionary forces which consisted of light infantry armed with two lances, a sword, dagger, and small shield; of heavy infantry armed with a long cut-and-thrust sword and protected by a heavy shield, a metal helmet, and cuirass; and of light cavalry which the Romans would come to reckon second only to the Numidian. In defence, however, the women played as important a part as the men. A less pleasant aspect of the Iberian ethos was that they killed those who through illness became a burden to the community.

The Phoenicians came to trade, for Spain was then rich in tin, copper, silver, and even gold. They were allowed by the Iberians to establish small colonies east and west of the Straits of Gibraltar.

About the year 500, Ionian Greek traders from Phocaea were

also allowed to settle along the coast, from Manakie (near present-day Málaga) northwards to Rhode (Rosas). Emporion (Ampurias) they developed as a double city to the model of their metropolis. Now Manakie was close to the Phoenician colony of Málaga. Rivalry between Phoenician and Greek was inevitable. The Greeks encouraged the local tribes to attack the Phoenicians. The Phoenicians called on Carthage to protect them. The Carthaginians took over the Phoenician colonies, beginning with Cadiz about 500 B.C.

The Carthaginians recognized the fighting qualities of the Iberians and began to recruit them as mercenaries as early as 480 B.C. They were an important element in the Carthaginian forces of the First Punic War. Like other mercenaries, they turned on their defaulting employers when Rome defeated Carthage. Hamilcar Barca had to subdue them. He was killed by the Iberians in the process. The disunited Iberians, however, were no match for Hamilcar's son-in-law and successor Hasdrubal. Hasdrubal founded Carthago Nova (Cartagena), a bigger and better colony than any previous, and pushed northwards along the coast, to the alarm of the Romans who sought and obtained from Carthage an agreement that the Ebro should demarcate their spheres of influence in Spain. Hasdrubal's successor, Hannibal, turned on the inland towns with considerable success. There was, however, one coastal city south of the Ebro which continued to resist Carthage – Saguntum. In 219 B.C. Hannibal decided to reduce it. It resisted assault. Hannibal deployed large forces in its siege. The Saguntini appealed to Rome to fulfil a treaty obligation to come to their aid. Rome either could not or would not. For eight months the Saguntini withstood the siege. When further resistance was impossible, the inhabitants set fire to their houses, their effects, and themselves rather than fall into the hands of Hannibal. The second war between Carthage and Rome followed. Roman legions under Publius Scipio and his brother Gnaeus invaded Spain primarily to fight the Carthaginians. However, they had to contend also with Iberians. The Carthaginians defeated the Scipios. The dead Publius Scipio's son, Publius Cornelius Scipio, was thereupon sent to Spain to avenge the death of his father. He cleared the peninsula of Carthaginians in four years, Carthago Nova submitting in one day. Thus in 206 B.C. Rome replaced Carthage as the dominant power in Spain.

Chapter 3

Roman Spain

IT IS THE PROUD BOAST of Spanish historians that it took the Romans nearly 200 years to subdue the whole of the Iberian peninsula. This is an exaggeration of the truth; the truth is impressive enough.

The first battles between Iberians of the eastern coast and Rome took place in 211 B.C.: the last in 197 – a period of fourteen years. Rome then rather prematurely declared the peninsula two Roman provinces, Hispania Citerior and Hispania Ulterior. The former covered roughly three-quarters of Spain – the whole of the north, the west down to the Douro, and the east down to Carthago Nova. The latter consisted of what is now the southern half of Portugal, Andalusia, Spanish Extremadura, and Castile up to the Douro. Each province was placed under a praetor with consular authority, in recognition of the importance Rome gave to them and the difficulties they expected to encounter.

When the Romans began to move inland they met with strong resistance. Powerful forces under the command of consuls had to be deployed. The reduction of the Celtiberian central tableland took eighteen years to 179 B.C. There was then a period of thirty years of comparative peace followed by a major rebellion. Roman general after general was defeated. The consul Quintus Pompeius had to reduce 876 towns or villages. However, he failed to take the city of Numantia in the north (close to modern Soria). Set on a hill and protected by walls six feet thick, its 8,000 defenders held out against Pompeius' 30,000. Pompeius' successor fared worse. The Numantians forced him and 20,000 Romans to capitulate. In 133 B.C., fourteen years after the beginning of the revolt, the Scipio who had destroyed Carthage with a small force was given an army of 60,000 men to destroy Numantia. The defenders of the Spanish city had by then been reduced to 4,000 men and women. Scipio surrounded the city with his massive army. The defenders would still not surrender. Their provisions began to fail: they ate their horses, then their dead companions, and then cast lots to kill and devour one another. They held parley with Scipio who demanded their unconditional surrender. They agreed to give him a definite

23

answer. Scipio then saw the whole city ablaze and the inhabitants throwing themselves into the flames. Some Roman historians maintain that not one Numantian was captured alive.

Spaniards have as yet not forgotten Numantia : no surrender in the face of impossible odds is a fundamental of Spanish honour. Rome herself long remembered it. For Tacitus two and a half centuries later Numantia was a *clades,* a name reserved for the severest of military defeats. A hundred years after the fourteen-year war, Horace would equate it with the bloodiest of those against the Carthaginians, and with those between the gods of Olympus.

> Nolis longa ferae bella Numantiae
> Nec durum Hannibalem nec Siculum mare
> Poeno purpureum sanguine mollibus
> Aptari citharae modis.[1]

With the destruction of Numantia Rome did not become the master of the whole peninsula : one region, that of the Astures and Cantabri, held out into the very times of Horace, who would write of the *bellicosus Cantaber* and the *Cantabrum indoctum iuga ferre nostra.* They were defeated in 25 and 24 B.C.; even then they remained for another four years *pertinaces in rebellando.*[2] Caesar Augustus then renamed Hispania Citerior the Provincia Tarraconensis, the capital city being Tarraco (Tarragona). Numantia was left in ruins, but a hundred miles to the east of it he founded Caesaraugusta (Zaragoza). Of Hispania Ulterior he made two provinces, Betica with an expanded Hispalis (Seville) as its capital and Lusitania with Augusta Emerita (Mérida) as its chief city. Over the next century and a half, Spain became the cradle of writers (the Plinys, Martial, Quintilian, Lucan, and Seneca) and of emperors (Trajan, Hadrian who manned his wall in Britain with the 'bellicose' Cantabrians and Asturians, and the philosopher-emperor Marcus Aurelius Antoninus).

Spain became as Roman as Rome. By the end of the second century A.D., it had a greater number of towns and smaller settlements, theatres, amphitheatres and circuses, and luxurious villas than any other comparable area outside Italy. It was in Segovia that the Romans built one of the two most imposing aqueducts of antiquity, and at Alcántara they solved the engineering problem of bridging a river in a gorge 200 yards across and 200 feet above the level of the water.

Such was the prosperity of Roman Spain at the beginning of the fourth century that Constantine limited the authority of Tarraco

[1] Odes II. 12.
[2] Odes II. 6, II. III. 8.

to the north and north-east of the Ebro. Of the rest of the Provincia Tarraconensis he made two new provinces – Gallecia (corresponding roughly to the northern half of modern Portugal and Spanish Galicia, Asturias, and old Castile) and Carthaginensis, so that there were in all in Spain nine provinces administered *separately*. There was throughout a common legal system and basis for law; but it would appear that the Romans made full allowances for local customs and traditions, a factor important in the future history of the peninsula with consequences into the twentieth century.

That Spain became as Roman as Rome was due perhaps to two factors. In the first place the Iberians and Celtiberians were not primitive tribes. They had a substantial civilization before the Romans ever set foot in Spain, so that the Romans, having conquered, did not have to build either metaphorically or literally from the foundations. Segovia was a Celtiberian and Ilerda (Lérida) an Iberian city before their development under the Romans. Secondly, and more important, the Roman conqueror offered no violence to the religious beliefs of the natives and no unacceptable social customs. The Iberian personal code of conduct and family life were very similar to the Roman at their best. It may well be asked how far Seneca based his code of ethics, so alien to the world of Messalina, Agrippina, and Nero, and in so many ways acceptable to Christians, on the teachings of his native Spanish mother. Seneca is classed with the stoics, quite rightly; but there is much in his philosophy which is not of the stoa yet akin to the mode of thought of Spaniards yesterday and today. True, he had no concept of the human soul as spirit, but he spoke of the conflict between body and soul. He maintained that every man, as a rational being, had the power to choose if he *would* the path of virtue. Marcus Aurelius laid even bigger stress on Divine Providence, on the close relationship between God and Man, and on man's duties towards his fellow men: 'love mankind, follow God'.[3] As a good Spanish monarch, let it be added, he persecuted those who were not of his state religion – in his case he persecuted Christians – but then he, like Seneca and Spaniards throughout the ages from Numantia to the present day, thought of death as a liberation.[4]

It is the unshakeable belief of most Spaniards that St James the Great was the first to preach the Christian faith in the peninsula. It is a tradition which can be neither proved nor disproved conclusively. If he did, it would have been to the Jews whose own tradition suggests that there were sizeable communities in Cadiz,

[3] Med. 7. 31.
[4] Med. 11. 3.

Cartagena, and Toledo, in Augustan if not in earlier times. St Paul expressed his intention to visit Spain,[5] but again there is proof neither that he did nor that he did not. Hadrian shipped several tens of thousands of Jews as slaves to the peninsula, and as his fury against the Jews was concentrated on those who had made their homes among the ruins of Jerusalem after its destruction in A.D. 70, of whom enough were Christian to warrant a bishop, it is a reasonable supposition that there were Christians among the Jewish slaves. There were certainly Christians among the slaves of the Romans and among the legionaries in Spain at the turn of the century, as elsewhere in western Europe. There were also early converts among their masters.

Spain had its fair share of Christian martyrs during the imperial persecutions. The one with the greatest popular appeal ever since is the twelve- or thirteen-year-old Eulalia of Mérida who suffered under Diocletian in 304. In Mérida the Temple of Mars became her shrine, and has survived as such to the present day. More villages are called after her than after any other person. There was one detail about her trial which typifies her as a true Spaniard and may have contributed to her popularity : she spat at the face of her judge, a detail recorded by her compatriot, the poet Prudentius, whom Erasmus considered the greatest of the Latin Christian poets. A year after Eulalia's death the Roman persecution of the Christians ended. A record of a Council of the Spanish Church, held in Iliberia (Granada) in 300 or 301, gives nineteen as the number of Spanish bishops attending, so the number of Christians must by then have been considerable.

Prudentius was in his early thirties when two Spaniards used Roman legions against one another. They were Magnus Maximus, commander of the Roman forces in Spain, and Theodosius, emperor at Rome jointly with Valentinian II and Gratian. Maximus proclaimed himself emperor in 383, backed by the legions in Britain, Gaul, and Spain. Gratian marched against him, was defeated and assassinated. Then, in A.D. 388, Theodosius outmanoeuvred and defeated Maximus. Theodosius went on to defeat the armies of Alaric the Goth in Thrace, but his victory was incomplete. Roman Spain was about to share the fate of the Roman empire, to whose downfall she thus partly contributed as earlier she had contributed to its greatness.

[5] Rom. 15 vv. 24 and 28.

Chapter 4

Visigothic Spain

IN 406 THE FIRST of the German barbarian tribesmen crossed the
Pyrenees. They were Alani who headed south and took over Lusitania. Close on their heels came the Suevi who turned west into
Galicia; and on the heels of these came the Vandals who split once
they had crossed the Pyrenees, one body turning westwards and the
other south to acquire Betica and the Provincia Carthaginensis.
Thereafter, in 415 the Visigoths, already masters of the Roman
province of Narbonne, crossed the Pyrenees and acquired the north-
east of Spain. Over the next fifty years the Germans battled
amongst themselves. The Alani drove out the Vandals from Andalusia, and were in their turn penned in a small area in the centre
by the Suevi. The Visigoths then defeated both the Suevi and
Alani, and by 467 were well on the way to becoming the sole pos-
sessors of the peninsula. They moved their capital from France to
Spain and were to be the masters of the whole peninsula for the
next 250 years.

Since the Visigoths did not conquer Spain in one single battle
as the Normans conquered England, the change of overlords did not
imply any violent revolution. The conquerors took two-thirds of
the land from the Hispano-Romans, but left them with a third.
They conceded to the conquered the right to continue to be tried
by their own laws, the laws of Roman times tempered by a hundred
years of amendment under Christian influence. They did not disturb the municipal organization which had been standardized by
Hadrian, except that the local Senate was made subject to a Visigothic *comes,* or count. They allowed the towns to retain their
collegia or *corpora,* the primitive Roman trade unions which were
eventually to develop into the guilds of the Middle Ages.

The Visigoths at their coming and for nearly two centuries kept
themselves apart. They did not marry the conquered. They judged
themselves in their own courts and by their own laws. These were
not altogether different from those of the Romans; for the Visigoths were already considerably Romanized before their coming.
Their official language was Latin, quite good Latin with a smattering only of German words or of some Latin words which had

meanings Cicero would not have understood. True, no man could aspire to kingship unless he was of Visigothic stock, whereas Roman Spaniards had become emperors; but the method of succession to kingship was not so different from that of accession to the imperial office of Rome. In theory a man became king by popular acclamation. In practice he did so either because he had been chosen as heir by his predecessor or because he had disposed of him. The king took titles not unlike the Roman, *Pius, Gloriosus, Victor.*

The Visigoths had almost the same Christian principles as the people whom they had conquered. Most were Arian, and as such, had been excommunicated under the decision of Nicaea in 325; but that did not lead them immediately to deny the conquered contact with the bishop of Rome : there was a Visigothic Catholic minority and it would seem also that there was an Arian minority among the conquered, for the *Filioque* clause had not been inserted into the Creed in the Spanish Church until 401, only shortly before the coming of the Visigoths.

In 554 the capital was moved from Seville to Toledo, geographically very nearly the centre of the peninsula. Leovigild, who succeeded to the throne in 568, now moved to unify his kingdom. He had the Suevi forcibly converted to Arianism. That he would next attack the orthodox Christians was foreseeable; but his eldest son, Hermenegild, married a Catholic and was converted. Leovigild disinherited him. Hermenegild thereupon rose in arms and was defeated and captured. He refused to give up the Catholic faith and Leovigild had him executed. In doing so, Leovigild created for himself both a personal and a public problem. He was filled with remorse at having killed his own son; and in addition, the execution of the second highest person in the land had encouraged his fellow Arians to challenge his kingship. Leovigild recalled Leander, the bishop of Seville whom he had banished for receiving Hermenegild into the Church, and recommended him to his next son, Recared, as a man to whose arguments he should listen. Leander converted Recared. Recared now argued with the Arian bishops and converted many of them. On his accession in 586 he declared himself a Catholic. The ordinary people accepted the change. It is possible that the nobility did not. The national councils of bishops held in Toledo were enlarged to include state officials. The councils became the Council, the national legislative body : and the state almost a theocracy.

In theory three principles underlay all legislation from this time onwards in Visigothic Spain. The first was that no man-made law should be contrary to divine or church law. The second was that human laws and the state should help the individual to fulfil his purpose as a created being, in other words, the good of the state should not be held as greater than the good of the individual which it was the duty of the state to promote. The third was that justice should be done and be seen to be done.

In the first thirty years of the seventh century the most influential member of the Council was Isidore, bishop of Seville, in succession to his brother St Leander. Isidore, 'the schoolmaster of the Middle Ages', to whom the Venerable Bede was much indebted, was a man of prodigious erudition and a prolific writer in clear Latin on Theology, Scripture, History, Geography, Astronomy, and Grammar. He steered through the Council a decree establishing about sixty schools open to all pupils of ability, where the liberal arts, Hebrew and Greek, were taught. Under Isidore it became the duty of bishops to ensure an adequate defence of the poor in the courts and to watch over the judges. Under his direction the process was begun of whittling away the differences between the *Leges Visigothorum* and those of the Hispano-Romans, a process which culminated in a codification known as the *Fuero Juzgo,* approved by king and Council in 671, thirty-one years after his death. The *Fuero* established complete equality before the law for all Christian free men irrespective of their racial origin. Two principles guided settlements by their courts – *talio* and *compositio. Compositio* was settlement by agreement; *talio* punishment similar and equal to the injuries sustained. A thief would have to make restitution according to his abilities, but no more. For wilful murder the punishment was death, but the victim's family had the right to claim from the murderer or his family compensation in kind as well. Similarly in all kinds of violence there was both a deterrent punishment and an obligation to indemnify the victim. The *talio* for taking away another man's wife was the reduction of the adulterer to the status of slave of the husband. False witness, being explicitly forbidden in the Ten Commandments, entailed the reception by the perpetrator of the same punishment as the man he had falsely accused would have received had he been found guilty. All evidence had to be given or presented orally in court, as until recently in English tribunals. In 683 the Council approved what was in all details an act of *Habeas Corpus.*

Such was the influence of St Isidore, an ascetic of clear mental vision and charitable to his fellow men. Yet he had one serious blind spot. He could not see how any Jew could persist logically in his ancient creed, and attributing bad faith to those who did, he argued strongly for their expulsion from Spain. They were not expelled, but their liberty of movement and choice of residence were curtailed. They were severely penalized in their commercial transactions. Later, the *Fuero Juzgo* codified an appalling injustice. It had long been argued that the children of parents of the Jewish faith should be instructed in both their parents' creed and the Christian, so that when of age they should make a free choice. The law made such double instruction obligatory, adding that the children should be taken away from their parents, a palpable negation of a Christian principle no less than a Jewish.

The followers of Mohammed were now in North Africa, where Spain had a base at Ceuta. In 674 or 675 they made an unsuccessful attempt to invade the peninsula. They tried again in 701 and 709. In that last year the king, Vitiza, died, having named one of his three children as his heir; but a count Roderick usurped the throne. Civil War broke out. Count Alban of Ceuta sought the help of the Muslims on behalf of the children of Vitiza. The Muslims, already assured by refugees of support from the persecuted Jews, took full advantage of the offer of Christian help in their invasion plans. With the blessing of Damascus, the Muslim Commander-in-Chief in North Africa, Tarik ibn Zeyad, organized a force of 25,000 men of whom only 5,000 were Muslims – Berbers, Syrians, and Yemenis. He landed by the Giber, or Rock, which since then has borne his name. The year was 711.

Chapter 5

Conquest and Reconquest

ON LANDING Tarik turned first on the Visigothic fort that in Roman times had been the Colonia Julia. He took it without difficulty. His mixed force of Arabs, Jews, and Christians was joined by the resident Jews who hated the Visigoths and by other Christian supporters of Vitiza's sons who assumed that the Arabs were not conquerors but allies in the civil war in which Spaniard was destroying Spaniard. This was not, let it be added, the first but the last of a series of civil wars over the previous seventy years to settle rival claims to the throne. Not till 713, when the Arab forces had been substantially reinforced by more Berbers, Syrians, Yemenis, and even Persians, were the Spaniards undeceived. To the natural delight of the Jews who had suffered much from the Visigoths and little from the followers of Mohammed, Spain was then declared an Emirate dependent on Damascus. Rather more than half the peninsula was then in the power of Islam. Zaragoza fell the following year. By 716, all that remained of Visigothic Spain was its province north of the Pyrenees and the lands protected by the Cantabrian mountains in the western Pyrenees.

The reconquest began before the conquest was over. In 718, at Covadonga, halfway between Oviedo and Santander, a Visigothic nobleman, Pelayo, defeated a force of Arabs sent to liquidate him. The Christians almost immediately afterwards lost what remained to them of Galicia, and in 740 Pamplona and au Navarre fell; but Pelayo's victory was to work wonders. As Pamplona was falling Pelayo's successor, Alfonso, was capturing León and Astorga, and was quickly to regain part of Galicia – in all an area the size of Wales. The Christian kingdom of León had come into existence.

The rapidity of the Arab conquest of the peninsula has been a cause for marvel to writers from the late eighteenth century onwards. The Arabs, however, did not sweep through as rapidly as the Alani, Suevi, and Vandals had done 300 years before them, nor as spectacularly as Napoleon's troops were to do eleven centuries after them. The Arab feat bears better comparison with that of the young Scipio. Between 711 and 716, they accomplished much the same as the Romans had done between 216 and 211 B.C. Both had to leave the Asturians and Basques unsubdued. The Arabs, like the Romans, did not have to battle with a coherent national military force, if we exclude Roderick's army of 50,000. This was defeated because a major part of it deserted him, thinking it was helping Vitiza's sons. The Arabs were at liberty to subjugate towns piecemeal, so that the issue was never in doubt however long the local defenders held out – indeed some local lords entered into pacts without fighting. (The Arabs, like the Romans, were prepared to allow an overlord a substantial measure of autonomy in return for collaboration.) No inhabitants of any Christian city hurled themselves into flames of their own making in the way that the Numantians did; but some fought hard; there were to be revolts against the Arab masters; and some Christians from time to time deliberately sought martyrdom at the hands of the Muslims.

It is customary to look on the period of Arab domination in Spain as being uniformly progressive and liberal, and also to consider Spain as being under Arab rule for seven centuries. This is to identify the whole with a part. The truth is rather more complex and more varied.

In broad outline, the Basque provinces and the lands between the Bay of Biscay and the Cantabrian mountains were never effectively in Arab hands. By the middle of the ninth century the Arabs had lost all land north of the Douro to the sea and as far east roughly as Aranda. Burgos was by then the capital of a new frontier province – Castile. In the western Pyrenees there was a Christian kingdom of Navarre, and in the east the outposts of Christianity which Charlemagne had earlier established had developed into what was called the county of Barcelona, comprising much of modern Catalonia. By the middle of the tenth century the kingdom of León stretched well south of Coimbra, Salamanca, and Ávila : the reconquest of Aragon had begun. Aragon would soon be a kingdom.

Two factors helped the Christians of Spain in their determination to reconquer their lands : one was the defeat of the Muslims by Charles Martel before Poitiers, at the moment when Alfonso was preparing to move into the attack in Asturias; the other was the disunity of the Arabs. In 741 the Spanish Arabs broke off their connection with Damascus and turned on each other. In the course of fifteen years of confused fighting and alliances, the ruler of Córdoba, Abderrhaman, emerged triumphant over his fellows. He called himself Emir of Spain, and for 130 years the dynasty he established successfully suppressed all challenges to its overall authority. From 886 there was a second period of political disintegration and inter-Arab warfare. From this, in 932, once again the ruler of Córdoba emerged triumphant, and called himself not Emir but Caliph of Córdoba. The Caliphate exercised effective control over Arab Spain for ninety-nine years, to 1031.

The first two centuries of Arab rule, therefore, were for the most part an era of wars between Arabs and Spaniards, and of wars among the Arab rulers. In the circumstances little development could or did take place. It was during the one period of co-ordinated government – the 130 years of the Emirate – that a beginning was made on the greatest monument of Arab Spain, the Mosque at Córdoba. Christian slaves built it on the site of their cathedral with the columns taken from Visigothic and Roman buildings over a wide area.

In their treatment of the defeated, the Arabs distinguished at all times during these two centuries between those captured in battle or in raids into Christian territories, and those who placidly accepted Arab rule; and between those who remained faithful to the old religion and those who embraced the religion of Mohammed. Conversion was a way out of slavery, and for the Christian renegade, the *maula*, there was theoretically no limit to the social and political status to which he could rise. In fact one reached the governorship of Toledo at the beginning of the ninth century, and tried to carve out a kingdom for himself, killing 3,000 of the citizens of Toledo in the process. Christian women slaves could not appeal against being chosen as concubines by the Arabs; their children were brought up Muslims, and as *muladies* were also politically and socially un-handicapped. The disabilities of other Christians varied in intensity at different times and in different places.

In the first place many Christians surrendered without battle because they had been promised freedom of religion. Their bishops were expected to collaborate with the Arabs in keeping the Christians docile and obedient. Here and there local rulers decided that the toleration promised was not the most orthodox interpretation of the Koran. The bishop of Zaragoza was burned alive in 724. Active persecution was national policy, however, only during two periods, 788–96 and 850–86. At other times, provided that the Christians did not parade their faith, that they lived quietly in ghettos in the cities, and did not attempt contact with the outside world, they were left free to practise their religion and to exercise among themselves their *Fuero Juzgo*. The lack of contact with the rest of Christianity, and in large measure between one city and another, gave rise to strange heresies and to deviations from the *Fuero* going back to pre-Roman and pre-Christian Germanic times. Trials by fire and water and by duelling replaced judgement by a learned judiciary on the basis of oral evidence and cross-questioning;

and these throwbacks came to be accepted as legitimate in the Christian kingdoms as they became extended to include cities and areas where these practices had already become habitual.

Understandably the Arabs encouraged the conquered to learn Arabic. In the year 800 they proscribed Latin.[1] With this, great impetus was given not to Arabic (even some of the converted were unable to learn the language of the Koran) but to debased or rather simplified forms of Latin which, it is generally assumed on the basis of scraps of written evidence, had existed even before the coming of the Arabs. These popular simplifications of Latin became also the languages of the new Christian kingdoms. By the end of the eleventh century they were grouping into three distinct tongues which in time developed into Castilian, parent of modern Spanish, Catalan, and Galician, parent of modern Portuguese. In these new languages case endings were discarded and compound tenses (already making their appearance in very late Latin) were developed further; but writers in them retained the classical Latin preference for the rounded period with its abundance of subordinate clauses in place of simple subject-verb-object sentences.[2] Arabic did not influence grammar or syntax in the slightest. The Christians adopted much of the Arabic vocabulary of the bazaar (the names of certain domestic utensils, vegetable products, textiles, and weights and measures), and of the terms relating to slavery (the names of bricklayer and other similar trades, trenching and other tools, and Arab law-enforcement officials); but the sum total of Arabic words adopted into what the Spaniards called *cristiano* was very small compared, say, with that of Norman words incorporated into English. To the Arabs the language of the Christians remained *romi*, the 'language of Rome'.

We have been speaking of Arabs and Spaniards, but the terms are really quite inaccurate in the context, for the *reconquista* was essentially a struggle between two religions and two cultures for the possession of the peoples of the peninsula.

The greatest military threat to the Christian was the creation in 932 of the Caliphate. For the first Caliph, Abderrhaman III, in his plan to make Córdoba a second Baghdad, determined on the reconquest of the reconquered lands. He made great inroads into the north, where the Christian kings and their nobles were almost as much at loggerheads with one another, and as ready to destroy each other, as the Muslims had been before their subjugation by the

[1] Latin would thereafter sometimes be written in Arabic script, possibly to deceive the casual inspector.

[2] Spanish is unquestionably closer than French to Latin: whether it is closer than Italian is a matter for fine judgement.

Caliph. His son and grandson had a great general to command their armies, Almanzor, 'the Conqueror', who carried off the bells of St James at Compostela and had León, Castile, Navarre, and Catalonia for a while at his mercy. Fortunately for the Christians, he did not know how to exploit his victory; unfortunately for them, they did not learn the lesson before the next counter-attack that together they could do more than singly and at variance with each other. Yet the Caliphs, or at least the first two of the three, were among the most tolerant ever of Muslim rulers.

To make Córdoba a second Baghdad, the Caliphs had to encourage the Christians to remain with them, and that meant the relaxation of their disabilities. The free were allowed to purchase privileges. The Arabic scholars among them were permitted to instruct the children of wealthy Muslims. The Caliphs relieved, too, the burdens of the native slaves by importing large numbers from wherever traders could bring them. With them Abderrhaman and his son Makim amplified the Mosque until it became the wonder that it is today.[3] They developed textiles, leather, iron- and other metal-working industries. Córdoba came to have half a million inhabitants. Above all, however, the Caliphs were determined that their city should outshine Baghdad as a centre of learning. To this end they gathered a library of 400,000 volumes which attracted from Europe and the Near East Jewish and Christian scholars. It was now that numerous scientific and medicinal terms were added to the vocabulary not only of Spanish but of other European languages.

Almanzor's death in 1002 heralded the end of the Caliphate. There was no one to stop a raid on Córdoba by the count of Castile seven years later, nor to keep the Muslims together. Fortunately Córdoba survived the Caliphate as a seat of learning, and as such reached its zenith 150 years later when its two chief luminaries were the Jewish philosopher Maimonides (1135–1204) and the Arab Averroes (1126–98).

The final collapse of the Caliphate in 1031 was followed by half a century of political confusion. From his accession in 1072, Alfonso VI of León-Castile sought to extend his domains. He captured Toledo. In 1082 he attacked Seville. The Muslim king of Seville thereupon asked for help from a new body of Muslim

[3] It should be noted that as St Sophia was to be the model of the new mosques in Constantinople, so also the inspiration of the Mosque at Córdoba is essentially Roman-Visigothic church-building. It is primarily nave after nave of columns, architecturally a multiplication of an idea and not innovation; in this multiplication there may perhaps have been a parallel in symbolism: counted longitudinally and laterally, these naves may be said to represent the hundred and more names of Allah just as the three naves of the Christian church represented the Trinity.

conquerors in Africa – the Almoravids. They saved the king of Seville, but they remained in Spain, taking Córdoba in 1102 and making themselves masters of almost all Moorish Spain. Their supremacy was short-lived. Another group of Muslim conquerors, the Almohades, judged the Almoravids' tolerance of Christians criminally wrong. They landed in Spain in 1146, and by conquest took over from the Almoravids. They persecuted alike Christians, Jews, and easy-going Muslims.

The persecution of the Christians gradually restored to the struggle its religious aspect. During the eleventh and twelfth centuries it had lost this to a considerable extent. How far can be judged from the history of Ruy Díaz, the *Cid*, the *Campeador,* or *Campidocti,* that is 'the skilled in arms' – a vassal of Alfonso VI of León-Castile. He helped the king to restore León-Castile to its pre-Almanzor lines, and then to establish a *cordon sanitaire* beyond of Muslim lords of cities and fortresses whose total inclusion into the kingdom would have been too costly to defend. Alfonso, however, quarrelled with the *Cid* and, in 1081, banished him. The *Cid* thereupon put himself at the service of the Arab king of Zaragoza, and thus he warred not only against the king of Lérida, a Muslim vassal of the count of Barcelona, but against the Christian count himself, Ramón Berenguer surnamed the fratricide, and the Christian king of Aragon, Sancho Ramírez. For over a decade the *Cid* pursued a personal vendetta against the count. Only after 1094 can he be said to have fought for the Christian cause—as opposed to that of Castile or Zaragoza – by capturing the kingdom of Valencia and maintaining it against the Almoravids till his death in 1099.

To point out that the historical *Cid* did not behave throughout his life as an exemplary Christian is not to belittle his feats of arms, the living memory of which has inspired Spaniards in battle throughout the ages to the present day. Now, the early twelfth-century epic which sings of those deeds, not the least of whose great literary merits is that it is realistic, portrays a society with an impure Christian morality. The *Cid,* like his German and Roman ancestors, and like his enemies, the Muslims, relies on auguries – Toledo became world-renowned as the centre for necromancy. He commends his soul to God and prays before great battles; but there is more a touch of the Muslim idea of a Holy War in the way he does so. He has at his side before Valencia the first warrior monk in literature, Jerome of Périgord, who asks to be in the vanguard of the attack to receive the first wounds, to kill Moors 'for the honour of his order' (that of Cluny) 'and his habit',[4] and

4 *Mio Cid,* vv. 2371–5.

who rejoices that he kills two with his lance and five with his sword. In his call to arms the *Cid* of the poem appeals equally to the crusading spirit and to the desire of men to have property and lands.[5] He himself battles 'to win his bread', and has his wife and daughters watch him fight that they may witness 'with their own eyes how hard bread-winning is'.[6] There is nothing 'Moorish' in the poem's treatment of women – quite the contrary; but the *Cid*'s dissolution of his daughters' marriages and their remarriage, in the poem, in the lifetime of their worthless first husbands is certainly not Christian.

Other twelfth-century poems, and in particular one which tells the story of the Seven Princes of Lara, have as their theme vengeance premeditated with Arab patience and executed with cruel refinement. Sometimes there are pagan overtones, as when the avengers heap stones on the dead 'to shut the soul from paradise for ever' : sometimes the protagonists accept Christian belief, as when they kill their enemies in bed to catch them, as Hamlet's father was, 'full of bread' that they should suffer for ever in hell.

It would be unfair to attribute to Arabic influence the recrudescence in Spain of the pre-Christian spirit of vengeance and cruelty or the development of a concept of honour which cut across most of the Ten Commandments and ignored the precept to love one's neighbour; for a similar recrudescence occurred wherever else there were wars between Christians and non-Christians. That indeed was the heart of the matter : that the wars, however worthy the motives of those who took part, brutalized whole peoples. Spain may owe to the Arabs some fine monuments (though it should be noted that some of the finest, for example the Alcázar at Seville, were built and decorated by Muslim craftsmen in post-Arab times); Spaniards would benefit through the ages in Valencia and Murcia from the expansion and development by Arabs of Visigothic irrigation systems and from the Arabs' introduction into Spain of new crops and breeds of cattle; many Spaniards would be thankful to the Moors for their establishment of bull-fighting; but all this must be weighed against the stultification, consequent on Arab conquest, of the growth of Spain into a political unit, and of the lowering of moral human values. In 711 Spain had been well on the way to political unity, even if at that moment she was in a state of civil war. She had had a code of law substantially in advance of any in the western world. In so far as it is possible to judge from the scanty records, it would seem that her society was one in which there had been no acute differences between the richer and the

[5] vv. 1189–92.
[6] vv. 1643, cf. vv. 834, 1173–5, etc.

poorer men. There had been a hierarchy of king, lords spiritual and temporal, lesser nobles, and people, but the gaps between them had not been unbridgeable. Non-Arab Spain, at the beginning of the twelfth century, presented a sorry spectacle of Christian killing Christian, of superstition debilitating religion, of private feuds, and of lords attributing to themselves the unlimited powers which Arab local rulers had exercised over their subjects. León, Castile, Aragon, Navarre, now came together, now separated, but most of the time dissipated their energies in fighting one another.

In 1177 Alfonso VIII of Castile concluded that there was no virtue and no sense in his fight against Navarre to the east of him and León to the west, and that the real and only enemy was to the south. He called on León and Navarre to join him, but they refused. He attacked the Muslims on his own and suffered a severe setback. Furious, he turned on Navarre and León and the county of Portugal, which was seeking to become an independent kingdom just as the county of Castile had broken off a hundred years earlier from its parent León. Repenting of his fury, Alfonso made peace with his fellow Christians. He prevailed on the Pope to call a Crusade. Knights came from England, France, Germany, and Italy. They left after the city of Calatrava had fallen, but Navarre then came to Alfonso's aid. On 16 July 1212, Castilians and Navarrese faced a vastly superior force by Navas de Tolosa. The Almohad Muslim commander had formed a barrier of 10,000 negroes bound with chains to form a human wall around his tent. The Navarrese crashed through them without counting the cost. The Castilians overwhelmed the enemy taking 60,000 prisoners.[7] 'To fight and not to count the cost' became sacrosanct to the Navarrese : and to remind them they chose as their armorial motif the chains of the battle.

Two years later Alfonso of Castile died. He was succeeded by his eleven-year old son, killed three years later by a tile from a roof; and then by his daughter Berenguela, who abdicated in favour of her eighteen-year old son Ferdinand. Ferdinand had to contend for years with rebel barons who were aided by his own father, Alfonso IX of León. Ferdinand, refusing to fight his father, persuaded him that their forces should jointly renew the battle against Arab Spain. The war was taken beyond Cáceres, Badajoz, and Mérida to the frontiers of modern Andalusia. Ferdinand was besieging Jaén when he heard the news of his father's death, whereby he became king of both León and Castile. He could now draw on the manpower of both kingdoms. Nevertheless, it took him three years to take Jaén, and a further three to reach and capture

[7] Doubtless 'rounded-up' figures.

Córdoba. James of Aragon now helped by taking Valencia which had fallen into Muslim hands after the death of the *Cid*. Ferdinand was thus able to concentrate on the great city of Seville, which he had long had as an ultimate goal.

Seville fell to Castile in 1249 after a sixteen-month siege, and henceforth El Andalus, Arab Spain, was reduced to the south-west corner of the peninsula.

The peninsula was now shared by five kingdoms – Granada, under a Muslim, Portugal, Castile (incorporating León, Asturias, and Galicia), Aragon (incorporating Catalonia and Valencia), and Navarre. James of Aragon, having taken the Balearics, became king of a Mediterranean power, captured Sardinia and Sicily, and called upon by the Pope to strike at the resurgent Muslim powers in the Near East, even held Athens for a while. In Spain itself, however, two and a half centuries were to pass between Ferdinand's reduction of El Andalus to such a small area and the final overthrow of the Moorish kingdom of Granada : but the re-Christianization and re-Europeanization of Spain was a process which continued all the time, even if military operations did not.

Chapter 6

The End of the Muslim Presence and the Political Union of Spain

THE FAME OF CÓRDOBA has obscured to many the fact that in the very year of Averroes' death (1126) Raymond of Sauvetat, archbishop of Toledo, established in that city a school of translators. From Arabic and Hebrew they turned into Latin the Aristotelean corpus (which the scholars at Córdoba had rendered into Arabic), and also the work of the great Muslim and Hebrew philosophers. Without Toledo, much of the thinking done at Córdoba would have been lost to posterity. By the time when Averroes was being hounded in Córdoba by the Almohades who were destroying the books which they judged an insult to Allah and his prophet, this school had become as important as Paris and Bologna to mediaeval Christian philosophy. One of its members, Domingo González, was the first to attempt a synthesis between the philosophy of Avicenna (itself a synthesis of the Aristotelean and neo-Platonic) and that of Augustine. By the end of the twelfth century Raymond of Sauvetat's foundation in Toledo was attracting English, Scots, French, and Italian scholars. Spanish scholars, too, were crossing the Pyrenees. Toledo proved too small. Other foundations were made. By the middle of the thirteenth century Salamanca and Lérida were as famous as Oxford and Padua. By the beginning of the fifteenth century Salamanca had the largest student body in the world. The reconquest did not diminish learning. Furthermore, the Pyrenees were no barrier to men or ideas at any time during the Middle Ages. There was a high road to Santiago. The Basques, Navarrese, and Catalans did not recognize the Pyrenees as national frontiers. There was a continuous interchange of men of learning between the Iberian peninsula and the rest of Europe.

The extent of the interchange of ideas can best be seen if we examine the religious aspect of those ages. In the twelfth century the monks of Cluny entered the peninsula to help in the re-Christianization of conquered Spain. In the thirteenth century priests from Spain played a most important part in the intellectual battle between orthodoxy and heterodoxy in the south of what is now

France. A kinsman of the king of Aragon, Dominic of Guzmán, founded the Order of Preachers specifically to combat the Albigensians whose doctrines were believed to encourage sexual perversion. All nations, and especially all the seats of learning of western Europe, welcomed these 'Dogs of the Lord' (or Black Friars as they were called in England), while Spain welcomed the Franciscan Order instituted in Italy, and the Carmelites, the hermits of Mount Sinai reconstituted as friars in England. All three Orders flourished in the peninsula and others also with more specific tasks, such as the Order of Mercy for the redemption of Christian slaves in the hands of Muslims. All three were to play a most important part in the development of ideas in Spain during the sixteenth and seventeenth centuries.

The Orders of Friars attracted in Spain, as elsewhere, both those who truly sought to imitate Christ in poverty and those who saw in their practice of begging alms an easier way of life than work. Admission to them was open to all classes. So was admission to the secular clergy. There was at the time the idea that if a man provided the money for a foundation he and his successors had a right of patronage; that is to say, if a man endowed a university college he could intervene in the choice of its incumbent. Inevitably, if not the founder himself, his successor would have an illegitimate son for whom to provide. The son might be named for the benefice even as a child. In due course he might be ordained with neither the necessary intellectual nor moral training. Concubinage was not uncommon. Side by side with great learning there was gross ignorance.

In all this the situation in Spain was no different from the situation elsewhere. Nor was Spain free from the influx of the heterodox undercurrents of the time. The family ties between the rulers of Toulouse and the Crown of Aragon and the proximity of the strongholds of Albigensianism in France to Aragon and Catalonia, the intercourse between the *Levante,* the eastern coast of Spain, and the Asiatic Levant, facilitated the development in north-eastern Spain of focuses of Catharism in various forms. Catharism was regarded not only as heresy and, by some, as encouraging sodomy, but also as a solvent of society. The Crown of Aragon accordingly allowed from the thirteenth century onwards the establishment within the kingdom of ecclesiastical tribunals of Inquisition, with the double task of discovering the leaders and of protecting those falsely accused. The tribunals passed over the unrepentant to secular justice, and in Aragon as in contemporary England heresy was held as a crime more heinous than treason, and therefore more worthy of punishment by death.

The Crown of Aragon had to contend with a problem, which

indeed faced most mediaeval monarchs, but which was almost nowhere else so acute : the spirit among the nobles of independence from, or non-subservience to, the king. On accession a king had to kneel before the four assembled Houses of the *Cortes* – the Men of Wealth, the Knights, Clergy, and Commons – and hear the Speaker say : 'We who are as good as you, swear to you who are no better than we, to accept you as our king and sovereign lord, provided you accept all our privileges and laws : but if not, not'. In consequence the rebel had merely to show a *prima facie* infringement by a king of some privilege to have popular support; treason, in the sense of rebellion against the king, could never – until very modern times – be regarded with the same horror that it came popularly to inspire in England.

The *Cortes* of Aragon were not the oldest in the peninsula nor the most democratic.[1] In 1130 *procuradores,* representatives of towns and cities, assembled in the courts (the *Cortes*) of the king of Castile to propose laws for the better government of the realm. By 1177 it had been established that without their approval no one could inherit the throne of Castile, no king could declare war or seek peace, and no king could levy taxes. In 1188 the king of León put a signature to an ordinance drawn up by the *Cortes* of León which established the right of the humblest peasant to kill any man, even the king, who entered his household uninvited. In the *Cortes* of Aragon the nobles were preponderant, as they were long to be in the Parliament of England. In those of Castile and León the towns and cities had the greater say, and the peasant in his own house was upheld as the equal of the king in his palace.

Moreover, throughout these 400 years the Pyrenees were no barrier to literature. The same forces and ideas were at work to produce on the one side *chansons de geste* and on the other *gesta*. Drama was reborn in the churches of Spain as in those north of the Pyrenees. In the poems of Alfonso X, *el Sabio,* the learned thirteenth-century compiler of laws and prolific writer on science and history, parallels can be seen between the rhyme patterns of the Arabs and his own (he was an Arabic scholar), but their subject matter and their title, *cantigas de Santa María,* are uncompromisingly Christian. In the undercurrent of lascivious writing exemplified in the fourteenth-century archpriest of Hita's *Libro del buen amor* (Ovid in a new guise) there are also Arabic undertones, but its approach presumes a Christian outlook, if not behaviour. In all this, of course, it must not be forgotten that what was written in the vernacular dur-

---

[1] Simon de Montfort developed his idea of a Parliament for England from the *Cortes* of Aragon with which he had come into contact as he fought under his father in the wars against the Albigenses – and others.

ing the period say from 1200 to 1500 was literature for the illiterate :
works to be read out loud. The intellectual leaders of Spanish
literature preferred to read and write Latin, to study the enormous
international corpus of writing in Latin, and to contribute to it.
So it was to be into the sixteenth century. Not until printing presses
had been at work for a hundred years did their output of Spanish
titles begin to draw level with that of Latin works.

The European traveller to Spain in the late Middle Ages would
have had far to go before coming across architectural styles strange
to him. At Calatayud he might have marvelled at the tower of the
church, originally the solid square minaret of the mosque; but the
cathedrals of Zaragoza, Burgos, and Compostela were uncompromisingly ogival. The liturgy in those churches was as in the
rest of western Europe; albeit some of its plainchant was derived
more directly from the Byzantine. In the treasure-houses of those
cathedrals he would have seen illuminated manuscripts which did
not eschew the human form as a subject; and as marriage was
proof of the rejection of Catharism, so may the portrayal of human
figures be taken as proof of the Christianity of the people.

The Spaniards were consciously Christian. The popular reaction
to the Muslim laxity of the courts was to make the people even
more consciously Christian. This reaction and this consciousness is
perhaps nowhere more marked than in the famous poem by the
young soldier Jorge Manrique who was killed in battle :

> 'O let the soul her slumbers break,
> Let thought be quickened, and awake;
> Awake to see
> How soon this life is past and gone,
> And death comes softly stealing on,
> How silently! . . .
>
> 'O Thou, that for our sins didst take
> A human form, and humbly make
> Thy home on earth;
> Thou, that to thy divinity
> A human nature didst ally
> By mortal birth,
>
> 'And in that form didst suffer here
> Torment, and agony, and fear,
> So patiently;
> By thy redeeming grace alone,
> And not for merits of my own,
> O pardon me!'[2]

[2] Longfellow's translation.

No poem is better known to Spaniards than this.

There were, nevertheless, differences between Spain and the rest of Europe. There were not only many castles and more walled cities, but villages were almost invariably sited on steep hills and fortified. South of the northern strip recovered in the early days of the reconquest there were no isolated farmsteads. Men preferred to walk long distances daily from the safety of the village to their fields. The ordinary unarmed peasant farmer had no interest in land beyond an hour or so's walk from the village. Increasingly larger grants of land had been made from at least the ninth century to the leaders of successful campaigns against the Arabs as rewards and as part of their ennoblement, and also to monastic institutions whose duty it was to Christianize again the reconquered regions. As sons followed fathers into leadership, and as new regions were conquered, some families came to have several large estates. Collectively the monasteries became the largest landlords, but of course 10,000 acres owned by a conventual house with a hundred members represented a state of greater distribution of property than a similar area owned by one noble. Furthermore, the monks were enjoined by their rule of St Benedict in all its forms, original, Cluniac, or Cistercian, to labour in the fields: the nobles were too busy at court or on the battlefield to do such work.

There was another difference to be seen in the countryside. The lands of Spain, even less than elsewhere in the Mediterranean, did not naturally provide all-the-year-round pasture for sheep, the staple meat diet. By the ninth century, the practice of *trashumancia,* the driving of huge flocks of sheep up into the mountains when the tablelands were parched in the summer, and back for the winter, had resulted in the establishment of a complex of lanes, usually ninety yards wide, running through hundreds upon hundreds of miles. The tillage of these lanes, after battles between the sheep-owners and the shepherds on the one side and the settled farmers on the other, was expressly forbidden by stringent laws. In 1482 the number of migrant sheep exceeded 2·25 million; in 1526 it was to reach its maximum, 3·4 million. As the owners and shepherds were prepared to share their profits with the Crowns of Spain, their guild, the *Mesta,* had the ears of the kings, and acquired from them not only the right to graze over a vast acreage, but a law and judiciary of their own.

To return, however, to the political history of Spain, by the middle of the thirteenth century the counts of Barcelona had become kings of Aragon and of Valencia. The counts of Castile had become kings of Castile, León, Asturias, and Galicia. The counts of Portugal had become kings of Portugal. The next logical step should have been the unity of the three and the liquidation of the surviving Muslim kingdom of Granada.

St Ferdinand's successors were not of his mettle. His son, Alfonso X, earned for himself the title of 'the Learned' – and he was; but he squandered money and effort in an unsuccessful attempt to acquire the title of Holy Roman Emperor. His great-grandson, Ferdinand IV, captured Gibraltar in 1310, but the son of this Ferdinand, Alfonso XI, lost it in 1333. Alfonso died trying to recapture it seventeen years later, leaving a legitimate heir, Peter, and five bastard sons. Paradoxically it was now when the Muslims had been bereft of their great military and political power that their culture began to have its deepest influence in the Christian courts. Peter had his five half-brothers, an archbishop, and even perhaps his own wife, killed, and had built for himself a palace in Seville, so 'Moorish' in its architectural style and inspiration that it is often mistaken today for an Arab building. In the next century there was reaction and counter-reaction. Henry IV of Castile (1454–74) modelled his own behaviour and that of his court on the morals of the laxest oriental potentates. 'The throne itself,' Menéndez Pidal has written, 'set the insensate example of belittling and insulting national values'. Moorish customs were openly adopted. The reconquest was deliberately impeded. The law was held to scorn with official encouragement. Corruption became endemic among all government officials and judges. Religion was openly held in contempt. People boasted of their bestiality and material outlook.

Henry's mode of life aroused antagonisms, not least on religious grounds. Momentarily in 1462 he acquired popular favour by capturing Gibraltar. Opposition then centred round the archbishop of Toledo, Alfonso Carrillo de Acuña. Toledo was well on its way to becoming the wealthiest diocese in Christendom and Carrillo's motives were not exclusively political. At a solemn ceremony in Ávila in 1465 Carrillo 'deposed' Henry, but he survived the deposition and the rebellion that accompanied it. Carrillo and the anti-Henry party bided their time. On Henry's death in 1474 Carrillo and others, including Cardinal Pedro González de Mendoza, archbishop of Seville, had Isabel, Henry's half-sister, proclaimed queen of Castile. Isabel, married on Carrillo's insistence to her cousin Ferdinand, heir to the throne of Aragon, emerged triumphant after five years of war against the king of Portugal and other supporters of Juana, daughter of Henry's queen, but probably not of Henry himself.

Once victorious and at twenty-three already a woman of remarkable determination, Isabel made sure that she would not have from nobles or even bishops the trouble her half-brother had had by establishing her supremacy over both estates. Her defeat of the Portuguese ensured her kingdom from foreign attack, and when Ferdinand inherited the throne of Aragon in 1479, the only danger that remained was from Granada, a potential bridgehead for much stronger forces from Africa. Castile had therefore to absorb Granada, and Isabel invited Ferdinand to co-operate in the venture.

In 1492, after ten years of fighting, the forces of Isabel and Ferdinand overwhelmed the kingdom of Granada. The Moors – the Muslim North Africans and Turks – were repeatedly to carry out raids on the coasts over the next eighty years, and even to attempt the invasion of the peninsula, but they never again succeeded in obtaining more than a temporary foothold. On Isabel's death in 1504 there was a moment of revolt when it looked as if the unity created by her marriage to Ferdinand might be dissolved, but Ferdinand defeated the dissidents and remained joint king of Aragon and Castile. In 1512 he moved successfully against the kingdom of Navarre south of the Pyrenees, and thus, at his death in 1516, he left to his heir and successor, Charles, the son of his mad daughter Juana, all the peninsula except the kingdom of Portugal. Finally, in 1580, when Philip II gained the Portuguese Crown, the unity which the Arab invasion of 711 had broken was restored. Such unity, however, was fragile, for the Portuguese had by this time developed their own national characteristics. Eighty years later, they broke away, never again to be part of Spain, an occasion welcomed by their British allies. The Catalans, too, maintained their independent spirit, looking more for French support until they learnt that Paris had no greater respect for their national consciousness than Madrid.

Indeed, nowhere in the peninsula did the union of Crowns lead immediately to a union of peoples. The nobles of Aragon could still call upon popular support for independence from Castile a century after the accession of Isabel and Ferdinand. In the twentieth century the Basques were still sufficiently conscious of their separate identity to fight for their independence from Madrid as tenaciously as they had done in their remote past against Arabs and Romans. Nevertheless, Isabel's conquest of Granada in 1492 and Ferdinand's of Navarre in 1512 established in the minds of the peoples of Castile and Aragon the idea that Spain was one, or ought to be one, in language, culture, and religion; and that thereafter there should be no king but the King of Spain.

PART TWO

The Making of Modern Spain

Chapter 7

Spanish and Foreign Views of the Period 1492–1701

⁀O THE MAJORITY of Spaniards, Isabel and Ferdinand are heroes,
he monarchs who unified Spain. They were certainly the first
ings for 700 years steadfastly to devote themselves to policies the
esults of which should have been the unity of political life and
dministration, of language and culture, and of religion. They con-
uered Granada; they destroyed the powers of local barons; they
upported Nebrija, whose work on Spanish grammar contributed
ore than anyone else's to the development of modern Spanish;
hey praised Cardinal Cisneros for his encouragement of learning
nd his reform of the clergy. Few Spaniards doubt that their title
f 'the Catholic kings' was undeserved; and, of course, Isabel and
'erdinand are remembered as the providers of the Spanish ships,
rews, and money necessary for Christopher Columbus (whose
¡enoese origin some learned Spaniards have doubted) to discover
⁀merica.

Nevertheless, the names of Isabel and Ferdinand recall to foreign
cholars and writers other facts. Some remember that Ferdinand
⁄as the model of Machiavelli's Prince, that he had a papal legate
anged, and threatened a schism with Rome such as his son-in-law
Ienry VIII of England carried out; others, especially in the Eng-
sh-speaking world, emphasize the expulsion of the Jews and the
stablishment of the Spanish Inquisition. In any reference to the
cquisition of the Spanish empire in the Americas, they quote
artolomé de las Casas, forgetting that the author was a settler
urned priest in repentance and that Isabel rewarded him with a
ishopric for the frankness of his report.

Isabel's and Ferdinand's grandson and successor, Charles I of
⁀astile, Aragon, and the other Spanish kingdoms, Charles V of the
Ioly Roman Empire, is a less controversial figure. Most foreigners
dmire his blatant erastianism, while Spaniards venerate him for
is retirement to the austerity of the monastery of Yuste. His son,
'hilip II, is credited by foreigners with heinous crimes. To most
paniards he was, and is, *el prudente,* the skilful, a man of many

49

sins perhaps, but also of great virtues. Although a few Spaniard
have indeed doubted whether Charles V and Philip II were sir
cerely champions of Catholicism, too much can be adduced i
evidence to show the contrary. Foreigners have for the most pa
accepted the Black Legend : that Spaniards were grotesquely cru
as colonists, and that the decline of Spain was due to their religiou
obscurantism and their persecutions of Jews, Moors, and Prote
tants. The legend continues to affect Anglo-Spanish and America
Spanish relations. It infuriates the Spaniard not only that the legen
is believed but that it was invented and propagated by Spaniard
penitentially; as it also enrages the Spaniard that popular idea
on the history of the Inquisition spring from the highly suspe
Llorente[1] who destroyed the records which did not support h
thesis. It should not surprise the British and Americans that the
beliefs have a counterpart. Spanish writers, too, have painted i
most sombre colours the persecutions in Britain under Elizabeth
and James I; British colonization; the American behaviour towar
the Red Indian, Negro, and Latin American; and today they prid
themselves that even Llorente admits that the Inquisition tende
to scorn those who accused people as witches, while norther
Europeans burned hundreds if not thousands for witchcraft. Suc
charges and counter-charges, however, only obscure the real im
portance of this period to modern Spain.

It was during the first hundred years of this period that Spai
came to have territorially a most extensive empire in Europe an
another in the New World; her infantry acquired a reputation fo
near invincibility; and she appeared to be economically mo
powerful. It was over the first 150 years that Spaniards achieve
remarkable artistic perfection, and that Catholicism became a pa
of themselves, even of the few who rejected it. It was during th
last hundred years that Spain's European empire cracked and the
collapsed, that she ceased to be a first-class military power (thoug
her fame as one long outlived the reality), and that the rulin
classes defrauded the people of their wealth; and it was during th
last fifty years that the inspiration of writers and artists declined, t
reach the nadir of the eighteenth century. Empire, military opera
tions, economy, originality in philosophy and the arts, and Catho
icity all interacted on each other, not always consistently. Th
interaction left imprints on the Spanish mind which affect th
thought and behaviour of the Spaniard today.

[1] 1756–1823.

Chapter 8

The Rise and Fall of Spain's European Empire 1492–1701

In two ways Spain has never recovered from the fact that she had a European empire from 1492 to 1701, or more exactly until the Peace of Utrecht in 1713. The first is that the acquisition, maintenance, and loss of that empire absorbed by far the greater part – and it could even be argued virtually all – of the economic benefits she obtained from her American empire. Certainly she survived the loss economically poorer than she had been before its acquisition. (It would be difficult but interesting to calculate how much of the Spanish bullion which is now a part of the treasure of Fort Knox, the Bank of England, Zurich, and other financial centres of Europe, was originally South American.) By the beginning of the eighteenth century when a French king came to the throne of Spain, she was economically in no position to pursue a foreign policy independent of France : she was dragged into wars not of her own making and from which, unlike her wealthier partner, she received neither territorial nor financial advantages, but rather yet again suffered severe losses in wealth and manpower; and so into the nineteenth century. As a consequence, in that century Spanish entrepreneurs lacked the capital necessary to take advantage of the industrial inventions of the time : so Spain became essentially a colony of other European powers, a source of raw materials and certain foods, and a market for the manufactures of those powers.

Spain is not the only modern nation to have had a European empire, but no other nation had one for as long as she; and during the century and a half of her hegemony a pattern of thinking was engrained into the Spaniard which rated the profession of arms, if not above all others, at least as incomparably superior to work in the fields, or when the time came, in factories.

Chapter 9

Military Spain 1492–1701

I SABEL KNEW HER HUSBAND WELL. In her Last Will and Testament
she implored him to take the war against the Muslim into Africa
but not to engage in wars of conquest in Europe. He ignored the
Will. He was already embroiled in Italy, having joined with Louis
XII of France in the carving-up of Naples. After bitter quarrels
between him and Louis he obtained all of Naples in 1503. By 1512
he had engineered the annexation of Navarre and paved the way
for his grandson's acquisition of Milan. Thereafter ceaseless war
between France and Spain was inevitable. French kings looked upon
Navarre as within their rightful sphere of influence, just as Spanish
kings considered Rousillon and Cerdagne as rightly Catalan and
therefore Spanish. France, too, wanted suzerainty over Italy. The
accession of Charles to the thrones of Spain and Austria in 1516
made Milan the vital strategic link between his west and central
European dominions. Charles's hereditary claims to the Netherlands, Flanders, Artois, Burgundy, and the Franche-Comté cut
further into France's territorial ambitions. His election to the
imperial throne landed Charles into the middle of the religio-
political warfare of Germany. His Austria was seriously threatened
by the Turks, as was the whole of Europe. The Muslims were out
of Spain, but the power of Soleiman was in the ascendant in the
Mediterranean, and Spain would not be safe unless at least Tunis,
and preferably Algiers as well, were in European hands. The possession by the King of Spain of an area of Europe greater than that
ever held by a single man since Roman times thus involved Spain
in years of war. On behalf of the King of Spain, though not
directly as King of Spain, Spaniards thus had to fight virtually
throughout Charles's forty-year reign : four times against France,
constantly against the Turks, and from 1544 against the Protestants. Charles, however, was catholic in his choice of enemies,
rather than Catholic in a religious sense, for his wars included a
three-year war against the Pope, and his troops – German Protestants chosen for this occasion – in 1527 sacked Rome as thoroughly
as any others before or since. Philip II did not inherit the German
empire, but he did succeed to the rest of his father's possessions in

rope. The French did not bother him quite so severely as they
d his father – they had their own internal troubles – but it was
his reign that the Turkish navy reached the apex of its power
the Mediterranean. He had to equip most of the armada with
ich his half-brother, Don John, won Lepanto in 1571. It was
his reign also that English pirates began to attack his ships in the
lantic and England started to intervene in the Netherlands. The
suing war lost him not only his 'invincible armada', estimated to
ve cost £9 million in gold, but other ships in the subsequent
vasion of Ireland about which English history text-books are
ore reticent.

Offsetting Lepanto against the defeat of the invincible armada,
anish armadas had in the sixteenth and seventeenth centuries as
e a naval record as that of any other power. To serve in them,
ecially when the cause was held to be just, was considered a
h honour. Cervantes fought aboard one of Don John of Austria's
lleons; Lope de Vega was a crew member of the San Juan, one
the survivors of the invincible armada.

Nevertheless, the Spaniards, like the Romans, were at their best
fighters on land. At the very moment when Ferdinand sought to
pand the frontiers of his rule, he had a military genius as a most
al subject, Gonzalo Fernández de Córdoba. As a youth at the
ad of a small body of cavalry, Don Gonzalo had fought for
bel against her rival for the throne of Castile, and Isabel had
varded him with a more important command against Granada.
rdinand placed him over all his forces for the invasion of Italy.
e history of Don Gonzalo's campaigns was of victory after
tory, in attack and in defence, and with numerical odds now
 him, now against him. He came to be known as 'the Great
ptain', a title said first to have been given him by his enemy, the
ench, who were no match for him. The secret of Don Gonzalo's
ccess was his evolution of new infantry tactics and his organiza-
n of the infantry into manageable, self-sufficient units: pikemen
resist the initial cavalry charge of a battle; arquebusiers to guard
 flanks and enfilade the attackers; and infantry armed with
elins and the Roman-Spanish short sword, and protected by
nd shields, to move through the pikemen into the attack. The
eat Captain died in 1515, but his tactics and his principle of the
lependent, self-sufficient infantry unit survived. Its organization
s more or less standardized around 1534 when it came com-
nly to be called the tercio. It consisted then of twelve com-
nies, each of about 250 men, six of them of pikemen, four of
rdsmen, and two of arquebusiers. In column of route they
rched; pikemen-swordsmen-pikemen, with the arquebusiers

guarding the flanks and in the vanguard. The arquebusiers we.
the 'crack men', the younger and more nimble. They were pa
extra.

Wherever Charles V or Philip II had these *tercios*, they had r
cause to fear defeat. They formed a spearhead of the attack
Pavia, Muhlberg, and Gueldres; they wiped out the great arm
headed by the Constable of France sent to relieve St Quentin
1557; and they could have taken Paris then had Philip not decid
to try to make a friend of his main enemy in Europe. They sav
Paris from Henri of (French) Navarre in 1590 and Rouen in 159
Spanish victories which contributed to Henri's decision that 'Pa
was worth a Mass'. The Dutch rebels wisely avoided open batt
with the *tercios* as far as they could, and appreciating that Spai
success with infantry had led to her comparative neglect at sea
in siege work, made the sea and the strong walls of fortresses th
allies in their wars for independence.

It was thanks to the *tercios* that in 1598 Philip III inherit
from his father almost as extensive a European empire as Philip
had inherited from Charles V; but he was heir also to war with t
French, English, Dutch, and Turk – and bankruptcy. The ne
king's Minister, the duke of Lerma, patched up peace with all b
the Turk. Hardly had this been accomplished when Spain w
embroiled with the rest of Europe in the Thirty Years War. Phil
III saw only the beginning.

It was in the course of that war, or rather complex of wars, th
the *tercios* suffered their first major defeat. As Frederick the Gre
was to write, nothing can contribute more to failure than succe
For over a hundred years the *tercios'* composition and deployme
had remained unchanged. At Rocroi in 1643 the great Con
pitched a larger new model army against them.

To Spain's further economic loss the Peace of Westphalia w
not the end of the war. France and Spain continued to fight for
further eleven years. At the Peace of the Pyrenees in 1658 Spa
had to surrender to France Catalonia beyond the Pyrenees – Rous
lon and Cerdagne. The following year Portugal, annexed by Phi
II in 1580, was able to break away. Philip IV, who had succeed
his father Philip III in 1621, was in his turn succeeded in 16
by his son Charles, a child weakling; while Louis XIV hammer
away at the Spanish Crown's dominions in Flanders, the Franc
Comté, and Italy. The *tercios,* now without the inestimable adva
tage of their reputation for invincibility but still with the tenac
of their nation shown at Saguntum and Numantia, clung to t
fortresses that stood in the way of the expansion of France. O
the years many were lost, yet fifty-four years after Rocroi, at

time of the Peace of Ryswick, the Spanish Crown had still not
yielded to France all that France wanted. France was to get her
way in the end, but not primarily through victory in battle.

The long supremacy of the Spanish *tercios* was not due wholly
to their organization or deployment, nor yet to the brilliance of
their commanders. Gonzalo Fernández de Córdoba apart, Spain
did not produce generals of the calibre of, say, Gustavus Adolphus,
Condé, or Frederick the Great. Other nations tried to copy the
organization and tactics of the *tercio,* yet failed. It is in the character of the Spanish infantryman that we must look for the
decisive factor.

The distinction must be made between the *tercios,* which were
almost entirely Spanish in composition, and the mercenaries –
employed by the Crown of Spain as by all the other European
powers and principalities. The truly Spanish infantry had a strong
stiffening of men who considered it a duty to fight for their king
or his cause, of men of noble blood or at least *hijos de algo,* of
men of intelligence and letters. The great lyrical poet Garcilaso de
la Vega fell mortally wounded as he scaled the walls of Nice at
the head of his *tercio.* Cervantes, the sailor at Lepanto, was earlier
in his very varied career a soldier in a *tercio* in Italy. Though
there were, doubtless, men of violence and evil life among them,
as a body they were renowned for their temperance, abstemious-
ness, resistance to disease and extremes of temperature, and phlegm
in victory and defeat. The mercenaries demanded prompt payment
for services rendered : to the *tercio* the sufferance of arrears of pay
was a point of honour. Yet even they had to be clothed, provided
with weapons, and fed.

Chapter 10

The Spanish Economy 1492–1701

THE TREASURY OF CASTILE was empty when Isabel ascended the throne. Henry IV's mode of life had not been thrifty. The conquest of Granada was expensive : the invasion of Italy by Ferdinand even more so. Charles V came to the throne of Spain not merely with empty pockets, but with a substantial debt to foreign bankers who had given him the money with which he had bribed his way to the imperial throne. Apart from engaging in the wars to maintain his European inheritance and to ward off the Protestant threat to his sovereignty over Germany, Charles had to fight two major revolts in Spain itself : one against the people of Castile who refused to let him have the money to pay the interest on his foreign debt (the usual rate was 14 per cent), and one against the Christians of Valencia who distrusted the Muslims among them at a time when the power of the Turks was rising in the Mediterranean. Charles left his son a debt to foreign creditors of over £6 million,[1] a figure equal to roughly one-fifth of all the gold and silver in existence in Europe before the discovery of America. Philip, who apart from going to war against the English, the Dutch, the French, Turk, and Pope, had to suppress a widespread revolt of the Moriscos, the Muslims of Granada forcibly baptized under a law of Isabel, left his son Philip III debts of £45 million. The revolt in the Netherlands cost Spain about £50 million : the war against England (armada and Irish invasion combined) about £15 million. Add to these the probable expenses of the several wars against France, in Italy, and against the Turk, say £100 million, plus the interest on the foreign loans, and we can begin to appreciate what the maintenance by Philip II alone of his European empire cost Spain.

Bullion to the value of £257 million officially arrived in Spain from the New World during the longer period 1503 to 1660, and a further £30 million may have been smuggled. The average, there-

---

[1] Even an approximation of purchasing power is difficult : say multiply by 50 in 1550 and by 25 in 1600, as against 1969 prices. Another way of assessing the real meaning of the debt is to consider it as equal to a year's national income.

fore, was £1·8 million a year, of which the Crown's share in the
first place was approximately a quarter. To service debts and to
finance new military operations alone it had to entice from the
people far more than the total value of the bullion. It did this
through several measures.

Possibly the most profitable was taxation. By 1551 Charles V was
netting more than £1·5 million a year; by 1573 Philip II was
milking Castile of approximately £2·5 million. The principal source
was the *alcabala*, technically a 10 per cent sales tax charged every
time a substance changed hands. To give an example : Spanish
gloves were in demand for their high quality; between the killing
of the kid and the sale of the finished article to the consumer, there
could be five or six transactions. A large percentage of the sale
price to the consumer was therefore tax. As can be imagined, the
alcabala killed many an industry.

The second method of raising money was the *ad hoc* forced
levy, from the nobles and the Church. Some of the loans were considerable sums of money. The Crown also consistently helped
itself to rather more than one-tenth of the Church's income.

A third method of raising income was by the virtual sale of titles
of nobility. Under Charles V, ordinary citizens were encouraged to
lend him money at 10 per cent in exchange for letters patent called
juros, non-redeemable bonds. These gave the buyers the right to
consider themselves *hijos de algo* and to use the prefix Don before
their name. In 1577 Philip II forced the holders of *juros* to accept
a reduction of the interest rate to 5 per cent. Bankers who had
bought *juros* from individuals at a substantial discount protested,
but by that time the right to *hidalguería* was so much in demand
that there was no shortage of new buyers.

The moral iniquity of Isabel's expulsion of the Jews in 1492 and
the later expulsion of the Moriscos in 1609 has pushed into the
background the immediate economic benefits which these measures
brought to the Crown. Behind both these acts there were religious,
religio-political, and political considerations. We shall consider the
purely religious later. The principle of *cujus regio ejus religio,*
formulated at Augsburg, was already implicit in the behaviour of
princes long before 1555; but so also among the people was the
principle *ut populus sic rex.* Isabel's title Queen of Castile belied a
deep disunity among her subjects : of language – Castilian, Galician, Asturian, Basque; of racial mixture; of social habits. There
was no national administration nor nationwide corpus of law. The
only bond between her and the majority of her subjects was that of
religion. Among this majority, there was no great love for either
Jew or Muslim. The memory was vivid of the important part played

by those of Jewish religion in the early stages of the Muslim conquest of Spain. While individual Jews had sided with and helped
Christian kings during the wars of reconquest, on the whole their
sympathy and aid had been for the Muslim rulers. There was no
guarantee of their loyalty to the Crown now that the Muslim had
been driven from Spain. Alfonso the Wise had sought to be king
over the 'three religions', but had not succeeded. In 1492 Jew and
Muslim alike were potential allies of the Arab powers in Africa
and were an offence to the principle of unity of faith between
sovereign and people. Accordingly Isabel should have dealt with
both alike. She did not.

On capturing Granada Isabel expelled the Muslims who were of
recent immigration : their loyalties were to Arab rulers. To those
who were not recent immigrants she promised respect for their
faith if they were loyal to her; but they rebelled in 1501. Isabel
thereupon gave them the alternative of baptism or exile. Once
baptized they would be subject to that superb instrument of the
Crown for ensuring its safety, the Inquisition. She made the conditions of exile as intolerable as possible.

The Jews, too, were given the alternative of baptism or exile, but
in 1492 and not in 1501. The conditions of exile were not quite as
harsh. Tens, even hundreds, of thousands were given asylum by the
Sultan of Turkey; thousands, even tens of thousands, were given
asylum by the Pope who saw no reason why he should bar them
from his dominions on the grounds of religion.

The logic of Isabel's action must be sought, therefore, in other
than religious or political considerations.

The Muslim industrial and agricultural worker was essential to
the economy of Granada. There were nobles in plenty willing to
accept from the Crown grants of ownership of vast tracts of land,
but too few productive workers were prepared to move southwards
to work in the fields or in industry for those nobles. The Muslims
had to be kept in the peninsula. After the forcible baptism, neither
the Crown nor its agents, the landowners, exerted themselves unduly to ensure that the conversion was more than nominal. Ferdinand, who had a whole region full of Muslims – the eastern coast
– did not go even as far as this. His policy was to leave the Muslims totally undisturbed in their faith and social practices, a policy
which should not credit the life-model of Machiavelli's *Prince* with
any liberal ideal. He could extract from the Muslim far more in
taxation than he could from his less wealthy and productively less
successful Christian subjects. On the matter of the Jews, however,
he was at one with his wife.

The position of the Jews in the economy was different from that of the Muslims. They were bankers, entrepreneurs, and merchants, men with money and urban property. Both Crowns were heavily in debt to them. Their expulsion, therefore, would rid the Crowns not only of potentially disloyal subjects, but of heavy debts, and thus bring considerable wealth.

Economic reality continued to dictate policy on the Moriscos, the forcibly converted Muslims, for a further hundred years. Charles V sided with them against the people of Valencia at the beginning of his reign. Later he momentarily ordered their expulsion on the grounds of 'his conscience', a conscience assuaged by large sums of money given to him by the industrious Moriscos. In Spain he was not prepared to enforce his principle of *cujus regio ejus religio* to its logical extreme. It was more profitable not to do so. Philip II continued his father's policy, though there were many to advise him that the rising power of the Turks in the Mediterranean made the presence of their spiritual allies on Spanish soil a danger to the security of his dominions. Thus the Moriscos survived in Spain until the next century. The old objection to their expulsion, that there would not be workers to take over the fields and industries, no longer held : taxation had ruined industry everywhere in Spain, and there was no shortage of labour. They were then also discovered to be in contact not merely with the Sultan of Turkey and the king of Morocco, but with Henri IV of France, and to have sent him some £50,000 as a token of the help they would give him if he invaded Spain on their behalf. Their expulsion would therefore now be justifiable on security grounds, and no loss to the economy. Indeed there would be a gain : for they were known to have considerable hoards of money. The state had twice debased the currency as a quick way of withdrawing money from the people, but the Moriscos had wisely hidden their gold and silver. Accordingly in 1609 their expulsion was decreed : 150,000 out of a possible half a million Moriscos were expelled, without the authorities considering whether their Christianity was genuine or not. This was left to the Arabs of Morocco to establish. The genuine Christians received short shrift.

Spain's rapid industrial decline during the seventeenth century has been too readily attributed to the Morisco expulsion and the fact that there were many fine artisans among those expelled. However, if the parallel often made with the French Huguenot expulsion were valid, the workers of which Spain deprived itself should have made good in the lands which received them, as the Huguenots did in England. In fact Spanish industry was already moribund well before the end of the sixteenth century, strangled by the

Crown's fiscal policy. So was Spanish livestock farming – again taxed excessively. By the beginning of the seventeenth century there were at least 150,000 unemployed in a population of about 8 million.

Such unemployment was involuntary: but there was another kind of unemployment even more ruinous to the economy. It became a convention early in the sixteenth century that an *hidalgo* should not work except as the king's servant. To serve the king in war or in the aggrandisement of his empire in the New World was not within the physical capacity or taste of every *hidalgo,* especially of those who had acquired their title by purchase. Spain thus came to have a new social class of hangers-on at court, of seekers of office: for the honour as often as the pickings. Only at the top did the pickings recompense the outlay with interest. *Poderoso caballero es Don Dinero* – a powerful gent is Sir Cash – ran the refrain of a satirical poem. Philip II did not allow his Ministers to grow rich at the expense of the general public. At any rate, he did try to keep corruption at court within a tolerable level. Not so Philip III, who permitted his Minister Lerma to make himself a millionaire in a short time. When Lerma fell in disgrace, Lerma's son, Uceda, enriched himself in a similar fashion. During the first twenty-two years of Philip IV's reign the count-duke of Olivares, a man of few principles, contrived to amass for himself an income of some £200,000 gold a year of public monies while the situation of the people went from bad to worse with the continuance of the Spanish military involvement in the wars of Europe.

In his imitation Versailles, the Palace of Buen Retiro, Philip IV was too engrossed in the welfare of his many mistresses to consider the consequences to the people of his Minister's acts. Over the remainder of Philip's reign power passed through many hands, falling finally into those of his niece and second wife, Mariana of Austria, whose four-year-old child by him succeeded as Charles II. Mariana's first preoccupation was to ensure for her infant son and herself an income which would enable them to live in the style to which her uncle-husband had accustomed them; and in due course to find her cretinous son a wife from Austria so that the Habsburgs should continue to rule Spain. All this occurred while France gnawed away at Spain's European empire, and Spaniards lost their lives on the battlefields of Europe. Coupled with the celibacy of a fair percentage of the population and the emigration of others to the New World, the result had been a substantial fall in the population of Spain. In Castile where there had been about 8 million people in 1560, by the second half of the seventeenth century there were under 7 million. Madrid, now established as the capital of

pain, had grown to house 350,000, but at the expense of the
ountryside. Food production was inadequate to feed the people.
here were riots among the starving in the towns. Bands of brig-
nds roamed the mountains. Spain's European empire and the
Habsburgs had brought ruin : and the Habsburgs themselves were
uined since Mariana's son was incapable of begetting a successor.

Chapter 11

Catholic Spain 1492–1701

HAD ISABEL EXPLAINED her expulsion of the Jews, or Philip III his
expulsion of the Moriscos, solely on the grounds that they were
security risk which the state could not tolerate, or more easily still
had the plea been one of 'economic necessity', the modern non
Spanish world would doubtless have been ready to sympathize. But
to have pleaded thus would have damned them in the eyes of their
contemporary fellow-countrymen, and even of most Spaniard
today. The Moriscos irritated Spaniards because, among other un
Spanish activities, they were preoccupied with the acquisition c
money. It is one of the major charges made against them by th
austere Cervantes in his *Coloquio de los perros*. In the literature c
the sixteenth century, the stock character of opprobrium was th
indiano, the man who returned from the Indies flaunting his wealth
The dismissal of Lerma and the prosecution of his henchma
Rodrigo de Calderón were popular because they too had spen
much effort amassing a fortune. That is not to say that it wa
acceptable that anyone, other than a friar or a professional beggar
should display his poverty to the world. The life of pretence live
by many a poverty-stricken Spaniard was the subject of a whol
literary genre, the picaresque. Accordingly it would have bee
unseemly for the Crown either to have admitted its poverty openl
or to appear avaricious.

For the Crown to have explained its policies on security ground
would have had some meaning within those areas directly affected
but not in Spain as a whole. The sentiment of nationalism had bee
growing in Spain throughout the Middle Ages. The Cid's remar
quant grand es Espanya, the late mediaeval battle cry *Santiago
cierra España,* may be quoted as milestones in its developmen
Nevertheless, when the Christian peasant farmers of the easter
seashore pressed their king to take action against the Muslims i
their midst, they did so more in defence of their own lands than c
Spain. Their fears were more basic than their feeling of nationalit
It was their fields, their houses, their women who were ravishe
when Turkish and other Muslim pirates raided the eastern shore
They were afraid, too, of being crowded out. Indeed, Cervante

62

noted that the birthrate among the Muslims was notoriously higher than among Christians : evidence perhaps that many of the Christians who took a vow of chastity also kept it.

The surest way to popular support at any time during the late fifteenth or the sixteenth century – and even long after – was through an appeal to religion. The phrase 'in discharge of the Royal Conscience' was built into the preamble of every major law.

The Pyrenees, as we said earlier, were no barrier to ideas or men in the Middle Ages. The undercurrent of heterodoxy from southern France crossed into Aragon and Catalonia from time to time. Aragon provided one of the Avignon anti-popes, Benedict XIII, alias Pedro de Luna; and Valencia provided the man to whom, more than to any other single individual, credit is due for the ending of the Great Schism – St Vincent Ferrer, who preached penance and religious fervour throughout the length and breadth of Spain, and extensively in Italy, Switzerland, and France. From there, at Henry IV of England's invitation, he would have crossed the Channel but for the Hundred Years War. Ferrer died in 1418. In 1419 was born another great preacher and ascetic, St John of Sahagun, whose chief field of activity was the influential city and university of Salamanca. John was thirty-six when a renowned ex-professor of law at Lérida, an ailing man in his seventies, was elected Pope as Calixtus III. His pontificate lasted only three years, enough for him almost to succeed in organizing an international force against the Turks, and to incur the implacable hatred of the citizens of Rome by appointing to high office in civil and religious administration a plethora of Catalans and Valencians. Among them were two nephews, both of whom he made Cardinals, one only twenty-four years old. This was Rodrigo de Borja, who later, as Pope Alexander VI, drew the line of demarcation between the lands to be explored and Christianized by Spain and those by Portugal; a line subsequently used by the two countries as a basis for discussion and agreement on a new line of demarcation of conquest. That in consequence Brazil is Portuguese-speaking while the rest of South America is Spanish-speaking is irrelevant to modern Spain; but there are two other acts of Don Rodrigo which are highly relevant.

In 1472, still a Cardinal, Don Rodrigo went back briefly to Spain as Papal Legate. One of his tasks was to settle the civil war between Henry IV and the supporters of Isabel. His arrangement proved only a temporary truce; but what he did do was to regularize in marriage the existing liaison between Isabel and Ferdinand, a *sine qua non* of their subsequent acceptance as kings by the peoples of Castile and Aragon. On the same occasion Cardinal Rodrigo, who had been granted by the Pope plenary powers in church affairs, summoned to Segovia a Council of all the bishops of Castile and León, and, inveighing against the appointment of 'so many ignorant clergy', thereupon began the purification of the mediaeval Spanish Church of laxity and abuses. The Council went on to lay down rules for more careful training and selection of candidates to the priesthood. Three new universities were founded over the next ten years, at Sigüenza (1472), Zaragoza (1474), and Ávila (1482). The Council decreed heavy penalties for concubinage and other breaches of clerical discipline, and sought by rules to curb plurality of benefices, though this was difficult since so many of them were the perquisites of noblemen. In 1484 an extreme ascetic Franciscan friar, Ximénez de Cisneros, was recommended to Isabel as her confessor. Eight years later he became archbishop of Toledo. In this position his influence was far-reaching. He used the wealth of Toledo to found the world's finest university city, Alcalá, which within a few years came to have 3,000 students and to produce a masterpiece of scholarship, the Biblia Complutensis, or Polyglot Bible, whose Greek text was sounder than Erasmus' later version and whose Hebrew was not to be bettered for four centuries. Moreover, Alcalá was a foundation which inspired others, so that by 1620 Spain had no less than thirty-two universities with at least 50,000 students in them, a remarkable figure when Spain's population did not exceed 8 million. Cisneros carried out also a thorough reform of the conventual houses of his Order, expelling the hangers-on. He brought back the clergy of his own archdiocese to a strict discipline. He had to spend his advanced years in politics and he died with the work of reform uncompleted; but his example inspired others to complete it.

It was this reform from within, rather than action on the part of the Crown, which made Spaniards almost entirely unresponsive to the ideas of the Protestant reformers. Indeed, the Crown's attitude to reform and to the Church was equivocal.

Isabel expelled the non-Castilian Catholic clergy from her realms of Castile and León in 1480, twelve years before she turned on the Jews. In spite of Pope and clergy, Ferdinand placed his bastard Álvaro in the See of his capital Zaragoza when the child was six. As they began to reconquer Granada, the 'Catholic Kings' claimed that in effect they were refounding all the churches of the area and were therefore entitled to 'present', or nominate, men of their own choosing to vacant benefices. Threatening now military action, now schism, they wrested from the Pope the powers which came to be known as the *real patronato,* not over Granada alone but over the whole of Spain and Spanish America. The pressures on the Pope were kept up by Charles and Philip. By the end of the six-

teenth century the Crown had obtained an administrative control
of the Catholic Church throughout the Spanish dominions such as
even Henry VIII did not have as Head of the Church of England.
The king defined diocesan and even parish boundaries. No church
could be built without royal consent. All tithes went to the king's
treasury in the first place; they were reissued by the king only in
part as salaries. It paid the king, of course, to keep Sees vacant as
long as he could. Except during one brief period under Philip II,
the re-Christianization of the south was discouraged or even hind-
ered. Thus the people, especially in rural areas, threatened with
dire penalties if they dared to practise the Muslim religion yet at
the same time left uninstructed in Christianity, reverted to a semi-
paganism. Indeed, the foundations were thus laid for one of the
divisions of modern Spain, the Christian north and the anti-religious
yet superstitious south.

Isabel and the Habsburgs can be said to have reversed the
Augustinian principle that it was the duty of Christian princes to
protect their people : their acts can be seen to have been logical and
consistent only if we postulate that they believed it to be even more
the duty of a Christian people to protect the interests of the prince.

Isabel's own foundation, the Spanish Inquisition, was like the
older Roman Inquisition in that it was a Court of Inquiry to establish the validity of accusation levelled against an individual of
bigamy, extortion, false witness, *usuria*,[1] sodomy, or heterodoxy. It
differed, however, from the Roman Inquisition in that its members
were neither appointed nor dismissed by the Church but by the
Crown. It could be used, and was used, by the Crown for its own
ends as, notoriously for example, in the case of Antonio Pérez,
Philip's traitorous Secretary and possible rival in a love affair. How
many persons the Inquisition handed over to the 'secular arm' for
burning at the stake, as irredeemable heretics or sodomites, will
probably have to remain a subject for speculation rather than
factual statement till Doomsday : the first historian of the Inquisition, Llorente, destroyed most of the archives deliberately.[2] What

[1] The mediaeval word rather than the English derivative, usury, must be
used. The mediaeval mind distinguished between the loan to further commercial enterprise where 4, 14, or 40 per cent could be legitimate, depending
on the returns the enterprise produced, and the loan to a person for his
sustenance or that of his family in distress, where even half of 1 per cent was
held to be sinful.

[2] Independent of Llorente there is evidence of the burning of only fifty-
two Protestants during the second half of the sixteenth century; and of very
few thereafter. The Inquisition's record is far worse, though in detail
debatable, as persecutor and prosecutor of the pseudo-convert Jews. From
1544 and into the following century, the Inquisitors kept on discovering
alumbrados, pseudo-mystics who indulged in every form of sexual perversion.
Towards the end of his reign Philip abolished the death penalty for sodomy.

is no less to the point is that many of the Church's most orthodox
and leading figures also faced the tribunal : for example Carranza,
archbishop of Toledo and himself Inquisitor-General; Ignatius of
Loyola and Francis Borgia, two of the outstanding Spanish saints
of the sixteenth century.

Ignatius, wounded in battle for his king, chose to study in Paris
when Alcalá was at its zenith, to beg for alms in England when alms
were more readily given to students in Spain, and to establish
his famous Order in Rome, binding its members to a special vow
to obey the Pope, when the emperor of half of Europe and Spain
was doing his utmost to make the Pope his servant. At the Council
of Trent Carranza distinguished himself by defending the spiritual
rights of the Pope against the emperor. The Pope's principal
theologians were the two Spanish Jesuits Salmerón and Laínez, the
former possibly, the latter most certainly, Jewish by race.

Jesuits from the beginning of their history in 1540 were the most
insistent and consistent opponents of the erastianism of the Habsburgs. Suárez in his *De Legibus* destroyed all claims of the sovereign
to Divine Right. He condemned colonial wars. He and his fellow-
Jesuit Mariana put forward the theory that if a king became a
tyrant, the people could rightfully judge him, and if guilty, execute
him. Mariana argued that it was the duty of a Christian Head of
State to ensure the proper care of the unemployed and unemploy-
able, the sick, the widows, the orphans, and the old. He urged the
nationalization of land which was not properly exploited.

The Jesuits were certainly the foremost opponents of Divine
Right, but they were not the only ones to criticize the Crown. The
Dominican Las Casas is universally known for his account of the
earliest methods of Spanish colonization. He, however, concentrated only on the immorality of the methods. A whole school of
Dominican theologians at Salamanca, headed by Francisco de
Vitoria, condemned as immoral the very act of conquest. To
balance Vitoria and to dispute with him and his fellow Dominicans,
there was a whole corps of civil jurists, Ginés de Sepúlveda chief
among them, to justify colonialism and conquest. Charles V tried
to suppress the Dominicans' teaching.

Philip II, long furious that the Jesuits should have defied him by
electing the Jew Laínez as general of their Order in succession to
Ignatius, did his best to foment dissension within their ranks, and
over substantial periods prohibited the departure of their members
to the New World. He was won over to allowing them a measure
of liberty of movement only late in life by the celebrated Englishman Father Robert Persons. Indeed, he then went on to recom-
mend Ribadeneyra's anti-absolutist *Tratado del príncipe cristiano*

to his son and successor; and it was to the same Philip III that Mariana dedicated his *De Rege et Regis Institutione* with its argument that a people could judge and execute an unjust king.

As in other European countries, so also in Spain books were subject to censorship, but in Spain the censorship was twofold, of the Church and of the Crown. Nevertheless, both passed the works of Mariana and of Suárez. It was in France that *De Rege* and in England that Suárez's not dissimilar attack on the theory of Divine Right were publicly burnt. The Spanish church censorship was in fact most liberal. So long as it was not on Lutheran or Calvinistic lines, very wide theological speculation was permitted. At the end of the sixteenth century, for example, the Jesuit Luis de Molina put forward a theory of Free Will and Grace ('predestination') which the Dominican Domingo Bañez challenged. A debate in word and print ensued between the two Orders which rapidly degenerated into acrimony and abuse, the Dominicans calling the Jesuits Pelagians and the Jesuits replying that the Dominicans were Calvinists. A papal commission found both Jesuit and Dominican doctrines tenable and forbade further insults. The Spanish Inquisition accepted the commission's findings on this occasion, but it did not always follow Rome. Indeed, the censorship was strictest where the document or book had a Roman *Imprimatur* : and the closest scrutiny of all was reserved for papal Bulls.[3] On the other hand, the Inquisition gave full rein to books on the natural sciences, the teaching of the Copernican theory being allowed a full hundred years earlier than in the Protestant North. Again satire of all aspects of life and customs flourished, and the censors were not oversqueamish. Literary merit could excuse realism bordering on obscenity.

Censorship or no, almost as many books were written between 1500 and 1650 in Spain as in the rest of Europe put together. It was between these dates that the greatest masterpieces of Spanish literature, painting, and music were produced, and there was deep religious fervour behind most of them. Human passions were strong, but so was the will to bring them under control, or to sublimate them. Men failed but strove again, and if the man was a poet like Lope de Vega, the struggle produced great poetry.

The Spanish reaction to the Lutheran dogma that faith alone mattered turned Spaniards towards good works. Hospitals, hospices, and orphanages multiplied (after theology, medicine became the most popular discipline in the universities). Men and women in tens of thousands sought to work for their fellow men. The number

---

[3] There were several Bulls prohibiting bull-fighting, one at least excommunicating the prince who allowed them to take place in his realm.

of conventual houses and their inmates has been grossly exaggerated, but certainly a large proportion of the population sought to
dedicate their whole lives to God, some by learning, some in
asceticism and contemplation leading to mysticism, some in more
practical ways. All social classes were affected with this religious
fervour. Among the men renowned for their virtue, Paschal Baylon
was a shepherd and Francis Borgia resigned a dukedom. The
notorious princess of Eboli was a Mendoza, but so was Doña Luisa
de Carvajal who gave all her money to help found a college for
Englishmen in exile; then herself journeyed to England to help
her co-religionists imprisoned in the Tower and other London
prisons. Nevertheless, religious fervour was not uniform. It was
from the north generally rather than the south that the men and
women of learning, good works, and piety came, though there
were notable exceptions: from the smaller provincial towns rather
than the large cities, and from those farther from rather than
nearer to the court. The court was pious towards the end of Philip
II's reign and for a time continued so under his son, but later it
became profligate under Philip IV (1621–65) who is said to have
fathered thirty bastards, yet left only a poor half-wit of a monster
to succeed him as Charles II.

It was now, a century and a half after Luther had nailed his
declaration, that religious fervour began to wane among Spaniards.
With their *real patronato,* their power to choose the holders of
bishoprics and other high offices, the Habsburgs had by no means
always avoided 'troublesome priests', but they had constantly kept
dioceses without a leader for long periods. The leaders when
appointed had on the whole been men worthy enough in their
private lives, but most of them were men who had set out to be
appointed by first making themselves known and trusted by the
Crown; and thus after appointment felt qualms of disloyalty if
they attacked the Crown's abuses too severely.

This lack of fervour at the top began to permeate down to
parish priest level. The economic bankruptcy of Spain started also
to have its effect on university attendance. From the start Spanish
universities had been open to all irrespective of means, but the
penniless scholar now began to find fewer alms-givers and patrons.
By the end of the seventeenth century the university population
was down to about 20,000.

Perhaps because of the dispute on Free Will at the turn of the
century, the number of original writers on theology in Spain
declined from, say, 1650 onwards. The one original work was the
Spiritual Guide written by a Spanish priest, Molinos. It established
the movement, of more importance in Rome and France than in

Spain, which is called Quietism, and which has been aptly described as 'a morbid growth on the healthy body of mysticism'. In
literature also inspiration began to flag. Calderón lived until 1680,
but he was out of his time. More typical was the discontented Jesuit
Gracián whose novel trilogy *El Criticón* was in time greatly to
influence Schopenhauer and Nietzsche. So as the seventeenth century drew to a close, Catholicism in Spain was noticeably weaker
than it had been even fifty years earlier. In the eighteenth century
it was to face a severe trial.

Chapter 12

Political Developments 1492–1701

IN NOVEMBER 1700 the Habsburg Charles II died childless, as had long been expected. As his end approached, he had willed all his kingdoms in Europe and overseas to his great-nephew Philip of Anjou, the second grandchild of his elder sister Maria Theresa. In 1701 the Bourbon Philip arrived in Spain to ascend the throne as Philip V of Spain and the Spanish dominions.

Philip's accession did not suit the commercial interests of Britain or Holland, nor the pride of the House of Austria. His grandfather was the still belligerent and active Louis XIV of France. It was not inconceivable that Philip might inherit France as well as Spain at a time when the economies of France and the Spanish empire were complementary.

There was also a strong legal argument against Philip's accession : in marrying Louis XIV, Maria Theresa had renounced all claims to Spain on her own behalf and that of any children she might have. Legally the man with the strongest claim was the Emperor Leopold I, Charles II's cousin and husband of his younger sister Margaret; but as Britain and Holland were as opposed to a reunion of the Habsburg empire and Spain as they were to the union of France and Spain, the emperor had passed his claim to his second son, the Archduke Charles.

Louis, though he had entered into treaties with Britain and the emperor to partition Spain and her dominions, now decided to accept the will of Charles II and support his grandson. In September 1701, Britain, Holland, and Austria declared war on Philip and Louis.

Blenheim, Ramillies, Oudenarde, and Malplaquet have no direct relevance to Spanish history. Those Churchillian victories won for Britain a place at the conference in 1713 which led to the Treaty and Peace of Utrecht. There, Britain achieved the ends for which she had gone to war – important trading rights with Spain and the New World, and the monopoly of the slave trade, and for good measure the possession of Gibraltar (and of Minorca) to make her a Mediterranean power. She also obtained from France New-foundland and Nova Scotia. The Archduke Charles, who had succeeded his father on the imperial throne, was given Spanish Naples, Sardinia, the duchy of Milan, and the Netherlands, and the duke of Savoy, a minor figure in the conflict, was handed Spanish Sicily. Spain gained nothing – unless the loss of the Netherlands, the retention of which had cost her so dearly over so long a period, could be called a gain. Philip V remained King of Spain and the Spanish dominions overseas.

Yet the war and its outcome was a turning-point of Spanish history. The armed struggle between the Grand Alliance and the Bourbons over Spain also involved a complex civil war in Spain, and afforded an opportunity for the eventual victor to effect a revolution under the camouflage of war, a revolution which, like so many others, had been preceded by a long period of mental gestation.

To this civil war there were three important aspects : legalistic, centrifugal, and religious.

Sides were taken on legalistic grounds by Spaniards according to whether they took the view that the will of a dying king had greater or lesser value in law than other traditional practices and theories, such as those of primogeniture and of acceptance by the people.

It was as no scholastic exercise that Suárez, Ribadeneyra, and Mariana insisted at the end of the sixteenth and beginning of the seventeenth centuries that the king had no authority save that given him by the people. Elizabeth of England and her successor, James, were claiming a Divine Right to rule. So also, though as yet not quite as blatantly, was the King of France. Yet what the Jesuits had principally in mind was not the ideas of British or French monarchs but contemporary trends in Spain itself. The Habsburgs of Spain theoretically rejected all claim to Divine Right, but in practice they had established the machinery of autocracy, and it was this which worried the philosophers.

Except in the north and east the people had been deprived of even the limited means they had once had to make their will known. Isabel had begun the process in Castile. The *Cortes* of that realm, once they had acknowledged her as queen, had been ignored. She had set up Councils to administer the country. She had nominated their members and they had been responsible to her alone. Charles V, in his search for money to satisfy importunate foreign creditors, had had cause to summon the *Cortes* more frequently than his grandmother, but he had ousted from them the *labradores,* the tillers of the land, and the *hidalgo procuradores,* members from the towns, had come to be for the most part men of his own ennoblement. Philip II had developed conciliar government, and by establishing a Council of State (*Consejo de Estado*) over the lesser

Councils, had further centralized effective power in the Crown. The Council was responsible to him alone. Its task was to advise him so that he could arrive at just decisions, and Philip did have a passion for social justice and for protecting the poor against the oppressor, the would-be oppressors being the nobles. Now given a king who took it upon himself to listen at length to advice from all sides and personally minutely to examine every problem before coming to a decision, the system had worked reasonably well, and soon after its establishment there had arisen within the Council two parties which could loosely be described as liberal and conservative. Philip would agree now with the duke of Alba, the leader of one party, and now with the prince of Eboli, the leader of the other, a concession to one being balanced by a corresponding concession to the other. While this situation existed, neither side did nor could achieve power, and the king was the champion of the people against both. He left the Basques, the Navarrese, the Catalans, and the Portuguese with their own laws and liberties; if he moved against the *Cortes* of Aragon, he did so because the Aragonese *fueros* were rather privileges for noblemen. The better to maintain contact between the people and himself, he appointed over each of his kingdoms, other than Castile, a viceroy charged with the duty to attend to regional needs. On the whole his choice of viceroys was excellent : many of them were men of great virtue. Nevertheless, what if a weakling should succeed Philip II, and an unprincipled nobleman make use of the machinery?

It was against the dangers inherent in this personalized and centralized system that the Jesuits wrote down what they considered the nature of authority to be and what they deduced should be the principles of government. Ironically it was in France and Britain and not in Spain that new constitutional structures akin to those principles were in time to develop. The dangers became reality in Spain in the very lifetime of Mariana. On the death of Philip II power passed not to his son but to the man with the dominant personality in the Council, the duke of Lerma. Lerma replaced opponents in the Council and among the viceroys with get-rich-quick noblemen like himself in character. He sent Mariana to prison for proving that his devaluation of the currency was nothing but a fraud on the poor. Philip IV on his accession was no more interested in ruling and governing than his father had been. He left that to the count-duke of Olivares. Olivares, seeing Castile already ruined industrially and economically, had to seek elsewhere for his personal fortune and the funds which he needed to indulge in war by which he could hope to present himself as the Defender of Spain.

The most promising area of Spain was the east coast. Valencia, still enjoying a degree of autonomy, had pleaded economic ruin after the expulsion of the Moriscos, and had escaped giving Castile tribute in any quantity for a generation. Catalonia's autonomy had also cushioned her. In 1640 Olivares demanded men and money from both. Threats that if the *Cortes* did not provide them, he would send armies to get them, intimidated the *Cortes* of Valencia, but not that of Catalonia, which pleaded exemption on the grounds that Catalonia was making a full contribution to the defence of Spain in defending herself against the encroachments of Louis XIII. In 1639 she had successfully beaten off an invasion force sent into Roussillon by Richelieu. Olivares, infuriated by the Catalan refusal and determined to establish that the command of the Crown was law, *Cortes* or no *Cortes,* sent Castilian troops to occupy Catalonia. He ordered the viceroy to 'spare no force, no matter how they cry against you'. In their despair the Catalans sought help from France. Catalonia now became the pit of nineteen years of war – beyond the deaths of Louis, Richelieu, and Olivares; but the Catalans discovered too late that the French were no less their enemies than the Spaniards. When eventually they were left in peace by Paris and Madrid, they had to surrender Roussillon to Paris and their fortresses to Madrid. As an army of occupation the Castilians came to be hated by the Catalans, as the English were by the Irish. It would be an exaggeration to say that Olivares and Philip IV were to Catalonia what Cromwell and William of Orange were to Ireland, for the Castilians were never as thorough in their oppression; there was no Drogheda or Limerick; nor were there religious differences to inspire atrocities. But with the generation of bitter war to separate them and the subsequent occupation, there was never again to be true peace between Barcelona and Madrid. Thus the deep wedge driven by Olivares between Catalonia and Castile proved to be the centrifugal aspect of the civil war which took place concurrently with the War of the Spanish Succession.

The likelihood from the moment of Charles II's accession that sooner or later a Bourbon would ascend the throne of Spain was a source of worry to a large body of Spaniards no less than to the rulers of northern Europe. This body was made up of well-informed churchmen. Gallicanism was then a growing force, and the French king, as its chief beneficiary, was its principal upholder. To Spanish churchmen in general the doctrine that a king had full power to do with the Church as he saw fit and was above any law of the Church was unacceptable; the Spanish *real patronato* was very much a lesser evil, for it did not claim quite so much. But by 1680, when it had become obvious that Charles II could have no direct heir, the situation had become confused. Even some French Jesuits, originally the staunchest opponents of Gallicanism, seemed to have compromised with it. They had come to consider Jansenism the greater immediate danger, and they had, as it were, done a 'package deal' with Louis XIV : if he showed disfavour towards the Jansenists, the Jesuits would not press the anti-Gallican arguments. Little was understood in Spain of the complexities of Port Royal : the names of Madame Guillon and Pascal were hardly known. What Spanish churchmen could not understand was how His Most Christian Majesty could have allowed the publication of such a book as Pierre Bayle's *Dictionnaire Historique et Critique* with its theory that truth was divisible and that religion was not compatible with reason. The prospect of a French king was therefore far from heartening : but presumably the Bourbons could be accepted, for otherwise the Papacy would have excommunicated them.

In the event the Spanish clergy and people (as yet still one) accepted Philip of Anjou as king. Philip took the trouble to summon the *Cortes,* though not so much to ratify his accession as to inform them that he had acceded. Gallicanism under the name of Regalism acquired adherents in Spain itself. Then there was a reaction. Philip proceeded to replace the Spaniards in the Council with Frenchmen : inherent in a belief in Regalism was a contempt for Spanish ideas and ideals. Such was the situation when England and Holland decided that it was not in their best commercial interests to have a Frenchman on the throne of Spain, and joined the emperor who believed that his grandson Charles had as good a claim to the Spanish throne as Philip of Anjou.

For Catalonia there was no problem as to which side should be backed. The emperor had come to the aid of the Catalans as recently as 1695 when the French had invaded their lands yet again. The leader of the imperial force, Prince George of Darmstadt, had in effect rescued Catalonia and thereby become a local hero. Charles II, grateful and at the same time anxious to conciliate Catalan opinion, had allowed him to remain in Catalonia as viceroy. The Archduke Charles now promised to restore Catalonia's lost autonomy. Every nation, theologians had said from Vitoria onwards, had the right to independence, and Catalonia was a nation.

For the other peoples of Spain there was no clear moral answer to the question which side to back. Nominally *Cortes* of a sort had ratified the accession, but had *the people* done so? If the answer was no, then Philip was in essence a tyrant, and to rise against him was legitimate; but if yes, then Philip had a right to rule until he should prove himself a tyrant by his acts. Now supposing that Philip was a usurper, would greater good or greater evil result from his substitution by the Archduke Charles? The emperor had as allies Britain and Holland, popularly credited with a catalogue of atrocities on the high seas against Catholic missionaries on their way to the Americas and the East. As against this, France was the hotbed of Jansenism and Regalism, doctrines as odious as those upheld by the British and Dutch Protestants.

Chapter 13

Spain in the War of the Spanish Succession

In NOVEMBER 1705 a British naval force landed in Barcelona as part of an imperial army with the Archduke Charles at the head. Catalans flocked to the archduke's standard, as did Aragonese and Valencians. Pope Clement XI recognized him as King of Spain. Shortly afterwards an Anglo-Dutch-Portuguese army crossed the Tagus at Alcántara and swept eastwards to capture Madrid with remarkable ease. The people of Castile did not interfere. The news of the Pope's recognition had, of course, been kept from them. What they now heard instead were the details of the behaviour of the British sailors after their capture of Gibraltar in 1704. The British admiral had allowed the inhabitants to move out, but the sailors had destroyed the much-revered shrine of Our Lady of Europe; that shocked Spaniards far more than the slaughter of the inhabitants would have done. The invasion force in their midst did violence to Spanish ideals. Who then had right on his side? The Pope supported the archduke, but the archduke had evil men as allies.

Ironically it was an Englishman who came to the rescue of the Castilians, the duke of Berwick, the exiled bastard of the English James II, who commanded an army of French infantry and Spanish cavalry. At Almansa, on 25 April 1707, he defeated the combined British, Dutch, Portuguese, and imperial forces and re-captured Madrid, Aragon, and Valencia for Philip. Then the tide of war changed again : a new British invasion force crossed into Castile from Portugal and again took Madrid. This time, however, the British commander, Stanhope, reported : 'We are not masters in Castile of more ground than we encamp on'. The population was hostile and fought the invaders in its own way. In December 1710 a Franco-Spanish army led by a Frenchman, Vendôme, forced Stanhope to surrender, and Charles was once more reduced to Catalonia. Three more years of confused fighting produced no change. A new Tory government in England then saw greater commercial advantages in peace with France than in further war, and began to negotiate with France secretly. Charles fought on, but when the French defeated his surviving ally, the Dutch, and his own troops in northern Europe, he had to withdraw his forces from Spain – on British ships. Catalonia's refusal to surrender meant that she could expect no quarter from Philip.

After Almansa Philip decreed the abolition of the separate legal and administrative systems of Aragon, Valencia, and Catalonia. For the first time they were required to pay tribute to Madrid. That, however, was not the whole story. The abolition of the treasuries of Aragon and Valencia was only part of a series of economic reforms which the Frenchman Orry, whom Philip had brought with him in 1701, devised to increase productivity so that the sovereign could levy heavier taxes. He and Macanaz, a Spaniard more Regalist than any Frenchman, also placed before the king a plan to despoil the Church which they insisted was not only wealthy but also the chief obstacle to the progress of absolutism. A part of this plan was deliberately to reduce the number of priests : in future the king would determine how many were to be ordained. The king accepted the plan, dismissing from his Council of State all who opposed it, and thus raised Macanaz from humble office to be the destroyer of the last remnants of Aragonese and Valencian autonomy. Macanaz went ahead with such Regalist zeal that the archbishop of Valencia excommunicated him.

Religious belief and separatist sentiments accordingly now combined in Catalonia to yield yet another example of Numantian tenacity in desperate circumstances. Philip organized his army on French professional lines, and the Catalans were no match for it in the field. Hard-pressed and defeated they fell back on their capital, Barcelona, to be besieged by 40,000 Frenchmen and Castilians. At Utrecht Britain, somewhat conscience-striken over her desertion of the Catalans, had promised to save them from the vengeance of Philip and had had built into the treaty a guarantee of the Catalans' rights. But far from helping Catalonia, she now sent ships to help Philip, and in September 1714, thirteen months after the beginning of the siege, Barcelona fell. Catalonia was heavily punished.

Chapter 14

The Wars of the Bourbons 1717–83

UTRECHT DID NOT USHER IN a long period of peace for Spain. The Bourbons squandered Spain's wealth in war as prodigally as the Habsburgs had done. Philip was like his more recent Habsburg predecessors in being a victim of mental illness and like them, too, in his desire to exercise nominal rule over as large a part of the Old and New Worlds as possible, while leaving all real authority to women or Ministers. Until 1714 the real ruler of Spain was the very pro-French princesse des Ursins, lady-in-waiting to Philip's wife, Marie Louise of Savoy. In 1714 Marie Louise died, and Alberoni, the Italian priest who represented the duke of Parma at Philip's court, suggested that Philip should marry his master's niece, Elizabeth Farnese. As she was reputed to be the quintessence of docility, 'a good healthy girl accustomed to hear of nothing but needlework and embroidery', the princesse des Ursins and her henchman, Orry, readily accepted the suggestion. Once married, Elizabeth as queen proved the very opposite of her reputation. She ousted the princess and replaced Orry with Alberoni. In 1717 the Pope, glad to see this enemy of the Church out of office, granted Elizabeth her request to give Alberoni a Cardinal's hat in the hope that the Orry-Macanaz plan to bring the Church under the royal heel might be rescinded. Elizabeth, however, had more urgent plans for Alberoni : she now had a son by Philip, a son with no prospects unless Alberoni created them. She prevailed upon him to despatch a Spanish fleet to take Sardinia from Austria. It was successful and so the next year Alberoni sought to retake Sicily from Savoy for Spain. Britain now reacted against such a show of Spanish naval power, and France likewise against the attack on her ally, Savoy. A British fleet, under Admiral Byng, destroyed the Spanish force off Sicily, and for good measure British troops sacked Vigo, Pontevedra, and much of Galicia. French troops overran the Basque provinces and Catalonia. Though Alberoni fell in consequence, nevertheless, by the terms of a peace signed in 1720, Elizabeth was promised the duchies of Tuscany and Parma for her son, Prince Charles. The people of Spain again gained nothing by war.

In January 1724 Philip, in one of his bouts of melancholia,

abdicated in favour of Luis, his elder son by his first wife. Luis, however, died of smallpox five months later and Elizabeth put her husband back on the throne. She now had a second son; and in Alberoni's place a Dutch Protestant-turned-Catholic, Riperdá. This new favourite was despatched to Vienna to obtain from the emperor for her elder son Charles the promise of the hand of his daughter and heir presumptive, Maria Theresa, with all the Habsburg possessions outside Italy, and for her younger son, Philip, the hand of his second daughter with all the Habsburg possessions in Italy. Popular reaction against the agreement and the war it might provoke would have been overwhelmingly unfavourable but for one supplementary point – the Emperor Charles VI was to help Spain to recover Gibraltar. In the event, however, Elizabeth caught out Riperdá in boasts and lies and dismissed him (he ended up, a convert Muslim, in Morocco), while the emperor, seeing all Europe prepared to oppose the marriage of his daughters to young men both so close in succession to the throne of Spain, himself quietly forgot his promises. Philip, however, ordered the siege of Gibraltar in a bid to regain the support of the people, but the siege failed. By the subsequent treaties of Seville and Vienna (November 1729 and July 1731), Elizabeth gained the assent of England, France, Holland, and Austria to the accession of Prince Charles to the duchies of Parma and Piacenza.

The emperor's failure to help Spain in the siege incurred Spanish anger. Elizabeth, for her part, was furious with the emperor when he failed to ratify his assent to Charles's title of duke of Parma and Piacenza, and she now turned to France for support. In 1733 the Bourbons of France and Spain entered into a *Pacte de Famille,* which enabled Charles to overrun, with the help of the Spanish fleet, the kingdoms of Naples and Sicily, and to keep them. The next war was of brief duration, and for once it was not of the Bourbons' making. In 1738 an English sea captain, Jenkins, returned to England, having had one ear cut off by the Spaniards for acts of piracy in the Spanish Main, and in 1739 England declared war on Spain. Honour was settled when an English assault on Cartagena and a Spanish one on Gibraltar both failed. Elizabeth, however, next involved Spain in the War of the Austrian Succession, which broke out in 1740, by advancing her husband's claim to the imperial throne. She sent Spanish armies into northern Italy on the side of the Protestant Frederick of Prussia and of France after renewing in 1743 the *Pacte de Famille*. At the subsequent peace of Aix-la-Chapelle, in 1748, she got Parma and Piacenza definitely for her younger son Philip, Charles keeping the Sicilies.

Philip V died in 1746 and Elizabeth's second step-son ascended the throne as Ferdinand VI. Ferdinand's wife, Bárbara of Braganza, believed that Spain should disentangle herself from European politics, as did Zenón de Somodevilla y Bengoechea, who had been created marquis de la Ensenada in 1736 for his organization of the navy with which Naples and Sicily had been acquired for Charles. Now Minister of War, Navy, Treasury, and the Indies, he addressed a long memorandum proposing a reform of Orry's earlier reform of taxation. Orry had so successfully organized the depredation of the Church and the taxation of such essentials as salt, that of Spain's 7½ million inhabitants, who would have been fewer but for a ban on emigration, 2 million were on starvation level. Hundreds of thousands of hectares of first-class land were uncultivated. Valencia had a textile industry which was flourishing, but this was only because it was geared principally to the needs of war and because the Catalan industry had been destroyed after 1714. Ensenada suggested the taxation of inessentials, such as tobacco, and the taxation of church property 'according to justice' and not with destruction as its end. (The battle between Church and state had by 1737 reached such a pitch that the Pope had been constrained to negotiate a Concordat, in the hope that the king would bind himself to respect some limit to his Regalism.) Ensenada also proposed free trade within Spain and measures to improve agriculture, especially beef-cattle farming, even at the expense of the *Mesta* whose thirty-metre wide sheep-runs still vitiated commonsense.

When peace came in 1748 Ensenada became Finance Minister Extraordinary. As a start to reform he determined on a *catastro*, a census of the life and wealth of the country, which was to run into 150 volumes and was to show Spain as a relatively poor but potentially wealthier country. He persuaded Ferdinand VI to end tax-farming, but the salt tax remained. Ferdinand would accept no reduction in the exercise of his personal power over the Church, and a new Concordat in 1752 gave the Crown control of the appointment to vacancies in all but a few benefices and the sanction to direct to the Treasury more of the Church's income. Little else that Ensenada proposed was carried out, for he saw as imminent a trial of strength between France and England in America and the Far East, and this he reckoned could be of profit, or a danger, to Spain according to how Spain intervened; and he was more prepared to trust France than Britain. To balance his views, however, there was at court a pro-British party whose leader, an Hispano-Irishman, Ricardo Wall, brought forward charges in 1754 that Ensenada was secretly negotiating with the French, charges which led to Ensenada's exile.

The Seven Years War should have been the first major European conflict for 250 years in which Spain should not have been involved. Ferdinand did his best. He refused to allow his fifty-six Ships of the Line which Ensenada had bequeathed him either to support the French (though in 1756 they offered him Minorca, momentarily in French hands), or to support the British in 1757, while Pitt the Elder dangled Gibraltar as a bait. Bárbara, however, died in 1758 and her husband, who dearly loved her, followed her in 1759. As they were childless, Elizabeth Farnese's elder son Charles, King of Naples and Sicily, succeeded.

Charles resigned his Italian thrones to his third son (his first was mad, and his second was now his heir to the greater kingdom of Spain), and then hastened to Madrid with a former Neapolitan shopkeeper who was his favourite, Squillaci. He negotiated a new *Pacte de Famille,* and, in high-handed fashion, declared war on Portugal in 1762. Britain hastened to Portugal's aid. British fleets captured Havana and Manila and Charles was lucky to get out of the war in 1763 with the loss of only a few Caribbean islands and Florida. France then presented Spain with Louisiana to ensure Charles III's loyalty to the *Pacte de Famille,* Choiseul, the French Chief Minister, persuading him that France and Spain together could conquer the world as soon as the economies of both countries had recovered from the recent war. To this end taxation was momentarily eased in Spain, especially as it affected agriculture. The opportunity for both countries to attack Britain came in 1779, for Spain, like France, supported the North American revolt against the government of George III. She recovered Florida and Minorca (now back in English hands), but her long siege of Gibraltar was fruitless. At Versailles in 1783 Britain officially ceded what she had lost in the war (and which she had won from Spain earlier), and Spain by inference agreed to the continued possession of Gibraltar by Britain.[1] Between 1717 and 1783 Spain had been at war on behalf of the Bourbons for over forty years.

[1] To Britain's *possession* but not *sovereignty* over: Charles III continued to call himself King of Gibraltar in all official documents.

Chapter 15

The Creation of the 'Two Spains'

CHARLES III IS NOT REMEMBERED by the Spaniard of today because he dragged Spain into the Seven Years War. So many other kings of Spain placed their own ambitions above those of the people over whom they reigned. Nor do Spanish history books stress the support he gave the nascent United States of America. To do so would be to absolve Britain, at least in part, from perfidy in the role she played a generation later in the creation of the disunited states of Spanish America. Rather it is for his internal policy that he is applauded by some Spaniards and vituperated by others.

Charles III, or rather a group of Ministers and civil servants whom he trusted, made yet another attempt to establish Spain as one administrative unit as France was, and to carry out such changes in agriculture, education, and religion as were necessary to that end. Spain was to be regenerated by the introduction of *luces,* enlightened ideas.

Philip V had succeeded in destroying the autonomy of Catalonia, Valencia, and Aragon, but the Basque provinces, Guipúzcoa, Vizcaya, Álava, and Navarre, had given him no excuse for action. Navarre had a viceroy, but government was in the hands of an elective body, the Provincial Deputation, while the other provinces also each had their own general assemblies. Madrid's laws and demands stopped at their frontiers. They paid tribute to Madrid, but they were exempt from conscription, taxation, and other dues. Charles III's Ministers now sought to put an end to this autonomy.

They tried hard without open warfare, but in the event the Basque provinces and Navarre succeeded in thwarting almost completely the attempts of the centre to destroy their autonomy. *Cortes* said to be representative of the whole country assembled in Madrid in 1760, but Navarre held its own *Cortes* in 1767. This area of Spain was thus largely to escape the changes effected elsewhere.

The agricultural reform proposed was complicated, but its underlying principle was that unemployed town-dwellers were to be given land which was not being cultivated. Some was scrubland, deserted during the seventeenth-century decline of the rural population. Much was land unused only in the sense that it was not tilled :

land held in mortmain, that is to say belonging to corporate bodies such as the religious Orders or to town and village councils, and thus in effect common land. In 1765 Campomanes, the Minister of Finance, supplied the king with a politico-philosophic-moral justification for the suppression of monasteries and the appropriation of land held in mortmain. Some of the common lands were expropriated from 1770 onwards and became the property of already large landowners. Almost the only successful colonization was that of some 6,000 Germans and Dutch in the Sierra Morena. The evils of *latifundia*, of insecurity of tenancy, of scrub pastures in Andalusia and Extremadura which irrigation could have made fertile, and the existence of hundreds of thousands of labourers unemployed except for a few weeks in the year were to continue until another age.

The reform of education and religion (the two inextricably mixed) was more thorough. Such had been the decline of education in the second half of the seventeenth century, that most of the *colegios mayores* (the university colleges of the Oxford-Cambridge type) had closed. The situation in Salamanca was typical. Where in its heyday, the middle of the sixteenth century, it had had 8,000 students, by the year 1700 there were only 2,000, and where there had been 200 tutors and professors in mathematics now there were none. The once great library of scientific works had been destroyed in a fire and no attempt had been made to replace it. Theology, philosophy, medicine, canon and civil law no longer occupied that order of importance. Such students as there were were mostly of canon or civil law, some of the well-to-do hoping for government posts or fat benefices. Philip V had had no use for the universities other than to provide him with lawyers to combat with legal argument the opponents of Regalism, and by the end of his reign, Salamanca had further declined to a mere 1,500 students. He had had the seven universities in Catalonia suppressed after his victory over Barcelona. The college he had founded at Cervera to take their place was small and limited to his loyal upper class. In Madrid he had established a College of Nobles to a French pattern. To similar patterns, he had had organized a National Library (1712) and a Royal Academy of Language (1713). The foundation of other learned academies had followed, open only to men of ability to whom the king showed favour because they showed him goodwill. Works of great erudition, and limited practical value, emanated from them in plenty, but they were mainly imitations of French models.

By the time of the accession of Charles III Spain was culturally French. There was little poetry, theatre, or fiction not subservient to the French fashion of the time. Lope de Vega and even Calderón had been understood and loved by the people. The new writers wrote for the court and intellectual coteries. Almost the only writer of originality of the time was a Benedictine, Benito Jerónimo Feijoó, a man of erudition as befitted the time and a prolific writer, yet possessed of an acute sense of humour, an enemy of superstition whether under the cloak of religion or of science who urged men to seek the truth. Out of context his works would provide quotations in plenty for a class of society which could not distinguish as he did between religion and superstition.

The Church still remained the one profession through which a man of humble origin might aspire to enter the circles of the wealthy – always provided that he accepted Regalist theory and practice. Up to the middle of the eighteenth century the Regalists had for the most part been men whose deviation from orthodox Catholicism consisted only in their substitution of the king for the Pope in church government. Thereafter, however, a new kind of Regalist, increasingly numerous, believed in the monarchy but not in religion. Nevertheless he considered religion necessary to keep the masses in their place. If the state could control the bishops, the bishops would control their clergy and the clergy the people. During the last three decades of the century there was yet a third type of Regalist – one who believed in the necessity of a king in society at that juncture of national development but not in the immutability of the institution of kingship. Squillaci and Campomanes were examples of the second group. The most notable of the third group was Pedro Pablo Abarca y Bolea, tenth count of Aranda.

Aranda was originally an army officer. In 1753, at the age of forty-five, he reached the top of his profession as Captain-General of the new Spanish regular army which had been created to the contemporary French model. He had then turned to politics. As a young man he had become a Freemason and in that capacity, or in carrying out one or other of the diplomatic missions with which he had been trusted, he had established a very close friendship with Voltaire, D'Alembert, and Raynald, then collaborating with Diderot. He read Montesquieu and shared Voltaire's vague deism and implacable hatred of all religion and of *l'infame,* the infamous beast of Rome in particular. As a good general, Aranda appreciated that an international Church could not be destroyed by a total frontal attack. The most active forces of the Church Militant and the most formidable opponents of Regalism were the Jesuits. As schoolmasters and professors in universities and other seats of learning (including Philip's Cervera) and seminaries, they had a powerful influence on the ideas held by churchmen and laymen both in Spain and in the New World. Jesuit mathematicians, physicists, and other scientists gave the lie direct to the contention of the French and Spanish followers of Voltaire that religion was in essence obscurantist and anti-progressive. Aranda in Spain saw with Voltaire in France that if the Church were deprived of this body of several thousand learned men, who somehow always reconciled the findings of scientific research and Christianity, the field would be clear for the new philosophy. Future generations of the secular clergy would be even less well instructed; society would be ruled by an élite of Voltairists; the end of the Church could be foreseen; but Aranda could not act without the king's authority.

It was easy to present the Jesuits as the enemies of Regalism, and even by quotation out of context, of kingship. The Jesuits had also established in the area of the Paraguay river a number of colonies of natives which were a living offence against the universality of the king's law. There they exercised a tutelage over 100,000 Guaranies in twenty townships by the rivers Paraná and Paraguay from which all Spanish traders were rigorously excluded. Each settlement was almost a Plato's Republic in practice, and much admired by the representatives of the Spanish Crown who visited them; but that was the scandal. Bourbon Spain was no Plato's Republic and the king's representative should not have admired what differed from that which Charles III decreed as uniquely right for all his subjects. Moreover, the Jesuits were popular. They had schools not only for the well-to-do, but for artisans and the poor. Aranda appreciated that premature action against them could ignite a popular revolt against himself and he knew that Charles III would not hesitate to save himself at the expense of a Minister. He bided his time while circulating rumours that the Jesuits were amassing fortunes in Paraguay and setting up an independent state there, and in Spain plotting against the king and justifying the plots on the grounds that he was a bastard.

In 1766 Squillaci issued an edict forbidding the wearing of the Spanish cloak, which had become a symbol of protest against French influence at court. Riots which assumed almost revolutionary proportions broke out as the edict was promulgated. Aranda suppressed them, Charles revoked the edict, and Squillaci was dismissed, but not before considerable damage had been done to shops and bourgeois property by the mobs. Aranda seized his opportunity and accused the Jesuits of being the instigators of the riots. In 1767 he put before the king a new edict and explained the strict security precautions which would be taken on the eve of its simultaneous publication throughout the Spanish empire. The Jesuits

were summarily to be expelled from all the Spanish dominions –
1,500 from Spain and 1,800 from Spanish America – and their
property confiscated. The army would be deployed to deal drastically with any show of disapproval of the royal sanction. The Jesuits
left meekly. The army had to act in some cities against the people.

There were members of the royally-appointed hierarchy who
praised Charles III, and there were members of some religious
Orders who wholeheartedly approved, if only because they assumed
that what had been Jesuit property and offices would be distributed
among them. In the long term they were to be sorry for their
attitude. The expulsion was only the first objective in a deliberate
plan, following Voltaire's slogan 'écrasez l'infame', to destroy the
Church – the enemy, as Aranda saw it, of human happiness in this
world.

It was the central tenet of the new philosophy that men should
seek to be happy in *this* world whether or not there was a next.
Only a few Spanish Voltairists followed their master in upholding
that 'la véritable sagesse est de savoir fuir la tristesse dans les bras
de la volupté' : but all agreed that a greater number of men
should have the means to be happy in this world – more men
should have wealth and a reserve of wealth in order to enjoy life.
To that end they preached revolution, a revolution from above,
maintaining that it was the duty of the king, his Ministers, and
the enlightened to encourage all human activity calculated to
produce more wealth, and to suppress all that did not. Accordingly,
during the last three decades of the century, great impetus was
given to the study of mathematics and physics, mining and agricultural methods. In 1795 a fifty-one-year old poet and playwright
turned agriculturist, jurist, politician, and avid student of Adam
Smith's *The Wealth of Nations*, Gaspar Melchor de Jovellanos,
published his conclusions on the ideal structure of Spain's agricultural economy, a work which continued to inspire advocates of land
reform into the second half of the twentieth century.

The state took over what remained of the once great mediaeval
universities. The study of Duns Scotus, Aquinas, and Suárez was
forbidden. Calderón was ruled jesuitical and performance of his
plays was banned. The arts had to have 'a social purpose'. Goya
was encouraged to portray as happy the industrious, especially the
lower classes at work and at play (after a hard day's work), and
as contemptible the beggars, mendicant friars, and priests. Aranda
and his followers quite logically considered that hospitals for the
poor, hospices, and soup-kitchens were grossly anti-social. By providing the poor with the means to assuage hunger, the religious
Orders were held to encourage idleness; but the good of society

required all men to produce wealth. As long as a man had the assurance that he would find a home, in his destitute old age, he would have no incentive to save to create a reserve of wealth.

In 1787, therefore, Aranda moved to suppress the 3,000-odd conventual houses with their 130,000 dependants and the whole Church now began to fear for itself. Aranda was too powerful to assail, but his collaborator Olavide laid himself wide open by leading a scandalous life and publicly mocking religion. He was denounced to the Inquisition and the Inquisitors who had recently distinguished themselves by condemning priests who were enemies of the royal prerogatives, had no alternative but to sentence him to prison for eight years. Aranda survived, but so also did most of the conventual houses.

This was the age of the Spanish enlightened despot, relevant to modern Spain only in one, but in one very important, particular. On hearing of the expulsion of the Jesuits, Voltaire had said of Aranda : 'half a dozen men like him, and Spain would be regenerated'. Whatever Aranda intended, and whether that major act of his public life be judged good or ill, he and his followers splintered Spain in a way so fundamental that a series of civil wars down to 1936 was almost inevitable. As men saw in his hatred of religion the driving force behind all his reforms, political, social, economic, and educational, excellent though many of them were, change came to be identified in the minds of many, even most, men of all classes, with an atheistic mind. There were henceforth to be 'two Spains', the one materialistic and anti-religious, the other inclined to ignore material values and reforms even when they were relevant to what was spiritual.

There were in fact to be more than two Spains, for each of the two was fissiparous. Thus 'spiritual' Spaniards included men who with Suárez believed in the Divine Right of the people and those who upheld the opposing Divine Right of Kings; those who with Vitoria doubted Spain's right to empire and those who saw in every war in which Spain was a participant a Crusade and in her generals reincarnations of the *Cid*. On the other side 'materialistic' Spaniards soon divided into those who with Voltaire or Diderot would have had revolution from above, and those who after Rousseau would look for it from below.

Chapter 16

The War of Independence

It WAS THE KING and his enlightened Ministers who first saw the danger of the newest ideas from France : it was one thing to say 'whether or no there is an after life, let us seek to be happy in this world', and another to say 'as there is no God, therefore there can be no Divine Right of Kings : and under natural law [that is in the French School's and not the Scholastic sense] republicanism alone is a tenable doctrine'. From 1783 Charles's Inquisitors began to hunt out on the king's behalf the anti-monarchists, and on their own account atheist literature.

In 1788 Charles III died. His son and successor, Charles IV, was a throw-back, dominated by his wife María Luisa, Elizabeth Farnese's grand-daughter, and she, in her turn, by Manuel de Godoy, a guards officer half her age. For the moment Aranda continued as Chief Minister, while another protégé of his, the count of Floridablanca, who had earlier distinguished himself in the persecution of the Jesuits, suspended all newspapers to prevent the diffusion of the news of events in France. The Inquisition was instructed to intensify its search for 'dangerous books', that is all books which might encourage Jacobinism. The new France, however, soon proved herself as imperialistic as the old. Late in 1792, the French Assembly demanded of Spain recognition and a close alliance like the *Pactes de Famille*. Aranda stalled, Charles began to suspect his loyalty, and he was dismissed. Godoy, aged twenty-five, was appointed to succeed him as Chief Minister and made a Grandee, with the post of Commander-in-Chief in the war which followed. What happened over the next twenty-one years to 1814 was in detail extremely complex, but it may be simplified without over-much distortion as follows.

There were popular demonstrations throughout most of Spain demanding war against the 'Godless' French revolutionaries. Charles IV tried to save his cousin Louis XVI by diplomatic means and when the news of the French king's execution reached Spain, many of the Encyclopaedists' disciples uttered cries of horror. This was not what they understood by enlightenment. They joined in the popular clamour for war, and in 1793 Spain went to war; but

Godoy, a poor courtier, was an even worse Commander-in-Chief. Over the next two years Spanish armies suffered defeat after defeat. Godoy's heart, it would be fair to say, was not in the war. In 1796 he made peace with France and declared war on the French side against England. He could with justice blame incompetent admirals for the subsequent loss of Trinidad and the severe reverse suffered by the fleet off Cape St Vincent. When France claimed back Louisiana, he handed it over. In 1801 Napoleon sent troops to Spain for a while to ensure Godoy understood who was the real master and to back him in an invasion of Portugal; and it was Napoleon who alone decided on peace with England in 1802. When the Consul went to war again in 1803, he allowed Godoy to remain neutral so long as he paid him 6 million francs a month out of Spanish Treasury funds. In December 1804 he needed the Spanish fleet for his plans to invade England, and Spain had duly to declare war again. Nelson's victory at Trafalgar in October 1805 destroyed Spanish and French naval power; but Napoleon's defeat of the Austrians and Russians at Austerlitz in December decided Godoy that his best interests lay wholly with Napoleon. In May 1806 he sent Napoleon 24 million francs on the understanding that when the emperor realized his intention of taking Portugal, Godoy would receive half the country and be crowned its king. For good measure he despatched an expeditionary force of 15,000 to fight for Napoleon in northern Europe.

Godoy's courting of Napoleon was not unknown to Charles IV, who had suffered a rebuff in his search for an alliance with England. A British force took Montevideo in 1807, and it looked then as if the South American continent was England's for the taking. Nor was Godoy the only Spaniard courting Napoleon. Charles's son Ferdinand wanted the emperor to depose his father and get rid of his mother and Godoy on his behalf. The Spanish Voltairists and Rousseauists, the *afrancesados* as they came to be called, saw in the emperor's outlook on religion (not as extreme as the National Convention's had been) greater hope for the fulfilment of their dreams than they could see in any Bourbon. In 1799 Charles, with the full support of his Ministers, had been on the point of establishing by law a national schismatic Church. He had not had the opportunity to carry out his intentions, but the *afrancesados* were not interested in any Anglican-type destruction of the old religion – they held Protestantism to be even more an insult to human intelligence than Catholicism.

Such was the situation when in November 1807 Napoleon despatched 26,000 Frenchmen across the Pyrenees. They duly took Lisbon. On their heels 100,000 more French soldiers crossed the mountains and fanned out over the whole of the north. Godoy and Ferdinand each thought that the French had been sent to advance his own ends and Charles publicly accused his son of treachery. The people refused to believe him. Godoy, reputed to be as *afrancesado* as the rest of the king's Ministers, was held to be the villain. Napoleon demanded all Spain north of the Ebro, and despatched Murat with an army to Madrid, whereupon Godoy and Charles fled to Aranjuez. There a mob organized by Ferdinand clamoured for Godoy's blood. He escaped but Charles abdicated. Ferdinand hastened to meet Murat who told him that Napoleon himself was on his way to recognize him as King of Spain, and advised Ferdinand to go north to meet him. Ferdinand was lured step by step to Bayonne, whither – surprise of surprises – Napoleon's troops also escorted Godoy, Charles, and María Luisa. There, Napoleon forced Ferdinand to abdicate in favour of his father and Charles to resign the Crown to Joseph Bonaparte, who was proclaimed king in June 1808. That there was little to choose between Ferdinand and his father in moral rectitude or loyalty to the people of Spain was not known to the people at the time. Charles became the popular symbol of turpitude, his son that of rectitude.

Joseph was welcomed in Madrid by the *afrancesados*, Meléndez Valdés, their poet, writing an ode in his honour. The Council of Castile decided to collaborate. The French army, however, proceeded to behave towards Spaniards with a savagery which has never been forgotten and which, with due allowances for exaggeration in the telling, can be compared only with that of the Russian and German armies in Poland in World War II. Joseph, on Napoleon's behalf, declared total war on the Church : all monasteries and convents were to be dissolved and their inmates scattered. This was to prove the last straw.

Already, on 2 May 1808, two young Spanish army officers had distributed arms to the people in Madrid, and the mayor of Móstoles, a village near Madrid, had issued a national call to arms. Murat suffocated the revolt locally with extreme severity. The people, led by priests and monks for the most part but not exclusively, now began to attack the invaders as best they could. In Asturias peasants and university students seized an arsenal and prevailed on the hitherto subservient provincial government to declare war on Napoleon; and an appeal for help was sent to Britain. *Juntas* of resistance were organized throughout the country. When appealed to, Britain, with easy conquest in mind, was about to send an army of 10,000 men to South America, but the troops were diverted to the peninsula. Thus began what English history books call the Peninsular War and Spanish books the War of Independence.

It was a long time before English soldiers could help the Spanish patriots; in the meantime, disorganized though they were, the Spaniards began well. A large French force was smashed at Bailén. A ragged peasant army of Valencians, bedecked with religious emblems, forced Murat and Joseph to withdraw from Madrid. The sympathizers and collaborators with the French, the upper classes and bureaucrats, now joined the rebels to save themselves from the popular fury against them for the people did not spare captured enemies. Napoleon poured more troops into Spain until their number reached 300,000. The Spaniards at Zaragoza withstood an assault in strength and in a siege which recalled Numantia the women distinguished themselves in hand-to-hand fighting in the streets; but Zaragoza fell. The British force under Sir John Moore, sent to help the Spaniards, was forced to leave Spain to the mercy of the French. The Spanish cause seemed hopeless. By 1810 the French were in possession of every major town except Cadiz. Undaunted, the *guerrilleros,* warrior people, some 30,000 in number, developed a type of fighting, that of *guerrillas* (little wars), which wore down the French as effectively as the snows of Russia.[1]

The land was not finally cleared of the invader till 1814, when Ferdinand was then invited by the Spaniards to return as their king, but to a Spain which was very different from that which he had left. It was not only that Spain had been devastated by six years of war, but that those who invited him back had sought in his absence to create a new Spain. He was to be something new to Spain—a 'constitutional monarch'.

[1] It is a myth of English history books that Wellington alone drove the French from Spain. It is a myth of Spanish history books that it was the *guerrilleros* that did so. In fact they could not have managed without each other.

Chapter 17

The Evolution of the Two Spains 1800–15

THE SPANIARDS who in the first place had sided with Napoleon were of two types : the wealthy who saw in collaboration the chance of survival with least damage to their property; and the intellectuals who saw in Napoleon a political, social, and legal reformer after their own heart. Those who had actively opposed him in the first place were almost exclusively those who in modern terms would be described as reactionaries : the clergy and people to whom Napoleon and the French soldiery were atheistic savages, bent on the destruction of all that was holy, all that had made Spain a great nation. They had, however, been joined subsequently by others. There were those who believed in Bourbon absolutism as divinely ordained, who held that Ferdinand's abdication had been forced upon him and was therefore illegal. There were those *afrancesados* who had come to regard Napoleon as no better than the Bourbons in the oppression of what they called Liberty. There were those whose fear of the people had become greater than fear of the French, and lastly, as in all human affairs, there were opportunists. Now the people were not given to fine distinctions as to who was a collaborator and who was not. If the rigid centralism of the invader was not to be replaced by anarchy, there had to be some authority : Charles IV's order had collapsed. A central *junta* was formed by September 1808. In September 1810 it summoned a *Cortes,* a body of 105 men who were to be held as representatives of 'all the Spains', the old kingdoms in the peninsula and the new kingdoms in the Americas.

As soon as the *Cortes* met at Cadiz it became evident that there were four major schools of thought. The first maintained that the Bourbon order of monarchy was divinely ordained and immutable. If the *Cortes* had any force at all, it was limited to the work of caretakers pending the return of *el deseado,* the Desired One, Ferdinand VII. This first group apart, the others believed that the moment had come for the people to reassert their sovereignty, and to assert Liberty, Equality, and right to property for all. What, however, was meant by 'the sovereignty of the people', 'Liberty, Equality, and the right to property'?

In the beginning the majority of the members of the *Cortes* were men anxious to restore the mediaeval Catholic concept and principles of society, holding that all men were equal in the sight of God. They believed that the Church was the perfect society, but that man was a political being, and as such free to form his own associations, whether village councils, guilds, religious communities, or universities. As a human being could surrender his own personal right to property in favour of a community, so also he could forgo wholly or in part his right to the control of his civil affairs beyond the village to his province, his region, the nation, or even a king. Experience had taught that the surrender of all rights to a king could lead to the suppression by the king even of those rights or freedoms which the individual or the people wished to retain. Hence those of this school of thought were prepared to accept that a king should be bound by a written constitution. Though the drafting of a constitution by an assembly (even if called by the mediaeval term *Cortes*) smacked too much of the French ideas which were anathema to them, none the less there was good mediaeval precedent for so binding a king. The Visigothic kings had been subject to the *Lex Wisigothorum,* and the *Partidas* of Alfonso the Wise had set limits on the king no less than on his subjects.

Present at the *Cortes* from the start, but more numerous as deliberations continued into 1811 and 1812 and the 'mediaevalists' preferred to pursue the enemy on the battlefield rather than the enemy within, there was a third group, one with radically different ideas. As they stressed Liberty, they came to be called generally *Liberales.*

Though Spanish *liberalismo* had its smattering of Bentham and Locke, none the less it was from the start very different from what liberalism means to the Anglo-Saxon mind. It was in the first place a philosophical religion capable of inspiring among Spaniards as impassioned a fanaticism as Islam or Catholicism. Only in a secondary sense was it ever a political doctrine or an economic theory. As a philosophical religion it shared with Catholicism the tenets that every man has a free will and every man certain rights. However, where the Catholic maintained that free-will and human rights were the gift of God the better to serve Him, and that in order to serve God better, men were free to surrender their rights in greater or lesser measure so as to form national or local societies, the Liberal held that free-will and human rights were of the very nature of man, whether or no there was a God. (Some *Liberales* were deist, others agnostic, and others atheist.) While in *liberal* theory every man was born free to think as he wished and to do as he liked, freedom without limit made life in society impossible, and man's need of society was evident. There had, therefore, to be authority to determine the limits. Ideally that authority should be exercised by all the members of a nation together, but that too was impossible in a practical sense. Hence authority had to be vested in a body held to be representative of the whole in so far as the people would be free to choose their representatives from among intellectuals; and these once chosen would form the sovereign state. Now since the authority of the state was the sum of the authority of the nation's individual members, the subtraction from it of any part was prejudicial to it. Hence there could exist within a country no society which in any way claimed for itself any authority except in subordination to the state's. It had to be an integral part of the state or be destroyed. Independent universities, guilds, or Churches were therefore a negation of the *liberal* principles of authority. The Church, if it was to be allowed to continue to exist, would have to be a Church subservient to the state. But again, the state being the sum of its individual members, and there being nothing to restrain the individual except what the individual decided for himself to be for his own benefit, so there could be nothing to restrain the state except what it decided was for its own benefit : or, more positively, Liberty was the prerogative of the state, and as far as the individual was concerned Liberty was a state-given gift.

Such a political philosophy pursued to its logical conclusion would, of course, make the state totalitarian, and subsequent generations of Spanish philosophers easily discovered the transition from *liberalismo* to Marxism, anarchism, and even the philosophically woolly Falangism.

Equality in the liberal spectrum was limited to equality before the law of all Spanish nationals and to insistence on one law for the whole nation, the whole nation being all those born on Spanish territory anywhere in the world. This had its splendid humanitarian side. It implied the abolition of slavery and of subservience to feudal jurisdictions everywhere in the Spanish dominions. It also implied the conversion of the Spanish empire into a single nation of equals. On the other hand, it also meant the perpetuation of centralism, the subjection to Madrid of the ancient nations of the Catalans, Basques, and the rest. To the *Liberales* equality also meant free commercial competition, equal freedom to amass wealth and to buy and sell in an open market. From Visigothic times in most parts of Spain, lands had passed from father to eldest child in unbreakable entail. As a result the amount of land available for free sale and purchase was limited, and being limited the price was high. Equality here, however, qualified liberty. While a man was to be free to sell his property, and his right to property was held to be one of the Rights of Man, the *Liberal* maintained that no man had any justification in surrendering a right which was part of his nature as man. There could therefore be no disposal of property to a community. A community could not own land. Thus there had to be an end to the common lands and the monastery lands which had survived the sequestrations of the previous centuries.

Between the strict 'mediaevalist', Catholic, politically centrifugal believer in the right of human beings to enter or refuse to enter into associations with wide or limited ends, and the full *Liberal* demanding one law, one all-embracing society, and one sovereign and omnipotent state, there could be no agreement. Nevertheless, the *Cortes* of Cadiz evolved a constitution and proclaimed it as that of Spain, peninsular and overseas, on 19 March 1812.

The Head of State was to be a hereditary king, but sovereignty would be embodied in the *Cortes,* a single-chamber body to be elected by universal male suffrage. The *Cortes* would make the laws and settle all questions relating to their interpretation. There would be provincial government on the basis of a division of Spain in the pattern of French *départements,* and there would be municipal authorities; but they would be subordinate to the central government and essentially the machinery for the execution of the commands of the *Cortes* with no influence on them. Each province would have its *jefe político,* the agent of the central power, one of whose tasks would be to make the arrangements for the elections of deputies to the *Cortes.* The king would have the power to defer but not veto new legislation, and he and his Ministers would be answerable to the *Cortes* for public order, justice, the armed services, and international affairs. To advise him the king would have a Council nominated by the *Cortes.*

To the *Liberales* the constitution appeared a reasonable compromise between their ideals and those of the other groups in the *Cortes,* and those of the masses. Ideally they would have had a republic; they accepted a constitutional monarch. They would have abolished the Church; they agreed to its continued existence as an integral part of the state – the constitution recognized the Catholic religion as official, but the Church in Spain was to be subject to the state of Spain.

Self-evidently such a constitution could not be accepted unconditionally in good conscience by any orthodox Catholic. The bishop of Orense, a member of the central *junta* (which now became the Council of Regency pending the return of the king from his captivity in France), accepted it with reservations. This was not enough for the *Liberales* who expelled him from Spain and deprived him of his citizenship.

The *Liberales,* a self-appointed majority in the *Cortes,* proceeded now to approve laws which were calculated to put into effect the *liberal* theories about rights to property – to enclose common land and to deny property rights to the monasteries. They also abolished the *señoríos,* the long-standing rights of the manor, not in order to protect the peasantry but to ensure that new landowners' titles were not hampered by some ancient custom or responsibility to tenants. In the name of the constitution they began to rule as tyrannically as any Bourbon. In 1813 they abolished the Inquisition – or rather, since Napoleon had already abolished it, they refused to revive it, or to take action against a near pornographic ridicule of religion entitled the *Diccionario crítico burlesco.*

The Bourbons had made of the Inquisition a Star Chamber for the pursuit of clerics who kicked too violently against the king's claims to spiritual overlordship. Towards the end of the eighteenth century the Inquisition had been useful to the sovereign through its restriction of the circulation of books containing Jacobinist ideas. Here the interests of the king had coincided with those of the Church. All this, however, did not touch on the affairs of the masses. To them the Inquisition was a tribunal where men could be fairly tried even if they were wealthy or powerful. It was, within its rules, a just tribunal, more so than the state's common courts. Ordinary men had long preferred trial by the Inquisition to trial by criminal courts for such offences as were within the jurisdiction of either. The men in power were now introducing into the state's tribunals a system which was basically Napoleonic and alien to the customs of Spain. When, therefore, the *Cortes* moved to abolish the Inquisition the masses rioted in protest and were rigorously suppressed.

With the enclosure of the common lands, with the abolition of the feudal jurisdictions which had imposed on the nominal landlord responsibilities even if they also gave him privileges, with the suppression of the one tribunal which did not appear to respect wealth or power, and with several *Liberales* no longer making any secret of their intention to complete the destruction of religion which Aranda had begun, a direct confrontation was inevitable between, on the one hand, the people and the clergy who were of the people and, on the other hand, the *Liberales* – essentially still a small body of bureaucrats whose system might have been intended to create a bourgeoisie but which was seen as a method whereby moderately wealthy bureaucrats might acquire the wealth of the old landed families.

The people of Spain refused to accept the 1812 constitution. So did the Spaniards of the New World who went their own way and with British help created independent states – a movement that had already begun even before the convention of the *Cortes*.[1]

The French released Ferdinand in 1814, to be greeted with frenzied enthusiasm as he made his way south. Delegations from the people and clergy and from the old gentry pressed him to reject the constitution and the subsequent legislation of the *Cortes*. General Francisco Javier Elío pledged him the support of his forces. The non-liberal members of the *Cortes* urged him to accept a constitution based on the traditional 'mediaevalist' theory of king and *Cortes*. On 4 May he declared his acceptance of this constitution, with modifications which made it largely meaningless. General Francisco Eguía, a man of the old authoritarian Regalist school, went ahead into Madrid to arrest the architects of the 1812 constitution and its strong supporters. As the king entered the capital the populace shouted 'Muera la libertad! Muera la constitución!' – for the liberty which they had been promised had been, in their opinion, a fraud.

Ferdinand, according to one school of Spanish historians, now proceeded to rule as tyrannically as any of his Bourbon ancestors, and to cover Spain with a cloud of obscurantism. It would be truer to say that to keep his throne he was prepared at all times for the rest of his life to bow to the prevailing wind, though not always quickly enough. In 1814 he satisfied popular fury by expelling both prominent *Liberales* and the 12,000 Spaniards who had collaborated with the French. He allowed the Jesuits to return, revived the Inquisition, and also forgot he had promised to establish a non-liberal constitutional monarchy. No *Cortes* were convened. The universities were brought even more under government control. There were, however, two internal problems which he could not solve – a country ruined by the years of war and an army whose officers demanded recompense for services rendered. The men with bureaucratic and especially economic ability whom he might have called to help him were *Liberales*. He could not trust them and the country's economy went from bad to worse. He just did not have the money to recompense his officers, yet he had need of an army. While on his arrival some army officers had hastened to his side, it soon became evident that others owed a primary allegiance to Freemasonry and that Freemasonry linked them with the *Liberales*. In the Americas the revolt against Spain was now in full progress : Bolívar, San Martín, and others were destroying piecemeal the Spanish American garrisons. Ferdinand had officers whose loyalty he could not guarantee posted to the provinces and passed over in promotion, and this did not solve his problems.

[1] The Regalists of course had denied the *Cortes* any right to meet at all.

In 1814 there was an army revolt under the ex-guerrilla leader Javier Mina in Pamplona and in 1815 General Juan Díaz Porlier revolted in Corunna. In 1816 an army paymaster tried to assassinate the king. In 1817 the Hispano-Irish General Lacy rose in Valencia. The leaders of these and other plots were Freemasons and *Liberales,* but they were supported in some measure by people whose cause against the new régime was its centralism. All the revolts failed and their leaders were executed, but they were harbingers of what was to come.

On 1 January 1820 a force of 22,000 men was under orders in Cadiz to embark for the Americas. On that day Major Rafael Riego 'pronounced' war on the king's absolutism in the name of the 1812 constitution. His lead and his commands were followed by officers senior to him, his higher grade as a Mason taking precedence over his lower army rank. His revolt was followed by others in Corunna, Barcelona, Zaragoza, and Pamplona, as much against Ferdinand's Madrid-centred absolutism as in favour of the 1812 constitution. The army in Madrid refused to move against any of the rebels. Ferdinand agreed to swear to the constitution and in theory over the next three years Spain was ruled by governments composed of *Liberales.* In practice there was no real government and the differences between the 'two Spains' deepened.

Chapter 18

Civil Wars 1820–68

WITH POWER IN THEIR HANDS the *Liberales* fought as much against themselves as against the Bourbon and the old Spanish orders. Some wanted to give the people time to change their traditional mode of thought. To them the 1812 constitution had seemed at the time as radical a change as was prudent. Studying the events of the eight years to 1820 they now concluded that concessions to the non-*liberal* mind would be politically expedient. Others, however, recalled that the 1812 constitution was itself a compromise. If change were necessary it should be away from the 1812 constitution towards the ideals of the French founders of their political philosophy. The former came to be known as *Moderados,* the latter, of whom Riego was one, were dubbed *Exaltados.* The *Exaltados* now pressed for the immediate destruction of king and Church. They established a network of action cells in Madrid and other cities akin to those of the later anarchist and communist movements, organizing riots in the streets to back their members in new 'elected' *Cortes* whenever there was any hint of a concession to the king. The *Moderados,* however, required no prompting from the *Exaltados* to expel the Jesuits anew, to restart the suppression of monasteries which had stopped with Ferdinand's return in 1814, or to forbid young men and women entry into religious Orders. Those measures were not enough for the *Exaltados.* In their meeting places, masonic lodges and coffee and lodging houses, they inculcated among the half-starved and illiterate a deep hatred of priests and monks. Murders followed and Riego himself urged a mob to burn down churches. The *Exaltados,* and their opponents, began to recruit militias from among the urban unemployed, now swollen in number. By 1821 a multi-sided civil war was in full progress. *Exaltados* fought *Moderados,* and both factions fought Catholic regionalists; yet *Exaltados* and *Moderados* at times worked together and *Exaltados* in some places posed as regionalists. By 1823 Spain presented to the outside world a state of anarchy in which the totally lawless were gaining the upper hand. The kingdoms of Europe, fearing a repetition in Spain of the events of 1789 in France, agreed (Britain dissenting) that France should send an

army into Spain to restore order. In April a force dubbed 'The
Ten Thousand Sons of St Louis' crossed the Pyrenees. The peoples
of the north who had hacked to pieces Napoleon's 'atheists' welcomed the Sons of St Louis with open arms as liberators from
liberalismo. Ferdinand was loath to spare from exile any person who
had too openly doubted his royal prerogatives. To the chagrin of the
victims, however, he displayed no zeal in bringing to justice those
who had merely persecuted priests or religious, and there arose
among laymen and priests groups as *exaltado* in spirit as those
who bore that name among the *Liberales*. In an unknown number of
cases they too took the law into their own hands.

As the king's Catholicism was seen to be little more than nominal,
those to whom religion meant more than king began to look to his
brother and heir presumptive, Carlos, who was reputed to be a
good Catholic. He was thought also to favour the restoration of
the mediaeval autonomies and liberties which still meant so much
to the peoples of the north, and to favour in addition strong
measures to scotch liberalism which they considered a religion as
false as, and more dangerous than, Protestantism, Islam, or
Judaism.

Carlos counselled patience. His brother, though he had had
three wives, was childless. In 1829, however, Ferdinand married
his cousin, the allegedly pro-*liberal* María Cristina of Naples;
and she was quickly pregnant.

Back in 1713 Philip V had allayed British and Dutch fears that
one person might again come to be heir to the Spanish and French
thrones with a decree introducing Salic Law and making birth in
Spain a condition of inheritance of the throne. Charles III's son,
born in Naples, should therefore not have become Charles IV of
Spain. Lest anyone should raise the matter of his foreign birth,
he had had the decree secretly abrogated by a subservient congress
in 1789. As no one did raise the matter, the secret was kept, and
the public believed in 1829 that Salic Law still applied in Spain.

The pregnant María Cristina urged her husband to make public
his father's act, in case their child should prove to be a girl. In
this she had the support both of the old Regalists and all *Liberales*.
The latter recognized that the accession of Don Carlos would
mean the end of liberalism. Don Carlos allowed his followers only
to impugn the legality of Charles IV's act of which, as they said,
there was no official record.

María Cristina's child did prove to be a girl, named Isabel,
and the 'Liberal Succession' now seemed assured. When in 1831
a number of republican *Exaltado* and *Moderado* exiles invaded
Spain they aroused no enthusiasm among their co-religionists, were

captured without difficulty, and executed. In 1832 it was the turn of the Carlists, with the king ill and believed to be dying, to force on Cristina acceptance of Salic Law; but the *Liberales* rallied to her support. The king recovered. He now had Carlist sympathizers ousted from army and government and replaced by moderate *Liberales* and *Cristinos,* men loyal to his wife and daughter. In consequence, when the king did die in 1833 the machinery of the state was firmly out of the Carlists' reach and María Cristina was named regent.

The Basque provinces (but not Bilbao), Catalonia (but not Barcelona), and Valencia after hesitations declared for Don Carlos even before he issued a general call to arms from exile in Portugal. *Liberal* enlightenment had created in Bilbao and Barcelona a powerful but not numerous class of entrepreneurs and manufacturers whose strongholds were these capital cities. When Don Carlos arrived in Navarre, men rallied to him in tens of thousands from throughout the north.

There followed six years of bitter civil war in which neither side showed mercy to its enemy. Carlos might have won but for three factors : first, his generals wasted the strength of their forces in an unsuccessful siege of Bilbao and hesitated until it was too late in going for Madrid; second, Britain sent 10,000 men and Royal Navy ships to help María Cristina; and third, neither Carlos nor his supporters had any clear-cut positive programme with which to appeal to the masses of Castile and the south. The Carlist battle-cry was *Dios, Patria, Rey* – God, Fatherland (in a regional sense), and King (in a mediaevalist way); but what period of the Middle Ages did they have in mind and what exactly were to be the relations between the kingdoms and the Kingdom? Carlos' followers seemed to be divided between the God of Justice and the God of Mercy. At Vergara in August 1839, General Rafael Maroto, a Carlist, openly embraced the *liberal* General Espartero, but the more intransigent Carlist General Cabrera continued fighting for a further eleven months until his defeat by Espartero in July 1840. For the moment, the Carlist cause was lost. The *Liberales* and Christina had triumphed.

Espartero's next major act was to depose Cristina, no longer considered trustworthy, as regent, for she had become religious with age and had secretly married a guards officer risen from the ranks, rather than be his mistress. In 1836 an anti-*liberal* attitude on her part had had to be brought to heel by the sergeants of her palace of La Granja.

During the six years of civil war Madrid had been far from politically idle. Extreme and moderate *liberal* politicians could not agree among themselves on proposals for constitutional reform, and there were several *pronunciamientos* by generals on behalf of one or other of the *liberal* groups. There was one point, nevertheless, on which they were nearly all agreed : that the time had come again to move from the piecemeal attack on the religious Orders to the spoliation of the whole Church. When, in 1834, a terrible cholera epidemic broke out in Madrid, the *liberals* spread among the mob the story that monks and priests had poisoned the drinking water, and over a hundred priests were killed out of hand. On the feast of St James, the National Patron, 25 July 1835, a new law decreed the confiscation of more monastic land. In November 1834 Juan Álvarez Mendizábal, a Jew with a long history of conspiracy in Spain and Portugal who prided himself in being a businessman, had been summoned from London to become Finance Minister. In September 1835 he became Prime Minister and stated rightly that to defeat the Carlists an army of 100,000 had to be recruited, trained, and provided with arms. To obtain the necessary funds he had earlier floated a loan in London the market value of which had fluctuated to the enrichment of Englishmen with advance information of day-to-day events in Spain and the impoverishment of those not 'in-the-know' – fluctuations which quickly discouraged new investors. He now proposed the wholesale confiscation of all church property, but since there was so much of it, he sought to sell only so much at a time. Even so it realized only about a third of its true value. The buyers were *Liberals* undeterred by the Church's excommunication of buyers. 'Surplus' church buildings were demolished to make room for new town houses for the rich, or turned into factories. Those with no ready buyers were converted into government offices, prisons, and barracks. Mendizábal survived in office for one year only, but his work was carried on by his successors. By 1844 the Church had been reduced to beggary, and there were more land-owners and manufacturers than ever whose interests bound them to liberalism of one kind or another.

By 1840 at least three *liberal* groups had in fact become discern-ible—the most extreme adumbrating socialism and deaf to com-promise; a centre body, to the left of the old *Moderados,* convinced of the inevitability of Progress if only *liberal* principles were followed, but prepared to compromise for tactical reasons; and new moderates, to the right of the old, the new men of property or of increased property perturbed by the power of mobs when incited to violence. The mobs had been promised wealth and prosperity if the Church were deprived of hers. This had been done, but all that had happened as far as they were concerned was that soup kitchens and free hospitals had disappeared. Covetous eyes might now be directed against the new rich, the new moderates, who now sought a *modus vivendi*, even an alliance, with the Church; but it was to be some years, many army *pronunciamientos*, several constitutions, three changes of régime, and another Carlist war before such a *modus vivendi* became practically possible. A new Concordat, signed with the Vatican in 1851 during a period when the moderates were in the ascendant, confirmed Catholicism as the religion of Spain. On the one hand, the state then undertook to pay the clergy fixed salaries (ranging from a few shillings a week to a curate to roughly £120 a month to the Primate to cover all expenses of his archdiocese as well as his own) and restored to the Church the right to acquire property; yet, on the other hand, Rome agreed to have no say in church affairs except with the approval of the government in power. The Concordat was a dead letter within three years as government passed to the progressives.

The political ins and outs of the twenty-nine years 1840–68 are irrelevant to modern Spain, except in that the most important political figures were General Espartero, who moved from liberalism to a personal dictatorship, and Generals Narváez and O'Donnell, who moved backwards and forwards over the *liberal* political spectrum : rule by army generals, the precedent for which Aranda had established, became commonplace. The squabbles between the generals left governments little time to attend to the ever-growing economic needs of the country.

The wide use of Jenner's vaccine, the virtual closure of Spanish America to immigrants from the beginning of the Napoleonic Wars to the end of the Spanish American wars of Independence in the third decade of the nineteenth century, and the government's discouragement of chastity as a mode of life, contributed with other factors to the extraordinary increase in the population of Spain from about 10 million in 1800 to 16 million in 1860. Substantial progress was made in mid-century in the industrial development of the Barcelona and Bilbao regions and in the exploitation of the mineral resources of the Cantabrian mountains and the Río Tinto area; but this was minimal compared with similar developments in Britain, France, or Germany. The country remained essentially agricultural, and for all the fine *liberal* theories that with monastic and common lands in private hands and with the creation of a free market in land by the disentailment of estates, Spanish agriculture would flourish, in fact it did so only for very short periods. In the long term the rich became richer and the poor poorer as the century progressed. The new rich were speculators, industrialists, landowners, lawyers, and generals, who having become men of wealth sought respectability, the respectability associated with

Church and Establishment. They were a very small group. Beneath them there developed a vast bureaucracy in government, army, and industry, men so ill-paid that to make ends meet they had to undertake two jobs. The sight of the junior army officer working evenings as a clerk in some small private enterprise became common. Such double employment was not open to the urban proletariat or to the agricultural workers. By 1868 they had learned to expect little or nothing either from their old defenders the clergy, or the politicians. They saw the clergy as officials of the state whose salaries were suspended if they did not fall into line with government policy, and as men who frequented the salons of the wealthy. That some did so in order to acquire by deed of gift property with which to refound schools and hospitals was not realized by the masses. For all the *Liberales'* talk of universal suffrage in the 1812 constitution, forty years later the enfranchised numbered hundreds, where they should have numbered tens of thousands : even so elections were rigged, and always won by the government in office. Governments arrived in office by virtue of military *pronunciamiento*. Changes in government were frequent only because the generals pronounced for radical, progressive, or moderate liberalism with tedious regularity. By 1868, the year of the First International, the mass of the people were ready for new leaders, neither *Liberales,* Catholics, *Cristinos,* nor Carlists, but men from their own unenfranchised ranks. As yet was no one to lead them, but there soon would be.

Isabel had been declared of age in 1843, when only thirteen. After much scheming among the foreign powers she had married an effeminate bastard cousin when barely sixteen. By nature afflicted with what a contemporary Englishwoman politely referred to as 'the Queen's terrible constitutional malady' she had had a large number of children whose putative fathers were a disparate lot, and alternated between moments of dissoluteness and periods of remorse and religious piety. By 1868 she had lost the affection of the people, to many of whom monarchy had lost all appeal. The old *liberal* republicans could, therefore, count now on a substantial measure of popular support and on the help of many who, while still monarchists, judged Isabel unfit to remain as queen. The feeling was shared by the progressive *Liberales* who after 1856 had held very few ministries under the queen. There was also a new breed of intellectuals prominent especially in the state-controlled University of Madrid. Disillusioned with French philosophy, these intellectuals had turned to the doctrines of a minor Austrian philosopher, Karl Krause, who had died in 1832. Within a pantheistic conception of the world the Spanish Krausists argued that what mattered was moral purpose and not utility : 'think right and you will live right and be right'. They had been expelled from the university in 1867. Two years earlier Emilio Castelar, a professor of history, had been deprived of his chair after casting doubts (with good reason) on the good faith of the queen when she had offered the royal estates to the nation as a means of raising money to pay for an ill-conceived attempt to bring independent Peru back under Spanish rule. Students now agitated against the state which had dismissed the professors of a philosophy which they hardly understood.

Students, professors, Krausist intellectuals, progressives, and republicans combined under Generals Francisco Serrano and Juan Prim, Admiral Juan Bautista Topete, and a professional politician, Práxedes Sagasta, to depose Isabel, who, in October 1868, left quietly at their command. Spain was now to experiment with the strangest of all régimes – a republic with a king at its head.

Chapter 9

'Democratic King'–Republic– Constitutional Monarchy 1868–1906

PRIM, THE IDOL OF THE REPUBLICANS and a self-appointed king-maker, hawked the Crown of Spain round Europe in search of 'a democratic king', thereby touching off the Franco-Prussian War. Spain was not to become a dependency of France or Prussia. He finally prevailed on Amadeo of Savoy, son of King Victor Emmanuel II who was then annexing the Papal States, to accept it. In December 1870 a disillusioned republican assassinated Prim as Amadeo was about to land. The others who had invited him tried to enlist the support of the republicans by engaging in a fresh attack on the Church, thereby once again driving the peoples of the north to war. In February 1873, faced with trouble both in Madrid and out of it, Amadeo washed his hands of Spain, and the kingless Liberals declared Spain a republic. In the first eight months of its existence the republic saw four presidents in turn and governments were divided within themselves. Some wanted a federal Spain and others a unitary state; some a revolutionary, others a mildly progressive programme; while General José Manuel Pavía wanted a military dictatorship under republican guise. In the event it was Emilio Castelar who took over government, to rule Spain with as iron a fist as almost any military man in Spanish history. By September 1873 Madrid had lost control of most of the country, but fortunately for the government there was total disunity also among its enemies. The grandson of Ferdinand's brother Don Carlos, himself also called Don Carlos, now heading the rebels in the north, defeated the government troops at Montjurra; but he was a young lad, a romantic, and militarily and politically inept. His armies should again have swept from Catalonia and the Basque provinces to Madrid; but on this occasion, too, there was no cohesion between Carlists east and west; and those in the west were once more obsessed with the idea of capturing Bilbao. The tens of thousands of volunteers, whose battle-cry this time was 'God, Liberty, and Country', lacked artillery. By 1874 it was evident that they could not win and men whose ideals were the defence of religion or local autonomies began to look elsewhere. Disillusionment in Madrid was widespread. The masses were not interested in bourgeois intellectual republicanism. Two new philosophies were now gaining adherents among the masses by the hundred thousand. Both were to reach their heyday in 1936 and provide a civil war within a civil war.

One of the two new philosophies began with Rousseau's principle that man is by nature good, and left to himself will strive for good. The crimes committed by the oppressed could be seen as the results of oppression : poor men stole because their children were hungry; they were moved to violence because the authorities used violence against them in the name of the law. The Liberals maintained that laws were necessary for the public good, but surely it was law made by man which wrenched man from his natural 'innocence'. What sanction was there then for law? Churchmen claimed that they taught what they did by the authority of an omnipotent God and that the laws of men were sanctioned by that God : but the laws were evil. Either God was evil, a contradiction in terms, or He did not exist. If He did not, then in truth there was no sanction for either Church or state. To restore man to his natural goodness, laws, state, and Church had therefore to be destroyed.

Such arguments were current in Spain when the Russian Bakunin was thinking elsewhere on similar lines. He sent his friend, the Italian Fanelli, to Spain. At the Bakuninist Conference held in 1873 in Geneva, the Spanish delegate claimed that he represented 300,000 converts to the new philosophy, anarchism, and that further converts were being made in 270 centres, scattered throughout Spain. Anarchism was indeed proving especially attractive to those in desperate straits in Andalusia, who were being hounded by the Civil Guard, a body established in 1844 to stamp out brigandage but one which tenants and labourers had already come to look upon as backed by the landowners. It spread from Andalusia as many Andalusians fled their native region. There was work there at best for only two months in the year and they sought work in the industries of Galicia, Asturias, and especially Catalonia. Barcelona, the port for the arrival and departure of foreign anarchists, had already become an anarchist centre in its own right.

Perhaps the delegate at the Geneva conference exaggerated. The Spanish socialist Francisco Mora put the number of anarchists at 60,000, but he had his own high figures to give for adherents to the other new philosophy of the people, Marxist socialism.

The Spanish Socialist Party, fully Marxist, was not officially founded until May 1879, but already by 1868 Proudhon and by 1873 Marx were widely known names. Such principles as 'to everyone according to his needs and from everyone according to his abilities' and 'the land should belong to those who work it' were not new in Castile : Jesuits had expounded such dogmas 300 years earlier, and the Castilian, unlike the Andaluz, was not averse to the strict discipline which Marxist socialism demanded of its converts. The masses of Madrid and Castile, therefore, turned towards Marx, while those in Barcelona and Andalusia looked to Bakunin.

Socialism and anarchism frightened the liberal property-holders of the First Republic. The Krausist intellectuals were now surprised at the fact that university students were interpreting their newly-given freedom to study what they wished as they wished, as meaning freedom not to study at all. The politicians were perplexed at their own disunity; and they had troubles abroad. Since 1868 Spain had been fighting in Cuba : the republic did not believe in independence for colonies any more than the Bourbon dynasty. If the Cuban war and the war against the Carlists were to be brought to a satisfactory conclusion (even though many a traditionalist no longer looked on Don Carlos as capable of recreating the Spain of the remote past), then there had to be strong and effective government at the centre.

All but a few Liberals had become convinced by 1874 that whatever else might be the answer, a republic did not provide it. A schoolmaster turned politician, Cánovas del Castillo, advocated a return to monarchy in the person of Isabel's son Alfonso, now a sixteen-year-old cadet at Sandhurst. A young brigadier-general, Martínez Campos, 'pronounced' in his favour. The Captain-General of Madrid, Primo de Rivera, informed the republican government that he could not guarantee the loyalty of the garrison to the republic, and Cánovas accepted the premiership from Sagasta. Alfonso called on Spaniards to rally to the cause of constitutional monarchy, defining himself as 'a good Spaniard, a good Catholic, and a Liberal'. In a bloodless revolution he became Alfonso XII. For the first time in a century of revolutions the conquerors did not wreak vengeance on the conquered. There was tolerance and mercy.

Cánovas now set about designing a new constitution, modelled on the British system admired alike by the king and Cánovas, in consultation with Sagasta. The country was to be governed by the king in Cortes, comprising an Upper Chamber (in part hereditary, in part nominated by the king or ex-officio, and in part elected) and an elected Lower Chamber. The king would summon, prorogue, or dissolve the Cortes, any dissolution being followed by the summoning of new Cortes within three months. Ministers would be appointed by the Crown on the advice of the Prime Minister, but they would be responsible to the Cortes. Catholicism was to be the official religion of the state, but other religions were to be 'tolerated' (as part of the persecution of the Catholic Church by Amadeo and republican régimes, Protestants had been given every encouragement to proselytize, and there were now between 10,000 and 20,000 in the country.) There would be civil marriage, not for all as the extreme Liberals had demanded but for the non-Catholic. Cánovas had to face bitter opposition from churchmen and Liberals over his proposals, but he was a persuasive speaker, and all but a few diehard republicans and the Carlists came to accept the new constitution, not as the ideal but as the best possible decision in an imperfect Spain. It was to survive, with modifications, till 1923; and it might have survived to the present day had it borne the fruit which Cánovas intended it to have.

Cánovas recognized that what he had done was to impose on the country a pattern of political life, which, acceptable though it was on paper to the majority in the upper and middle classes, presupposed a willingness on the part of the opposition to allow governments to govern : and this was something which no Spaniard not himself in government had been prepared to allow since the Habsburg period. He saw in the British alternation between Gladstone and Disraeli, Liberal and Conservative, the conductor for the frustration generated whenever men were too long in opposition or could see no way to power except by armed rebellion. There were in *Cortes* conservative Liberals like himself, Liberals of various persuasions, republicans and Carlists. He had his own substantial body of adherents. It was up to Sagasta to bring together as many dissidents as possible and form them into a coherent opposition which in course of time, and for a time, could take over from Cánovas and his conservative Liberals. Sagasta succeeded by 1881. Cánovas thereupon duly stepped down and Sagasta duly took over. They changed round again in 1884, 1890, 1892, and 1895. In 1897 an Italian anarchist shot Cánovas dead, but the system survived and Sagasta was returned to power.

Under the constitution the Prime Minister had to have a working majority in *Cortes* to govern. To ensure the regular changeover elections to *Cortes* had therefore to be arranged. Sagasta and Cánovas agreed upon the changeover and the method. The old *jefe político* organization of earlier liberal gerrymandering was improved upon. What was intended here was not that elections should be falsified thereafter for ever, but that the people should come to realize for themselves the virtues of the two-party system, and learn to choose for themselves between non-extremist parties. What happened was the establishment in the country, especially in the south, of *caciquismo*, of political bosses managing elections, seen ever more clearly as time passed to be a fraud and so exasperating to the electorate.

It can be said that developments up to 1892 were roughly 'according to plan.' Attempts at revolution by republican generals failed dismally in 1883, 1884, and 1886. The constitution survived the death from consumption of Alfonso XII in 1885 and the accession of his posthumous son as Alfonso XIII in the following year. His mother, the Habsburg princess María Cristina, was a radically different person from her grandmother-in-law and namesake, and she acquired for the royal family a love and respect among the people such as Spanish kings and queens had not enjoyed since the early Habsburgs. The system even survived the publication in the newspapers of the results of the election held in 1886 before polling-day. Yet the two large parties failed to recognize that they would never appeal to the masses of the people unless they were prepared to dedicate their energies in full to the betterment of social conditions. Spanish liberalism produced no Lord Shaftesbury, nor for that matter did Spanish Catholicism. Those who were appalled at the conditions of workers in factories or on the land did not have the know-how to press for legislation against the abuses of employers and employees. They wrote pamphlets. They put into practice in their own enterprises advanced social principles, but their example was not widely followed.

Money and not social reform was the principal concern of *Cortes*. It may be said in the defence of both the major parties that they were heirs to an inefficient system of taxation. The cost of tax collection was a third of the amount gathered. The very people who could afford to pay were the ablest at avoiding payment. Governments were also heirs to an overstaffed civil service which they could not pay adequately because they could not gather the revenue. Again, though Cánovas in 1878 had succeeded in halting Cuba's advance towards independence, the maintenance of the *status quo* there required an army which by 1896 numbered 100,000 men, inadequately armed and inadequately paid, yet still costly. Advocacy of independence for Cuba was not popular and governments had to find the money to prevent that independence.

All governments failed also to recognize that the industrial and agricultural development of Spain would be minimal so long as literacy was the privilege of a tiny percentage. At a time when in Britain the Churches had been establishing schools 'for the deserving poor', Spanish governments had been destroying the schools run by religious Orders, which were almost the only ones there were. Now that the war between Liberals and the Church was officially over, each side adopted a dog-in-the-manger attitude. On the one side the Church insisted either that education should be in its hands or that children in state schools should receive at least elementary religious instruction under its control; on the other side the Liberals would rather have had no schools at all than schools in which religious instruction was permitted.

In the meantime anarchism and Marxist socialism gathered momentum. The socialists established among workers the *Unión General de Trabajadores* in 1888, the primary object of which was not to improve working conditions (indeed it would have been contrary to true Marxism to work for that bourgeois end), but to foment a revolutionary spirit among the workers so that at the propitious moment they should take over the country. The anarchists set up their own workers' organizations on a local basis to prepare anarchists for the eventual takeover by syndicates of the land and the factories. While waiting for the millennium, anarchists were to carry out acts to 'register a protest' against the existing order. Bomb explosions became frequent, especially in Catalonia from 1883 onwards, and on 5 January 1892 anarchists managed momentarily to take over the city of Jérez. Cánovas saw no reason why the leaders of this revolt should not be executed, an attitude that was to lead to his assassination in 1897.

On 25 March 1892 a body of Catalans demanded home rule for Catalonia. This, the force of regionalism, was the third popular force that the two major parties failed to appreciate. Like anarchism and Marxist socialism, it grew rapidly as the century neared its end. A fine renaissance of Catalan literature renewed the dormant awareness of the Catalans that they were different from the rest of Spain. There was a similar revival of Galician literature with similar, though not so militant, consequences. The Basques did not require literature to remember what they had never forgotten – their separate nationhood. However, so long as Madrid left them alone in the practice of their religion and allowed them to gather taxes for Madrid in their own way, they would not go as far as the Catalans.

As the century neared its end an event occurred which was to have the most curious and far-reaching repercussions. The United States of America, which had expanded earlier at the expense of New Spain, now the United States of Mexico, picked an excuse in 1898 to go to war with Spain. In a three-month campaign both in Cuba and off its coast, a quarter of a million well-equipped American soldiers and sailors in modern warships crushed a Spanish army of 100,000 ill-armed, ill-shod, and ill-clothed troops, and sank a navy in which the only modern ship had not yet been fitted with its main armament. Another American task-force of modern ships then sank the even older Spanish Pacific fleet off the Philippines.

Sixteenth-century Spanish writers had gloried in the fact that mere handfuls of men had won the New World against astonishing odds. The shameful aspects of that conquest had also been given publicity by Spaniards of whom Bartolomé de las Casas was only one and not the most accurate, but thereafter the Spanish empire had become established fact. Because it was so very Spanish in culture, it had disintegrated politically at the very moment when there had been a legal excuse for it to do so. Originally, indeed, Buenos Aires and Caracas had declared themselves independent of French-occupied Madrid, and not of the Spanish Crown. Then other legal arguments had been advanced for the complete breakaway. How little the loss of continental Spanish America meant to the Spaniards as a whole can be seen from the fact that the army which might have recovered them for Spain followed Riego in his revolt against Madrid. O'Donnell had meddled in 1861 in the affairs of Mexico jointly with England and France, and in 1864 there had been an expedition to seize the guano islands off Peru; a few writers had bemoaned the loss of the empire but there never had been any popular enthusiasm to recover what had been lost.

The retention of what remained of the empire—the Philippines, Puerto Rico, Cuba, and a few bits of Africa—was another matter.[1] The suppression by the Amadeo, republican, and Alfonsine régimes of attempts at Cuban independence during 1868–78 had been rigorous and it had had wide support. When Cubans renewed the battle in 1895–6 Cánovas sent General Valeriano Weyler, an admirer in his youth of Prim, to deal with them and he did so in a way which which earned him the title of 'the Butcher'. Yet Cánovas granted Cuban autonomy in 1898, and it had seemed reasonably safe in Spanish hands when the U.S.A. stepped in and took it, and Puerto Rico and the Philippines into the bargain. That the upstart U.S.A. should have acted in so aggressive a manner was what irked Spaniards most of all.

Politicians blamed the armed services for what had happened and vice versa. The politicians had neglected the armed services : the armed services had directed into private pockets the money which should have gone into new equipment. The army had turned to politics no longer as republicans or Liberals but as a political force in its own right, a force to be reckoned with and mollified by whichever government was in power. Aranda had shown that the army was a political ladder to the top; though not entirely in the same way, so had Godoy, Riego, Espartero, O'Donnell, Narváez,

---

[1] A rough parallel may be seen in British reaction which accepted the loss of India, yet strained at the gnat of Gibraltar.

Prim, and others. Riego and those after him had acted on behalf
of political groupings of civilians as much as on their own account.
The army now began to think of itself as the guardian of the
nation's honour with the right to act on its own account. Its officers
evolved a political code which may be summarized: 'where a
government by its actions brings the nation to dishonour in the
eyes of the world, either by proving itself unable to maintain order,
or by placing it under the control however remote of a foreign
power, then it is the bounden duty of the army officer to rise in
defence of the country against the government: for however lawfully instituted, it has ceased to be lawful by its bringing dishonour
to the nation'. Army officers as guardians of the honour of the
fatherland therefore came to consider themselves, singly or collectively, above any constitution or government.

In 1906 a task was found for the army by the politicians – an
adventure which would cost the lives of tens of thousands of Spaniards over the following twenty-one years and bring in its train
major political changes.

Chapter 20

The War in Africa and its Political Repercussions 1906–23

WITH THE LOSS of Cuba and the Philippines, Spain had been left with no overseas possessions except some unimportant islands off the west coast of Africa, a portion of the Sahara Desert, the cities of Ceuta and Melilla, and a few fortresses on the coast of Morocco. France was now coveting all Morocco as well as Algeria. She realized, however, that Spain could harass her lines of communication if she attempted any action there without Spain's goodwill. In October 1904, after much wrangling, France agreed that Spain should help her in her self-appointed task of 'protecting' the Sultan of Morocco. Spain was to be allowed to expand into the hinterland of Melilla and Ceuta, and the agreement was welcomed by Liberals and conservatives alike. The liberal count of Romanones stated the party's general view that Morocco was Spain's last chance to keep her position in the concert of Europe. It was also an opportunity for him and other politicians to invest heavily in a mining company to which the Spanish government gave rights to be 'protected' in the hinterland. Intellectuals who after the 1898 disaster had maintained that Spain could not be regenerated unless it had a will to empire, also welcomed the agreement.

Moroccan tribesmen naturally resented the arrival of the foreign miners. There were minor skirmishes; resentment grew; and on 9 July 1909 a force of Moroccans attacked a military outpost protecting Spanish workers building a railway to serve the mines. Four workers and one sentry were killed. Here now was a chance for the politicians and the army. They were urged to avenge the dead as O'Donnell had done in 1859, when tribes had attacked Melilla, and he had sent a punitive expedition. War fever spread among the upper classes. When on 13 July 6,000 Moroccans fell into a skirmish with 2,000 Spaniards, the demand for action became overwhelming and Spanish battalions in Spain were ordered to stand by in readiness for service overseas. On 23 July there was a third skirmish. The Spanish commander in Africa now estimated the rebels at 16,000, against whom he could muster only 15,000 soldiers, and he requested the immediate despatch of reinforcements totalling 40,000. The Prime Minister, Antonio Maura, ordered the call-up of reservists. As war hysteria spread among the upper classes, so among the proletariat was anti-war hysteria encouraged by Marxist socialists and anarchists. The socialists now called for a general strike in Barcelona unless married reservists were exempted. Maura maintained, with the army, that without obedience there could be no discipline, without discipline no army, and without an army no state. Anarchists and socialists concurred – and that was why they acted as they did. On 26 July Barcelona became a city of barricades. Within a few hours the strike called by the socialists had become an orgy of destruction, murder, and rapine. Maura ordered the army to restore order. It took them four days, until the 30th. The dead were then buried by the cartload.

Possibly the most active of the destroyers were the gangs of toughs organized by a young journalist, Alejandro Lerroux, who was moving from various 'protection rackets' into politics as an anti-Catalanist and republican, and for years had been preaching class hatred and nihilism. However, it was the anarchists alone who were blamed for what had happened, and the internationally famous anarchist intellectual Francisco Ferrer was arrested on the charge of being the instigator-in-chief. He was executed in spite of protest meetings all over Europe. Maura, then a Liberal of the centre, was deserted by those to the left of him, by his fall making way for a more left-wing liberal government which sent the notorious General Weyler to pacify Barcelona. Weyler showed as little mercy to his countrymen as he had earlier shown to the Cubans.

Spanish enterprises in Cuba had been largely in the hands of Catalans. The loss of Cuba, therefore, had been a particularly heavy blow to Catalonia. Cuba could no longer provide a protected market for Catalan produce, and the poor people of the south and the rest of Spain could not pay the relatively high prices of Catalan textiles and other manufactures.

Free trade was to the interest of Spain but not of Catalonia. Thus the industrialists came to the conclusion that the arguments of the Catalan intellectuals and solidly Catholic smallholders who dreamt of the autonomy which had once been theirs had good business sense behind them. A century earlier it had been contradictory for a Liberal to be a Catalanist, but henceforward this would be so no longer. Catalan home rule had, from now on, Catholic and anti-Catholic, monarchist and republican advocates, and also industrialists and workers. The splintering of Spain was also of course seen by anarchists in Catalonia as a move towards their ideal : the more pronounced the divisions among the ruling classes and within the state the easier it would be to destroy the state.

Those who felt the shocks of the 1898 disasters most keenly, however, were not the Catalans nor the officers of the armed services nor yet the politicians, but the intellectuals. To what depths had Spain sunk that she had been outwitted by the upstart United States? Once her philosophers, men of science, and creative artists had inspired the world : for over a century and a half none of her philosophers, men of science, or writers, except for one painter (Goya), had acquired international renown. What had gone wrong? The Catholic intellectuals attributed Spain's decline to the acceptance of Regalism and the rejection of the philosophy whose last great Spanish developer had been the *doctor eximius*, Suárez. In their view Spain's hope for the future lay in her return to the principles, though not the practices, of her great past. The intellectuals belonging to the 'other Spain' were as dogmatic though less unanimous. Some Liberals argued that it was because the men in power had failed to act consistently according to the principles of the 'incontrovertible' French eighteenth-century philosophers that Spain had dropped to where she was : had there been consistency, then the second-class mid-eighteenth-century Spain would have risen again to her rightful place. This, in essence, was the message of the most prolific of Spanish novelists, Pérez Galdós. Man, he assumed, was by nature good, and would be good if given the opportunity : let Spaniards rid themselves of superstitious beliefs and social practices, and of priests and religious maniacs, and let the state give encouragement to engineers and men of science, and Spain would be regenerated and renew the face of the earth. Other representatives of the 'other Spain' had different solutions. The cleverest of the Krausists, Giner de los Ríos, had established in 1875 a sort of avant-garde open university, the *Institución Libre de Enseñanza*, a focal point for all the intellectual anti-Establishment. At the turn of the century it was now the *alma mater* of the sons of the wealthy beneficiaries of the nineteenth-century expropriations. Voltaire and Rousseau had proved as inadequate as the mediaeval philosophers; the situation in France was different from the Spanish only in degree; the Germany of Nietszche, Kant, and Hegel and not France should be the model to follow.[1] In due course for many of the pupils of the *Institución* the passage was easy through Kant and Hegel to Marxism and other totalitarianisms and through Nietzsche to Bakunin. Galdós, educated in the *Institución*, progressed, under the influence of friends, from the liberalism

[1] This philosophy was to be developed by Ortega y Gasset, see below, pp. 163, 167 for the consequences.

of his early years to revolutionary socialism. So did many a university professor. More important still, many of the pupils of the *Institución* in the early years of the twentieth century were destined to become the political leaders of the second and third decades.

By 1909 the alternation of conservative and liberal governments had become difficult to engineer secretly. Each of the two major parties had developed deep internal divisions. Though they combined within themselves to make difficult the return of socialists, republicans, or Carlists, no Prime Minister could command for long the support of a sufficient number of conservatives or Liberals (they were so divided among themselves) to remain in office for any length of time, and the average term was under a year. The ablest and most honest of them, Maura, had removed by law the worst election abuses and had done his best to make his countrymen realize that the country needed unity and stability for progress. At the same time he had hoped to make government representative, but got little support from right or left. Politicians continued to behave as in the previous century and crisis followed crisis. In succession to Maura, José Canalejas became Prime Minister in 1910 at the head of a group which called itself radical-liberal. For years he had toured the country preaching against the admission into Spain of refugees from the French religious persecution. Like other Liberals to the right of him, he was particularly perturbed by the success which old and new religious Orders had been having since the end of the nineteenth century in the re-Christianization of the *haute bourgeoisie* and professional classes, hitherto the preserves of liberalism. During the twenty-two months he held office he concentrated on anti-Church legislation. This inflamed the Basque Catholic *petits bourgeois* and peasant who now began seriously to consider the advisability of a break with Madrid.

There had been in existence since 1894 a Basque Nationalist Party; but unlike Catalan nationalism, Basque nationalism appealed to few intellectuals or captains of industry. Unamuno, Baroja, and Maeztu, the three leading Basque writers associated with the intellectual questioning which followed the 1898 disaster, disassociated themselves from the aspirations of their race. Basque nationalism was essentially middle and lower class, and essentially religious. It was in the Basque provinces alone that the Catholic trade union movement, begun by a Valencian Jesuit, Antonio Palau, at the turn of the century, constituted a rival to other workers' associations.

The spread of the free Catholic trade union movement worried the socialists in the Basque provinces. The anarchist hold over the workers in Catalonia worried them much more. Anarchist intellectuals and terrorists had paid dearly for their part in the 1909 Barcelona Tragic Week. By 1912 they had, however, recovered sufficiently to renew their 'acts of protest' : they assassinated Canalejas, and thereafter they moved on to kill members of the bourgeoisie with such regularity that assassination ceased to be news. At the same time they had come to realize that the 'daily revindicative tasks' which they urged upon workers were not enough. If there was to be revolution aimed at the abolition of the state, some form of national organization was required. In any case, when the new age dawned workers' syndicates would have to be prepared to take over fields and factories; thus there was a case for their immediate formation. Accordingly they had established in 1910 a new nationwide workers' organization, the *Confederación Nacional del Trabajo* (CNT), whose success in Catalonia and Andalusia astounded the socialists. The CNT's membership rapidly outstripped that of the tighter-knit socialist UGT, which had been founded in 1888.

Spain opted for neutrality at the outbreak of the 1914–18 war. The operations which had been taking place since 1909 in the hinterland of Ceuta and Melilla (Spain since 1912 had been expected to 'protect' roughly a quarter of the country while France reserved for herself the economically more profitable remainder), were proving that the equipment and leadership of the Spanish armies were too inferior for those armies to be of value either to Germany or Britain. The king had married Princess Ena of Battenberg, Queen Victoria's granddaughter, but his mother was an Austrian. There were pro-British, pro-French, and a few pro-German army officers. There were also a number who were opposed to alliances and who considered that operations in Morocco would have been easier if Spain had had Tangier; but Britain and France had made it 'international'. Intellectual Spain was also divided; Kant and Hegel battling with Voltaire and Rousseau. The clerical mind balanced Elizabeth of England and Cranmer with Luther and Bismarck, and the middle-class mind the Sons of St. Louis with Napoleon, and Canning with Wellington. To socialists and anarchists the war was between imperialists, and no concern of theirs. The industrialists were on the side from which they could get most.

In spite of socialist-inspired strikes and anarchist sabotage the Cantabrian region was able to provide the allies with the raw materials of war and the Catalan mills with the cloth for uniforms. The new prosperity momentarily relieved tension and wages were more than doubled in these areas; but then the profits of the industrialists were enormous, profits which they failed to plough into their businesses. Early in 1917 the leader of the centre and right-wing Catalans, Francisco Cambó, a man of progressive ideas, originated a nationwide movement called *Renovación*.[2] Its aims were akin to those of Maura – the replacement of the sham electoral system by free elections, the cleansing from the royal court of lickspittles, and the overhaul of the civil service to put an end to the corruption which poor pay had made general. He called for the establishment of *juntas*, action groups to bring about the 'cleanup'.

It was within the army that such *juntas* had the widest appeal. The Prime Minister, García Prieto, resigned when they petitioned for reforms in army administration. The new Prime Minister, a moderate conservative, Eduardo Dato, promised to consider the petition, but politicians to the right and left of him protested, and by June 1917 there was general unrest within the army, the *juntas'* action and proposals being highly controversial. Civil service *juntas* now petitioned for better pay, but Dato stood firm. In July sixty Catalan members of the *Cortes* met in Barcelona to demand not only home rule but 'the renovation of the Spanish constitution, public administration, the armed services, justice, and the national economy'. Dato would not hear of it. The Catalans called on the *Cortes* as a whole, or on those members who sympathized, to attend an 'Assembly' in Barcelona to demand renovation of the constitution. Seventy-one defied a government threat to take action against them as 'subversive'. This was, possibly, the last chance that the Spanish right had to set Spain in order, but they let it slip and the initiative now passed to revolutionaries.

Socialists and anarchists had hailed the news of the events of March 1917 in Russia as the dawn of their rival millennia. Though Pablo Iglesias, the founder of the Spanish Socialist Party, thought otherwise, the professor of logic Julián Besteiro ('the Spanish Laski') and Largo Caballero, later to be called by the Comintern 'the Spanish Lenin' and at that time head of the 200,000-strong UGT, came to the conclusion that the situation in Spain was not unlike that of Russia. The time, they thought, was right for revolution : among the ruling classes, civilian and army, there was confusion worse confounded over *Renovación*, over the war, over economics. Admittedly the wages of the Catalan, Basque, and Asturian workers had doubled, but food prices throughout the nation had risen in proportion, and discontent was general.

The socialists established an alliance with the CNT whose membership now exceeded half a million. Both anarchists and socialists thought they could count on the support of convert N.C.O.s and

---

[2] Literally 'Renovation', but more accurately 'Redecoration' or 'clean-up', as of buildings.

officers, and Marcelino Domingo, a radical-socialist Catalan, believed that they could establish soviets within the army.

The date for the paralyzing of the railway system was fixed for 10 August and on 13 August a nationwide general strike was to follow. A manifesto calculated to appeal to republicans, radicals, and even Liberals was prepared. The strike was to lead to a republic, a 35-hour working week, the replacement of the army by a Workers' Militia, separation of Church and state, closure of all churches, divorce by mutual consent, nationalization of 'the means of production', and the running of factories by workers' syndicates. (The anarchists wanted bullfighting and indecent cabarets banned, but the socialists would not agree.)

Pablo Iglesias, however, was proved right : the government declared martial law; the army decided to back the government; and N.C.O.s and private soldiers did not hesitate to fire on the workers. In Barcelona the strike was over in a week. Only among the miners of Oviedo did the strike last as long as three weeks. The army had saved the establishment—but only temporarily.

German *agents provocateurs* now took a hand in events. They provoked anarchists to acts of sabotage in order to disrupt Barcelona's exports of textiles to the allies, then denounced them to the authorities; but able lawyers defended them. Employers began to hire gunmen to shoot anarchists as the quickest method of disposing of them; and Lerroux had guns for hire. By the time the Armistice was signed in November 1918, there was such a back-log of scores to settle that no one could call an armistice in Barcelona. In 1920 Dato sent an army general nearing his sixties, Martínez Anido, to put an end to the battles. His methods over the next two years may be imagined from his own confession that he was but a surgeon and that a doctor would have to come after him. In March 1921 three anarchists killed Dato in Madrid. Some workers were sorry, for they owed to his initiative factory and other laws bettering, albeit modestly, their working conditions. Nothing changed.

By 1921 the war in Africa had been in progress for twelve years, yet Spain could protect the Sultan only over a small part of that quarter of his kingdom which was now officially called the 'Spanish Protectorate'. South of Ceuta the real ruler was the tribal leader Raisuni. South-west of Melilla another chieftain, Abdel Krim, had declared war on the Sultan and on Spain. The Spanish generals continued to be hampered by the poor equipment and inadequate training of their troops, and by the refusal of governments, whether conservative or liberal, to give definite orders as to how far they should extend their counter-rebel operations. The socialists had kept up pressure for a withdrawal from Africa or for purely peaceful penetration, backing their demands with occasional strikes and showing solidarity with Soviet Russia by supporting Abdel Krim.

Back in 1911 Spain had established the *regulares*, a corps of Moroccan soldiers officered by Spaniards, with the idea of using them in forward positions so as to reduce the numbers of Spanish other-rank casualties. On 1 June 1921 a Spanish outpost south-west of Melilla was overwhelmed by Abdel Krim's forces. On 7 June one thousand *regulares* on their way to recapture the outpost murdered their officers and joined Abdel Krim. During the lull which followed there were further desertions. On 17 July Abdel Krim surrounded the main forward post of the Spanish army at Igueriben to the west of Anwal. The commanding general, Silvestre, moved his main force to relieve the besieged, but on 21 June 4,000 Spaniards died in the attempt, whereupon his fellow officers sentenced Silvestre to death by suicide. What remained of the force panicked. Abdel Krim did not take prisoners. By the evening of 23 July his forces were threatening the city of Melilla and they had killed 14,000 Spaniards in their advance. Meanwhile the Spanish Foreign Legion, which had been founded in 1920 with Major Francisco Franco as second-in-command, was rapidly switched from the west where it had Raisuni cornered. It arrived in Melilla with other troops just in time to save the city and stabilize the situation.

Back in Spain the news of the disaster stunned army, politicians, and people, the army blaming the politicians and the politicians blaming the army. In an orgy of accusation and counter-accusation as to who was to blame for Anwal, the political life of Spain was reduced to a state of chaos. In 1922 Maura, who had moved to the right since his early days and had become an ardent monarchist, did his best to calm passions by appointing a committee of inquiry. The inquiry revealed such irregularities in both political and army administrative circles that Maura was appalled. When pressed by the army to publish only the revelations of political corruption, he resigned. His successor, Sánchez Guerra, appointed a parliamentary committee to study the report, but he would not accept responsibility for what might happen if it were published. A third government, formed in December 1922, decided that the best course was to divert public interest, and it proposed the appropriation of all church funds and property which had accrued since the last appropriation had taken place, a ruse which proved successful. As the archbishop of Zaragoza, Cardinal Soldevila, protested too loudly, a gunman was found to silence him in June 1923. The rumour then spread that the person really to blame for the disaster was the king himself, since he was said to have given Silvestre the orders to extend his lines beyond what was militarily prudent.

Alfonso XIII, although in a precarious position, had nevertheless gained the affection of many army officers. On 13 September Primo de Rivera, Captain-General of Barcelona and the nephew of the Captain-General of Madrid who had ushered in the 1875 restoration, with two of Spain's sixteen army divisions under his command, announced that he had formed a government under the king. The 1876 constitution was suspended.

Chapter 21

The Dictatorship 1923–31

EVEN THE SOCIALISTS backed Primo de Rivera's move to end the political and social chaos reigning at the time, and they had two good reasons. The post-1917 Barcelona gun warfare in which the CNT had played a prominent part had given the UGT a measure of respectability. In 1922 the party as a whole had refused to join the Third International and while most of its leaders still believed in revolution as a *sine qua non* of progress towards their Marxist ideal, others had come to believe either that time was not ripe for revolution or that socialist ideals were not impossible of realization through co-operation with the state. Primo de Rivera promised a new social order and offered a hand of friendship to Largo Caballero, still head of the UGT, who accepted it. He also promised that he would surrender his dictatorship as soon as order had been restored, which won him the support of a wide variety of politicians. He appeared to say, too, that in the new order Catalan and other regional aspirations would be respected. With that the powerful Catalan *Lliga* headed by Cambó decided to back him.[1] His other promises were to put an end to the costly war in Africa, to bring new prosperity to Spain which had the essentials to become the haven for European tourists, to stamp out corruption, especially in local government, and ensure that individuals would quickly get redress for grievances, to improve the laws relating to working conditions.

He started well by undertaking a vast programme of public works, removing some of the grievances of the civil service, studying the war in Africa, and deciding that Spain's interests would be best served by the surrender of the Protectorate. During his visit to Morocco in 1924, however, he discovered that the Spanish army in Africa was of a different opinion, and he accepted a plan of which Colonel Francisco Franco was the chief exponent to bring the war there to a successful end. By the beginning of 1926 this had been done, but for minor mopping-up operations, with some help from the French.

By the beginning of 1926, however, Primo de Rivera was

[1] See below, pp. 135, 158.

proving very different from the man many had imagined him to be. He had brought some order out of chaos, destroyed the political bosses who had 'managed elections', cleaned up local government offices, and set up a not inefficient machinery for better labour relations. There was now far less unemployment than at any time before in the twentieth century (though it was still very high). He had also set up arbitration boards to settle disputes between the workers and employers, and in consequence there was industrial peace. But it had become evident that Primo de Rivera could not conceive of liberty within order.

The first liberty he attacked was that of the Catalans, a liberty which was hateful to him. In 1924 he dissolved the Catalan *Mancommunidad*, the limited local government granted Catalonia in 1912, and forbade the teaching of the language, its use in churches, the flying of the Catalan flag, and even the dancing of the *sardana*. By doing so he brought discredit on the centre and right-wing Catalans who had earlier collaborated with him, and Catalans turned away from the moderate Cambó, who had hoped that Catalonia would regain her lost autonomy without recourse to arms, to an ex-army colonel, Francisco Maciá, politically a radical republican, and within the Catalan context a separatist *à l'outrance*.

Primo's distrust of intellectuals underlined still more his dictatorial tendencies. He had their private letters opened and their telephone conversations tapped; dismissed Unamuno from his chair of Greek at Salamanca because of his criticisms of Primo's régime to a personal friend in Buenos Aires; and closed the *Ateneo*, the meeting-place of the famous in arts and sciences. Nor would he brook criticism in the press. Press censorship was not new; both liberal and conservative governments had used this instrument, but Primo used it bluntly where others had been subtle. As a result, persecuted intellectuals became convinced republicans where before some had considered progress possible under either a monarchy as in England or a republic as in France.

In military matters he thought as an infantryman, holding no brief for the other branches of the army, but he thus aggravated grievances felt by the artillery. One reason for the prolongation of the war in Africa had been the Spanish army's lack of artillery – a deficiency going back to the Napoleonic Wars, when the *guerrilleros* had had next to no cannon. The regular army as reconstituted by Ferdinand VII had incorporated many of the *guerrilleros*. Moreover, one of the conditions of the 'Embrace of Vergara'[2] had been the admission of Carlist officers and men into Isabel's army; and the Carlists had also had few artillerymen. Riego, Espartero,

2 See above, p. 101.

O'Donnell, Narváez, and Prim had all been infantry officers, pampering their own arm, and when artillery units had sought their fair share of the pickings of victory they had been worsted. Now one of the sops to encourage service in Africa where officer casualties were particularly heavy had been promotion in the field for acts of bravery; but the artillery rarely had the opportunity to take part in the hand-to-hand fighting which led, where not to death, to quick promotion, and considering themselves all equally brave, the gunners who had had the 'good fortune' to face the enemy in close combat, had concluded as early as the mid-nineteenth century that there was no reason why they should be promoted above those on whom fortune had not smiled—and vice versa. They had, therefore, steadfastly refused such promotion in Africa.

Primo de Rivera now demanded that they should. There could not be two sets of rules in the army, one for gunners and one for the rest, any more than there could be two sets of laws, one for Catalonia and one for the rest, or two religions, languages, or anything else. On 27 July 1926 he issued his decree. On 5 September the artillery moved into its barracks and closed the gates. When Primo sent infantry to arrest the whole regiment – about 20,000 – there was no resistance except in Pamplona where one officer, one sergeant, and one gunner were killed. After the regiment had been dissolved, with re-employment offered only to those ready to accept his decree, Primo knew he had the upper hand : no civilian would dare incur his wrath by offering ex-artillerymen employment. He had thereafter a discontented body in the army, whose discontent would spread beyond their corps.

In the beginning Primo had made a name for himself as a man who when presented face to face with an injustice would cut through all red tape to redress it. In time the very arbitrariness of his decisions began to irk the public. As the dissoluteness of his private life was not generally known at the time, he made much of his attendances at church, insisting, too, on his Ministers going to church and being respectful to the clergy. He allowed new church schools to be opened and removed from the state syllabus textbooks offensive to Catholic sentiment. Yet increasingly from 1926 onwards the Church seemed cool towards him, and not only because he had excluded from his labour dispute settlement boards representatives of the Catholic trade unions, recognizing only the UGT. Too many churchmen for his liking pointed out in pulpits and elsewhere the differences between Spanish practice and papal writings on social questions; yet his attempted recognition of degrees granted at two centres of higher learning run by religious Orders failed to win him new supporters : on the contrary, students and staff at the state universities rioted. The competition for government posts open only to men with university degrees would be fiercer if graduates of these colleges were recognized as eligible. Thereafter student rioting became a feature of Primo's Spain.

In 1926 Primo obtained the services of a man who was generally considered to be a brilliant economist, Calvo Sotelo. Calvo proposed a capital tax and an all-embracing income tax. The banks and millionaires opposed the former, and the middle classes the latter. The campaign against the income tax became a campaign against the government. Primo next set up new semi-state banks to free Spanish foreign trade from dependence on foreign credit.[3] He now, on 27 June 1927, decreed the surrender to a state-controlled banking monopoly, CAMPSA, of the refineries and petrol-distributing stations of Standard Oil, Shell, and other foreign companies. When, in reprisal, they refused to supply Spain with crude oil, Primo secured supplies from Russia; but unknown to him the foreign oil companies had in fact admitted capital from Spanish millionaires, so that the confiscation lost Primo the support of Spanish as well as foreign financiers.

While Primo failed to understand Catalan and Basque nationalism, he did sympathize with the desire of people everywhere to manage their own affairs. He sought, therefore, to give the municipalities power such as they had not enjoyed for centuries. The municipalities, once freed and given credit from the centre, entered into a spending spree which further weakened the economy of the country, for while some of the schemes would eventually improve the economy locally, others were no more than grandiose show-they had had in the general originally.
pieces. Foreign businessmen and bankers lost the great confidence

By 1928 there were still no signs that Primo would fulfil his promise to step down now that order had been restored. The ousted politicians were by now more than anxious to return to power. The lawyers did not know where they stood with Primo's reversals in the courts of decisions which he considered unjust. Measures against the students to keep them in order merely provoked more demonstrations and riots. He now proposed a national assembly by limited suffrage; but the socialists (whose UGT was now in a dominant position, Primo having emasculated both the CNT and Catholic unions) would have none of it; nor would the

[3] For some years there had been a campaign against the enormous influence which through the years foreign companies had come to exercise in Spain. The country had indeed long been a victim and beneficiary of what a later age would call 'neo-colonialism'.

representatives of most other political organizations. The end, however, came from the same 'state within the state' from which
General Primo de Rivera had come.

In July 1929 a unit of the newly constituted Royal Regiment
of Artillery rose in revolt at Ciudad Real. It proved to be more
than a sign that the new regiment was no more to be trusted than
the old. The conservative ex-Prime Minister Sánchez Guerra voluntarily surrendered himself to the authorities, claiming that the
rising had been a premature start to what had been planned as
a nationwide rising of which he was the head. Primo had Sánchez
Guerra court-martialled. Willingly the ex-Prime Minister gave the
court every minute detail of his subversive activities and the tribunal of brigadiers found Sánchez Guerra not guilty of sedition.
The dictator knew now that the army as well as the nation was
against him, but he clung to power.

The economic situation went from bad to worse, the peseta drop-
ping in the foreign money markets to an all-time low in spite of
all Calvo Sotelo could do to restore confidence in it. The king was
advised to get rid of Primo de Rivera and on 28 January 1930
summoned him to explain how it was that two days earlier he had
sent a telegram to all the captains-general of the eight military
regions, asking them point blank whether he still had their support, without the knowledge of the Commander-in-Chief of the
Spanish Army, the king himself. Primo had no answer but to ask
the king to relieve him of his duties. The king did so, and entrusted
the government to an ageing man with a distinguished record in
the African War, General Damaso Berenguer.

Berenguer, a kindly man, saw his task as the restoration of the
1876 constitution following free elections over which he would
preside, but he never got the chance. General Mola, another
African campaign soldier whom Berenguer chose as his Director-
General of Security, warned him that a revolution was being
planned by many politicians and intellectuals; that socialists were
buying arms; that the revolutionary elements had supporters in the
armed services, including the cavalry General Queipo de Llano
and the extremely popular trans-Atlantic flyer Ramón Franco.
Berenguer pooh-poohed the signs of an armed rising. He believed
that if he was to fulfil his duty to hand over to a freely elected
government, then he should allow politicians full liberty to form
political parties. The plotting continued unhampered.

In August, at the suggestion of the Socialist Party, an assort-
ment of politicians, representing a wide range of ideals and calling
themselves a revolutionary committee, met at San Sebastián. They
were agreed only upon two points : that the king should be ousted

and a republic established; and that the change should be done by a *coup d'état*. The day on which they would proclaim the republic was fixed by the National Revolutionary Committee for 15 December. On that day, General Queipo de Llano would take command of all the armed forces in Madrid on behalf of the new régime and Ramón Franco would shower leaflets over Madrid to inform the public of what had happened. Republican army officers would take over command throughout the country and would confine their troops to barracks so as not to prejudice the action of the workers who would come out on strike. The revolution would be bloodless as far as possible. However, if the king did not surrender immediately, Franco and his squadron would threaten to bomb the royal palace.

The plot misfired because of the premature action on 12 December of a captain in distant Jaca, Fermín Galán. Berenguer, who had refused to believe that a man such as Ramón Franco, whose exploits as a flyer had brought prestige to Spain and whose brother, General Francisco Franco, was the youngest and most able general officer, could be a member of a revolutionary committee, let alone an anarchist organization, now gave Mola authority to arrest civilians and army officers involved in the plot.

Those arrested were brought to trial before a military tribunal in March 1931. In their defence it was argued that if the accused were guilty of violating the constitution, so also was the king in that he had accepted Primo de Rivera's dictatorship. The president of the court and several fellow generals were for the acquittal of all the accused, and they were in fact all released.

The question now was not whether there would be a republic, but when. Berenguer still wanted to call elections for *Cortes,* and to this end had the municipal electoral rolls and machinery overhauled. When party leaders refused to take part in an election with him in office he resigned and the king called on Sánchez Guerra to form a ministry but this government was also unacceptable to the San Sebastián committee. The king then called on an old admiral, Aznar, who suggested holding *municipal* elections on 12 April. In theory their purpose was to determine whether the machinery existed for subsequent elections for new *Cortes,* and whether the machinery could work in the prevailing climate of strikes and student riots. In practice republican and monarchist politicians agreed that the elections should be used to determine whether the people wanted a monarchy or a republic.

The monarchists were so certain that republicanism was a disease which had affected the minds of only a few intellectuals, university students (too young to vote), and a part only of the urban pro-

letariat (less numerous in any count than the agricultural population which was conservative by nature), that most monarchists stood
for election unbacked by any electioneering organization. The republicans covered over the differences among themselves, dismissed any
questioning as to what they intended to do having once got rid
of the king, and with a perfect understanding of the Spanish
mind concentrated their propaganda on the one point which could
win the millions over to their side. These were the millions who
were still conditioned by the mediaeval concept of man as one
who should be *liber et legalis*. On being declared of age Alfonso
XIII had solemnly sworn to uphold the 1876 constitution; in 1923
he had put himself outside the law by engineering, or condoning
(it did not matter which), the destruction of that constitution;
whether or not Spain should be a republic, Alfonso XIII had
forfeited his right to be king.

On the day following the election, all the captains-general in
the country received a telegram from Berenguer, now Minister of
War, telling them that the monarchist candidates had been defeated in the principal cities. In a roundabout, yet clear enough,
way he ordered the army to accept without demur an impending
change to a republic.

When the final results were known, 41,224 monarchists had in
fact been elected as against 39,248 republicans, but the republican
vote was essentially the urban vote; the cities were the key to Spain;
and this was clear enough by 13 April. Berenguer acted to avoid
civil war. Sanjurjo, in command of the para-military Civil Guard,
thereupon informed the king that he could not guarantee the
loyalty of his men to the monarchy. The choice before the king
was now clearly to call for war between one half of his subjects
and the other half or to surrender. His physician, the internationally famous heart specialist Dr Gregorio Marañón, his Secretary
of State the crafty old politician Romanones, and Berenguer and
others advised the king to leave the country.

Even before the king had finally made up his mind, a republic
had been declared in Barcelona, and in Madrid the centuries old
red and gold flag of royal Spain was being replaced in public
buildings by the republican purple, gold, and red, and the royal
arms in stone were being defaced.

The National Revolutionary Committee had for months been so
certain of victory that they had already agreed among themselves
that they were to constitute the first government of the Second
Republic and which individual was to take over which Ministry.
When, therefore, they received word that the king had ceded them

the right to rule, they were ready. At the top the changeover was orderly.

In a farewell message to Spain Alfonso XIII confessed that he might have erred. He forbade anyone to use force on his behalf. He was not abdicating, but he was leaving the country to see whether new men under a new form of government could find solutions to the complex problems which had eluded absolute monarchy and republic, controlled democracy and dictatorship.

The Second Republic was to have a life little longer than the first, but Spain was to be without a king for longer than ever before in her history.

PART THREE

Modern Spain

Chapter 22

The Republic: The First Phase April 1931 to November 1933

ON 14 APRIL THE MEMBERS of the National Revolutionary Committee made their way through wildly cheering crowds to the Puerta del Sol and *Gobernación,* the Prime Minister's office. They had already settled among themselves who was to have which Ministry, so they were ready to go into action as the provisional government almost immediately. Their actions and reactions to events over the next six months established a pattern of political life which in retrospect can be seen as having made the subsequent Civil War almost inevitable.

There were three socialists in the government: Indalecio Prieto, the party leader, aged forty-eight, a brilliant orator and journalist; Largo Caballero, at sixty-two in the prime of life, head of the Socialist Workers' Organization, the UGT; Fernando de los Ríos, sixty-two, brought up in his uncle's *Institución Libre de Enseñanza,* who, far from being a pantheistic Krausist like his uncle, was a Marxist with an abiding hatred of all religion. Prieto, in deference to his business acumen as a newspaper proprietor, was given the Ministry of Finance; Largo became Minister of Labour; and de los Ríos Minister of Justice – all Spanish church matters being a matter for that Ministry.

Between Prieto and five others in the Committee, there was the bond of solemn oaths of Spanish Freemasonry. All had therefore sworn to destroy Catholicism; but in personal background and political ideas they differed among themselves. The oldest was the sixty-seven-year-old Lerroux who became Foreign Secretary. Even since 1909 he had been in the thick of every plot and riot against the Establishment, but with age he had ceased to appeal to rebellious youth; and his Radical Party was now one of middle-aged *petits bourgeois* with grievances against officialdom. For some time the Radical Party's one coherently expressed purpose had been the propagation of republicanism, but with the advent of the republic, the party had no further *raison d'être* and would now have to seek a new role. Lerroux himself had begun to have doubts about the validity of his Masonic oaths. Nevertheless, he had brought into the Committee the Grand Master of the Spanish Orient, the forty-eight-year-old Diego Martínez Barrio, who had never previously figured in politics and for whom a Ministry of Communications was created. Two others in the government, Álvaro de Albornoz, aged fifty-two, a lawyer-journalist, and Marcelino Domingo, forty-seven, a schoolmaster bound to Martínez Barrio as his second-in-command in the Spanish Orient, were ex-associates of Lerroux. When Lerroux had become more temperate, they had broken away, taking the younger generation with them to found a Radical Socialist Party – ideologically Marxist, Jacobin in word and deed. Domingo was allotted the Ministry of Education and Albornoz that of Development. The fifth Mason friend of Prieto was Casares Quiroga, aged forty-seven, a substantially wealthy lawyer, coldly calculating and cynical, yet closely associated with the romantic liberal literary society of Galicia which had been inspired by the poetry of Rosalía de Castro to dream of an autonomous Galician republic and to found a party to work towards its realization. The important naval base of El Ferrol is in Galicia, so Casares Quiroga was the natural claimant to the Ministry of Marine.

There was another man, himself not a Mason until 1932, but looked upon by Martínez Barrio, Albornoz, Domingo, and Casares as their intellectual leader – Manuel Azaña, aged fifty-one, another rich and successful lawyer. More to the point, he was a persuasive speaker and writer who bore his considerable erudition lightly. Between 1913 and 1920 he had been Secretary of the *Ateneo,* the meeting-place in Madrid of intellectuals and professional men, especially the Liberals and those inclined to be critical of the Establishment. At the time of the San Sebastián meeting he had been the *Ateneo*'s president, in which capacity he loved to be looked upon as a Spanish Mirabeau, for he had achieved his ascendancy over others in spite of his repellent physical appearance and private appetites. Later he cast himself in the role of a Robespierre. In his ideas he was more truly a second Aranda, especially on religion, except that his second engrossing hatred was of the army. Azaña claimed for himself the key post in the incipient republican government of Spain, that of Minister of War.

Prieto came from Bilbao but was in no sense a Basque, and neither the socialists nor Azaña nor the Masons had any sympathy with Basque aspirations to autonomy. Basque nationalism was Catholic; there was no place for it in government. But they did find a Catalan historian of republican and agnostic views, Luis Nicoláu d'Olwer, aged forty-three, who seemed to confirm the Catalan reputation for business acumen and as the youngest member of the government became Minister for Economic Affairs.

There were two 'odd-men-out' in the Revolutionary Committee whose membership of the *Ateneo* was their only link with the others : Miguel Maura, the forty-four-year-old son of Antonio, Alfonso's great Minister; and Niceto Alcalá Zamora, fifty-four, a professional politician of the old liberal-conservative school – both practising Catholics. Maura believed in a moderate and steady reform of social conditions in Spain. Alcalá Zamora believed in himself. Azaña and Prieto saw in them two men who by their inclusion in the government could give respectability to the new régime; for the new government could in no way be considered representative even of those who had voted for the republic unless it included non-socialists and non-Masons. Maura was given the Ministry of Home Affairs and the vice-premiership, and Alcalá Zamora the nominal premiership and office of Head of State combined.

In Madrid enthusiasts renamed the Calle de Alcalá, the old principal street of Madrid, the Calle de Alcalá Zamora, overturning a few statues as they proclaimed their loyalty to the republic. In Seville anarchists let out all prisoners and opened fire on the police. Martial law had to be declared before the authority of the republic was imposed and order restored. In Barcelona the new republic's authority was challenged in a different way.

Back in 1923 the Catalan home-ruler Cambó had helped Primo de Rivera to power, believing that Primo would grant Catalonia autonomy. The dictator's subsequent treatment of Catalonia had discredited Cambó and his party, the *Lliga*. Francisco Maciá had gone into exile having run foul of Primo, and from exile had thereupon organized a new party, the Catalan *Esquerra,* or Left. Its members were mostly shopkeepers and minor officials. Surfacing after Primo's fall, the *Esquerra* hastily put up candidates for the municipal elections in greater numbers and with better organization to back them than any other party. Before all the votes had been counted, Maciá's lieutenant in the *Esquerra,* Luis Companys (an associate of Domingo), declared Catalonia an independent republic, the *Estat Catalá.*

This was altogether too fast for the republicans in Madrid and Domingo, de los Ríos, and the Catalan d'Olwer hastened to Catalonia to bring Maciá and his *Esquerra* to heel. He was promised that the new *Cortes,* to be convened shortly as a constituent assembly, would have a statute placed before them granting Catalonia autonomy. After a protracted discussion Maciá agreed that the *Estat Catalá* should be renamed the *Generalitat,* the Catalan Commonwealth, pending the promised statute. The republican General

López de Ochóa kept the two divisions in Catalonia on the alert until Maciá agreed to respect Madrid.

In the municipal elections roughly one out of every two of the Spaniards who had gone to the polls had voted *against* the king, and therefore it could be said that one-half of Spain had sanctioned the establishment of a republic under the men who had taken over government. It was their duty now to summon a constituent assembly and this they did for the following June; but in the meantime they were not disposed merely to govern.

In 1931 nominally 90 per cent of Spaniards were Catholic: nine out of ten had been baptized and eight out of ten received elementary instruction prior to First Confession, Communion, and Confirmation. After an all-time low in the mid-nineteenth century there had been some return to the practice of religion. Regular attendances at church varied from about 3 per cent in the Málaga area to 80 per cent in the Basque provinces. For the whole of Spain the average was about 20 per cent. There were over 30,000 priests and at least 45,000 lay brothers and nuns, men and women mostly of the urban and rural proletariat, a pointer to the strength of the Church among the less wealthy members of society. Thus, three adults in every 400 had chosen the religious life. The Church was weaker among the lower-middle classes but among members of the liberal professions there had been a Catholic intellectual revival to balance the influence of the *Institución*.

The fact that only one adult in five frequented church did not mean that the other four hated the Church – far from it. The men who made of their atheism a militant religion totalled at most 10 per cent of the population: the anarchists, the Marxists (the leaders of the Socialist Party and the UGT, but only a few of the rank-and-file members), and the Masons. There were perhaps another 10 per cent who were really anti-clerical. The remaining 60 per cent, who were neither regular churchgoers nor anti-clerical, were far from anti-religious, considering themselves Catholics and hoping that after a death-bed repentance they would be buried by a priest. They insisted on the baptism of their children whom they sent to church rather than state schools. There were church-school places for about 25 per cent of all children between seven and eleven and for about an equal number in state schools. The Church, crippled after the depredations of the eighteenth and nineteenth centuries, had secondary schools for under 10 per cent of the children of relevant age, but in secondary education the state had done next to nothing. The alternative to fee-paying church secondary schools was lay fee-paying schools in a few of the larger towns. On the other hand, the state had a virtual monopoly of education at university level.

The anti-religious minority suffered from certain legal restrictions consequent on the identification of Church and state under the 1876 constitution and the 1851 Concordat. The state regarded consummated marriages as indissoluble.[1] The best cemeteries, or parts of cemeteries, were church-consecrated ground from which atheists, and those who died without visible sign of reconciliation with the Church of their baptism, were excluded. In church schools children were taught with a crucifix on the classroom wall and by teachers to whose appointment the local church authority had had no objection. They had to say prayers with their classmates and learn a catechism which explicitly condemned the irreligious ideas of their parents as sinful.

Not all atheists were republicans nor were all Catholics monarchists. Alcalá Zamora and Maura were far from unique as Catholic republicans. It was widely held among Catholic intellectuals, schooled in Aristotle, that all things being equal a monarchy had practical advantages over a republic, but none held a republic to be contrary to Catholicism. Prieto and Azaña knew this. They were not so certain, however, that the inclusion of Alcalá Zamora and Maura would be sufficient to gain for the government its acceptance by the hierarchy. The hierarchy, under the Concordat, had been appointed by the king and was well informed about the views on religion of socialists and Masons.

So were the Catholic intellectuals and professional men. Their newspaper, the daily *El Debate,* had been founded years earlier, by the Jesuit sociologist Angel Ayala and the lay journalist Angel Herrera, to diffuse Catholic progressive social doctrines. In 1931 Herrera was editor and on 15 April *El Debate* carried a long article on the change of régime. The king was thanked for his past services to Spain, but readers were urged to accept the republic – so strongly, indeed, that for many years monarchists asserted that Herrera and his staff had long been secret republicans and conspirators against the king. Over the next two weeks the bishops of several dioceses added their plea that their flocks should respect the new authorities and be loyal to them.

The First of May was celebrated as never before by the Socialist Party and the UGT. Priests were harassed by insults and mob violence. Socialists recently nominated to local government by Madrid arbitrarily arrested known opponents of Marxism 'to

---

[1] *Divortium a mensa et thoro* was legally obtainable, but not divorce in the sense of dissolution of a bond and therefore freedom to make a new contract.

protect them from the righteous anger of the people'. Some property was damaged, but there were no major incidents.

On 7 May, Cardinal Segura, archbishop of Toledo and Primate of Spain, published a pastoral, written on 1 May. He reminded his readers that, although the Church had no preference for any particular form of government, under Alfonso XIII there had been peace between Church and state, and he thanked the king for it. He warned Catholics that difficult days lay ahead for the Church, and that it was the duty of all Catholics to unite in her defence, but he instructed them to render the government 'respect and obedience in the maintenance of order for the common good'.

On 9 May Maura was informed that there was a plan to set fire to churches and religious houses in Madrid and other cities. This information he passed on to the Cabinet, advising his colleagues that city police forces lacked the means to prevent the execution of the plan; but when he asked for authority to call out the Civil Guard to defend the threatened property, Azaña replied that he would rather all the churches of Spain should burn than that harm should come to a single republican head. The Civil Guard was ordered to take no action whatever happened.

When on 10 May, contrary to Alfonso XIII's wishes, a few monarchist aristocrats and army officers who wanted to establish a monarchist centre gathered in a house in the Calle de Alcalá, an angry crowd set fire to their motor-cars. The Civil Guard dispersed the crowds by firing over their heads.

On 11 May the radical socialist Rada, the man who had been Ramón Franco's mechanic on the first flight across the South Atlantic, led a group of men to the main Jesuit church and residence. Police and Civil Guard watched them pour petrol round the buildings, while firemen intervened only to save neighbouring property. The fire-raisers then went on to sack and burn down a convent; a non-fee-paying school for 500 boys; one for 300 girls; an orphanage; and Madrid's best equipped technical college. A colonel of hussars who wished to intervene to save the last was warned from Azaña's Ministry of War that there was a dossier against him as an enemy of the republic. In Madrid a total of twelve religious buildings were razed to the ground and another thirty-six damaged, while in Málaga, twenty-two were destroyed on that day and on the following day; and churches and conventual houses were burnt in over a dozen other cities. There would have been more had all the local authorities obeyed Madrid; but with private property now in danger, the government was forced to think again. On 13 May the orders to the Civil Guard were reversed. The first government of the Second Republic had failed in its primary purpose as a government, the protection of all citizens irrespective of creed or party. Reading foreign reaction to the event, it sought to attribute the burnings to monarchist and even church *agents provocateurs,* and suppressed the monarchist paper *ABC* and *El Debate* for a while. Apologists of the left tried to explain away what seemed to many a deliberate plan as 'spontaneous popular reaction to the Cardinal's anti-republican pastoral': foreign public opinion, unaware of the real sequence of events, was satisfied. Within Spain, however, no one was deceived.

The government, in fulfilment of the Cardinal's warning that Catholics were to be severely harassed, expelled the bishops of Vitoria and Málaga who had spoken against its recent inaction. The formal expulsion of the Cardinal had to be delayed for a month because on 13 May he had hastened with the other Spanish archbishops to report to the Vatican on the government's antireligious intentions. Fernando de los Ríos declared freedom of worship : government officials and serving officers were forbidden official attendance at religious functions. Marcelino Domingo had crucifixes removed from schools and forbade prayers and religious instruction in them. The government made it clear that it intended to secularize cemeteries, introduce divorce by mutual consent, establish 'a lay system of education', and separate Church and state.

There were still Spaniards who opposed the separation of Church and state on Regalist grounds. There were others, however, who knew history too well not to know that on balance the Church had suffered as much as it had benefited from its close link with the state. But there was one very practical matter to be settled : if Church and state were to be separate, would the state continue to pay the small salaries it had been paying since the middle of the nineteenth century as compensation for the properties it had confiscated earlier from the Church? Clergy in wealthy town districts might be able to rely on the generosity of their parishioners, but not those in slum areas or in the countryside.

The promise of 'a lay system of education' was even more ominous. The Church in Spain, as elsewhere, maintained as a right that it should continue to have a measure of control over education, insisting that while a man's conscience was his own affair, no man had the right to propagate error. Hence it had in the past fought for and obtained the power to veto the appointment to state schools of teachers of scandalously immoral lives or heterodox views. Now the term *enseñanza laica* (lay education) had come to mean not merely the exclusion of religious instruction and practices in schools and the creation in them of an irreligious atmosphere, but the inculcation in children of anti-religious views. The Church, therefore, could not be impassive to the government's declaration of intent. On 3 June the hierarchy issued an official protest.

The anti-religious 10 per cent rejoiced at the new measures; and with reservations so did the liberal intellectuals and the anti-clericals; but the church-going 20 per cent and a great part of the 60 per cent non-church-going Catholics were affronted by what was being planned. As they saw it, they were to be deprived of any guarantee that their children in state schools would not be taught atheism; their cemeteries were to be 'defiled'; marital unions were to be reduced to farmyard level. Nevertheless, the official protest having been made, Catholics were advised at parish level not to disturb the public order and 'to respect authority'. The Petrine *etiam dyscolis* was as much quoted in defence of the republic as it had been earlier of the monarchy and was to be of a later régime.

The Church was no danger to the republic, nor were the monarchists, disorganized and their morale shattered, at that moment a security risk. Nor was the army. Serving officers had accepted the change of régime without more incident than a symbolic delay in running down the old flag of Spain by the young General Franco, then Commander of the Royal Military Academy, and his senior, the Captain-General of the Zaragoza region. The real danger to the republic was from another quarter.

Largo Caballero, once in power, had made it plain to his UGT that while he was Minister of Labour as well as their leader it was the duty of socialist workers to create wealth. The financiers, unlike the monarchists, had not been surprised by the strength of the feeling against Alfonso. They had seen the change coming ever since the outcome of the court-martial of the Jaca politicians and had taken their capital out of Spain. That capital had to be replaced or the new republic would be in economic trouble which would create political difficulties. The republic, with its new educational system, was promising school-places for every child. It was also promising the dispersal of the large estates among the landless : but the new kulaks and co-operative farmers would have to be provided with working capital. If, within a reasonable time, the urban workers who had long thirsted for sufficient schools for their children saw no new buildings and the rural proletariat found themselves owners of little plots which they could not work for lack of capital to acquire tools and seed, inevitably both classes would turn to the men who argued that the world would be better without capital – the anarchists. As it was, there were 800,000 in the anarchist CNT as against 400,000 in the socialist UGT. The Socialist Party could not establish the dictatorship of the proletariat until it had either converted a substantial proportion of the workers from anarchism to socialism or had at its command a people's militia or army with which its will could be enforced. Here, then, was the problem for the socialists : how to appear the most revolutionary party and yet not to destroy the new régime and themselves with it.

The socialists could offer no immediate and quick solution to the problems of the working classes. The anarchists, on the other hand, particularly the intellectuals who had formed themselves in 1927 into a body called the FAI (*Federación Anarquista Ibérica*), did have a solution to offer. To them, republic or monarchy, the 'daily revindicative task' and the fomenting of 'a revolutionary atmosphere' by 'strikes and direct action' was a duty, and if accomplished, the day of 'libertarian communism' would dawn within a brief period. They would have no part either in the government or in the Constituent Assembly and in its election. Little strikes in June 1931 became greater strikes in July. One in Seville began to assume revolutionary proportions and seemed part of a plot to spark off a widespread rising. Azaña, as Minister of War and with the approval of all the Cabinet, ordered aircraft to machine-gun and artillery to shell the insurgents in their redoubt, a bar in the suburbs. Thirty were killed and 200 wounded.

The government thereby proved that it was after all prepared to use force to suffocate disorder (or, put another way, as monarchists, Catholics, and anarchists did, to destroy its enemies) and that it had the force to do so. The army officers had unquestionably obeyed the orders of Azaña, even though, not without reason, they were already convinced that he was intent on destroying the army. In May he had given all officers the choice of retirement on full basic pay if in conscience they could not swear loyalty to the republic—an offer not as generous as it appeared, for the Spanish officers' basic rates of pay were among the lowest in Europe. Five thousand mainly elderly officers had accepted the offer of retirement. Azaña had then declared that he would 'triturate' the army and had already decreed its reduction by nearly 50 per cent. As the new half-size body would require far fewer young officers and N.C.O.s, he had therefore just ordered the dissolution of the Military Academy. Moreover, by sending to the bottom of seniority lists all officers whose promotion had been in the field and not on a time basis, he had 'frozen' them in their ranks. And yet, at Seville in July, the army obeyed him.

The government was then preparing the fulfilment of its promise to hold elections for a Constituent Assembly. The socialists, with their unique nationwide organization and network of propaganda and electioneering centres, agreed to contest them in alliance with their republican colleagues in the government. One of Pablo Iglesias' master-moves in the early days of the party had been to harness the working-class thirst for education through the foundation in cities of *casas del pueblo,* Workers' Colleges, Working Men's Clubs, and socialist propaganda centres. Under the dictatorship the number of *casas del pueblo* had been multiplied and the networks had been spread into rural areas, to wean the rural proletariat from anarchism as well as to make it conscious of its political exploitation by landowners. In the election campaign they proved invaluable.

The left-republicans had no such national network, but as Masons they had the lodges at their disposal, and most large cities had one or more. Maura and Alcalá Zamora had only their personal resources and friends. The right had no organization. Herrera tried to rally under one banner, *Acción Nacional,* all men prepared to accept the republic as a fact but who did not equate republicanism with Marxism or with any of the forms of nineteenth-century liberalism. He received little support. Neither he nor the clergy at any level wanted to identify the Church with a particular political organization, but he and the clergy hoped that Catholic laymen would support him. The middle- and lower-class laity, however, had been cowed by the events of 11 May. In the León–Castile regions those inspired by Herrera did manage to obtain some co-operation from a hastily organized 'agrarian' party, but elsewhere conservatives joined socialists in denouncing his ideas on the distribution of wealth and the practicability of the encyclicals on social justice.

Right-wing and *Acción Nacional* candidates were harassed severely by the left during the election period : meetings were broken up and some candidates were personally assaulted; their families were threatened; some were offered bribes to withdraw their candidatures. Most of them stood their ground, but in many areas of Spain there was no choice outside the republican-socialist lists.

All Spanish males aged twenty-three and over, about 6 million in number, were entitled to vote; but fewer than one in two actually voted, an abstention not satisfactorily explained by the fact that most anarchists had no use for elections. As expected, socialists topped the list of successful candidates with 116; the combined supporters of Azaña, Albornoz, Domingo, and Casares Quiroga totalled 103; the Catalian *Esquerra* won a further forty-three seats. Other smaller groups expected to agree with the socialists and Azaña brought the total left-wing strength to 311. The surprise of the day was the success of Lerroux's radicals, who gained ninety-two seats. Ever an opportunist, Lerroux had realized early in May that he could benefit from the disorganization of the right and had urged moderation on his supporters. Many had followed his lead, and where there was no strong right-wing opponent to the socialist and left-republican candidates, scores of thousands had voted for the radical as less obnoxious. Lerroux could foresee from this a future, and profitable, role for the radicals – to appear as the political centre. For the present, once elected, he aligned his radicals with the left and the centre was formed only by Alcalá Zamora's twenty-one republican progressives. To help them oppose the socialist and left-republican bloc there were twenty-six members (five *Acción Nacional* and twenty-one others of similar views) who for simplicity's sake were called the 'agrarian bloc', fourteen Basque-Navarrese autonomists, and a few independents.

The extreme left had, therefore, an overwhelming majority with or without the radicals. Even so, the first debate in the *Cortes* was on the validity of the agrarians' election, Albornoz's radical socialists pressing for their expulsion. The young professor of constitutional law at Salamanca, Gil Robles, in defence of all the agrarian bloc, delivered an unanswerable speech which earned him the respect of the liberal intellectuals in the house. Ideologically he and they were poles apart, but before the end of the year Gil Robles, the *Acción Nacional* members, and the Liberals saw that they and only a few others had any understanding of what a parliament should be. The sessions had by then been marred by prolonged noise to prevent minority views from being heard and by physical assaults on the more intrepid opponents of the majority. As disturbance had succeeded disturbance, and the left had made it ever clearer in speech, procedure, and act that to them democracy was the unquestioning acceptance of what they, and they alone, decided, so such men as Madariaga, Ortega y Gasset, Unamuno, and Marañón had become disillusioned, and one in despair cried out 'No es ésto' ('this is not the Republic of our dreams').

Following the first meeting of the *Cortes* on 14 July, two committees were quickly constituted, one to prepare the impeachment of the king and Primo de Rivera's associates, the other to draft the new constitution. A socialist, Jiménez de Asúa, was appointed the president of the second committee, and the draft which he tabled before the full *Cortes* on 18 August was his in all but minor detail : a mixture of Mexico 1917, Soviet Russia 1918, and Weimar 1919. It declared Spain 'a Workers' Republic', to be ruled by a President, a Prime Minister, and Cabinet, with a one-chamber assembly to be elected by universal suffrage. There were the usual clauses, as in all West European constitutions, guaranteeing the liberties of the individual, and in all 121 articles; for it went into extraordinary detail on such subjects as how Spain's revenues were to be collected.

It took the *Cortes* three months to pass the constitution – not that in its final version it differed in more than minor detail from the draft; but the *Cortes* were in no great hurry and interrupted their work repeatedly to deal with 'urgent matters'. The term 'Workers' Republic' was modified to read 'a democratic republic of workers of all classes'. There was some discussion as to how far the liberties of the individual would be nullified by the proviso that they would be permitted 'subject to the security of the state'. The non-socialists were pleased to see the right to private property recognized in principle, but feared the possible implications of the limitation 'if not contrary to the national interest' and of specific references elsewhere to the state's power to sequestrate private property. Jiménez de Asúa had in fact made constitutional not merely a radical reform of the whole social structure of Spain but the creation of a socialist state. The non-socialists pinned hopes on the fact that it would not be unconstitutional to delay that process and that given time they might acquire the two-thirds majority needed to change the constitution.

Article 3 defined Spain as a 'lay' state, thus breaking Spain's traditional bonds between Church and state; but Article 26 read : 'all creeds will be considered associations subject to the general laws of the country. In no circumstance will the state maintain, show favour to, or help financially churches or religious associations or institutions. The state will dissolve all religious Orders and nationalize their property'. Jiménez de Asúa explained what this meant : those who so wished would still be free, as he said, 'to *think* Catholic thoughts', but the Church, separated from the state, would be subject to the laws of the state and its priests would have to rely entirely on the alms of their faithful. This did not mean that the property taken in the nineteenth century by the state would be restored to the Church, but that the state would suspend the notional compensation it was paying the clergy. As the Spanish republic was a Workers' Republic, there could therefore be no place for the contemplative monastic Orders. Only workers would be allowed; but freedom of religion was incomplete if a man were not freed from religion. Therefore, priests and nuns would not be permitted to engage in any social welfare work, and particularly no work which brought them into contact with the sick or infirm since it gave them an opportunity to proselytize or reconcile men and women to religion. Azaña went further : Spain had ceased to be Catholic; there was to be no religious teaching; the religious Orders were definitely to be disbanded; and the Jesuits, who with their fourth vow owed an allegiance to a foreign power, were to be banished.

This Article was opposed by the few Catholics in the *Cortes,* while the Liberals considered that the proposal went too far. Azaña, however, threatened them : if they jeopardized its passage he would help the Socialist Party to seize power. After a continuous and acrimonious seventeen-hour debate, which lasted from 4.30 in the afternoon of 13 October until 7.40 the following morning, the decree was passed, the Azaña – socialist faction mustering 175 votes, the Catholic opposition fifty-nine. Alcalá Zamora and Maura resigned; thereupon, at Prieto's suggestion, Azaña took over as president of the government from the former, without giving up the Ministry of War. Casares Quiroga was given the key Ministry of Internal Affairs and a sixty-one-year-old pharmacist Mason friend of Azaña's, Giral Peteira, the Ministry of the Navy. The government passed completely into the hands of the anti-religious and socialist extreme.

The left-socialist group went on to enshrine divorce by mutual consent and explicitly 'lay education' in the constitution. Thereafter, as a Basque deputy, Father Pildaín, pointed out, Catholics in Spain could in conscience adopt one of only three attitudes : passive resistance; legal opposition within the law; or active resistance. As Alcalá Zamora wrote years later, the constitution had become 'one which incited to civil war'. The Basques became more convinced than ever that their only hope of survival as a Catholic nation[2] lay in autonomy. Spain could go on its own road to damnation for all they cared.

The Constitutional Assembly (*Cortes constituyentes*) did not dissolve itself as it should have done, having approved the constitution in December. It merely shortened its title to *Cortes.* The government had no intention of putting its actions to the test of elections. Alcalá Zamora, having in the meantime overcome his scruples over Article 26, accepted the Presidency. Azaña went through the formality of sending his resignation as Prime Minister to the President and was duly asked to form a new government; but Lerroux

[2] Among them and the Navarrese the proportion of practising Catholics to non-practising and anti-religious combined varied from 40 per cent in Bilbao to 80 per cent and over in rural districts.

refused to sit with socialists, and Azaña formed a new government of Masons and socialists alone.

The outcome was predictable. In January 1932 Azaña began to reinforce the anti-religious clauses in the constitution with specific laws and decrees. The Jesuits were declared dissolved and expelled, their 184 schools and ten centres of higher learning were closed, and their property was confiscated. Yet the government made much of its educational plans and achievements in this field, especially before visiting journalists from abroad, promising to increase the number of state 'schools' by 27,000 in five years and announcing in February 1932 that it had 'created' 8,000 new schools since the fall of the monarchy. (Under the monarchy the yearly average had been 500.) This figure, however, was grossly misleading, for a high proportion of the 'schools' were new only in the sense that they were schools previously run by country parishes reopened as 'lay' schools.[3] For the moment religious Orders were allowed to continue teaching in schools so long as they taught no religion and removed all religious symbols. The state specifically forbade children to come to school wearing the crucifixes with which their pious mothers had provided them when the crucifixes were removed from the walls. For the moment religious Orders were also allowed to carry on in hospitals, for while the country had a reserve of unemployed teachers, there was no reserve of nurses, nursing being an unpopular profession among laywomen with the necessary education.

Azaña was well pleased with the republic's record, and not least with the progress of his army reforms. He boasted that his 50 per cent cut had made it as efficient as any in Europe. Nothing was farther from the truth. He had approved the creation of a Service Corps, but otherwise his new model was essentially a half-scale replica of its predecessor, ill-organized, ill-fed, badly clothed, poorly housed, and under-paid. There had been army officers who, only too aware of the army's shortcomings, had hoped for its modernization even at the expense of the reduction in size. They were, therefore, now seething with discontent. In March 1932 Azaña further exacerbated this feeling by decreeing a measure designed as much to force an extra thousand or so officers to retire as to be rid of anyone who displayed his feelings too openly: the forcible

[3] The term *escuela* (school) was at the time very vague. It was used both of a single classroom and of educational buildings with several classrooms. The government calculations of Spain's needs were based on a simple arithmetical formula: the number of children without classrooms was estimated to be about 1·35 million; on the basis of one 'school' and one teacher per fifty pupils, 27,000 'schools' would be required. Thus, in official figures, 'schools' meant schoolrooms.

retirement of any officer not found a definite new posting within six months of being declared redundant. Thereafter an unwise word was frequently followed by a notice that the culprit was *disponible* – 'disposable'.

In May 1931 four discontented army officers had founded a secret society, the *Unión Militar Española,* to further counter-revolutionary activity in the army, but they had then met with little support. Azaña's 'trituration' gained the *Unión* many recruits among serving officers.

At the same time, the officers who had accepted Azaña's offer of retirement on full basic pay were discovering that without private means to supplement that pay they could not maintain more than a lower-middle-class standard of civilian living, and that their army training had given them no qualifications for civilian employment. Those who voiced doubts on Azaña's justice now found that their pensions could be suspended very simply under one of the provisions of the Law for the Defence of the Republic, proposed by Azaña as of 'utmost urgency' and approved by the *Cortes* on 20 October 1931, within days of his assumption of the premiership from Alcalá Zamora.

This law contradicted the constitutional guarantees of civil liberties as much as the whimsies of Primo de Rivera had done and explicitly made the 'defamation of the republic' punishable by fines of up to 10,000 pesetas (roughly $1,200 gold), deportation to the island of Fernando Póo, dismissal from government employment, and cancellation of all pension rights. Any criticism of a government official could be construed as defamation of the republic. Furthermore, the law gave the Minister of the Interior the power to prohibit on his own judgement any assembly or publication and to hold persons indefinitely without trial. It established a new secret police force and a uniformed body of tough, well-armed men called *Guardias de Asalto,* whose task was to break up meetings and demonstrations, and who had authority to shoot on sight anyone committing an act of sabotage. They were officered by ex-army officers and N.C.O.s of known left-wing republican or socialist views.

The law was supposed to last only for the duration of the Constituent Assembly, but as the Constituent Assembly turned itself quietly into the *Cortes,* the law remained in force. True enough, the republic was threatened not only by monarchists and others who believed that Pildaín and Herrera were reaching for the moon in thinking that resistance to the constitution and the government 'within the limits of legality' alone could lead to change, but also by the ever more active and numerous anarchists and indeed by the socialists who were nominally part of the government.

The threat became serious on 19 January 1932 when anarchists took over the valley of the Llobregat in Catalonia. Azaña spoke of a 'plot supported by a foreign power to overthrow the republic' and, having mobilized the greater part on an army division to recover the valley, ordered the arrest of prominent anarchists and communists in Barcelona and Valencia, 104 of whom were immediately transported to Spanish Guinea. The news sparked off a demonstration in the *Cortes,* one of the leaders of which was Franco's brother Ramón, then a radical socialist deputy. There were strikes and gun-battles in several cities.

The masses who had been led to believe that their wrongs would be redressed with the establishment of the republic were indeed disillusioned. The assembly had spent its time drafting and approving a constitution and laws which were irrelevant to their immediate needs, and workers in despair joined the CNT whose membership passed the million mark. Belatedly Prieto and Largo had devoted part of their attention to the improvement of social conditions, especially in the rural areas of anarchist-dominated Andalusia, and had intensified their development of rural *casas del pueblo* and recruitment of members for their Federation of Land Workers. They had begun to establish wage arbitration boards which appeared to be preoccupied with local practical problems and not with questions of principle or national policy. The socialists had in a few months gained considerable influence; but they had achieved this not merely by establishing the arbitration tribunals but also by encouraging class warfare in rural areas; and this had caused an incident which had far-reaching consequences.

A firebrand, Margarita Nelken, had sought in 1931 to gain rural adherents to the Socialist Party by stirring up feeling against the Civil Guard and branding it as the agents of the landowners and their bailiffs. On 31 December at Castelblanco near Badajoz a group of unemployed labourers killed all the members of a Civil Guard detachment and mutilated the bodies – an incident which shocked the country. Six days later a crowd of workers in Arnedo in Castile taunted the Civil Guard. This time the Civil Guard fired into the crowd, killing six and wounding thirty persons, and the *Cortes* demanded the removal of the Commander of the Civil Guard, that same General Sanjurjo who had told the king bluntly that he should leave the country and whose prompt action against the radical socialists and anarchists in July 1931 had saved the infant republic.

On 5 February 1932 Azaña sought to pacify the *Cortes* by transferring Sanjurjo (who held the rank of Lieutenant-General in the army) to the command of the corps of *Carabiñeros* (customs guards); but this added insult to injury. Sanjurjo thereupon repented of his republicanism – or rather he began to see the government of Spain as one which by incompetence or design was allowing a state of affairs to develop which could only end in total anarchy.[4] The general went to see Lerroux – now established in the national mind with his radicals as the only effective opposition to the Azaña-socialist government. His party rallies were attracting masses of supporters and he believed that power was well within his grasp if only the President could be persuaded to dissolve the *Cortes* and call a general election, as he was bound to do sooner or later. Let Sanjurjo bide his time as Lerroux was doing.

By the summer of 1932 UGT membership had grown to 900,000 and CNT strength was nearing 1,500,000. The Marxist ideal of the union of all workers was farther from realization than it had been a year earlier. The UGT could no longer afford the policy of discouraging strikes in urban and industrial areas, though Prieto continued to warn the country that strikes were ruining it. In 1931 the number of workdays lost through strikes in the Vizcaya metallurgical industries was 4,000, nearly all before the advent of the republic; in 1932, following the socialist reversion of policy, the number exceeded 90,000. In 1931 Prieto had proved to the railway-workers that the railways were losing money, but of this they were already convinced. In 1932 men still living on a bare subsistence wage began to ask how it was that, however hard they worked, their productivity per head was among the lowest in Europe. They had been told for so long that capitalists were enjoying enormous profits at their expense : now they were being told there were no profits. The situation in the Asturian coal-mines was even more incomprehensible to the workers. During 1931 they had worked hard. In 1932 they were being told to work for only four days a week, because coal was accumulating at the pit-heads. It could not be sold abroad because it was too expensive and it could not be used at home because it was of too poor a quality for locomotives or steel-works.

The statutory publication of statistics put the government in a more perilous situation. Although the government could not be blamed for the fact that foreign trade had dropped in 1931 to 30 per cent of what it had been in 1928, Spain could not escape some of the consequences of world depression and there was a

---

[4] It was an undeniable fact that in the ten months of republican rule more people had been killed in the streets of Spain than in the preceding forty years of monarchy.

reduced market for its excellent iron-ore. But international economics were comprehensible only to a few : the majority blamed their own government. The decline in Spain's other major export of the time, citrus fruit, was not the government's fault either; but the growers who had failed to reorganize themselves and improve their products to compete with the post-1914–18 war development of the Palestinian industry would not admit to their shortcomings. They, too, blamed the government. Yet economists could not understand the government's internal economic policy either. The budget which was approved at the end of March foresaw a deficit of 200 million pesetas (say $25 million), and more if all the public works suggested were to be undertaken. As it was, where under the monarchy every two paper pesetas had had a backing of a peseta in gold or silver, each of the latter now backed three paper pesetas. The government was making much of the doubling of agricultural wages to two pesetas per day, yet prominent socialists, left-republicans, and radicals were shown to be *enchufados* ('plugged-in') to sources of revenue running into between 5,000 and 10,000 pesetas a month per person. Suspicions of corruption and economic difficulties added to the general unrest. Unrest bred unrest, strike bred strike.

Lerroux continued to watch the government's discomfiture with some glee. His public speeches had voiced precisely those anxieties entertained by Sanjurjo, who again approached him : the republic of their dreams had become a nightmare of chaos; Azaña was destroying the army and the morale of the Civil Guard; the *Cortes* were discussing the Catalan Statute which would effectively make Catalonia a state over which Madrid and the *Cortes* would have no control except in anti-religious legislation and foreign policy; it was almost certain that the *Cortes* would approve of this dismemberment of Spain. Was it not, therefore, the duty of Lerroux and Sanjurjo 'to save Spain'? Lerroux preferred to await a further deterioration in the situation, so that any armed rising should have wider popular support, but Sanjurjo believed there was no time to lose. He sounded out army friends and monarchists. Further consultations among army officers revealed that the youngest general in the army, and the only one of that rank who commanded the respect of junior officers, Francisco Franco, did not believe a rising at that moment either morally justifiable or militarily opportune. Encouraged on the other hand by monarchists and promises of support from other officers (discontent with Azaña was now widespread), Sanjurjo went ahead with plans for a *coup d'état,* to overthrow the government, though not necessarily the republic. In true nineteenth-century style and with the minimum of preparation and security, Sanjurjo issued at 0400 hours on 10 August 1932 a *pronunciamiento* from Seville.

It was an utter failure and was all over in twenty-four hours, for the government, never in any real danger, knew the minutest details of the plan. The only fighting was between supporters of Sanjurjo and government troops together against anarchists in Seville who would not miss the opportunity for a show of *their* strength. Nevertheless, 145 monarchists were deported to Africa. Sanjurjo was sentenced to death, but as he was a hero of the African War, the sentence was commuted to imprisonment for life.

Battles between anarchists and socialists became commonplace in Madrid and to the south and resulting deaths were considerable : sixteen on Labour Day, 1 May. In the north the socialists were also coming face to face with other enemies. The Basques and Navarrese had split on how they were to combat the central power's anti-religious policy. Most of the Basques believed that they could wrest from Madrid without warfare the autonomy that Madrid was prepared to give Catalonia, even though Prieto made it clear that he would never countenance the establishment of what he called 'a Vatican Gibraltar'. Most of the Navarrese, on the other hand, rejected the idea of autonomy, thinking it their duty to 'save Spain' and not merely a part of it. The old spirit of Carlism revived among them. Inspired by a romantic and never clearly defined 'traditionalism' (in which the restoration of the Carlist pretender was only one aspect), they became a political force again, almost a party, one by no means convinced of the virtues of the parliamentary systems they had experienced under Alfonso or the republic, and certain that it was their duty to prepare for armed rebellion against the destruction of Spanish traditions and in defence of their Catholic religion. The socialists would have neither the pacifist Basques nor the warlike traditionalists, and clashes with one or other sometimes resulted in deaths.

The failure of the Sanjurjo plot boosted the prestige of Azaña among all to the left of the radicals and aided the passage through the *Cortes* of two controversial measures – the statute giving Catalonia autonomy and an Agricultural Reform Law.

For Azaña the former was a matter of honour, since he had promised Companys that he would grant Catalonia a measure of autonomy. Following the original declaration of the Catalan republic in April 1931 and the establishment of the *Generalitat* as the *de facto* Catalan government and House of Representatives, a statute of autonomy had been drafted by a committee of all Catalan parties and approved in a referendum held in August 1931. It referred to Catalonia as a self-governing state within the

Spanish republic, entitled to its own flag and all that implied, even if conceding to Madrid management of customs, tariffs, and foreign affairs, including relations with the Vatican. Catalan was to be the official language and the language of education, and Catalonia would be mistress of her educational system. Catalans would serve in the Spanish armed forces but would not be used except in defence of Catalonia. Laws passed and financial provisions demanded by the central government would be enforced in Catalonia only through the *Generalitat,* which alone would be responsible for public order.

This, in effect, meant virtual independence. It was opposed in Madrid as implying 'the dissolution of Spain and over four centuries of history' : if the flag and language of Spain were not to be official in an integral part of Spain, then a complete break would be only a matter of time. The defence of Spanish interests would be deprived of a major source of manpower and war materials. Moreover the statute was as bitterly offensive to non-Catalan industrialists and economists as it was welcome to their opposite numbers in Catalonia; for Catalonia was the most advanced industrial *and* agricultural region of the peninsula, and the most prosperous. Thus the Spanish treasury would be deprived of 25 per cent of its revenue. Socialists, and Prieto in particular, abhorred the statute because it would leave their Catalan colleagues in difficulties. Catalonia was a stronghold of the CNT, but not of the UGT. Socialism, they considered, would lose Catalonia either to the anarchists or to the bourgeoisie. And if an autonomous Catalonia, all opponents of the measure asked, why not an autonomous Basque country, Andalusia, Galicia, and the rest? Opposition to the statute thus cut across all frontiers of class and politics.

Discussion of the statute in the *Cortes* began on 6 May 1932 and passions ran high. Against a background of mass meetings called to oppose the statute in Castile and Aragon, Azaña nevertheless piloted through the *Cortes* the definition of Catalonia as 'an autonomous region within the Spanish state'. The powers of the *Generalitat* were confirmed except in that Catalan was to be no more than the official equal of Spanish and Catalonia was not to be in sole control of its educational system. To get that much through the opposition of socialists and even of his own supporters cost Azaña the best part of three months' labour. After the Sanjurjo rising, however, he had his party fully behind him and the socialists were prepared to suspend their opposition. Catalonia was given control of local finances, radio, railways, roads, harbours, public works, and civil law.

Simultaneously with the discussion of the Catalan Statute, the *Cortes* had been discussing an Agrarian Reform Bill. The basic facts of Spanish agriculture as seen by politicians in 1932 were these : the natural fertility of the land, together with the rainfall, went from extreme to extreme; nowhere was the land efficiently exploited; vast areas were owned and worked as single units while other areas had come to be subdivided into tiny holdings; security of tenure was precarious; there were zones with crops which required tens of thousands of men to harvest, men for whom there was no work for ten months in the year. In short, there was in-efficiency in husbandry and social injustice, a situation generally recognized by men of the right and left. On neither side, how-ever, was there any agreement as to what should be done, or what could be done; and on both sides an oversimplification of an extremely complex problem.

The right tended to see the problem as essentially one of eco-nomics and climate. They accepted that irrigation of the dry lands would result in increased crops, but irrigation would require, as it had in the past, a vast programme of dam- and canal-building. Neither the landowners nor the state had the capital. More could be done for the economy of the country by rationalizing the over-tiny holdings than by dividing the *latifundia*. The left saw the problem primarily as one which could be solved by a change of ownership. The *latifundia* (farms of 2,500 acres and over) should be taken from their owners with or without compensation and, according to the socialists, should then be administered as state or collective farms; according to the non-Marxist left, they should be divided and distributed to the landless as smallholdings.

Greed, idealism, and ignorance obfuscated thinking on all aspects of the subject; but the revolutionaries of San Sebastián had pro-mised land reform, and on 10 May 1932 a Bill was put before the *Cortes*. It proposed in emotional terms the abolition of the *lati-fundia*, the punishment of absenteeism, and adequate remunera-tion for workers in the fields. In the first year some 70,000 to 75,000 families were to be settled on expropriated land at a cost of 50 million pesetas, with compensation for the original owners out of profits to be paid in instalments over a long period of years. Even such a pusillanimous and inadequate law provoked sixty-eight amendments in the first place and a further seventy in June. This inadequacy becomes particularly glaring when one considers the situation in southern Spain alone, where there were half a mil-lion landless families and where even in those days $100 would hardly have sufficed to stock a smallholding.

The Bill was still under discussion when Sanjurjo's rebellion

misfired. A Bill to confiscate the land owned by those implicated in
the plot was then rushed through the *Cortes,* and this at long last
eased the way for the passage in September of the long-discussed
Agrarian Reform Law, in its final form a lawyers' paradise. The
one clause which could be understood without discussion was that
all the lands owned by 'the extinguished nobility' were declared
the property of the state without compensation : 127 dukes and in
all 390 men and women were thereby deprived of hundreds of
thousands of acres. Yet over the next thirteen months a mere
12,260 landless families were settled.

As the winter of 1932 approached, the number of unemployed
rose alarmingly, topping half a million, about 15 per cent of the
labour force; strikes multiplied; several dozen churches were set on
fire; and not a few local government officials were murdered. The
prisons were full both of men suspected of being involved in deeds
of violence and of those too critical of the régime and not protected by parliamentary immunity. In Extremadura and Andalusia
extensive areas were in the hands of anarchists. The explosion of a
detonator in Barcelona led the police to the discovery not merely of
a bomb factory but of plans for a nationwide anarchist rising. The
government alerted its security forces and on the night of 8/9
January 1933 an anarchist rising was suppressed with the loss of
between fifty and 200 lives.

The suppression was complete except in the village of Casas
Viejas near Cadiz where a Captain Rojas, in command of a force
of ninety Assault Guards sent to help the local Civil Guard detachment, set fire to a house in which some anarchists were holding
out, even though they held an Assault Guard as a hostage. Rojas
then gave orders for the village to be sacked. When twelve men,
secured by ropes, were brought before him he ordered that they
should be shown the body of the dead Assault Guard. As they
stood beside the body Rojas shouted 'Fire!' Some of the Assault
Guards and two Civil Guards obeyed and Rojas then ordered
another two villagers to be killed in cold blood.

When the news of what had happened at Casas Viejas became
public, there was general indignation. Rojas claimed that he had
received strict instructions to act ruthlessly, to take no prisoners,
and to 'shoot in the belly', and he was widely believed. The radical
Martínez Barrio called the Azaña régime one of 'mire, blood, and
misery' and both left and right began to clamour for the dissolution
of the *Cortes.* In the municipal elections of April 1933 much to their
discomfiture, Azaña and the socialists gained between them only
35 per cent of the seats. The radicals and Gil Robles, whose
Acción Popular and associates had gained 30 per cent, demanded

Azaña's resignation. Azaña, however, knowing the anti-religious fervour of Martínez Barrio and a good majority of the radicals then in the *Cortes,* reminded them that the Bill to put into effect one part of Article 26 of the constitution was not yet law. The Bill of Religious Congregations, then long under discussion, expressly made it illegal for members of religious Orders to engage in commerce and industry, or to teach in any school even as private individuals. In spite of protests from agnostics as well as Catholics, the deputies rallied to Azaña, and in May the Bill became law by a solid vote of 278 to fifty. Over 300,000 children were to be deprived of primary, and 17,000 of secondary, schooling by 1 October. About half a million people in hospices and orphanages were to be left not homeless, but at the mercy of day-to-day begging, since the religious Orders looking after them would have been denied all other sources of income.

Once the Bill was passed, the left fell to renewed infighting. The socialists' acute problem remained unresolved – how to persuade the rank-and-file of the UGT, especially the new members in the rural districts, that orthodox Marxism had more to offer them in the long run than anarchism. This rank-and-file set fire to harvests in Extremadura and Andalusia in July and August. In Seville the socialists could now see a new rival at work. At the proclamation of the republic the Spanish Communist Party had numbered at most a thousand members. In 1932 its leaders, Nin and Maurín, had seceded from it to found a Trotskyite party; but by 1933 it had discovered new leaders. In terms of membership it was still very small, but tightly organized and able to exert an influence among workers which astonished and frightened the socialists. In August the first gun-fights between communists and socialists occurred in Seville, while anarchists and gunmen hired by the landowners made the battles quadrilateral. If the socialists were to gain the leadership of the workers they would have to break with Azaña.

The constitution-makers had rejected the idea of an Upper House for the *Cortes* in favour of a Tribunal of Constitutional Guarantees whose members were to be elected by municipal councillors, universities, and colleges of lawyers, and the elections for it were held in September. Two out of three of the government nominees were defeated, and in their place men of the centre and of the right were elected, including the exiled monarchist Calvo Sotelo and the previously imprisoned financier Juan March. Lerroux challenged Azaña to test the confidence of the *Cortes* in his government and in the votes that followed two-thirds of the

Cortes abstained. Azaña handed in his resignation. On 12 September the President called on Lerroux to form a new government, but his attempts to gain support for an administration based on the radicals and radical-socialists failed. Alcalá Zamora appointed a caretaker government to supervise new elections. The first, left-wing, phase of the republic was over.

Chapter 23

The Republic: The Second Phase
November 1933 to January 1936

THE SOCIALISTS had few illusions about the November 1933 elections. The municipal elections of the previous April and those for the Tribunal of Constitutional Guarantees had revealed that there was a strong popular feeling against Azaña and the other non-socialist leaders of the left. There were two imponderables : how severely would the socialists be defeated and how far would the disunity of the right enable the left to assert itself within the *Cortes*?

Angel Herrera's *El Debate* had been suspended from time to time by the Azaña government and meetings of *Acción Nacional* had often been banned. The party had had to be renamed *Acción Popular* following a decree denying the term 'national' to any political organization – other than the CNT, against which the government had neither the will nor the courage to move. Nevertheless, *Acción Popular* had grown rapidly and by the end of 1932 could boast over 600,000 known supporters. There had then been an internal crisis. Herrera had continued to insist that to Catholics monarchy and republic were equally acceptable as structures of government, and maintained that it was even morally wrong at that moment to press for the restoration of the monarchy because such pressure could provoke the left to violence, and the only hope of a victory over the left was by constitutional means. In all that Gil Robles, though a monarchist at heart, fully supported him. Not so, however, another prominent member of *Acción Popular*, Antonio Goicoechea. He had seceded in January 1933 to found *Renovación Española,* a party whose declared purpose was to work for the re-establishment of monarchy by democratic and bloodless means. Two months later in March 1933, however, Gil Robles, now the recognized leader of *Acción Popular,* had brought together into a loose confederation a number of scattered non-left groups, the *Confederación Española de Derechas Autónomas,* a title which suggests that on its executive there was no one with an understanding of the elements of advertising or propaganda. It was too long and therefore from the start people referred to it by its initials, the pronounceable combination CEDA; but *ceda,* the Spanish for the letter 'z' and the imperative 'yield', was hardly an inspiring alternative. The programme was essentially a negative one – perhaps the only one possible, for the confederation was properly one of 'individualistic anti-left parties' and not what a literal translation of the Spanish title might suggest. Its member parties undertook to seek election to the *Cortes* in order to remove from the statute book and the constitution the anti-religious laws and clauses and to uphold 'the traditional values of motherland, family, property, order, and work' against the Marxist offensive on them. It was a most liberal organization in that it allowed its members as individuals or component parties to advocate whatever else they wished.

CEDA, like *Acción Popular,* was Catholic in inspiration, but it did not appeal only to practising Catholics. Nor did it comprise all practising Catholics. The Basques were not satisfied with Gil Robles' own sympathy with regional autonomy, for they were now no longer home-rulers but separatists. CEDA did not appeal either to most latifundists, for *Acción Popular,* reckoned as its major and leading component, was preaching the justice of the distribution of land-ownership which would have almost the same effect on their interests and themselves as the socialist plans for the nationalization of the land and its management as state or collective farms. Nor would CEDA's acceptance of the republic make it tolerable to the not inconsiderable portion of the population which still held monarchy to be divinely ordained. Some still wanted Alfonso back; others (the traditionalists) the Carlist pretender. CEDA was not nationwide either. Anti-Marxist activity in Catalonia was in the hands of the Catalan *Lliga,* too closely linked with business interests to have a wide appeal.

To the new *Cortes* of 470 members only fifty-five socialists were returned – a severer blow than they had expected. In the dissolved assembly of just over 500, they had had 116 seats. The other left-wing parties had only sixty-three between them (including twenty for the Catalan *Esquerra*) and Azaña's private party was down from twenty-seven to five. Of the architects of the constitution only the Lerroux radicals, who had so assiduously cultivated their image as reasonable middle-of-the-way men, could be said to have held their ground. Their share of seats in the *Cortes* had been reduced, but they still had seventy-nine deputies. A maze of other more genuinely centre parties gained eighty seats between them. The parties of the right outside CEDA totalled ninety-seven. CEDA had 115 seats, but even so could not claim victory – a prize no party could claim.

The combined strength of CEDA and the right did not add up to 235 seats: that of the left (ninety-eight) together with the radicals (seventy-nine) and about fifty of the centre who would follow Lerroux in his new image of a centre leader could just do so, as could CEDA with the radicals and as few as forty of the centre. Lerroux, anxious to be Prime Minister, was prepared to accommodate CEDA on the relaxation of the anti-religious legislation and on other matters. When, therefore, President Alcalá Zamora decided that CEDA could not be held to be a single party and that he was bound by the constitution to offer the premiership to the leader of the largest party in the *Cortes* – Lerroux – Gil Robles promised Lerroux CEDA's support. The alternative would have been a Lerroux-left coalition.

The anarchists celebrated the advent of a new government with what was intended to be a nationwide rising and declarations of 'libertarian communism' in several localities to the accompaniment of the solemn burning of churches. Lerroux's Minister of the Interior, Martínez Barrio, ordered the Civil Guard to take immediate action and the rising was suffocated in four days of battle. In the new year Lerroux faced an internal crisis: Martínez Barrio, true to his masonic oaths, resigned from the Cabinet when he discovered that Lerroux was not prepared to put into effect the Law on Religious Congregations and close the Catholic schools still open. In April 1934 Lerroux began to fulfil his promise to Gil Robles by introducing – to the horror of Martínez Barrio – a Bill to restore to the clergy two-thirds of their pre-republic stipends. Amid uproar the left opposed it as unconstitutional. So it was, in that as from 1933 the constitution had absolved the state from the obligations it had contracted in the nineteenth century. Over twenty radicals followed Martínez Barrio in abstaining. Nevertheless, 280 members from right and centre combined to vote the Bill through – only six left-wingers bothering to vote against it formally.

The result showed the socialists that they could not hope to stop the nullification of the left-wing legislation of the Azaña régime by parliamentary means. The situation which they faced was therefore more serious than that which had confronted the Catholics after the passage of the anti-religious Articles 3 and 26 of the constitution. If there was to be no retrogression from, let alone further progress towards, socialism, neither passive resistance nor opposition within the law would suffice. There had to be active resistance and without waiting for any party decision, individual socialists embarked on it. In the *Cortes* CEDA members called on Martínez Barrio as Minister of the Interior to punish flagrant violations of the law by socialists in rural districts. The socialist leader Prieto thereupon warned the assembly that the socialists were 'being pushed out of the limits of legality towards revolutionary stances'. He demanded a vote of confidence in the government. Monarchists, Catalanists and Basques, and some radicals abstained, and still Lerroux got 235 votes against fifty-four.

The National Committee of the UGT and Executive Council of the Socialist Party met to consider the situation. Professor Julián Besteiro argued that it was the socialists' duty to allow the government to govern; but Largo Caballero would have none of it. He wanted the party to dedicate itself to the creation of the classic Marxist 'revolutionary situation'. Thereafter, whenever he addressed union meetings he called on the workers to arm and be prepared for 'street warfare'. The daily *El Socialista* preached against peace and called upon workers to watch out for 'the red disc', the signal for revolution. On 4 February Prieto came out on the side of Largo. At a meeting of socialist leaders, he stated that the Socialist Party and workers' organization would soon have to fulfil 'the destiny which History has reserved for you ... Nothing can stop the phalanxes of the party and the UGT ... Let the proletariat come to power and let it do with Spain what Spain deserves. The proletariat must not falter, and if bloodshed is necessary, it is its duty to encourage that bloodshed'.

Azaña, in disapproval of their policy, remonstrated with his old allies, but they were not prepared to listen. Lerroux's reaction to the vote of confidence was belief that he could cope with any attempt at revolution. He continued to appease Catholic sentiment. His new Minister of the Interior allowed the Holy Week processions to be held – they had been banned in 1932 and 1933. After witnessing them in Seville, on 1 April Martínez Barrio broke finally with Lerroux, taking with him thirteen other radicals to found a new party of the left, in opposition on church matters, thoroughly bourgeois on economics, and politically an embarrassment to Lerroux, who was now forced to seek votes of members to the right of CEDA.

To attract the votes of the electorate, always ready to sympathize with men imprisoned for political offences, Gil Robles had pledged himself to seek amnesty for those summarily convicted as participants in and accessories to the Sanjurjo rising. So had some radicals, and of course all monarchists. On 20 April Lerroux introduced a Bill of Amnesty, which proposed the release of several hundred men in prison for political offences and concerned principally, but not exclusively, the men sentenced by the republic for collaborating with

Primo de Rivera and the supporters of Sanjurjo. It was passed by 269 votes to one, the Basques abstaining on the grounds that it was no concern of theirs, the left-republicans because they could not forgive those who had risen against them, and the socialists because they had no further use for the *Cortes*.

That a few men more or a few men less should be amnestied was of little consequence to the socialists. What mattered was that Gil Robles could pull together 268 members of the *Cortes* behind him even on such a controversial subject. In Gil Robles and *Acción Popular* they saw their major enemy – and with good reason.

In two years *Acción Popular* had become almost as numerous as the Socialist Party after two generations. The latter comprised only two classes : a few intellectuals and a mass of manual workers; the former appealed to a much wider range. To the workers whose habit of mind was still Catholic, *Acción Popular*'s social doctrines made more sense than those of Marx. To the landless of Castile and Aragon especially, Gil Robles' advocacy of the distribution of land in *ownership* was far more attractive than the socialists' now officially declared intention to abolish all land ownership and make *latifundia* and *minifundia* alike state farms. (The peasants saw the hated landlord's bailiff merely putting on a new hat as the state farm-manager.) Now the action taken against the socialists by Dr Dollfuss in Vienna on 12 February had been given full publicity in the Spanish press, independent and liberal no less than left-wing, and whatever the rights and wrongs of the event, it had aroused deep sympathy for the defeated socialists. Gil Robles had from time to time publicly argued that the principle of one man one vote had philosophically less to commend it than a principle consequent on the corporative theory of representative government, of relating the individual citizen's voting power to his responsibilities. (Thus, for example, a steel-worker, married with a family, might have three votes : one as a citizen, one as a worker, and one as the head of a family.) Mussolini was then paying lip-service to corporative political theories – and thereby discrediting them. Gil Robles had no love for Mussolini, being rather better informed than most Catholics about the philosophical and theological implications of Fascism – but Dr Dollfuss was a Catholic and Gil Robles was a Catholic. The socialists now took up the cry that Gil Robles was a Fascist – worse, a 'clerico-fascist'. If Gil Robles and CEDA were to come to power the fate of the workers in Spain would be that of the workers in Vienna.

Deep though Gil Robles' hatred of Fascism was, he was not averse to copying some of the propaganda methods of Fascism and socialism. The founders of *Acción Popular* had decided early

11

on that though their social and political doctrines had been spelt out before any of them had been born, there was little hope of converting the older generation in mass to them. That older generation was for the most part irretrievably conservative or liberal, monarchist or republican. The future lay with men and women still in their twenties. Accordingly they had organized a youth section, the *Juventudes de Acción Popular,* or JAP, rivalling the better-organized and more military-minded Socialist Youth, which like the UGT was now under Largo Caballero. JAP early in the spring of 1934 became politically embarrassing to Gil Robles. Its leaders began to argue that CEDA was now a united single party and therefore constitutionally entitled to government, or at least to a share in government. They pressed Gil Robles to demand his 'rights' of the President; but he continued to argue that the promises CEDA had given the electorate were being fulfilled as rapidly as was prudent; as they were supporters of but not collaborators with Lerroux, they would benefit most in the long run; governments were subject to 'wear and tear'; the opportune moment for CEDA to enter government would come in due course. Besides, Gil Robles knew that Alcalá Zamora would never willingly call on him to form a government.

Both to demonstrate their strength to the President and to move Gil Robles from his policy, JAP organized a congress in the Escorial, north-west of Madrid, which was to culminate in a mass rally on 22 April. Immediately it was announced, the socialist press called on the government to ban such an act of 'Fascist provocation'. Lerroux saw no reason why he should. The UGT thereupon called on all its members to go on strike. Blue-shirted Socialist Youth groups picketed *Acción Popular* offices, giving the clenched-fist salute and assaulting those wanting to leave or enter. They killed one JAP member. In spite of the general strike no fewer than 30,000 attended the rally, several thousand young men and women walking the twenty miles from Madrid to the Escorial. Placing their right hand on their left shoulder they acclaimed a statement of ideals and aims : the participation of youth in politics; the protection of the Christian family; freedom in education; the distribution of wealth; war on class-warfare; war on the idle and rich among youth, Marxism, dictatorship, and false parliamentary systems. In their declaration, however, they included a phrase which out of context was to give the socialists one of their best weapons in their presentation of JAP as a Fascist organization : *los jefes no se equivocan* – 'leaders never make a mistake'. Gil Robles took the intended hint, meant as a challenge to his leadership. Addressing the rally, he called on the President to hand power over to CEDA;

he also spoke at length against Fascism with the argument 'the more Spanish you are, the more Catholic and therefore the more anti-Fascist', but in reference to the fact that socialists had shot and seriously wounded two youths on their way to the rally and held up vehicles at pistol point, he added : 'we have always acted within the law, and this rally reaffirms that we are the firmest defenders of the established law : but if the revolutionaries fight in the street, then we shall have to fight them there'.

JAP, however, did not seek battle with the Socialist Youth. They left that to the *Falange,* which by the spring had a membership of 4,000 and a score of deaths to avenge.

The *Falange* may be called the Spanish Fascist Party, with some reservations in that it had been born in reaction to anarcho-syndicalism and not Marxism, and sought to wean anarchists from Bakunin rather than socialists from Marx.

In October 1931, six months after the establishment of the republic and when the chief threat to it was anarchist-syndicalist activity, two twenty-six-year-old university graduates, Ramiro Ledesma and Onésimo Redondo, had come together to found a new revolutionary movement. It was to consist of groups of young men forming themselves into Committees of National-Syndicalist (as opposed to anarcho-syndicalist) Militant Action, *Juntas de Ofensiva Nacional Sindicalista* (JONS).

Ledesma, the son of a schoolmaster in Zamora, had studied German philosophy under Ortega y Gasset in Madrid, and like his master had become an ardent disciple of Nietzsche. In 1931 he was editing an intellectual magazine with the provocative title *La Conquista del Estado* (The Conquest of the State). He advocated the syndicalization of all the means of production; rejected state-ownership (for in his opinion the state would prove as damnable an employer as the capitalist); was convinced that workers' syndicates alone could 'regenerate the nation'. He saw the syndicate as the natural unit of society, and the syndicated nation as itself a syndicate. With the anarchist, he saw the interests of the syndicate as greater than those of the individual, and logically put the nation above the individual. Religion, and especially Catholicism, he judged enervating and therefore to be eradicated. He admired the anarchists' determination and outlook on death and violence.

Onésimo Redondo had been a law student at Salamanca, and then an assistant lecturer at Mannheim where he had come to admire the discipline of the Nazis but not their ideals, except in so far as they coincided with his own Hegelianism. On his return to Spain he, too, had taken to dilettante journalism and in 1931 was editing a weekly paper, *Libertad,* in which he vented his hatred of the bourgeoisie and extolled the virtues of the working classes. He too had empathy with anarcho-syndicalism, but again he faulted the Bakunin-Sorel idealism of the CNT for not giving sufficient value to the regenerative power of patriotism, the 'sense of nation'. Redondo's thought was acutely Castilian: 'Castile through bloodshed and violence can regenerate Spain,' he wrote.

The JONS, Redondo and Ledesma decided, were to be 'small groups of young men avid for deeds of daring and violence, trained for war and disciplined'. Members were to wear blue shirts and red ties, and their flag was to be the anarchist black and red. Their symbol was to be Ferdinand and Isabel's Yoke and Arrows. They took as their battle-cry, *España, Una, Grande, Libre,* four words which would come to summarize a whole political structure in whose construction the JONS had a part, but which on completion they saw as quite different from what they thought they were building. The JONS grew slowly, but they grew all the same. By the beginning of 1933 there were perhaps 400 university student members ready to do verbal battle with Marxists, separatists, and anyone else who doubted 'the greatness and dignity' of Spain.

In March 1933 what was to have been a new weekly – *El Fascio* – had made a brief appearance. The public never knew what it contained because it was confiscated immediately. Ledesma was one of its contributors, but its chief editor was José Antonio, the thirty-year-old son of the late Primo de Rivera, a doctor of law from the University of Madrid, but better known in literary than in legal circles; for he wrote good verse. He had felt his father's death in 1931 keenly, and had then taken to politics, so he said, to vindicate the memory of his father. The monarchists assumed that he was one of them and welcomed him into their ranks. The dictator's son was indeed no republican; but he regarded Alfonso and the monarchists, whom he considered to have betrayed his father, with distaste. He had his own ideas. He had assiduously studied Spengler, Marx, Lenin, and Ortega. In 1933 he was reading Hitler and Rosenberg, and despising them as fools if not worse. He admired Mussolini because he had brought 'order out of chaos', but saw in Fascism as such little of particular relevance to Spain. Like Ledesma and Redondo he believed that Spain had 'a historic mission'. Spain to him was the sum of all its parts, or rather the synthesis of all individuals of all classes which thus synthesized became a new organism whose parts could never be greater than the whole, and must be disciplined or adjusted to the well-being of the whole. What was required in his view was the homogenizing of all Spaniards into a well-ordered society. All Spaniards were to be workers and classless : class-warfare would then be impossible. The right to private property would be recognized, but the means of production, and especially capital, would have to be nationalized. The individual would be left free to be religious, but the state would have no religion. All political parties would be abolished because parties led to divisions : in Spanish history they had been responsible for the *pronunciamientos,* revolutions, and civil wars of the nineteenth century. José Antonio Primo's ideology was thus a hotchpotch of Hegel, Nietzsche, and Marx.

To guide Spain towards its 'well-ordered unity', José Antonio had launched on 29 October 1933 a new 'movement' (he eschewed the word 'party'), with the name *Falange Española* and funds provided by monarchists. The lower-middle class and even some workers, faced with the chaos of the republic, were beginning to look back on the Primo de Rivera régime with nostalgia and the monarchists were looking on that development as a first step towards the rehabilitation of Alfonso XIII. Admirers of Mussolini because he had diverted numbers of workers from socialism and republicanism, they had decided that this young man of great personal charm, the poet in a land where poets were not admired only by narrow coteries, the bearer of a famous name, might well do in Spain what the *Duce* had done in Italy. At the inaugural meeting José Antonio had inveighed against 'Rousseaunian liberalism' and Marxism as fissiparous forces. He had spoken of his movement gathering momentum 'by dialectic'; yet, he had added, in the defence of justice and the motherland, the only dialectic would be that of 'fists and pistols'. To his monarchist backers what he had said had not mattered so much as the fact that he had said it well, and that he had proved his capacity to enthrall an audience.

At top Socialist Party level the *Falange* looked insignificant enough on 29 October 1933 : a group of monarchists had financed a meeting of university men headed by a poet. At youth movement level, however, a more serious view was taken of it. Three days later, on 2 November, an encounter between a group of Socialist Youth and Falangists ended with the stabbing to death of one of the Falangists. José Antonio, a monarchist candidate for the *Cortes,* gave strict orders that there should be no reprisals. During December socialists shot dead two young Falangists distributing the *Falange's* new newspaper *F E,* but José Antonio, now a member of *Cortes,* again forbade reprisals. During January 1934 five more Falangists were killed and on 9 February yet another Falangist was shot dead. Primo de Rivera attended the funeral but demanded of his followers that they should be prepared to die but not to take vengeance. The *Falange* murmured and recalled their leader's phrase about the 'dialectic of fists and pistols'. There were now about 2,000 Falangists, nearly all of them undergraduates and junior teaching staff of the universities, for the movement was essentially one of protest by this younger generation against its immediate precursor. (It was to become historically interesting that the older generation had preached what a later age would call 'a permissive society' as well as political liberalism, and that the younger was the one demanding order, discipline, and restriction.) José Antonio now allowed Falangist students to attend lectures with pistols hidden in hollowed-out books; but he was about to cease to be sole master of the *Falange*. For months *Falange* and JONS, so similar in ideas and programme, had been discussing a merger, even though José Antonio had disliked Ledesma back in the days of *El Fascio*. In Ruíz de Alda, the navigator in Ramón Franco's pioneering South Atlantic flight, they had now found a go-between.

On 13 February 1934 the two quasi-Fascist organizations fused into one under the triumvirate of Primo de Rivera, Ruíz de Alda, and Ledesma. It was called the *Falange Española de las JONS* or, more simply, *Falange*. From March to the following October Falangists and socialists wreaked assassination on one another. In October, however, José Antonio became sole leader of the *Falange* once again.

The gun-battles between the Falangists and socialists were only one factor in the disorders of the period. Back in Madrid after the Escorial rally Gil Robles was informed by Lerroux that President Alcalá Zamora was considering sending back the Amnesty Bill to the *Cortes* unsigned. He signed it on 24 April, but sent the *Cortes* a long statement which was in essence an attack on the integrity of Lerroux. Lerroux refused to join Gil Robles in a proposal to censure Alcalá Zamora and so obtain his removal, but resigned the premiership. Alcalá Zamora called on another radical, Ricardo Samper, a personal friend of his but otherwise insignificant, to form a new government. Another factor which led to trouble was that under Azaña works tribunals had been established with the purpose of ensuring reasonably just contracts between landowners and casual agricultural labourers. Their weakness lay in the fact that the arbitrators were government appointed and under Azaña they had favoured the workers. Decisions had been made more with an eye to approval at anti-landlord government level than with reference to the facts and contracts where justice had been so more by accident than design. With Lerroux in power and anxious to obtain the support of landowners or the friends of landowners in the *Cortes* among his own radicals no less than on the right, the arbitrators had become monstrously biased in favour of the landlords. The new contracts were unjust to a degree that outdid what had been done before the republic. Nothing could have suited the socialists better. During early May they called for token strikes in several industries in various parts of the country to test the strength of the UGT and its co-operation with communists, Trotskyists, and individual anarchists which Largo Caballero had been negotiating. On 25 May a combined UGT-CNT committee announced that agricultural workers would go on strike on 5 June in support of certain demands being made by the Socialist Federation of Land Workers. The harvesting of the most abundant wheat crop ever known in Spain was due to begin at that time. By then Largo Caballero had convinced all but a few intellectuals in the party that as no further progress towards socialism seemed possible by constitutional means, the time had come for a socialist revolution. Arms and ammunition were being obtained by stealth and purchased and stored in the *casas del pueblo* which were being prepared for siege. The Socialist Youth was being organized into militia units and their members were being refreshed in conscript service training. Socialist newspapers carried regular inflammatory articles; but preparations for the classic Marxist pre-revolutionary strike were far from ready. The agricultural strike was intended only to gain the confidence of the agricultural workers in socialist leadership by obtaining for them high wages and employment even where landlords had bought machines to replace hand-harvesters; but Samper's Minister of the Interior, with many others, read the signs and declared the strike political in purpose and therefore illegal. The government supervised the work of a tribunal which by 5 June had granted most of the original demands. Strike leaders countered these concessions by making new demands. With the original demands granted, however, 80 per cent of the workers refused to fall into line. The militant 20 per cent, anarchists and communists for the most part, attacked machines and farm buildings. The Minister, calling on the Civil and Assault Guards, had several hundred workers and socialist village schoolmasters, and even two *Cortes* members, arrested, whereupon the strike collapsed. There were complaints in the *Cortes* against the arrest of the socialist deputies and the socialists redoubled their smear campaign against CEDA and intensified their para-military training of militia.

The government and *Cortes*, however, were more concerned with a simultaneous crisis, unconnected with the agricultural workers' strike. In the November 1933 elections the regionalist right-wing Catalan *Lliga* had won twenty-five seats from the *Esquerra*, reducing their number in the *Cortes* to nineteen. In December the moderately left Maciá died, and the extreme left Companys inherited the leadership of the *Esquerra*. In January 1934 elections for the *Generalitat* were held, and with the anarchists participating on behalf of the *Esquerra*, the *Esquerra* won a large majority of the seats. On 11 April the *Generalitat* passed an Agrarian Reform Bill presented by Companys to enable tenant farmers of small vineyards to acquire title to land which they had cultivated for at least fifteen years. The landlords instantly challenged the law under the clause in the republic's constitution which reserved to the national *Cortes* all laws affecting contracts. The *Generalitat* thereupon justified its position under an article in the Catalan Statute giving it the right to legislate in matters of agrarian social policy.

The matter was put to the Tribunal of Constitutional Guarantees, ten of whose members upheld the *Generalitat's* reading of the statute, eighteen the landlords' allegations of unconstitutionality. The *Generalitat*, refusing to accept the decision, made plans to defend Catalonia's frontiers; the *Esquerra* members left the *Cortes*; and the Basque nationalists followed suit.

On 5 November 1933 a Statute of Basque Autonomy had been put to the vote in Navarre and the Basque provinces proper – Guipúzcoa, Álava, and Vizcaya. Socialists and monarchists (both Carlist and Alfonsist) had abstained, but of those who had voted an overwhelming majority had approved the statute. The Basque nationalist leader, José Aguirre, had brought it before the *Cortes* late in December. Neither Lerroux, nor Samper, nor the Catalan *Lliga* leader Cambó, nor Gil Robles from whom, as a Catholic, they expected understanding, had shown any willingness to sponsor its discussion, and the twelve Basque members had become by April disenchanted with the centre, the Catholic centre-right, and the Catalan right.[1]

The Catalan assembly, standing firm in its defiance of the *Cortes*, approved a new Law on Farming Contracts in line with its regional Agrarian Reform Act. Samper decided not to press the issue. The *Cortes* adjourned on 1 July for the summer holidays with the matter in abeyance and the government moved, as had been the custom under the monarchy, to San Sebastián. Under its very nose, the Basques proposed to hold elections as yet not sanctioned by any law emanating from Madrid. Under the constitution a new Law of Municipalities to establish the limits of the central government's powers over local governments should have been prepared, but neither Azaña nor Lerroux had bothered. The towns

[1] Like most Castilians to the right and left of him Gil Robles underestimated the strength of Basque nationalist emotion; he judged its strength only on the 1933 election results when right-wing candidates had received 37 per cent, the nationalists 34 per cent, and the left 28 per cent of the votes cast.

were to choose delegates to negotiate with Madrid the future taxation of Basques.[2] The government despatched armed police to Bilbao, Vitoria, and San Sebastián, the capitals of the three provinces, to prevent these illegal elections. The Basques went ahead on 12 August in fifty out of their 180 towns and some Basque aldermen were arrested. The Basques' consciousness of race and nationality now rose to a point unequalled in centuries. Prieto, who though not a Basque had lived most of his life in Bilbao, appreciated the strength of that consciousness. Hitherto he had been as ill-disposed to Basque nationalism as the most extreme Spanish nationalist of the right, but he now began to back and even encourage the Basque defiance of the central government. This defiance was useful in itself as creative of the required Marxist 'revolutionary situation'. The Basques, being tough fighters, would be useful allies. At the beginning of September he and other socialist leaders made a point of attending and speaking at Basque rallies. They promised to support the Statute of Autonomy and even invited the Basques to discuss the matter jointly with representatives of the communist and socialist parties on 2 November. The Basques were grateful for this socialist support, but they were too concerned with their own affairs to notice that in the rest of the country their new socialist friends and the left generally remained as anti-Basque as ever.

By the beginning of September the socialist plans for revolution were in a sufficiently advanced state for their newspapers to hint that the signal for revolution would be given in October. On 29 August there had been a significant sign. Communist Youth members had stood side by side with socialists at the funeral of a socialist murdered by Falangists. Earlier in the year communists and socialists had battled one against the other as arduously as socialists had done against Falangists, the communists calling the socialists Fascists. Henceforward communists were to co-operate with socialists : Moscow had grudgingly approved the entrance of the communists into a *Frente Unico* proposed by Largo Caballero, for the official line of the time was 'action through the bourgeois parliamentary democracies'. Moscow did not want revolution in Spain or anywhere else at that moment; but the Spanish Communist Party's future was at stake. It would be ruined if it failed to participate in plans for a revolution which appeared to have a chance of success even though, in communist eyes, amateur-led.

[2] Almost the only 'ancient liberty' still left to the Basques was their exemption from *direct* taxation by Madrid. Each town council contracted to pay a lump sum to the central government and to do its own tax-gathering.

Over in Catalonia, Companys, the leader of the *Esquerra,* was moving well to the left and the socialists had no difficulty in enlisting his support. Catalonia's importance lay not only in its inherent strategical position, but in its apparently good militia organized by a curious character called Dencás, a militia which had acquired its arms from the *Somatén,* the Home Guard which the *Generalitat* had abolished.

Everything seemed set fair at the beginning of September for revolution. The socialists then suffered some severe setbacks. The French intercepted a second shipload of arms on its way to Asturias. The police raided the *casa del pueblo* at Madrid and removed its arsenal, and discovered many of the socialist arms dumps in the capital and provinces. Those who like Besteiro had always had doubts of the feasibility of seizing power by revolution began to voice their doubts again. Within the tactical alliance arranged by Largo Caballero, the communists and anarchists seemed to be proceeding in too independent a way. There was indeed much to be said for the communist contention that the socialists were bungling amateur revolutionaries; but they were revolutionaries; and their newspapers had made it clear enough at the end of September that the revolution was at hand, and that it was the duty of all socialists to support it.

The pressure on Gil Robles to demand at least a share in government had grown during the summer months. On 9 September he had to face another mass rally of JAP at Covadonga, the starting-point of the reconquest of Spain from the Muslims. JAP felt that Samper's government had been one of 'do nothing' even now when the unity of Spain was being threatened by Basque and Catalan separatism. It had initiated no constructive legislation. It was incapable of keeping order : guns had been fired at CEDA supporters on their way to Covadonga; the frequency of bomb incidents was increasing; there was growing lawlessness; there were at least three-quarters of a million and possibly a million unemployed. His supporters urged Gil Robles to demand the premiership; he continued to justify his policy of keeping out of government till then but was now prepared to agree that circumstances had indeed changed.

When the *Cortes* reconvened on 1 October, Samper had no plans for dealing with separatism, the country's economic problems, or the growing disorder. Gil Robles announced that CEDA could no longer support Samper's ineffectual government. Neither could Lerroux. Samper resigned, *resentido* (with a chip on his shoulder). Alcalá Zamora again refused to call on Gil Robles to form a government, at least not until Gil Robles had publicly and unequivocally stated that he was wholeheartedly a republican. He would not accept Gil Robles' assurance that he would be loyal to the republic as sufficient guarantee since he wanted from a premier a declaration not only of loyalty but of belief in a republic as the only system for Spain. Gil Robles' belief that a republican system was the only one possible for Spain at that moment of history was too lukewarm. The President again turned to Lerroux who agreed to retain Samper as Minister of State but insisted on giving CEDA three places (out of fifteen) in the Cabinet, the Ministries of Agriculture, Justice, and Labour – not precisely key posts.

Alcalá Zamora agreed to Lerroux's list on 4 October. Azaña, Martínez Barrio, and Maciá thereupon accused the President of handing over the republic to its enemies and explicitly stated that they were cutting off all their connections with the institutions of the state. Here now was the *casus belli* which the socialists required to begin the revolution. Their newspapers announced that the hour had come to seize power; the UGT declared a general strike in orthodox Marxist fashion; workers chanted 'Better Vienna than Berlin'— which could be taken to mean 'better a fight with Fascists than destruction without a struggle'. At dawn on 5 October the strike appeared to start well in Spain's major cities. In Madrid armed revolutionaries drew fire from Civil Guard and Assault Guard detachments. There were gun-battles, too, in other cities. The news was heartening to the government : for it was evidence first of indiscipline among the revolutionaries and secondly of the loyalty of the police forces.

Lerroux was made of sterner stuff than Samper. By the morning of the 6th he had the President's signature on a document authorizing the promulgation of an *estado de guerra,* a state of full emergency, enabling him to call out the army in support of the civil power. His Minister of War, Diego Hidalgo, had established a special operational headquarters in the Ministry of War in Madrid under General Franco, in whose loyalty to the republic and ability to defeat the revolution he had every confidence. By the evening of the 6th Madrid was back to normal, although earlier in the day there had been attacks by armed bodies on various government buildings. A tour of Madrid by two platoons of infantry posting up notices of the promulgation had sufficed to persuade the revolutionaries, who had expected a 'people's rising', to go home. In fact the people, and in particular JAP members, were running essential services well; the news from the provinces was satisfactory; and there appeared to be no conflagration which local army units could not be expected to suffocate – except in two regions, Catalonia and Asturias.

In Barcelona the UGT and the CNT had jointly come out on

strike on the morning of the 5th. Dencás had stood by in command of about 7,000 militiamen : the Civil Guard, the Assault Guards under their commander, Colonel Ricart, Catalonia's own new para-military police force of *Mossos d'Esquadra* under Major Pérez Farras, the socialist militia, and Dencás' own militia, the *escamots*. Companys had authorized the distribution of arms to the latter and to the tenant farmers. At 1930 hours he had proclaimed 'the Catalan State within the Federal Spanish Republic' in a crowded main square, and ceremonially hoisted the striped red and yellow flag of Catalonia, to cries of protest from socialists clamouring for 'the Red Flag with the Star'.

All this happened while people were wondering what General Batet, a Catalan and a republican, in command of the army division quartered in Catalonia would do. In Barcelona itself he had under 5,000 men; but, to the dismay of Companys and Dencás, at 2130 hours he ordered a company preceded by a military band to make a sortie from barracks and post up the Madrid proclamation of the *estado de guerra*. The Civil Guard changed sides and the company met with gunfire from other organizations. Batet brought into action the rest of the troops in Barcelona, including their light artillery pieces. Companys and the *Generalitat* formed barricades. The fighting continued till midnight, when Batet ordered a cease-fire which he knew would allow the less determined to slip back home quietly. Firing was resumed at 0400 hours on the 7th. After two hours Companys surrendered, Dencás fled, and Pérez Farras and Ricart were captured. Isolated incidents occurred later, but when a company of the Spanish Foreign Legion and a battalion of light infantry sent by Franco from Africa to reinforce Batet arrived in the evening, there was nothing left for them to do. The attempt to establish an independent Catalan state had cost about sixty lives, Batet's success having been achieved with the use of the minimum force necessary.

In Asturias the course of events was very different. In Barcelona the anarchists had quickly decided that they were not interested in setting up a Catalan, a Spanish, or any other kind of state. The enthusiasm of the socialists had waned the moment they had realized that a victory for Companys and Dencás would not be a socialist but a Catalan victory. In Asturias there were no nationalist complications. The CNT was not a serious rival to the UGT. While the French had intercepted a shipload of arms and ammunition, another had previously reached the socialists in Asturias. The army garrison in Asturias was smaller than the one in Catalonia. The Asturian miners were not merely ex-conscripts, but also men who used dynamite in their daily work. Their valleys had bemused invaders from Africa and from across the Pyrenees time and time again. Here, then, a straight fight was possible between socialism and 'Fascism' in favourable conditions; and it had in fact begun some hours earlier than elsewhere in the peninsula.

Revolutionary committees of socialists and communists, here and there in association with anarchists, had been established during the year in all the towns. They moved to action-stations during the night of 3/4 October, so that at dawn they proclaimed the end of the Spanish workers' republic and the establishment of the socialist (in some places Soviet) republic. On the 5th forces totalling at least 10,000 well-armed men overwhelmed the local Civil Guard detachments, set fire to churches, schools, and other religious institutions, and shot 'capitalists'. Local units united to form a column which marched on Oviedo, where they took over the artillery works and arsenal with twenty-nine guns and some 400 machine-guns. They then drove back army units sent to intercept them and in Oviedo penned the garrison of 900 men in their barracks. Other revolutionaries manned the passes from León—Castile. By the morning of the 7th they held the entire region with the exception of parts of the city of Oviedo and the nearby port of Gijón. With their haul of weapons captured from defeated units and arms depots their armed strength had risen to between 20,000 and 30,000 men. That evening, however, a surprise awaited them. Their forces in Gijón were subjected to shell-fire from a cruiser despatched there from El Ferrol by Franco : the government's counter-attack had indeed begun.

Franco had ordered army units from Galicia to close in on Oviedo from the west and had sent General López Ochóa to take over their tactical command. He had also despatched from Africa two battalions of the Foreign Legion, and one of Light Infantry and another of *Regulares,* the Spanish Moroccan forces, under the command of his old friend of the African war years Lt-Colonel Yagüe, who landed with his troops on the 10th. On the 11th López Ochóa and Yagüe both reached Oviedo. The revolutionaries fell back, blowing up the old university and burning down much of the city. They concentrated on the mining towns of Sama and Mieres, this last their operational headquarters. López Ochóa and Yagüe pursued them, but the advance was painfully slow and costly against men conducting a rearguard action with efficiency and superb courage. The revolutionaries in their triumph had shown no pity towards their enemies and now that they were being defeated they were being given no quarter by Yagüe's legionaries and Africans. (Thus both sides would have atrocity stories to tell the world.) López Ochóa, a centre-republican, was the nominal commander, but then

as later Yagüe, already under the influence of José Antonio's
Falange, had his own ideas as to what was to be done with 'rabble'.
By mid-October Franco had provided López Ochóa with 15,000
soldiers. The main body of revolutionaries surrendered. Some few
thousands continued to fight, but they were now desperately short
of ammunition, having lost the factories. The original leader of
the revolution, the socialist González Peña, was ousted by, or
resigned in favour of, a communist committee. On the 18th the
communists allowed a socialist to sue for peace on behalf of the
remainder. The revolution had failed.

The attempt to establish a Spanish socialist republic was over.
For years to come communists would condemn its socialist leaders
as incompetent : had communists been the leaders, they would
argue, then it would have succeeded. At the time the Comintern,
giving full publicity to real and imaginary inhumanities, helped
Spanish socialists to mobilize European public opinion against the
Spanish government. The Spanish Foreign Legion and Moroccan
units were accused of shooting unarmed civilians and prisoners, and
of raping infants. Acts undoubtedly occurred contrary to good
order, military discipline, and common humanity. When casualties
were officially counted, there were said to have been 855 revolutionaries killed, with 200 soldiers and some 160 civilians killed
by the revolutionaries. The last two figures could be taken as substantially correct; the first as a minimum, with a possible maximum
of 3,000. Left-wing propaganda swelled it to 14,000.[3] The government and the right took the view that what had happened was no
concern of the outside world or that, in so far as it was, the outside
world was stupid not to see that the left had attempted by revolution to overthrow a government elected legally according to the
rules established by the left. It was now the duty of the government,
they maintained, to punish those who had broken their own rules.

According to those rules Spain was not a federal but a unitary
state. Catalonia had been entitled under its statute to a substantial
measure of autonomy, but the *Generalitat* had had no right to
make itself the equal of the *Cortes.* Companys, the *Generalitat,* and
all who had borne arms on their behalf were therefore traitors to
themselves. Again, Spain was a workers' republic, but not a socialist, and much less a Soviet, republic. Therefore, all who had borne
arms against that same workers' republic in the hope of creating
a socialist republic were guilty of treason, and worthy of

---

[3] The official figures alone were an indictment of the behaviour of the
victors : for a 4 : 1 ratio of deaths was not to be expected where one side
had been of conscripts and only a reinforcement of professional soldiers
and the other of ex-conscripts given 'refresher' training.

punishment according to their degree of responsibility. By the end of October some 20,000 – 40,000 according to the left – were being held pending trial throughout the country.

These were the rank-and-file. Proceedings against the military leaders of the Catalan uprising had begun as quickly as courts martial could be convened. Ricart, Pérez Farras, and eighteen others, army officers on the active list when they had rebelled, had done more than rebel against the republic : they had broken their oath dutifully to obey their army superiors. They were found guilty of a degree of treason for which the only permitted sentence was death. The Cabinet unanimously confirmed the sentences, but Alcalá Zamora immediately intervened, with the argument that all death sentences had to be reviewed by the Supreme Tribunal. Gil Robles objected vehemently. He based his strong opposition to the exemption of these officers from the rigours of the law on the principle that the non-enforcement of the law could only bring it into general contempt, and contempt of law would lead to the destruction of all rule of law.

In this opposition to the President's intervention, Gil Robles had the support not only of fellow lawyers but of other groups. The first was the army, which maintained that if men were not to be disciplined for indiscipline, then there could be no discipline and therefore no army. The second was the ultra-nationalists. For the nationalists the Catalans had committed a more serious crime than the socialists. Largo Caballero had sought to make Spain 'red'; but Spain could be red, white, or any other colour so long as it was still Spain. The monarchist Calvo Sotelo, Primo de Rivera's Minister of Finance (who had been forgiven his past association by the Amnesty Act and so enabled to return to Spain), was to voice succinctly the ultra-nationalistic opinion in the *Cortes* before the end of 1934 : 'Better a Red Spain than a shattered Spain'. The third group was the anti-Marxists, mainly but not exclusively CEDA, who supported Gil Robles because they were convinced (as Gil Robles was himself) that if the Catalan officers were reprieved, then there was no chance that the socialists, guilty not only of treason against the republic but of many crimes in common law, would not be punished as they deserved. Now was the time, for political reasons, to give wounded socialism the *coup de grâce*. If such a *coup* were not given, socialism, better organized, would revive to attack again, and with greater ferocity.

Such arguments only served to alarm still more the more vociferous supporters of Alcalá Zamora. Prieto had escaped to France; but if socialists were to harbour any hope that Largo Caballero and González Peña, whose experience of failure could teach them how to succeed another time, might be saved from the firing squad (there was no question of their guilt), then it was essential that the Catalans should be spared – and a pardon for the Catalans would be the precedent for a pardon for the socialists. Alcalá Zamora did have other supporters, men of peace like Cardinal Vidal, archbishop of Tarragona, and many thousands of petitioners for clemency who believed that forgiveness would be more conducive to peace than punishment, however legally justifiable; and yet others, men of the left, the centre, and the republican right, who like Cambó considered it politically expedient not to create 'martyrs'.

Government was brought almost to a standstill as the Cabinet argued with the President over a period of more than two weeks. The three CEDA Ministers, acting in accordance with their leader's instructions, would not give way even when one by one the others became prepared to do so. On 1 November, at the end of a three-hour address, Alcalá Zamora issued an ultimatum – if the present government refused to commute the death sentence on Pérez Farras, another one would. In other words, he threatened to dismiss the government and hand over power to an administration of the left, though Azaña was under arrest, allegedly as an accomplice of Companys.

Gil Robles now acted in a way which did honour to his principles and practical political sense, but which was to bring on him for a generation the opprobrium of those to the right of him in politics. The right considered that Gil Robles was faced with the choice of a *coup d'état* to depose the President or a sell-out to the left, which would then be able to carry out the very aims of the defeated revolution. Gil Robles saw the choice as one between civil war or a compromise in order to keep out the left. There were plenty of hot-heads in the army who would have backed him in a *coup d'état*. He had, however, through a third party asked his personal friends Generals Fanjul and Goded what the chances were of unified army support; and he had been advised that the army was too ill-equipped and that too many of its officers were either supporters of the left or totally demoralized after the Azaña 're-forms.' Accordingly the three CEDA Ministers bowed to the President's will. The sentences on Pérez Farras and the others were commuted.

After the commuting of the sentences Gil Robles sought from Lerroux greater influence in the Cabinet and the drafting of over-due legislation on reafforestation, land reform, tenancies, agricultural credits, and hydraulic works, on local government and the machinery of elections, on freedom of the press and association, on the reform of the Supreme Tribunal to which Alcalá Zamora had nominated friends who were not lawyers, and measures against usury and to combat unemployment. Lerroux was ageing, and the right, having been baulked of the deaths of the Catalan officers, were seeking other victims. They engineered the dismissal of Samper and Hidalgo from the Cabinet attributing to them gross negligence in not scotching the preparations for the Catalan rising and the socialist revolution. They also sought the abrogation of the Catalan Statute; but Gil Robles opposed the move as unconstitutional. The eventual compromise 'suspension' of the statute pleased no one. Henceforth the right called Gil Robles a 'traitor to Spain'.

With Azaña and Largo Caballero and other socialist deputies awaiting trial, Prieto in France, no socialists attending the *Cortes*, and only a few left-republicans present, there could now have been many changes in the law. Salvador de Madariaga was later to comment that in Spanish politics the left repeatedly betrayed the left; but it was equally true that the right betrayed the right. It was the right which now prevented the radical—CEDA coalition from governing – it was unable even to prepare a budget. Both radicals and right-wing deputies raised objections to proposals, thus bringing on a situation which could not last. Giménez Fernández, the CEDA Minister of Agriculture, introduced a Bill to postpone, as a matter of urgent justice, the eviction of squatters who had taken possession of lands in the early days of the republic, only to be called by the right 'a Marxist with a mask', and its passage took four weeks, a period vital to the squatters who needed some security before starting to sow. Giménez Fernández then put before the *Cortes* the first of his proposed Land Reform measures, a simple matter to give tenants decent security and redress against the greed of landlords. The monarchist and republican right combined in vehement opposition. When the Minister, in private life the Professor of Canon Law at Seville, tried to win support by emphasizing that its basis was Catholic doctrine and papal pronouncements, the cry arose from the right 'if you take away our land with your encyclicals, I'll avow myself a Protestant'. Amendments were pressed to division and even this part of Giménez Fernández's great scheme for land reform was passed only in a heavily truncated form after three months of debate.

Meanwhile in Asturias, Major Doval of the Civil Guard, sent there by the radical Minister of the Interior, had been seeking out the principal participants in the revolution. By the end of the year he had consigned 2,000 men to prison, including González Peña and Largo Caballero. In the pursuit of the wanted men he

12

had used tortures which the right sought to excuse on the grounds
that substantial quantities of weapons stolen from army and government depots had not been recovered. Although he was posted to
Morocco in January 1935, his actions served to strengthen the
resolution of the families of victims to fight again at the first
opportunity.

The trials of Asturians began in November and went on throughout December. Where men were condemned to death, the Supreme
Tribunal automatically recommended a reprieve, and the Cabinet
accepted the recommendation. In the last days of December there
was a sensation when the Supreme Tribunal confirmed the death
sentences on a sergeant who had deserted with arms and a brigand-
turned-revolutionary. If the executions raised any hope in the
minds of those anxious to discourage revolutions, they were soon to
be disappointed. González Peña was brought to trial on 14 February.
There was no doubt that he had been the commander-in-chief of
the revolutionaries in the field, even though Largo had been their
national organizer, and he was sentenced to death. The Supreme
Tribunal recommended a reprieve. So did Alcalá Zamora, his
argument being that González Peña had personally stopped his
men from shooting one hundred Civil Guards who had surrendered.
CEDA, on the other hand, argued that if a pair of mere under-
lings had been shot, it was unjust to reprieve the leader. This time
two other Ministers in the Cabinet agreed with the three CEDA
men, but the remaining seven tired after a month of discussion
against the President. They carried the day on 29 March 1935.
The minority resigned and the government fell.

JAP now clamoured for 'full power for Gil Robles', but Alcalá
Zamora would still not dream of it : he did not want even one
Minister in power from the largest single party. After six days of
crisis Lerroux agreed to resume the premiership at the head of a
Cabinet eight members of which were not deputies but personal
friends of the President. The *Cortes* had been adjourned for Easter
and the anniversary celebrations of the republic, and Alcalá Zamora
and Lerroux knew that the government could not survive once the
Cortes reassembled. It could be expected to last for one month, and
so it proved. During that month it confirmed the Supreme Tribunal's findings that there was no case against Azaña. It was a pure
coincidence that he had been in Barcelona during the rising and
he had had no part in the Asturian affair. However, during that
month one other interesting event occurred. Soon after Azaña's
acquittal a series of articles by the still exiled Prieto, advocating a
United Left Front to fight what were then thought to be imminent
elections, was published. Prieto admitted frankly that the socialists

on their own could not come back to power constitutionally and that further revolutionary action at that moment in time could only turn the people further away from socialism.

Gil Robles, for his part, had ordered *Acción Popular* to prepare itself for an election campaign when his Ministers had resigned at the end of March. He seemed determined then to force on Alcalá Zamora the dissolution of the *Cortes*; but he came to realize that Alcalá Zamora was quite capable of calling on left-wing politicians to govern during the election period. His experiences of 1931 undermined his determination. Electioneering under a caretaker government of the left was likely to be extremely difficult; Gil Robles was sufficiently a realist to appreciate that even if the campaign were free and the voting unhampered, CEDA was not likely to get an overall majority.

Lerroux, too, was aware that his Radical Party was not likely to do well in any further election. Those who had voted radical in 1933 were moving either to the left or to the right. The only solution was to insist that the President should allow CEDA back in a new coalition. Gil Robles demanded five places in any new Cabinet under Lerroux and Lerroux thought the demand reasonable.

On 6 May Lerroux announced his sixth, and the two-year-old republic's tenth, government, the most broadly-based to date : four radicals, two 'agrarians', a Liberal, and five CEDA. Five out of twelve, however, did not give CEDA the controlling power, but it did hold the Ministries of Communications, Industry and Commerce, Labour, Justice, and War. Gil Robles was himself Minister of War – an important, but not the most important, post. The key post (after the premiership), that of Minister of the Interior, went to Portela, nominally a radical, in fact Alcalá Zamora's personal representative, whose task it was, over the nineteen weeks that this government was to last, to ensure that the repression of the left did not go too far.

It did not. Azaña was given every opportunity to hold mass meetings attended by left-republicans and socialists; and he spoke, acting on Prieto's behalf, even at meetings composed entirely of socialists. By July Azaña and Prieto had established their United Front. Prieto had repented of his support of Largo's revolution; but Largo had not himself repented of his revolution – on the contrary, in prison he had become more convinced of the value of revolutionary methods in the pursuit of socialism and his Socialist Youth began to talk openly of the sovietization of Spain and the fusion of the Socialist Youth and the as yet quite small but highly militant Communist Youth.

Spain's most urgent needs at that moment were twofold : financial

and social. Spain had to set its financial affairs in order – misgovern-
ment, or rather non-government, over so many months was having
its serious economic consequences – and work or relief had to be
found for the unemployed. At the end of July the CEDA Minister
of Labour got through the *Cortes* before the summer adjournment a
vast programme of public works, at village, rural district, and town
level, to absorb many of the unemployed.[4] The Minister of Finance,
Chapaprieta, once a Minister of Industry and Commerce under
the monarchy and an adviser to commercial firms, pushed through
a balanced budget. But the only major piece of legislation was a
reform of the Azaña Land Reform Act, a most retrograde step
calculated to appease all those of the right and centre whom
Giménez Fernández's proposals had infuriated. It legalized a distribution of land which, as José Antonio Primo de Rivera pointed out,
would take 170 years to complete. The new Minister of Agriculture
was a representative of the landowners and CEDA did not seriously
oppose the measure, though it recognized it as alien to its principles
of social justice, because Gil Robles was anxious at the time to get
as wide a backing as he could for the reform of the constitution.
The time when such a reform might be possible was not far off.
The constitution would be four-years-old in December. Until then
any changes required the vote of two-thirds of the *Cortes,* over 300
votes, a number which no side could command. Beyond that date a
simple majority only would be required and Gil Robles calculated
that a simple majority was attainable if the radicals still loyal to
Lerroux, CEDA, and the agrarians (the landowners' party) combined. On the reform of the constitution Gil Robles was prepared
to risk anything and, much to his satisfaction, before the *Cortes*
adjourned they appointed a commission of twenty-four to draft
changes to forty-five of its 121 articles, to remove from it all that
was offensive to Christian doctrine and sentiment, and to make the
machinery of government more workable. As Alcalá Zamora was
himself to say of it in retrospect, the 1931 constitution was one
which made for civil war. 'It had not been drafted', as Madariaga
commented, 'as a practical instrument of government for any
nation', but as a stepping-stone to the socialist state desired by at
most 30 per cent of Spain.

Already many Liberals and other men of the centre feared that
civil war was inevitable. Right and left were preparing for it. In
the north the heirs of Carlism, the traditionalists, were secretly
organizing their young men into military units and drilling them.
Though Prieto was opposed to it, the Socialist Youth were doing

4 There were at the time in Spain 900 villages and 8,700 hamlets cut
off but for footpaths.

the same. The *Falange* had its *centurias*. Gil Robles' own JAP was becoming militant, urged on among others by a young lawyer called Serrano Suñer. The sad fact was that nearly every Spaniard believed in the absolute truth of his own particular political philosophy. The arithmetic of parliamentary democracy was irrelevant to anarchists, communists, and socialists, the republican left, Falangists, and monarchists. Even the Basque nationalists did not believe that the will of the majority should necessarily prevail, for in fact they represented at most 40 per cent of their electorate.

No one in government was unaware of the plotting and planning on the left and right. Gil Robles was especially conscious that Spanish political divisions were reflected within the army, where clear dangers presented themselves. One was that the army might return to politics to 'save Spain' from the chaos into which its politicians were reducing it; another was civil war. The *Unión Militar Española* was growing in strength and there was a corresponding organization on the left. The army had indeed rallied to the support of the established republic in both Catalonia and the rest of Spain. In Asturias the conduct of General López de Ochóa had been exemplary, as was to be expected since his sympathies had always been republican; and so had the conduct of Fanjul and Goded. Fanjul had been elected to the constituent *Cortes* as a right-wing man prepared to accept the republic, though not a republican by conviction; Goded had been Azaña's Inspector-General and was known to have become anti-left in consequence, but that did not make him anti-Catalan. Franco, a former Gentleman of the King's Bedchamber, had made known his opposition to the replacement of the ancient flag of Spain by a tricolour, but he had thereafter kept scrupulously clear of all plots and all politics, and not even his closest associates could tell what he thought. He seemed to sympathize with the social plight of the Asturian miners, but had not hesitated a moment when called upon to suppress the rising. There was, then, a body of officers loyal to their oath. The Catalan rising, however, had also revealed that there were officers in the services who did not consider it their duty to obey orders – not merely the Catalan Ricart and Pérez Farras. Franco's own cousin, La Puente Bahamonde, commander of one of the air squadrons ordered by Franco to make a sortie in support of the beleaguered Oviedo garrison, had refused to carry out his orders. When the cruiser *Cervantes* had had to put into El Ferrol on its way from Africa to Gijón, the commander of the battalion of light infantry it was transporting intended to order his troops not to fire on the revolutionaries. Yagüe, however, had acted and spoken in a way which made legitimate the question whether Falangism was now seeping into the army.

Gil Robles decided that as Minister of War it was his duty to do two things : first – what Azaña claimed he had done – make the army into a modern small fighting force; second, ensure that anyone whose loyalty to the established republic was suspect should not gain a strategically important post. He made Fanjul his secretary, Goded his Inspector-General, and Franco Chief-of-Staff; raised morale by restoring the old regional names of the infantry regiments – a small detail but one which meant much to the men serving in them; 'unfroze' promotions (merit was to count no less than seniority); ordered a thorough investigation into the real state of the army's equipment and organization; and transferred the arms factories from civilian into army ordnance hands.

Chapaprieta, the Minister of Finance, acting with similar energy, investigated the antiquated and never efficient revenue system, and planned a complete reform, reckoning it would take three years to bring into effect. Of more immediate concern, by September he had ready a plan to reorganize the civil service, streamlining it from top to bottom and making for greater efficiency with very substantial economies. But in September there was yet another government crisis.

Lerroux had given the Ministry of Marine to a second agrarian whose one love was his land and his one hate Catalonia. The members of the *Generalitat* who had taken part in the rising had been condemned to various terms of imprisonment. Both Gil Robles and Lerroux were now anxious to restore Catalonia's autonomy. Over a small point, however, the transfer of authority in the conduct of public works in Barcelona and Tarragona, the Minister of Marine resigned and with him the other agrarian, the Minister of Agriculture, still piqued because CEDA members had spoken so vehemently against his alteration of the Land Reform, even though they had not stopped its passage on 20 September. For reasons which no one could understand at the time Lerroux resigned as well.

Alcalá Zamora now offered the premiership to Chapaprieta, under whom Lerroux agreed to serve as Foreign Minister. Chapaprieta, now in a position to put his economies into effect, cut the number of remaining Ministries from eleven to seven, but retaining Gil Robles as Minister of War and two other CEDA men. The other portfolios were given to a Catalan home-ruler, an agrarian more liberal than the two whose resignations had caused the crisis, and two radicals.

When the new government met on 1 October, Chapaprieta

announced his plans : the streamlining of the administration; an Electoral Law; a law to encourage reafforestation; another to give agricultural credits to the small farmer; a balanced budget for 1936; and neutrality in the Italo-Abyssinian conflict.

The reaction of the left to the new government was to call it Fascist, and though a few days later Spain voted for sanctions against Italy and put its armed forces at the disposal of the League of Nations should more action be voted against Mussolini, the left persisted in their use of the term. Gil Robles ordered Franco to strengthen the defences of the Balearics and Cartagena and keep on call a mobile independent brigade. By the end of November Franco had completed the work preparatory to the modernization of the army; but by the end of November the right was determined to destroy Chapaprieta before his fiscal reforms and promise of heavier taxation for the wealthy could become effective; the left was ready to present a common front to the electorate; and Lerroux and the radicals were in the middle of a major political scandal.

Ever since his election as President of the Republic, Alcalá Zamora had taken full advantage of the equivocally worded clauses relating to his powers in the constitution. He had intervened in politics as much as any king. He had presided over cabinet meetings. Since November 1933 he had called upon whom he willed to be premier. His choice of Lerroux instead of Gil Robles had been doubtfully constitutional in the first place. The government which lasted a month over the Easter 1934 recess had been his personal affair even though Lerroux had headed it; while Samper's administration which followed was unjustifiable except that Lerroux and Gil Robles had condoned it. In choosing Chapaprieta, an independent Liberal, he had acted as autocratically as any king. Yet he had intervened in government in other ways too. He had packed the Supreme Tribunal with his personal friends, some of them lawyers, many of them not; and it was to his credit (or his discredit) that the leaders of the October revolution had all been absolved. (On 30 September the tribunal dismissed as insufficiently conclusive all the evidence against Largo Caballero.) He had forced his personal friends on Lerroux as Ministers, for example Portela, a sick man of weak character, who became Minister of the Interior in April 1935 and again in May–September, during that period when the youth of the left and the UGT were embarking on demonstrations and strikes calculated to disrupt the peace. In June there had been a serious outbreak of anarchist trouble in Catalonia, quickly suppressed only because Gil Robles, with the approval of Lerroux, had again promptly declared a state of full emergency, and under his personal supervision the military had been called out in aid of the civil power. Lerroux had thereupon compelled the President to agree to the exclusion of Portela. Alcalá Zamora had always shown disdain for Gil Robles, treating him at interviews as a stupid boy requiring counsel from a concerned parent. From the time that Lerroux ejected Portela, the President had begun openly to show hatred towards Lerroux as well. Why he should have had such antipathy towards Gil Robles can only be surmised; what evidence there is suggests that he looked on the young Catholic lawyer, leader of a powerful party, as an image of what he would have liked to have been. Envy, too, might well have accounted for his feelings towards Lerroux. Alcalá Zamora had a small circle of friends and a greater number of enemies. The aged Lerroux, in spite of his nefarious youth, was now recognized widely as a man worthy of reverence.

On 16 September Alcalá Zamora received evidence which, properly used, could destroy Lerroux, his party, and even any other person or party closely allied to him, such as Gil Robles. The evidence concerned Lerroux's middle-aged adopted son, and two of the many people whose membership and support of the Radical Party had been rewarded with high civil service office. Licences had been obtained for two men called Strauss and Perl to operate in the San Sebastián casino a gaming device which was as fraudulent as it was ingenious. No sooner had this gone into operation than suspicious police had confiscated it. Strauss and Perl had spent money in obtaining the licences; now they wanted their money back, with substantial interest. Lerroux refused to be blackmailed. Strauss then contacted Prieto in Belgium, at a moment when Azaña was visiting him and solidifying their United Front. They redrafted and touched up the 'evidence', and posted it to Alcalá Zamora who showed it to Lerroux on the 18th.[5] Though insisting that the sins of the son could not be visited upon the father, Lerroux thereupon resigned. Alcalá Zamora appeared content, even encouraging Chapaprieta to give Lerroux the Ministry of Foreign Affairs in the new government.

On 9 October, radicals, agrarians, *Lliga,* and CEDA, who knew nothing of the background and thought that Alcalá Zamora had grossly insulted Lerroux by replacing him with Chapaprieta as premier, held a banquet in Lerroux's honour. Gil Robles spoke of him with warmth and affection, and his speech was fully reported. CEDA and the radicals, Gil Robles and Lerroux, were now identi-

---

[5] The envelope was postmarked 'The Hague' and dated 5 September. It was received by the GPO, Madrid, on 10 September and delivered to the palace on 11 September. Yet its contents were seemingly not shown to the President till the 16th (Gil Robles, *No fué posible la paz,* pp. 298–9).

fied as collaborators as never before and the President seemed mortally offended that Lerroux should have been acclaimed as he himself had never been. On 12 October, with a great show of secrecy and melodramatic showmanship, Alcalá Zamora handed Chapaprieta, Gil Robles, and Martínez Velasco, the leader of the agrarians, the evidence 'he had just received', alleging corruption against members of the Radical Party and even perhaps Lerroux himself. The news was given full publicity seven days later and a government commission, appointed to examine the evidence, cleared Lerroux though not other radicals. The party had been successfully ruined. The left had got rid of a rival. A second scandal involving more radicals was published a month later, an unsuccessful attempt being made by the left to implicate CEDA and Gil Robles in it. More telling in the long run were innuendoes in and outside the *Cortes* in October and November that Gil Robles was planning a military *coup*.

The scandal had spelt the ruin not only of the radicals but also of the whole centre-right coalition. Chapaprieta refused to carry on after 9 December. Gil Robles could certainly now have commanded a majority in the *Cortes*. Alcalá Zamora offered the premiership to half a dozen men of the centre and right in turn – but not to Gil Robles. On 11 December Gil Robles found the Ministry of War surrounded by Civil Guards (dependent for orders on the Ministry of the Interior and only in a state of emergency on the War Minister). On his arrival at the palace for an explanation, Alcalá Zamora intimated that he might dissolve the *Cortes*. Gil Robles warned him of the probable consequences. To the right of CEDA there was now substantial agreement that if the left won the elections, the left would rush on to the establishment of the dictatorship of the proletariat; and the right would rise in rebellion. If the left lost the elections, then the left would seek by revolution what was otherwise unobtainable. Either way elections meant civil war. Two days later Alcalá Zamora called on his friend Portela to form a caretaker government, combining the duties of premier with those of Minister of the Interior. The French communist newspaper *Humanité* joined the Spanish left-wing press in praising the President, who duly dissolved the *Cortes* on 7 January 1936 and called elections for 16 February. The conviction that Spain was now set for civil war was widespread.

Chapter 24

The Republic: The Last Phase
February 1936 to 18 July 1936

In 1931 THE LEFT had refused to listen to the reasoning of liberals. Men representative of not more than at most a quarter of the nation had forced on the remainder not merely an unworkable constitution but one which 'made for civil war'. In 1934 the right, or rather that half of it which represented one-eighth of the nation, had shut its ears to the logic of papal encyclicals. Laws had not been passed which would have redressed some of the grosser injustices inflicted by the wealthy on the poor. By 1935 politicians of the left and right had drowned reasoning in rhetoric, then rhetoric with demagogy. In 1936 they vied with each other in urging their compatriots to 'join us to fight the other half of Spain, the obscurantist – the godless, the Marxist – the capitalist, the enemy of the republic – the enemy of Spain' even as they disguised their meaning in the form 'vote for us'.

There were in existence over thirty distinct political parties at the beginning of 1936, when five of them agreed to form an alliance under the name Popular Front. The five were : *Izquierda Republicana,* under Azaña,[1] itself a coalition of the 1931 Azañists, radical-socialists, and others; the *Unión Republicana,* the party founded by Martínez Barrio (Azaña's superior in Freemasonry) after his break with Lerroux over the relaxation of the anti-religious laws; the Socialist Party; the Communist Party; the Trotskyists; and, in so far as collectively they could be called a 'party', groups of anarchists joined at the last moment. The only factors they had in common were hatred of religion and hatred of monarchism. The anarchists, as before, abhorred all government and abominated Marxism in all its forms. The Trotskyists loathed the Stalinism of the communists; the communists loathed the socialists for their independence of Moscow; the socialists, while divided among themselves into 'socialism tomorrow' and 'socialism now' factions, despised the *petit bourgeois* mentality of the *Izquierda* : the *Izquierda*

---

[1] In Catalonia the *Esquerra* under Companys.

despised the grand airs that the *Unión Republicana* gave itself as the linear descendant of the oldest republican party.

The genius behind the union of such a disparate collection was Largo Caballero. Azaña had said as early as 1933 that he considered himself 'in and out of government united for always to the socialists'. While no connection was ever established between him and either the Catalan rising or the socialist revolution of October 1934, he was proved to have provided Portuguese socialists with arms for use against Salazar, the Portuguese Prime Minister. During 1935 he had kept the Socialist Party together for Prieto and Largo in exile and in prison respectively. He had established the United Front of his party and the socialists early in the year. Largo, on the other hand, had forced the communists into a Union of Proletarian Brothers for the October revolution. His initiative had been duly noted and highly commended by the Bulgarian communist leader Dimitrov at the VIIth Comintern Congress (in July 1935), to the embarrassment of the Spanish Communist Party delegates. The Comintern called him by the name which Spanish socialists had called him two years earlier – the 'Spanish Lenin'. His name was linked with such avowed communists as the German Thälmann and the Hungarian Rakosi. At that Congress in 1935 Dimitrov had ruled that the political alliances made by Largo or by Azaña were not wide enough. Communist parties were to seek agreements with *petit bourgeois* organizations and form Popular Fronts. The tactic would be to seize power from within governments, 'the tactic of the Trojan Horse', as Dimitrov called it. In Spain, the Communist Party was to accept Largo's leadership, for in the long term he would either become a communist himself or be easily replaced by a communist after he had established his supremacy over the less militant Prieto and Azaña. To begin with, the Marxists would hide behind Azaña; while Largo, with his Lenin-like record and image, would win over the Trotskyists. His revolutionary zeal would also commend him to anarchists. Largo had himself confirmed Dimitrov's trust in him when, on being released from prison in November 1935, he had declared that he had a clearer understanding of Marxism than before his imprisonment, words echoed a generation later by Fidel Castro. Not that Largo was ever an avowed communist in the Stalinist sense of a man obedient to, and at the service of, Soviet international policy.

The parties outside the Popular Front might have presented an equally united counter-revolutionary front. Suggestions to this end came from leaders of centre, CEDA, and right-wing parties. Local agreements were entered into, with varying but on the whole inadequate success except in Madrid. The general idea was that the anti-Marxist vote should not be divided, but whereas the Popular Front, in spite of all its internal divisions, managed to bring out a joint manifesto, and to present Azaña as its leader, no such cohesion was possible among the anti-Marxists. Even in Madrid they had two potential leaders : Gil Robles on the one side and the monarchist Calvo Sotelo on the other. The differences on the right went much deeper than differences on the left. Professor Besteiro's 'socialism tomorrow once the masses are educated to it and not by violent means', Prieto's 'socialism now whether Moscow likes it or not', the communists' 'socialism when Moscow says so', the Trotskyists' 'international socialism now but not Stalinism' were all differences of method, not of principle; and with these slogans went Azaña's 'even socialism if it is the only way to destroy religion' and Martínez Barrio's 'better socialism than the re-establishment of the Church'. There was no parallel on the right. The Navarrese traditionalists, the Basque nationalists, and CEDA supporters were Catholics; but the traditionalists wanted the restoration of the Carlist line as an authoritarian monarchy over a united even if regionalist Spain; the Basque nationalists would be satisfied with nothing short of independence from Spain (except possibly in matters of defence); and CEDA considered late mediaeval political theories irrelevant to the twentieth century and Basque nationalism chimerical. CEDA and the Catalan *Lliga* were close in many ideals, but the *Lliga*'s preparedness to accept social reforms as a matter of common justice was too limited for CEDA. On social justice in rural areas, the points of view of CEDA and the agrarians were diametrically opposed. For some members of CEDA collaboration with the monarchists was welcome, for they were monarchists at heart; but others were as sincerely republican. Between the ardent nationalists of *Renovación Española,* founded by Calvo Sotelo on his return from exile as *the* Alfonsist party, and the regionalists of *Acción Popular* and the Catalan *Lliga* there was no hope of co-operation . . . and so on. The result, on the right, was the ineffectual negative slogan 'vote counter-revolutionary'.

On the Popular Front there was a solid, soundly bourgeois, manifesto calculated to wall-paper the fundamental cleavage between the Marxist and non-Marxist conception of Utopia and to appeal to very human and humane desires and emotions. The Popular Front pledged itself to give workers a happier future and a greater reward for their labour, always provided that there was greater productivity, but without regard to what it might cost the privileged. The socialist principle of working-class control of industry was noted, but soft-pedalled. The land would be for those who worked it : whether the method would be by nationalization or distribution in ownership was glossed over. The Popular Front promised wider and greater educational facilities : the Jesuit and other religious establishments which Gil Robles and Lerroux had allowed to reopen would again be shut; but working-class boys of ability would be able to go to the universities from which the wastrel sons of the wealthy would be barred. Above all, it undertook a general amnesty for the '30,000 prisoners languishing unjustly in Spanish gaols'.

The last promise was calculated to appeal to the Christian sentiment of Spaniards – and even anarchists were still recognizably Christian in much of their thought; but '30,000' was a gross exaggeration, for the whole prison population of the time was under 35,000 and there could hardly have been as few as 5,000 serving sentences for non-political crimes when the population of Spain was 24 million. 15,000 to 20,000 would have been nearer the truth. Communist publications abroad gave figures of between 45,000 and even 150,000. *Treinta mil* (30,000) was chosen because it had a resounding ring lacked by *quince* (15), *cuarenta y cinco* (45), or any other number. The promise was to prove a winner, though the Popular Front Victory was not as large as the outside world was led to believe.

In considering the results of the February elections, the historian has to face several sets of 'official' and semi-official figures with more than insignificant variations. They fascinated commentators at the time and they continue to fascinate writers on Spain anxious to prove one or other iniquity. Before any attempt is made to use any of them as evidence for or against any conclusion several factors must be kept in mind. The first is that the mechanism of the elections was most complicated. Many Spaniards did not understand it themselves. Nearly 10 per cent of the votes cast were declared null and void because of spoilt papers in both the 1933 and 1936 elections.

The socialist-Azañist government of 1931 had made the boundaries of the provinces and certain cities of Spain the boundaries of electoral districts. Each district had been allotted a number of seats in the *Cortes* in the ratio of between 1 per 25,000 and 1 per 27,500 electors. The electors of Madrid were entitled to return fifteen members; but they could not all be from the same party or coalition; twelve seats went to the party (or allies of the party) to which the person polling the highest number of votes belonged : the remaining three went to 'opposition' parties. So, if a socialist came in first, eleven more seats went to the party. Each *Madrileño* could therefore vote for up to twelve candidates (not necessarily of the same side) and, incidentally, a person could stand for election in more than one district. (José Antonio Primo de Rivera figured as a candidate in no less than five places – and failed hopelessly everywhere.)

The allocation of seats per district was reasonably rational. Not so, however, the division into 'majority' and 'minority' seats. As Prieto admitted, it was done deliberately in such a way as to favour the socialists. This was the case in Madrid and also in Valencia, where the socialists could also expect a small majority. The allocation here was ten to the 'majority' and three to the 'minority', irrespective of any other considerations; whereas in Salamanca, where the anti-Marxists were overwhelmingly more numerous than the left, the ratio was 5 : 2.

There were two other important stipulations in the Electoral Law : where no candidate obtained 40 per cent of the votes cast, there had to be 'a second round'; and all allegations of irregularities had to be considered by those already elected in the *Cortes*. Thus, if the right won, then the right would pass judgment on all allegations whether from the right or left, and vice-versa. Hence the side to be declared the victor first had an opportunity to increase its lead, in the 'second round' and again by declaring results unfavourable to itself as having been irregularly obtained.

During the election period there were numerous complaints, mainly from CEDA candidates, of assaults on themselves and on their supporters. Two working-class CEDA members were shot dead by socialists. Though officially all press censorship and other limitations on liberty were removed, the police, under orders from Portela, seized JAP news-sheets and here and there prevented speakers from addressing public meetings. Nonetheless, the campaign was orderly.

So was the polling on Sunday 16 February, until 1600 hours (lunch-time), when the booths closed. In the cities Marxist militias stood by polling-stations, but so did police. Three hours later the streets of Madrid began to fill with bands of men and women giving the clenched-fist salute, shouting 'Long Live Russia' and other Popular Front slogans, and acclaiming the Front as the undoubted winner of the elections. Fearing a repetition of the holocaust of 1931, Franco, still Chief-of-Staff with an office in the Ministry of War in the heart of Madrid, informed the Inspector-General of the Civil Guard, General Pozas, by telephone of what he could see from the Ministry. Pozas, later to become a prominent Communist Party member, pooh-poohed Franco's fears. The counting of the votes was still in progress.

Lines of communication in the Spain of 1936 were, to say the least, poor. Nevertheless, Portela's secretary announced soon after

2100 hours that the Popular Front had won an overwhelming victory in Barcelona and that the Governor-General of Catalonia and president of the *Generalitat* had resigned. The news reached the Ministry of War that in many cities Popular Front crowds were attributing to themselves victory without waiting for any official pronouncement. Mobs were in fact attacking and here and there setting fire to opposition party and newspaper offices, private houses, churches, and convents. Franco pressed his Minister, General Molero, to prevail on Portela to ask the President to declare 'a state of full emergency' lest the crowds should destroy urns which might contain unfavourable results. Others asked the same of Portela who telephoned the President, but Alcalá Zamora curtly dismissed the proposition.

On the morning of 17 February Largo Caballero and the crypto-communist Alvárez del Vayo visited the main Madrid prison to inform the prisoners that they would soon be released. There were large crowds outside all the prisons; the Socialist Party executive proclaimed the day as 'a new dawn'; and the papers of the left banner-headlined the still unknown results as 'an overwhelming victory' for the Popular Front. The state of disorder grew. Franco saw Portela personally. The President had agreed to the declaration of a state of partial emergency, the principal provision of which was the reimposition of press censorship. At lunchtime Franco implored Portela to realize that more was required. Unknown to Franco, Alcalá Zamora had already authorized his Prime Minister to proclaim even a 'full emergency', but sparingly and locally, wherever he saw fit. Portela said he was too old to do anything and put the question to Franco, then aged forty-one – why couldn't the army act on its own initiative? Franco answered to the effect that the army would split unless the orders came from the government. Portela promised to 'sleep on it' : he wanted his *siesta*. Back in the Ministry Franco found Goded and Fanjul, who were of the opinion that a military rising was now justifiable. He asked them to enquire of the garrison commanders if they would obey an order to rise in defence of the republic if the army High Command gave it. The majority answered that they would not.

On the 18th news came of prisoners in several cities disarming their gaolers and taking over control. There was further news of attacks on property. Portela asked Martínez Barrio to come to see him and, totally demoralized, asked the Popular Front to assume control. The Inspector-General of the Civil Guard, General Pozas, and General Núñez del Prado, Commander of the Assault Guards, burst in on them to announce that Goded and Franco were on the point of a military *coup*. Pozas and Núñez dramatically pledged the loyalty of their forces to the republic and Martínez Barrio left. Portela, cowering in his Ministry, telephoned the President to say he was quitting the following day – and quit he did in spite of visits by Gil Robles, Calvo Sotelo, and Franco to raise his morale. With-out further ado, Alcalá Zamora called Azaña to the premiership.

On the 20th, with Azaña in power, the first official results of the polling were published. Of 13,528,609 electors, only 9,226,000 were said to have voted : one voter in three had not gone to the polls, an extraordinarily high proportion when every party, even the anarchist CNT, had urged everyone to vote. The abstentions appeared to be mainly from the *right*. In Madrid, curiously enough, hardly anyone in the aristocratic Buenavista ward seemed to have voted and in Badajoz province, where the Popular Front had won by only 20,000 votes, the absentees numbered over 100,000. In Badajoz city the results were even more curious. There 172,710 had voted, 142,886 for the extreme socialist firebrand Margarita Nelken, 124,733 for a centre and 124,007 for a CEDA candidate, figures which make no sense unless an astounding number of voters did so at once for left and right or left and centre. Notwithstanding such curiosities an official breakdown of voting was given on 20 February into left, centre, and right for the whole country :

Total 'valid' votes	8,566,051
Right	4,187,571
Centre & independents	325,197
Basque nationalists	141,137
Popular Front	3,912,086

This was hardly the 'overwhelming ... indisputable ... decisive victory over Fascist reactionaries' which the left wing had been publicizing since the evening of polling-day and on which the crowds had been acting. Even leaving the equivocal Basques out of account, the anti-Popular Front vote was 52·5 per cent of the total and the Popular Front's only 45·8. In terms of seats the results were only marginally more encouraging. The Popular Front seemed certain of only 220 seats. Elections for nearly fifty candidates would have to be held again under the 40 per cent rule. Nor was the out-look particularly bright, for the reason why no candidate had re-ceived 40 per cent of the votes in nearly all those fifty cases was because monarchists, right-wing republicans, Basque nationalists, CEDA supporters, radicals, and other candidates had split the anti-Popular Front vote over and over again. If, therefore, right and centre now co-operated in the 'second round' the composition of the *Cortes* was likely to be : Popular Front 225 (at most); Basque nationalists ten, and anti-Popular Front 238 (of which at least 120 would be CEDA). Under the protection of Azaña's government, which consisted of nine of his friends, his masonic brother Martínez Barrio and one friend, and another left-wing republican (the socialists had promised to give Azaña full support but refused to be implicated in any governmental responsibility), the 'second round' was held on 1 March. New voting figures were issued on 3 March. Rounded off they were:

Popular Front	4,540,000
Others	4,200,000

The seat distribution now was: Popular Front 266; others 207.

When the *Cortes* met, socialists and communists sang the *Internationale*; left and right raised accusations of irregularities in the election of all but 187 deputies; and the left 'majority' now proceeded to behave as in 1931. Over the month of March it rejected virtually all the objections raised by the right, while it upheld those from its own ranks. CEDA's original holding of 120 seats began to be whittled away, vacant seats being given to originally defeated socialists and friends of Azaña and Martínez Barrio. The Popular Front increased its holding to 277. New official figures of votes cast were issued:

Right	3,996,931
Centre	449,320
Popular Front	4,838,449

The left was still not satisfied. New elections ordered for Granada and Cuenca, where CEDA had had resounding victories, were held in circumstances of extreme violence in April. The right gave up the fight in Granada, but pressed for a third election in Cuenca. In this third Cuenca election, held in May, the Popular Front was stated to have won—in circumstances we shall examine later.[2]

The final composition of the *Cortes* was settled. The Popular Front had, at long last, an overwhelming majority and CEDA strength had been reduced to eighty-eight seats.

It may well be asked why the Popular Front was so anxious to present itself as the winner of the elections. A distinction must here be made between the motives of the Marxists (one-third of the Front) and of Azaña. As Calvo Sotelo once said 'better a Red than a shattered Spain', thereby showing that he gave priority to the concept of 'the nation-state Spain', so at any time Azaña might have said 'better a Red Spain than a Catholic Spain'. Azaña was favourably disposed towards the Laski-type academic socialism of

[2] See below, p. 199.

Professor Besteiro and towards Prieto personally, but he had rather
less use for the – to him – uncouth Largo Caballero and his revolutionary socialism. He would, however, have supported Largo
rather than that Catholicism should survive his generation. The
1936 elections had disappointed him more than those of 1933. However much juggling was done with the figures, the fact remained
that 900,000 more Spaniards had voted for the right than in 1933
and that of these at least 600,000 extra votes had gone to the Catholic party *par excellence*. If the process of destruction of the Church
in Spain which he had begun in 1931, which Lerroux had stopped,
and which Gil Robles had then reversed during the 'Black Bien-
nium', were not to stay in reverse, a narrow majority in the *Cortes*
was not enough. To stop the reversal he required a majority. To
recommence the process of destruction he needed a large majority,
and the larger it was, the quicker he could make it go. To explain
the socialist motive fully, it would be necessary to digress at length
on the thought behind the concept 'socialist legality', but there was
another more immediate factor. Sooner or later the socialists had
to establish the dictatorship of the proletariat. (The sooner the
better, according to Largo.) Five years of labour unrest had had
serious economic effects. Spain's output per working man had fallen
steadily. Other nations were beginning to recover from the economic slump of the early 1930s : not so Spain, and the fact was
reflected in the falling value of the peseta. Spain's best customer
of the little she had to offer – citrus fruit and iron-ores – was Britain.
Britain had ostracized revolutionary Russia where her interests were
not directly involved : *a fortiori* the possibility that a Red Spain
could provoke the United Kingdom to any form of intervention
had to be considered. For a Red Spain could conceivably become a
strong or at any rate a non-neutral Spain which could upset the
balance of power in the Mediterranean and endanger the security
of Gibraltar. Government in Britain was in the hands of men whose
normal sympathies were with the Spanish monarchists, but the
British government had its hands tied by 'bourgeois' democratic
principles : it would never act against the sympathy of any large,
even if minority, body of opinion. It was essential, therefore, that
the Spanish socialists should cultivate the support of the powerful
British Labour movement. To that end Largo Caballero came personally to Britain in February 1936 to be fêted and heard by Attlee
and the other British Labour leaders of the time. Largo – and his
mentor Álvarez del Vayo – were as aware of the virtual irrelevance
of Marxism to British Labour as British Labour politicians were
ignorant of the thorough Marxism of Spanish socialism. Attlee was
no less 'subservient' – as Álvarez del Vayo would put it – to 'capital-

ist democratic' principles than the British Prime Minister, perhaps more. If Spain was to be converted into a dictatorship of the proletariat, and yet retain her economic links and sympathy with Britain, then it was most important that the conversion should be seen as one which had the sanction of the majority expressed in 'free elections'.

Within three days of taking over government, Azaña fulfilled his election promise that he would release all those serving sentences for 'political activities'. A day later he ordered the suspension of payments of rents by tenant farmers in Extremadura and Andalusia. There and elsewhere as far north as the province of Salamanca the order was interpreted as authority for the seizure of land and property, and the establishment locally of anarchist 'libertarian communism'. He revived all the anti-religious legislation; the Jesuits were expelled a second time; and religious services were banned in hospitals. He ordered police to guard religious buildings, but they were not always successful. Franco, dismissed from his post as Chief-of-Staff, saw palls of smoke from burning churches as he passed through Cadiz on 9 March on his way to his new appointment, G.O.C. the Canary Island garrisons.

Violence in the cities and in the countryside was now an everyday affair. Azaña maintained a strict press censorship, forbidding any mention of riots, arson, and assassination other than local incidents, about which the people could get to hear with or without newspapers. The victims were CEDA supporters and republicans of the centre and right. There were daily socialist victory parades in which the demand for the dictatorship of the proletariat 'Now' became ever more insistent and cries of 'Viva Rusia' more frequent than 'Viva la República'. On 11 March Azaña ordered Largo to stop the parades, but Largo claimed that all the violence was provoked by Fascists, and the *Falange* in particular. The parades, called 'demonstrations of working-class solidarity', continued. On 13 March Falangist students did indeed attempt to assassinate the socialist deputy and editor of the 1931 constitution Jiménez de Asúa, as a reprisal for the assassination by socialists of *Falange* workers and two students. Azaña thereupon ordered the arrest of Primo de Rivera and the *Falange* executive. The Socialist Youth and the *Falange* Youth now really got to grips with each other; by mid-May when the *Falange* was outlawed and some 2,000 Falangists were imprisoned, the number of deaths resulting from the socialist-*Falange* battles probably exceeded one hundred, 'honours' being roughly even. No action was taken against any socialist or communist.

Those deaths were not the only ones, nor were all the people killed connected with politics. Two episodes showed most vividly how far a truly 'revolutionary situation' existed by mid-May. On Labour Day several tens of thousands of the anti-Fascist Workers and Peasants movement, carrying banners demanding the immediate establishment of a Red Army, marched through the streets of Madrid and other cities in formations which would have done credit to the Spanish Foreign Legion. They had been undergoing training under Spanish army officers and N.C.O.s secretly affiliated to the socialist or communist parties. On 3 May two women and a man (known communists) ran through the streets of Madrid shouting 'murderers, they have poisoned my child'. A crowd, readily believing that nuns and Sunday-school teachers were giving poisoned sweets to workers' children, attacked several churches and lynched some nuns and pious women – the exact number is unknown for the government took no action. The episode showed clearly that a mob could be roused to any action to which a few directed them.

By then the government was indeed in no position to take any action which did not meet with the approval of the Spanish Lenin, Largo Caballero. Prieto might still figure in the Socialist Party hierarchy and in speech and printed word influence intellectual socialists and retain the respect and reverence of Azaña and other republicans; but over the masses he had no authority whatever. The $1\frac{1}{2}$-million-strong UGT was solidly behind Largo and at his command the 200,000-strong Socialist Youth had united with the 30,000-strong Communist Youth. In Catalonia the parties had fused. What Largo had in mind now was the establishment in Spain of the type of régime which Josip Broz was to set up years later in Yugoslavia – communist but independent. He believed (and he was encouraged in the belief by Álvarez del Vayo) that his national communists in the Socialist Party, the UGT and Socialist Youth, could dominate and convert the Moscow-minded. He was to discover his mistake too late – but that was a year ahead.

Prieto had served his purpose as link-man between the Marxists and the *petits bourgeois* the moment the elections were over. Largo's full-scale offensive to destroy him as a socialist leader began almost immediately, and yet on 3 April Prieto tabled in the *Cortes* a motion seconded by Largo Caballero to have Alcalá Zamora deposed, a motion taken up with alacrity by Azaña and the whole of the Popular Front. Here was the irony of it all : Alcalá Zamora was to be deposed for dissolving the *Cortes* 'twice within his term of office as President' – and therefore unconstitutionally – and for calling the elections through which, by one means or another, the Popular Front had come to power. Alcalá Zamora's justification that his dissolution of the *Cortes* in 1933 did not count as they had been constituent *Cortes* was brushed aside, and the Popular Front proceeded almost unanimously to remove the President. Azaña, Martínez Barrio, and the left-republicans generally were moved possibly by a personal dislike of the man; Prieto's motives are difficult to guess. Largo indirectly owed his life to Alcalá Zamora : had Pérez Farras been executed, so would González Peña have died, and if González Peña, then the real leader of the October revolution also. One possible explanation is that Largo did not want as President any man in whose name the army might be tempted to rise. The colourful General Queipo de Llano was related to him and he had many other good friends who were senior officers. There may have been purely personal reasons – and personal reasons figured very prominently in the workings of the republican hierarchy irrespective of political ideologies. One of Alcalá Zamora's sons had been a close friend of one of Largo's daughters.

By May Largo's preparations for taking over power were well advanced, but the right had been far from inactive. As CEDA members had been excluded one after another from the *Cortes* more and more CEDA supporters had drifted away. They had done their best to work within the law and the constitution, to be democratic, but in the name of the law and constitution the most undemocratic things were being done. The JAP began to disintegrate in April, many of its members veering towards the *Falange*. In Navarre the traditionalists were looking for weapons to use in the armed struggle they now saw as inevitable.

As Chief-of-Staff, Franco had discovered that one in four of all new recruits were under the influence of, or members of, the socialist or communist parties, the FAI or CNT. Individual army officers had watched the political events of 1935 with misgivings. Some had in consequence established contact with the monarchist *Renovación* and the traditionalists, and others with the *Falange*, organizations which upheld three principles dear to army officers whether republican or monarchist : authority, discipline, and the unity of the nation-state of Spain. All Spanish officers had had two principles inculcated in them as fourteen- to sixteen-year-old cadets : the first was that the honour of the motherland was to be defended as ardently as the honour of a mother – and this principle meant more to a Spaniard in the first half of the twentieth century than to any member of any other nation; the second was this : *where a government by its actions brings the nation to dishonour in the eyes of the world, either by proving itself unable to maintain order, or by placing it under the control however remote of a foreign power, then it is the bounden duty of an army officer to rise in defence of the country against the government.*

Army Intelligence attributed to Largo's actions much more Moscow inspiration than was justifiable on the evidence; but there was the evidence of the VIIth Comintern Congress on Popular Fronts. Largo's closest associates were Álvarez del Vayo, Santiago Carrillo, and others who were in constant and direct contact with Dimitrov. Was the government therefore placing the country under a foreign power? Azaña in 1931 had done his best to 'triturate' the army and he was now back in office. Since December 1935 left-wing speakers and authors had inveighed against the army and Civil Guard. With the coming of the Popular Front, both army officers and other ranks had been insulted by socialists with impunity. Back in December 1935 army officers had been divided in opinion whether they could in conscience rise against Alcalá Zamora because his choice of Portela rather than Gil Robles as Prime Minister seemed unconstitutional or because it seemed probable that Portela was not capable of keeping order. In February 1936 an insufficient number were prepared to support the few who earlier made up their minds that the decline of the country into anarchy could not be tolerated much longer. In March several officers decided that if the government carried out the socialist demands for the disbandment of the Civil Guard and the organization of a Red Army, they would rise immediately; but that otherwise they were to wait until action could be co-ordinated within the army so that all garrisons rose simultaneously, and in concert between the army and all organizations in the country which thought that the Popular Front was an illegitimate government or one which by its actions and omissions had forfeited all right to government. The preparations were entrusted to Brigadier-General Mola, the commander of a brigade with headquarters in Pamplona, the heart of traditionalist country; but it was understood that in the event the rising would be under the supreme command of Sanjurjo whom they all still recognized as a lieutenant-general.

By the end of April the number of officers who had become convinced that it was their duty to rise was gratifying enough to the plotters. Mola, however, had encountered opposition. The Falangists were prepared to co-operate, always provided the army allowed them to keep their formations under their own command; but no army officer wanted freelance amateurs. The traditionalists insisted that they would follow no flag save the traditional red and yellow. Mola knew that many of his fellow officers were as republican as they were anti-Popular Front. Sanjurjo was a man whose name commanded trust and loyalty among senior officers, from, say, lieutenant-colonel upwards : but the one man among the generals whom junior officers, N.C.O.s, and men really trusted was Franco – and Franco would not commit himself.

Franco had been contending as long as anyone that whatever the tactics of the moment, the capture of Spain was important to Russia's strategy. The Popular Front was a façade. Azaña was no match for Largo Caballero, but when the test came Largo Caballero would be no match for the real communist. As Chief-of-Staff he was more aware than most that the Spanish army was not a caste but an integral part of Spain. There were communist and socialist no less than Falangist, CEDA, republican, and monarchist officers in it. He did not share the optimism of those who argued that the army had but to issue a *pronunciamiento* and the Popular Front would collapse. He saw a long and costly civil war ahead, for the anti-Fascist militias were no untrained rabble and their precursors, the October revolutionaries, had been almost the match of the crack Foreign Legion. The role given him by the plotters was to take over command of the Spanish army in Africa – peninsular units, Foreign Legion, and Moroccan troops. He might get it across to the peninsula, but it could well be seriously outnumbered. Was the provocation of an armed struggle the only way? He asked his friend Fanjul to enquire of Gil Robles whether for the Cuenca third election in which there was to be a joint anti-revolutionary list of candidates, Gil Robles would be prepared to surrender one of the CEDA candidatures to him. Gil Robles agreed. Franco was a persuasive speaker and might be useful in the *Cortes*. The news provoked violent socialist reaction. Franco's candidature was over-ruled on a technical point and he withdrew; but he would still not say yes or no to the plotters.

In normal circumstances the Cuenca third election would have been considered as providing 'safe' seats for the right. The plotters were anxious to have Primo elected in order to get him out of prison; and he would have steadied the extreme elements in the *Falange*. Gil Robles would have liked him in the *Cortes* not only because he was an able and persuasive speaker but also because Prieto was showing signs of breaking with Largo. Giménez Fernández had established a dialogue with Popular Front men who now saw what Largo Caballero was really trying to do. At Cuenca, however, the extreme left threw all caution to the winds. Militia stood menac-ingly by polling booths; voters were attacked; there was no pre-tence at a fair election. The results announced deceived few, the Popular Front candidates being awarded over twice as many votes as any left-wingers had got in 1933, and those of the right less than a half. This convinced many a doubter that there would never

again be free elections in Spain unless the Popular Front were
ousted from power by force.

The question which Spaniards, with a few naïve exceptions,
asked thereafter was when would the civil war begin. A few days
later the 1½ million-strong CNT ended a congress in Zaragoza.
Largo Caballero had asked it to consider amalgamation with the
UGT, which had now, at long last, numerical parity with the
anarchist group. The CNT announced that it was prepared to
co-operate with its rival provided one condition were fulfilled : the
UGT and Largo had definitely to break with the Popular Front.
This did not suit Largo, for openly to have done so would have
lost him his considerable though indirect control of the springs of
power, and lost him the support of the Communist Party whose
militant members now numbered about 80,000. (The Communist
Party had instructions not to be less revolutionary than Largo, but
action through a Popular Front was a major Comintern policy
decision.) The CNT programme proclaimed at Zaragoza had its
similarities with the socialist : it demanded the dissolution of the
armed services of the state, the end of private property, and the
teaching of the virtues of free-love eugenics and atheism in schools;
but it parted company with the Marxists in its advocacy of 'arms to
the people' (not a Red Army of disciplined fighters) and the
abolition of all authority except at local syndicate or village level in
an Iberian Confederation of Autonomous Libertarian Communes;
and most Marxists thought too drastic or idealistic the anarchist
contention that there should be no prisons – those not conforming
being either subjected to medical treatment or education or else
eliminated as incurable and uneducable.

The CNT continued in its own way to add to the chaos and
disorder that afflicted Spain, as did the government by its actions
and omissions. Azaña, chosen as President in succession to Alcalá
Zamora, gave the premiership to his intimate friend Casares
Quiroga on 10 May. Casares retained for himself the Ministry of
War, the closer to watch officers suspected with good reason of
plotting. With Azaña's commendation, and as an answer to the
many complaints from Gil Robles and leaders of other parties
made during his period under Azaña as Minister of the Interior
that his police forces were not doing all they could to protect life
and property, Casares closed all church schools 'for their own protection' and had all nuns and lay brothers working in hospitals and
other charitable institutions driven out. Locally, mayors in Valencia
province, not to be outdone by the central authorities, closed
churches and expelled priests. From Salamanca Unamuno reported
that mobs were threatening magistrates and desecrating churches.

Provincial left-wing newspapers urged their readers to disembowel and hang the clergy. The disorders increased as Largo socialists, Prieto socialists, UGT, and CNT fought each other when not attacking jointly or severally Falangists, CEDA members, monarchists, and even men of the centre. By the beginning of June even politicians of the *Izquierda* and *Unión* began to press Casares to act against the real troublemakers. He promised action on 13 June.

There was no action. On 16 June Casares was confronted by the right in the *Cortes*, the one place where they could now speak without fear. Gil Robles challenged Casares' contention that all was now well, following his orders on public peace. He gave details of eight assassinations that had occurred during the preceding forty-eight hours and listed the acts, of which he had evidence, committed against public order since the advent to power of the Popular Front: 160 churches had been totally destroyed and attempts had been made to set fire to another 251; 269 persons had been assassinated and 1,287 had been wounded; there had been 146 bomb explosions; ten newspaper offices had been gutted; 138 travellers had been held up at pistol point and robbed by people who claimed to be agents of the Red Aid International or anarchist bodies. The British Royal Automobile Club had issued a circular to members advising them against motoring in Spain. There had been 341 strikes of varying intensity and breadth for political ends. The British police had had to board Spanish ships in Workington to cope with mutinous crews. Spain was in a state of anarchy and democracy had died.

Gil Robles was heard with respect. A socialist then spoke briefly to state that for most of the disorders the right was to blame. Calvo Sotelo added further details of 'disorder, pillage, destruction' and referred to Asturias where Largo Caballero had admitted that government orders were being obeyed only where they coincided with 'the spirit of the October revolution'. The armed forces were being publicly insulted and men in uniform assaulted while the Minister of War did nothing. The debate got heated. Casares Quiroga lost control of himself and made a remark that perhaps he was later to regret, an involved and cryptic remark which sounded like a threat of death. The communist Dolores Ibarruri ('La Pasionaria') and the one anarchist member in the *Cortes* spoke warmly in praise of the disorders. The government received a vote of confidence from 207 Popular Front members.

It was one of the rare occasions on which there had been a quorum. The 'civil war' within the Socialist Party was over: Prieto had lost (even though he had survived machine-gunning by Largo's men) and Largo made no secret of his opinion that parliament was a useless adjunct. By 1 July it was he and he alone who ruled in Asturias; though in wide areas of the south it was his rivals, the anarchists, whose word was law.

On 23 June Franco had written to Casares Quiroga, drawing his attention to the unrest caused by the policy upon which the Prime Minister had embarked earlier in the month, of replacing army officers of merit with others who had voiced approval of the October revolution or Catalan rising. Franco waited in vain for an answer. At the beginning of July Franco told Mola to count him as one of 'them'. Sanjurjo had already written to Mola that 'with little Frankie-boy or without little Frankie-boy we shall go ahead and save Spain'.

Early in the morning of 13 July a posse of government Assault Guards in a police car set out to kidnap and assassinate Gil Robles and Calvo Sotelo. Gil Robles was away; but they left a dead Calvo Sotelo in the keeping of the night watchman at a cemetery. The names of the assassins were known. The government lamely arrested the driver of the police car 'as under suspicion'. The commander of the Assault Guard posse was the lover of Margarita Nelken and Nelken had long been a supporter of Largo Caballero, but Largo was in no way responsible. He was at the time extremely worried. At the beginning of June he had got the Madrid UGT and CNT to co-operate in a strike of building-workers and lift operators. Then the CNT had let him down, ordering workers to obey the principles of libertarian communism, to live off the small shopkeepers without payment, and this had won them many converts from the UGT. Largo, who had first spoken of the strike as 'mighty ramblows at the gates of power', had then urged the workers to accept the higher wages, forty-hour week, and paid holidays offered by the Ministry of Labour, but the CNT would not follow the UGT back to work. With that Largo's power suffered a temporary relapse. On the other hand, Prieto's stock rose and there was even talk of a 'government of national conciliation'. Whether or not talk would have become reality as the defenders of the Popular Front have since argued (back in April—May there had been similar talk), the murder of Sotelo put an end to it.

The revolt of the army officers, planned as a *coup* which would bring quick results, began prematurely on 17 July in Morocco. By the 20th the insurgent officers knew that it had failed. Their action had sparked off the long-expected civil war.

Chapter 25

The Collapse of the Republic and the
'Two Spains' at War 1936–9

As HUGH THOMAS SAYS PITHILY in his standard work on the Civil War: 'The Second Spanish Republic failed because it was from the start not accepted by powerful forces politically both to the Left and to the Right. Furthermore . . . it estranged many who had at first contemplated collaboration with it'.[1]

It was never accepted, and could never have been accepted, by the anarchists: they made war on the republic from its first day almost continually to its last. Nor could it be accepted by the heirs of French Regalism (the Alfonsist monarchists); though Alfonso ordered them to obey the new dispensation, in 1932 some did their amateur best to destroy it. The republic was equally anathema to the traditionalists (the Carlist monarchists), who saw in kingship the sole effective protection for the liberties of human beings. It was accepted by the Marxists, but only as a necessary and a fleeting step towards the ineluctable destiny of human society – the dictatorship of the proletariat; and in 1934 a substantial number thought that the time had come for the final step to that goal. Anarchists, monarchists, and Marxists, of course, never made much secret of their opinions or intentions. If judgement is to be made, then the severer censure must fall on those who pretended that they believed in the principles of liberal democracy and when in power were false to them: the left-republicans who rejoiced when churches were set on fire in 1931 and who made laws offensive to the hearts and minds of one-half of Spain; the men of the centre who from 1933 used office to personal monetary advantage; and those of the right who were as blind to the principles of social justice as the left had been earlier to true freedom of religion. They, no less than the anarchists, Marxists, and monarchists, destroyed the republic, the dream of the liberal philosophers who had seen it as a 'pretty girl', a good fairy who with the wave of the magic wand of education would cure the thousand ills to which Spain was heir.

By May only a few intellectuals still clung to the belief that

[1] *The Spanish Civil War* (London, 1961), p. 111.

203

Spain could or should be a liberal democracy. By then the republic was anything but that. The government in Madrid was effectively in the hands of a minority – the Largo Caballerist – within a minority, the Popular Front; no Popular Front man seriously maintained *at the time* that the majority of the people of Spain had sanctioned what they were about. By the beginning of July 1936 the central government had lost control of wide regions of the country— Asturias, Valencia, much of Extremadura and Andalusia. They were about to lose control of another portion. Whether the last-minute attempts on the part of the left-republicans and Prieto to govern within the law and to restore order might have succeeded or not had the military not risen on 17–18 July cannot be known : but there is one fact which must not be forgotten. In 1936 more individual Spaniards than in 1931 believed with deeper intensity that their beliefs, religious, philosophic, economic, and political, were right, and their neighbours' right only in so far as they coincided with their own.[2]

The events of the weekend 17–20 July surprised both the government and the insurgent officers : the government because they did not immediately realize how widespread the army rising was; the insurgents because the answer to their call for revolt was not as widespread as they had expected.

The plan in which Franco had concurred at the eleventh hour was a simple one. The Spanish standing army consisted of eight infantry divisions quartered over wide regions and with headquarters in eight cities : Madrid, Seville, Valencia, Barcelona, Zaragoza, Burgos, Valladolid, and Corunna. There was also a cavalry division in Madrid. Of the divisional commanders only one, Cabanellas of Zaragoza, was in the plot. On D-Day he was to declare for the rising, and the other divisions were to be taken over by colonels or unemployed-list generals who were in the conspiracy. At lower levels, where the commander was in the plot he was to declare for the rising; where not, officers of the same rank or junior were to take over command. The divisions in Madrid, Seville, Barcelona, and Corunna were to stay put; the other four were to be concentrated round their town headquarters. On D plus 1, the Burgos division would join the Valladolid division and as one column they would advance southwards, the Zaragoza division would set off south-westwards and the Valencia division north-westwards, all towards Madrid. Franco would by then have flown from the Canaries to Morocco, taken command of the Spanish African army (which was supposed to rise on D plus 1), transported it to the peninsula, and subsequently advanced northwards to Madrid.

[2] cf. Gil Robles, *No fué posible la paz* (Madrid, 1968), p. 792.

The plan miscarried. There was confusion worse confounded as to which day was supposed to be D-Day. The only division to fall intact into insurgent hands was the one from Valladolid. By Monday 20 July the insurgents had lost the Valencia and the Barcelona divisions completely and they knew that the Madrid division was also lost. The other four were partly theirs and partly the government's. On the same day General Sanjurjo was killed. The aircraft which was to take him from Lisbon to Burgos and the supreme command of the insurgents crashed minutes after take-off. The rising was thus without a commander-in-chief. Mola had an army consisting of a division and parts of others in the north; Queipo de Llano held Seville with a few hundred men; Franco had the African army but inadequate means to get it across the Straits.

The history of the republic is encrusted with many a legend : that of the Civil War with many more, the first being that 'the army rose against the government'. The accurate fact is that a small number of officers rose against both their superior officers and their government, that they were followed by a majority of their fellows but only by three-fifths of the men under them. The casualties in the first seventy-two hours were extremely heavy. The situation in the peninsula thereafter was :

Loyal to the *government* : 2,000 officers; 23,000 other ranks
With the *insurgents* : 3,500 officers; 33,000 other ranks.

The army, however, was only one of the armed land forces of Spain : there were also the Civil Guard, the Assault Guards, and the Carabiniers. The split here was approximately :

Loyal to the *government* : 13,500
Supporting the *insurgents* : 14,700

The second legend is that the army rose against 'a determined but unarmed people'. At the outbreak of the war there were in the country trained and armed militia. There were :

Against the *insurgents* : 12,000 socialists and communists
15,000 Trotskyists and anarchists
(total 27,000)
With the *insurgents* : 8,400 *Requetés* (traditionalists)
4,000 Falangists (total 12,400)

Thus, the trained armed land forces immediately available in the peninsula to each side were :

government : 65,500
insurgents : 63,600

All this meant stalemate. Franco in Africa had a force of 24,000 men – of whom 6,000 were 'Moors' and 6,000 'Foreign' Legion[3] – an important factor only if Franco could get them across the Straits, and on the morning of the 20th this looked unlikely. By far the greater part of the Spanish air force (such as it was : fearless and skilful pilots, but old machines) had remained loyal to the government. The greater part of the navy had fallen into government hands : Giral, the Navy Minister, had issued orders which the crews of most of the warships had interpreted rightly or wrongly as a command to murder any officer whom they so much as thought to be disloyal and to pitch his body overboard.

The long-term outlook was bleak for the insurgents. They had in their hands only one of the four major mobilization centres (Zaragoza, Valencia, Barcelona, Madrid) with all their contingent arms and other military supply depots – and there were in Spain enough weapons, albeit antiquated, to mobilize up to three-quarters of a million men. The Popular Front or its nominal supporters held, as Prieto in a broadcast told the insurgents : 'the major cities, the industrial centres, all the gold and silver of the Bank of Spain, limitless reserves of men. . . .' These 'reserves of men' were not wholly inexpert in arms, for they were ex-conscripts. With the exception of a small artillery factory in Seville, all the arms and munitions factories, motor vehicle and aircraft-assembly plants, iron and steel works, and textile mills were in Popular Front hands.

Why then did the insurgents not listen to 'reason'? On the evening of 18 July Martínez Barrio who had inherited the premiership earlier in the day from a frightened Casares Quiroga, had offered amnesty to all the insurgents and the redress of many army grievances. Mola, with whom he talked and to whom he offered the Ministry of War, refused all blandishments. To have accepted would have been contrary to the Spanish concept of honour in which any amount of commonsense is irrelevant. Martínez Barrio understood. The generals and the colonels could have saved themselves, they could not have saved the many thousands of civilians who had shown their willingness to support them.

In the cities and towns of Old Castile, Aragon, and Navarre the rebellious troops had been loudly acclaimed as liberators from

[3] Another of the Civil War legends is that the Spanish army in Africa was of 'Africans and foreigners'. The Legion, when founded by Millán Astray and Franco in 1920, had admitted a large number of World War I veterans, but by 1936 its foreign element was not more than 5 per cent. The Legion was superior in military discipline, skill, and armament to the rest of the Spanish army, which was of conscripts. The 'Moors' were also tough and ruthless professionals. The remaining 12,000 were no less Spanish and conscripts and no better trained or armed than those in units stationed in the peninsula.

tyranny. Such resistance as showed itself had been limited to militant socialists and anarchists. In Pamplona, where Mola had his
headquarters, the people had been wildly enthusiastic. More to the
point, the government's last-minute offers did not change the situation. The insurgents had not risen out of personal advantage but
because they sincerely believed, however mistaken they may have
been, that it was their duty to rise because the government had by
its actions and omissions forfeited all right to govern.

Most army officers, on declaring themselves at war with the
government, had shouted 'Long live the republic', only a few the
less specific 'Long live Spain'.[4] All had explained their action as
being 'in defence of Spain'. Franco, abler than most at self-expres-
sion, had spoken of the bad example Spain was giving the world;
of the prevailing anarchy; of the ruination of the economy by
strikes and sabotage which could only bring hunger to the nation;
of a government whose very agents and officials were fomenting
hatred between classes and between the inhabitants of one region
and another, which applied the law arbitrarily, paid scant respect
to its own constitution, and was allowing Soviet agents to help in
the destruction of Spain. A cabinet reshuffle did not make the
government more legitimate and did not guarantee that law and
order would be respected.

By the morning of the 21st news of what had been happening
since the 17th in the areas where the revolt had failed and especially in Madrid, was percolating to the insurgent areas generally.
The immediate reaction of the UGT and CNT to the news of the
rising in Morocco had been to demand the distribution of arms to
the 'workers', which could only mean themselves. In Madrid the
Anti-Fascist Workers' Militia already had 8,000 members armed
with rifles and automatic weapons, and the socialists controlled the
thousand-strong Assault Guards with their armoured cars. There
was no sign of any rising among the Madrid troops. Fanjul was
supposed to be leading it, but the news of the Moroccan rising
seems to have been even more of a genuine surprise to him than the
government pretended it was to them. Casares Quiroga had refused
to hand over government weapons; but the UGT and Marxist
Youth had insisted, and by the afternoon of the 18th, with the help
of an artillery colonel, had acquired 5,000 rifles. Casares then
resigned. Azaña proposed a new government which would take in
the left with Prieto and a good part of the centre as well. Largo
thereupon threatened to bring out his forces in open war against
the republic. That night Martínez Barrio took over as premier, but

[4] Here yet another legend—that the rising was against the *republic* as
distinct from the Popular Front (see below, p. 214).

by the morning he, too, had resigned. Azaña then summoned Giral and Giral did as Largo wished. General Miaja, the commander of one of the two brigades of the Madrid division, stood by his side as weapons were issued to 'the people', while Fanjul was trying to rally the Madrid troops (in the Montaña barracks) to the insurgent cause. During the night exultant Marxists and anarchists set fire to some fifty churches; indulged in indiscriminate murder; and on the following day stormed the Montaña barracks. Madrid was theirs. Trigger-happy militiamen and some 55,000 UGT and CNT soldiers looted, burnt, and killed all day long, their special victims, as a matter of principle, being priests and members of religious Orders. Others were killed to satisfy old grudges.

It was even worse in Barcelona; and as bad in many other cities and towns where the insurgents had succeeded. Here, in the name of the insurgents, were many deaths to be avenged. They began to shoot prominent Marxists, anarchists, and Masons.

After that weekend there was no possibility of an end to the war except after a long period of attrition or a spectacular local victory.

Giral could have achieved such a victory. He had the requisite equipment, the men, and the officers rapidly to have organized at least four divisions in Madrid. (At most only 1,500 from the Madrid infantry and cavalry divisions joined the insurgents; for the Communist Party had long made the Madrid garrisons the *Schwerpunkt* of their proselytizing activity.) These could have advanced north against Mola – whose men had no more than a handful of rounds apiece – or south to Seville which Queipo was holding with a few hundred men. He could have concentrated his air force on the ports and airfields through which Franco was beginning sporadically to reinforce Queipo. Instead he chose to use his aircraft in useless raids of one or two machines at a time, on insurgent and Moroccan cities, which killed a few civilians and increased their determination to fight him and what he represented. By the end of July he had thirty modern bombers and fighters, sent him by the French Popular Front government which had come to power on 4 June. Franco by then had nine Italian bomber-transports. On 5 August, under the umbrella of six of these and the eleven Spanish fighters he could muster, he loaded 3,000 men on cross-channel steamers and smaller boats, and ferried them to the mainland. Giral's navy could have blown them out of the water. Instead he allowed those 3,000 to make their way north to Cáceres and establish contact with Mola and so provide him with the ammunition he lacked.

The next opportunity for a quick victory was Franco's. By 21 September his ex-Africa army, which had suffered heavy casualties before Mérida and Badajoz, but had been reinforced by local volunteers and further units ferried from Africa (in twenty Junkers-52 transports sent to him by Goering), now numbered about 8,000 effectives. It was then at a road-fork. One fork led to Madrid, forty-five miles way, the other to Toledo, twenty-four miles away. In the Alcázar at Toledo, one hundred officers, five cadets, 190 other ranks, 800 Civil Guards, and 200 civilians had been holding out since 18 July against odds which recalled Numantia, Saguntum, and Zaragoza – a siege that was making headlines in the newspapers of the western world. Short of food and water, subjected to aerial and artillery bombardment and dynamiting, they could not be expected to hold out much longer. Franco had to choose between the remote possibility that he might frighten Madrid into surrender by the presence of 6,000 to 12,000 troops at the gate (only he knew that what he could muster were so few – the world at large accepting his and the Popular Front's propaganda that he had a *grande armée*), and the less remote possibility that they might scatter the 16,000 besiegers of the Alcázar. He chose to go to the relief of his friends, as a matter of 'honour', and the Alcázar was relieved. Franco's troops did not reach the outskirts of Madrid until the beginning of November. On the 7th an assault force of 6,000 tried to storm Madrid across a river and uphill, but Madrid was then defended by an army of 24,000 which could call on perhaps a further 60,000 'irregulars' to aid it. It would have been a miracle if the attack had succeeded. After this there was no further possibility of a quick victory : the war had to continue until one side crushed the other, or one side destroyed the will of the other to continue the war – not to occur until 1939.

The principal reason why, by the beginning of November 1936, there was no further possibility of a quick victory was that the character of the war was changing rapidly. It was ceasing to be a war of columns engaging in pitched battles and of siege set-pieces – the Napoleonic or more recent colonial war pattern – and was becoming one of continuous, even if lightly manned, fronts with trenches and barbed wire – the 1914–18 type, but on a smaller scale. Fronts had become continuous because each side had made a new army out of its half of the Spanish army. The new armies had become feasible because of outside help and internal reorganization, which in its turn had been possible because of important political changes on each side.

The republican[5] scene had changed radically since July. Of the period immediately following the news of the rising Manuel Azaña was to write straightforwardly : 'There was a proletarian rising,

[5] I use the terms republican and nationalist from here onwards for clarity, while fully conscious that they are misnomers.

14 • •

though not against the government. Goods and persons were
sequestrated; many died without trial; the bosses were driven out or
killed – so were technicians who were not trusted; and the unions,
cells, "libertarian" groups, and even political parties took possession
of buildings, factories, shops, newspapers, current accounts, shares,
etc.'[6] Up to 1 September not less than 20,000 and perhaps as many
as 40,000 persons had been killed[7] in the republican zone. The
Marxist militias and armed anarchist groups had indeed been far
more anxious to kill the 'enemy' in their midst than to sally against
the enemy armies. The workers in the munitions and arms factories
likewise had done as they pleased. Giral had immediately appealed
to León Blum to send him arms, and a handful of French pilots had
flown in machines while others had been despatched in crates.
Russians and Central Europeans attending the Workers' Olympiad
in Barcelona (the communists were boycotting the Berlin Olympics)
had stayed on as members of the Catalan anti-Fascist forces under
the anarchist Durruti, and they had been joined by young writers
and university students from western Europe. In all their numbers
came to no more than a few hundred. The French had quickly
despatched fifty-five bombers and fighters but had then entered
into the international non-intervention scheme. Giral needed much
more : and there was one nation prepared to give that much more
– at a price. The price was : gold, the restoration of order in the
republican zone, and the acceptance of direction on political
matters from expert advisers. The country was Soviet Russia.

Complex but logical reasoning[8] had led the Kremlin to conclude
that Britain should not be frightened into thinking that a 'communist' revolution was taking place in Spain. The majority of the
popular British newspapers of their own accord were guiding
popular opinion into support of 'republican' Spain. British insularity
could be trusted to look on foreign countries as imitations, even
if inferior, of Britain and the revolt in Spain was duly seen as one
against a government lawful because chosen in free elections.
Nevertheless, in Russian eyes, the 'ruling classes' were reading too
much about 'the terror'. They were not impressed by the popular
tribunals which Giral had set up halfway through August to give

[6] Manuel Azaña, *La velada en Benicarló* (Buenos Aires, 1939), pp. 95–6.
[7] No greater precision is possible. I concur with Hugh Thomas's estimate
of 60,000 for the whole war rather than the official *Causa General's*
total of 85,940. The only careful study is Antonio Montero's *Historia de
la persecución religiosa en España 1936–39* (Madrid, 1961). He gives 13
bishops, 4,317 secular priests, 2,489 male religious, and 283 nuns as the
number killed by the republicans. Accuracy was possible because nominal
rolls of all priests and religious existed in diocesan and conventual archives.
[8] Cf. B. Bolloten, *The Grand Camouflage* (New York and London, 1968),
pp. 221–2, for Vidali's version which was intended for foreign readers.

semblance of legality to the mass executions still taking place : proof of membership of the now defunct CEDA was still enough for a death sentence. British business interests were not further to be alienated. Besides, no war could be successfully conducted without rigorous order behind the lines and discipline at the front.

Vidali, the Italian communist, had very quickly after the rising taken over the conversion of communist militia into an army. He established what was called the Fifth Regiment, as the depot of battalions properly organized to Red Army patterns, complete with commissars. While others wasted petrol and ammunition in *chekas*, Vidali had despatched 8,000 men against the insurgents, and where the discipline of the Marxist militias had broken before determined attacks, and they had fled leaving their weapons, these communist-organized units had been trained to perfection. Togliatti had become a frequent visitor to Spain and Duclos, Gerö, Stepanov, and Codovila had taken up residence, but they were all non-Russian Comintern men and needed Soviet experts to advise them. Giral had therefore agreed to the appointment of the old revolutionary Antonov-Ovscenko as consul-general in Barcelona, with a large staff, and the trusty Stalinist Marcel Rosenberg as ambassador in Madrid, with an even larger staff which included General Berzin and army officers of all ranks. Marshals Rokossovski, Koniev, and Malinovsky were among the several hundred 'experts' to follow.

The first piece of advice to Giral was that he should send gold to Moscow and over 510 million grammes were duly despatched. The Russians were so true to their word that already on 24 October Franco's troops pressing on Madrid heard a new noise, that of Russian Vickers tanks under General Pavlov which promptly destroyed the Italian tankettes which Franco had pressed into service with even greater speed; and on 8 November the people of Madrid welcomed a fine body of men whom they hailed as 'Rusos' but who were in fact of many other nationalities – the first of the International Brigades organized by the Comintern.

The despatch of the gold and the acceptance of Russian advisers, however, had not satisfied the Kremlin. Order had to be restored and kept. The only way to bring the anarchists to heel was to install as Head of Government the one Marxist whom anarchists respected, Largo Caballero, and he suited the Kremlin in two ways : he was still under the influence of the communist Álvarez del Vayo and still admired by the British Labour Party as a Ramsay MacDonald if not quite a Clement Attlee. Accordingly on 4 September Giral stepped down and Largo became Prime Minister with a Cabinet in which there were only two avowed communists, Álvarez del Vayo and Juan Negrín posing as socialists. The inclusion of four left-republicans gave it middle-class respectability in the eyes of Britain and the United States; and from now on the hunting and shooting of priests and 'Fascists' declined very sharply. Men were made to work in factories, especially those concerned with the war, and sabotage was rapidly and violently punished; in short, order was restored in most of the republican zone. On 27 September a government was established in Catalonia under Companys, similar to the Madrid government under Caballero and with anarchist, Trotskyist, Marxist, and *Esquerra* members. The only problem areas were the south, in the hands of anarchists who were still opposed to co-operation with anyone else but who, having got rid of 'enemies', were anxious to prove that 'libertarian communism' was the ideal way of life, and in the north the Basque provinces.

The fact that the Basque nationalists had sided with the Madrid government at the outbreak of hostilities, and had effectively suppressed the rising in San Sebastián, Bilbao, and other garrison towns, had surprised Madrid almost as much as the insurgents. Behind the Basques' decision there were many factors : the principal one being that they were Catholics, the best instructed of all the inhabitants of the peninsula; the next that like other 'minority nations' they were absorbed in their own affairs. What happened even in the neighbouring provinces of León or Asturias was no concern of theirs. They had always been more interested and therefore better informed about what happened in Biarritz than in Santander or Oviedo, so that even if there had not been press censorship since the eve of the February elections which prohibited news of other than local disorders, many would not have noticed the news. The February elections in the Basque provinces had been exemplary in comparison with the rest of Spain and after the 'second round' ten nationalists had been returned. Bilbao was a socialist stronghold, but Prieto's own, and Prieto in Bilbao was even more a 'moderate' than Prieto in Madrid. There were few communists and only a few hundred anarchists among the fishermen and villagers. After the elections the Basque provinces had been a model of order : strikes and acts of violence had been limited to Bilbao where, at the best of times since it was a major port, a modicum of disorder was to be expected. Accordingly, the claim of the various army officers that they had risen to save Spain from anarchy and chaos had had no bearing on the facts as the Basques knew them. Had the army leaders mentioned the defence of religion, that might have struck a chord : but *not one of them in their original declarations had spoken of the redress of Catholic grievances.* Their language had been identical with that of the great liberal generals of the nineteenth century who had persecuted the Church. Only days and weeks later was there talk of a *cruzada*, and though individual parish priests sided with the rebels, no Spanish church dignitary was to speak on their behalf till late in November – except as we shall see in a moment.

The conditions making legitimate a rising against authority, as thought out by Mariana, Ribadeneyra, Molina, and Suárez (Jesuits, though not Basques, like Ignatius of Loyola) just did not exist in the eyes of the Basques. The rising succeeded in Álava, but prompt action by the Basque nationalist leaders led to its failure in Guipúzcoa and Vizcaya. Prompt action by the same men prevented anarchists and Marxists from burning down more than two churches in San Sebastián and killing off more than 500 private citizens. They would not admit Marxists into their police forces. Now Mola, prior to his attack on Guipúzcoa, which was designed to seal off the western end of the French frontier and thus prevent the supply of weapons by that route to the republicans, had prevailed on the bishops of Pamplona and Vitoria to call on the Basques to lay down their arms. The Basque priests had guided their people to judge for themselves whether the bishops had spoken under duress. A few days later the same bishop of Pamplona was protesting from the pulpit against executions in the nationalist zone. As Mola's troops advanced, anarchist and Marxist troops, sent through France from Catalonia to help the Basques, set fire to religious buildings, so that at the last moment the Basques had to fight the men sent to help them as well as Mola's troops : but then Mola's troops were imprisoning priests. On religious grounds, therefore, there was nothing to choose between the two sides; but there was on nationalist grounds. The Popular Front had promised the Basques their Statute of Autonomy. The insurgents made no secret of their strong anti-separatist and even anti-regionalist intentions. On 1 October the Popular Front was to fulfil its promise. Later it would even give a Basque nationalist the Ministry of Justice – which he accepted in the hope that he could mitigate some of the injustices of which his Marxist overlords were guilty. The Basques were to suffer much, for help that the Madrid government gave them before they were overrun by Mola's and Franco's forces in the spring of 1937 was cynically opportunist and inadequate. They were never to be forgiven by the victor for backing the losing side.

Their cousins, the Navarrese, ran wild with enthusiasm on hearing the news of the rising, primarily because to them all Madrid governments had been illegitimate for a century. Mola had raised again the red and yellow flag of Spain. That was enough for them to know that he was better than 'the others'. There were few Freemasons, socialists, communists, or anarchists among them. They had proceeded to put to death those who were almost as quickly as if they had been priests in the republican zone – almost though not usually quite so quickly because they normally had scruples about sending a man to his Maker without giving him a chance to confess his sins. The Navarrese were alone among the peoples of Spain not to divide for and against the insurgents. Even among the Basques there had been quite a few secret supporters of the rising, and many a family had sons killed on either side. The Civil War was, in a literal sense, fratricidal.

In this respect the Basques shared the tragedy of the rest of Spain. Neither in the beginning nor subsequently was the Civil War a struggle between the privileged and the unprivileged. Azaña was a wealthy man before as President he began to live as a king. Many a penniless proletarian sided with the insurgents. It was not, as we have seen, a war of the army against the civilians. (All monarchists were with the insurgents but not all republicans were against them.) There were advocates of dictatorship and of democracy on either side. There were Catholics and atheists. There were men dedicated to all the seven capital sins and others to their contrary virtues. There were opportunists and there were idealists. It was idealism, romantic idealism, which inspired the defenders of the Alcázar on the one side and of Bilbao and Madrid on the other, and on both to suffer the heroic privations of the winters in the *sierras*; and just as there was an irreconcilable difference between anarchism and socialism, so on the other side pure traditionalism and pure Falangism were irreconcilable – and traditionalist and Falangist were but two of the many ideologies to be found among the supporters of the insurgents.

The single common factor among them all was that they had had enough of the anarchy and chaos that had preceded the rising. Accordingly within a few days it had been possible to establish order in the nationalist zone. Men and women could dress as they wished and go about their daily business. Food was plentiful – the armies lacked factories, but the area to fall immediately into their hands included some of the best wheat lands. (In the republican zone there were serious local shortages owing to bad organization, for this zone had wheat lands and the rich farming country of the eastern coast.) They could go to Mass (forbidden in the republican zone). They were convinced that they would win.

Romantic idealism is of its nature undisciplined and intolerant. Therefore Falangists and traditionalists, like anarchists and socialists, sought out real or imaginary enemies in their midst and shot them. Mola, disturbed by such violence, would not have the *Falange* and *Requetés* acting independently of the army. In given circumstances, where the insurgent armies could not effectively guard prisoners-of-war, they shot them after the briefest of 'trials'. Thus Colonel Yagüe, in command of the troops from Africa which captured Badajoz, had about 200 leaders killed out of the 4,000 or so who survived the battle.[9] He was afraid of the potential threat to his lines of communication of the mass escape of such a large body with their leaders. The insurgent officers, where successful, court-martialled their fellow officers and N.C.O.s who had not sided with them as men who had failed in their duty to defend the nation. The nationalist side set up its tribunals (of army and civilian members) as quickly as the republicans had their popular tribunals. These proceeded to judge rapidly and to sentence to death any man who had been a leader of anarchists, communists, socialists, Catalan or Basque separatists, and any Mason, as one who had betrayed his country – and the penalty for treason was death. Rank-and-file members could expiate their 'crime' by joining the *Falange* or the army – and tens of thousands did. It was argued in their defence that they had been misled, and they were even often excused responsibility for criminal acts; but there was no easy reprieve for the man of letters, wealth, law, or medicine whose name appeared in captured nominal rolls of the proscribed societies, and their priesthood proved no protection for fourteen Basques.[10] As on the republican side so on the nationalist the number of deaths away from battlefields exceeded tens of thousands before the end of 1936; by the end of the war the nationalists must have shot at least 40,000. As victors they were to kill another 40,000 between then and 1943, bringing their total in all to 80,000, in the long term thus exceeding the 60,000 for which the republican side was responsible.[11]

[9] The *Chicago Tribune* reporter's, Jay Allen's, '2,000' does not stand up to mathematical analysis and the whole report must be considered as a brilliant piece of imaginative writing, of which there was as much in the Spanish Civil War as in other wars. What I read in newspapers of the war in the Far East (1944–5) bore little resemblance to what I knew to be happening. Over 2,000 republicans were killed at Badajoz, but *not* executed. It was a very bloody battle. My own investigations of army records (and there is a surprisingly good collection from *both* sides in the archives of the *Servicio Historico Militar* in Madrid) have led me to concur with Thomas's estimate.

[10] It was, however, for about another 400 who were imprisoned. It is yet another legend of the Civil War that the nationalists were fighting merely to preserve the privileges of army, Church, and wealth, and that the men they shot were exclusively working-class. The executed included a first cousin of Franco's.

[11] For the estimates up to the end of 1939, cf. Thomas, p. 631. In my *Franco the Man and his Nation* (London, 1967), referred to hereafter as *Franco*, p. 331, I gave 10,000 as the figure of executions between the end of the war (April 1939) and the appointment of Serrano Suñer as Foreign Minister (October 1940). It was severely attacked by Herbert Southworth and others who spoke of various figures up to 200,000. I have since seen evidence to convince me that I should increase my estimate *between those*

Not that in the long term, had it won, the republican side would have been more merciful. In the whole course of the war it was to capture only one major city, Teruel, and it dealt with civilians who did not share its views as summarily as had the nationalists after each advance. In all this there is one point which must be emphasized, that there was hard Spanish logic on both sides, whatever the numbers; except in the early stages there was little passion whether of anger or envy. The logic was this: a proposition cannot both be and not be; it is either true or a lie; no man has the right to propagate error, to mislead others into error; if he does so, he is guilty of a crime against the mind of the person he misleads, worse than such crimes as theft or violence which affect merely the body of the victim. In propagating error (Catholicism or Freemasonry, Fascism or communism, capitalism or communism, nationalism or separatism) the accused has become an enemy of society. What the courts had essentially to decide was not only whether the accused was guilty but how dangerous his continued existence would be to society. For the anarchist the answer was simple: could the man be redeemed from his error? If it was thought possible, he was safe. If not, he was executed. For all the others it was more complex because with them it was axiomatic that punishment was a powerful deterrent. In the period after the October 1934 revolution the right had argued that clemency towards the culprits would encourage other revolutions and other risings. The left had agreed with them: they had been most anxious to save the lives of Largo Caballero, González Peña, and the other leaders not merely so that they should survive to lead another revolution, but that their followers should not be afraid to side with them again. The right could now say: if the leaders of the 1934 revolution had been executed, then in 1936 the situation immediately preceding the Civil War would not have arisen. The nationalists were determined that there should be no clemency this time; and in their determination they condemned to death many a man who constituted no danger to their society and even many a friend. Locally there were barbarous and absurd extremisms. Giménez Fernández came near to being shot because he maintained that extreme though the provocation had been, the rising was still morally unjustified. Another CEDA deputy, Manuel Saco Rivera, and many lesser known CEDA members were shot by nationalists for maintaining that same point of view.

In their pursuit of the enemy among them, the nationalists, then, were as ruthless as the republicans. As the French philosopher

dates to about 15,000 but not more. The figure 40,000 for the period to 1943 inclusive is based on that evidence. See below, p. 450, note on deaths.

Jacques Maritain wrote,[12] the nationalists 'behaved with the same primitive instinct as the masses whom they feared'. In the pursuit of the enemy before them and the development of the necessary political and military structure necessary for victory, their love of order was to be a decisive factor.

The original plan—concentration of four columns of troops on Madrid, fall of Popular Front within days, possibly by 25 July, the feast of the Patron Saint of Spain, St James – had envisaged the establishment of a military *junta*, with civilian members, under General Sanjurjo, which would supervise elections for a constituent assembly. Its failure and the death of Sanjurjo left the insurgents without a plan. Mola's immediate reaction to its failure was to think that the insurgents would do well to concentrate on Navarre (where the population was so wholeheartedly with them) and carry on indefinitely a guerrilla war, as the Carlists had proved to be possible in the nineteenth century. Other generals had been more sanguine as it became apparent that the Popular Front had thrown away its chance to smash the insurrection. A military *junta* had therefore been formed under the senior general present, Cabanellas of Zaragoza, and Franco had joined it as soon as he had got his column proceeding northwards; but the situation was militarily unsatisfactory. Queipo de Llano was in military (and therefore political) control of the south and Mola of the north. Franco's immediate reaction to the unexpected loss of the navy had been to seek aircraft from Britain, Italy, and Germany. Quite separately, Mola had also got in touch with Italy and Germany. There had to be a unified control of contacts abroad and of operations in Spain. Which was to be given priority, the north-western front with its potential harvest of steelworks and arms factories, the northeastern with Barcelona as its objective and the closure of the overland supply of weapons for the enemy, or the southern route offering Madrid as a possible prize? There had to be, as a matter of military principle, concentration of effort and economy of force, mobility, the possibility of effecting surprise and avoiding surprise. There had to be a *generalissimo*; but there had to be also a Head of State and a Head of Government. If the reason for the rising had been to put an end to disorder, then there had to be order where the insurgents were in power. An army could not conduct a war without civilian backing. The insurgents had to have a government and, to express their confidence in victory, a Head of State of their own.

The choice of *generalissimo* was the easiest of the three tasks. There were three major-generals and a brigadier from whom to

[12] Introduction by Jaques Maritain to A. Mendizábal, *Aux origines d'une tragédie* (Paris, 1937).

choose : Cabanellas, Queipo de Llano, and Franco, and Mola. Cabanellas at sixty-four was past his prime. Queipo had a distinguished record : he had risen from the rank of bugler and had once led a spectacular cavalry charge in Africa. As a cavalryman he had little idea of the use of infantry and by September it already looked as if it was going to be an infantry war. Mola had planned the rising, but he had left many ends untied and was junior in rank to the others. He favoured Franco, and so did all other generals, brigadiers, and colonels, let alone the younger officers, all, that is, save Cabanellas himself who was the odd man out. At a *junta* meeting organized by the senior air force officer Kindelán[13] on 21 September to appoint a C-in-C, Cabanellas stated that he did not see why a war could not be run by a committee as efficiently as by a *generalissimo*. On a vote being put, all but Cabanellas voted for a C-in-C. Franco's name was proposed and all but Cabanellas voted for him. Days passed, but Cabanellas as president of the *junta* did not promulgate the result.

The insurgents were divisible into monarchists and republicans; the monarchists could be subdivided into Alfonsists and Carlists. Therefore there could be neither King nor President as Head of State. Nor could there be a civilian Head of Government, for what sort of government could there be? Only those political parties with militia had survived the rising : *Renovación* (with a few hundred), the traditionalists, and the *Falange*; the former wanted the restoration of the liberal-conservative 1876 constitution, but this was unacceptable to the other two. The traditionalists, then as ever, wanted an authoritarian government of a pattern which would give individuals maximum liberty.[14] The *Falange* wanted a nationalist, authoritarian, version of anarcho-syndicalism. With about 20,000 *Requetés* (traditionalists) and 5,000 Falangists at the front, and a further 25,000 Falangists in the rear areas, the army *junta* could not afford to offend either traditionalists or *Falange*.

While Cabanellas sat on the nomination of Franco as *generalissimo*, Kindelán, an Alfonsist monarchist to the marrow, Yagüe, a thorough anti-monarchist Falangist, and Nicolás, Franco's elder brother, agreed to act together on their own initiative. They reconvened the *junta* and provided it with a 'guard of honour' of a hundred armed Falangists and a similar number of *Requetés*. Kindelán read a draft he had prepared – a decree appointing the already chosen Commander-in-Chief Head of Government as well. Mola opposed this : a C-in-C would have enough to do without

---

[13] One of the last of the descendants of the 'Wild Geese'.

[14] Not a contradiction, though it might so appear to a modern political theorist.

having to meddle in politics. Cabanellas was incoherent with rage. Kindelán, no unworthy descendant of a refugee from Cromwell, won over all opposition. Franco, neither to be pigeon-holed as a monarchist or a republican nor to be classified as a believer in any specific political ideology, was the ideal man for that particular moment.

On 1 October in Burgos Cabanellas formally bestowed on Franco all powers of C-in-C, Head of Government, and Head of the new State of Spain. The new state extended at that time over two-fifths of the territory of Spain. Its 10·5 million inhabitants recognized him each in his own way : as a *locum tenens* for Alfonso XIII or the Carlist pretender, for José Antonio de Rivera imprisoned by the republic in Alicante, for Gil Robles now in Portugal after being expelled from France by Blum; in a word as a stop-gap by nearly everyone who supported the insurgents; and as a usurper by those who did not. Franco did not then see himself either as a man who would rule Spain for the rest of his life. His immediate task was to unite Spain, by winning the war. He was Commander-in-Chief of about 150,000 troops – a force numerically inferior to the enemy. However, he planned to increase his strength to 200,000 by the end of the year and to 400,000 by the end of 1937. He had his 200,000 by the end of 1936, plus 6,000 Germans with aircraft and anti-aircraft guns, plus the advance guard of Italian 'volunteers', who by March 1937 totalled 35,000. By the end of 1937, even after sustaining heavy losses in the capture of Bilbao in June, Santander in August, and all of Asturias in mid-October, in resisting an offensive calculated to break his siege of Madrid and another siege to take Zaragoza, he had 650,000 men, excluding the foreign element of Germans, Italians, and Moors, amounting to another 60,000.[15] By the spring of 1938 the figure was higher still. More to the point, he had a strike-force of a quarter of a million men. With these he proposed to cut the enemy in two by driving a broad-based wedge down to the Mediterranean. In six weeks he added to his area of Spain a mountainous region roughly the size of the Netherlands, or of Wales and Northern Ireland combined – a considerable feat, when it is remembered that his was not a mechanized army and that the overall as opposed to the local superiority of his forces had not been overwhelming at the start of the offensive.

The fact that Franco had a total of about 750,000 men in the

[15] The distinction must be drawn at all times between those who served on one side or the other in foreign units and their effective strength at any one time. Thus, over 40,000 served in the International Brigades, but there were seemingly never more than 18,000 in Spain at any time. So again, the number of Germans who served in Spain was about 15,000, but never more than 6,000 at any one time. The Italians never numbered more than 35,000 at any one time.

spring of 1938 was due to the order which he had established in the area which he controlled; but the fact that the opposing republican army numbered 450,000 organized troops was also the result of order – the order established by the Russian, Comintern, and Spanish communists. Advised by the Russians, Largo Caballero had decreed the incorporation of anarchist and other freelance militias into the army. The whole army had been reorganized to the interesting pattern of mixed brigades and infiltrated by communist officers watched by commissars. The efficiency of the Fifth Regiment in the early days had converted even such regular army generals as Miaja and Pozas to communism. Germany was providing Franco with good aircraft and anti-aircraft artillery, but Russian tanks and anti-tank guns were supreme. The supply of other weapons was more than adequate. The Comintern's International Brigades were as good as if not better than Franco's Legion and any one of them better than a whole Italian division. By the end of 1936 the republican army had been 250,000 strong. During 1937 Franco had deprived it of 120,000 men in capturing the Basque and Cantabrian regions, and it had suffered heavy casualties in other battles; yet its strength at the end of the year was around 450,000. Not that Soviet advice and military organization was all to the good, for in July 1937 it was the Russians who overruled other plans and suggested an attempt to break Franco's Madrid siege. The non-communist General Vicente Rojo thereupon planned what could have been a decisive victory; but the operation (Brunete) failed because at the crucial moment commissars overruled military orders, causing utter confusion, and Miaja lost his nerve. It was the Russians who in August advised an offensive to capture Zaragoza. It failed and though Franco must be given some credit for the victory their battle tactics were grievously at fault. In December they were to advise the most costly of failures, the attack on Teruel, which, though it led to the capture of the city, ended with the advance of Franco's forces to their bases for Franco's spring 1938 offensive.

It was not only the army that communists had infiltrated thoroughly by the end of 1936, but every department of government in Valencia (henceforward the seat of government), Madrid, and Barcelona. Rosenberg, the Soviet ambassador, attended cabinet meetings and regularly called on Largo, at the end of December 1936 taking him a most important directive from Comrade Stalin himself. Stalin recommended Largo 'the parliamentary way' to revolution : the 'violent' way was not for Spain, he said; Largo should seek to befriend the republicans, especially Azaña, to protect the property of the bourgeois and foreign interests, and mind the real wishes of peasants.

The Communist Party had already been championing peasant proprietorship in Barcelona and Valencia. Henceforward, Largo decreed, there were to be no more new collectives, whether UGT or CNT : those already in existence were to be brought under government control, since the regular supply of food to the army required it. Further collectivization of industry was also stopped.

Thus far Largo was prepared to obey Stalin. Moscow, however, also wanted the union of the socialist and communist parties, and was displeased with his non-communist Minister of War, General Asensio Torrado. In arranging the union of the socialist and communist youth organizations, Largo Caballero had naïvely imagined that the more numerous socialists would absorb the communists, but the opposite had happened. In Catalonia where the parties had coalesced, there was no doubt which was the master. Largo was still a nationalist though an ideological communist. He refused to consider the proposed fusion. Asensio was his last protection against the communist domination of the army through the commissars and he refused to dismiss him. Rosenberg insisted unsuccessfully and was duly recalled by Stalin. In April 1937 Largo tried to dismiss the commissars, which prompted Moscow to decide on the political destruction of the 'Spanish Lenin'.

It was done in May. Largo was blamed for a very bloody battle of mysterious origins between UGT, CNT, communists, and Trotskyists in Barcelona over the possession of the telephone exchange. The two communists in the Cabinet resigned and the socialists walked out on Largo Caballero. Negrín, Moscow's choice, took his place and remained premier till the end of the war.

More than one view is possible of Negrín and his relations with Moscow and the Spanish Communist Party. Nominally a socialist, he has had both his defenders and accusers.[16] In May Moscow was particularly anxious to liquidate the Trotskyists.[17] The NKVD achieved this either with or without the collusion of Negrín, who established his own *Servicio de Inteligencia Militar*. With or without his co-operation, it became a Spanish NKVD, with torture chambers. Soon after taking office he arranged for discussions to be held on the possible union of the Socialist with the Communist Party, but in October he abruptly declared that this was undesirable. It was certainly unnecessary. The Socialist Party was permeated with crypto-communists. He abolished the commissars, yet the army remained firmly in communist hands. He made Prieto his

---

[16] Jackson defends him : Madariaga who knew him well is more critical. His ablest defender was the communist Alvarez del Vayo in *Freedom's Battle* (London, 1940).

[17] i.e., the *Partido Obrero de Unificación Marxista* (POUM).

Minister of War, but Prieto had to do what Soviet advisers told him. In the spring of 1938, as Franco hurled twenty-one divisions to the Mediterranean coast to cut what was left of republican Spain in two, Prieto believed that the war was lost and advocated peace to prevent further bloodshed. Negrín, in unison with the Communist Party, insisted that the war should continue and got rid of Prieto. Prieto, it would appear, did not know that Russia was at that moment shipping prodigious quantities of war material which Daladier allowed to be transported through France, while at the same time Hitler, having decided that 'a white Spain might be on the side of Italy's enemies' and that it was in Germany's interest to prolong the war in Spain,[18] had stopped the supply of arms to Franco. In July 1938 those Russian arms were used to good effect. Franco, closing in on Valencia, saw his whole army threatened as a republican strike-force of over 100,000 broke through across the Ebro to the north. But it was a flash in the pan, albeit a brilliant flash. By October the line had been restored. Out of the 100,000 only 30,000 remained. Momentarily, in September, as victory became defeat, Negrín himself had faltered; all order in the split republican zone, the quarter of the country still not in Franco's hands, was collapsing. Food was becoming scarce in Barcelona and Valencia, though they were surrounded by fertile areas. There was famine in Madrid and the south-east. Franco was demanding unconditional surrender. The war was now certainly lost : then, as never before, Negrín and the communists insisted that it should continue.

Negrín, it must be admitted, was widely admired in the democratic countries; but then since he had come to power, efforts to present the government as a bourgeois parliamentary democracy had been redoubled. A dozen or more books and hundreds of newspaper articles had been written describing it as one, and quoting impressive statistics to support the thesis that in spite of the war, the republican government had marvellously developed social services and educational facilities, figures which were so presented as to arouse doubts only in the minds of sceptical mathematicians.[19] Negrín was a linguist; he entertained foreign journalists, especially

[18] *Documents on Germany's Foreign Policy* (London, 1951), Series D, Vol. I, pp. 36–7. International Military Tribunal, *The Trial of the Major War Criminals* (Nuremberg, 1947–9), Vol. XXV, pp. 413–14, and other references to the Hossbach Conference of 5 November 1937.

[19] One of the cleverest and most plausible was *Education in Republican Spain* (London, 1938). Negrín appeared also to be a man of peace in that on 1 May he had stated that he was prepared to negotiate a peace if Franco accepted thirteen points which did not seem unreasonable when read by an Englishman. No Spaniard, however, could really have expected the nationalists to take them seriously. He did not restate them during his moment of doubt in September but on 1 October, when his nerve had been restored.

British and American, sumptuously; he was a doctor of medicine; he dressed for dinner; he was respectable; he was 'a good chap'.

Life in the nationalist capital, Burgos, was somewhat different. Until the middle of 1938 there was no shortage of food and never any breakdown of supplies to the fronts or to cities and towns. Seemingly there were no disorders. The only inefficiency was that of the nationalist press officers who had no idea how to make the best of their case and fabricated palpably false evidence.[20] The government consisted of military officers unused to answering questions. In Burgos and in Salamanca, the military HQ, Franco lived ascetically. He neither smoked himself nor tolerated smoking about him and he drank little. Except that he now had priests visiting his household, he was still the Franco of the War in the Rif who had had the order put up in barracks *ni copas, ni mujeres, ni curas,* 'no cups, no women, no priests'. Beneath the surface, however, since his appointment as *generalissimo*, he had had difficulties similar and as intense as Largo or Negrín with their foreign helpers and internal allies. And there had been important political changes.

Hitler sent to Spain an air force (the Condor Legion) and provided Franco with anti-aircraft units, instructors in anti-tank gunnery and aircraft, guns, and ammunition. He also sent an ambassador to Spain. The relations between Franco and the Germans were as involved as those between the republican government and the Russians.[21] There were similarities and important differences. Franco would listen to no advice from any foreigner on how to conduct the war—'la guerra era lo mío', 'war was my *métier*', he was to say. However, just as the Russians used their aircraft and tanks, the Germans used their aircraft and guns to suit their research and training programme for World War II, not directly to aid Franco. No sooner was a pilot or air-bombardier trained than he was replaced by another. The Russians got payment in advance for the arms they sent. The Germans expected mining and trading concessions. What they got was a pittance compared with what they expected.

Mussolini sent Franco aircraft, tanks, guns, ammunition, and 35,000 'volunteers', and based some air squadrons in the Balearics. The Italian aircraft proved no match for the Russian (or the American sent by Mexico). The tanks were worthless. After the famous rout of the Italians at Guadalajara in March 1937, Franco used them sparingly and never where another rout could occur. The Balearic squadrons bombed without reference to Franco : it was

[20] Not that it was wholly unsuccessful. Cf., e.g., Arthur F. Loveday, *World War in Spain* (London, 1939).

[21] See *Franco,* chapters 9–11, for a fuller history based on German and other documents.

Ciano's way of venting his fury at the fact that Franco spurned Italian advice from beginning to end. If the Italians expected anything in return for the help given, they were completely disappointed.

Franco was never anything but master in all military (if not air force) affairs. He had handled Germans and Italians serving in the Legion, and for one who had explored the labyrinths of the Arab mind, the simplicity of the German and Italian was no match. The handling of his own people was not so easy.

In the beginning, as we have seen, the insurgents had the military support of traditionalists, *Requetés*, and Falangists. These were not represented in the military *junta* and were not consulted when Franco was chosen *generalissimo* and Head of State by the *junta*. They just had to accept the choice as did the Alfonsists and everyone else in the nationalist zone. With the advance to Madrid still in progress and most people still confident that the war would be over in a matter of months if not weeks, no one bothered much with politics—except the *Falange* which opened its doors wide to accept anyone, ex-CEDA, ex-radical, ex-socialist, anarchist, even left-republican. By the end of 1936 it could claim one million members. The *Falange* programme was in its social and economic aspects very similar to that of the British Labour Party : the nationalization of banks and certain basic industries; 'fair shares for all'; equal educational opportunities; state-run social services. Towards the end of 1936, however, it was evident that the war was not going to be over quickly. The *Falange* began to think ahead, as did the traditionalists. Fal Conde, their leader, conceived a plan to found a Royal Carlist Military Academy, an act of gross insubordination in Franco's eyes, and Franco banished him. At the same time he ordered the *Requeté* and Falangist militias to be subject to regular army discipline, to accept regular army officers, and in effect to be incorporated into the army. He would have no private armies.

In the meantime the Falangists had found a firm ally in the German ambassador, Faupel. The totalitarian overtones of Falangist authoritarianism appealed to his Nazi mind. So did the Falangist programme point 'separation of Church and state', though he and his master would have preferred 'institution of national state Church' as the more wounding to the Vatican. Franco listened attentively to this counsel, yet rejected it. What he wanted was unity in his camp. Nothing would have helped his military operations more against the Basques in the winter of 1936–7 than a Vatican declaration in his favour. All the Pope had done was to condemn the co-operation of Catholics with communists and all violence; to urge peace; to commiserate with the victims of perse-

1. The Family of Philip V, by Louis-Michel Van Loo – the formidable Elizabeth Farnese dominating the picture. *From left*: Bárbara of Braganza (*2nd from left*); the future Ferdinand VI; Philip V; Luis, third son of Philip and Elizabeth; Elizabeth Farnese; Philip, future duke of Parma; Marie-Louise of France, Philip's wife; Maria Amalia of Saxony, wife of Charles (*2nd from right*); the future Charles III

2. Manuel de Godoy (1767-1851) – guardsman, royal favourite, and 'Prince of Peace' (portrait by Goya)

3. Gaspar Melchor de Jovellanos (1744-1811) – reformer and civil servant

4. Juan Antonio Llorente (1756-1823), luminary of the Enlightenment and 'historian' of the Inquisition (portrait by Goya)

5. General Juan Prim (1814-70) – revolutionary and kingmaker

6. The Lady of Elche – Hispano-Phoenician sculpture of great
antiquity

7. The Ruins of
Numancia – des-
troyed by Scipio
Aemilianus in
133 B.C.

8. The Roman
bridge at Alcántara

9. The early Romanesque Cloister of Santo Domingo de Silos

10. The Castle of Manzanares el Real—one of the hundreds of castles built in the progress of reconquering Spain from the Muslims

11. Philip II's Escorial—royal palace and mausoleum, monastery and school

12. The Bourbon Royal Palace at Aranjuez

13. Barcelona Cathedral

14. One of the new housing estates in Madrid

15. The launching on 17 June 1968 of the 100,000-ton tanker *Montesa*. In 1969 Spain was building three ships of 250,000 tons each and began to build four 325,000-ton tankers

16. Spanish cars awaiting shipment to Yugoslavia, 1969

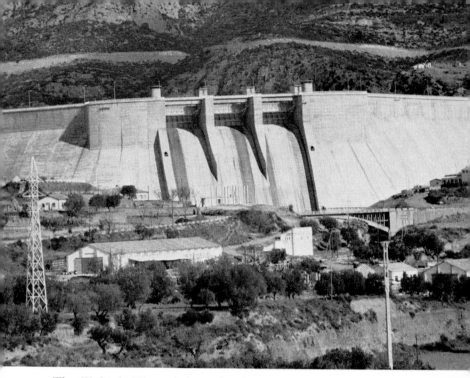

17. The *El Grado* (Huesca) dam, shortly before it went into service in 1969 as part of the major irrigation works in Aragon

18. The oil refinery at Cartagena – Spain became an exporter of petroleum products to the U.K. in 1967

19. Vineyards in La Rioja

20. Foreign tourists on the sands at La Linea opposite Gibraltar

21. The 'economic overlord' Professor Laureano López Rodó

22. Gregorio López Bravo – former Minister of Industry, appointed Foreign Minister in October 1969

23. José Solís Ruíz – general secretary of the *Movimiento* until October 1969

24. Manuel Fraga Iribarne, Minister of Information and Tourism until October 1969, (*left*), greeting Jack Valenti, President of the (U.S.) Motion Picture Export Association

25. The illustrious polymath, Ramón Menéndez Pidal (1869–1968)

26. Professor Joaquín Ruiz Giménez

27. Fernando María Castiella, Spanish Foreign Minister until October 1969, with General Franco and the French Foreign Minister, Michel Debré

28. Prince Juan Carlos takes the oath as Prince of Spain, and heir apparent to the office of Head of State, July 1969

cution and war; and to help exiles, Basque and Spanish alike. The Vatican would agree to mediate, but it would treat President Aguirre of Euzcadi (the Basque region) as Franco's equal, and Franco would not accept that. Nevertheless, any suggestion of a break with Rome would have alienated to the point of warfare the traditionalists and a great many supporters. Franco would never allow the exiled Cardinals Segura and Vidal access to him, but he was doing well with the Church of Rome at home. His earliest experience of war had been against the Moroccan el Mizzian who had preached *al-jihad*, 'holy war', against the infidel Spaniard and he knew that in battle men fight most bravely and fiercely when they are convinced that they are doing so for God. His use of the word *cruzados* to describe his troops (Muslim and Christian) on 24 July and the description of his war as 'a crusade' on the following day had been taken up by the people of Seville and then all his propagandists. On 15 August the aged Cardinal Ilundaín had stood by his and Queipo de Llano's side as the red and gold flag of Spain had been ceremonially unfurled. The Catholic Basques might disagree with him about who was on God's side, but on 23 November Cardinal Gomá, archbishop of Toledo, for all his Catalan autonomist history, had finally spoken clearly in Franco's favour after a long study of the reports of the murders of priests in the republican zone.[22] For his part, Franco had then confirmed the general assumption that the republic's anti-religious laws were to be considered null and void. Books contrary to Christian faith or morals were expunged from school syllabuses and the crucifix was restored to classroom walls. Nurses in hospitals dressed again as nuns. Chaplains were appointed to the forces. He and other officers made a point of inviting church dignitaries to all public functions. Whatever his private views, and however much Faupel might object on Hitler's behalf, it was militarily and politically expedient that the Church should be seen as his supporter, and vice-versa. Franco's one concession to Hitler was to forbid, in March 1937, the circulation in Spain of the encyclical *Mit brennender Sorge*. The fall of Bilbao in June cleared him of the final obstacle. On 1 July the forty-one bishops in his zone issued a joint declaration in his favour. It did not matter to him that some of them signed with reservations, and one at least in the belief that it would be easier to guide the new régime by behind-the-scenes admonition rather than by open opposition in an atmosphere removed from extremes, including the Falangist desire for separation of Church and state and Hitler's idea of a national state Church.

By 1 July 1937 Franco had won his first major political victory.

[22] Gil Robles, op. cit., p. 796.

15 * *

His thought was always incisive, his objectives always simple, however complex and sinuous his ways to them. The war had to be
won. It could be won only if there was unity at the front and in
the rear. Whatever contributed to unity was good : whatever did
not, was bad. The peace would also have to be won. As he saw
Spanish history, had there been unity there would have been no
war. Nothing had contributed more to the disintegration of Spain
than the multiplication of political parties. There were representatives of over thirty among his supporters apart from the two major
ones, the traditionalist and *Falange*. The Germans counselled the
formation of a single party—a Nazified *Falange*, but not, of course,
under Franco because Franco had sold himself to the Church (in
Faupel's view) and because, while willing enough to accept weapons,
he did not seem prepared to pay for them. Franco had a different
idea. *One* party was as bad as many. He would have no party; but
to have no party he had first to bring the two major ones under his
control. The exile of Fal Conde had put the traditionalists in his
hands, in fact if not in theory, and he ordered their new nominal
head, the count of Rodezno, to investigate the possibilities of a
merger. Negotiations lasted three fruitless weeks, until 1 February.
Franco himself studied their programmes : there was enough in
common between them for him to force a union. He waited, as he
would always wait in all matters, for a suitable opportunity.

It came sooner than he expected. The *Falange* was being run by
a *junta* with a Santander mechanic, Manuel Hedilla, as its Secretary-General. Faupel cultivated him, considering that for want of a
better man here was a lower middle-class little Hitler. At the end
of February, Franco's brother-in-law, Serrano Suñer, turned up at
his headquarters, having escaped from prison in the republican zone
and bringing confirmation that Primo de Rivera had been shot the
previous November. Franco ordered him to investigate the possibilities of the desired union, which was becoming militarily important.
Clashes were occuring in the rear areas between Falangists and
traditionalists. Serrano reported that the union was not only possible
but desirable. The *Falange* itself was showing signs of disintegration
between the 'old shirts', those who had joined Primo in the early
days, and the newcomers. They could not agree on who was to be
Primo's successor. Serrano's idea was more or less the German idea,
casting Franco instead of Hedilla as its head. His experiences in
prison had turned Serrano into a pathological hater of 'democracy'
and all its works and pomps. He wanted a dictatorship of one party
and the *Falange* suited him. Franco summoned Faupel on 11 April
to tell him in effect to stop interfering in Spain's internal affairs
and that Hedilla was no leader. On the night of the 14th, there

was an affray between Falangists. Leading Falangists were arrested but released on bail to take part on the 18th in a *Falange* National Council meeting, at which Hedilla was elected the new head of the *Falange*. That evening, however, Franco broadcast a speech of 2,000 words, partly in praise of all his supporters but principally a call to unity. What it all meant puzzled most listeners. They understood it the following day. In a brief decree all political parties were declared abolished. There was to be 'a single political party' which *for the moment* was to be called the *Falange Española Tradicionalista y de las Juntas de Ofensiva Nacional-Sindicalista,* to act as intermediary between society and the state, the channel of communication between them. Its head was to be the Head of State himself, its Secretary-General, Serrano Suñer. Hedilla was sent to gaol and Faupel was replaced.

In years to come Franco would regret his choice of Secretary-General. For the moment what astounded observers was the ease with which Franco got his way. There were only a few whimpers and disgruntled murmurs as the traditionalists put on the hated *Falange*'s blue shirt and the *Falange* the Carlist red beret. Franco gave them an *idearium* of twenty-six points, superficially similar to Primo's twenty-seven, but capable of traditionalist interpretation, especially since any suggestion that Church and state should be separate was expunged. He never referred to his creation as a party, but gave it the name *Movimiento,* movement, a movement towards national unity. Ten years later Serrano was to say of it: 'the *Falange* never came to be the single ruling party, the exclusive power-platform—far from it. There was always opposition, *even at the source of government*';[23] that is on the part of Franco himself: but then, Franco never wanted a party but the machinery of government for a nation of 24 million individuals. The real unity could only come about, Franco appreciated, when the Civil War generation should pass.[24] It was Serrano who had long been an admirer of Mussolini, and whom terrible experiences in prison had undermined physically, who wanted a single party, a Spanish equivalent of his own devising of the Italian Fascist Party. In using his position of Secretary-General to that end, he deepened the differences not only between traditionalist and Falangist, but between 'old shirt' Falangist and 'new'.

In military matters Franco had showed himself on several occasions a master at exploiting lack of cohesion among the enemy. It

[23] R. Serrano Suñer, *Entre Hendaya y Gibraltar* (Madrid, 1947), p. 127. Stanley G. Payne, *Falange* (Stanford, Calif., 1961; London, 1962), pp. 186–7, for the *Falange* version.

[24] It did not, even then. Hence the *Falange* anti-government riots in 1966 and 1968.

was so at Brunete and again at Teruel. It would be so again on the Ebro. The deepening of the divisions in his own political camp would be used by him to his own advantage.

In February 1938 Franco dissolved the *junta* of technicians who had been running his part of the country. He formed what was recognizably a government on a principle he was to follow for many years : that of balance between the various 'parties' in his region of Spain. He made a retired general, Jordana, a nobleman and a monarchist of liberal views, his vice-premier and Foreign Minister. This was a slap in the face for his German allies, for Jordana was notoriously Anglophile. However, he balanced Jordana with Serrano as Minister of Internal Affairs. Serrano was becoming increasingly Germanophile : he hated Britain because be believed that the British embassy could have saved his brothers from execution. Serrano the Falangist was balanced with the traditionalist count of Rodezno, a young Carlist with a young Falangist, a 'new shirt' with an 'old shirt', and both by another general and an admiral.

It was at this moment that Franco was planning what he hoped would be the final operation of the war, the driving of the wedge to the sea. It succeeded in that his troops did reach the sea. It failed to end the war for the reasons we have given, the decisions of Stalin and of Hitler, and Negrín's own determination to continue the struggle. It was not till the eve of Christmas 1938 that Franco was in a position to attempt once again to end the war. Negrín had made Barcelona his capital (making a mockery of its autonomy) – so Franco decided to absorb Catalonia. On 26 January 1939 his troops took Barcelona. Negrín fled the country. The nationalist army swept up through Catalonia. Negrín went back to Valencia. The republican army had perhaps 80,000 troops left. Franco now had 879,000. Britain and France recognized Franco. Azaña, a fugitive in Paris, resigned the Presidency. Negrín and the Communist Party ordered 'fight on' and Negrín promoted the communist officers; but the commander of the Madrid sector, Casado, was not one of them and he had had enough. In the republican zone (the rough square Valencia—Madrid—Almería—Valencia) people were dying of starvation by the tens of thousands. Casado's own troops were in rags. There occurred then a second civil war within the Civil War, Casado versus Negrín, non-communists versus communists. Franco's troops entered Madrid on 28 March.

On 1 April Franco issued his last war communiqué. The last republican unit had surrendered. The war was over.

Chapter 26

Spain under Franco: The 'Fascist' Phase 1939–44

THE WAR WAS OVER. The cost could be counted.

A quarter of a million houses had been totally destroyed and another half million damaged. About 4 million were homeless. Three out of every four railway passenger coaches, two out of every four locomotives, one out of every five goods-waggons had been damaged beyond repair, and as many needed repair. Nearly a quarter of a million tons of shipping had been sunk. The Catalan and Valencian factories were in ruins. Such agricultural machinery as there had been in July 1936 had been smashed wherever anarchists had practised 'libertarian communism'. In the desperate effort to cover the losses of the battles of Teruel and the Alhambra river in winter 1937–8 and against Franco's spring offensive, Negrín had ordered the call-up of all able-bodied men from the age of fifteen. In consequence little farming had been done. In the face of starvation, all livestock had been slaughtered in the republican zone, one-third of all Spain's livestock.

Restocking required time, and time was not on the Spaniards' side. The 1938 harvest in Franco's zone had been fair. There were stocks to supply the starving in Catalonia, Madrid, and the east and south-east for about eight months, not more : and already in May it was evident that the 1939 harvest would be poor. Franco toured the country urging people to grow the food that would be required, but nothing could be done against the weather. There was enough unskilled labour to repair railways and roads, and to begin on the reconstruction of the 183 heavily damaged population centres; but the skilled labour to repair the factories and keep them going was lacking. A quarter of a million people had fled into France as Catalonia had been overrun, mostly men and mainly the skilled industrial workers. As a class the skilled had provided the leaders of the UGT and CNT, and they had the most to fear from the victors.

The material damage was assessed at a figure roughly equal to a year's gross national income. Thus, even if miraculously the gross national product had been increased immediately by 10 per cent above its 1935 level, it would take ten years to make up what had been lost; and this assessment did not take into account the loss in production during the three years of war. Around 1·2 million Spaniards had served in Franco's armed forces, and 600,000 perhaps 700,000 in the republican armed forces.[1] The war had cost over 300,000 million pesetas – the national income of six years. Military and civilian deaths attributable to the war exceeded half a million,[2] far the greater number being of men aged between eighteen and thirty-five, in terms of the national economy the most productive.

Nothing would have helped more at that moment than enormous credits to buy replacements for the missing machinery. Russia was not going to return the 510 tons of Spanish gold which Negrín had sent. Italy and Germany wanted payment for the military aid they had given to Franco. Franco did not want any more military aid. The Germans were despatched to embark from Vigo for Germany and the Italians from Cadiz to Rome as soon as they had taken part in the victory parade. What Franco wanted was machinery – and no one was prepared to give it him except for cash down – or in the case of Germany, in exchange for mining concessions.

Franco ratified existing mining concessions with Great Britain and was prepared to give the Germans no more rights than the British had. He believed that he had fought a war to 'save Spain', to keep Russia out, and he would therefore not let in Germany; and in the event he confounded his enemies in the English-speaking world who had prophesied that he would surrender the Balearics to Italy, Spanish Guinea to Germany, and bases on the peninsula to both.

The victors went on between 1939 and 1943 to execute over 40,000 of the defeated and to sentence a quarter of a million to varying terms of imprisonment, if not for murder, rapine, arson, and other crimes, then under the provisions of Franco's Law on Political Responsibilities. Tens of thousands were to die in prison from malnutrition and disease.

This was a most iniquitous law. It made anyone over the age of fourteen who at any time since 1 October 1934 was judged to have 'helped to undermine public order', or after 18 July 1936 'to have impeded the national *Movimiento*' even by being 'grievously pas-sive', and anyone who at any time had belonged to any of the Popular Front bodies, or to regional nationalist organizations, or to the Liberal Party, or to a masonic lodge, liable to have all his goods

[1] These figures to include all three services, militia, and para-military police.
[2] See below, p. 450, note on deaths.

confiscated, to be deprived of his nationality, to be exiled to Africa, or to be sentenced to up to fifteen years imprisonment. Trials under this law were to be by special tribunals of Falangists usually with army officers to help them.

The *Falange* were out to avenge the deaths of many thousands of their fellows at the hands of the Popular Front and the desire for vengeance was widespread. The tales of crime and atrocity multiplied and grew in the telling among the victors in Spain no less than among the conquered in exile. As in October 1934 and in February–July 1936, so in April 1939 too many men were not prepared to listen to reason. Two arguments were advanced to justify the repressive measures : first, that a policy of mercy just did not pay; the leniency which had been forced by Alcalá Zamora on the Lerroux government in 1934 had encouraged, it was said, the disorders of 1936 which in turn encouraged the atrocities committed on the outbreak of the Civil War; secondly, that if 'justice' were not done by organs of the state, then individuals would take the law into their own hands and there would be anarchy again. There was evidence in plenty that among the defeated were many who did not believe their defeat final for a minute. The convinced Marxist had not changed his beliefs because he had become the prisoner of 'Fascist hordes'. Fascism could have no permanence. As a 'capitalist reaction' it was bound to disintegrate. The advent of the dictatorship of the proletariat and the disappearance of the state in communism was as ineluctable for humanity as death for the individual mind. Besides, it was obvious that 'Anglo-French capitalist reaction' was about to go to war with Fascist Germany and Italy. Negrín's determination to fight on after his moment of doubt in September 1938 had been largely based on the hope that the powers to the north of Spain would go to war over Czechoslovakia. At worst the war would have deprived Franco of German and Italian supplies while Russia would have continued to supply the Popular Front from Odessa, even if not via France; and at best Britain and France would have declared war on Spain as well as on Germany.

All of this was true; there were many Spaniards prepared to risk their lives in sabotaging the new Spain which Franco was set on creating, and the desire to avenge brothers was widespread. It was also true that among men who had faced each other in battle, there was empathy; though on opposite sides, both had suffered the same privations and both had been prepared to sacrifice their lives : and the new Spain which Franco was creating was supposed to be, in his own words, Catholic, and if Catholic then surely bound by the precept on the forgiveness of enemies.

Cardinal Gomá, who, in November 1936, had been the first

important cleric to speak on his behalf, sought to change the mind of the man who was now referred to as *El Caudillo* (the 'Military Hero' rather than Leader); but he failed. He wrote a pastoral to be read in all the churches in his archdiocese on Christian forgiveness and on the social duties of Catholics. Serrano Suñer, whose appointment in 1937 had been opposed by 'old shirts' in the belief that as an ex-CEDA member he was a 'Vaticanist', and who was now Minister of the Interior and ruler of the press, ordered its suppression. On 19 April 1939 Pope Pius XII, who like his predecessor had never once spoken for or against the nationalists, broadcast a message to 'his very dear children of Catholic Spain'. He congratulated them on the peace and victory. He spoke of the 'most noble and Christian sentiments' of the Head of State and he included him in his blessing. However, two-thirds of the address was devoted to an explicit order to the victors to receive back into the fold with goodwill all who had opposed them. The speech was heard only by the very few who had wireless sets and were used to listening to Vatican Radio. Again, the people of Spain were allowed to read only the passages which received Serrano Suñer's *imprimatur*.

There were other voices raised in Spain on the Christian forgiveness of enemies : bishops in pastorals, priests in pulpits, and laymen in conversation urged those in power at all levels by love and understanding to win over the minds and hearts of the defeated. They argued thus : however worthy of the severest punishment such men might be in the abstract, they were being judged by the victors, and no defeated man could look upon his victor as a competent or impartial judge. Therefore, such infliction of punishment was *contraproducente*; for the feeling that an injustice had been done would destroy the possible effect of the punishment as a deterrent to rebellion. Again the defeated had no sense of guilt, rather a certainty that they had fought for a better cause than that of their victors. To inflict punishment on them was unjust, for it was a basic principle of Catholic theology that a man was not guilty of a sinful act when he had no consciousness that it was a sin; these men were therefore not to be imprisoned, much less shot. There were, on the other hand, priests who saw what was being done and thought it well done, to their subsequent shame; and the laymen responsible were Catholics, even if only nominally. A far greater number of priests, however, maintained silence, some perhaps out of fear of what might happen if they spoke, some out of a feeling of hopelessness, and many out of a mixture of both. Would anyone listen, they asked themselves? If in spite of exhortations in season and out of season to the contrary, men still took the name of the Lord in vain, dishonoured parents, committed murder and adultery, bore false witness, and stole – with cold premeditation; if experience showed that it was even more useless to reason with a man or woman at the height of the passion of an illicit love, was there any point in speaking now to men inflamed with a passion for vengeance which took the form of an incorrigibly perverted sense of justice? Was there any point in speaking merely to arouse anger against themselves? In the long term there was to be violent anger because they did not speak, strongest, curiously, among those who would not have listened, and among those most insistent that bishops and priests were not the whole Church, but who as laymen had also kept silence. So, the Law of Moses rather than Christian Law, Roman Law rather than Law of Rome, prevailed.[3]

Franco was prepared to be a Catholic and a Falangist after his own fashion, and not that of the Church or the *Falange*. As he intended a synthesis between Falangism and traditionalism, so he wanted a synthesis between Catholicism and Spanish nationalism. He had himself set the pattern. On the very day of the start of the spring 1938 offensive, on the outcome of which he had had such high hopes of final victory, he had issued his first major piece of legislation, the Labour Charter.

Though he had entrusted Serrano Suñer in 1937 with the details of how the *Falange Española Tradicionalista* was to become a unified *movimiento*, this piece of legislation was very much his own. He had commanded a company in Asturias during the attempt at a revolution in 1917 and what he had seen had led him to study social conditions. Through the years he had come to see the need for the regulation of working hours, paid holidays, minimum wages, decent working conditions, with all that Catholic sociologists called 'the dignity of man'; but he recognized that all these in themselves would not necessarily lead to industrial peace. As he saw it, much of the trouble between workers and employers was due to the stratification of society. Men in the army did not talk of 'them' and 'us': in army terms 'us' meant all the members of one unit; 'them' meant those of another unit. Rankers, N.C.O.s, and officers felt more solidarity with each other within a given regiment or arm than

[3] There was nothing 'Spanish' or 'Latin' in the extremes to which vengeance was taken; one has but to recall Cromwell at Drogheda. There was an important difference between the Spanish and English Civil Wars to account for the less violent aftermath of the latter. In England the masses were outside the conflict between Royalists and Parliamentarians. In Spain the whole nation was involved, roughly one-half on one side and the other half on the other; and in any case one has but to remember the aftermath of the Monmouth rebellion in England in 1685, the Pilgrimage of Grace in 1536, and the Rising of the North in 1569. After the latter one in ten of all the males in Durham were hanged.

with the corresponding members of another unit. The army was organized vertically and the *Falange*'s idea of vertical unions of employers, managers, and workers therefore appealed to Franco as an ideal solution. He had made a draft of what he called a *Fuero* – a Charter, or Liberty in the mediaeval sense – discussed it with priests, traditionalists, and Falangists, given it to Serrano Suñer to obtain the *Falange*'s reaction, had him apply his legal mind to it, made the final emendations, then presented it to his government, who had dutifully endorsed it.[4] Its preamble, which was to remain unchanged for twenty-nine years, began as follows :

> Restoring the Catholic tradition of social justice and of giving man a high position (in the order of creation) which inspired the laws of the Spanish empire, the state which is national in as much as it is an instrument totally at the service of the whole country, and syndicalist in as much as it rejects liberal capitalism and Marxist materialism, undertakes, in a military, constructive, and deeply religious spirit, the revolution of which Spain stands in need in order to restore to Spaniards for ever more their country, bread, and justice.

Here was a masterpiece of multivalence, a chord whose overtones coincided with the fundamentals of the erstwhile parties in nationalist Spain. *Renovando* has three meanings : to restore; to bring up to date; to replace one thing with another. Traditionalist, Falangist, new and old, monarchist, republican could each interpret it to his liking. 'Syndicalist' pleased Falangists, but qualified as a rejection of liberal *laissez-faire* and Marxism, it was acceptable to others. Other key words were *totalitario*, of which 'totalitarian' is a completely wrong translation,[5] and *Imperio*, empire.

To the ordinary Spaniard *totalitario*, then as now, meant 'that which is the sum of all its parts without exception'. Hence an *estado totalitario* was one which accepted that it could legitimately concern itself with all the activities of society for the benefit of its individual members. Hence it could regulate the conduct of commerce and industry, nationalize industries, redistribute landed and other wealth, intervene in education – activities previously denied

[4] See Payne, *Falange*, pp. 186–7, for an account which gives greater credit to the *Falange*.

[5] Contrariwise it is equally inadequate to translate 'totalitarian state' and its equivalents in German, Italian, etc., as *un estado totalitario*; for the Spanish word lacks the essential meaning of 'a state which subordinates the rights of the individual and the individual himself to the state'. Therefore, at this period and much later, Catholic arguments against and condemnation of 'totalitarianism' by theologians did not impinge upon Spaniards – to the delight and benefit of the Nazis, Fascists, and Nazified Falangists. The 'perfect' *estado totalitario* in Spanish terms is post-World War II Britain.

the Spanish state as of right, here by Liberals, there by conservatives, and in the case of education by the Church. It must, however,
be added that Falangists who had travelled in Germany or Italy
rejoiced in the use of the term as their means of guiding the state
to their less Spanish ideal; and for the same reason it horrified
others, in particular Cardinal Segura who had become familiar with
the international meaning of the word during his Roman exile. On
his return to Spain, late in 1938, as successor to the now dead
Ilundaín, he had denounced the *Falange* in the same breath as the
Nazis. Over the next nineteen years to his death he was to be the
most outspoken critic of Franco's anti-democratic policies.[6]

By 'empire' was meant the Habsburg empire, whose Laws of the
Indies had indeed been inspired (in spite of the emperors) by Catholic ideas on the dignity of the human person, irrespective of race,
and on social justice (and not observed because of the emperors as
much as anyone else). But 'empire' had a very special meaning to
Falangists, for their founder had made 'will to empire' one of his
principles. Here Franco was not ahead of his time. In 1924 he had
publicly defied his senior, General Primo de Rivera, who toyed
with the idea of giving up the Moroccan Protectorate,[7] because he
believed Spain had a divine mission in the Protectorate. Furthermore, he believed that Britain and France had deprived Spain of
her rightful place in Africa; and with all Spaniards (save Catalans
and Basques who did not consider themselves Spaniards anyway)
that the possession by Britain of Gibraltar was an injustice and
insult to Spain.

Gibraltar and Africa could wait. The immediate task was the
unification of Spain, the destruction of the stratification of society.
Workers, as he saw it, were not only to be protected from their
employers but from each other. The value of work to society had to
be stressed no less than the dignity of labour. The Charter therefore
stated not merely that workers would be entitled to 'a wage sufficient to give the worker and his family the means to live with
decorum and decency' but also entitled to family allowances, holidays with pay, and social services; that tenant farmers would be
protected from eviction and labourers allotted a plot sufficient to
their needs; that employers would have duties in justice towards

[6] Having talked to him at length, and with his close personal friend
Viscount Templewood, I have no doubt that the Cardinal's opposition to
Franco was based entirely on Christian principles, as was his opposition to
the republic – and that his personal affection for Alfonso XIII had nothing
to do with it. I found him a critic of Spanish monarchism no less than
republicanism.

[7] See *Franco*, p. 136. The Spanish edition (Madrid, 1968), p. 139, gives
more details.

employees; and the Charter also attempted to define the nature and purpose of work itself.

The whole Charter and the whole subsequent body of legislation on labour evolved from these axioms :

(b) God has imposed on man the duty to work that he may fulfil his individual ends, and increase the prosperity and greatness of his society (significantly called *patria*, fatherland, in the Charter).

(b) As it is inherent in the nature of man that he must work, work cannot be just 'manpower', a commercial asset, but always related to other aspects of man's nature, his need for periods of rest, etc., his dignity, and the decorum of his family.

(c) As work is essential in human nature, every man has the right to work.

(d) As work is a social duty, any man not incapable is bound to contribute with his work to the common weal.

(e) Therefore, on the one hand it becomes the duty of the state to ensure that there is work available for every man and training to enable him to do it, and on the other the state (representing the nation) can expect of a man to work as befits a human being.

(f) Again, it is the duty of the state to ensure that work is regarded with the esteem that should be given it : it should be 'exalted' to receive its due veneration; but it is equally the duty of the state to see to it that the work available is worthy of a human being, carried out in fit circumstances and adequately rewarded, and that the worker is protected in involuntary unemployment, in sickness and old age.

All this was a combination of Catholic philosophy, nationalism, national-syndicalism, and traditional Spanish paternalism : and the resultant mixture was not a smooth emulsion. The elements of the compound were nowhere more apparent than in clauses such as this :

(XII.1) 'The state recognizes and will protect private property as a natural means to individual, family, and social means. All forms of ownership are subordinate to the supreme good of the nation, whose interpreter is the state.'

While Catholic doctrine was clear in sentences such as 'the state shall act ruthlessly against usury in any form', authoritarianism, not to say totalitarianism in its international sense, was inherent in the clauses on the organization of all workers (intellectual, professional, managerial, craft, manual) into syndicates. Quite bluntly it was stated : 'The vertical syndicate is an instrument at the service of the state to enforce its economic policy. The syndicate must inform itself on the problems of production and propose solutions – but these must be subordinate to the national interest'. Again : 'All individual or collective acts which in any way disturb normal production or affect it adversely, shall be considered crimes against the country . . . Any wilful lowering of output shall be punished'.

The syndicates, then, were intended to be the means whereby the state would be enabled to work towards the fine goals it had set for itself and the country. Neither in 1938 nor in 1939, any more than at any time over the previous two centuries, would any government have been able to provide an income in cash or in kind sufficient to give every family the means to live decorously, even if every man had given all he produced, earned, or received as rent or interest to the state for the state to distribute 'to every man according to his needs'. This was the tragic reality of Spain – that neither communism nor socialism nor anarchism nor Falangism could give what was not there. In man-hours everything from an olive to a set of clothes cost several times what it did in any other country of western Europe.

The organization of the syndicates was put in hand when the war ended and officially established by a law promulgated in December 1940. All activities were grouped in the first place as agrarian, industrial, or 'services', and in the second into twenty-two syndicates, according to the essence of the product, e.g., cereals, olive, vine, textiles, metal, chemicals, or the product used, e.g., paper, vehicles, etc. The agricultural and industrial syndicates were each divided into the following sections : primary producing, processing and manufacture, sales (some having also export and import sections). Thus, the men who worked in, managed, and owned breadshops, bakeries, flour-mills, and wheatfields were all made members of the same syndicate.[8]

During the war strikes were illegal : anything short of maximum production was contrary to the nationalist war interest. The war over, it was in the national interest that there should be no strikes the sooner to have the damage repaired. When all the damage was made good (around 1955), it would be argued into the late 1960s that strikes denied others their right to work; that Spain could not afford strikes; that the machinery existed within the syndicates for all conflicts on wages, management, etc., to be resolved without any need for strike action.

Given that after the war Spain had need of men to repair the

[8] The structure remained basically unchanged for thirty years, see below, p. 382.

damage and make good as soon as possible the loss to the economy consequent on the dedication of over half the labour force to the conduct of war and the provision of its materials, what was to be done with the hundreds of thousands of Spaniards sentenced to imprisonment by courts martial or the tribunals under the Law of Political Responsibilities? Franco's own view had long been that 'by accepting his punishment a guilty man becomes a new man'.[9] However, work dignified a man more than punishment. The imprisoned were therefore given an opportunity to 'redeem themselves through work',[10] as unskilled labourers in reconstruction, for which many were physically unsuited, and in which thousands died. They might have been used 'according to their abilities', for here was Spain's real problem (recognized in the Labour Charter) : that there was a shortage not of manpower but of skills and of men to teach the skills.

This, however, was not done. It is unbelievable that the quarter of a million and more sentenced to imprisonment were all of the calibre of leaders and therefore a real as opposed to a remotely potential danger to the security of the new state. In fact the really gifted were those who covered up their membership of the proscribed societies, joined the *Falange,* and became prominent members of it. There were many such. As for the rest, for those who survived imprisonment or the rigours of labour under the 'redemption through work' scheme, the treatment they received at the hands of the victors strengthened their resentment and their hatred of the new order. Few of the families and relatives of men who were punished believed that justice had been done. If it was done, it was not seen to be done.

The Labour Charter looked to the distant future. The immediate future as from August 1939 looked very grim. In a world at peace Franco might have been able to have played Britain, France, and Germany against each other to give him on credit the machinery Spain required and even the technicians to pass on skills. In war that would be possible only in token form.

Franco had been impressed by the German artillery he had seen but not by German armour.[11] If, he reckoned, the Russian copy of the Vickers tank was anything to go by, then Britain, the land of Liddell Hart and General Fuller, would surely outclass Germany in armoured warfare. The German bombers he had had to support his operations were excellent, but German fighters had been outclassed by Russian and French. France had, he thought, a near-

---

[9] *Raza,* a film script by Franco himself (limited edition, Madrid, 1942).
[10] See *Franco,* pp. 331–2, for details of how this was a distortion of a liberal penologist's theory.
[11] Nor were British and French 'observers'. A surprise lay in store for all

invincible army, Britain an invincible navy. The military attaché in Paris had warned him in 1936 that French army morale was at a low ebb; nevertheless actual war would surely raise it. At worst (and alas most likely) a new war would be a repetition of 1914–18 : a triumphant Germany to begin with, a war of attrition, entry of the United States as in 1917, final victory for Britain and France; alas, for Europe would then consist of an exhausted Britain and France and a shattered Germany. Russia, having watched western Europe destroy itself, would then invade the ruins. Spain would again have to defend herself as best she could, but to be able to defend herself at all, she would have to maintain neutrality.

Franco believed profoundly in the 'supreme destiny of Spain' and in the 'supreme reality of Spain', phrases common in his speeches. Whether he was right or not, he sincerely believed that he had risen on 18 July 1936 'to save Spain' from the foreign domination of international communism. Now apart, from any long-term planning, there was the reality of the Spanish situation. Spain was in no condition, economically or politically, to go to war on anyone's behalf. She could provide manpower for others, but she lacked the resources to equip even one division to the level required in international war; but even if she were reckoned economically capable of entering the war, he had to consider the views of his generals. Varela, the ablest of them and the best-loved by the rank-and-file, was warmly pro-British; so were Aranda, Moscardó of the Alcázar, and Solchaga. Yagüe and Vigón alone were enthusiastically pro-German.

In preparation for the war which he was convinced was coming, Franco reorganized his Cabinet. Jordana, his pro-British Foreign Minister, was sixty-three and ageing; he was replaced by the equally pro-British Colonel Beigbeder (who, having been at the Berlin embassy, 'knew how to deal with Germans'). For the rest, except that the average age was much lower, the Cabinet was as before a carefully balanced one between Falangists and non-Falangists, monarchists and republicans, civilians and military. But there was one important change. The office of vice-president of the Cabinet was abolished, and many of his duties were passed to Serrano Suñer who survived from the old into the new Cabinet as Minister of Internal Affairs. He controlled the press, even directed it. He continued with his plan to fashion Spain to his ideal of 'one leader, one party, and a mass organization directed by a minority of devout believers'. He became very friendly with the German ambassador and German residents in Spain who were members of the Nazi Party. Serrano believed the Axis invincible. He promised to 'influence' the press in favour of Germany.

Shortly before the end of the Civil War, Franco had yielded to
German pressure to sign the anti-Comintern pact and a cultural
agreement. The latter had a very brief life. The Catholic hierarchy
opposed it violently. News of what was happening in Germany to
Catholics in opposition to Hitler was not known at all: Serrano
Suñer, through postal as well as press censorship, made certain it
did not reach churchmen especially; but they did have a knowledge
of the philosophical implications of Nazism and its incompatibility
with Catholicism, and they would not have their flocks contam-
inated. Spain's adherence to the anti-Comintern pact, on the other
hand, was a different matter. Only communists could oppose it and
they, of course, had no say in the conduct of affairs in Franco's Spain.

To the real rulers of Spain in 1939, Franco and the generals,
the news of the signature of the Ribbentrop—Molotov pact was a
shock, the violence of which cannot be overemphasized because it
was contrary to their whole concept of honour. (For how much
'honour', or rather *honor,* still counted in Spain, one has but to read
the speeches of deputies to the republican *Cortes,* or, in the 1945
Fuero de los Españoles, the clause 'The personal honour of Spaniards and that of their families is to be respected as of right. Whoever shall offend against it, whatever his position, shall be liable to
prosecution.') Here was a man, Hitler, who had sworn an agreement
with other nations to combat communism, now making a pact with
the very leader of communism. Hard though Serrano Suñer was to
try thereafter, he was never able to persuade his brother-in-law
to more than words, mere words, even words which would be
'used in evidence against him', but which remained words. The
invasion of Catholic Poland destroyed in non-Falangist Spanish
Catholics whatever feeling of obligation to Germany remained.

Franco formally declared Spanish neutrality on 4 September
1939, and until June 1940 it was adhered to in spirit and letter. The
press – with the exception of *Informaciones,* the Madrid evening
paper which Serrano Suñer had 'given' the Germans – carefully
balanced the communiqués of the one side with the other and
commented impartially enough on events. Spain strengthened an
earlier mutual defence agreement with Portugal, but otherwise kept
out of international politics. She continued to sell to whoever was
prepared to buy her products and to buy from whoever was ready
to trade with her. What worried her government was where to get
the food for Spain's 24 million inhabitants. By the end of 1939
hunger began to manifest itself.

The 1939 harvests had proved even more disastrously inadequate
than expected. It was not just that the fields in the last areas to
fall to Franco had been 'liberated' too late, but rather that Spain

had entered into one of her periodic cycles of drought. Trade agreements with Portugal and France negotiated in January 1940 allowed for the importation of small quantities of wheat, but not enough. The wheat would have to come from Argentina. Britain, fearful lest Spain should be a loophole in her economic blockade of Germany, was not prepared to allow more through than she considered a reasonable quantity. What Britain considered reasonable was based on economic intelligence which must have been singularly erroneous. British 'experts' could not or would not believe that Spain's needs were as great as they were. Spain might have proved her necessity by inviting inspection. That, however, would have been an admission of the fact that her word was being doubted, that her 'honour' was being impugned; and, once admitted, 'honour' would have required 'satisfaction'. As it was, Navicerts alone seemed to Spaniards not only an insult to their country's sovereignty but dishonourable to the country which, in enforcing them, was denying her age-old doctrine of 'freedom of the seas'. The hunger in Spain, however, was too serious for her to make a stand on a point of honour. Livestock was being slaughtered, not only to assuage hunger but also because there was a lack of fodder. The prospects for 1940 were even more serious than the present in January 1940. Even if rain fell the harvest was bound to be poorer still because Spain was in no position to import the fertilizers from Chile on which she was traditionally dependent. She had neither the money to buy them nor the ships in which to bring them. Her merchant fleet had been sunk by the two warring sides. Spain needed credits of a size then unheard of to eat, let alone to buy capital equipment with which to restart her industries. Long-drawn-out negotiations with Britain resulted in an agreement in March 1940 which seemed very generous to Britain at war, but rather less so to hungry Spain. At the outbreak of the Civil War Spain had had £2 million in the Bank of England. There were also then £7 million outstanding in debts to British firms. Britain now made Spain a loan of £2 million 'with strings'. Spain was to use the money in the Bank and the loan to repay 50 per cent of the debts (the balance to be paid with interest by instalments). The remainder was to be spent on the purchase of goods from British firms in Britain or the sterling area – subject to the hated Navicerts. £500,000 worked out at fivepence per head, even in 1940 hardly a princely sum.

Spaniards passed not only a hungry winter in 1939–40 but a cold one. Bad though it was, Spanish coal was used in locomotives and industry; Britain, the traditional supplier, had none to export. The spring brought no relief to the hunger. By June everything edible was rationed. In October black-marketeering was made

punishable with fines of up to $50,000 (£12,500) and hard labour.
Among those convicted was a general who was also a duke, and
who was dismissed from the army into the bargain. In Barcelona
£250,000 in fines was collected within a month. Britain agreed that
same month to allow Spain to purchase £600,000 of food – 6d. per
head; but it could not go far. In November the bread ration was
reduced according to the individual family income, the poorest
getting 150 grammes per person per day, the richest 75 – on the
grounds that the wealthy would be able to supplement their ration
with dearer foodstuffs. But the October concession was a timely
one. It gave Franco a bargaining counter, in the toughest situation
that he ever faced, to keep Spain an independent country.

In mid-June German troops reached the Pyrenees. On 12 June,
when Franco had to admit that he had been proved wrong, that the
Germans had defeated the French army, and that there was no
'buffer' between Berlin and Madrid, he moved from neutrality to
'non-belligerency', the jargon word of the time to indicate that Germany (and Italy) had a non-warring ally in Spain. Neutrality had
not saved any of the states of northern Europe. On 14 June, with
the consent of Britain and Pétain, Spain took over Tangier. Serrano
Suñer tried to press Franco into the war, going out of his way to
satisfy the German embassy's request for a favourable press. The
Falange was inspired to beat at the doors of the British embassy with
demands for the return of Gibraltar; but the *Falange* was not Spain,
nor was Serrano Suñer Franco. Franco and all but two of his
generals still believed that Britain would not be defeated, and the
knowledgeable Catholics of Spain were now aware that Nazism was
as anathema to their Church as Bolshevism. In May 1940 the dying
Cardinal Gomá had explicitly told them in a pastoral that Britain
and France were fighting to uphold the Christian spirit of morality
invoked by Pius XII. Serrano Suñer had forbidden the publication
of a single word of it, but this time its text was being widely circulated.

Franco henceforth to September 1942 had to play a clever game.
In the best interests of his country he had to keep Spain out of the
war. Hitler needed Gibraltar, or rather the control of the Straits.
Spain could not in honour allow foreign troops across her territory
without being formally at war on the side of those troops : if Franco
said 'yes' to Hitler, he would have led Spain into war against
Britain; if he said 'no', Hitler would deal with him and Spain as
he had with all who had said no to him before. Franco kept on saying 'yes', adding 'but . . .' in the same breath. He sent the pro-German General Vigón to tell Hitler how much Franco admired him,

how many difficulties he too was having with the Vatican (which was true), and how ready he was to enter the war, if only he could be sure that Britain could be prevented from taking the Canaries and that Germany would let Spain have the whole of Morocco in any new post-war carve-up of Africa. Of course Spain wanted Gibraltar, but as it was an integral part of Spain only Spaniards could possibly be allowed to capture it. Next Franco, having allowed Serrano Suñer to accept an invitation to visit Germany, briefed him to stress Spain's economic difficulties, and he returned with an invitation : would Franco meet Hitler at Hendaye? Franco agreed. He went further. He made Serrano Suñer his Foreign Minister, a change which the Germans interpreted as a gesture of goodwill and a promise that Hitler's long journey from Berlin would not be in vain.

They were to be disappointed. What Franco was in effect doing was to apply the techniques of the war in Africa to international politics. There the Spaniards had learnt that the best troops, especially in defence, against the Moors had been Moors, provided they were officered by Spaniards; so now he was putting the most pro-German of his colleagues in the vanguard of his defence against Germany. At that moment Serrano, however, was lacking much of his previous pro-Nazi fire. Ribbentrop had not treated him with the respect that Serrano considered his due during the September visit.

At Hendaye, on 23 October, Franco allowed Hitler to talk at great length without interruption. Then, after a pause, he replied at great length, seeing to it that he also was not interrupted. He agreed with each point Hitler had made, except that he qualified the accuracy of each point. Of course he would come into the war whenever Hitler wanted him to do so, that is to say when Spain thought the moment opportune and she was economically in a position to do so. He then went on to make demands on Hitler which he knew Hitler either would not or could not meet – among them one million tons of wheat. He gave Hitler a history lesson about the Spanish War of Independence and how the remnants of an army and an ill-armed peasantry had defeated the best troops which Napoleon could send. He was most grateful to Germany for the help given in the Civil War, but could a friend extort payment from a friend not in a position to repay? ('He made *me* feel like a Jew', Hitler complained after hours of talk of which in retrospect the Führer was to say : 'I would rather have three or four molars out than meet that man again'.)[12] Over the next six months there

[12] Count Galeazzo Ciano, *L'Europa verso la catastrofe* (Milan, 1948), pp 603–4.

were hours and hours of talk, at lower levels, and a volume of diplomatic correspondence – and on Franco's part always demands and an excuse for not entering the war – the economic situation, the will of the people, the bad roads, etc.[13] Hitler informed Franco that he should declare war on Britain in January 1941. Franco spoke of Spain's 'bad weather' in January and moved troops to Irún, and not, as Hitler expected, towards Gibraltar. Hitler made a final appeal. Franco promised a reply after he had seen Mussolini at Bordighera. Mussolini was instructed to 'bring back home the prodigal son'. The 'prodigal' asked the faithful : 'Duce, if you could get out of the war, would you?' Mussolini cried out, 'You bet I would'. Hitler shelved his Operation Felix, the sweep through Spain to Gibraltar, and invaded Russia instead.

That invasion of Russia, in June 1941, was to benefit Franco in two ways other than the slackening of the pressure on him to declare war on Britain. In the first place it enabled him to rid himself of a number of Falangist civilians and army officers whose loyalty to himself had become doubtful; secondly, it gave him an opportunity to repay his 'debt of honour' to Germany.

The initiative was not his. It was his brother-in-law who set in motion a train of events which Franco cunningly guided on to lines he and not the *cuñadísimo*[14] desired. Among the many facets of the development of the *Falange* about which Franco had had his doubts, but which fitted Serrano Suñer's concept that 'the *Falange* should be to Spain what the Fascist Party is to Italy', had been the establishment, in August 1940, of a 'militia' to which all boys were to belong on reaching the age of eighteen until being called up for military service, and again from their discharge from the army until no longer liable for military service. As it would create and maintain 'a military spirit', Franco had approved it wholeheartedly, as he had the *Frente de Juventudes* – in Serrano's plan the equivalent of the Fascist *Ballila* – membership of which was to be compulsory from seven to eighteen and for girls from seven to seventeen and which was to impress discipline and a sense of social service into the community, and to be the school for the inculcation of fascio-Falangism. Where the militia did not meet with Franco's approval was in its potential rivalry to the army itself. There could only be one army, with the chain of command direct from him, the *generalissimo*. The militia's loyalty was to the *generalissimo*, but only via the president of the *Junta Política*, the *cuñadísimo* himself. Early

---

[13] For fuller details based principally on *Documents of German Foreign Policy,* Series D, Vols. II–XIII (London, 1950–64), see *Franco,* pp. 338 et seq.
[14] 'Brother-in-law-in-chief', i.e. Serrano.

in 1941 General Yagüe had confessed, in the face of evidence Franco had shown him, to participation in a plot against him organized by a Colonel Tarduchy and encouraged by the Nazi chief in Spain, Thomson. Franco had taken no action against Yagüe or any of the plotters, accepting their plea that they had acted in what they thought were the best interests of Spain;[15] all he did was to remove from any strategic point any army officer whose allegiance to the *Falange* was stronger than his allegiance to army discipline.[16] Such was the situation when the German ambassador communicated to Foreign Minister Serrano the news of Hitler's invasion of Russia. Serrano Suñer at once offered Germany Falangist militia to help fight the Russians. Franco's reaction was rapid. No militia could earn battle honours other than as part of the Spanish army. He was ready to sanction the raising of a volunteer force open alike to the army and to the *Falange*, but officered by regular army officers. Enough volunteers were forthcoming to form the famous Blue Division; General Varela, the traditionalist and pro-British Minister of War, encouraged the Falangists in the army to volunteer, and Franco appointed as the Division's commander the young General Muñoz Grandes, whom Franco had named Secretary-General of the *Falange* in August 1939 to keep an eye on its president. It was to repay 'Spain's blood debt to Germany' nearly twenty times over.[17]

The divisions which Hitler had held for many months poised beyond the Pyrenees now moved eastwards. Franco could attend to the internal situation, and this, by June 1941, was worse than ever. There was still no rain. The import of fertilizer was pitifully inadequate. In April Britain had relaxed her economic blockade to some extent, but even what the Economic Warfare experts thought adequate for Spain's needs was well below real needs. The Spanish people were now in their third year of hunger, the worst yet. Argentina was prepared to supply Spain, on credit. In sheer anger, and now that no one was demanding that he should do so, Franco came very close to declaring war on Britain after all. Instead, on 17 May, he delivered a splenetic speech to the National Council of the *Falange* and Serrano was given full backing in his attacks on Britain and everything British in the press.

The few with plenty of money could buy a luxury meal. There

---

[15] Franco never once punished anyone who plotted against him *personally*, clearly distinguishing such an individual from one who plotted against him in order to bring to power a person, a party, a situation which he considered injurious to *Spain*. The distinction may appear subtle but it is nonetheless fundamental.

[16] Conversations with General Barroso, 1966.

[17] 6,286 Spaniards were killed fighting against the Soviet Union.

was a smugglers' line of communication from Switzerland and France to the expensive hotels, and always provided that they kept clear of staple foods, bread and olive oil, which they did willingly for the former was black and unpalatable, the latter mixed with substitutes and often rancid, they were rarely disturbed. In the rural districts of Galicia, the Basque provinces, Navarre, and Cata-lonia, smallholders could keep their produce to themselves; but in the large population-centres men and women starved. Beggars thronged the streets of Madrid in numbers not seen since the republic had closed down the hospices run by the religious Orders, and their numbers increased. It became impossible to enforce the black-market laws. Policemen themselves received what had become a pittance and with families and dependants to support, few had the heroic virtue to resist bribery. In November 1941 (after another bad harvest) the scale of sentences for black-marketeering was ex-tended to include the death penalty, and as civil courts were so slow, judgment of alleged offenders was passed to military courts. Once a person was arraigned before them, he had little hope of not being sentenced; but in the first place the man had to be brought before them. One who was arraigned and executed was a Falangist participant in the Tarduchy-Thomson plot. In January 1942 Britain's economic experts, coming now to believe that Spain's food crisis was indeed serious, began to issue Navicerts more freely. The 1942 harvest was fair and by the end of the year it became possible to increase the maximum bread ration to 350 grammes – still well below normal consumption of course, but enough to assuage hunger. Another nine years were to pass before food supplies returned to pre-1936 levels.

It was to be twelve years after 1941 and seventeen years after 1 October 1936 that Franco succeeded in getting from the Vatican the Concordat which he had envisaged on the earlier date as one which would 'respect that national tradition and the religious feel-ings of the huge majority of Spaniards'. It seems that in the first place Franco was prepared to accept the Catholic view of relations between Church and state : on the basis of rendering to Caesar the things that are Caesar's and to God the things that are God's, it was the duty of a Christian Head of State to ensure that state law did not contradict divine law or the Church's laws, especially in such matters as marriage annulment and divorce; that though the state had a legitimate right to demand efficiency in the educa-tion of citizens, it should recognize the Church's own right to pro-tect its children from heterodox teachers; that just as the state alone decided on its own officials, so the Pope alone should decide on who should be bishop and over what territorial area, and the bishop should decide who should be parish priest and where. Opposition to the last point, however, was provided by those Falangists who differed from José Antonio Primo's view that Church and state should be separate, and who wanted the state to control the Church like any other society within the state, and those monarchists who upheld the view that the *real patronato* was 'the most precious jewel in the Spanish monarch's crown',[18] and not one which a mere *locum tenens* like Franco could surrender to the Pope. This opposition, coupled with Franco's experience that though during the Civil War he had repealed the anti-religious laws of the republic, had restored the clerical stipends, had readmitted even the Jesuits, had had the crucifix put back on classroom walls and religion taught in schools, and had affirmed that his Spain was to be a Catholic Spain, he had been criticized nevertheless by churchmen and not openly supported by the Vatican – all this made Franco change his mind. If he surrendered the royal prerogative to choose bishops, he could be faced with many more bishops like Cardinals Segura, Vidal, and Mujica, or Gomá, whose criticisms of the new Spain had been all the more damaging because he had been Franco's earliest clerical supporter. Accordingly Franco demanded of the Vatican recognition of his entitlement to the *real patronato*. The Vatican refused.

On the one hand, Franco knew well that to accept German advice to set up a national Church, or even merely to break with the Vatican, was to invite a revolt of Spaniards against him; on the other hand, thirteen of Spain's fifty-seven bishops had been killed by republicans and by the end of 1940 another six had died from natural causes. When Cardinal Ilundaín of Seville died, Franco had agreed to Segura's recall to take his place, but when the war was over and Tarragona was in Franco's hands, he had vetoed the return from exile of Vidal,[19] and Mujica he refused to have at any price. The position, therefore, was that there were nineteen vacant sees and in addition two vacant because Franco would not have their holders back in Spain. The Vatican, realizing the truth of the maxim 'strike the shepherd and the flock shall be scattered', held out until June 1941, when it signed not a Concordat but an interim agreement, to the following effect : the nuncio, in consultation with the government, would send the Pope at least six names as possible candidates for a vacant see. From these the

[18] See above, p. 64.
[19] Letter from Sra. Rita Vidal Barraquer de Humble (a niece of the Cardinal) to author. He died in Fribourg on 13 September 1943. His tomb bears the inscription *Dilexi justitiam et odivi iniquitatem propterea morior in exilio.* For the affection in which those who remembered him held Cardinal Vidal, see *Cuadernos para el diálogo,* No. 61 (October 1968).

Pope would select three, if acceptable. From these three the Head of State would choose one whom he would 'present' to the Pope for the Pope to name him as the bishop (or archbishop) elect. But, if out of the six there were less than three acceptable, the Pope could make his own list of three. If, however, any on the Pope's list were unacceptable to the Head of State on *political* grounds, then the process was to begin all over again.

Quite how distant Pope Pius XII's views were from those of Franco on who should be bishop may be gathered from the speed with which the vacancies were filled. The *move* to the Primatial see of Toledo of Plá y Deniel, the bishop of Salamanca, took five months until November 1941; but that still left nineteen vacancies. Only four were filled during 1942; and indeed at no time thereafter, while Franco was Head of State, was there to be a 'full house' of bishops.[20]

Franco had other graver matters to preoccupy him during 1942. The entry of the U.S.A. into the war had put him in an interesting situation. There were, as he saw it, three separate wars now in progress.

(1) Germany and Italy versus Britain, France, etc., a war he considered madness, a civil war of western culture: the West committing suicide. He would keep Spain out of it so long as neither side attacked Spain – or Portugal. (In December he came to an even closer alliance with Portugal.) There were disturbing rumours that the Allies were as prepared to invade Spain as the Germans had been – and indeed such plans were made and discussed by the Allies.

(2) Germany versus Soviet Russia. Against 'the barbarous hordes of communism' he could not be neutral. On 14 February 1942, after meeting Salazar to ratify the December treaty, he made the statement which was long to be used as evidence against his neutrality in War No. 1: 'if ever the road to Berlin were open, then not merely one division of Spanish volunteers but a million Spaniards would go there to bar the way'.

(3) The U.S.A. and Britain versus Japan. Franco offered Spanish troops to fight against 'the Asiatic hordes', for in attacking the Philippines, Japan had attacked an outpost of Spanish culture. The offer was not accepted.

His views did not change till the end of the war and it must be recognized that they were shared by a large body of Spaniards.

[20] The text of the 1941 agreement is given in an appendix to *Concordato entre la Santa Sede y España* (Madrid Oficina de Información Diplomatica, 1953).

Critics of these distinctions were the Nazified Falangists like Serrano Suñer, to whom Britain was no less an enemy that Soviet Russia, and Catholics following their bishops who maintained that Nazism was evil and had to be fought. Among them there were some who, with Cardinal Segura,[21] believed that Nazism was even worse than communism. Communism in preaching atheism left a void of which the normal man became conscious, but (other than in its atheistic aspect) was no more than an exaggeration of very sound principles. Nazism, on the other hand, was the deification of Nationalism, etc., a religion which left no void and which was based on principles diametrically contrary to Christianity. Hence, humanly speaking, the conversion of a Nazi was impossible. There were also the defeated republicans and socialists who hoped that the Allies, having defeated Hitler and Mussolini, would turn out Franco for them – a belief in which, it would appear, they were encouraged by Spanish republicans in both the Americas and nearer home in Britain, who had access to microphones and whose supervisors were people with an inadequate knowledge of how subtle the Spanish language can be in the hands of Spaniards. Only Spanish communists believed in Russia and hoped that Russia would win. War No. 3 was too remote for most Spaniards to be concerned one way or another.

In 1942 Franco still feared invasion by German troops, but he also believed that an Allied invasion was by no means out of the question. The Spanish republicans in the U.S.A. had a power quite disproportionate to their numbers[22] and he distrusted Roosevelt's political judgements. He knew of Allied plans to invade Spain.[23] However, it was the enemy or potential enemy within Spain which concerned him more. On 24 June 1941 Falangists who had attended a meeting at which Serrano had appealed for volunteers against Russia had gone straight from it to attack the British embassy, quite unaccountably if Serrano's word is to be believed that he did not inspire the attack. To Franco Serrano's friendship with the German ambassador had long seemed altogether too close and Serrano too ready to please the Nazis. In February 1942 what had started as a demonstration by students in protest against the delay – as they put it – in the restoration of the monarchy took on anti-Franco aspects. Franco still took no action, but several hundred demonstrators were put in gaol as demonstration succeeded demonstration and riot succeeded riot until the end of the scholastic year in June. Among the rioters several groupings were discernible : monarchist,

[21] Conversations with Cardinal Segura, 1950.
[22] They had a powerful influence on American journalists close to the White House.
[23] See Churchill, *The Second World War* (London, 1948—), Vol. IV, p. 345; cf. Vol. II, pp. 460, 552–63, 625, 639; Vol. III, pp. 388–9.

traditionalist, Nazi—Falangist, 'old shirt' and 'new shirt' Falangist. Franco ordered José Luis Arrese, a young man who had made a name for himself through his planning of new workers' housing in Málaga and was now Secretary-General of the *Falange,* to get rid of what were politely described as anarchists and Marxists. He did so, but they were not the real troublemakers, as quickly became clear.

Franco apart, the main stumbling-block to the German invasion of Spain had been General Varela, the Minister of War, now married to a daughter of a notoriously pro-British family. On 14 August, a traditionalist by conviction, he attended a Requiem for the Carlists fallen in the Civil War. As he left the church a bomb exploded, missing him but killing seventy-two bystanders. All that can be said for certain is that the culprits were Falangists and close associates of the Nazi Party. Two weeks later, Franco announced a new Cabinet, excluding Serrano, now out of office for the rest of his life, and also, to show Franco's non-belligerent neutrality, Varela, who was given an important army command. The very pro-Allied General Jordana was appointed Foreign Minister and the mildly pro-Axis General Asensio was made Minister of War. A new situation was developing. The Allies were bound to strike at the Axis somewhere – and Franco hoped their target would not be Spain. At the end of October Franco had word that the Allies were massing aircraft and ships in Algeciras Bay, which to him meant one thing only : that the Allies were going to land in North Africa, not Spain (wrong rendezvous) nor the Canaries (too large a force). He gave orders that the Allies were not to be molested. This was all part of a war which was madness to him anyway. He did his best to persuade the Allies to come to terms with Germany, holding before them a picture of Europe in which Poland, Czechoslovakia, and Romania would be 'so many more states of the Soviet Confederation' if Germany were destroyed or sovietized. The Allies, however, were now committed to the policy of 'unconditional surrender', just as in mid-1938 Franco had pledged himself to that policy. Furthermore, to Allied ears his pleas sounded as if they were German-inspired, though in fact they embarrassed Germany no less than they annoyed the Allies. In 1943, after another German plot to oust Franco had failed, Hitler made a final appeal to Franco to declare war on his side or at least against Russia. Franco's reaction was secretly to order his Minister of War to organize the withdrawal of the Blue Division. Grand-Admiral Doenitz pressed Hitler to invade Spain. Hitler's reply is recorded, and it indicates how successful Franco's lecture to him on the War of Spanish Independence had been : 'they are the only tough Latins and they would carry on guerrilla warfare in our rear'.[24]

With Hitler Franco had played a clever game, and he had won. He had kept Spain out of Germany's clutches at a cost of no more serious breaches of neutrality than those committed by Switzerland, Sweden, or Turkey, on whom the pressures had never been as heavy as they had been on Spain. As part of the game, however, he had made the most committed of statements which would long be used in evidence against him, and for which he, or rather Spain, was now to be made to pay dearly.

The republicans in exile had the sympathy of the American and of much of the British press, and Roosevelt was counselled to invade Spain. Churchill, whose background included a period spent with Spanish troops in the very campaign in which Theodore Roosevelt had been on the opposite side, knew Spaniards better, and it was well for the Allied cause that he did, for otherwise Allied divisions would have been faced with the same guerrilla opposition, the thought of which had unnerved Hitler. Instead, and in spite of Foreign Office advice, Roosevelt decided to bully Franco.

By 1943 Spain was beginning to make a little money out of the war, money wherewith to buy food, medicines, vehicles, fuels, fertilizers, and even capital equipment. She had a commodity which had suddenly become precious – wolfram, essential to the manufacture of aircraft and jet engines. Pre-war Burma, now in Japanese hands, had been its chief supplier; there were small quantities of the right quality in Saxony and Bohemia and on the Pacific coast of the U.S.A.; but neither side had enough for its own purposes. As much and more than was required was available from Spain, who in her trading had maintained a strict neutrality on the basis of cash and carry. The two sides now began to outbid each other. The price of wolfram rose from a few hundred pounds to £7,500 a ton. Each side was anxious not only to cover its needs but to deny the substance to the other. The Allies, buying during the first eleven months of 1943 3,313 tons while the Germans bought a mere 690 tons, were more successful for two reasons : first, it was easier for the Allies to carry the material out of Spain; secondly, Franco was prepared to sell only against payment in the goods which Spain needed. Germany had neither fuel nor food to spare; Allied bombing was having its effect on German factories; and Germany could not provide Spain with the machine-tools which Spain listed as the *sine qua non* of transactions to pay for more wolfram. Britain saw Spain's point of view and had no objection to the sale to Germany

[24] *Führer Conferences on Naval Affairs* (London, Admiralty, 1947), pp. 38–9.

of small quantities because such a sale was depriving Germany of goods she could ill spare, whereas Spain's demands from the Allies were for oil, of which there was no shortage, and of food from Argentina. There was perhaps a greater knowledge now of what really had been Spain's plight from 1939 to 1942 and amends were being made. It was the Americans who now would not be convinced that Spain did not have the railways nor the roads needed to send to Germany vast quantities of war material, even supposing she wanted to do so; and Franco certainly wanted no such thing, for it had been obvious to him after the success of the Allies in Africa and the collapse of Italy that Germany had lost the war. It was in his country's interest to favour the side that was going to win. This did not mean that he would accept dictation from the Allies any more than he had from the Germans. He had been on the point himself of withdrawing the Blue Division in July 1943 when that had been demanded of him by the British and American ambassadors. He had thereupon delayed withdrawal and the reaffirmation of neutrality which he had planned to make before going on holiday at the end of July he also delayed till his return on 1 October. Roosevelt now threatened to stop fuel supplies from the end of January 1944 unless Franco undertook not to send Germany another ton of wolfram. (Portugal incidentally had long been sending Germany much more than Spain, but that did not seem to worry the United States.) Roosevelt's threat sounded like an ultimatum—and the Spanish reaction was foreseen by the Foreign Office. Monarchists and republicans, anti-Franquists and pro-Franquists, pro-Allied and pro-German elements, all rallied behind the *generalissimo*, the *Caudillo*, the leader, for the first time since 1 October 1936. As the oil embargo began to create real hardship (food could not be adequately distributed), the Spaniards' determination to stand firm against the Americans increased. Churchill made Roosevelt change his mind by warning him that if the U.S.A. did not renew the oil supplies, Britain would do so. When the supplies were renewed, Franco undertook to reduce the wolfram exports to Germany.

The year 1944 was one in which fantastic rumours circulated in western Europe and the Americas about what was happening in Spain. Franco was said to be manufacturing V.1s and V.2s, and other secret weapons for Hitler; yet there were also said to be half a million workers in gaol. In August a republican army of 50,000 was said to have crossed the Pyrenees; and in advance of their rapid progress the people were said to be rising against their hated oppressors in Barcelona, Asturias, and Andalusia. In fact at most 1,500 *maquisards* did indeed cross the Pyrenees. They met with no sympathy from the inhabitants, and a small army and Civil Guard force deployed against them killed about one hundred, captured 500, and drove the rest back without difficulty. For many years afterwards handfuls of men did carry out daring raids from bases in Toulouse, but there was never more than a nuisance value in such activity.[25] The reality of the Spanish situation was indeed very different from what the exiles believed or hoped for. Spain was indeed beginning to manufacture for herself goods which had previously been obtainable only from abroad, but in the field of 'armaments' she manufactured nothing more modern than field-gun shells and light aircraft. Through the years there had been several amnesties. By mid-1943 the number of political prisoners had been down to 49,000 and, by the spring of 1944, to 25,000, a figure which included at least one thousand violent opponents of the régime from within the *Movimiento*. The dangers to the régime, mostly from within, were real enough, though perhaps not as great as they appeared to be at the time. The Movement had been pushed in one direction by Serrano Suñer; and since his fall in a different direction; and it was still moving, though not towards the unity which Franco desired.

It was to be one of the ironies of modern history that in seeking to overthrow Franco, the United Nations in fact strengthened his position in 1946 to a degree which in retrospect can be seen to have ensured his survival as Head of State into old age.[26]

[25] See Appendix A.

Chapter 27

Spain under Franco: The Isolation of Spain 1944–53

ON 17 APRIL 1946 Oscar Lange, Foreign Minister in the post-war government of Poland, called on the Security Council to declare Franco an immediate threat to world peace. According to him, Franco had a mechanized force of 250,000 massed on the point of invading France; Spanish factories were turning out in quantity German-designed tanks, artillery, and aircraft, and Spanish ship-yards powerful surface and submarine warships; uranium was being processed and heavy water produced. No one asked openly how such a transformation of Spain into the highly industrialized coun-try which all this presupposed had been effected so secretly and rapidly. Incredulity found expression in no more than the appoint-ment of a sub-committee to study the evidence. Giral, now 'Prime Minister of the Spanish republic', submitted a seventy-seven-page memorandum, purporting to be the evidence behind the 'facts' Lange had given. Giral stated that the Spanish army had a strength of 840,721 and equipment superior to that of the *Wehrmacht* on the western or eastern fronts. He made Spain the possessor of an armaments' industry of which Krupps would have been envious.

The leaders of the 200,000 or so Spanish exiles had not been daunted by the defeat of the 1,500 *maquisards* who had crossed the Pyrenees in the autumn of 1944. They had gone into exile in 1939 with very considerable funds. They had entertained the right people. They had the services of able propagandists in the United States, Britain, Mexico, and France. In February 1945 at the San Francisco Conference of the United Nations, the Mexican govern-ment obtained for them a ruling that 'any régime established with the aid of the armed forces that had fought against the United Nations' would not be admitted into their organization. In August at Potsdam Stalin called on Britain and the U.S.A. actively 'to help the democratic forces in Spain'. Churchill persuaded Stalin that it would be enough to state that the Big Three would not favour any Spanish application for membership. All this happened while Negrín was living in England in a manner which reminded those who knew of its details, more of the stories of debauched Renaissance princes than of Lenin. Casado, however, was also in Britain and could tell of the second civil war within the Civil War. The exiles could never have acted together under even the nominal presidency of Negrín. Exiled Popular Front *Cortes* delegates met in Mexico (about a hundred of them) and elected Martínez Barrio 'President of Spain'. Negrín accordingly resigned from whatever office he was supposed to hold, President and/or Prime Minister, and Mexico thereupon accorded Martínez Barrio the honours of a Head of State. He appointed Giral 'Prime Minister' and Giral chose a Cabinet which carefully excluded communists – except for Álvarez del Vayo who was still pretending in public that he was a non-revolutionary socialist.

This government met with Stalin's approval – but Stalin was in no position himself to install it in Spain. This could only be done with the consent of, or directly by, Britain and France.

The moment seemed propitious. In France de Gaulle was still nominally in power, but that power was being strongly contested by the vociferous communist element in the government and Constituent Assembly, and by the French Communist Party generally. In Britain Attlee had succeeded Churchill; but Attlee had such an idealized and simplified view of Spanish affairs that within 48 hours of the rising of 1936 he had pledged the Labour Party and the Co-operative Movement to give 'all practicable support' to 'Spanish democracy' in its 'fight against Fascism'; in December 1937 he had visited the International Brigades, greeting them with the clenched-fist salute and shouting 'Workers of the World Unite'; a year later he had 'reviewed' the surviving 305 members of the British Battalion on their arrival back from Spain; and in February 1939 he had opposed Britain's recognition of the Franco government as 'a gross betrayal of democracy'. In the winter of 1945 British Labour men and women could be stirred to passionate outbursts against Franco as a Fascist and imperialist while they remained impassive before the advance of the Soviet empire into Europe. Bevin, however, a more astute man than Attlee, had already learnt to distrust any move prompted by Stalin. Furthermore, Truman was less naïve than Roosevelt.

In December 1945 the French invited the Americans and the British 'to discuss Spain' jointly with them, but the invitation was declined. In January 1946, with de Gaulle out, the French Assembly called on Britain and the U.S.A. to break off diplomatic and trade contacts with Spain. Britain and the U.S.A. would go no further than to support a resolution at the United Nations Assembly in London on 9 February to act 'in accordance with the letter and spirit of Potsdam in the conduct of their future relations with Spain'. At the end of February France closed her frontiers to trade and normal traffic, and began to allow guerrilla and saboteur train-ing-schools to operate openly in the Toulouse-Pau area, and trained bands to move freely so as to cross into Spain from whatever point would give them the initiative of surprise. Radio Paris joined Moscow Radio in reiterating the dogma that Franco was a menace to peace, that there were daily riots against him, and that the people of Spain were on the point of 'general revolt against his barbarous tyranny'. France then declared its intention to raise 'the case of Spain' as a 'menace to world peace' in the Security Council. On 4 March Britain and the United States persuaded France into a milder declaration : Spain would not be admitted into the U.N. while Franco was in power, but they would not intervene in the internal affairs of Spain. It would be up to the people of Spain to bring about 'a peaceful withdrawal of Franco' and to establish a government of their own choice. France none the less went on to insist on Security Council handling of the matter. The new guerrilla groups were meeting with even less success than before, for the Spaniards would not support them. If Franco was to be overthrown on behalf of the Spanish government in exile, it would have to be done by armed intervention, for which, in the climate of immediate post-war Europe, U.N. permission was desirable; even the French communists thought so.

The sub-committee appointed to investigate Oscar Lange's accusations (Poland, France, Brazil, China, Australia) refused Span-ish offers to lay Spain open to inspection by members of countries with which she had diplomatic relations and heard only what the exiles had to say. They concluded in June that the Franco régime constituted a *potential* menace. The U.S.S.R., Poland, Mexico, and France thereupon demanded the imposition of sanctions against Spain; but the rest of the Security Council would not stand for that. In November the General Assembly took up the subject, which dominated the discussions of that month and December. The Soviet Bloc, France, and Mexico dropped the demand for sanctions but still pressed for a full diplomatic break. The voting was twenty for the resolution and twenty against, thirteen coun-tries abstaining. A U.S. resolution expressing the pious hope that Franco would gracefully retire also resulted in a draw, twenty-two against twenty-two. Finally on 12 December, by thirty-four votes to six, with thirteen abstentions, the U.N. agreed to exclude Spain from all its agencies as well as the General Assembly and recom-mended members 'to withdraw their ambassadors and ministers plenipotentiary'.

Franco, to use a vulgar expression of the time, 'could not care less'.[1] When on 9 December the Soviet Bloc was moving for a mandatory break in relations, between one in three and one in two of all the people of Madrid congregated outside his office in the Royal Palace. They acclaimed, in a spontaneous demonstration, the like of which had never been seen in Spain, their solidarity with him against 'foreign intervention'. The U.N. had indeed united the people under Franco to a degree which he himself had never achieved.

The U.N. dubbed his régime Fascist; but it was so in 1946 only in the communist sense that what is not communist or socialist is Fascist. There were prisoners serving sentences for having belonged to proscribed political associations, for distributing anti-régime propaganda, for holding unauthorized meetings, for seeking to inspire workers to strike, as well as others who were not only members of the proscribed parties but who had attempted or carried out acts of sabotage, robberies with violence, homicide – in all about 15,000 on 31 December 1946.[2] The only permitted political association was still the *Movimiento* and the only workers' association the *sindicato*. There was no freedom of association or meeting; the printed word was subject to the strictest censorship; a man could rail against the régime in the privacy of a café, but woe betide him if when sober he directed his attack against the person of any Minister or the Head of State. A plain-clothes political security force[3] could break into private property and arrest on suspicion, and its methods of interrogation were often savage. There was also a uniformed force, the *Policía Armada*, which like its republican parent, the *Asaltos*, believed in the use of the charge with weapons in dealing with difficult situations—but no more so than the French *Compagnies Républicaines de Sécurité* or the Royal Ulster Constabulary in those periods when opponents of de Gaulle or the Belfast parliament took to the use of explosives to further their aims. Nevertheless, by December 1944, let alone December 1946, Spain had been moved in intent and in fact away from the Serrano Suñer Fascist-Nazi goal.

The first public announcement had been in an interview given by Franco to an American news agency in May 1943. Spain was to be a Christian state, authoritarian perhaps, but not totalitarian. The family was to be its fundamental unit, the syndicate and

[1] The British ambassador was the only ambassador of a major power in Madrid.
[2] During 1946 2,543 persons were detained as accomplices of the *maquis* or 'bandits' (see Appendix A), bringing the total since 1943 to 5,000.
[3] The *Brigada Social y Política*. Their interests are not exclusively political. They deal with 'vice' as well.

17

municipality its political expression. Franco's conversation and attitude to *Falange* (as opposed to *Movimiento*) doctrine had prompted
no less than eight of the thirteen lieutenant-generals to petition him
that September to restore the monarchy in the person of Don Juan,
the now dead Alfonso XIII's son.[4] Franco had considered the move
inopportune, to the delight of the Falangists; but they had received
a heavy blow that December with the abolition of their militia. It
had become the complaint of 'old shirts' during 1944 that new
men, admittedly members of the *Movimiento* but hardly Falangists
in thought or word, were being repeatedly preferred in such offices
as mayors of *municipia,* and that adherence to Falangist doctrine
counted for little in the civil service or appointments to universities :
indeed some of the professors who later showed strong Social
Democrat leanings were men given chairs about that time.

During 1945 the reorientation of the Movement had been more
public. Early in the year Franco had instituted a body of mainly
apolitical senior citizens to which he had given the mediaeval name
'Council of the Realm', whose task it would be, in the event of his
demise, to decide on the fitness of pretenders to the throne, if the
monarchy were to be restored, and to choose a king from among
them. On 19 July he had reshuffled his Cabinet, bringing into it a
man closely associated with the late king, General González
Galarza. King and *Falange* did not go together, so the inference
was legitimate that other than in the *sindicatos,* Falange influence
was to be reduced still more. Shortly before the reshuffle an important law had been decreed, the *Fuero de los Españoles,* or
Charter of Liberties of Spaniards, and in October there was to be a
Law of Referendum. It was easy to ridicule these measures as
worthless and meaningless and the left in exile did so. Under the
latter law, the Head of State bound himself to refer any far-reaching legal proposal to the direct vote of all men and women twenty-
one-years-old and over. However, he reserved to himself the decision as to what was to be considered important enough for such
a process. Under the Charter the Spaniard was guaranteed freedom
of expression and freedom to correspond with whom he willed,
secrecy of the mails, freedom of residence anywhere, and freedom
to meet and to form associations for lawful purposes. His house
would be held inviolable without a search-warrant and if arrested
he would have to be brought before a judge within 72 hours, and
set free unless a *prima facie* case were established that he had
broken some law. However, by the simple procedure of a decree,

---

[4] Full text of letter in Payne, *Politics and the Military in Modern Spain*
(London, 1967), pp. 433-4.

the government reserved to itself the right to suspend any or all of these freedoms.

None the less the laws were important in themselves and cardinal to the way in which Spain developed over the next twenty years. To have judged them for what they were worth, the non-Spanish world would have had to have realized :

1. That Spain has ever been a nation of jurists.
2. That with the exception of the 'enlightened' Charles III, and Ferdinand VII, all rulers, having committed themselves under a law of their own creation, considered themselves in honour bound to work within that law thereafter.
3. That Franco had been rigorously schooled in the legalistic aspects of *honor* no less than the others.
4. That laws in Spain often look to a desirable future rather than the present.

In 1942 Franco had decreed the establishment of *Cortes*, seemingly at best a revival of the mediaeval rather than the modern institution; their powers advisory rather than legislative. Approximately fifty of the members (*procuradores,* the mediaeval term) were to be expressly nominated by the Head of State by virtue of their distinction in ecclesiastical, military, administrative, intellectual, and other fields. Another fifty were to be the mayors of the provincial capitals—and as mayors nominees of the Head of State. Cabinet Ministers, twelve rectors of universities, and over one hundred National Councillors of the *Movimiento*, all of them also nominees of the Head of State, were also to be members. Various learned societies and professional colleges were to elect some twenty members, the *sindicatos* around 150, and local governments another fifty, but no one could be elected to office in local government or *sindicato* without the approval of the Head of State – so it had all seemed a carefully chosen body and hardly, as it was claimed, 'the highest organ of the peoples' participation in the tasks of state'. However, the preamble to the 1945 *Fuero* had stated unequivocally that the Spanish *Cortes* 'as the supreme organ ... etc.' had drafted it. Was it all pretence? Or were the *Cortes* to evolve into a parliament which would satisfy men's desire to participate in government, so that Franco could have as much right to call his régime a democracy as any of the new East European régimes? If they were to do so, then the British and Americans might come to be less dissatisfied with the régime.

As far as the Charter was concerned, the extreme left, being as Spanish as Franco, understood it for what it was, a declaration of intent. The clauses on the freedoms of the individual were not the ones which worried them. The republican constitution had guaranteed the same freedoms and had as carefully reserved to the government the right to withdraw them at a moment's notice; just as did the United Nations' own Declaration of Human Rights, approved some months later than the *Fuero*. It was the other clauses that committed Franco to working towards the disappearance of the proletariat by converting it into a class of capitalists, towards the ideal of as many families as possible being owners of their own houses, their own plots of land, their own reserves of capital. If that goal were approached, it would become impossible to set up the dictatorship of the proletariat.

All these considerations were present in the minds of the highly intelligent Spanish extreme left. They realized, as none of their allies with an imperfect knowledge of Spanish thought and history could, that the longer the western powers delayed in bringing down Franco by direct intervention, the less chance there was of their return to power. To them the tripartite declaration of 4 March with its clear-cut statement that Britain, the U.S.A., and France would not intervene directly, yet hoped that Franco would withdraw peacefully, was as severe a disappointment as it was a source of strength to the *generalissimo*, who never in his life had done and never would do what others told him to do. Nor was the Giral government in exile, which the U.S.S.R. backed, at all pleased with the probes which British officials made at about that time to bring together right, centre, and left (possibly under Gil Robles) as a shadow government to which Franco might hand over power if, as appeared not unlikely to the British embassy, he offered the Headship of State to Don Juan, the Dartmouth-educated descendant of Queen Victoria. The only restoration the exiles desired was of themselves, and only themselves. Here indeed the British embassy and Giral had read Franco's mind correctly, in that he did intend at some moment he thought opportune to restore Spain to the status of a monarchy. The Law of Referendum was also a declaration of intent : that he was minded to put to a plebiscite some major point; and the only one which made sense was whether the new Spain should be a monarchy or not. In 1946 Franco might have considered the moment opportune had first the three powers and then the United Nations not 'offended the very honour of Spain' by discussing her internal affairs. As it was, on 20 February Franco at long last proclaimed his personal standpoint, declaring categorically that he was a monarchist. He cut the National Council of the *Movimiento* to fifty members and gave the fifty vacancies in the *Cortes* to local government representatives. He made several subtle but legally substantial changes[5] within which the *Cortes* did in fact evolve out of their 'rubber-stamp' beginning into a chamber which in sub-committee could and did sometimes fundamentally alter drafts submited by the government, and originate legislation.

In 1938 Franco had pledged himself in the 'Labour Charter' to work towards social justice. In 1946 workmen were being paid wages the purchasing power of which was not enough 'to enable the worker and his family to live decently and morally', but they were, even if marginally, better proportionately than they had been in 1936; and though their administration left much to be desired, the family allowance and national health insurance schemes introduced in 1942 and 1944 respectively were improving the lot of some hundreds of thousands. Under the republic unemployment had oscillated between a half and a full million. It was now the policy of the government, as it had been under Primo de Rivera, to have men building houses, schools – not always wisely – in fact anything rather than have them idle. By 1941 the government had become convinced that the primary need in rural areas was irrigation and in urban areas electric power for industry. It therefore embarked on plans for hydroelectricity, at which the enemies of the régime laughed. The dams completed by 1946 held no water. While workers complained that they were forbidden to strike, employers were equally bitter over the law prohibiting them from dismissing staff without long legal proceedings. There was still hunger in Spain, for harvests had continued to be ruinously bad. There was still no rain; but the government was convinced that the rains would come to feed the dams to provide the power for factories and the water for crops. In the meantime, Spain had perforce to import foodstuffs and animal fodder. (This indeed had been by no means the least of the factors behind the pressure of the Giral government and of the Soviet Bloc for economic sanctions when the western powers had rejected what they most desired – direct intervention; though whether Spaniards would have been starved into submission is doubtful in the light of their history and tradition.)

Fortunately for the Spaniards they had a friend in Perón of Argentina – not that he was acting entirely without self-interest, for his most unruly subjects were *Gallegos* who, Argentine though they had become, were not prepared to see their relatives starve. In October 1946 he promised Spain a further 600,000 tons of wheat and 120,000 tons of maize, on credit at a low interest-rate. When

5 The amendments bear the date 9 March but they had been under discussion for some months.

the United Nations 'recommended' its members to withdraw their ambassadors, Perón ignored the United Nations. At the time there was no Argentine ambassador in Madrid, but he immediately sent one; and he stood by his promise to send food. It began to arrive in December, and though there was not enough of it, its effect on the morale of the people was considerable. A daughter-nation was seen coming to the help of the mother-country.

Mexico had been a protagonist in the United Nations' battle but the six who voted against the motion were all Spanish American countries. Three others had abstained, which was very gratifying. Uruguay's and Paraguay's votes for the motion were explained away (not without a grain of reason) as an act of defiance against Argentina rather than Franco; those of Bolivia, Chile, Guatemala, Panama, and Venezuela as subservience to the U.S.S.R. Liberal and right-wing Spain had long looked on Mexico as a very wayward daughter who had repudiated its mother even as early as 1917 with its cult of Aztec-ism. The attitude of the nine abstainers and opposers was quoted as proof of the success of the policy of *Hispanidad*.

This had been a cultural movement begun under Alfonso XIII to strengthen the bonds between Spain and Spanish America which only a man totally insensitive to history could deny existed. It had fitted well with the *Falange* 'will to empire' and Franco had established in 1941 a *Consejo de Hispanidad* with motives no more sinister than the British Council. Though far from racialist – there were certain similarities with *négritude* – it was born of the feeling that the only way to combat British and American cultural and economic 'imperialism', to reduce the dependence of Spanish America on the U.S.A. and of Spain on Britain, was to bring together all the Spanish-speaking world.[6] With Argentina under Perón and up to 1950 it was to pay good dividends. Argentina in April 1948 concluded a trade agreement which was as beneficial to Spain as prejudicial to Britain. To enable Spain to repay old credits and further credits to a total of £110 million, Argentina ordered from Spain a fleet of modern cargo-passenger liners and railway rolling-stock. After that these good relations deteriorated; largely because the President's wife, Eva, fêted in Spain in 1947 like a princess of royal blood, later came to imagine that certain jokes about her current in Spain were government-inspired and also that the Spanish ambassador in Buenos Aires had slighted her.[7] Such

[6] The 'empire' of which the *Falange* dreamt is that outlined in J. M. de Areilza and F. M. Castiella, *Reivindicaciones de España* (Madrid, 1941): Gibraltar, North Africa, and what was French Indo-China.

[7] I was myself resident in Buenos Aires at the time. Señora Perón was hypersensitive.

trivialities could always change the course of international relations as easily as economics, principle, or deep reflection.

Franco was incapable of action without long reflection, but having reflected he could act suddenly. The solidarity which the United Nations had created for him gave him the opportunity to try out his Law of Referendum. First the *Cortes* were required to consider a new Law of Succession, which they amended in detail and sent back to him. On March he called on the nation to vote on 6 July yes or no to the following clauses :[8]

1. That Spain was a political unit, Catholic in religion, and a *Kingdom*.
2. That Franco was Head of State.
3. That in the event of the office of Head of State becoming vacant, a Council of Regency consisting of the Speaker of the *Cortes,* the senior prelate in the *Cortes,* and the senior serving officer in the armed forces should assume power.
4. That the Council of the Realm should in future consist of the Council of Regency, the Chief of the General Staff, the President of the High Court of Justice, the Council of State (a sort of Privy Council), the Institute of Spain (a body of learned men), and seven members of the *Cortes.*
5. That the Head of State should bind himself to hear the Council of the Realm whenever he was not prepared to accept any bill drafted by the *Cortes,* before declaring war or negotiating peace, and before putting before the *Cortes* anyone's name as a successor to himself.
6. That the Head of State should be free to put before the *Cortes* the name of anyone whom he would like them to consider as king or regent in succession to him as Head of State.
7. That if he were to die after the *Cortes* had approved his suggestion of a successor, then the Council of Regency should administer the oath of succession and proclaim the successor king or regent.
8. That if the *Cortes* had not approved of any nominee at all, the Council of Regency should summon within three days the Cabinet and the Council of the Realm and select a person of royal blood and propose him to the *Cortes* as king (or if no one so proposed proved acceptable to the *Cortes,* to propose as regent any worthy person).
9. That king or regent should be male, Spanish, at least thirty

---

[8] This is a summary of what was put to referendum.

years old, a Catholic, 'with the necessary qualities to fulfil his high calling', and swear to uphold the constitutional laws.[9]

10. Such laws were the *Fuero,* the Labour Charter, the *Cortes* Law, the National Referendum Act and the Act of Succession now at referendum, and the 'Principles guiding the National Movement'.

11. That if a king succeeded, thereafter succession should be by primogeniture, excluding females, through whom, however, the right of succession could be transmitted.

12. That the approval of the *Cortes* should be necessary for royal marriages and abdications.

13. That the Head of State should propose to the *Cortes* the exclusion of his natural heir if unfit or unworthy to rule.

14. That by a two-thirds majority the Cabinet should be able to bring to the notice of the Council of the Realm and they to the *Cortes* the 'incapacitation' of the Head of State.

15. That all decisions of the *Cortes* under this proposed Act of Succession should require a two-thirds majority of the members present and a simple majority of the nominal total membership.

Here was a proposal which in a very true way summed up the whole history of the kings of Spain. Had such a clear-cut law existed in 1827 as was now being proposed, the Carlist wars would have lacked their dynastic aspect; had it existed in 1647, certain depraved or mad princes would never have ascended the throne, and the ruinous War of the Spanish Succession would not have occurred. The process of election, coupled with selection and nomination subject to assembly approval, recalled almost the Visigothic system. Here, however, Franco was tying down any future king and himself in a way in which no Bourbon nor Habsburg had been bound to *Cortes.* The law tied him down too, of course, to the principles of the National Movement : quite what these were no one was any longer quite sure, except that they were not Primo de Rivera's twenty-seven points as such. They were to be defined in 1958 under twelve headings in terms which still allowed substantial elasticity of interpretation.

Don Juan called the referendum a fraud and stated that the proposed law was totally unacceptable to him as heir to the throne. The count of Rodezno agreed with his first point but not with the second – that Don Juan was the heir. 17·2 million were entitled to vote – all men and women of twenty-one years and over who had no prison record. 15·2 million did so. According to the official re-

9 *Leyes Fundamentales.*

sults, 14·1 million, 82 per cent of the electorate, approved the proposals. The *Cortes* formally accepted the 'will of the people', and the proposals became law on 26 July. Thereafter, for far longer than anyone anticipated or believed possible, Spain was officially a monarchy, with a *Caudillo* as Head of State, 'by the Grace of God', instead of a king.

Though the official results were unlike those of any elections ever held previously in Spain or in any of the western democracies, there is no evidence that at the time the majority of the people did not favour the restoration of the status of a monarchy. In 1931 the king had given up his throne not because the majority of the nation had expressed republican views, but because the majority of the inhabitants of the cities had done so. More than half a million 'republicans', including all the leaders, had either been killed or gone into exile. Within Spain there was little support for the republican leaders other than for Prieto or Gil Robles. Prieto had come to believe that there was much to be said for a monarch as Head of State and Gil Robles had always been a monarchist at heart.[10] Of course, not all those who voted for the Act did so because they were monarchist: many voted 'aye' for no other reason than to show what they felt about United Nations 'inter-ference'.

Three or four years later the results might have been substantially different. The Soviet Bloc kept up its cold war against Franco throughout 1947, seconded by the Giral government and Mexico. They continued to present a picture of Spain under a White Terror and still seething with revolt. A Spanish Republican Army of Liberation had been established under the communist hero of the Civil War Enrique Lister, who claimed during 1947 1,317 armed encounters with the Spanish army and Civil Guard, an average of more than three a day, a number which must be accepted with no less reserve than other 'news' items broadcast at that time, among them that as a result of miscalculation an atomic device had accidentally exploded at the Cadiz naval base. Spain was excluded from the Marshall Plan, although countries rather less neutral during World War II and less affected by war damage like Sweden or Turkey, were to receive $22 million and $105 million respectively. On the other hand, Argentina's example of sending an ambassador to Madrid was being followed by other Latin American states, who in May 1949 tried to reverse the U.N. recommendation. They were then unsuccessful, for though their motion was carried by twenty-six votes to sixteen with sixteen abstentions, a two-thirds majority

[10] Robles, op. cit., passim. See also Welles, op. cit., pp. 345–6.

was required – the number of votes in favour had to be double those against.

The climate of opinion was changing, not so much in favour of Spain as against the U.S.S.R. In 1948 the U.S. War Department advocated the association of Spain in western defence plans and Congress was recommending economic aid. Britain bought Spanish produce to the value of £31 million and exported £13·8 million worth of goods to Spain as against £12·7 million and £6·1 million in 1946. The withdrawal of the ambassador in 1946 could be said to have been highly beneficial to the Spanish economy. In February 1948 France reopened her Pyrenean frontier and the French wine industry was welcoming all the cork Spain could send it. This reopening was to have a disastrous effect on the credibility of anti-Franco propaganda. Ordinary men and women began to tour Spain. Lister still claimed for his army no less than 983 battles, more than two a day, while Giral still insisted that Franco had a well-equipped army of 800,000. No tourist ever saw any battle and the observer with a knowledge of military affairs could find no weapon of later design than 1938. The army had a few dilapidated lorries whose maintenance in service was a tribute to the ingenuity of the Spaniard – an ingenuity for which many a tourist could be thankful when some vital part of his car broke on the appallingly ill-maintained roads of Spain, roads over which no modern army could have advanced with any rapidity. The tourist would generally find that a local mechanic could make him on a local forge whatever new part the car required. The army was the same happy-go-lucky conscript force of pre-republican days, clothed in ill-fitting uniforms and poorly fed. Tourists went back to France, Britain, and especially South America. The British remarked on the presence everywhere of the *Caudillo*'s portrait, on the large numbers of men in uniform, especially police, and on the large numbers of beggars. The French only on the *Caudillo*'s portrait, for they too had various police forces at home and a conscript army, and the beggars were what they associated with Spain anyway. The South Americans noticed the austerity of the lives of their cousins whom they had gone to visit and the absence of large American cars, indeed of cars generally except official cars with the letters PMM or ET on them.[11] They heard tales of atrocities before and during the Civil War, of executions as late as 1943, and of arrests till about 1944; but they

[11] These were even more noticeable from 1950 onwards. PMM stood for *Parque Movil Ministerios* (Government Ministries' Pool) and ET for *Ejército Terrestre* (Land Army). Popularly PMM stood for *Para Mi Mujer,* (for my wife) and ET for *Este También* (this one too). The tourists were for the most part wealthy Argentines, Peruvians, Venezuelans, Cubans, and Colombians.

neither heard nor saw anything to warrant the term 'White Terror'. On the contrary, by contemporary Argentine and other South American standards, the government seemed reasonably liberal. On 10 December 1948 Churchill spoke bluntly against the continued ostracism of Spain. He was sure that there was more freedom there than anywhere beyond the Iron Curtain and that so far from leading to the downfall of Franco the continued ostracism of Spain had in fact consolidated Franco's position.

As the East-West Cold War was intensified, so 'the case of Spain' ceased to be a major preoccupation of the western powers; and in communist propaganda the iniquities of Franco had to take second place to those of the western powers. Truman was now prepared to lend Franco a small amount of American money to help out Spain's economy, while Britain was anxious to recover her lost trade. Spain was beginning to court the Arab states and appeared to be doing so remarkably successfully and even to Britain's discomfiture, for the Middle East had been Britain's private sphere of influence since the defeat of Germany. In October 1950, the South American countries again moved in the United Nations the reversal of the 1946 resolution. With the full backing of the Arab states this time, they obtained thirty-seven votes, including that of the U.S.A.; only the Soviet Bloc, Mexico, and Guatemala voted against; Britain was one of the twelve abstainers – a Labour government was still in power. Spain was now free to join the U.N. agencies, though not as yet the U.N., and countries were at liberty to send ambassadors.

Between 1949 and 1953 the yearly number of tourists increased from 750,000 to 1·7 million. It was the dictator Primo de Rivera who had first realized the economic potential of turning Spain into a tourists' paradise. Visitors to Spain in the 1920s had been either upper-class west Europeans who demanded first-class roads and a line of good hotels as they journeyed in large and sturdy cars to fashionable resorts, or serious-minded school-teachers and students from West and Central Europe prepared to pass the night anywhere so long as it did not cost too much. The newcomers of 1950–53 were people of much more varied economic means and occupations, and much more numerous. The state carried out a survey of every hotel and lodging-house, classified them, and bound them rigorously to fixed tariffs. It developed the Primo de Rivera plan of converting disused castles, palaces, and conventual houses into state-owned hotels for motorists, and gave private enterprise every encouragement to build hotels in cities and near beaches, especially on the Costa Brava. Now the tourists not only brought money into the country, but also made the railway system economically less ruinous. Much of the money obtained as 'aid' from the U.S.A. in 1950 went in the purchase of new rolling-stock. It was to be a decade before locomotives made a century earlier were taken out of service and fifteen years before the railway system could cope with the ever-increasing tourist traffic and ordinary traffic; but a good start was then made – and the authorities learnt from mistakes.

These early tourists had to cope with inconveniences – especially the British. Frontier police scrutinized documents closely. While resident foreign correspondents had long been free to send de-spatches without censorship, visiting reporters were discouraged : in the opinion of the authorities too many came not merely with a critical eye but with the intention of 'writing up' what they saw or heard which satisfied their prejudices and gave body to their pre-conceived theory that Spain was a 'clerico-Fascist dictatorship'. Few of the reporters spoke Spanish and those who thought they did had no more than a smattering. It was easy to contact the 'under-ground', especially the socialist and left-republican. Though the top leaders were all in exile, many who had occupied even high posi-tions had remained behind. They had not all been condemned to death (or if they had, their sentences had been commuted), and many sentenced to twenty and thirty years were now at liberty (under the age-long Spanish system of amnesties to celebrate national and religious feasts or events). Equally in the privacy of their rooms in universities or private houses, or in the publicity of restaurants or crowded wine-bars (where a glass of white wine then cost a quarter of a U.S. cent or a halfpenny), they would answer at length any questions that were asked of them. 'Redemption through work' had not converted them to the régime – quite the contrary.

What irked the socialists and left-republicans most was the evi-dent return to a position of influence of the Church. In the worst days of the persecution of the defeated (1939–43), a good word on the part of a cleric had often meant the difference between death and prison, or a long sentence and a short one. What those who served sentences in prison had hated most about it, was not the harshness of the labour they had had to do nor the occasional brutality of their warders, but compulsory church attendance. Out-side prison the people had flocked to the churches : a practising Catholic could not be a Marxist, or vice versa; therefore it had been politically wise to be seen attending church services. (The alternative, which many preferred, had been to profess ultra-Falangist views – the 'life buoy' as Queipo de Llano had called it.) Cardinal Gomá had not been deceived by the apparent return to

Catholicism.[12] Nevertheless, there was a genuine return as well, and by 1953 those who went to church did so voluntarily and no longer for their own personal safety. Figures varied from area to area. In the Basque provinces – excluding Bilbao city – there could hardly have been much improvement on the pre-war figures, for the Basques had then been practising Catholics with few exceptions, and the war had made no difference to their religion, any more than to their conviction that they were not Spaniards except by political accident and defeat in war. There was little change either in Navarre; but elsewhere there was, on average, an improvement of over 100 per cent. Where in Madrid practising Catholics had numbered about 10 per cent, now it was 25 per cent :[13] in Málaga province and diocese the figure was about 4 against 2 per cent, and rising.

The spleen which the left showed when talking of the Church's influence in the new Spain was moderate compared with that of the genuine Falangist. In very real ways the Church was in direct competition with the *Falange* for the allegiance and soul of the people, especially the young. The organization Catholic Action had a third of a million active members, 240,000 of them young men and women. In the *Falange* Youth there were not so many activists. Catholic Action groups engaged in charitable and social welfare work in competition with the *Falange*'s own *Auxilio Social*. The *Falange* Youth units had chaplains attached to them and they were not all men convinced by Falangism. The *sindicatos* had Catholic sociologists, Jesuits in particular, to advise them at national level, and at local level, especially in the Basque provinces, managers of factories were readier to be advised by priests on social matters than by Falangists. The strength of church influence varied from province to province, and within provinces : strongest in the north and weakest in the south, strongest in such provinces as Santander where there was a high degree of literacy, weakest where, as in Jaén, the percentage of illiteracy was much higher than the national average of 20 per cent.

Not all Catholics agreed with the Church's permeation of the official state institutions. Clergy and laity could be grouped into believers in the régime and opponents of the régime on matters of principle. The opponents could be further divided into those who made their opposition known on every occasion – the most vocal being Cardinal Segura, with whose views on subjects other than the

[12] Cf. Juan de Iturralde, *El catolicismo y la cruzada de Franco* (Toulouse 1955, 1960, 1965), Vol. III, pp. 530–1.
[13] As elsewhere, by 'practising' I mean men and women fulfilling the commandment of the Church to hear Mass on Sundays.

régime many Catholics disagreed – and those who accepted it as 'the best in the circumstances', in that no radical change could be brought about without further bloodshed. These were in their turn separable into those who believed that in collaborating with the régime, the Church would be held responsible as a whole for its sins of commission and omission and never given credit for the way in which it had directed the state towards social justice and Christian values, and those who maintained that whereas overt opposition had been proved sterile, their apparent collaboration had been fruitful. There was, finally, another group of whom Angel Herrera, now bishop of Málaga, was the most notable. His background was sufficiently well known for no one to doubt that he was fundamentally opposed to the régime. He had given up journalism and politics at the outbreak of the Civil War to become a priest and had been named bishop by the Pope in 1946 after a long tussle between the Vatican and Madrid. During the early 1940s a young Falangist, José Luis Arrese, had made a name for himself in Málaga planning new suburbs to replace slum dwellings. The plans had brought him to the notice of Madrid and in 1941 Franco had made him Secretary-General of the *Movimiento*. As the plans had remained plans and neither *Falange* nor government was prepared to act, the bishop had on his own initiative begun a housing programme of substantial magnitude, but the Falangists put difficulties in his way. Eventually the government was forced to act in its own interests and build; but the bishop, rather than the *Caudillo*, remained the man on whom the masses looked as their leader.

Churchmen had a say in the censorship of the printed word, films, and plays. It was their task to examine all manuscripts prior to publication and all plays and films before public showing, and to prohibit any which presented as morally good what the Church had ruled morally evil or any dogma as true which the Church had anathematized. Such churchmen were employees of the state and on the whole they were far more cautious than the *censores diputati* of bishops. There was plenty of reading material. Books, especially works on history, the arts, and sciences, were being produced in relative quantity : much poetry and many novels not without literary merit were being published. In the literary cafés of Madrid and other cities, dilettantes would rail against the censorship, but the critic, shown manuscripts which had been forbidden publication, could be left wondering after reading them whether they were in fact the masterpieces that their authors proclaimed them to be. Foreign publishers rejected them as thoroughly as the Spanish censors. On the other hand, rather as in the days of the Inquisition, artistic, literary, or historical merit could mollify the officials. As during the war, lay state censors continued to stop the publication in newspapers of papal, pastoral, or other ecclesiastical pronouncements containing or even remotely implying criticism of the régime. There was one periodical exempted from censorship – *Ecclesia*, a weekly with limited circulation, which took the authorities to task severely, especially on their wages policy.

Under the Labour Charter the government had promised a minimum wage for all workers. Although large families received subsidies and had priority for new housing, beds in hospitals, and school places, wage-earners found it quite impossible to make ends meet on that wage. Workers in cities had to undertake two jobs, to the detriment of their efficiency in both, and to their family life, which still meant much to the Spaniard. Those in rural districts and fishermen, however, had no such opportunity. *Ecclesia* argued that wages should be higher : the government that the economy could not stand it. The gross national product of the country was almost up to the 1935 level by 1950, but this overall figure covered up the fact that taking the 1935 level as 100, agricultural production stood at 86·5 per cent and that half Spain's labour force was engaged in agriculture.[14] Furthermore, in 1950 there were almost 28 million to be fed, nearly 4 million more than in 1935. The hard economic fact was that the production of a ton of wheat, a litre of olive oil, a crate of fruit, took three or more times the number of man hours that it took elsewhere. Until that could be improved, there was little which could be done. The government added that it was doing its best by encouraging the growth of industries.

In 1941 Franco had established a national development corporation – the *Instituto Nacional de Industria*. Falangists had welcomed it because it fitted in with their founder's socialist outlook on the ownership of the means of production. It was empowered to acquire controlling shares in private firms and to establish state-owned enterprises. Inevitably after a few years of working it had aroused the antagonism of private entrepreneurs who accused it of unfair competition in that it had the control of raw materials in short supply. It had undoubtedly squandered money on ill-conceived and costly plans; but it had also opened new shipyards and mines. The efficiency of its workings varied, but private industry itself had no brilliant record, being unwilling to plough back profits and to renew its capital equipment. INI engaged in enterprises of national prestige and doubtful economy (it took over Iberia airlines which would not pay for many years), but at the same time it must be recognized

[14] The comparison is not strictly fair, for the years 1931–5 had ideal weather for bumper harvests and the 1935 industrial output was considerably above that of 1934, the year of the 'October revolution'.

that the government was forced into the uneconomic production
of many an article because Spain could not otherwise acquire it
during World War II. With the country ostracized by the U.N.
and denied any help from the Marshall Plan, the policy of economic
autarky was inevitable, Falangist principles or no.

Strikes and demonstrations remained illegal. Nevertheless, in
March 1951 the régime had to face a disturbing demonstration
when over a quarter of a million Barcelonese boycotted public
transport for over two days after fares had been raised. The local
police fired on the demonstrators, killing three and wounding
twenty-five others – altogether a new experience for the régime.
Somewhat in panic the government rushed 3,000 of the *Policía
Armada* into the city. The bishop's appeal for order was more
effective in quieting a population which was not concerned so much
with the small rise in the uneconomically small fare as with the
belief that, as of old, Madrid was milking industrial Catalonia to
benefit the rest of Spain. In April a quarter of a million Basques
downed tools and demanded a 50 per cent wage increase. Their
clergy supported them and *Ecclesia* openly stated that the strikers
had every right in natural law to go on strike.

Prophesies were plentiful that the régime was about to fall, but
this did not happen and then, after ten years of drought, it began
prodigiously to rain. The many dams which had been built under
the supervision of INI began to fill. In 1950 they had been down
to 10 per cent capacity and factory after factory had had to close
for lack of power. By the end of 1951 they were two-thirds full. By
mid-May 1952 the water-level was at 85 per cent. The 1951 harvest
was good; the 1952 harvest a record. Between 1949 and 1950 the
cost of living had risen by 18 per cent and during the next year it
rose by 28 per cent; between 1951 and 1952 the rise was under one
per cent, the cost of food declining rapidly. There were substantial
increases in wages, especially for agricultural workers, though even
then they remained well below what *Acción Católica* statisticians
worked out as sufficient for a decent standard of living.

The régime nevertheless was now in a better position than at any
time since 1939. The nightly call to arms on Radio Moscow and its
Prague-based satellite *Radio España Independiente* had become
sporadic and they claimed victories for the Republican Army of
Liberation only intermittently. Regular visitors noted that in travel-
ling they were asked only most infrequently for identity papers.
Monarchists (Carlist and Juanist), Catalanists, Basques, Catholics,
Falangists old and new, left-wing republicans and socialists, all
criticized the régime from their various standpoints, but they all
recognized at heart that the time to act had passed, if ever it had

existed. The army (in which all the political and national divisions of Spain could be found) was loyal to its *generalissimo*. Spain was not absolutely united, but more united than it had been for half a century. It was not a great power, but Britain, the U.S.A., and France had made the first moves towards the exchange of ambassadors after the withdrawal of the U.N. resolution. King Abdullah of Jordan had visited the country. The heads of other Arab states were to receive in 1952 the Spanish Foreign Minister almost as a Head of State. The new British ambassador had been told bluntly that Spain wanted Gibraltar back. The new American ambassador was asking for bases for American ships and aircraft, and the U.S.A. was prepared to pay for them – Congress dangling $100 million 'aid' as a carrot. Franco was no donkey; he reckoned he could get more; and on 26 September 1953 he did.

Chapter 28

Spain under Franco: The End of
Isolation 1953–59

ON 26 SEPTEMBER 1953 the Spanish Foreign Minister, Martín Artajo, and the American ambassador, James Dunn, signed three agreements on behalf of their governments. Spain authorized the U.S.A. to develop and make use in the first place for ten years of one naval and four air-bases, provided that the Spanish flag flew over them and they remained under Spanish command. The Americans undertook to spend $191 million on the installation of the bases and new equipment for the Spanish forces and to make $85 million available to Spain for the purchase of food and industrial equipment.[1]

Most army officers welcomed the agreements. As they saw it, Spain was being brought back to her rightful place in the concert of Europe. Acutely conscious of the deficiencies in organization, training, and equipment of the Spanish army, they looked to the agreements as an opportunity to modernize it and make it an efficient, even if reduced, force.[2] There were some officers who worried lest in social intercourse with American equals in rank they should be at a disadvantage. (At the time an American corporal, for example, received as much pay as a Spanish colonel.) Others hoped that when such disparities became apparent, Spanish service rates of pay would be increased. Shopkeepers looked forward to the influx of well-paid soldiers and their families; but the non-commercial middle class were apprehensive lest that very influx should make commodities scarce and so lead to a rise in the cost of basic necessities. The experience of both was then limited to rich

[1] For a fuller account (by an American) see Arthur P. Whitaker, *Spain and the Defense of the West* (New York, 1961), pp. 28–44, on negotiations; on the agreements pp. 44–5; description pp. 56–70. See also Benjamin Welles, *The Gentle Anarchy* (London and New York, 1965), pp. 285–92. Anticipating the agreements, and that with a part of the money the army might be modernized, the Cabinet made provision in June for the retirement of 2,000 officers.
[2] The Cabinet decreed the reduction in June. The army was to be reduced in strength gradually to 250,000 and in organization from twenty to eighteen divisions.

tourists and they did not know about the American Post Exchange which would largely deprive the shopkeepers of the realization of their hopes, and the housewives of their fears. Churchmen and the lower-middle classes in general were more apprehensive and critical of the agreements on other grounds. Keen cinemagoers, they imagined Americans as a nation of trigger-happy gangsters, drunkards, swindlers, and men and women unfaithful in marriage. The 'old shirts' looked upon the agreements as yet another betrayal by Franco of José Antonio's Falangist principles. Franco, they said, was creating 'five Gibraltars'. They divided mentally the $85 million by Spain's 30 million inhabitants and asked what benefit to the economy could be expected from such a pittance per head. Traditionalists judged the agreements to be the beginning of a new period of embroilment in Europe and, with memories of the wars of the Habsburgs and Bourbons, murmured forebodings of impending disaster. However, by 1953 a new group, later called 'technocrats', was coming to the fore, for the most part university professors and ex-university men, inclined to believe with the Head of State that the current European ideologies were neither noxious nor irrelevant to Spain, and firmly of the opinion that Spain had much to learn from Europe and America in national administration and industrial and business management. They considered the agreements as the opening for a substantial flow of foreign capital into Spain and an exodus of men who would study beyond the Pyrenees or overseas how the national and individual business economy could be better run.

Many of those who disapproved of the agreements on the day of their signature came to approve of them within a few days.[3] They changed their minds, affronted by the comments of British politicians, editorial writers, and broadcasters. These upbraided the U.S.A. for aiding 'a Fascist régime' and for entering into an alliance with 'an enemy of democracy' : but, the Spaniards objected, there had been no word of censure when American aid had been extended to communist Yugoslavia or to Portugal, whose régime was far from democratic; indeed, Portugal's 'Fascist' rule had been no bar to her membership of the North Atlantic Treaty Organization. To Spaniards the conclusion was inescapable that the British were cloaking the truth with fine words; that the truth was that Britain hated Spain rather than the régime; and that the British were motivated by no nobler sentiment than envy of another's material good and by no morality but that of the narrowest nationalist self-interest. For the strengthening of western defence a prosperous Spain was desirable; for Britain's more immediate private ends a weak Spain was preferable. The right revived memories of

[3] Observations from conversations in Spain.

Britain's pro-left attitude during the Civil War and the Navicerts which had contributed to the hunger of the 1940s. The left recalled convictions that the British government had promised sometime during World War II that it would destroy Franco once it had defeated Hitler.[4] If, therefore, the U.S.A. had within the agreements strengthened Franco's position, Britain could blame no one but herself, for if Britain had kept to her promise, Franco would not have been there to make the agreements.

Almost the only Spaniards who continued to look favourably on Britain were monarchists: the traditionalists because to them Queen Elizabeth II, happily married, embodied their ideals of a sovereign; the others because she had invited their king, her cousin Don Juan, to her coronation in June 1953. Several thousand monarchists journeyed to London to cheer the two of them and all other persons of royal blood gathered for the occasion. That they had been granted passports and visas infuriated the Falangists, whose newspaper, *Arriba,* thereupon published articles, not always in the best taste, criticizing Britain, British colonial policies, and British products. The announcement at the end of July that the queen would visit Gibraltar at the end of her forthcoming Commonwealth tour gave the paper the opportunity to vent its anti-British spleen as it had not done since Serrano Suñer had ceased to be its mentor a decade earlier. The press had indeed already been given the directive not to praise Britain but to press Spanish claims to the British colony. British commentators explained the furore over the announcement as engineered by the *Falange.* They would have been nearer the mark had they known what Spanish writers had written on Gibraltar over the previous 200 years and had they not been British. For the engrained courtesy of the Spaniard inhibited him from displaying openly to an Englishman how vehemently he felt about Gibraltar unless he could be made to forget that the man he was addressing was British; but for that to happen the Briton had to speak indistinguishably from a native, and in order to realize that republicans and monarchists, men of the left as well as the right and of all classes, were affronted by the projected visit of the queen to a 'piece of Spain in alien hands', he had to go outside the circles of diplomacy and business. Only Catalans (who with some historical humour maintained that Gibraltar had been captured in 1704 for Catalonia, and more seriously that Gibraltar was no concern of theirs since they were not part of Spain) and the southerners who benefited economically from the existence of the naval dockyards,

---

[4] The British government never made such a promise: the idea that it had seems to have arisen from 'readings into' what a regular broadcaster of the time said.

disapproved of the government's revival of the claims for the Rock. Gibraltar was, as Franco said in an arranged interview with *Arriba,* 'a feeling deeply rooted in the soul of Spain'.[5]

Nevertheless, it was not till the British comments on the U.S. agreements became generally known that public opinion turned against Britain on all points and not just the subject of Gibraltar, and it was not till the late autumn and winter of 1953-4 that the agitation over Gibraltar reached effective strength. British commentators then explained it as an effort on the part of the Spanish government to divert the people's attention from local evils; but this explanation was as untenable as it was sincere.

In the late summer of 1953 Spain presented a picture of desolation : there was drought again; the harvests were poor; the water-level in the hydro-electric reservoirs was down. Madrid's residential districts were without electricity for several hours daily and those of Barcelona for three days a week. Work in Barcelona's factories dependent on electric power was severely restricted. Then in the second week of October, it began to rain, and as in 1951 it rained heavily for a long time. The wells filled, ensuring the next year's harvest—which in the event proved to be a very good one. Factories began to work by night as well as by day to make up for lost production. The Americans started recruiting local labour on the construction of their bases and the necessary roads to them. The government decreed an increase in wages. The police captured the leaders of a new, clandestine, Socialist Party acting on information seemingly supplied by workers.[6] There were, as we shall see, other political ferments, but nothing with which the authorities could not cope with ease, for they were of interest to small groups rather than the nation. It was then that demonstrations over Gibraltar began to assume the popular – as opposed to the *Falange*-stimulated – intensity which the Spanish ambassador in London, the Duke Miguel Primo de Rivera, had said the queen's visit to Gibraltar would provoke when he had made his official protest to the Foreign Office over the visit on 30 July 1953.[7]

There was another aspect of Anglo-Spanish relations at the time which escaped the notice of most British commentators. Spain was still pursuing her war- and isolation-imposed policy of economic autarky and industrialization. She was exporting all the primary produce she could spare in order to have the foreign currencies with which to buy capital equipment and machine-tools. At the

---

[5] *Discursos* (1951–4), p. 360.
[6] The Secretary-General was a forty-year-old architect's draughtsman, Tomás Centeño. He died when being interrogated. The police alleged that he committed suicide.
[7] *Spanish Red Book on Gibraltar* (Madrid, 1965), pp. 57, 285.

time Britain was anxious to export just such goods. The pattern of
Spanish imports from the U.K. during the years 1949–55 was as
follows :[8]

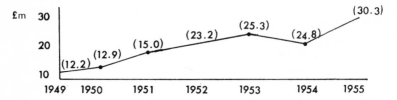

All these years Spain had millions of pounds sterling to spend.
The dip in 1954 is noticeable. On the basis of the 1952 figure it
was confidently expected in mid-1953 that the year's imports from
the U.K. would be higher than the £25·3 million realized, and that
by 1954 Spain would be importing around £30 million worth of
goods from Britain. Behind the drop towards the end of 1953 and
during 1954 was the little-publicized fact that industrialists in Spain
found it more than usually difficult to obtain the necessary permits
to import goods from Britain from September 1953 onwards : they
were encouraged to satisfy their requirements from elsewhere in
the sterling area.[9]

More noticeable and therefore more readily the subject of comment were the restrictions on the passage of goods and of people
from Gibraltar to Spain which were imposed as the date of the
queen's visit approached, restrictions which were not to be lifted
until 1960. In this year the régime was faced with internal strife
above normal, but the restrictions were reimposed, with additional
limits in October 1964 when the Spanish economy was rising
on a wind more favourable than ever in history and the political
seas of Spain were relatively calm.

This is not to say that the régime did not have internal problems
in 1953–4. The *Falange* never needed outside stimulus to be anti-
foreign and Falangists were restless, and not only because of the
alliance with the villain of the war of 1898. The U.S.–Spanish alliance had been signed within a month of another agreement which
to them was even more explicitly a betrayal of their founder's
principles. On 27 August 1953 the Vatican ratified the Concordat
for which Franco had been waiting and negotiating for fourteen
years.

The value of the Concordat to Franco was manifold. In the first
place the Vatican did not enter into peace treaties (for that is all

[8] Board of Trade exports ex-U.K. f.o.b.
[9] Conversations with industrialists, Bilbao, Madrid, Barcelona.

that Concordats are) with régimes so long as it considered them transient. Therefore the signature could be taken as a recognition by the Vatican that Franco was firmly a Head of State, a conclusion to which it had come as the U.S.—Spanish negotiations had progressed. For by mid-1952 any intelligent appreciation of the future was bound to conclude that an agreement was probable and that with American economic aid Franco's position would be unshakeable;[10] and in the early summer of 1953 it was common knowledge within official circles that the agreements were ready but for minor details. In speeches Franco was making lightly veiled references to the fact.[11] Thenceforward, therefore, the Vatican had to weigh, on the one hand, the evils of having its lines of communication with its bishops cut off at the Spanish government's will and of the state's control of the appointment of bishops and parish priests, against, on the other hand, the evil of appearing to place the chrism of legitimacy on a régime which it knew was not to the liking of a large number of the people, for Franco had come to look upon a Concordat rather as Napoleon had looked upon his anointment by Pope Pius VII.

Under the terms of the Concordat Franco recognized the Catholic Church as the Church of Spain – an irksome recognition for Falangists and Spaniards of the left at home and in exile, who all described the Concordat as capitulation to the Vatican. Franco agreed to give the clergy salaries more in keeping with 1953 than 1851. Church buildings and non-productive property were to be exempt from tax. The Church was to be allowed to acquire property; to be at liberty to open new schools in which religion was to be an integral part of the curriculum. Church holidays were to be national holidays. The police were to be forbidden entry into church property in pursuit of suspects without express permission from the ecclesiastical authorities. No priest was to be tried in a civil or criminal court without the knowledge of his ecclesiastical superiors. The state was to recognize church marriage as enough for civil purposes and as null and void any apparent marriage so declared by an ecclesiastical court. The findings of ecclesiastical courts in matters of Canon Law were to be accepted by the state. The Church was to have freedom of speech, meeting, and association for religious purposes. The state promised not to impede in the future direct communication between the Vatican and the bishops.

In Spanish republican and Falangist terms all this was a surrender

---

[10] The very observant could have deduced this even earlier. The Ministry of War's *Diario Oficial* (26 January 1952), ordered all small arms and gun calibres to be converted to U.S. army standards.

[11] Cf. *Discursos*, pp. 324 (16 May 1953), 338 (9 June), 349 (23 June).

to the Vatican. In fact the Concordat gave the Church in Spain nothing of importance that it did not have *de jure* or *de facto* in any of the English-speaking countries which had not concluded Concordats. On the other hand – and here is why internationally Catholics viewed the Concordat as the Vatican's capitulation to Spain – the Concordat ratified the 1941 arrangement on the appointment of bishops and a further agreement of 1946 giving the Head of State the power of veto over the appointment even of a parish priest 'on general political grounds' – and this was more important to the régime than the concessions.

On the whole, churchmen welcomed the Concordat, which appeared to protect the activities of the all-embracing organization *Catholic Action* whose meetings and very existence could have been challenged under the laws of association and decrees prohibiting gatherings of persons above a small number. One branch of that organization, the *Hermandades Obreras de Acción Católica*, the Catholic Action Workers' Brotherhoods,[12] was becoming particularly active, spreading not merely Catholic views on social justice, but the statements of bishops who were critical of the government's labour policies. The substance of a forthright pastoral on what constituted a living wage issued by the archbishop of Valencia was clandestinely circulated during October 1953 in the Basque and Catalan industrial areas. The Concordat had freed communication between Rome and the bishops, but communication between bishops and people was still subject to the will of the Ministries of Justice and of the Interior.

That month the National Council of the *Movimiento,* or *FET y de las JONS*, was summoned in congress. The Council then consisted of ninety-five members, representative of the *Falange*'s various elements, traditionalists, monarchists, and others, carefully selected and appointed by Franco in 1942. The congress duly endorsed what had been done with the resolution 'Spain associates herself in a definite and contractual manner with the defence of Europe and, above all, the defence of Western Christianity'. It then went on to discuss other themes and to pass other resolutions. There was to be no suppression of private property nor wholesale nationalization. There was to be a better distribution of the national income and of land, more and better housing, and higher wages tied to a cost of living index.

These resolutions reflected the true nature of the *Movimiento* and its National Council. It was the only authorized political association, but it was no more united as a party than it had been when Franco had declared the *Falange,* the traditionalists, monarch-

[12] Founded by Cardinal Plá y Deniel in 1947.

ists, and all his other supporters a single body. On its Council was to be found a minority who looked to modern Europe for inspiration, others who looked to mediaeval Spain, liberals and conservatives, clericals and anti-clericals, monarchists and republicans. The sole factor common to all its members was that they were in the Council because Franco had willed it, a Council supposed to be the inter-mediary between society and the state, the channel of communica-tion between them. Its sole purpose to date had been to act, as it were, as the government's mouthpiece of declarations of intent. The government in the face of the agitation from church circles had decided already to raise wages, but it could not be seen to be subject to any political pressures except from within itself, and by definition, or lack of it, the government itself was supposed to be interlinked with the *Movimiento*. In so far as the *Movimiento* was distinguishable from the government, it had up and down the country shabby offices, some youth and sports clubs, a women's branch (a sort of Women's Voluntary Service and Citizen's Advice Bureau combined), and a chain of newspapers, magazines, and radio stations. The radio stations were inferior in equipment, transmitting power, and professional standards to the commercial and the state stations which existed at their side. The newspapers had to compete with independent papers and these attracted more advertising and more readers. Compared with the prestigious offices and power of the government all that the *Movimiento* had was a Secretary-Gen-eral with a place in the Cabinet, an unknown number of members, and nominal control of the *sindicatos*. However, in 1948 José Luis Arrese, the *Falange* theorist, had been removed from the post of Secretary-General and the man who had taken his place, Raimundo Fernández Cuesta, for all that he was a *camisa vieja* and a com-panion of Primo de Rivera in prison, was no model of energy. Membership of the *Movimiento* did not carry any special advan-tages. On being commissioned service officers became members automatically, but they did not have to be members to be com-missioned. Similarly, on appointment to the higher echelons of the civil service and local government, a man was expected to be-come a member; it cost nothing and committed him to nothing more than loyalty to the country and the régime; but to reach the higher echelons membership was no advantage. It was only in the *sindicato* organization that membership did matter. All *sindicato* officials had to be 'militant members'. But the *sindicatos* had their own head (appointed by General Franco) and the authority of the Secretary-General of the *Movimiento* over them was nil; for they were 'instruments of the state's labour and economic policies', instruments of the Ministry of Labour. Franco had chosen as Minister in 1941 one of the most fiery and revolutionary of the Falangists, José Antonio Girón, the man of humble origin who had organized the *sindicatos*. The following year he had logically put them directly under the Minister. Girón was still Minister of Labour in 1953 and was to remain in office until 1957, sixteen years in all, a longer term than any other Minister; but then no other man served Franco more conscientiously.[13]

Those whose views were Falangist rather than *Movimiento* had to act outside the *Movimiento,* and even outside the *sindicato* organization as such. There was an 'odd man out' in that organization. This was the *Sindicato Español Universitario,* the University Students Syndicate or SEU. By reason of its very composition it could not be an instrument of economic policy. It did not fit into the pattern of employers—*técnicos*—workers. It had a historical link with the organization of the same name founded by Primo de Rivera and on its reconstitution after the Civil War and thereafter it had retained dedicated Falangists as its officers. In 1943 membership of the SEU had been made compulsory to all university students. Most paid their dues, but grumbled at having to do so and otherwise ignored its existence. The militants were not displeased with the apathy of the majority, so long as it paid dues. They welcomed recruits to pure Falangism and there would always be a minority of young men ready to accept the essentially revolutionary character of the ideology and to take part in demonstrations.

The *Falange* proper was as averse to monarchy as ever. In November 1954 Franco allowed municipal elections and four monarchist candidates contested seats in Madrid. Falangist gangs broke up their meetings and harassed known monarchists with impunity. Nevertheless, in December Franco invited the man whom the monarchists called John III, Don Juan, count of Barcelona, to meet him in Spain. The count of Barcelona's eldest son, Juan Carlos, then sixteen years old, had just completed his secondary studies. Don Juan and Franco agreed on the boy's future. He was to attend the three service academies in turn and then do a course in politics and economics at Madrid University, six years of study in all. When he arrived the following January, the SEU led demonstrations against the prince – and against Franco by inference. Franco replied to his critics through the *Falange* newspaper *Arriba* :[14] the Law of Succession, approved by referendum, had established that Spain was

---

[13] Girón knew about the Tarduchy—Thomson plot of 1941 (see above, p. 245), but it is impossible to say up to what point he was implicated.

[14] *Discursos* (1955-9), pp. 7-11. For interesting details of the monarchist moves see Welles, op. cit., pp. 352-4.

to have a king after him. The SEU went on to distribute leaflets accusing the Bourbon monarchs of a long inventory of crimes and Alfonso XIII of more of them than all his ancestors put together. Franco again replied through *Arriba* :[15] the young people, half the nation, knew no more about the Spanish monarchy than the lies they had been told; Alfonso XIII had been a great man but the victim of a thoroughly bad system of government, liberal parliamentary democracy; the monarchy would be restored in due course, but not the party system of old.

The *Falange* was not satisfied – especially as during the rest of the year Franco, as they saw it, went out of his way to offend Falangist sensibilities. At public functions he never appeared except in army uniform – and army uniform had had monarchical emblems restored to it – and he eschewed *Falange* (*Movimiento*) uniform.

Moreover, the Falangists had other reasons to be critical of the *Caudillo*. Franco welcomed with great ceremony John Foster Dulles, the U.S. Secretary of State. Spain established trade contacts with eastern Europe and full trade agreements with France and Britain. She sought, and in December 1954 obtained, entry into the United Nations, and there were well-founded rumours that she was seeking admission to, and help from, the technical experts in the International Labour Office, the International Bank for Reconstruction and Development, the International Monetary Fund, and the Organization for Economic Co-operation and Development. All this could only mean that the government was planning to end its attempt to make Spain economically self-sufficient. Economists began to state publicly that Spain's nationalistic economy was hindering development.

Indeed, the director of INI became the chief critic of that policy. So extensive had the activities of INI, the state's own development corporation, become by 1955, that it not only owned steelworks, fertilizer, synthetic fibre, and cellulose plants, but also had acquired substantial holdings in private companies. INI, however, was killing private enterprise and in any case what Spain needed for quicker development was foreign capital investment. The Falangists were horrified. To what purpose had the Americans been bought out wholly from the Telephone Company and the British partly from the Rio Tinto mines? Again the state seemed prepared to reverse its policy of trying to make Spain linguistically and culturally one. In 1954 chairs of Galician and Catalan studies were established in the University of Madrid. By 1955 the lists of books available in Catalan and Gallego were substantially long. In 1955 a chair of Basque was added at Salamanca. Basque language academies

15 *Discursos,* pp. 13-23.

were allowed to open in the Basque provinces and the strict limits on the use of Basque and Catalan in sermons were relaxed. The Church was allowed to air its criticisms of government policy to a degree unthinkable even a year previously, the secular press printing references to more protests against wages and housing shortages. *Ecclesia*, free from disabilities, carried an all-out campaign against press censorship; there was nothing new in that, but what was new was that a long exchange of letters between Bishop Angel Herrera and the Minister of Information, Arias Salgado, on censorship was published in the secular press. All this in Falangist eyes was giving the Church too much importance and power; and to crown everything, in October 1955 the first of the new workers' universities was opened in Gijón, with an intake of 2,500 pupils, 1,000 of them resident – under the control of the Jesuits.

The head of the SEU was removed in September to ensure that the academic year would begin without trouble from the students; but there was trouble all the same. On 20 November a *Falange* youth insulted Franco to his face;[16] José Antonio Elola, an old shirt, who since 1941 had been the *Falange (Movimiento)* Youth's director, was ordered to resign. In his customary New Year message[17] Franco appealed to parents to control their children and urged all Spaniards to concentrate on the ideas which united them rather than on what was of no importance and yet caused disunity; but the Falangists, and in particular those in the SEU, were now fully aroused. So, however, were other members of SEU, the non-Falangist students with Christian Democratic, liberal and socialist, monarchist, traditionalist, and republican ideals, who objected that the SEU was no union of students but an organization imposed by the state on the students and to whom the payment of dues was irksome. On 9 February 1956 the Falangists in Madrid again organized a demonstration against Prince Juan Carlos, which became a battle between them and the rest. A Falangist fired a pistol, the shot wounding one of his fellows. The police belaboured both sides and there were arrests. The anti-Falangists protested against the arrests and made overt demands for the abolition of the SEU. The rector of the university, Dr Laín Entralgo, wrote an open letter to the Head of State declaring himself on the side of the abolitionists. The Falangists drew up a list of army men, government officials, and intellectuals whom they regarded as being their special enemies and armed themselves. Shortly after noon on 10 February Generals Muñoz Grandes, then Army Minister, Rodrigo, the Captain-General of the Madrid Military Region, and Martínez Campos, on whom

16 Accounts vary as to what he did.
17 *Discursos*, pp. 122 et seq.

Franco and Don Juan had agreed as tutor to Prince Juan Carlos, called on the *Caudillo* to acquaint him of the gravity of the situation. In the university campus it looked as if matters were getting out of hand and as if the riots might reach the proportions of the student riots which had set in motion the fall of the monarchy in 1868 and of Primo de Rivera in 1930. The generals urged action.[18] After his customary hesitation Franco ordered the arrest of the Falangists and the suspension in Madrid of the Articles in the *Fuero* guaranteeing freedom of movement, and the appearance in court of an individual within 72 hours of arrest.

The university was closed until Easter. Dr Laín Entralgo, who had been a prominent Falangist in the 1940s, was dismissed and so was the Minister of Education, Ruíz Giménez, whose membership of the *Movimiento* had been purely nominal. Like Laín, Ruíz Giménez was a lawyer, but his principal extra-professional interest had been the international Catholic university graduates' organization, *Pax Romana*. The Foreign Minister, Martín Artajo, prominent in *Acción Católica*, had once suggested to Franco that Ruíz Giménez would make a good ambassador to the Holy See, and Ruíz Giménez had himself come to the conclusion that he could do more good, as he saw it, working within the régime than in opposition. In July 1951 Franco had transferred him to the Ministry of Education, though it was known that his views on education and politics were more liberal and international than those of the régime; he was able and he was young. His subsequent election to the presidency of *Pax Romana* was held to bring prestige to Spain, but his head had to roll because a *Falange* head had to roll. Franco rarely dismissed a man representative of one view without dismissing one of contrary opinion; and the *Falange* head was that of the Secretary-General of the *Movimiento* and *ex-officio* cabinet Minister, Fernández Cuesta.

There had been one political development within the *Movimiento* in the eight years during which Fernández Cuesta had been its Secretary-General. In 1955 the nominated Council of ninety-five had been replaced by a 160-member body, of which fifty had been elected to it by the local *FET y de las JONS* associations, the rest

[18] Cf. the events of February 1969. *Le Monde's* correspondent, Jean Créac'h, *Le Coeur et l'épée* (Paris, 1959) has the generals declaring that if any of the Falangists' intended victims were harmed, the army would be forced to take over Madrid to restore order. From my knowledge of the involved situation, I would think it more likely that they said to Franco that the army was prepared (i.e., in a state of readiness) to restore order. Not too much, however, should be read into this. Franco had the custom of maintaining an open door to his senior officers, and at audiences with general and even field officers of inviting them to speak their minds; how freely they did so depended on individual nerve.

being cabinet members *ex-officio,* senior service officers, other state officials, and Franco's nominees.

Franco now put José Luis de Arrese back in the post of Secretary-General and charged him with two tasks. First he was to bring the extremists under control. He managed to quieten them down, but not before some army officers of the Madrid region had informed the Captain-General and made it known to Arrese that in the event of further trouble from the Falangists, they would not wait for orders to bring them to heel.[19] Secondly Arrese was to examine anew whether the *Movimiento* could be given a definite shape, closely defined idealism and purpose, and determined unity.

Arrese summoned Falangists to a national conference to discuss what the *Movimiento* was and what they wanted it to be. What Franco had said in the past about the *Movimiento,* when closely analyzed, provided no clear or coherent picture of what he intended it to be. He had repeatedly obfuscated meaning with rhetoric. He had frequently distinguished between *Movimiento* and *Falange,* referring to the latter as just a part of the former; but when the new Council had been sworn in, he had said : 'You know that the *Falange* is a movement; that it is not a party; and being a movement at the service of the Motherland, you know that it aspires to unite the peoples and the lands of Spain. We are not a sealed organization. We are a community whose spirit is of service, whose doors are open to all Spaniards who will work with us, whose hearts are ready to welcome to it all who have patriotic yearnings, all the desires of our brothers . . .'[20] Was the *Falange,* then, the *Movimiento* after all? What was to be made of Franco's repeated phrase 'the successor of the *Movimiento* is the *Movimiento*'?[21] Did this mean that it should be an institution, for only organized institutions could be said to be self-renovating?

Through February and March 1956 Franco was silent. The word *Movimiento* was noticeably absent during his speeches in April. Arrese now had definite orders to prepare *Leyes Fundamentales* (Basic Laws – the régime's open-ended substitute for a constitution). Franco had decided to give the *Falange* yet one more chance to lead Spain into unity behind him. Arrese was given till the end of the year. He worked away on his own theories as to what the *Movimiento* should be, how it could be made into an institution,

[19] There was some talk at the time in left-wing civilian circles in Spain and abroad of *Juntas de Acción Patriótica.* The Madrid region officers who made their anti-Falangist views known, may possibly have called themselves a *junta,* though I have doubts whether they did. They were too amorphous a body to be worthy of the name.

[20] *Discursos,* pp. 41–2.

[21] Ibid., p. 61.

and what its position should be then in relation to government. He had no patience with its actual position, a nebulous body of men vaguely subscribing to twenty-six points which defined aims so loosely that almost anyone could swear to uphold them without violating his conscience.

On 1 May Franco was called upon to address a gathering in Seville of 25,000 non-*Movimiento* Falangists. His speech, in which he challenged anyone present to pinpoint any deviation on his or on the government's part from those twenty-six points, was in essence a warning to Falangists who would not accept a monarchy and to monarchists who would not accept the *Falange*, and especially to anyone seeking to set the *Falange* against the army or fostering speculation as to who would succeed him as Head of State. The Movement was 'faith in Spain', 'discipline', 'and a desire to serve the motherland'. The shape of the vessel containing that spirit did not matter. 'What is our political movement? A movement of unity, of hierarchy, of authority : we are like a pyramid at whose apex is one person, and we have one discipline and one obedience'.[22]

All this did not help Arrese; for on the one hand 'the shape did not matter', and on the other hand it was 'a pyramid'.

On 17 July 1956, the twentieth anniversary of the rising in Morocco, Franco addressed the National Council of the *Movimiento*. This time he went through the twenty-six points one by one.[23] As he did so he reviewed what he had done to fulfil them and where so far, especially in social justice, much had still to be done. But the Movement would be self-developing and to that end the Council would soon have to consider new *Leyes Fundamentales*. What these might contain in a final form no one knew. Arrese had had one, or possibly two, drafts of a *Ley Fundamental* on the *Movimiento* rejected at cabinet and higher levels.[24]

It was often said that the Franco régime rested on three pillars, the army, the Church, and the *Falange*. If so, it would have collapsed quickly. It would have been brought down by the *Falange* suborned by the Germans or by the Church before 1953 (or again after about 1960). The one pillar – if this metaphor must be used – was always the army; and even the army had its Falangist, Yagüe, pro-German followers of Tarduchy, and monarchist

[22] Ibid., pp. 181–90.
[23] Ibid., pp. 201–30.
[24] The left-wing New York based *Ibérica* (October 1956), Vol. IV, No. 10, published what was said to be a document from an army *junta*. I should like evidence that it was genuine or that on 1 July a delegation of generals went to tell Franco that Arrese's proposals were unacceptable. Individual officers did so in the normal way — see above, p. 285, note 18.

generals. Apart from those who in 1943 had 'humbly petitioned' Franco to restore the monarchy,[25] others had from time to time secretly pledged their fealty to Don Juan. An apter metaphor would be to compare Franco to the driver of a troika drawn by three horses each trying to go a separate way; restlessness in one immediately causing restlessness in one of or both the others; a pull in this or that direction being immediately controlled by curbing the rein on one side or loosening it on the other – and on occasion by using the whip.

In February 1956, as we have seen, the most restless was the *Falange* and its friskiness came near to making the army rear and kick it. Almost immediately afterwards an event took place which the enemies of the régime hoped would make the army bolt and overturn the troika.

On 10 January 1956 France suddenly announced that she intended to begin giving up her protectorate of Morocco on 2 March. Spain had granted to her zone of Morocco partial autonomy in 1952, and since 1953 had been harbouring the supporters of Sultan Mohammed bin Yusuf, whom the French had deposed, allowing them to broadcast independence propaganda from Radio Tetuan and to organize, or at least to form up, before the major assault on the French in October 1955.

Franco had long been fully aware that sooner or later Spain's control over her part of Morocco would have to be surrendered. Even in his African days he had urged his fellow Spaniards to recognize the Moroccan way of thinking;[26] and it was because he himself had done this so completely that in 1936 he had been able immediately to command the loyalty of the Moroccan troops in the Spanish army and the support of the Moroccan authorities, and that although the Spanish zone had not been as developed as the French, it had long been the more peaceful and known to the Moroccans as the 'happy' one. From 1951, when he had appointed one of his old corps commanders, García Valiño (perhaps his best tactician), High Commissioner, his object had been twofold : first, to appear to be ahead of the French in leading Morocco to independence, so that when independence came Morocco would look to Spain and not to France for 'spiritual' inspiration; and secondly, to go no faster than was absolutely necessary to give the officers and N.C.O.s in the army (the young rather than the older who like Franco appreciated the reality of Moroccan thought) time to reconcile themselves to the consequences. Service in the army, once

[25] See above, p. 258.
[26] *Revista de Tropas Coloniales,* No. 1 (January 1924); cf. other subsequent articles.

the Spanish Protectorate had ceased to exist, would be limited to garrison duties in the peninsula or the essentially Spanish cities in Africa, Ceuta and Melilla, or to patrols in the unpleasant Spanish Sahara and Guinea. As the Moroccan units of the Spanish army would presumably pass into a new Moroccan army, their Spanish officers would have to be found new posts in the peninsular army. For nearly fifty years, service in Morocco had been popular among the many officers with no private means, for there alone, with the special allowances provided, could an officer live on his pay. Naturally the more Spain could befriend Moroccan nationalists, the more disposed they would be to have Spanish rather than French advisers – but even the advisers would have to leave in the end.

Franco's policy was naturally displeasing to France. By her announcement of 10 January she had jumped ahead of Franco who the previous December had made his position clear – that he supported Sultan Mohammed bin Yusuf; that the man the French had put in his place, Mohammed bin Arefa, was a 'quisling'; that he sympathized fully with the 'natural desires of the Moroccan people'; and that the French formula 'independence within independence' was Protectorate 'writ large'.[27] France had outmanoeuvred him and Franco had rapidly to arrange the liquidation of the Spanish Protectorate. This he did, by 9 April 1956, but not before skirmishes had occurred in the hitherto 'happy zone'. His Muslim colleague of the African war and corps commander during the Civil War, General El Mizzian, became one of the three generals in the new Moroccan army, and was soon to be the army's inspector-general, but Spain's influence in the newly independent country was to be less than France's, who had more money to offer.

On 29 April Franco addressed the officers of the Seville Military District – and in effect the whole army. The first twelve minutes of his short speech were devoted to two themes : fire-power, not size, is what counts in a modern army; the Spanish army of the future is going to be smaller than it was in the past. The last four minutes were a reminder that Spain had accepted 'the bones of Morocco, an inhospitable coast and a few arid mountains' in temporary trust and an explanation that he would have liked to have handed the Protectorate back to the Sultan better developed (implying 'a little later').[28]

Franco's civilian and military critics believed that he could have

---

[27] *Ibérica*, of course, and Elena de la Souchère, *Explication de l'Espagne* (Paris, 1962) give quite a different interpretation and, following them, Payne in *Politics and the Military in Modern Spain* (New York and London, 1967), pp. 440–1. Whitaker, op. cit., is sounder.

[28] *Discursos*, pp. 115–20.

kept the Spanish zone.[29] For Spaniards who had lived or served in Africa it was as difficult to realize that the colonial era was over as it was for the British who lived or served in India. There were murmurs, especially in army circles where officers (and N.C.O.s) spoke their minds, but they were a handful. The troika was not upset as republican exiles had confidently expected that it would be; it cannot even be said that it was rocked. The cabinet decision of June 1953 to retire gradually 2,000 officers of the army had not been done without an eye on the Moroccan outlook; but there was still the loss of pay to consider. Army salaries had last been raised, by 40 per cent, in 1949. Since that date the cost of living had almost doubled. In July 1956 new salaries were announced. The pay of majors and lieutenant-colonels was raised by 103 per cent; that of second lieutenants was increased by 77 per cent; and that of lieutenant-generals by 62 per cent.[30]

The régime's troubles were still not over. In April 1956 the government had decreed a 20 per cent increase in the basic wage (the first big increase since 1953). Workers in Pamplona had thereupon gone on strike because the percentage was not enough; a Catholic Action inquiry in 1954 had proved that the minimum necessary if workers were to live with a minimum of 'dignity' was then 50 per cent, and the cost of living had risen sharply since the inquiry. Priests justified the workers' action from their pulpits. Police, drafted to Pamplona, met with a unique method of resistance, for the workers congregated in the main square and, as the police advanced, knelt down and began to recite the rosary. Having thus stopped the police in their tracks, they went back to work. With the breaking-out of strikes in Basque and Catalan industrial plants, the Church now took up the workers' case officially. On 15 August 1956 the hierarchy, in an unwonted display of unanimity, declared 'the right and duty of the Church to intervene in social problems' and indicted the whole of Franco's labour and wages policy.[31]

The government gave way on the wages issue and instead of 20 per cent, increases were allowed of 30 per cent and in some cases more. In granting them the government knew that it had solved nothing and that within months higher prices would have absorbed the increases. What was required was a thorough examination of all aspects of industrial and economic policy, fiscal methods, such investment in industry as was based on the hope of making

[29] Having asked the critics 'how?', I never heard a realistic answer.
[30] Lt.-Gen. 68,000 ptas. a month (worth, say, $1,100,, or £400), Lt.-Col. 37,100 ptas. ($550, £200), 2nd Lt. 16,150 ($270, £95).
[31] Full text was published as an appendix, pp. 173–92, in *El momento social de España* (Madrid, 1959).

Spain self-sufficient, and the monetary policy of keeping the peseta at a value in the international money market quite unrelated to the facts of the situation. All this had to wait, however, for by October 1956 the political situation was again becoming critical. Arrese presented a third draft of the *Leyes Fundamentales*, the new constitution.

Copies of the proposals went into wide and possibly unauthorized circulation in October. What Arrese proposed showed remarkable resemblance to Soviet socialist constitutions – especially the Czech, for he envisaged Spain as a truly totalitarian one-party state. The party was in theory to be supreme but in practice ruled by an élite in a National Council (Central Committee) which would appoint its own Secretary-General, the Head of State, the government, and the Cabinet, and consider, veto, or approve laws. There was to be a *Cortes* akin to the Supreme Soviet and politically powerless.

Opposition to the proposals was voiced by all who read them (other than extreme Falangists) and most outspokenly by prelates and army officers.[32] The Cabinet considered the drafts officially only immediately after Christmas. Arrese defended his proposals heatedly against their critics, vehemently supported by the Minister of Labour, Girón, and opposed by the Foreign Minister, Martín Artajo, and the Minister of War, Muñoz Grandes. The proposals were offensive to monarchists and unacceptable to the Church. (The Primate, Cardinal Plá y Deniel, was said to have informed the Head of State in audience that this was the hierarchy's opinion.) The drafts were shelved.

The rapid growth of a minor into a major incident showed how sensitive the whole political situation had become. Fares were raised from 60 to 80[33] centimos on Barcelona's heavily subsidized transport. On 14 January 1957 the inhabitants of that city walked to and from work in protest not only against the fares but against fuel shortages caused by administrative mismanagement. In the university a young Carlist, Modolell, delivered to a large audience a violent attack against the régime; portraits of Primo de Rivera and Franco in the lecture halls were torn down; and police invaded the university area on horse and foot to bring the students to heel. The archbishop of Tarragona (senior cleric in Catalonia) protested

---

[32] I am not sure that the 'leak' was not deliberate and that it did not occur at the highest level. As Head of State Franco had to be 'above party' (or above the 'no-party' of the new Spain). This was very much a partisan document, so its rejection had to come from 'the people' – and that the 'people' would reject it was obvious except to Arrese and the Falangists proper.

[33] At the time, at unofficial rates of exchange, from the equivalent of one penny to a penny-halfpenny.

against the brutality of the methods used, as did the captain-general
of the Catalan military region, General Juan Bautista Sánchez.
After further police—student encounters during the next few days,
the civil government appealed in the press and on the radio for
order, but did not restrain the police. Sánchez confined all troops to
barracks, a move interpreted by the people as a sign that they had
his sympathy. He died from a heart attack on the 20th. Inevitably
the rumour ran through the city that he had been assassinated[34]
and his funeral was attended by a large body of angry but leaderless
civilians. Car-owners and taxi-drivers gave free lifts to the old and
infirm; some factories organized lorry services. Nevertheless by the
29th, the boycott was over.[35]

The official Gazette published briefly the news of the Barcelona
troubles on Monday 4 February. Leaflets calling for a boycott of
Madrid's public transport on the following Thursday and Friday
'in solidarity with the citizens of Barcelona' and 'in protest against
the corruption of government officials' were rapidly circulated. The
press was ordered to eulogize the régime and its accomplishments,
to speculate on what horror might have been perpetrated had the
losing side in the Civil War been victorious, and to make widespread accusations against foreign countries, and France in particular, of engineering the unrest 'to cover up for their aggression in
Suez and their betrayal of the Hungarian Revolution' and of seeking to undermine the Spanish national economy. On the Thursday
Madrid's normally overcrowded trams ran virtually empty. From
the old university building in Madrid city a column of Falangist
students marched to attack those walking to work. From the
university city itself a column of anti-Falangists hastened to repel
the attack. Both came into contact with the police.

The Falangists had been weighed in the balance and found
wanting. Falangist ideas on the rationalization of the *Movimiento*
had been proved once again unacceptable to the other bodies with

[34] As on many other occasions a people denied accurate information by
censorship listened to wild rumour. One version of events had Sánchez
writing to Franco to complain about army pay; Franco sending Muñoz
Grandes to Barcelona to dismiss Sánchez; Sánchez threatening rebellion if
removed. The left cast Muñoz Grandes in the role of an ogre when he was
appointed G.O.C. the Blue Division : so did the Falangists who knew that he
had been appointed as part of Franco's moves against Serrano Suñer's idea
of a *Falange* (not an army) volunteer force to fight in Russia; and the
Falangists always looked on Muñoz Grandes as responsible jointly with
Franco for the frustration of their hopes that they would achieve complete
power in Spain. For a kinder and vivid picture of Muñoz Grandes see
Welles, op. cit., pp. 57–62.

[35] During the week preceding the boycott leaflets from the French-based
Partit Socialista Unificat de Catalunya began to circulate : they were not
welcome to the original organizers of the boycott.

political power or influence in the state. Furthermore, the policy of economic nationalism so dear to the heart of the Falangists, necessary in 1940 and until 1953 because of the international situation, had brought the country to near bankruptcy – just how near would not be fully known till 1958. Prices were still rising : a pound of good meat was costing as much as a day's basic wage. It was now to be the turn of the army and the new men, the 'technocrats', to set the country right.

On 25 February Franco announced a new Cabinet. A change had been expected since the previous June but never such a radical one as this. Girón was out and so was Martín Artajo. Muñoz Grandes was promoted to the *rank* (as opposed to the appointment) of captain-general (Franco himself having hitherto been the only other holder); but he too was out of the Cabinet. Arrese was relegated to the Ministry of Housing; but he was, after all, a town-planning architect by profession and one of the causes of popular unrest was the shortage of low-priced housing. In place of Arrese Franco made the head of the *sindicatos*, Solís, Secretary-General of the *Movimiento*. Artajo's replacement was Castiella, still nationalist but by no means now Falangist, whose writings on Gibraltar had made him *persona non grata* to the Court of St James when he had been proposed Spanish ambassador some years earlier. In the Ministry of War Franco put the pro-British and pro-French General Barroso – not a typical Spanish officer, for he was a member of a very wealthy family, but Franco's talented chief of operations during the war, the republican General Rojo's erstwhile tutor, and now singularly well-informed on the strategic and organizational needs of western defence.[36] Castiella would be the man to lead the attack against Britain for the recovery of Gibraltar : Barroso the Minister to plan the modernization of the army with the money accruing from the lease of the bases to the U.S.A.[37] The power of the army was strengthened at the *Falange*'s cost with the substitution as Minister of the Interior of General Camilo Alonso Vega, a close companion of Franco since schooldays, for the ineffectual Falangist Blas Pérez. Falangist students were to be stopped from making trouble as rigorously as were their opponents. The severest blow to Falangism, however, was the appointment of three men without

[36] Whitaker's implications, op. cit., pp. 140–2, that Barroso made use of his position to become a rich man are quite unwarrantable. He was a rich man : and a highly intelligent one. He was also generous, especially to the 'enemy'. One of his first acts as Minister of War was to arrange the return from exile of the republican Chief of Operations, General Rojo, have him 'promoted' lieutenant-general (at the outbreak of war he had been a lieutenant-colonel) and given the corresponding retired pay. Later it was he also who obtained Colonel Casado's return without sanctions.

[37] See above, p. 272.

political antecedents to the Ministries of Finance and Commerce and to a new post without portfolio. The new Finance Minister, Navarro Rubio, was a career banker (incidentally an ex-army officer); the Minister of Commerce, Alberto Ullastres, was a professor of the history of economics in the Madrid faculty of economics and political science. These two men had in common lay membership of the religious society *Opus Dei* and as such were above suspicion of corruptibility. Possibly also an *Opus Dei* member, the new Minister without portfolio, Gual Villalbi, Professor of Economics at Barcelona, was set to examine the national economy and to co-ordinate the demands upon it from the various Ministries. The new Ministers settled down to work quickly.

It soon became apparent that there were going to be changes in foreign policy. On 6 February France and Morocco, where there were still 250,000 French and 100,000 Spanish residents, had signed an administrative and technical co-operation agreement, much to Spain's annoyance. Four days later the Sultan flew to Madrid to meet King Saud of Saudi Arabia who was paying a state visit to Spain. On 11 February came the news (to French annoyance this time) that a Spanish-Moroccan diplomatic agreement had been concluded and, on the following day, that Spain would represent Morocco's interests throughout Latin America (except in Mexico which still recognized the locally based 'Spanish Republican Government in Exile'). The honour of Spain, offended by the agreement with the French, had been more than satisfied.

On 15 February Spain surprisingly abstained in an anti-French resolution on Algeria at the United Nations, thus showing her annoyance with Morocco for not putting a stop to broadcasts from Rabat claiming the Spanish territory of Ifni and for backing the Algerian 'freedom fighters'. In May units of a 'Moroccan Army of Liberation' began attacks on Spanish army posts in Ifni. Diplomatic notes to the government in Rabat drew disclaimers of responsibility for the activities of Ait ba Amran tribesmen. France, possibly sensing that Spain might be persuaded to her side over Algiers in the United Nations, began to provide her with news of movements of these 'irregulars' through what had been the French Protectorate. Castiella met the Moroccan Foreign Minister Balafrej at Tangier, but he again denied Morocco's responsibility and urged his country's claim to the territory. Then in August Castiella met his French opposite number, Christian Pineau. Thereafter Spanish press criticism of French colonial methods ceased and Spanish republican propagandists were denied the use of Radiodiffusion Française's microphones. The French then warned the Spaniards that the 'irregulars' were massing to attack the town of Sidi Ifni and the attack duly took place on 23 November. Barroso rushed up reinforcements, but Franco would not permit more than a defensive operation. He did not believe that the Sultan, who hastened home from an official visit to the U.S.A. on hearing the news, would be unwilling or unable to command the 'irregulars' to leave Spanish territory; but Franco's judgement was wrong and there was another attack near Villa Cisneros on 3 January 1958. This settled the matter. Ifni and the Spanish Sahara further south were declared 'provinces of Spain'. Spanish troops counter-attacked in force on the night of 12/13 January. France, harassed by 'irregulars' in adjoining Mauretania, now agreed to act jointly with Spain; and ignoring the frontiers of Ifni, Spanish Sahara, French Sahara, and Mauretania, Spain and France together forced all the 'irregulars' back to Morocco by the end of February. A month later, on 1 April, Castiella and Balafrej met again. Spain handed over to Morocco a part of Ifni, declaring the new frontier final; but Morocco reserved the right to further revisions. There was a further minor flare-up in 1959. Franco's friend General El Mizzian was then appointed Inspector-General of the Moroccan forces. Thereafter Moroccan (and Mauretanian) claims to the Spanish territories in Africa were made annually, but not backed by armed conflict. Spain clung on to the areas in the hope that important quantities of valuable raw materials would be found there. Over the next ten years soundings were made and uranium, other minerals, and oil were found, but up to 1969 not in large amounts.

With the troubles in Morocco Spain's support of Arab aspirations cooled. The Presidents of the Lebanon and Pakistan and the Shah of Persia paid state visits to Spain in 1957, but Spain's real triumph of the year was John Foster Dulles's visit to Madrid after the December 1957 meeting in Paris of the NATO Atlantic Council.

From the signing of the U.S.—Spanish agrements onwards Franco had repeatedly stated that he had no intention of seeking membership of NATO. He had all the connections he wanted with western defence through his long alliance with Portugal and through the U.S. agreements. He, no less than the U.S.A., insisted that there was no *military* alliance between them. Nevertheless, the northern European members remained far from convinced that the U.S.A. would not come to sponsor Spain's obvious claims for real incorporation into western defence. Dulles called on Franco to report on the Council's proceedings and the call set northern tongues wagging; but Franco was further convinced that at least for the moment membership of NATO would not be to Spain's advantage. Earlier in the year he had angered the U.S.A. by allowing the press to belittle the American space programme and had himself gone out of his way to speak of the successful Russian Sputnik as an achievement possible only to régimes 'based on discipline and order'.[38]

There was no reason to suppose that the change of government in February 1957 would lead to the relaxation of the curbs on freedom. Quite the contrary. One of the few to keep his post was the Minister of Information, Arias Salgado, who, the more *Ecclesia* argued for freedom of speech and in the press, argued the more fiercely against it. The removal of those Falangists in the SEU who had been the troublemakers of 1956–7 did not mean that their opponents would be free to opt out of SEU, let alone form their own university union. Falangists, ex-Falangists, monarchists, Catholics, and the left wing were now all to be brought into line throughout the country – and they were to be reminded that the régime had a very long memory. There was a recrudescence of sudden detentions, searches, and interrogations by the police. On 5 March forty-four Catalan nationalists were tried at Tarragona for political offences alleged to have been committed in 1945 and all were sentenced, at least nominally, to fines and various brief periods of detention. On 13 March six men were sentenced to from eight to three years' imprisonment for alleged communist activities; on the 30th the police announced the arrest of fourteen alleged communists and on 12 April and 13 May the arrest of two groups of unknown size on a similar charge. On 5 May a certain Adolfo Reguilón was sentenced to death, this being the first death sentence for some years for political activities, and on the 17th the Prosecutor asked for a similar sentence on one Jiménez Aparicio, a Marxist socialist, for killing a Civil Guard in 1937. Also in May the police arrested a group of socialist-minded students and lecturers headed by Enrique Tierno Galván, a professor of constitutional law at Salamanca. But the arrests which caused the greatest stir were of Dionisio Ridruejo in April and Francisco Herrera in May.

Dionisio Ridruejo was widely known as the author of the verses of the Falangist hymn *Casa al Sol*. A *camisa vieja* and a close friend of José Antonio, he had served under Serrano Suñer as Director-General of Falangist propaganda. Disillusioned with the régime and the *Movimiento,* he volunteered for service with the Blue Division, and his experiences in Russia had inspired verses not without merit. Rethinking Falangism, he had passed from Falangism to socialism as easily as in the past others had moved in the opposite direction. In 1956 he issued and circulated a manifesto of his own creation about a *Partido Socialista de Acción Democrática* and he thereafter called himself a Social Democrat, going on to express his strongly anti-Franco views in an interview for a Cuban

[38] Not in *Discursos,* but widely quoted in the world press.

magazine. His Falangist past had protected him until the change of government.[39]

Francisco Herrera Oria was the brother of Angel, the editor of the pre-war *El Debate* and inspirer of the Catholic *Acción Popular* which Gil Robles had led. With him was arrested Antonio Menchaca, an industrialist who found that the labour and economic policies of the government did not correspond with his ideas on social justice. Ridruejo, Herrera, Menchaca, and Tierno Galván were kept awaiting trial, for the most part on bail, till 1961. By then the internal political situation was quieter and the Spanish economy was doing well. Except for Menchaca, who was fined 25,000 pesetas, the rest were acquitted. Ridruejo, however, had in the meantime published other anti-Franco remarks and he was in and out of gaol during the 1960s, and regularly fined; but nothing serious ever happened to him, because the régime held that his brand of socialism was not particularly dangerous and that he was not the man to attract a large following.

The organizations of which the Minister of the Interior and his Special Branch of the police, the *Brigada Social y Política*, were rather more afraid were those which might appeal to the masses, at the time the communist and socialist organizations directed from abroad, a *Frente de Liberación Popular* founded in 1956 but whose leaders were then unknown, and the *Hermandades*. Best at avoiding detention were the communists. They had no need to come out into the open or engage in any spectacular activities to acquire recruits. The government's policy of attributing all disturbances, suspected acts of sabotage, and labour unrest to 'communists' made their task easy : men who had any grievance against bureaucracy came to look favourably upon this seemingly omnipresent and 'active' party.[40] Quietly the communists infiltrated the *sindicatos*. Official attribution of subversive activity to socialists, on the other hand, was rare. Their help in the distribution of the leaflets calling for the boycott of the Barcelona trams had never been acknowledged by the state. Such reticence forced them into the open when there was a similar but briefer boycott in March 1958; and from information possibly supplied under torture, the police came to know the identity of the socialist leader in Spain, the successor to Centeño, arrested in 1953.[41] He was a thirty-nine-year-old lawyer, Antonio

[39] For more on Ridruejo, see Welles, op. cit., pp. 216–19.

[40] But few were prepared to show their admiration publicly. The Communist Party called for general strikes on 5 May 1958 and 18 June 1959. Both were fiascos.

[41] See above, p. 277. In all between eighty and one hundred persons were arrested that November 1958. Of these about fifty were socialists proper – the remainder moderate opponents of the régime. The government tried to label them all communist. Most were released fairly quickly, Amat himself in 1961.

Amat, arrested on 6 November 1958 (whose code name was Guridi). The *Frente de Liberación Popular* (FLP – whence its members and sympathizers came to be known as *Felipes*) had been known to the police for a long time only through cyclostyled literature. Apparently a widespread organization, in the event it proved to be a grandiloquent title for small groups of Catholic young men led by a junior member of the diplomatic service, Julio Cerón Ayuso, who had earlier organized in his university a rival to the SEU which he called the New University Left. Cerón and sixteen associates were brought to trial before a military tribunal a year later in November 1959 on a charge of 'military rebellion'. The *fiscal*'s allegations that he was a communist did not satisfy the court and Cerón was sentenced to three years' imprisonment, whereupon the *fiscal* appealed to the Supreme Court and demanded a twenty years sentence. The Supreme Court agreed to eight years after a spirited defence by Gil Robles who had returned to Spain after World War II and had since become prominent as the defence lawyer of those accused by the régime of subversive activities.[42] The police could take no action against the *Hermandades* as such, for they were officially part of *Acción Católica* and therefore protected by the Concordat. Over the next ten years they were to prove a thorn in the side of the régime.

The *Hermandades* used as textbooks the works of a young cleric, Rafael González Moralejo. In a series of lectures delivered to the Chamber of Commerce of Madrid during April 1957 he expanded the bishops' declaration of 15 August 1956 into a highly reasoned comparison between papal pronouncements on social questions and the government's *sindicato* system, to the detriment of the latter. His conclusion was that the *sindicatos* were neither trade unions nor Christian. Much could have been adduced in their favour in 1939; in 1957 they were perpetuators of social injustice, of the unjust distribution of wealth, and a major factor in 'the great sin of the century—the apostacy of the workers'.[43]

As if in reply to these charges responsibility for the *sindicatos* was passed from the Ministry of Labour to Solís, the Secretary-General of the *Movimiento*, who had been active in their organization from the beginning. In 1957 real elections were held for the 350,000 junior posts (*enlaces*, roughly shop-stewards) in the *sindicatos* and as from 24 April 1958 under a law on *Convenios Colec-*

---

[42] The sixteen others were given lighter sentences. Cerón was released in 1962. International Commission of Jurists, *Spain and the Rule of Law* (Geneva, 1962), gives a very full account of the Cerón trial, pp. 121–9.

[43] Mgr González Moralejo was soon afterwards chosen by the social-minded archbishop of Valencia, Marcelino Olaechea, as his auxiliary. The appointment of auxiliaries did not require the Head of State's *beneplacet*.

tivos Sindicales, the principle of collective bargaining was legalized. In 1959, the first full year of the law's operation, 205 agreements were made, affecting 67,980 enterprises and 433,229 workers.[44] Though the Church was not satisfied, in time the law on collective bargaining was to have important social, economic, and political repercussions. At the time the law, to which the régime gave maximum publicity, was one which was held to justify Franco's frequent references to Spain's having 'an open constitution' and his promises of new *Leyes Fundamentales.* Franco promulgated on 17 May 1958, in a long speech to the *Cortes,* his 'Law on the Principles of the National Movement as a Basic Law of the Realm'. Henceforward twelve principles, and not Primo de Rivera's twenty-seven or Franco's own twenty-six, were to be those to which every man would 'swear on investiture into a public post'. In substance these were the twelve :

i. Spain is a unitary state and it is the sacred duty of all Spaniards to serve the unity, greatness, and freedom of the motherland.

ii. The Spanish nation believes it the essence of honour to accept the Law of God according to the doctrine of the Holy Catholic Apostolic and Roman Church.

iii. Spain will work for justice and peace between nations.

iv. Spain's present frontiers are inviolate and the armed services must be able to defend them.

v. The nation is made up of human beings and families : but individual and group interests must be subordinate to the common weal. All Spaniards are equal before the law.

vi. The natural units of society are : the family, the local council (*municipio*), the *sindicato.* However, other institutions and organizations necessary to society should be given protection if the common good is their purpose.

vii. Spain is a 'traditional, Catholic, social, and representative' monarchy.

viii. The people must participate in legislation – through the family, the local council, the *sindicato,* and other 'well-ordered' representative bodies. Public office will be open to all Spaniards.

ix. Spaniards have a right to an independent judiciary; to free legal aid if necessary; to education and welfare services, free wherever necessary.

x. Work for Spaniards is an honour, a duty, and the sole criterion of rank in society. Private property is recognized but

44 *Sindicato* figures.

subject to its social function. Private enterprise is to be encouraged but supplemented by state enterprise where necessary.
xi. The [commercial, industrial, etc.] enterprise constitutes a
community of people and interests. There should be loyalty
between its members and justice in their relations : economic
interests must be subordinated to social and human associations.
xii. The state will do all in its power to improve the moral and
physical health of Spaniards; to make their conditions of work
worthy of human beings, to press for economic progress in
agriculture and all industry.

At first sight Catalan and Basque separatists would be unable in
good conscience to accept clauses i and iv; anti-Falangists clause vi
(unless *sindicato* was made to mean 'trade union'); true Falangists
clause vii, and so on. But were these principles statements of fact
or aspirations; or a mixture; and if so which were to be read or
sworn to as one or the other? Given the vagueness of the whole
(vaguer still in its original wordier form), it could be argued that
even an arch-enemy of the régime and all it stood for could work
his mind and conscience over the lot and swear to them in 'good'
faith. Many did.

By May 1958, however, the government as a whole was not
interested in constitutional or political developments, though Franco
had still much to say about them and even found time to warn
the country through the *Cortes* : 'the army is much more than a
simple instrument of defence : it is the bulwark of what is permanent and the [spinal] column of the motherland'.[45] The government and the bankers were perturbed about economic realities. The
cost of living had risen a further 10 per cent since the beginning of
the year on top of the previous year's 16 per cent. In March there
had been strikes for higher wages in Asturias, the Basque provinces,
Catalonia, and Valencia – serious enough in the suburbs of Barcelona for the *Fuero de los Españoles* to be suspended and armed
police to patrol the streets. By May the Catalan textile industry
was being forced to cut production because there was no demand
for its produce; even by working at two jobs 16 to 17 hours a day,
a man had little left for essentials of less immediate urgency after
buying the food for his family.[46]

In June 1958 the Bank of Spain published its report for 1957,
revealing that by the end of 1951 foreign reserves had fallen to a
mere $96·8 million. Public expenditure was described as 'very high
for a country with a low productive capacity'. There had to be

[45] End of year speech 1963. *Discursos*, pp. 611–40.
[46] For a more comprehensive list of strikes see *Annual Register 1958*,
section on Spain.

'an open door to foreign capital'. In 1957 the Minister of Commerce, Ullastres, had imposed heavy duties on the import of luxury goods. They were now raised and a levy was imposed of 25 per cent of their f.o.b. value on all imports except a few necessities. The Minister of Finance increased direct taxation to draw money away from the wealthy, and after an investigation into the outflow of capital, he discovered over one thousand holders of money in Swiss banks. The outflow was checked and heavy fines were collected.[47]

All those measures were stop-gaps and preparatory for what was ahead. Spain had sought and obtained associate membership of OEEC, ironically the body of international economic technicians which had evolved out of the administration of the Marshall Plan from which Spain had been excluded. She invited international inspection of her economy. The report of OEEC and the World Bank, published in mid-1959, made far-reaching recommendations. Spain was indeed bankrupt : her reserves were virtually exhausted. Industrialization had been planned too haphazardly and on unsound economic principles. The new industries were dependent on materials obtainable only from abroad; but Spain had far from increased her capacity to earn more foreign currency with which to buy those materials. Her once profitable citrus fruit output could no longer be marketed in competition with that of other countries. Industrialization had drawn workers from agriculture. That in itself was not to be condemned; but what did matter was that the growers had not invested capital in mechanization to replace the lost labour force and increase food production. Spain was having to import food which she could well produce herself. Nor were the new industries as efficient as they should be and they were not likely to become so as long as industrialists were protected from foreign competition. The country needed to be open to foreign investment and foreign goods. To make Spanish produce immediately competitive in price abroad there was only one solution – devaluation. If Spain were prepared to abandon her nationalistic economy and devalue, then, the World Bank stated, international help would become available to help her out of bankruptcy.

Franco gave his *Opus Dei* Minister technocrats a free hand and Spain accepted the recommendations. Ullastres and Navarro Rubio proposed a drastic Stabilization Plan : heavy increases in taxation; dearer bank credit; cuts in government expenditure; planned reduction of import tariffs; and a perceptible opening of the door to foreign investment. On 18 July 1959 the peseta was devalued

[47] The illegal exporters of currency lost heavily. They had bought dollars at up to 80 ptas. a dollar: the money was 'repatriated' at 42.

from 42 to 60 to the dollar (116 to 167 to the pound sterling). In consequence on 20 July Spain was admitted to full membership of OEEC and simultaneously granted by the IMF and U.S. banks $418 million in support of the devalued peseta and the Stabilization Plan. Spain had ended her isolation from the rest of the world.

On 30 April 1959 the Madrid evening paper *Pueblo* carried a long 'interview' with Franco. The questions were as interesting as the answers :

> *Q.:* Workers know that with the establishment of industries these last few years, unemployment has been absorbed; that except in a few rural areas where work is seasonal, it has ceased to exist; that the standard of living has risen. They know that the enterprises of the state have been mainly responsible. How far are we with industrialization. . .?
>
> *Ans.:* . . . We have laid the foundations. In the future advance will be faster . . .
>
> *Q.:* Salaries and wages have always been controlled. It is the job of the government to sanction changes, even now with collective agreements, which undoubtedly has made negotiation simpler. Nevertheless the feeling remains that . . . the government does not keep the same watch on rising prices . . .
>
> *Ans.:* . . . Higher salaries without a corresponding increase in productivity is a nonsense . . .
>
> *Q.:* Foreign press and radio systematically broadcast news of the imprisonment and sentences of people they call 'workers' simply . . .
>
> *Ans.:* In 1935 there were 34,526 persons in gaol. Today with 5 million inhabitants more there are 14,890 . . .
>
> *Q.:* . . . Common Market . . .?
>
> *Ans.:* OEEC is not the Common Market . . . too early to talk about the Common Market.

The rest of the interview was a restatement of worn themes : class warfare is destructive of life and property; the *sindicato* is superior to all other forms of labour organization; it was the party system which shattered Spain in the past and brought down republics no less than the monarchy in violence and anarchy.

After a question had just been raised in the House of Commons on Gibraltar, Franco reasserted the Spanish claim : neither its capture nor the Treaty of Utrecht give Britain the title to its ownership nor to its retention by force; its inhabitants are British, Spaniards, or Jews, and other foreigners happy under any flag; the legal population of the Rock is that in San Roque; the United

Kingdom has abandoned far greater numbers; Gibraltar's economy is parasitic – it lives by smuggling; the base no longer has strategic value. 'Gibraltar is not worth a war, but it shatters the sincerity of friendship.'[48]

On 24 April, after brief consultations with all concerned, Spain abolished entry visas for all citizens of all western European countries and they, with the exception of the United Kingdom, readily reciprocated. With this and with the subsequent devaluation the tourist traffic into Spain rose substantially. In 1959 it reached the then extraordinary total of 4·2 million. As a result tens of thousands of Spaniards came into contact, however slight, with men, women, and children from beyond the Pyrenees, and though the foreigners had strange social habits and did not speak – *cristiano,* they were discovered to be human beings. Though Spaniards avidly asked of their paying guests what life was like in their countries, the language barrier limited the passage of information to superficialities and conversation tended to be more on practical than on abstract subjects. More Spaniards began to be preoccupied with material wealth and its acquisition than before. The labourer in the field had had time to think as he walked the long distances from his hovel to his scattered half-acres, to contemplate life. Unable to read or write though he might be, he had a wide culture and a habit of abstract thought. If he should leave his fields, he could study enough to be able to become a lift-boy or a waiter; but, working long hours, he had no time for thought beyond the looks and the dress of the people he was serving, 'the ways of pagans'; and at all levels of book-learning and income more men began to concern themselves with the acquisition of material things. Fewer and fewer Spaniards became concerned with political theories and more with practical results.

At the end of 1959 Spain went out of her way to entice a very special 'tourist'. Castiella flew to London, capital of the country which had not accepted him as an ambassador, to invite President Eisenhower, then on a tour of Europe, to Madrid and Eisenhower accepted. Franco greeted him on the airfield of Torrejón, near Madrid, the base built at a cost to the U.S.A. of $120 million, but flying the Spanish flag in precedence to the American. Eisenhower stayed overnight. According to the official communiqué, the two generals talked 'in an atmosphere of cordiality and understanding'. They parted with a warm embrace in public. Eisenhower had given Franco 'a review of his European trip including the Western Summit Conference'.[49]

[48] *Spanish Red Book on Gibraltar,* pp. 61–2, 290–7.
[49] Welles, op. cit., pp. 247–52, gives a splendidly written account of the meeting. See also Whitaker, op. cit., p. 81.

Chapter 29

Spain under Franco: The Economic 'Miracle' 1959–67

Spain in 1959

THERE WAS NOTHING in the Stabilization Plan to make it welcome to anyone except a banker or an exporter – and there were not many of those. The wealthy grumbled against the increase in taxation and their wives, accustomed to luxury goods from abroad, against the devaluation of the peseta. Manufacturers of goods protected by high customs tariffs worried over the possible effects of the promise that tariffs were to be reduced. Those who relied on foreign supplies for raw materials complained that they would have to pay more for them. Stabilization required a wage freeze : wages frozen at 1957 levels meant that millions of workers would have to continue to do without all but basic necessities. One hundred 1957 pesetas had the purchasing power of only 80 in 1959 : to buy what 100 pesetas had bought in 1957, 125 were now necessary. The plan, they were assured, would prevent any further appreciable rise in prices, but that would still leave them short of cash.

The public in general could not understand the necessity of the plan. How could the country be bankrupt? Was this a trick of international financiers? Admittedly prices had been rising, but was Spain in such dire straits? It was hard to believe that she could be.

At the beginning of the year there had appeared to be no economic crisis on the surface. In the cold days of January and February, in Madrid, Barcelona, Bilbao, Valencia, and other cities, the windows of clothes-shops were full and there was brisk trade over counters, not only in the fashionable areas but even in the less prosperous suburbs. There were long queues outside cinemas. The people, even in slums, were clothed and shod well against the cold, as never before in Spanish history. The workman drank his glass of wine and the clerk his coffee.

Workmen, clerical workers, civil servants, and even army officers up to field rank, undertook two jobs and worked weeks of 60 and more hours to make their particular ends meet – but this was nothing new.

Spain was beginning to acquire one of the characteristics of the modern materialistically developed society – the traffic jam, not only in the summer with tourist traffic, but also in the winter, with local vehicles. The *haiga*,[1] the Detroit-built vehicle which South American tourists in the early 1950s brought with them, and then illegally sold at black-market prices, no longer stood out in the virtual absence of other conveyances. Popular at the time was a light four-wheeled vehicle of simple construction and austere comfort, known as a *sin-sin*, the owners being reckoned by the populace '*without* the ready to buy a proper car, and *without* the nerve to ride a motorcycle'. Cars, of course, were still beyond the means of all but a privileged few, the 200,000 who already possessed them, and a further 400,000 on waiting lists—say one 'head of family' in twenty-five.[2]

Where in 1954 workers could be seen at change-of-shift times coming and going out of factories on foot or bicycle or on top of lorries provided by their firms, by 1959 a fair proportion were doing so on light motorcycles. The renewal of licences at the end of the year confirmed the changes which had noticeably taken place during that five-year period:[3]

Vehicles	31 December 1954	31 December 1959	Increase per cent
Commercial vehicles	94,700	131,700	39
Omnibuses	8,500	10,900	28
Private Cars	95,600	204,300	114
Motor cycles, *sin-sin*, etc.	77,300	476,200	503
	276,100	823,200	198

There had been Spaniards among the pioneers of the automobile and the aeroplane, but car-production before the Civil War had

[1] So called because many South Americans confused the present subjunctive of *haber* (*haya*) with that of *hacer* (*haga*) into the barbarism *haiga*.

[2] Doctors, officials, and businessmen were being given priority in the acquisition of new vehicles. Inevitably there was corruption in the preparation of the priority lists. Many a recipient of a new vehicle with 'contacts' would run it for a day then sell it at an uncontrolled (and uncontrollable) price as 'second-hand' on the following day – a situation which had existed in Britain, France, Germany ten years earlier.

[3] Official vehicle registrations.

been limited to the specialist vehicle assembly and aeroplane construction to light aircraft. After World War II, the economics of aircraft construction had become such that it would have been madness for Spain to attempt any advance. She was, however, convinced that she could invade the automotive industry. In 1952 INI had entered into partnership with FIAT and later with other vehicle manufacturers. Since then the industry had developed at a remarkable rate :[4]

Year	Tractors	Cars	Lorries
1953	47	648	418
1954	60	6,381	420
1955	850	14,422	1,737
1956	750	17,478	4,677
1957	1,508	23,225	7,060
1958	2,943	32,626	7,552
1959	3,341	37,763	12,556

To back this and other industrial development Spain had substantially increased her output of steel and electric power. Steel production was in the hands of the old, powerful private company *Altos Hornos*, a new INI company, ENSIDESA, and seven medium and 137 small companies. Their combined output had increased as follows :[5]

Year	(Thousand metric tons) Iron	Steel
1934	362	648
1939	473	587
1953	799	896
1957	962	1,344
1958	1,302	1,651
1959	1,704	1,823

ENSIDESA had established its new mills at Avilés in Asturias, not so much to make use of Asturian coal as to provide work for the area. Asturian coal was not particularly suitable, being of too poor quality for most purposes. Hence coal output had been increased hardly at all through the years and in 1959 was running at only 207 per cent as against pre-war. But by 1959 Franco's

[4] *Instituto Nacional de Estadística* (INE).
[5] Ministry of Industry.

'paranoiac mania', as his enemies had called it, for building dams and hydro-electric power-stations was yielding quite astonishing dividends. Together with the thermoelectric product, electricity output was nearing six times the pre-war output. Spain's grid had been linked to France's to the mutual advantage of both countries; and on balance it was now exporting power :[6]

Year	Total energy in million kwh	Export	Import	Balance
1957	14,532	73	89·7	− 16·7
1958	16,350	104·4	119·2	− 14·8
1959	17,353	304·1	130·3	+ 173·8

The export was a useful source of foreign currency.

Mistakes and errors in planning notwithstanding, the increase in overall industrial production was encouraging :[7]

Year	Index of Industrial Production	Important events
1929	100	1936–9 Civil War
1935	103	1941 Creation of INI
1939	72	1953 U.S.-Spanish agree-
1953	206	ments. Spanish entre-
1957	279	preneurs begin studying
1958	305	U.S.A. & industrial
1959	319	Europe.

The amount of food being produced in Spain in 1959–60 was about 25 per cent above the 1930–35 level; but the population had increased from around 24 to 30 million, an increase of 25 per cent. The amount of food available had been grossly inadequate before the war and it was therefore inadequate now.

Critics of the régime worried over the decline in the rural population which had begun around 1950 and was now becoming quite marked. Surely, they said, had the government encouraged agriculture, the emigrants would have stayed on the land and would have produced more food. There was no actual evidence that more people on the land would necessarily have produced more food. Over the decade 1940–50 the number of adult workers (including

[6] *Economic and Social Development Program for Spain 1964–67* (Baltimore, 1965; hereafter referred to as *Plan*), p. 133.
[7] INE and Ministry of Industry.

wives and children) on the land had risen from 4·75 to 5·33 million, or 12 per cent, yet productivity had barely risen, remaining at roughly 14 per cent below the pre-war level. Over the decade 1950–60 it had not merely regained the pre-war level but, as we have said, it went on to surpass it by 25 per cent : and it was during this period that the number of rural workers dropped from 5·33 to 4·62 million. Agricultural output, therefore, had not suffered from the emigration and the country had benefited in two ways : first, some of the emigrants had gone into industry and had therefore helped in the raising of the industrial production figures; secondly, some had gone to work beyond the Pyrenees, whence they sent home money and foreign currency. This is not to say that there were not valid objections on moral or sociological grounds to the drift from agriculture – but in economic terms alone what was happening was not to be condemned.

How well off were the people of Spain? The official – and true – answer was 'better than ever in history', but the general answer covered gross inequalities. Of Spain's 6 million families, 100,000 lived well or extremely well, 3 million well enough, 2 million poorly. *Acción Católica*, after a survey in 1959, came to the conclusion that about one million families were suffering acute hardship.[8] It was no answer to argue that this was only 16 per cent of the population and that the pre-war proportion had been above 50 per cent; the fact remained – one million families did not have enough clothes, food, or drink. In general the people of the north were better off than those of the south, and those in the cities better off than those in rural areas. The 4·6 million agricultural workers constituted nearly 40 per cent of the total labour force, while the contribution of agriculture to the national income was approximately 25 per cent,[9] two figures which when taken together showed how much poorer the people in the countryside were than those in the cities. In 1959 the average income of an agricultural worker was 100 pesetas a day,[10] and statistically it was true that this was more than twice as much as the 1953–4 average, and at constant prices 60 per cent more. Nevertheless, that average of 100 covered two extremes – that of the smallholder in Catalonia who might make 160 or more and that of the labourer in southern *latifundia* who was lucky if on average he got 60. The situation was still one which could satisfy no one with a social conscience.

[8] Cf. Welles's quotations from another study, op. cit., p. 328. *Acción Católica* had wider and more truthful sources of information on such matters than the government.
[9] *Plan*, p. 106.
[10] Ibid. On wide local variations see Juan Anlló, *Estructura y problemas del campo español* (Madrid, 1967), pp. 167–83.

In 1959, the emotionally inspired answer to the inequalities was to say, as in 1939 or 1929 : divide up the *latifundia* and nationalize the large firms, the *monopolios*, and there will be no poor. The economists' answer then as before was to say : granted that the 'cake' is unequally divided, it remains true that the cake is not big enough; and this, it must be remembered, was the socialist Largo Caballero's answer when he was Minister of Labour, whatever he may have said before or after.

The only realistic way to consider how well-off or how poor the Spaniard was in 1959 is to relate the cost of goods to working hours, and for a better perspective still to compare the situation with that in another country – say Britain.

Meat, fish, bread, and dried vegetables cost the Spanish worker on average three times as much in hours of labour as they did a British worker. Cars (taxes paid) cost in cash more than twice as much as in Britain : in terms of labour (to produce) nearly four times as much. It was not that the Spanish worker did not put into his work as much effort as the British. He put in far more : doing without breaks for refreshment – the *siesta* was a myth; rarely going on strike; and having fewer holidays a year, for there was no long week-end for him.

Food cost so much because :

1. So much cultivated land was subject to extreme climatic variations – droughts, frosts, etc.; drought especially.
2. The physical divisions of agricultural land were uneconomic. Some holdings were too large (*latifundia*) to manage or exploit efficiently : others too small (*mini-* and *minimifundia,* even of one are, the hundredth part of a hectare, a fortieth of an acre).
3. There was a lack of 'know-how' at all levels.
4. The right seeds and breeds of cattle were only just being developed.
5. There were tens of thousands of holdings without so much as a cart-track to a village, and thousands of villages inaccessible except on foot or animal-back.
6. Communications between regions were still grossly inadequate.
7. Fertilizers, either imported or manufactured locally, were expensive.[11]

Such was the state of communications that in 1959 an orange from Valencia could be shipped to London more easily than by road to Galicia. It was sold in London (after devaluation had made its price competitive again with the Jaffa or South African oranges)

[11] For more details on agriculture, see Appendix B.

for what a British skilled workman earned in five minutes. It cost the worker in the shipyards of El Ferrol (Galicia) what he earned in fifteen minutes.

The situation with regard to agriculture in the previous decade and in 1959 was one of the factors which induced the international bankers in 1959 to advance Spain large credits, bankrupt though she was. They welcomed the emigration from rural areas. A smaller force was producing 25 per cent more and this meant more output per man. The mechanization of agriculture was proceeding at a good pace. In 1940 there had been a mere 4,300 tractors on Spain's 12·6 million hectares (31·5 million acres) of arable land. By 1959 there were 37,000 tractors and by 1960, 40,000. That was still only one per 315 hectares, when in France there was one per 35 and in Britain one per 15. The value of irrigation was perhaps better understood by the Spaniards than by farmers elsewhere in western Europe, since their dry land could be made up to six times as productive by irrigation. The magnitude of the work to be done, its cost, and the poor prospect of financial return in the first place had deterred one government after another in modern times, and many a great plan had remained a plan. For political and social reasons the present government had bought a number of large dry-land estates under a decree of 1939 and a few more under a law of 1946 'authorizing the compulsory expropriation of land for social reasons'; and the government now had a showpiece in the vicinity of Badajoz. Out of near wasteland they were converting 120,000 hectares (300,000 acres) into a complex of irrigated and very fertile smallholdings, with villages for the settlers and depots and processing plants for the produce. The work was well under way by 1959. By 1965 nearly half the zone was to be occupied and in production, and by 1969 all of it. There were irrigation and reafforestation works elsewhere. The face of Spain was changing. More important to the economy of the country than the division of large estates, a start had been made on the rearrangement elsewhere of scattered smallholders' plots into contingent and consolidated areas, and of the consolidated farms into co-operatives, so that by 1964 there were to be 2,000 co-operatives working some 400,000 hectares (one million acres) and yielding harvests and profits undreamt of by their thousands of owners.

The reasons why manufactured goods cost so much labour in 1959 accounted, too, for the high cost of food.

1. Bad communications.
2. Out-of-date plant; bad management of resources; ignorance of production control methods; complicated accounting.

3. Paucity of medium-sized enterprises; undercapitalization.
4. No government 'stick' or 'carrot' to make private entrepreneurs more efficient; too much control of production by the state's bureaucracy; in state enterprises too much bureaucracy.
5. Poor siting by the state of new industries and not enough study by the state of the relative economic value of their investments; lack of accuracy in the statistics necessary for good planning.

An often-quoted example of poor siting at the time was the placing of the new automobile plants in Catalonia. Much of the criticism was based on envy : other regions felt that Catalonia was industrialized enough already and should not have been so favoured. Nevertheless, it was true that in the secondary stage of development of those plants, when cars began to be built with local steel and not merely assembled from imported parts, the steel would have to come from far-away Avilés across difficult mountain passes by road or through a single-line railway mountain pass. The steel, already costly to make, would be made dearer by heavy transport costs.

There was much politically based criticism then and later of the large capitalist ventures loosely called *monopolios*. The state-owned ENSIDESA and the private *Altos Hornos* between them accounted for nearly 50 per cent and, with the seven 'medium'-sized plants, 80 per cent of the total steel production. The economist's answer was that the 137 small companies were far too small, that they should be scrapped or amalgamated. The pattern of near *monopolio* at one extreme and overfragmentation was common to most industries.

Undercapitalization was also a major obstacle to development. Trustworthy figures for 1959 are not available, but the situation must have been worse in 1959 than in 1966 (when an effort was in train to make small companies amalgamate or form co-operatives). In the latter year there were in the country 17,027 limited companies. Together they had a paid-up capital of a mere 376,414 million pesetas, an average of 22 million a company (say $360,000 or £124,000 after devaluation). Again this national average covered wide regional variations. The average for companies in the Madrid region was 40·1 million pesetas ($675,000; £220,000), for the Bilbao area 36·8 million, and for Barcelona 9·5 million (say $160,000; £56,000). If we leave aside 103 large companies with a paid-up capital of over 500 million, the national average dropped to 11·4 million ($190,000; £68,000).[12] Capitalist economists dis-

[12] Arturo López Muñoz and José García Delgado, *Crecimiento y crisis del capitalismo español* (Madrid, 1968), p. 158; on the 'iniquity' of *monopolios* cf. Ramón Tamames, *La lucha contra los monopolios* (Madrid, 1961).

approved. So did the would-be organizers of labour outside the state *sindicatos* : for the corresponding manpower was equally fragmented. The average number of employees per firm was eleven.[13] Again, apart from the few large firms, the average fell : in textiles to under ten, in chemicals to three, in metallurgy to under three. An observer of neither 'capitalist' nor 'socialist' persuasion might have described the situation as one in which the proportion of capitalists to workers was substantially higher than elsewhere in Europe or the Americas; indeed he might have judged it to be far from undesirable and one in which social justice might be more easily assured than in either a mammoth capitalist or a socialist state, assuming instruments more subtle than either state or party controlled labour unions.

In both government propaganda and criticism of government policy there was a certain amount of confusion. Thus many an advocate of nationalization and state-ownership (both Falangist and socialist) attacked INI, which since its foundation in 1941 had spread its tentacles into industrial undertakings to such an extent that by 1954 it was the 'capitalist' body *par excellence* in power production and mining, in steel, in metallurgical, fertilizer, cellulose, chemical, food processing, and automotive production, and in shipbuilding. Of all the capital invested in limited companies, 54 per cent was INI capital. Harold Wilson's Labour governments of the 1960s might have been well pleased had a similar situation existed in Britain. INI had showy offices, a large bureaucracy, and complicated paperwork. It did not lay enough aside for the renewal of equipment; but it was neither more nor less efficient overall than the older private companies.

In the very inefficiency of Spanish industry – under INI or in private hands – there was hope for the future. If it were made more efficient – and there was no intrinsic reason to prevent this – then the rapid economic development of Spain was likely. This thought lay behind the willingness of international bodies with capital to lend Spain money in her hour of need.

The Effects of the Stabilization Plan

One of the immediate effects of the Stabilization Plan may be seen from this graph, published by OEEC a year later on information supplied to it by the Bank of Spain.[14]

---

[13] *La dimensión de la explotación industrial en España* (Sec. Gen. Técnica, Ministerio del Trabajo, Madrid, 1960).
[14] OEEC report on Spain (1960), p. 17.

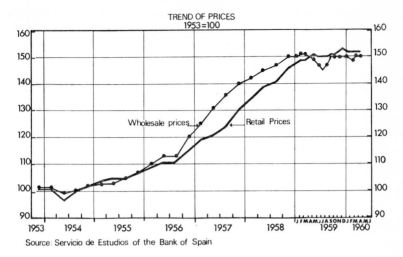

TREND OF PRICES
1953=100

Source: Servicio de Estudios of the Bank of Spain

In April 1959, 150 pesetas had been required to purchase what a mere two years earlier had cost 120; now both wholesale and retail prices were being kept at a fairly even level; the retail price had increased slightly but the wholesale price had dropped.

The following table showed another result:[15]

OFFICIAL GOLD AND FOREIGN RESERVES $ MILLION

Year	1958	1959 First half	1959 Second half	1960 First half	
Credits	65	63	217	442	—
Debts	63	67	109	94	—
Balance	+2	—4	+108	+348	—

– a reversal of fortunes greater than anyone had dared to hope: and by the end of 1960 the balance reached $500 million.

The visible trade figures changed radically:[16]

[15] OEEC report (1961), p. 39.
[16] Ibid. (1960), p. 28.

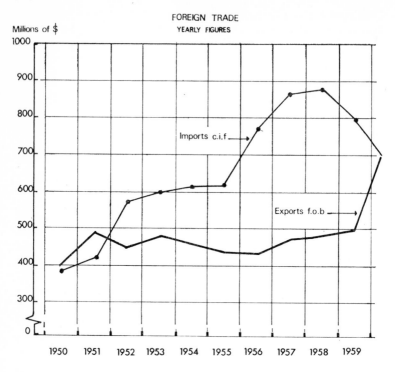

FOREIGN TRADE
YEARLY FIGURES

Millions of $

Imports c.i.f

Exports f.o.b

1950 1951 1952 1953 1954 1955 1956 1957 1958 1959

In consequence, after a year's working of the plan, OEEC, the World Bank, and Spain's international creditors were well pleased, but Spain was advised to reduce her tariffs further and by the consequent introduction of competition force manufacturers and industrialists – state and private alike – into greater efficiency, and also to open her doors wider to foreign investors.

Within Spain individual opinions on the plan had crystallized. Bankers and financiers welcomed the plan and the advice received from abroad, and were delighted with the results for several reasons. The nationalization of banking had been one of the principal points of Primo de Rivera's *Falange* : Primo de Rivera ascribed responsibility for the fall of his father not only to the politicians, but beyond them to the bankers as well; this apart, the young José Antonio's study of Marxism must also be remembered. Prieto the socialist had been a no less enthusiastic denouncer of international capitalism than the founder of the *Falange*, and the nationalization of banking had remained a project very dear to the real Falangists. If ever they had been allowed to hold real power under General Franco, or had seized power from him, the takeover of the banks would have been one of their first steps – and they would have had popular support for such a move; for the banks had foolishly built up a palatial public image of themselves in the principal cities of Spain. Now, thought the bankers, if the possibility reappeared of their nationalization, international bankers and organizations would exert pressure on their behalf.

The banks had done well under the régime, though not as well as their enemies imagined. During the republic their dividends had fallen from 12–14 per cent to 8 per cent, not because of any attack on the banks – the republic made no move against financiers – but because of the general contraction of the economy. After the war their dividends had risen slowly to 10 per cent by 1945 to remain thereafter at between 10·5 and 11 per cent. They invested heavily in industry as a safeguard against inflation; but they also had to extend substantial credit at the government's behest, and in an inflationary situation the principal, when they got it back, was always worth far less than when they lent it. With inflation brought under control, the leaders would be the recipients of greater dividends in real terms. Through their investment in industry they had to some extent been able to exert pressure towards greater efficiency, but they had not always been able to do as they wished, or invest where they wanted. The government directed money into projects whose ends were primarily social, political, or for prestige. Following international direction, the government was now giving the bankers greater freedom.

The industrialists' reactions after a year of the plan were subjective. Though they claimed to be advocates of 'free enterprise', they did not welcome competition from abroad. The Catalan textile manufacturers were perhaps the least pleased of any : some indeed sold out, the average size of enterprises thus growing slightly. But perhaps what irked the industrialists most was that they were now encountering a new spirit among the officials of the Ministry of Commerce. Men who had been well *enchufados*, 'plugged-in' to the current of securing permits for the import of raw materials for inessential consumer goods, now discovered that the *Opus Dei* Minister was cutting the wires behind the plug.[17] He did not care who was the brother, nephew, cousin, or in-law of an applicant for a permit or concession. In future efficiency was to be the sole rule to economic success.

Not that there were not still cases of corruption at lower levels or that all who 'wangled' permits were rogues. Much of the trouble was not corruption at all, but the inefficiency of bureaucratic and

[17] The industrialists praised his integrity while damning him for being what he was.

centralist methods dating back through the republic and the dictatorship and monarchy to previous centuries. One instance will illustrate the point. Spain was not at the time manufacturing marine engines needed for the Basque trawler fleet. Officially no spare parts could be bought from abroad without Ministry of Commerce and Bank of Spain approval. Between the request being made by the trawler-owner and the arrival of the permit up to six months could elapse. In the meantime the trawler-owner would have acquired the spare part, using funds lent to him by exiled but wealthy friends outside Spain, or from bank accounts secretly held in Hamburg or London. The permit, when it did eventually come, was kept against a future occasion or to show 'understanding' officials examining the trawlers too closely. Nor did Spain have the people at the right level with sufficient knowledge to know whether what they were told by industrialists was true, and the *vivo*, the quick-witted industrialist, could use the same permit to import, for example, a ton of nickel several times over. One thing that the tightening of credit showed was that industrialists had far greater stocks of raw materials than could be accounted for against permits issued.

Agricultural workers were not affected by the deliberate deflation of the economy consequent on the Stabilization Plan and associated measures. Their incomes rose a further 17 per cent (against the 1953 level) during the year following their introduction. There was no corresponding increase in the wages and salaries of the 60 per cent of the labour force in industry, commerce, and services; and they therefore could not look with favour on the plan. The Church took up their case – without success on wages – but the government did concede improved benefits to the unemployed whose numbers had risen from 0·7 to one per cent of the labour force of 11·6 million.[18]

The Church also looked with disfavour on another aspect of government policy connected with the Stabilization Plan, the encouragement given to German, Swiss, French, and other West European firms and individuals to recruit workers from Spain, and the encouragement of workers to leave. Between 600,000 and 750,000 did so in the four years 1959–62. By 1962 those workers were sending to their dependants in Spain $146 million, which meant they were earning for Spain that amount of foreign cur

[18] These figures relate only to the officially registered unemployed. Estimates as to how many did not register vary and bring the total to between 1·5 and 2 per cent. Ministry of Labour and OECD reports (1960), p. 16, (1962), p. 8. See also OECD reports (1963), p.11, (1967), pp. 10–11 on migrations.

rency, a valuable 'invisible'.[19] The Church considered it a serious social evil that a man should be separated from his family. The government recognized that this was so, but, they argued, there was not and could not be for some time work for those men at home. The net rate of increase in the population was running at 395,000 a year : which meant that around 200,000 jobs a year had to be created annually to maintain the *status quo*, let alone improve it. Surely, it was argued, it was preferable that a man should suffer separation from his family than starve with them; South America's doors were no longer as open as they had been in the past to the immigration of a man and his family.

The raising of the discount rate from 5 to 6·25 per cent, the demand for an advance deposit of 25 per cent on all imports from abroad, the restrictions on new credit were matters of no concern for Falangists. What they did object to with vehemence was the opening of the door wider to foreign investment. How could Spain be *Una, Grande, Libre*, if put at the mercy of the capitalists of other nations, of nations such as Britain, France, and the United States, Spain's traditional enemies? How far was she being called upon to surrender her sovereignty? The international organizations had recommended severe cuts in government spending. In March 1960 Arrese resigned from the Ministry of Housing and was said to resent strongly this 'surrender to foreign capitalists'.

In 1959 of all Spanish industries the structurally most chaotic, fragmented, undercapitalized, and undermechanized was the building industry. There were between 25,000 and 34,000 separate firms; and the number engaged in building varied between 550,000 and 700,000.[20] There were plenty of Spanish architects to design anything from a worker's cottage to a palace and as designers they were among the most creative in the world, but what Spain lacked

[19] There are no reliable figures on emigration in those years. Some estimates have put the total as high as one million. I prefer the middle figure in view of the amount of the remittances, the figures of which can be taken as more accurate since except for insignificant amounts they had to go through banks. From Britain, to which only a few thousand Spanish workers came and where the jobs open to them were not as remunerative as in France, Switzerland, or Germany, the usual amount was between £5 and £10 a month ($14 to 28). Accordingly, if there were as many as one million by the end of 1962 working in exile, one would expect the remittances to be higher. In 1963–6 officially a further 236,000 (net) workers left. According to official census figures the population in 1960 was 30·9 million; according to other official (Bank of Spain) figures 30·5; and there are two sets of 'official' estimates for 1967, 32·1 and 32·3. So one million as the total net emigration 1959–62 is possible. But even if there were as many as one million in 1962, it must in fairness be pointed out that quantitatively and even more so proportionately, there were more Italians, Yugoslavs, and Irishmen then working in exile than Spaniards.

[20] *Plan*, pp. 239–40.

were the constructors to give effect to those designs efficiently and quickly. The government had under construction at the time about 300,000 houses for renting at cheap rates, but the rate of completion was about 110,000 a year – thus it took up to three years to complete a 'housing unit'. The reasons given for the slow rate were 'slow industrialization ... traditional methods and techniques ... lack of investment in capital equipment'. This last shortage was borne out by the following table on the 1956 position :[21]

Country	Value of machinery (in million ptas.)	Number of workers	Value per worker
France	136,500	1,357,180	100,570 ptas.
Germany	106,000	1,217,000	87,099 ptas.
Spain	6,452	730,000	8,838 ptas.
U.S.A.	650,000	2,993,000	217,173 ptas.

The situation, however, must be considered in relation to political and social, as well as economic, factors.

Spain prior to about 1950 had been in no industrial position to manufacture any but the simpler tools of construction. Thereafter the government could have insisted on mechanization, and it could have bought machinery abroad, giving its purchase priority over, for example, railway rolling-stock, necessary though that was. Had it done so, the urban populations would have been better housed but they would have been worse fed and clothed. The government record can be criticized for devoting so much effort in the 1940s and into the 1950s to the construction of architectural showpieces like the University of Deusto in Bilbao and the Air Ministry in Madrid, and to technical schools and hospitals in several major cities, in which functional requirements were subordinated to outward appearances. But, these were buildings, like banks and cinemas, which did not require as many plumbers, electricians, and carpenters in relation to labourers as ordinary house-building did, and Spain's real shortage was of skilled men rather than machinery. Then, pressed by churchmen like the bishop of Málaga around 1953–4, the government did step up its construction of residential blocks of flats for workers and the instruction in mobile centres of men in the skilled building trades. According to official figures[22] only 31,000 dwellings for letting at low rentals were completed in 1951. The rate increased slowly over the next two years – 34,500

[21] *Plan*, p. 240.
[22] As OECD repeatedly stated, housing statistics were not very accurate; but as they were calculated on the same basis throughout these years, they serve to illustrate relative efforts.

in 1952 and 36,500 in 1953. There were then some impressive leaps : [23]

1954	47,500
1955	57,900
1956	73,100

Over the difficult years 1957 and 1958 the rate of *increase* was drastically reduced :

1957	75,200
1958	77,000

– but there was in 1959 a large leap, to 111,800, and another in 1960 to 127,800. Nothwithstanding Arrese's resignation as Minister of Housing (allegedly against a rumoured cabinet decision to cut the housing programme) the one branch of construction in which there was no reduction was in this type of house-building, as the following table shows : [24]

1960	127,800
1961	134,500
1962	147,800

– and in 1963 the figure leaped to 187,900.

It is to the credit of the government that in following international advice to cut down government spending, it did not reduce the house-building programme. The natural increase in population and the emigration from rural into city areas made it socially imperative that so far from being a cut-back there should be growth.

Towards Planned Development 1960–64

The stabilization programme had succeeded in spite of all the pessimistic prognostications that it would fail.[25] By June 1962 Spain's gold and foreign reserve holdings had risen to the healthy level of $992 million, IMF and the other creditors who had come to her aid three years previously having been repaid. Both OECD in July and IBRD in October emphasized in their surveys of Spain's economic situation that she was ripe for rapid economic development. The Bank believed that a growth-rate of 5 per cent *per capita* per annum in the gross national product could be maintained

[23] Ministry of Housing.
[24] OECD report (1966), p. 11, correcting earlier figures. Bank of Spain (1967 report) gives the Ministry of Housing figures, 143,052 for 1962 and 184,611 for 1963.
[25] Assurances given author by industrialists, Madrid, Catalonia, Bilbao, 1959.

for many years to come, but only, they said once again, if the government abandoned its continued practice of laying down tight rules for every aspect of economic life and made its role, like that of the French government, one of 'indication'. That meant abandoning all vestiges of nationalist socialism advocated by the *Falange*. Entrepreneurs, both organizations recommended, should be given more encouragement to invest and to expand : the doors should be opened yet wider to foreign companies and investors.

Up to a point Spain accepted the recommendations for liberalizing imports. From a position of virtual equality between exports and imports in the early months of 1960 trade had been allowed (because of the partial liberalization demanded by the international bodies) to go out of balance to this extent :[26]

	1960		1961		1962
Figures in $ million	First half	Second half	First half	Second half	First half
Imports c.i.f.	343	378	498	594	715
Exports f.o.b.	374	352	375	335	389
Balance	+31	−26	−123	−259	−326

In the second half of 1962 exports were to come to $345 million and imports to soar to $855 million, resulting in an adverse balance of $510 million for the half and $836 million for the full year; but this was a small difference compared with the 1963 adverse balance of $1,219 million. Notwithstanding the increased purchases of all kinds (more food, fodder, and machinery accounted for most of the increases), Spain's reserves continued to rise – to $1,030 by the end of 1962 and to $1,104 by the end of 1963. The balances came with tourists, remittances, and foreign investors who saw in Spain a great future. The remittances rose to $116·2 million in 1961, $146 million in 1962, and $195 million in 1963.

Nothing proved to be paying greater dividends for the economy than the decision taken at the very height of the nationalistic and socialist period to allow banks to give big credits to private entrepreneurs to build tourist hotels – the decree of 27 March 1942 on *Crédito Hotelero*.

[26] Ministry of Commerce and Bank of Spain.

Year	Number of Tourists	Money spent or invested by them in Spain in $ million
1931	276,300	—
1946	83,568	—
1950	456,268	—
1955	2,522,402	(90·7 estimated)
1960	6,113,255	246·5
1961	7,444,262	330·5
1962	8,668,722	465·8

During the years 1959–63 agricultural production had risen by an average of about 15 per cent, good results in 1959 and 1963 more than balancing the poorer results of 1960–62. The 1959 results had helped Spain to recover from bankruptcy; the 1963 receipts meant more food for the inhabitants. In 1963 Spain produced.[27]

811,000 metric tons of meat	1956–60 average	499,000
579 million dozen eggs	„	262 million
3,732 million litres of milk	„	3,207

Once the brakes had been eased on industrial expansion after 1960, the increase in production had been high. Spain at the end of 1963 was producing 42·3 per cent more manufactures than in 1960, the only industry showing a decline being coal-mining.

Steel had the following record :

1960	1·9 million tons
1961	2·3 „ „
1962	2·3 „ „
1963	2·8 „ „

This was not enough for her needs; so she was still importing. Power output had risen :

1960	18·6 thousand million kwh.
1961	20·8 „ „ „
1962	22·9 „ „ „
1963	25·9 „ „ „

On the land there were now :

114,400	tractors
10,200	*motocultores*
8,900	harvesters

[27] Ministry of Agriculture; Ministry of Industry.

In industrial areas bicycles and motorcycles were still popular, but the car was replacing the motorcycle in cities. Vehicles registered on 31 December 1963 were:

Lorries	244,599
Buses	16,322
Cars	529,700
Motorcycles	216,821

(the *sin-sin* had disappeared : their erstwhile owners could now afford proper cars whose number was $2\frac{1}{2}$ times that of 1959.)[28]

In 1963 the income *per capita* in Spain exceeded for the first time in history $500 – the demarcation level then imagined to distinguish between countries considered underdeveloped and countries in 'intermediate' development. During 1964 it rose to $565.

That year the income *per capita* in other OECD countries was :

Greece	$588
Portugal	$343
Turkey	$242
U.K.	$1,705
U.S.A.	$3,272

As OECD noted in 1967–8 when it came to study how Spain, the recipient of technical aid, could now help other countries as well as herself, 'the comparison of real incomes is notoriously delicate. The conversion into one common unit of estimates of *per capita* income or consumption derived from national accounts does not lead very far. Exchange rates are very inadequate indicators of the parity of purchasing power, except perhaps in international trade'.[29] OECD then gave two tables as more indicative of living standards than income *per capita* in terms of dollars. One table is shown opposite.

OECD commented on these figures : 'the general picture which they give of Spain is that of a country on the whole more "developed" than Greece, Portugal, Turkey, or Yugoslavia'.

OECD also applied Wilfred Beckerman's more ample criteria[30] to Spain and achieved the following indices of real private consumption *per capita* 1960 and 1964 (U.S.A. = 100).

[28] Official vehicle registrations.
[29] OECD, *Problems of Development: Technical assistance and the economic development of Spain* (Paris, 1968), p. 15.
[30] Ibid., p. 16. Cf. Wilfred Beckerman, *International Comparisons of Real Incomes* (OECD, 1966).

TABLE I.I. NON-MONETARY INDICATORS OF LIVING STANDARDS[1]

	Infant mortality rate[2]	Population per doctor (1963)	Calories per day			Annual production of steel per capita (kilos)	Sale of newspapers per capita	Number of domestic letters per capita p.a.	Telephones per 1,000 inhabitants	Illiteracy of the population 15 years and over	
			Year	Total	Animal origin					Year	%
Spain	37.9	820	1963–4	2,850	18	109	3.1	68	80	1960	13.3[8]
Greece	....	750	1962	2,910	15	84	3.6	20	51	1961	19.6
Portugal	69.0	1,200	1964	2,670	16	60	2.7	40	57	1960	38.1
Turkey	....	3,300	1960–1	....	10	26	1.1	9	11	....	....
Yugoslavia	76.0	1,400	1963	3,130	17	121	3.0	54	19	1961	19.7
United States	24.8	690	1964	3,120	40	615	37.9	354[7]	462	1959	2.2[9]
United Kingdom	20.6	840[3]	1963–4	3,280	44	438	26.0	197	171	....	....
Japan	20.4	920[4]	1963	2,280	9	324	12.5	91	65	1960	2.2
Chile	114.2	1,800[5]	1962	2,370	22	74	4.3[6]	13	29	1960	16.4
India	....	5,800[4]	1962–3	1,940	6	16	0.3	13	2	1961	72.2

.... Not available.

1. Year 1964, unless otherwise stated,
2. Infant mortality under one year per 1,000 live births.
3. Excluding Northern Ireland.
4. 1962.
5. 1960.
6. 1963.
7. Including parcels and foreign mail despatched.
8. 1965: 4.2% of the population from 15 to 60 years (Ministry of Education, Madrid).
9. 14 years and over.

SOURCES: U.N. Statistical Yearbook, 1965.
U.N. Demographic Yearbook, 1964.

	Beckerman 1960	Applied Beckerman 1964
Spain	19·5	23·1
Portugal	17·0	18·2
Yugoslavia	13·5	16·4
Greece	12·7	15·4
Turkey	9·8	9·2
U.S.A.	100	100
U.K.	61·7	61·6
Japan	28·7	34·7
Chile	16·9	15·7
India	3·1	3·1

Spain was thus forging ahead of her one-time fellow under-developed countries of the Mediterranean, and was now about twelve years behind Italy. As in Italy, national averages covered gross imbalances between one area and another, as well as between social classes. And there was evidence that the gap between the richer and the poorer regions was widening.

The First Development Plan 1964–7

Spain's economy at the end of 1964 was being directed in accordance with a four-year development plan, the first essay in Spanish history in co-ordination and long-range growth planning.

In 1962, as we have said, Spain had accepted in some measure the recommendations of OECD and IBRD. She had done more. In July of that year Franco reorganized his Cabinet. He brought back into the Cabinet General Muñoz Grandes in a new post – that of vice-premier and *ex-officio* heir apparent. More important for the future, he replaced the not over-efficient Minister of Industry with a man of the Ullastres—Navarro school, Gregorio López Bravo. In 1957 he had brought into the presidency (the Prime Minister's office) the then thirty-five-year-old Professor of Administrative Law at Barcelona, Laureano López Rodó. López Rodó then began to carry out a drastic reform of the civil service at top level. In 1962 Franco raised him to the second highest post in the presidency with the special task of looking to the future of the Spanish economy. López Rodó thereupon asked the World Bank to do a survey, which was completed early in 1963 under the chairmanship of the British economist, Sir Hugh Ellis-Rees. Franco accepted its recommendations (though not to rile the Falangists more than necessary he did not accept its condemnation of the nationalist policies of previous

years). López Rodó next set up twenty-two commissions to work
out in detail the implications of those recommendations and in particular the targets to be adopted in each sector of economic life,
and the possible social side-effects of development.[31] In October the
plan was made public. Its general aim was to achieve a 6 per cent
rate of growth and to raise the *per capita* income in real terms by
a third. An investment by the state was envisaged over the four
years 1964–7 of 334,900 million pesetas ($5,600 million; £2,000
million approx.) in education at all levels from primary to university, in low-cost housing, communications, heavy industry, agriculture, and indeed generally in all branches of the economy. Private
enterprise was to match the state's contribution to the value of
$8,400 million. For the state the growth targets were to be obligatory
(but 'flexible'), for private enterprise 'indicative'.[32] The state was to
allow 'the free operation of market forces'. It was to offer incentives
to private entrepreneurs in seven 'growth points' – Corunna, Vigo,
Huelva, Seville, Valladolid, Burgos, and Zaragoza – to spread industry beyond its traditional Bilbao—Madrid—Barcelona epi-
centres. The state and provincial or municipal authorities were to
undertake enterprises only where private investors showed no interest or private restrictive practices made such a course of action
socially necessary.

Here are some of the plan's targets for the state :

Agriculture : the consolidation of one million hectares (2·5 million acres) of tiny fields[33] into economically viable units on the lines

[31] For adverse criticisms of the plan see numerous articles in *Cuadernos
para el diálogo, Promos. El Europeo, Anales de Economía,* etc., by Prados
Arrarte, López Muñoz, García Delgado, Enrique Barón, Funes Robert,
Fuentes Quintana, and especially Ramón Tamames, *Estructura Económica
de España* 2nd edition, Madrid, 1964), chapter 38; and J. Prados Arrarte,
El Plan de desarrollo de España (Madrid, 1964); for favourable, government
statements, passim.; for generally favourable, OECD and IBRD reports,
articles in *B.O.L.S.A. Review.*

[32] 'As in France', as the IBRD had recommended earlier. López Muñoz
and García Delgado, *Crecimiento y crisis del capitalismo español,* pp. 29–40,
write at length on the similarities of this Spanish plan with the French
development plans from 1946 onwards, in support of their thesis that the
plan was unsound : Spain was not France. Whatever blame or praise is due
must be shared between the Spanish government or the Spanish technocrats
on the one side and the international advisory organizations or their British,
American, French, etc., members on the other. Once the plan was launched,
'OECD . . . contributed to many of its targets, especially in education and
regional development . . .' (*Technical Assistance and the Economic Development of Spain,* OECD, Paris, 1968, p. 26. See also pp. 78–82).

[33] Land passes from one generation to the next in Spain according either
to Visigothic *mayorazgo* or 'Napoleonic' rules : under the former 'eldest takes
all' and so some of the large estates have been created through the centuries;
under the latter by equal division among the children. But the 'equality' has
to be in all aspects. To ensure it each field has to be divided. So in the

of the 577,000 consolidated already; the improvement of the soil in 385,000; the irrigation of a further 300,000; the reafforestation of half a million hectares; heavy investment in agricultural research towards the improvement of pastures and livestock, of seeds and control of pests; the nationwide expansion of a network of vocational training centres for those engaged in agriculture.

Housing : the construction of 720,000 new dwellings.

Education : the building and equipping of 16,000 new primary-school classrooms, of 75,000 new places in secondary and 107,000 in vocational schools.

Given the right response from the public, average agricultural production was planned to rise progressively by at least 6 per cent per annum – by over 25 per cent in the four years; the diet of the Spaniard was expected to improve marginally from an average of 2,850 to 3,100 calories per person per day, but it was to be a diet with a marked drop in carbohydrates and increase in animal proteins. Big credits were to be available to agriculturalists to mechanize their farms rapidly so as to reduce the uneconomically over-large labour force by 340,000. Thus the output from the land was to be increased by over a quarter, but by a labour force little greater than 3·6 million.[34]

For the emigrants from the land, and to provide employment also for the ever more numerous population of working age, 970,000 new jobs were to be created in industry and services.

Opposition to the development plan came from many quarters : root and branch from nationalists because there was to be even freer entry of foreign capital; from the nationalistic left because they feared that capital would be mostly American – the penetration of American and other foreign capital was already considerable and the plan was expected to encourage further investment; from socialists simply because the plan was 'capitalist' in conception; from economists either in detail, or, if not consulted by López Rodó and not of his particular school, in general and far from precise terms; from the disinterested because the statistical foundation of the plan had a high content of the sand of supposition and rather less cement of fact; and from financiers, industrialists, and men of

---

course of generations thousands have come to be owners of say 5–10 hectares scattered in tiny parcels over a wide radius — even as many as twenty. See Appendix B.

[34] One man in the fields would thus be providing food adequate for nine other human beings: nowhere near the situation in Great Britain where one man provides for 27, but approximately three times better than the 1931–6 situation, all factors considered.

commerce if they considered their particular interests prejudiced or less favoured than those of others.

The planners' answer to the nationalists was twofold : first, economic autarky, the attempt to 'go it alone', had led to bankruptcy – expansion had been carried out by eating into capital and using on day-to-day needs foreign aid which would have been better spent on capital equipment; and second, the world's most developed country had risen from its backward colonial past with money invested in it by the then more developed and wealthy United Kingdom, and the same was true of Canada. To the economists of the left they replied that if they really cared for the well-being of the masses and not for an intellectually satisfying theory, they should look at the recent economic history of Poland, Czechoslovakia, or Yugoslavia where development had taken place only in so far as Marxist economic theory had been tacitly abandoned. Their reply to those who pointed out the obvious weakness of available statistics was that some planning was required there and then, and could not wait for the elaboration of more reliable figures. The targets of the plan would be adjusted as these became available. Official statistics might be right or wrong, but what proof was there that the estimates of private individuals or organizations were any more accurate? It was Spain and not the government of Spain which lacked men with expertise in statistical techniques.

Because of the plan, or in spite of it, and in spite of an economic crisis which developed during the last eighteen months of the plan, the target of 6 per cent growth was reached – and exceeded. The final figure was 6·3 per cent.[35]

Half-way through 1967 one of the sternest critics of the capitalist basis of the Spanish economy wrote with emotion of the plan :[36] 'the results are eloquent testimony [of its inadequacy] : targets unfulfilled, disjointed growth, total indiscipline of the forces operating within the system . . . glaring surpluses, eloquent deficits'.

It would have been an historical event without precedent had Spain's first attempt at medium-term programming gone entirely 'according to plan'. There were in the final results successes and failures.

The *per capita* income increased from about $500 at the end of 1963 to $850 at the end of 1967, an increase of 70 per cent. The general index of the cost of living went up by 42 per cent on this pattern :[37]

[35] INE.
[36] García Delgado, *Cuadernos para el diálogo*, No. 45–6 (June–July 1967), pp. 17–18.
[37] OECD report (January 1969), p. 25.

B. COST OF LIVING

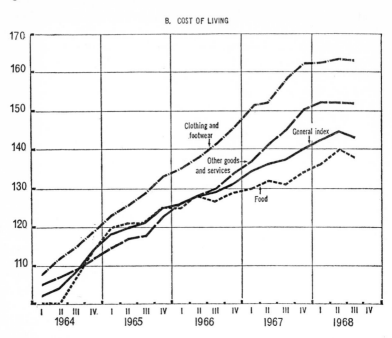

— so on this basis the *per capita* income rose in real terms by an amount below but not widely below what the planners had hoped for. In terms of calories the diet remained altered hardly at all, but in composition radically.[38] Here, of course, the plan was to enable a process already begun to continue. Thus in 1960–1 51·8 per cent of the calories were derived from cereals and potatoes, 36·6 per cent from other vegetable products, and 11·6 per cent only from animal products. By 1963–4 the pattern was : 46·7 per cent from cereals and potatoes; 36·8 per cent from other vegetable products; and 16·5 per cent from animal products. In 1967–8 the distribution was: 41·8 per cent from cereals and potatoes; 37 per cent from other vegetable products; and 21·2 per cent from animal products. The animal protein composition of the diet had increased over the period from 22 grammes per head per day to 35·8. Spaniards were eating in 1967–8 more than twice as much meat as in 1960–1 (37 kilos per person per annum as against 18) and 42 per cent more than in 1963–4 (when they ate just over 26 kilos a head).

[38] OECD gives 2,850 for 1963–4 and 3,100 for 1967. *La Agricultura Española* (Madrid, Ministry of Agriculture, January 1969), p. 219, agrees for 1963–4 but gives 2,813 for 1967–8. Percentages quoted are from this work.

However, it could be said with justice that this desired change in diet did not have the planned backing it merited. In spite of all the encouragement given to growers (subsidies, guaranteed prices, loans at rates as low as 2·75 per cent) agricultural output did not develop according to plan. The increased consumption of meat should have been met by increased production in the country. It was not. The production of meat did rise from 810,000 tons in 1963 to 1,058,000 in 1967, an increase of 31 per cent to meet the 42 per cent demanded. The deficit had therefore to be met that year as in previous years by imports. Milk production in 1967 was down by over 10 per cent compared with 1963 to 3,355 million litres and eggs from 579 to 546 million dozen, the drop here being marginal. Admittedly 1963 had been an exceptionally good year. These and other food deficits had also to be made up by imports.[39]

YEAR	1963	1964	1965	1966	1967
FOOD in $ million					
IMPORTS	417	394	581	681	658
EXPORTS	374	505	457	546	621
Balance	−43	+111	−124	−135	−37

The production of feeding stuffs for animals also failed to rise to anywhere near the required level. On the other hand, there were large and unforeseen surpluses of cereals. A new record for wheat, 4·8 million tons, was established in 1966 and the government did not know where to store it all. Every available barn, disused church, and warehouse was used. The record was broken again the following year with 5·6 million tons. Spain became an exporter of wheat to Argentina in exchange for meat – a curious turn of history.[40]

Overall agricultural production was a grave disappointment to the planners, and statistics could easily be used as evidence of their 'inefficiency'.[41]

[39] OECD report (1969), pp. 34–5, cf. p. 63; *B.O.L.S.A. Reviews* (May 1967 and May 1968).
[40] And of rice to Indonesia.
[41] *La Agricultura Española* for food statistics. López Muñoz, García Delgado, and other articles in *Cuadernos*, etc.

INDEX OF TOTAL AGRICULTURAL PRODUCTION FOR HUMAN
CONSUMPTION

YEAR	1963	1964	1965	1966	1967
1953 = 100	154·3	139·6	141·1	154·9	162·2

The extent of the failure could be better illustrated on the basis
1963 = 100 :

1963 = 100	100	90·5	91·4	100	105

the last figure, according to the planners, should have been 125.

Obviously any improvements consequent on the plan would not
begin to show immediately, but after a time lag of at least one or
two years. Thus, the figures for 1964 (a bad year for harvests) and
1965 belonged more properly to the pre-plan five-year period
1961–5 when the production index (in 1953 = 100 terms) averaged
139·3, this figure being just over 23 per cent above the previous
five-year average of 112·8 per cent. No accurate measurement was
therefore possible until the figures to 1970 were known, but 1966,
1967, and 1968 (172·1 estimated) yielded an average of 163, an
advance (if maintained) of 16·5 as against the 25 expected.

So the plan had partly failed. Once again voices were raised
blaming the inefficiency of the large landowners who, so long as
they had guaranteed prices for their wheat, had little reason to
increase livestock or intensify farming; and there was some truth in
what was said – but not the whole truth. The *minifundia* and the
scattered holdings of little fields widely separated were still as great
an obstacle to agricultural development.

In the concentration and *ordenamiento* (setting to rights) of the
countryside the government had fulfilled its target and no one
criticized the fact that it had gone beyond it. The area sorted out
totalled 1.27 million hectares (3·17 million acres) – with a further
382,000 in 1968. Reafforestation (393,200 hectares) had fallen short
of the target by 20 per cent. Work on soil improvement and irrigation also did not proceed as fast as expected. But by 1967 the
government did have an admirable network of training centres,
and the improvement of seed and stock continued.

The mechanization of farming also continued. On the land there
were now :

191,300 tractors   as against 114,400 in 1963
41,100 *motocultores* „   „   10,200   „
22,300 harvesters   „   „   8,900   „

The planned reduction of the agricultural labour force had been carried out. At the end of 1967 the labour force, now 12·57 million, was distributed : [42]

in agriculture   3·69 million 29·4 per cent
in industry   3·50   „   27·8   „
in construction   1·06   „   8·5   „
in services   4·32   „   34·3   „

As far as the Ministry of Housing could ascertain[43] the rate of subsidized housing went faster than anticipated, the target of 720,000 dwellings being reached early in 1967. So did primary-school building and the provision of educational places at all levels.[44]

The reason why the growth-rate reached during the four years 1964–7 passed the 6 per cent target in spite of the failure of agriculture was that the industrial and services growth-rate was correspondingly higher. The increases per cent were 12·9 in 1964, 12·5 in 1966; and though the rate was severely retarded for 1967, to 4 per cent, the average for the four-year period of the development plan worked out at 11 per cent per annum, cumulatively double (51 per cent) what the planned 6 per cent would have yielded (25 per cent).[45]

The figures for various key commodities and manufactures were as follows : [46]

	Unit	1963	1964	1965	1966	1967
Steel	million tons	2·8	3·2	3·5	3·8	4·3
Cement	million tons	7·1	8·1	9·8	11·8	13·3
Electricity	thousand million kwh	25·9	29·5	31·7	37·7	41·2
Motorcycles	thousands	178·0	179·0	175·0	182·0	157·0
Cars	thousands	79·4	119·5	155·0	249·4	276·0
Lorries	thousands	48·1	59·9	73·9	92·3	88·5
Shipping	thousand tons launched	188·4	219·6	278·4	343·1	389·8

[42] OECD report (1969), p. 56.   [43] Cf. ibid., p. 9 footnote.
[44] In all 900,000 state-subsidized houses were built. No reliable figures are available on private building.
[45] INE.   [46] INE and Ministry of Industry.

On 1 January 1964 Spain's reserves totalled U.S. $1,093 million. During the first year of the plan the total increased to $1,407 million; foreign tourists and remittances from Spanish workers abroad more than made good the adverse trade balance of $1,071 million, and foreign investors and money-lenders also added to the reserves. In 1965 the imbalance between imports and exports increased to $1,759 million. Tourist earnings went up from $852 million to $1,027 million, but the other sources of money were not quite so generous as before, and the reserves dropped to $1,268 million. Over the next six months to the end of June 1966 they dropped at an even faster rate, to $1,026 million. International advisers warned Spain of the dangers while acknowledging what had been accomplished. Thus, for example, OECD reported in July 1966 :[47] 'The boom in industrial development continued [during 1965] enabling substantial improvements in productivity and industrial structure. Moreover important programmes of public investment in recent years have gradually been modernizing the transport system and other basic facilities'. Elsewhere the report stated that living standards had risen 'remarkably'. Nevertheless :

> the process of development has been accompanied by increasing internal disequilibrium. . . . The inflation developed because insufficient action was taken, when demand began to approach capacity level, to prevent excesses in particular sectors. . . . The Development Plan . . . spelt out certain constraints (e.g. on the rate of increase of public consumption and on the volume of resources to be devoted to housebuilding) in the interest of financial equilibrium. The constraints have not been applied. And inflation was also generated by . . . price support measures for farm products [in 1964]. These pushed up the cost of living and intensified the price–wage spiral in a labour market which was tightening both because of expanding activity and emigration.

Therefore, OECD advised : '. . . Postpone less urgent investment projects . . . reduce the growth of demand for goods and services' – by taxation, not by raising tariff barriers to imports; '. . . any artificial reduction of imports would only serve to intensify the strains on the price level, and it is of primary importance that the Government perseveres in the direction of liberal import policies, attacking the cause of the inflation [excessive demand] and not the symptom [the foreign deficit]'. It advised Spain 'to reorientate agricultural policies so as to stimulate increased production on a sound economic basis of the types of food items which correspond to the changing pattern of demand, at the expense of some of the tradi-

[47] OECD report (1966), pp. 40–1.

tional crops'. In other words, the Spanish government was being advised to cut down on house-building and to abandon its full employment policy, to increase taxes and to stop 'mollicoddling' its food producers.

In the third quarter of 1966 there were 106,300 registered un-employed – 28,400 in agriculture, 17,200 in construction, and 60,700 in industry and services – 0·85 per cent of the population, a low figure. Even allowing for the continuing unwillingness of some workers to register, the ignorance on the part of others of the monetary benefits accruing from registration, and the inaccuracy of bureaucracy, and allowing for those not accounted for because they were in between emigrating from the countryside into industry or abroad, it could be reckoned as well within the 1·5 per cent internationally accepted as 'full employment'. However, to cut down on house-building or to abandon the 'full employment' policy would then as in 1959 have been politically undesirable as well as socially wrong. More so politically than before, for the nation was to be called upon at the end of the year by referendum simul-taneously to approve a new constitution and give a vote of confi-dence to the Head of State, now entering his seventy-fifth year. It was no less politically expedient that the wealthier landowners should not be irritated by changes in guaranteed prices with a bumper wheat harvest being collected. They were angry enough that the emigration of labourers was in their view making agricul-tural labour dear. Spain still lacked the machinery for the efficient collection of income tax, of direct taxes from employers and land-owners in particular. What could alienate the public more than increased direct taxation? And again, more indirect taxation aimed alike at the poor and at the wealthy was socially undesirable. The measures taken in 1966 were therefore more token than effective.

Up to a point the government could afford to wait until the end of the year; for indeed, the second six months included the greater part of the profitable tourist season. The growth of tourism and of earnings in foreign currencies from tourism had enormously exceeded the planners' expectations. In expecting 1966 to be yet another record year for tourism they were not deceived.

	No. of tourists in millions	Earnings in $ millions
1963	10·9	611
1964	14·1	852
1965	14·2	1,027
1966	17·3	1,202

Spain in the summer of 1966 appeared to be booming. To a

Russian visitor who had not toured the country since 1959[48] the improvement was 'unbelievable'. In 1959 he had gone there expecting Spain to be not only politically oppressed but also economically backward. What he had seen in 1959 had therefore been a surprise to him, though Spaniards had then had far fewer comforts than the rest of western Europe. Now he discovered that the gap had narrowed to an extent that he would not have believed possible. There was visibly a sharp drop in living standards between one side and the other of the Spanish-Portuguese frontier, but not between the French and Catalan or the French and Basque borders. There were regional differences, and wide variations between the purchasing power of one individual and another – but were they all that much greater than elsewhere in Europe? Not more than in his native Soviet Russia; they were to be pointed out, condemned, and combated, yes; but credit should be given where credit was due. Spain as a whole could not be considered a nation of poor people any more, even though poverty could still be searched out and found. There were still 1·6 million families 'on the other side of the poverty curtain'. In 1959 there had been between 2 and 3 million depending on where one put the curtain. The claims made both officially in Spain – that the people were 'better off than before' – and by the opposition – that 'the gap between the poor and the better-off has widened' – were both true.

How well was Spain off now compared with other countries? Since 1964 she had advanced much faster than any of the other OECD Mediterranean countries (Italy apart), so the application of Beckerman's criteria[49] to 1966 would show Spain even further ahead of the others than in 1964 – with a figure of about 28 points (U.S. = 100; U.K. about 60). It was a temptation now to compare Spanish living standards with those of France[50] – an unconscious tribute to the advances made.

In 1959 only one person in every 150 had a car : in 1966 it was one person in every 45. Television sets were rarities in 1959. By 1966 every ten inhabitants had access to a set. It was the same with mechanical aids to household comfort. Consumer goods still cost the Spaniard many more man hours than they cost a Briton, but substantially fewer than in 1959.

[48] A political economist, there in 1959 as a student and in 1966 on an extended holiday tour with his wife.
[49] See above, p. 324.
[50] Cf. article by M. Gómez Reino in *La Economía* (*Cuadernos para el diálogo*, num. IX *extraordinario*, Madrid, July 1968) the object of which was to show that the social inequalities of Spain were greater than those of France.

The movements of workers in and out of Spain showed that work abroad was no longer as popular as it had been in earlier years :[51]

In thousands	1964	1965	1966
To Europe	182·8	181·3	130·7
of which to France	69·6	55·9	42·6
Germany	47·4	65·1	38·6
Switzerland	49·1	28·1	30·7
Returns	99·0	120·7	131·7
of which from France	40·6	29·9	18·4
Germany	25·9	33·5	60·3
Switzerland	27·1	31·0	31·3
Balance	83·8	60·6	− 1·0

The decline in the demand for foreign labourers in France and Germany had a bearing on these figures; but not entirely. There were more jobs available at home in industry and services than had been anticipated, and many a man home for Christmas decided to stay at home. With what he could now get at home if he was a skilled workman, he and his family together could live as well as they had previously been able to do when he was working abroad, separated from his family.

The End of the Economic Boom

At the end of 1966 Spain's foreign reserves position was better than it had been half-way through the year, with $1,039 million in hand compared with $1,026 million on 30 June. Five months later, in May 1967, the balance was down to $982 million. Spain looked like heading towards the precipice of bankruptcy as in the period before 1959. She was still some distance away from it; but there was no longer any reason to pretend that all was well. The new constitution and continuing Headship of State by Franco had been approved in referendum. The government now released for publication an IBRD report which it must have held since before the end of 1966. The following were its main points :

[51] OECD report (1969), p. 57.

Agriculture. Production and exports of the traditional export commodities must be increased. The decline of the active population engaged in agriculture is a desirable trend – provided that it is combined with greater productivity and lower costs. The country must itself produce its meat and animal feeds, and not import them.

Industry. The structure must be improved and productivity increased in preparation for an eventual link with EEC. The iron and steel industry must be modernized. Spain should produce more chemicals, machinery, and motor vehicles. More manufactured goods must be exported. INI should not be allowed to expand.

IBRD also recommended less government spending, less building; it approved of the credit squeeze then in force and urged more direct taxes. For the new development plan, then being prepared, it suggested a target of 5·5 per cent annual growth – 3 per cent in agriculture, 8 per cent in industry, and 5 per cent in services.

In July OECD noted that during 1966 'industrial exports [had] exceeded by an appreciable margin the value of the traditional agricultural exports' – not because the latter had dropped in value or quantity, but because Spain had become a maker and exporter, even if only yet on a small scale, of capital equipment, ships, and cars; even lorries to Poland and petroleum products to Britain. OECD warned Spain not to lay too much trust on invisibles to balance the trade deficit : the warning here was prompted by the economic difficulties developing in Germany which were likely to lead to a lessening of their requirements from foreign labour, and in Britain and other countries which might prevent tourists from spending as much money as before on holidays in Spain. These warnings were to be proved right on both points. During 1967 only 3,900 left Spain to work in Germany; 43,900 returned.[52] Remittances from workers abroad fell from their peak of $345 million in 1966 to $320 million. 17·8 million tourists (a new record) went to Spain; but they spent there only $1,110 million, whereas in the previous year 17·3 million tourists had spent $1,202 million. Here was a trend to be watched.

OECD agreed with IBRD that Spain should invest more in agriculture, replace obsolete machinery, and limit government spending to essentials. Surely, it said (though not so pointedly), government subsidies for housing could be limited entirely to low-cost housing and inessentials could be taxed. 'Further progress', it continued, 'could surely be made in improving the assessment of

[52] The figures for all Europe were : departures 59,900; returns 85,900; balance — 26,000

personal incomes for tax purposes'.[53] Spain had still to control the total growth of demand.

OECD, however, accepted that whatever advice they gave, there would be that year 'an appreciable rise in wages', and 'a new expansion of house-building'.

When the government decreed the putting-up of the minimum wage from 60 to 96 pesetas a day in September, an economist critic[54] called it a 'mini-salary'; higher wages, he argued, could stimulate consumer demand and so bring prices down if only management was more efficient. Antonio Añoveros, bishop of Cadiz, in a most outspoken plea for social justice on 1 August, described the 'dark panorama' presented by the condition of workers in his part of Spain.

The sunshine of the economic well-being of a majority was putting an unprivileged minority in darkness.

[53] OECD report (1967), p. 33.
[54] Pablo Canto in *Cuadernos para el diálogo* No. 49 (October 1967).

Chapter 30

Spain under Franco: Political Evolution and the Ups and Downs of Freedom 1959–66

WHEN THE NEWS WAS RELEASED on 11 November 1959 that President Eisenhower was to visit Spain, a number of people went quietly to the American embassy in Madrid and delivered petitions calling on the President to ask Franco to grant an amnesty for political prisoners and exiles.

Spanish exiles had long been assured that if they had committed no common law crime, the fact that they had been on the losing side would not be held against them : they had nothing to fear; and it was true that if the police had no dossier the returned exile was left in peace; but the police had dossiers compiled in the period immediately after the war when culprits were being hunted. Then, to save a neighbour whom the victim had forgiven, the victim had named a person as culprit whom he thought dead or safely in exile. So the exile could now not return.

At the time there were some 950 persons serving prison sentences, convicted of distributing in printed form political doctrines at variance with the principles of the *Movimiento*; for doubting too publicly the integrity or infallibility of government officials; for holding assemblies of more than twenty people without police permission; for organizing or taking a prominent part in a protest against the government's conduct of social or industrial relations. A few, though only a few, belonged to the proscribed communist or socialist parties, or anarchist bodies.

Not all who broke the law were imprisoned or brought to trial. The law worked slowly. There were in November 1959 about a hundred awaiting trial for offences allegedly committed as far back as fifteen years before. There was no saying when they would be tried; but sometimes the 'due process of law' could be quite quick. On 29 January ninety-seven persons had dined together in a hotel in Madrid, the *Menfis* – lawyers, doctors, university professors, industrialists, and even army officers among them. They had announced the formation of an association, the *Unión Española*,

338

recognizing Don Juan as King of Spain. With Don Juan on the throne a government would be formed 'representative of the people', upholding Catholicism but allowing liberty of conscience, giving freedom of speech and association, and subject to a *Cortes* representative of the people. The organizers had been arrested and held briefly by the police. But was there a valid case against them? What they had proposed had been made sacrosanct by the referendum and the *Fuero de los Españoles*. The only charge was unauthorized assembly – and for that their leader, the industrialist Joaquín Satrusteguí, had been fined 50,000 pesetas.

No such defence could be adduced by some fifty-three young men, aged between nineteen and twenty-six, brought to trial by court martial between August and the end of November. They were charged with 'military rebellion' in that they had circulated, or caused to be circulated, in Barcelona, Valencia, and Madrid during the months of May and June, leaflets calling for a 24-hour 'passive resistance' act of protest on 18 June against the economic hardships being suffered by workers and against the authoritarianism of the régime.

Most of the fifty-three shared either the ideals of the *Hermandades Católicas* or the ideology of socialists. The defence recalled the fact that the protest had been a failure because the organizers had withdrawn the call for it when communists had attempted to take over its control : they could surely not be held guilty of military rebellion. The plea was rejected and the accused received sentences of between six months and ten years. One, however, who avowed himself a communist, was tried in November and on 1 December received the extraordinary sentence of twenty-three years. It looked less like an act of justice than the government's retort to those who inside and outside Spain were then asking President Eisenhower either not to bolster the régime's morale and cancel his trip or else when there to do his best for the imprisoned. Whether he did do his best or not, there was no amnesty.

By the end of the year, with the number of political prisoners standing at a higher figure than for some years, the more thoughtful were asking themselves what had become of the promise implied in many an official speech that 1959 would be a year of reconciliation. Much had been expected of the inauguration in April of the monument to the fallen on both sides in the Civil War, the monastery and church of the Valle de los Caídos. The abbot, Don Justo Pérez de Urbel, was a man closely identified with the régime, a Benedictine no less than Escarré of Montserrat.[1] He had on 18 June forwarded to the Minister of Justice a petition signed by an

[1] See below, p. 340.

imposing list of eminent Spaniards for a general and complete amnesty for all political prisoners and exiles; yet his public utterances were rather of support for the victors than of forgiveness of enemies. But then the speech of the Head of State at the inauguration had hardly been conciliatory. He had praised the dead of his side : the men and women who had died steadfast to their religion. This attitude could perhaps be excused; but his references to the Civil War, now long over, as a crusade, to his opponents as 'anti-Spain', and to the *Movimiento* as the only vehicle to peace, were still the words of a victor in battle and not of a peacemaker.[2]

No sooner had the heavy sentence on the young communist been pronounced than the military trial began of twenty Catalans on various charges – mainly unlawful assembly and propaganda over a period of fifteen years. This, too, appeared to be the government's reaction to an episode in Barcelona earlier in the year – an episode which at one time had begun to assume dangerous proportions.

For some time the Catalan provincial authorities had been dealing rigorously with young men belonging to boy scout troops formed under the aegis of parish priests, who thought that Baden-Powell's movement offered ideals more in keeping with Christian doctrine than those taught in the *Falange* Youth assemblies. One such boy scout troop had connections with the abbey of Montserrat. The Civil Governor of Barcelona, General Felipe Acedo, publicly accused the abbot, Aurelio Escarré, of fomenting subversion. The abbot replied obliquely in a sermon with a reference to 'men calling themselves practising Catholics yet ignorant of the Church's fundamental teaching on liberty'. The Governor then rushed to Madrid to demand Escarré's forcible removal. Such an act, however, would have been directly contrary to the Concordat, and Castiella, himself a good Catholic and liberal-minded, would not have stood for it. As it was, action against the boy scouts was doubtfully legal, for if they were, as claimed, a church organization, then they too were protected by the Concordat. The Governor returned discomfited to Barcelona. Taking heart from the episode, young men smeared the walls of buildings in Barcelona with the letter P for protest against the lack of freedom, B for *basta,* enough of the régime, and R for reconciliation. Beards became fashionable – after Fidel Castro – and beards could not be declared illegal.

With the new year 1960 there was no change in government policy on the freedoms of the individual. With the authority of their bishop, the Bilbao HOAC held a meeting on 1 May, the proscribed international Labour Day, which was neither subversive nor revolutionary. Nonetheless, the two principal speakers were arrested and

[2] *Discursos* (1955–9), pp. 593–9.

fined. To the consternation of the local authorities the bishop wrote them a letter confessing to being present, to having applauded the speakers, and to having himself addressed the meeting. He protested, therefore, at the sentences and the presence of police in a note-taking capacity at a 'church meeting'. On 30 May 339 Basque priests put their signature to a very closely reasoned article on the wide gap between the Spanish official and Catholic doctrines on the functions of the state, social order, and the rights and freedoms of the individual. Franco's reply – apart from allusions in speeches on the excellence of the Spanish state and its policies – was his signature on a decree issued in September reinforcing the definition of 'military rebellion' to include strikes 'inspired by political motives' or which led to 'serious disturbances of the public order', spreading false or tendentious information with the aim of disturbing public order, provoking international conflicts, 'damaging the prestige of the state, its institutions, government, army, or other authorities ... planning or taking part in meetings, conferences, or demonstrations with such ends in view ... strikes'.[3]

In November 200 signatories addressed a petition to the Ministers of Information and Education. The list of names was formidable. It included the names of nearly every leading academician, novelist, poet, playwright, scientist, philosopher, and writer for film and radio. Monarchists and Catholics signed together with suspected socialists and agnostics. They appealed not for the abolition of censorship but only for its clarification, for explicit regulations so that writers should know where they stood : 'what is authorized one day may be forbidden the next – a text may be passed for publication in a magazine yet banned as part of a book and vice versa'. The Minister of Information promised a review of the situation; but censorship continued as before, capricious, inexplicable, in moral matters as well as political.

Yet public protest could sometimes succeed, as an incident in Barcelona proved. At the time no newspaper could have an editor or leader-writer not appointed or at least approved by the Minister of Information. Luis de Galinsoga of the Barcelona paper *La Vanguardia,* a man who could be trusted to follow the official line without reference at every phrase to higher authority, for he wrote from conviction, got involved in the thorny subject of the use of Catalan and Basque, which had been forbidden after the war. The Church had objected that it could not do its apostolic work properly unless it spoke to people in the vernacular and concessions had been made. Sermons in Basque and Catalan were now permitted, or at

---

[3] For further details on the Basque priests' protest see International Commission of Jurists, *Spain and the Rule of Law* (Geneva, 1962), Appendix 8.

least 'tolerated'. Galinsoga was either unaware of the practice or else had had enough of it. Suddenly, after being subjected in February 1960 to a sermon in Catalan, he rushed to the sacristy to complain in strong language. He did not go to church, he said, 'to hear dogs barking'. The incident quickly became public knowledge. *La Vanguardia* was boycotted; copies of it were publicly burned in one of the main boulevards; student-led demonstrations met with mass public support; and Galinsoga's dismissal from the newspaper was decreed from Madrid.

In what was supposed to be a gesture of conciliation, Franco then spent most of May in Catalonia with his Cabinet. On the one hand, he sought to satisfy Falangist susceptibilities by attending various 'strength-through-joy' functions, but on the other he gave the Barcelona city council a new charter, granting it a measure of independence of action from Madrid unknown since the overthrow of the *Generalitat* at the end of the Civil War; and he had the Castle of Monjuich, regarded by all Catalans as the constant visible reminder of Castile's domination of Catalonia, demilitarized for conversion into a museum.

The effect of these conciliatory moves was to be diminished within weeks by the Civil Governor, General Acedo, who gave permission for a public function to celebrate the centenary of the birth of the Catalan poet Juan Maragall, but not for the singing at the function of the poet's *Cant de la Senyera,* venerated as the Catalan national anthem. In spite of the ban, it was sung. Police invaded the assembly in a tumultuous fashion and carried off about a hundred people. In detention those under arrest were roughly treated. The abbot of Montserrat, who had received Franco at his monastery in May, now wrote to him direct. Of those under arrest, all were released except one, Dr Jordi Pujol Soley, a leading Catholic and the prime mover in the centenary celebration, who received a seven-year sentence for breaking the law. Nevertheless, Acedo's retirement was announced in October.

With his removal the publication of books and magazines in Catalan became easier; programmes of Catalan verse began to be broadcast; there was even talk of a new daily newspaper in Catalan, talk which came to nothing through lack of capital rather than official opposition. Catalonia was to be trouble-free for nearly two years until 1962, and then the causes were social rather than political. Not until 1967 was there to be any recurrence of persecution by Madrid of what Pope John XXIII called *nationes minores* in his 1963 encyclical *Pacem in Terris.* The government accepted in due course, without demur, the saying of Mass in Catalan, Basque, Gallego, Valencian, and Mallorqín when the use of the vernacular Mass was sanctioned by Rome. But not all the freedoms were to be won so easily; and some not at all.

By 1960 HOAC had a membership of 100,000 men and women, influential in the industrial areas of the north, weaker like the rest of the Church in the south. In the same year the bishops issued a joint statement calling on the faithful to co-operate with the Stabilization Plan, but drew the government's attention to the way in which it was imposing a heavy burden on the poor. The Church was particularly perturbed over the plight of the unemployed and, as we have noted,[4] the government raised the rates of unemployment benefit.

By the end of 1960 HOAC was making serious inroads into the authority of the official representatives of the workers. The *Falange*'s immediate reaction was to seek from local government authorities the banning of HOAC meetings, but not every local official was prepared to oppose the local church authority. Falangist strong men then took to disrupting such meetings. In January 1961 the Primate, Cardinal Plá y Deniel, addressed himself officially to the Secretary-General of the Movement and head of the *sindicatos*, José Solís Ruíz : what HOAC members were doing was apostolic work; Solís' Falangists had no right to interfere. Furthermore, Plá argued, workers had a right to strike and to form their own unions, whatever Spanish law said.

Not to be outdone by HOAC, Solís summoned to Madrid a congress of *sindicatos* in March, which under his leadership passed resolutions advocating land reform, higher wages, and improved housing. Franco addressed them : he was pleased with their discussions – 'without dialogue there can be no policy' (*política*, which also means politics) 'but not anarchic dialogue, not the artificial dialogue of political parties.... The *sindicato* is the channel for your worries, your desires.... But these are not boom times. I must say to you again, we are living in difficult times'[5] – and the congress changed nothing.

Four months later, on 14 July 1961, John XXIII issued his encyclical *Mater et Magistra,* but the Spanish papers did not publish it in full. The régime made much of those passages in it which could be used in support of their contention that the vertical union made for class peace and gave the workers a share in management : Spain's institutions were in accordance with papal teaching. *Acción Católica* published the full text and it became the handbook of HOAC. The less eclectic readers argued that whatever the theory, in practice it was the employers and the government who alone

---

[4] See above, p. 316.
[5] *Discursos* (1960–63), pp. 127–31.

had any say in the vertical union : by law the *sindicatos* were 'instruments of government economic policy' and as such contrary to Catholic teaching. They, for their part, stressed such passages as those which spoke of the rights of workers to a share in ownership and control, and to the benefits of socialization in specific instances. To Spanish Catholic readers it was Spain which the Pope had had in mind when he had written passages such as these :

> In harsh and offensive contrast to the wants of the great majority, there is the abundance and unbridled luxury of the privileged few. . . .
>
> The present generation is compelled to undergo inhuman privations in order to increase the output of the national economy at a rate of acceleration which goes beyond the limits permitted by justice and humanity. . . .
>
> A notable percentage of income is absorbed in building up or furthering an ill-conceived national prestige, or vast sums are spent on armaments. . . .

In speeches to the *Cortes* in June, to the National Council of the *FET y de las JONS,* and to the nation at the end of the year, Franco had numerous passages which sounded like replies to his 'papally' inspired critics. He insisted on his own Catholicism and that the Movement was Catholic in inspiration. But for his victory, he asked on occasions when the Church had appeared 'ungrateful', where would the Church be? What was the fate of the Church in Iron Curtain countries? Communism had taken advantage of the excess of freedom allowed in them when they had been liberal democracies to destroy all liberty. He made much of what had been done to better the lot of the poorer classes – in the construction of new housing and schools. He was bound neither by liberal, capitalist, nor Marxist economic straitjackets. Where socialization was beneficial he accepted it; where private enterprise was more promising he encouraged it. There had been difficulties, and sacrifices had had to be called for and made, but the worst was over.[6]

Franco made no concessions to his clerical critics, save one during 1961 when he again raised unemployment benefits.

In January 1962 the bishop of Bilbao, the Basque Pablo Gurpide Beope, issued a pastoral criticizing the general level of wages in industry and the whole governmental machinery of labour relations, so slow that it could only bring workers to desperation. Two months later the archbishop of Seville, Cardinal José Bueno y Monreal (Segura had died in 1957), surprised the many who expected him to be docile to the civil authorities with a strong condemnation of

[6] *Discursos,* pp. 207–53, 317–41, 357–82.

the low level of agricultural wages : to be tolerable, he said, wages would have to be increased by 50 per cent.

On 6 April the miners of Mieres in Asturias went on strike. (Mieres was a name which still frightened the older generation which could remember the October 1934 revolution.) A good while previously they had put in a claim for a wage increase under the rules for *convenios colectivos,* but months had passed and nothing had been resolved. From Mieres the strike spread throughout the mining district, then to the steelworks at Avilés, the steel- and iron-works in Bilbao, the many little factories in the Basque valleys, over to Catalonia, and down to Valencia. By the beginning of May there were between 100,000 and 150,000 men defying the law against strikes. The newspapers and radio spoke on government orders of communists at work, and certainly there were Soviet broadcasts urging the Spaniards to turn the strikes into revolution. The workers, however, wanted no more than higher wages and an admission on the part of the government that their wage negotiation machinery was inefficient and needed renewal. For every activist who was communist or socialist, there were at least twenty who were not. Members of the *Hermandades* issued leaflets urging the workers to stand firm and in the Basque provinces, where the owners of small enterprises sympathized with the workers, they obtained funds from those owners.

In a speech to the *Hermandad de Alfereces Provisionales* (the Brotherhood of ex-Emergency Officers) on 27 May, Franco included a minatory paragraph : 'Our prosperity and internal peace hurts and irritates [communists and fellow-travellers], and therefore they have sought to infiltrate all our national bodies, even those opposed to their ideas such as the lay institutions of our Church'.[7]

HOAC could not see communists in their midst. *Ecclesia,* not a lay publication, insisted in editorials that the right to strike was 'a natural and Christian right'. The Catholic daily *Ya,* with a far wider circulation, courted government displeasure in milder but nonetheless intelligible articles which were not stopped by the censor. Other papers picked up courage. There were demonstrations of sympathy with the workers by women and students in Madrid. High churchmen in audience with the Head of State implored him in the name of justice to allow a general wage increase.

Two Catholic Action leaders were arrested, but the Cardinal Primate intervened on their behalf, and after inconclusive talks with Franco he wrote a letter to the Foreign Minister. Accepting that the Church should not intervene in political matters, as

7 *Discursos,* p. 392.

prohibited by the Concordat, the Cardinal argued that HOAC was not intervening in such matters but carrying out its social and doctrinal tasks. Was the Spanish state not acting like a communist state, he asked, in maintaining that it was no apostolic work to propagate 'a doctrine contained in the encyclical *Mater et Magistra* just because it clashes with state legislation? Would it not be more logical rather to reform what ought to be reformed, in order to bring it into harmony with this encyclical, in a state which calls itself Catholic and social and whose leader has declared in many speeches that it follows the social doctrine of the Church?' That the letter was addressed to the Foreign Minister and not to the Head of State was significant. The Cardinal was putting the matter out of the national into the international field.

The government was moved to raise the minimum wage to 60 pesetas ($1) a day, a 25 per cent increase, a start at least.

When on 10 July 1962 there were cabinet changes, the Ullastres – Navarro team remained, as did Solís, but there was a new Minister of Labour – a less committed Falangist – and a new Minister of Education, Manuel Lora Tamayo, a university professor of science of some eminence and a man prominent in Catholic Action; and Arias Salgado, identified with a hard line on the censorship of the press, left the post of Minister of Information (and Tourism). In his place there was appointed Manuel Fraga Iribarne, the holder of the Chair of the Theory of State and Constitutional Law in Madrid, who was also Spain's urbane and reputedly liberal-minded representative in UNESCO, a man who had travelled widely and had expressed admiration for British parliamentary democracy and politically independent trade unions. Much was hoped from these changes.

On 15 July the government promised to pursue policies giving 'due attention to the social doctrines of the Church' and 'to perfect the instruments of conciliation and labour jurisdiction'. Two days later at the 'inauguration' of a large new working-class housing estate in Madrid, Franco made a speech containing phrases the like of which he had never used before : 'To reach these hours of plenty, we had to sacrifice many Spanish lives. That blood had to be fruitful. *And I don't mean the blood of just one of the sides,* but all that was shed that one motherland should be free'. And victory as he then went on to speak of it was not his victory but of all, a recognition that both sides had hoped for a better future. He then continued :

From the beginning we sought to build our social edifice on the principles of that papal encyclical of Leo XIII, *Rerum Novarum.*

Indeed we went further than its proposals ... and when the voices of the Pontiffs reach us in that magnificent encyclical *Mater et Magistra* of John XXIII, we receive it with personal joy because that was the path we had been following for the previous twenty years. Just a few days ago, the *Cortes* approved a law of great moral importance, on the participation of workers in management. ... [8]

He sincerely expected much from that law. However, few enterprises were willing to implement it and it was a law without teeth – making it possible but not mandatory for workers to take part in management. More important were the instructions given that the high pile of pending *convenios colectivos* should be rapidly despatched. Wage increases of up to 75 per cent were allowed; and there was extraordinary expedition. The number settled that year reached the figure of 1,538, affecting 2·3 million workers as against 800 in 1961 affecting a third only of that number of employees. Through the years 1963 to November 1967 new *convenios* averaged a thousand a year, and wages were allowed to rise almost on a par with the cost of living, though productivity was still a factor in their calculation. Unemployment was kept at an average of 1·4 per cent of the labour force. Managements complained that on the one hand they were expected to improve their efficiency, while on the other it was difficult to dismiss under-employed staff. Workmen complained that management took advantage of its preponderant position in the *Jurados de Empresa* (Company Joint Dispute Settlement Tribunals) to dismiss the more forthright critics.

Another still more important change occurred in September 1962. The penal code was modified to legalize strikes or stoppages 'for non-political ends'[9] and no action was taken on the following occasions during the years 1963-7 : [10]

1963	777
1964	484
1965	232
1966	179
1967	567[11]

[8] *Discursos,* pp. 435-9; cf. p. 602.

[9] *Boletín Oficial del Estado* (20 September 1962). Modification of Article 222 of *Código Penal* of 1944.

[10] Statistics given by the *Secretariado General de la Organización Sindical* at the IVth *sindicato* Congress, Tarragona, 1968.

[11] Of the 567 in 1967, 203 were in solidarity with dismissed workers.

All these were substantial concessions on the part of a Head of State who had sincerely believed for years that the vertical *sindicato,* uniting employer and employee in a single organization, would produce mutual understanding and peace between them; just as he had hoped that Falangist and traditionalist and the rest would learn mutual understanding and come to work together in harmony in his *Movimiento.* Maybe in theory the *sindicatos* had much to commend them : in practice they failed to make either the employers understand that the best interests of the workers were also their own best interests or the employees to realize that not all employers were out to exploit them all the time.

Undoubtedly the preponderant and decisive factor behind the change of heart and mind which these concessions and the cabinet reshuffle indicated was the action taken by the Primate. Nevertheless, two other events may have contributed slightly to the cabinet changes.

First, over Christmas 1961 Franco's hand had been injured when a shotgun had exploded as he fired it. Secondly, Franco was now in his seventieth year. Though his father and maternal grandfather had lived to a great age, seventy was the biblical span of a man's life and prudence had always been a virtue, some would say a vice, of the Head of State. With the Act of Succession he had laid down what should happen in the event of his death or incapacitation; but he was now of an age at which he could expect lesser ills to beset him constantly and at which he should be able to shed some of his routine tasks. There was to assist him the Secretary of the Cabinet, Admiral Carrero Blanco, a younger man than he and an able interpreter of his thought, but he was a staff officer rather than a commander. During the few days the admiral had been away from his duties, Franco had called upon Generals Muñoz Grandes, Alonso Vega, and Barroso to act on his behalf in day-to-day decisions. Barroso, however, had since advocated his replacement by a younger man as Minister of War : he felt himself too old, even though he was a year younger than Franco.[12] Alonso Vega was three years older than Franco, his lifelong friend. Muñoz Grandes was only three years younger, but in every way suited to head the government if the Head of State were indisposed, and even if worse were to happen. By disposition a monarchist but not identified with the monarchists, he had been Secretary-General of the original *FET y de las JONS* and as such kept Serrano Suñer and the extremists in check. As com-

[12] In 1966 I found General Barroso the clear thinker he had always been, but he did believe his memory was failing him.

mander of the Blue Division he acquitted himself well – foreign Russophils hated him, but the Spanish army respected him for it; he was liked although he had been a disciplinarian; foreign army officers in recent years had found him easy to understand and they, too, liked him. Accordingly, in addition to conceding Barroso his retirement, and replacing the Ministers of Information, Education, and Labour, Franco instituted a new post. Muñoz Grandes, promoted to the rank of Captain-General, the same as Franco's, was named deputy Prime Minister.

There was a third event which may also have had some bearing on the cabinet changes, and in the introduction of a more liberal atmosphere. In February 1962 Spain had applied for associate membership of the European Economic Community and the reactions of some of its members and of western Europe generally had not been promising.

Since Britain had refused in 1959 to reciprocate Spain's abolition of visas for British subjects, British relations with Spain had become more 'correct'.[13] Britain then took three months to reply to the Spanish invitation for a reciprocal agreement. When the reply came, she explained the delay on the grounds that in the reply 'it was desired to include all the British territories which wished to enter an agreement'. Britain welcomed the Spanish initiative, but, the reply continued, 'the various measures against Gibraltar adopted by the Spanish Government in 1954 are unfriendly measures ... not consistent with relations now existing between the two countries.' Britain could not conclude 'a visa agreement which ratified, even indirectly, the existing situation at La Linea...' Spain and Britain, Spain was reminded, were now partners in OEEC; in 1956 Britain had voted for the entry of Spain into the U.N. and now into OEEC.[14]

For eleven months until June 1960 the matter had remained thus. La Linea thereafter had become an entry point for British visitors to Spain but not an exit point for Spanish subjects, and visas had then been abolished. It had worried neither government unduly that Spaniards had needed visas to enter Britain: few Spaniards had the money to travel; they wanted work, and Britain could not afford to be as generous as other countries. British workmen had not welcomed Italians as colleagues in the immediate post-war years and there was no reason to suppose that they would be more welcoming to Spaniards. Britain was not prepared to issue labour permits to Spaniards except within a limited range

[13] The Foreign Office stock phrase whenever diplomatic correspondents asked spokesmen what was Britain's policy towards Spain.
[14] *Spanish Red Book on Gibraltar.*

of employment – as hospital orderlies, maidservants, or waiters; many a Spaniard with a university degree and anxious to improve his English could be seen scrubbing floors in the mental hospitals of Surrey. Germany and Switzerland welcomed foreigners as industrial workers and even taught many of them skills which they were later able to use back home.[15] The only people affected by the La Linea restriction were the wealthy Spaniards of the south who could not make a quick trip into Gibraltar to smuggle luxury products back to Spain.

Early in 1961 the British Home Secretary, R. A. Butler, visited Spain as a tourist and dined informally with Castiella. He was reported as having said to his host that it was a pity that Spain had been kept out of international life when she represented an essential factor for the West against the communist danger. In spite of the storm which this remark aroused among left-wing members in the House of Commons, the Foreign Secretary, Lord Home, later went to Spain on an official visit with the object of improving trade relations though not, as the left wing suggested, to discuss Spain's entry into NATO. General Barroso, Anglophile and Francophile, may possibly have been attracted to NATO, even though Franco had often publicly stated that Spain had no desire to join NATO, being already integrated into western defence through the treaties with the U.S.A. and with Portugal. Spain indeed had nothing to gain from membership – and this was not appreciated by the British M.P.s who made their abhorrence of the Spanish régime clear in the House of Commons – except that in NATO the younger generation of Spanish officers, men who would be the general officers commanding military regions and divisions in a few years time, would have come into constant and daily contact with their opposite numbers in other countries, and their political and military breadth of vision would have been widened considerably.[16]

Lord Home's visit was intended to counterbalance that of Ludwig Erhard, then the West German Minister of Economy, who had offered Spain technical assistance and long-term credits worth

[15] The Federation of British Industries had a splendid scheme of scholarships, and some British firms were far-seeing enough to realize that a manager who as a youth had been trained in Britain, was likely to be well disposed towards capital equipment from that country. Where Germany and other countries had the advantage was that there were men well disposed at all and not just the top levels.

[16] In talking to Portuguese army officers in Angola and Mozambique in 1964, I was conscious of a wide gulf in thought and ideas between those who had served in NATO HQs and those who knew nothing of the world outside Portugal.

DM 200 million :[17] Britain could do no more than point to technical assistance through OECD and to the fact that she was Spain's best customer. Spain did begin then to look to Britain more frequently as a source of her needs. Over the years 1961–6 the pattern of Spanish trade changed completely. Spain's exports to Britain grew slowly from £69·1 million in 1961 to £79·1 : but British exports shot up £9 million in the very year of the Butler–Home visits to £39·5 million, to £60·9 million the year later, and thereafter by leaps and bounds to £115 million in 1966. The change would have been more marked still had Britain transferred Gibraltar and had Harold Wilson in 1964 not had qualms of conscience over the proposed sale of some frigates to Spain, qualms which he did not seem to have experienced when selling arms to other equally or more authoritarian governments.

With de Gaulle as President relations between France and Spain also improved substantially by 1962. Spanish exiles with subversion in mind were now being denied the use of French radio stations. The French police watched carefully the activities of socialists, communists, and anarchists in their headquarters in Toulouse and other towns. The days when a handful of terrorists could organize a raid into Spain, carry out their plan, and then feel safe once they had crossed back into France were over. One of the few survivors from earlier days, Francisco Sabater, had met his end spectacularly in January 1960, when, pursued back over the frontier by the French police, he had been killed in a gun battle by the Civil Guard 50 kilometres from Barcelona. In August 1961 the Civil War republican general *El Campesino* organized two incursions from France with a small band of followers, but the second attempt ended with casualties to his followers in Spain and his internment in France the moment he recrossed the Pyrenees.

It was in this atmosphere of better relations with western European powers, and especially with France, that Spain formally applied in February 1962 for associate membership of the EEC – just in time for the matter to be discussed at a congress of the European Movement held in Munich. (Britain, too, was then exploring ways of entering the Common Market.) Some eighty Spaniards went to Munich from Spain, Gil Robles and Satrusteguí, and a professor of political economy at Madrid, Jesús Prados Arrarte, among them, and met there some forty exiles, including Salvador de Madariaga.

These were Spaniards of democratic views afraid that if EEC were to accept Spain even as an associate member, the chances of liberalization under the régime would be severely jeopardized.

[17] $50 million; the agreement was concluded on 23 February 1962.

Membership might, on the other hand, be made conditional on such liberalization. Gil Robles, recently active as defence counsel for men accused of political offences and feeling the restrictions on liberty keenly, exchanged views with Madariaga, who felt the same way. They agreed that the establishment of truly representative and democratic institutions must be a prerequisite of Spain's association with 'the integration of European countries'. The congress, at their suggestion, passed a resolution 'that Spain's application to join the European Community was welcomed : that such membership necessarily implied acceptance of the democratic principles and practices on which the Community is based' – and it expressed the hope that Spain would evolve towards democracy without violence.

Meanwhile in Spain it was alleged that Gil Robles and his companions had consorted with exiles to denigrate the name of Spain. On their return he, Satrustegui, and Prados were offered the choice of exile or enforced residence in the Canaries. Gil Robles chose the former, the others the latter. J. B. Hynd, the British Labour M.P., who went to see Franco on their behalf, was left with the impression that Franco was 'genuinely interested to secure [EEC] associate membership.'[18] Nevertheless, it was not until much later, after the Primate's letter, that a more liberal view found favour. The exiles were not allowed to return home until July 1964, by which time Spain's application for EEC associate membership had floundered as deeply as Britain's for full membership.

There were two more cogent reasons why Muñoz Grandes should return to the Cabinet. First, he knew how to bring Falangist belligerents to heel. Franco could expect as stiff opposition from the old-style Falangists to his approaches to Europe as from any Dutch, Belgian, or British left-winger. The Spaniards at Munich had wanted Spain in Europe once she became a democracy : the Falangists wanted Spain to have nothing to do with Europe. Further, the U.S. bases agreements were due for renegotiation and Muñoz Grandes had been Minister of War at the time of their original negotiation.

The Falangist opposition reached fever-pitch on 23 January 1963 – belatedly and unnecessarily, for in fact, internal political considerations apart, the success or failure of Spain's request for associate membership depended from the start on the fate of the United Kingdom's negotiations for full membership, and after President de Gaulle's press conference on the 14th it was obvious that France would veto Britain's entry. On that day the old-style Falangist newspaper *Es Así*, which did not have to go through

[18] John B. Hynd, M.P., on 11 July 1962 in the BBC's European Service.

the usual channels of press censorship, published a violent attack on Franco's policy of Europeanization as the great betrayal of the cause for which Falangists had fought a civil war. It went on to demand a republic and dismissed the 1947 referendum on a monarchy as meaningless. A meeting of the National Council of the Movement was hastily summoned and its members spoke with surprising freedom. The Falangists publicized the results of a public opinion poll they had taken among the youth of Spain and claimed that 58 per cent favoured a republic.[19] The meeting closed with a long speech by the Head of State and nothing of moment decided. It was 9 March and by coincidence the twenty-fifth anniversary of the promulgation of the Labour Charter, a circumstance which gave Franco the opportunity to review all the ways in which the social conditions of workers had improved, to admit how much had yet to be done for agricultural workers, to ride again the hobby-horse that the *sindicato* organization was the model of what trade unions should be, and to declare how prejudicial to all societies were class warfare and strikes. Spain was not, and was never to be, either totalitarian or subjected to the 'tyranny of political parties unrepresentative of the people', nor again 'an anarchy of proliferating parties'. It was, on the contrary, an organic (that is well-ordered) democracy, with its existing institutions and the instrument of the referendum at hand whenever matters of importance had to be decided.[20]

Now one body of opinion, now another, could be pleased with what he said. His reference to the referendum could be interpreted in two ways : 'the future of Spain as a monarchy has been decided'; or 'a new referendum could reverse the first'. The republican Falangists quietened down. What the speech had in fact meant was that now as on other past occasions Franco was quite capable of dealing with mutiny aboard; that he would choose the course. The speeches at the National Congress of the Movement had revealed that beneath the surface there were still floating all the mines of twenty-five years earlier, monarchist of various sorts, republican, Catholic and anti-clerical, capitalist and anti-capitalist, liberal-minded and authoritarian, and even totalitarian.

The renegotiation of the U.S. agreements was protracted over several months, but it was concluded on the day of expiry of the

[19] One should like to know the composition of the 'representative sample' on which these results were based. The futility of the operation (as indeed of the 1947 referendum, though to a lesser extent) lay, of course, in the many basically different structures of government all called republics, e.g. the Soviet, the West German, the French, American, etc., and of all those called monarchies.

[20] *Discursos,* pp. 505–39.

originals – 26 September. Spain granted the U.S.A. the use of the bases for a further five years, but as before at a price. The U.S.A. was to help substantially in the re-equipment of the Spanish armed forces and to make $100 million available through the Export-Import Bank. Spain was to have greater control of the bases and to be kept informed on all matters relating to the defence of the West. She had no need to join NATO : and for the moment at any rate it was not to her economic advantage to be linked with the EEC.

The U.S.A. was not the only country prepared to help Spain financially. France advanced Spain in November 750 million New Francs (well over $150 million). The loan was due in April 1964, when an event occurred to show that Spain in 1963 was no different from Spain in 1947, 1940, or any other year back to 1939 in her reaction to outside pressures.

In November 1963 the Communist Party sent into Spain Julián Grimau, a Central Committee member, but almost immediately he was located by the police. According to them he jumped out of a first-floor window to escape. On 18 April he was brought before an open court martial which in four hours decided that he had been responsible for numerous executions and tortures during the Civil War and therefore condemned him to death. The Cabinet considered appeals from western diplomats, French Cardinals, and others. It was touch-and-go whether the sentence would be commuted, General Muñoz Grandes arguing that Grimau's execution would be *contraproducente*. Khrushchev sent a personal appeal to Franco for clemency, so Grimau was executed on 20 April – and Muñoz Grandes was proved right. The outside world refused to believe the story of the fall from the window or the evidence on Grimau's Civil War record. There was widespread revulsion anyway that a man should be condemned for crimes so far away in time. During the rest of the year there were a number of bomb explosions, the work of amateurs.[21]

The number of people being brought before courts martial for political offences was nevertheless diminishing. Two weeks after the Grimau case, on 4 May, the announcement was made that a new civilian Tribunal of Public Order would be established to try all political offences except those involving the use of firearms or explosives[22] and this was done the following November. The transfer of cases from the military courts to this new civilian

---

[21] On Grimau see *Franco*, pp. 435–6.
[22] Under the republic as under the monarchy from the early years of the century, the use of explosives resulting in death rendered the accused even if a civilian liable to a court martial.

tribunal gave defence counsels for the accused much more time to study the charges and prepare answers, and to bring witnesses on their client's behalf. At the time it was hailed as another advance towards liberalization, and it was hoped that the next step would be for this tribunal to be abolished, all cases being transferred to ordinary tribunals; but that was not to be for many years.

The demand for the removal of restrictions on common freedoms grew bolder following the publication of John XXIII's encyclical *Pacem in Terris.* So much of it, as of *Mater et Magistra,* seemed to Catholics in opposition to be particularly applicable to Spain. Among many other passages, activists underlined the following paragraphs :

> By the natural law, every human being has the right to respect for his person; his good reputation; the right to freedom in searching for truth and in expressing and communicating his opinion; and in pursuit of art, within the limits laid down by the moral order and the common good. *And he has the right to be informed truthfully about public events.*

(If the Spanish state did base its policies on Catholic doctrines, readers asked, how then could the existing censorship be justified? The Ministry of Information promised a new press law and in the meantime censorship was relaxed to some extent.)

> From the fact that human beings are by nature social, there arises the right of assembly and association. They also have the right to give the societies of which they are members the form they consider most suitable for the aim they have in view, and to act within such societies *on their own initiative* and *on their own responsibility* in order to achieve their desired objectives.

(This struck at one of the constitutional or *Fundamental* laws, in particular the clause defining the *sindicatos* as instruments of government economic policy.)

> It is impossible to determine once and for all what is the most suitable form of government, or how civil authorities can most effectively fulfil their respective functions, that is, the legislative, judicial, and executive functions of the State.

(Here the government could point to the many references by the Head of State to the imperfections of the régime's institutions and to his consciousness that they could be improved – but the answer did not satisfy all objectors, especially in the light of the following passage :)

To safeguard the inviolable rights of the human person, and to facilitate the fulfilment of his duties, should be the essential office of every public authority.

This means that, if any government does not acknowledge the rights of man or violates them, it not only fails in its duty, but its orders completely lack juridical force.

It must not be concluded because authority comes from God, that therefore men have no right to choose those who are to rule the State, to decide the form of government and to determine both the way in which authority is to be exercised and its limits.

(And those who had suffered trial by military courts underlined :)

Any human society that is established on relations of force must be regarded as inhuman, inasmuch as the personality of its members is repressed or restricted, when in fact they should be provided with appropriate incentives and means for developing and perfecting themselves.

(Catalans and Basques thought of their disabilities when they read) :

It must be made clear that justice is seriously violated by whatever is done to limit the strength and numerical increase of [national] minorities; the injustice is even more serious if such sinful projects are aimed at the very extinction of these groups.

On the other hand, the demands of justice are admirably observed by those civil authorities who promote the natural betterment of those citizens belonging to a smaller ethnic group, particularly when that betterment concerns their language, the development of their natural gifts, their ancestral customs, and their accomplishments and endeavour in the economic order.

But what shook official Spain most were the passages which encouraged Catholics to look for the good in non-Catholics and even in communists.

Outside Catholic activist circles *Pacem in Terris* was not mentioned. In his customary end-of-year message for 1963 Franco spoke of the sorrow and pain felt in Spain at the death of John XXIII, but much of the speech appeared to be a defence of his system against what the encyclical taught. Communism was the enemy. The countries enslaved behind the Iron Curtain had not suffered military defeat : they were the victims of liberal democracy in which communism could corrupt and buy minds. Indeed it worried him that 'so many worthy persons ruling the countries of the West' should not see the heart of the problem and plan for the future; but then they were so involved in party wars that they could not see the horizon. The development plan could be realized only in the peace made possible by the *sindicato,* which joined together entrepreneurs, management, and workers. Of course there was always human weakness and abuse of power; but there were independent tribunals to redress wrongs. There was unity, and he wanted unity but not uniformity. There was room within the law for *una variedad de pareceres,* a variety of opinions. There were in the world many types of government. He criticized no one else's solutions for their own domestic problems : let them not criticize Spain's. Spain, he reaffirmed, was Catholic. In Spain there was no battle between Church and state, each a perfect society. The 1953 Concordat was a treaty of friendship. The state imposed no curb on the Church's liberty.[23]

Fourteen days earlier Franco had answered questions put to him by *Le Figaro*'s correspondent. He was asked whether the Church, in the light of *Mater et Magistra,* had a say in Spain's social policy : if the answer was yes, what did he think of the *Hermandades?* In his reply, Franco said the *Hermandades* helped the religious advisers of the *sindicatos* : 'if sometimes they do otherwise it is because they have not disassociated themselves from the part being played by trouble-making agents infiltrated into their ranks.'[24]

The answer was an obvious warning that if the *Hermandad* and other Catholic activists continued with their advocacy of freedom of association, especially of workers, and to co-operate with men of socialist and communist tendencies, as they were doing within the limits established by *Pacem in Terris,* then they would be considered communists themselves. Nevertheless, they continued as before.

There was now in existence an *Alianza Sindical Obrera* to unite all workers, irrespective of creed or political ideology, who advocated the establishment of trade unions independent both of the state *and* of party. (This was anathema not only to the Spanish state, but also to the socialists in exile who wanted the re-establishment of the Marxist sectarian UGT.) And there were also *Comisiones Obreras,* Workers' Commissions, recognized at factory level as much more representative of the workers than the official representatives and brought in by many a management in discussions on collective agreements and other disputes. Their members were *Hermandad,* socialist, communist, and other activists, in many

[23] *Discursos,* pp. 611–39.
[24] Ibid., pp. 599–609.

cases dismissed *enlaces*; and there were a few who, in spite of being officially appointed representatives in the *sindicato* structure, were recognized by the workers as 'of them' and welcomed into the commissions.

All this was well known to the state, which decided for the moment to condone the existence side by side of legal and illegal workers' organizations. Students who demonstrated in February 1964, demanding freedom of association, were treated with unprecedented mildness. A trial was held, in civilian courts, of thirty-three of the socialists arrested six years earlier in 1958 and on bail pending trial ever since. They were accused of attempting to revive the banned Socialist Party. Eighteen lawyers were given complete freedom to defend their clients' political beliefs and actions, and in effect publicly to rehabilitate Spanish socialism. The court dismissed twenty of the accused and gave the thirteen convicted of having broken the law sentences which were cancelled by the amnesties granted on such occasions as the accessions of John XXIII and Paul VI, subsequent to the commission of their offences. A new generation of *Felipes*[25] (Peninsular Liberation Front) planted a handful of hand-made bombs in various places in 1963 and during May and June 1964 they renewed their activities; but this time they were detected. Their leader proved to be an embittered army officer, Ruíz Marqués, who claimed that their mentor was the crypto-communist Foreign Minister of the republic, Álvarez del Vayo. He was condemned to death – one at least of his bombs having killed an innocent civilian – but as his trial was open to the public and conducted unimpeachably, there were no protests at home or abroad.

The Communist Party proper was no problem. The state knew well enough that it was limited in number to a few hundred activists and maybe 4,000 or 5,000 sympathizers; and that the party was split – a split that produced a curious episode. The police received the names of twelve pro-Moscow communists, including the name of Juan Lacalle Larraga, son of the Air Minister. Six weeks later the police received the names of a hundred pro-Peking communists. All were sentenced under the law for their membership of the party, but none for any length of time.

There were small ripples in the generally unruffled surface of Spain in the year 1964 during which the government celebrated 'twenty-five years of peace'.[26] In doing so it repeatedly drew attention to its record; and its record in the material development of Spain was something of which it could be proud. In those twenty-five

[25] See above, p. 298
[26] 'Of peace—or victory?', asked the abbot of Montserrat.

years, in spite of World War II and of Spain's subsequent ostracism, improvements dreamt of but never achieved by any other Spanish régime had been realized. Spain was moving out of her endemic state of underdevelopment in which she had need of outside assistance, into a condition of medium development in which she was becoming able to help the less fortunate. In providing technical aid in this way her performance, proportionate to her means, was already somewhat better than that of many a more developed and more wealthy country. In the academic year 1964–5 7,000 first-degree foreign students were admitted into her universities. There were nearly one thousand in advanced technical schools and in schools of a similar level, and another 6,000 doing post-graduate study. In the year 1965–6 the figure was even higher, the foreign student body in the universities alone reaching 15,500, of which, as could be expected, 12,000 came from the Spanish-speaking world and the rest from the U.S.A., the Afro-Asian countries, and from Europe both sides of the Iron Curtain. These, plus another 3,000 non-university students, cost the Spanish government some 555 million pesetas ($92·5 million), a figure 'several times greater than the *total* technical assistance received by Spain from all sources since 1954.'[27] Even as early as 1959 there were some 5,000 students from Latin America, and in helping the less developed countries to the best of her ability Spain had anticipated one of the recommendations of *Pacem in Terris*.

The Spanish government's record in subsidized housing was one of which a British government might have been proud. All factors and ratios taken into consideration, perhaps no country could substantiate a claim to a better.[28] Where the government could be attacked was in that it had done little to disturb the complacency of the latifundists of the south, whose labourers lived in hovels.

Between 1956 and 1964 the government built 25,600 classrooms to accommodate a million children of primary-school age, six to thirteen, and there was room now in state and private establishments for 3·9 million. In the state universities there were over 75,000 Spanish students. The weakness lay in secondary education, but Spain was now participating in the OECD Mediterranean Regional Project, one of whose objects was to correct imbalances and another to expand and improve the quality of education throughout the system. In 1964 for the first time in living memory expenditure on defence took second place in the budget to housing and public

---

[27] OECD, *Technical assistance and the economic development of Spain* (Paris, 1968), p. 87. The figures quoted are rounded off; details on pp. 88–97.
[28] See above, pp. 319, 331.

works, and less was spent on the army than on education; the state had committed itself, by agreeing to participate in the OECD project, to ever-increasing expenditure on education – at fixed peseta values from 14,000 million pesetas in 1962, 1·8 per cent of the gross national product, to 35,100 million in 1967, 3·3 per cent of GNP, and rising thereafter to 65,900 million, 4 per cent of GNP.[29] Illiteracy among women had fallen by 1964 from 28·4 per cent in 1940 to 11·2 per cent, and among men from 17·2 per cent to 4·2 per cent[30]; though as in other aspects of life there were wide regional differences.[31]

The republican Azaña had in his day made much of his reduction of the Spanish army to 121,000 men in the peninsula and 30,000 in Africa. Thus 23 million Spaniards had to provide and support 150,000 soldiers. As Minister of War, Barroso also quietly reorganized the army. By 1961, when the country's population was almost 31 million, it had been reduced to 200,000. Azaña's ratio of civilians to soldiers was 154 : 1; Barroso's 155 : 1. The organization of Azaña's nine divisions made no sense in post-1914 terms, or indeed, it might be argued, in post-Franco–Prussian War realities. Five of Barroso's twelve divisions were of 'pentomic' structure and all capable of integration into the defence of the West at short notice. In 1964 there were plans for further cuts in the overall size of the army.[32] Opponents of the régime spoke of the armed services as 'patridophagous' (fatherland-eating), but in truth they were not more so than those of any other European power and less than most. The police forces – Civil Guard, *Asaltos,* and *Carabineros* – numbered in 1935 72,000 men. In 1964 there were 85,000 Civil Guards and *Policía Armada (grises),* uniformed and plain clothes. Thus the police forces were, proportionately to population, slightly smaller too. The *grises* acquired a reputation for brutality, but no worse than the *Asaltos* before them. The Civil Guard were now becoming 'highway patrols' rather than 'rangers'.

The government's claim that never in modern times had Spain enjoyed such political stability or general tranquillity is historically

[29] OECD, *The Mediterranean Regional Project—Spain* (Paris, 1965).
[30] Ministry of Education.
[31] The figures were lowered after 1962 with an intensive campaign in the army and in courses for adults. General Rafael Cavanillas Prosper in *El ejército de tierra y sus nuevas unidades* (Madrid), p. 404, states that during the period 1955–60 the percentage of recruits found to be illiterate varied between 12 and 15 per cent – nearly double the official national average for youths of call-up age. That is not entirely surprising if it is remembered that the 'call-up' was more thorough for rural than urban boys and for those in the south than in the north; and that most of the recruits of the time were boys with no more than four years schooling.
[32] Bringing reality and paper strength closer together.

true. The cost in terms of violent death, imprisonments, and curtailments of civil liberties demonstrably falls far below the proportionate cost to the country in the turmoil of the hundred years before the Civil War. In that century three kings were dethroned, two regents exiled, two republics and two dictatorships established and overthrown, three civil wars fought, four Prime Ministers assassinated, to say nothing of twenty major military revolts and a change of government on average every eleven months.

Perhaps the majority were reasonably well satisfied; perhaps they were not—there is no means of telling. The majority wanted to live in peace, and in general they lived peacefully; nevertheless there was always a minority who would have been more satisfied had much more rein been allowed to basic freedoms and thus more opportunity to spur officials to energetic action against social injustice.

In the last week of 1964 the official bulletin of the Brotherhoods carried an article on the desirability of democracy. Spain, it said, was ready to have a true parliament with a minimum of two parties. That was to be the high water-mark of HOAC daring against the established order. The *Cortes* had just had placed before them a new Law of Association. No society which advocated free trade unions or plurality of parties was to be permitted : no organization would be allowed to affiliate with international bodies without prior cabinet approval. Members of the HOAC had been in touch with the International Confederation of Free Trade Unions. The Boy Scout movement which had been growing under the protection of Catholic Action or parish priests wished for closer links with France and Britain. Within the *Cortes* the Bill was strongly opposed by Ruíz Giménez, who still had a seat as an ex-cabinet Minister. He argued that its provisions, whatever the Bill said to the contrary, contravened the Concordat. His views as a professor of law and an ex-ambassador to the Vatican carried weight, but not enough weight. *Ecclesia* called it 'a legal instrument for future violation ... of a basic human right'. How could it be reconciled with the relevant passages on man's right to freedom of association in *Pacem in Terris*? The Bill nevertheless became law and Ruíz Giménez resigned in protest.

The Head of State had often said that he welcomed dialogue and a variety of opinions, so long as they were presented without violence, and evolution so long as it was not revolution. In 1963 Ruíz Giménez founded a journal, *Cuadernos para el diálogo,* which, while editorially Christian Democrat, welcomed contributions from anyone with a reasoned approach to any political or social problem. Its object was 'to create a channel for dialogue between people of different religious, social, and political views'; 'to make easier the communication between men of different generations of beliefs and attitudes to life, of ideas and feelings, about facts and events and about the pressing religious, economic, social, and political problems of our changing moment of history.'[33] *Cuadernos* became within months as important in the education of opinion among young lawyers, economists, and other intellectuals as in their day were the ideologically very restricted bulletins of the *Institución Libre de Enseñanza*. Through *Cuadernos* Ruíz Giménez now hoped that he would be able to continue provoking argument and counsel to make youth think and the régime evolve, as it could possibly have done, into a democracy, a real democracy, such as Spain had never had. He came to be looked upon if not as Leader of the Opposition, at least as its mentor.

After the passage early in 1965 of the new Law of Association, the HOAC were advised locally 'not to press their luck too far', and not to put to the test the question whether the new law did or did not contradict the Concordat, and if so which had the greater force. This was perhaps a mistake, for where they stepped back from the vanguard, in the Workers' Commissions and elsewhere, others whose sincerity in advocating free trade unions was doubtful and who were more interested in disrupting the established order, took their place. On 13 March a thousand Asturian miners, shouting 'Liberty, Liberty', stormed the police headquarters in Mieres. No shots were fired, and only one demonstrator was arrested; and in April there was a clash between police and workers shouting the same slogan outside the *sindicato* headquarters in Madrid. The government as usual attributed the episode to 'communist conspirators'; for once they may have been right, though the thought lingered in the minds of observers whether the leaders should not be looked for within the official *sindicato* organization itself, among old-style Falangists anxious to regain the ground that their inactivity had lost them to Catholic or socialist activists, or among others wanting to say to a government which had been behaving with moderation since 1962 : 'look what happens when you give these people a bit of freedom – it leads to violence, and violence will lead to anarchy' – and so to provoke the government to repressive measures. The government was circumspect and conciliatory. It did not use its new law against either the HOAC or the *Alianza Sindical Obrera*. While attributing the Mieres riot to foreign communist conspirators, it

[33] For Ruíz Giménez's own reasons for the *Cuardernos* see *Cuadernos para el diálogo*, VII *extraordinario* (February 1968), pp. 5–9. The professor was a lay representative at Vatican II.

had observed that the basic cause of the miners' brief burst of anger had been bureaucratic inefficiency in the prompt payment of cabinet-approved benefits to victims of silicosis. And here too the government was perhaps nearer the mark than those who from abroad believed firmly that there was then a *widespread* desire among the workers of Asturias or elsewhere for independent trade unions. Behind the demand for free trade unions there were two separate motivations. One was religio-philosophic: the reasoning given in *Mater et Magistra* and *Pacem in Terris*. Men so motivated believed it immoral that the state should appoint so much as one man in authority over a trade union organization. It would be wrong to say that more than a few tens of thousands were so motivated. What irked the hundreds of thousands of workers was that the men whom they saw every day, the *enlaces* or shop-stewards, and the officials immediately above them, were not men of their choice, not their champions against management. Had these champions been dismissable by them rather than by some remote government official, and because they proved themselves weak negotiators and not because they were tough, had there been no immediately visible representative of government or manage-ment, then probably they would have been reasonably satisfied; and very satisfied if decisions made at factory level had not had to wait months for government ratification and if government deci-sions in the workers' favour had not taken so long to percolate back to the shop-floor. For it must not be forgotten that there was no tradition in Spain of free trade unions: the UGT and CNT had been the fighting instruments of a party and an ideology, their officials doing whatever they were ordered by the Socialist Party in the one case and by the natural leaders of the anarchists in the other, subordinating the genuine local grievances of workers to the creation of a revolutionary atmosphere.

The Mieres and a few other insignificant incidents apart, 1965 passed peacefully. Some 200,000 *enlaces* and other *sindicato* officials were due for re-election in September 1966. The Madrid mass-circulation evening daily *Pueblo* (*sindicato*-controlled) carried articles by its editor, Emilio Romero, demanding that this time the elections should really be free. He claimed that 1,800 of the *enlaces* elected on the previous occasion had been ejected and victimized for acting subsequently in the service of their com-panions: this should not be allowed to occur again. Solís, as Secre-tary-General of the Movement and head of the *sindicatos*, announced that any man, whether or not 'a militant member of the movement', would be permitted to stand for election. No hindrance was placed, at any rate in the larger enterprises, to canvassing by or on behalf of known members of the *Alianza Sindical Obrera,* the HOAC, and known members of the Workers' Commissions.[34] The elections were free. Solís spoke of the need for a new Sindical Law – which, it was assumed, would liberalize the whole system.

While there was less labour trouble during 1966 than 1965, there was plenty of trouble over those years in another department of Spanish life. Increasingly since 1960–61 there had been agitation against the government's *Sindicato Español Universitario* or SEU. The government dismissed the Falangist militants from office, but the students remained unsatisfied. They wanted no part in an organization the expressed principal aim of which was to inculcate a particular political philosophy. The government thereupon instructed the new officials to concentrate on the SEU's social aims and eschew politics. Students recalled the SEU's historical connections with the *Falange* in its infancy and the Fascist phase of the *Movimiento* and founded their own clandestine organizations. The government had encouraged them to surface and as the 1964–5 academic year began, the SEU began a withdrawal from the universities of Madrid and Barcelona.

In February 1965 a last-minute ban was imposed on a series of lectures, intended to cover an exegesis of *Pacem in Terris,* in the Madrid Faculty of Philosophy. Students organized a procession in protest and four professors were among those arrested for taking part in an illegal assembly. Student protests against the arrests led to more demonstrations and more arrests. The early cry 'we want free unions' gave way to 'we are fighting for a democratic union in a democratic state'. The students moved from the campus on the edge of the city into the city proper. The *grises,* called out against a crowd estimated at 5,000, beat the students with truncheons and had water-hoses turned on them.

The vice-Secretary-General of the Movement, Herrero Tejedor, asked representatives of the independent unions to meet him and discuss their grievances. Some were suspicious, others were convinced that no good could come from discussion; but the majority decided that the invitation to a meeting was sincere. So it was, in that Herrero Tejedor listened to all that they had to say. Any decision, however, would have to be left to the Cabinet, but when it met the Ministers were divided. Some argued that the SEU was a *sindicato*; if the student demand was met and the *sindicato* was dissolved, where then would the other *sindicatos* stand from a legal point of view? The *sindicatos* were an integral part of the state; dissolve one and all would have to be dissolved : dissolve all

[34] *Instituto de Estudios Laborales* (Barcelona), Bulletins 4 and 5 (1968).

and the régime would dissolve. Others counselled prudence. To concede nothing could have equally serious consequences. Professors had joined the demonstrations. If support grew like this workers might join the students and there was the precedent of Primo de Rivera's downfall on what student demonstrations might lead to. A compromise was reached : the moribund SEU was to be allowed to die; in its place there were to be new *Asociaciones Profesionales de Estudiantes* (APE), whose officials were to be freely chosen and elected.

To establish this in law a decree was issued on 5 April 1965. The students had called a truce at the time of the meeting with Herrero Tejedor. Easter was now upon them and the summer term was too near examinations for a renewal of hostilities – and there would surely be a renewal. Many of the activist students were angry at having been called by the government 'a handful of agitators who follow Moscow's orders'. Anger was more widespread when they saw the rules decided upon by authority for elections of officials to these new associations : voting was to be obligatory; first-year students were barred from standing for the higher posts.

The elections held in November were a fiasco. In some schools and faculties no candidate would stand when candidates marked as having taken part in demonstrations were declared ineligible. In others blank and spoiled papers outnumbered votes cast for candidates.

The truce was over and 3,000 students petitioned Franco direct to dismiss the Minister. He was dismissed, or at least he resigned after a decent interval the following year. In the meantime the four professors under arrest were fined, two being suspended and two, one of them a Catholic philosopher of standing, José Luís Aranguren, were expelled. So also was the socialist Tierno Galván, who in fact had advised the students to present their grievances in the prescribed manner and go home.

In its April 1966 number[35] *Cuadernos para el diálogo* suggested the changes in the legal position and organization of Spanish universities without which agitation was likely to continue. The universities would have to be autonomous. This meant that the state would have to surrender its powers over the nomination of deans of faculties and rectors, the deans thereafter choosing the rectors, the staff the deans. The universities would have to be left by the state to run themselves and their studies in their own way; and the students would have to be allowed to form their own national and local associations with freely elected representatives of

[35] *Cuadernos*, No. 31, 'La Universidad como Problema', p. 5.

their choice. What a student did within or as a member of an association should have no repercussions on his academic life or vice versa, although rectors and deans might have the power to intervene in the activities of an association in exceptional circumstances. Finally university education would have to be made really available to everyone capable of benefiting from it, irrespective of the economic means of the family.

The students and professors were asking for nothing revolutionary, but rather the return of the freedoms which the universities had had taken away from them by the *Liberales* and the Bourbons. Not all students and professors by any means, but at any rate a large enough number, had shown themselves ready, by taking part in public demonstrations, to risk their chance of entering the liberal professions, and thus to justify the supposition that those who shared these views were not a tiny group of malcontents 'inspired by communist agitators'.

The dissatisfaction with the legal position of the universities and their inability to form free associations simmered on throughout 1966 without reaching boiling-point except on one occasion. In March between 400 and 500 university men and women held a conference in a Capuchin friary on the outskirts of Barcelona. Their theme was freedom of association as a natural right. They drew up a constitution for a free *Sindicato Democrático de Estudiantes de la Universidad de Barcelona* (SDEUB). Police invaded the friary after a two-day siege and thirty-four of those who had attended were fined. There were demonstrations in their support in Madrid and other university cities throughout April and into May. In Barcelona 150 priests presented a protest against the ill-treatment by the police of one of the arrested students. The police cudgelled the priests in return.

The affair was the talk of the town for a fortnight in Madrid and Barcelona as well, for it was briefly reported in the press, as was the police defence that 'the priests had started the fighting'. News of that kind would not have been printed even six months earlier, but in April a new press law had come into force changing the system of press censorship.

The new law provided that any editor or publisher was now free to print what he wished; but he had to deliver the printed text to the censors at the Ministry a number of hours before the moment of public sale, the number depending on the length of the text. The censors were not authorized to take action unless in their opinion the text amounted to a lie or the publication of something immoral; scorned the principles of the National Movement or any of the Basic Laws; imperilled national defence, the security of the state, the maintenance of public order, or peace with other nations; brought into contempt institutions or individuals in the course of criticizing political or administrative measures; questioned the independence of the courts; or invaded privacy or offended personal or family honour. The censors, if so satisfied, could order the newspaper, book, or periodical to be withdrawn from sale or distribution, but if they did so, the publisher could bring the matter to court. The court would then find either for the censors or for the publishers; and if for the censors, then the publisher could be proceeded against for a breach of the law or any other law of the land.

It was not liberty of the press, but it was, as a writer in *Cuadernos* put it, a 'miniliberty'.[36] Newspapers began to give news of many more events in Spain than before. They carried satirical cartoons. There was fair criticism of institutions and even officials for their acts of commission and omission. Books giving independent judgements on numerous social, political, and economic subjects began to appear. The censorship, which had previously been neither thorough nor consistent, now seemed to be even less firm in its attitude; but overall it was substantially less arbitrary than it had been and more open to argument.

While Christian Democrats and Social Democrats took full advantage of the limited new freedom of the press to consider social and economic subjects, and advocate other freedoms, monarchists did so likewise to urge the restoration of the king and the Falangists to urge the fulfilment of the José Antonio nationalistic and socialistic programme. At the end of June an incident occurred which puzzled foreign observers to whom the distinction between *Movimiento* and *Falange* was unknown. The Madrid police dispersed a crowd of youths carrying banners, *Movimiento no, Falange sí* and even *Franco no, Falange sí*. There were not many of them but they were vociferous. In Barcelona groups calling themselves *Escuadrones Negros*, Black Squadrons, attacked Catholic liberal centres and individuals.

The *Falange* was again chafing against recent developments. Their doctrines had now little appeal to youth beyond a small minority, a minority prone to violence. Falangist candidates in the *sindicato* elections had fared badly wherever up against Workers' Commissions' men. The government appeared to be giving too much attention to the Church and the decisions of the Vatican Council : even a Law of Religious Liberty was being drafted.

In this atmosphere of relaxation of controls, unparalleled in the

36 Francisco José Ruíz Gisbert in VII *extraordinario* (February 1968), p. 9.

thirty years since the outbreak of the Civil War, and with a feeling of economic well-being without equal in the country's history, Spain intensified her campaign to force Britain to give her back Gibraltar.

After the visa agreement of 1960 Spain and Britain had conferred sporadically, Britain continuing to press for the conversion of La Linea into an 'ordinary frontier post', while Spain complained of the changes, already made or proposed, in the government of Gibraltar on the grounds that they were contrary to the provisions of Utrecht. She complained, too, of the opportunities that the creation of a free port in Gibraltar had given to smugglers. Spain had managed to discourage smuggling by sea. In 1959 coast patrols intercepted goods to the value of 1,794 million pesetas (£1·1 million); in 1961 to the value of only 840 million (£0·5 million). After 1954 Spaniards other than genuine workers were not allowed to enter or leave Spain by La Linea. In 1953, 144,000 had done so and presumably would do so again if La Linea became a point of exit for Spaniards. It would be impossible to search such numbers for smuggled goods without long delays. On 31 July 1963 Britain offered a 'package deal'. If Spain allowed Spaniards to cross over to Gibraltar by La Linea, Britain would provide the Spanish authorities with information on smugglers, especially those operating by sea. At that moment, however, Spain heard that 'the decolonization of Gibraltar' would be taken up again in September by the U.N. Committee of Twenty-four on Decolonization. The subject had previously been adjourned for a year after fourteen speeches had been heard and Britain had then quietly suggested to Spain that in their mutual interests they should jointly ask the U.N. to drop it. Now, however, Spain was jubilant. The committee on analysis had seemed more impressed by the Spanish than by the British arguments and Spain was not now prepared to deny herself such a good platform. How good a platform it was became apparent in September and October 1964. After listening to the representatives of Britain and Spain, Gibraltarians and Spaniards, the committee issued a long communiqué and instruction :

The special Committee . . . notes the existence of a disagreement, even of a dispute, between the United Kingdom and Spain over the status and the situation of the territory of Gibraltar. In these circumstances, the special committee invites the United Kingdom and Spain to undertake negotiations without delay, in order to find, in accordance with the principles of the Charter of the United Nations, a negotiated solution, taking duly into account the opinions expressed by the members of the

Committee ... and bearing in mind the interests of the population of the territory.

The views expressed had been varied and inconclusive; but Spain could feel encouraged by the fact that of ten members who had spoken only one, Australia, aligned herself behind Britain, whereas four, Venezuela, Uruguay, Syria, and Tunisia, supported Spain.

No sooner had this communiqué been issued than Spain imposed new restrictions on the passage of people and goods through La Linea. Until then there had been about half a million tourists a year visiting Gibraltar, of whom 150,000 landed there and then crossed over to Spain, and upwards of a quarter of a million were car- and coach-borne visitors who after a day or two in Gibraltar, went back into Spain. Tourists now found that Spaniards took a long time over each traveller at the customs, so that crossing the frontier involved hours of delay. The Spanish government insisted that the restrictions were no more than measures to curb smugglers. In the British view they constituted in effect an economic blockade. They were vicious and unnecessary and no other explanation of them was possible than that Spain was trying to force the issue by attempting to destroy the economy of Gibraltar which had been built over generations on the basis of interdependence between the two territories.

There was nothing that Britain could do. Spain was acting within her rights, however mercilessly. Britain assuaged the fears of the Gibraltarians by drawing up a plan for the Rock's development as a self-contained tourist centre – for about £30 million spread over fifteen years. Spain went one better. The hinterland, that part of the province of Cadiz called the *Campo de Gibraltar,* had long been disgracefully neglected. As part of the 1964–7 development plan seven cities[37] were selected as 'growth points' to bring industrial prosperity to depressed areas. The *Campo* was now decreed a new priority growth point in which the state undertook to invest 3,921 million pesetas (£23·5 million) and to encourage private enterprise to invest another 5,000 million (£30 million) during the two years 1966 and 1967. Mid-way through 1966 the investment was going more or less according to plan.

Throughout 1965 Spain increased the restrictions on traffic to and from Gibraltar. In January non-Spanish commuters were told that only carriers of workers' passes would be allowed through La Linea; in March that only Spaniards could have those passes; and Spain refused to accept passports issued in the name of the

[37] See above, p. 325.

24 • •

government of Gibraltar whose existence she did not recognize. A thousand Gibraltarians had to migrate back to the Rock. Next Spanish workers were told not to spend any part of their wages in Gibraltar. Only fresh fruit, vegetables, and fish were allowed to pass through La Linea out of Spain.

In November 1965 the British delegate at the United Nations reported all this to the committee, adding that overland tourist traffic had been cut by delays at the frontier by 95 per cent and that tourists were being made to pay heavy duties on any purchases they made in Gibraltar. Britain was not prepared to negotiate under duress and least of all to discuss her sovereignty over Gibraltar. On this occasion Mauretania, Syria, Tunisia, the Philippines, the UAR, and Zambia declared outright that Gibraltar should be returned to Spain. The committee enjoined Britain and Spain to settle their differences.

British and Spanish representatives met in London in May 1966. Britain was prepared to discuss joint measures to curb smuggling – anything but sovereignty : Spain nothing but sovereignty. The Spanish Foreign Minister brought with him the following proposals : having agreed to give Gibraltar back to Spain, first Britain would be allowed to lease Gibraltar as a military base; secondly, the present inhabitants of Gibraltar would be allowed to retain their British nationality; thirdly, they would be at liberty to remain there and would be guaranteed against discrimination.

No progress was made then, nor in June or July. In August Spanish workers in Gibraltar obeyed orders from their Spanish government-controlled unions to strike for higher pay. The Spanish government forbade the RAF to fly aircraft over Spain. In September there were further Anglo-Spanish talks as inconclusive as before. Spain still wanted the legality of Britain's sovereignty reviewed and imposed further restrictions on passage through the frontier. In October Britain proposed to Spain that the whole legal question of Gibraltar should be referred to the International Court of Justice at The Hague. Spain rejected Britain's proposal on the grounds that it was a contradiction of the U.N. resolution that the matter should be discussed by Britain and Spain.

The reaction of British commentators to Spain's rejection of the proposal was to assert that Spain was too aware of the strength in law of Britain's case to risk a judgment by the International Court. On the other hand, no Spaniard doubted that Britain had now no legal claim to Gibraltar if she had ever had any. The facts were so self-evident that even to submit the case to international judgment was to imply that Britain might have some vestige of reason on her side. Moreover, experience showed that the

International Court was one in which proceedings could be prolonged for years – and Spain (Franco especially) wanted Gibraltar then and not at some future date.

The U.N. General Assembly then discussed Gibraltar as the Committee of Twenty-four had done in the previous November; and though the Assembly went on to pass a resolution calling again for further negotiations to bring the colonial status of Gibraltar to an end bearing in mind the wishes of the inhabitants, it could be sensed that a growing number of countries believed that the solution lay in Britain's return of Gibraltar to Spain, Spain giving the inhabitants the guarantees that she had proposed in May. In the committee Venezuela, Tunisia, Syria, Iran, Tanzania, and Uruguay told Britain bluntly that in their opinion she was impeding the negotiations. On 12 July 1966 Britain had formally claimed sovereignty over the piece of land on which the airstrip lay. Up till then it had been described by Britain as a sort of no-man's land over which she had acquired rights in default of any Spanish objections to the building of the airstrip. Uruguay's representative, while expressing his admiration for 'that great country which is Great Britain', had called it 'usurpation'. In its report to the Assembly the committee had been less polite in describing this as 'a very serious act of aggression by the United Kingdom against Spain'.[38]

Spaniards laughed sardonically as they recalled that exactly twenty years earlier the same United Nations had voted to ostracize Spain as a danger to peace and potential aggressor.

Franco and his government could feel well pleased at the end of 1966; and they had another reason for their elation. What was in effect a new constitution had been put to a referendum and approved – a constitution which appeared to promise a more liberal future for the people than they had had for thirty years.

[38] British White Papers and *Spanish Red Books on Gibraltar* (U.N. Doc. A/6300/add. 8).

Chapter 31

Spain Thirty Years After the Civil War

The Opposition 1946–66

In 1946 FRANCO was expected by many of his supporters as well as his enemies to give up his position, but he disappointed them. In the 1950s monarchists, parliamentarians, and socialists, not to mention Falangists and traditionalists who looked upon Franco as a traitor to their two opposed ideals, desired his fall so ardently that they believed it imminent from one day to the next. So convincing were they when they talked to foreigners that even those not hostile to Franco assessed his chances of survival as slender. When the Germans withdrew from southern France, *maquisards* crossed the Pyrenees confident that the people would turn to them as liberators, but they received minimal help. Lister, the Civil War leader, thought there had been some misunderstanding. For years he continued to send small groups. They, likewise failing to find supporters, were driven to adopt the terror tactics of communist guerrilla warfare.[1] Spanish mountain villages refused to be cowed. Socialists sent in men of peace to re-establish the UGT clandestinely. They won over a few supporters, but only a few.

What held the people back? Franco's survival during the twenty years 1946–66 has been explained as based on the fear of another civil war, the army, the police. This explanation is inadequate. Against a mass rising not even the most efficient police force would have been effective. There would assuredly have been bloodshed as a rising gathered momentum. That alone would not have deterred Spaniards, among whom, after the Civil War as before, the age-long ideas of death as liberation was prevalent, of death for a good cause as the worthiest crown to life, and of cowardice as the most abject *deshonor*. If not the police, what about the army? The army was of the people : many of its officers were ex-rankers; there had been no *pronunciamiento* but civil war in 1936 precisely because the divisions of the nation permeated the army, because one army side had begun to fight the other before ever civilians had put on uniforms. What then did they fear about civil war?

[1] See Appendix A.

Not death, not even the shattering and putrefaction of battle. The front-line combatant had no desire to see again such scenes as he had seen, but front-line combatants constituted only a small percentage of the population.

If the enquirer pressed his questions below the surface, he found two other fears besides those of the police, of the army, or of going to the front. There was the fear of oneself, of what crimes any man might commit when driven by hatred or by lust for vengeance. The Spaniard, even the atheist, has a strong sense of what the Christian calls the consequences of original sin; and of his duty to avoid 'the dangerous occasions of sin'. Whatever his faults he does not hide from himself his human nature. He knows himself. This was the real fear. And there was another, quite as strong as all the others, fear of a return to the chaos and anarchy of the pre-war period in which men could not really live.

* * *

Because of the way that the landowners and the industrialists behaved in victory, there was little enough reason why their labourers or workers should be well-disposed towards them. Few workers spoke with favour and many with hatred of the Franco régime; but those who had experienced the republic remembered vividly the hardships of the unemployment of that period in which at times the rate had reached as high a proportion as 15 per cent. The wages they were now getting might be grossly inadequate, but there was work and there were wages. Why should they rise against the régime to exchange it for the tyranny of the dictatorship of the proletariat, or the Soviet state, or 'libertarian communism'? Where men looked back to the 'good old days' – and what literature contains a better poem on the theme than Spain's *Coplas* of Jorge Manrique? – the 'good old days' in the 1940s and 1950s were those of the dictator *par excellence,* the General Duke Primo de Rivera, another period of full and even more underpaid employment.

But apart from fears, there was another reason why the people would not rise against Franco. They knew their history. The only hope for a successful rising at any time was that some section of the officer corps should have decided to oust him and the others to condone the act. No change of régime, to the left or right, had ever occurred in the past without the help or connivance of a considerable part of the army, officers or N.C.O.s and rankers; in the imposition on the people of governments sometimes liberal, sometimes reactionary, during the nineteenth century; in the overthrow of Isabel II; in the interregnum of Amadeus of Savoy; in the establishment of the First Republic and its dissolution; the restoration of 1875 – in all these events army generals had been the protagonists. Had the army not connived at it, there would not have been a Second Republic. Yagüe the Falangist, Kindelán the monarchist, and other generals had been tempted to be disloyal to Franco, and had allowed their thoughts to succumb; but at the 'moment of truth' they had all repented and rejoined his side. Never in the history of Spain had any man in power who was not a king inspired such steadfastness, and only very few kings; and his ability to inspire this loyalty extended over civilians also, even in spite of themselves.

By 1960 the number of people who spoke of Franco's departure as imminent had diminished noticeably. A few continued to weave plots over café tables, but they could have no serious intention of carrying them out. The ageing Franco was beginning to command respect among people of all classes and ages. *Ese tío* (or more politely *ese hombre*) was a phrase which had acquired overtones of admiration even on the lips of men who had no natural cause to wish him well. By 1966, with Franco in his seventy-fifth year, all but a few extremist opponents talked of what they would do 'when he goes' and no longer 'when we have thrown him out'. What most Spaniards wanted was not fundamentally different from what Franco had often said he wanted for them – peace, prosperity, social justice, and a greater say in the management of affairs. Where they differed from him and among themselves, was how that greater say could be achieved, to what end, and how quickly.[2]

There was one sector which in 1966 as in 1946 wanted peace and prosperity, but which as a group was not zealous for social justice or democratization – the monarchists. With Franco in the natural course of events having only a few more years to live, Spaniards asked themselves 'after Franco what?' : the monarchists asked, 'after Franco who?' Some said Don Juan, count of Barcelona, the son of the late Alfonso XIII; a small number Carlos Hugo, a young man descended from the original nineteenth-century Don Carlos, but indirectly and through a female, and therefore as disqualified on Salic principles as Don Juan; yet, said his supporters, preferable to Don Juan because he was not descended from the hated Isabel II. It was generally assumed that Franco wanted Don Juan's son, Juan Carlos, to succeed him as Head of State; and that was why he had had him brought up in Spain. In fact, Franco never said so publicly, and even privately,

[2] Cf. editorials and articles (1966–7) in *Cuadernos para el diálogo, Destino, Triunfo, Promos,* and other opposition journals.

as far as is known, had said no more than that he hoped Juan Carlos would be a worthy wearer of the Spanish Crown – a successor, not necessarily *his* successor. The only relevant public statement had been that of Don Juan himself : that he, Don Juan, would never accept the Crown from Franco's hands.

Thus most Spaniards by 1966 were concerned about what would succeed Franco rather than who; and there were perhaps fewer monarchists at the end of 1966 than at the beginning. Following the passage of the Press Law in April, many newspapers, and in particular the Madrid *ABC* and the Barcelona *La Vanguardia,* had worn to death the theme of monarchy – and in the opinion of many a reader done the monarchy to death,[3] if only because so many of the advocates of monarchy had written in terms which recalled 1866 or even 1766, and hardly the present day.

Publicly socialists were now among the strongest supporters of the restoration of the monarchy : privately they referred to the king to come as *Juan el Breve,* John the Brief – either Juan or Juan Carlos, it did not matter who. Their reasoning was on these lines : the departure of Franco by death or incapacitation must be allowed to take place smoothly, for violence then would either favour the extremists, Falangist or communist, both better organized than the socialists, or else provoke the army to a *coup.* If army, Falangists, or communists should win, socialism would have lost. On the other hand, given a peaceful transition, a king restored without violence would be unlikely to resist pressures to permit the formation of moderate political parties. The Socialist Party then surfacing would have the chance to organize itself nationally. Once calmly organized, the masses throughout the nation could be told the virtues of Marxism which they would understand more easily and therefore accept more readily than in 1931 because more workers could now read and write, and Spain was more industrialized and urbanized. Accepting Marxism, the masses would vote the party to power, by a real majority and not as in 1931 or 1936. The party would then have what it had not had during the republic – the sanction of the people to establish the dictatorship of the proletariat; the king would see the implications and leave peacefully.

Let no one be deceived : the Spanish socialist of 1966 was wholeheartedly Marxist. It was one of the results of twenty-seven years of press censorship that the people of Spain missed the experience of other countries where Marxist economics was practised and

---

[3] Cf. Alberto Miguez, *Cuadernos,* No. 42 (March 1967), p. 24: 'in the few months of "liberty of the Press" the monarchists have created ... more anti-monarchists than did the whole of the troubled history of monarchy in Spain'. Having read the articles, I can sympathize with Miguez's reaction.

found wanting, and thus Spanish socialists were largely out of touch with the newer interpretations of the writings of Marx and Engels. The Spanish socialist mind was stuck in 1936. If a questioner penetrated behind the first reassuring answers, and pressed socialists to consider what they would do if post-Franco socialism failed to appeal to the majority as it had in the pre-Franco era (socialists in Spain were readier than those in exile to admit that socialism had never won over more than a quarter or a fifth of the people whatever the election figures), then some would confess, with regret, that they would have no choice but to proceed to revolutionary methods – but that was a long way ahead.[4] For the present they were doing well enough in their proselytizing among workers and intellectuals. Even Catholic intellectuals were being influenced by Marxism. Between 1964 and April 1966 books by young Spaniards, undisguisedly Marxist in approach, had been printed, passed by the press censors, and put on sale. Either the press censors were victims of their own censorship and ignorant of Marxism, and did not realize they were authorizing Marxist literature, or else they had decided that Marxist principles were not contrary to the principles of the *Movimiento*; perhaps the latter, for after April 1966 and after the passage of the Press Law, they began to authorize Spanish translations of the works of Marx and Engels, and even (oh the irony!)[5] the works of Oscar Lange, no longer a prophet in his own land.

Vatican II's *Gaudium et Spes* and John XXIII's *Mater et Magistra* and *Pacem in Terris* were for radical social change, but without violence; so the Catholic activists were bound in conscience to work in peace for social justice and democratization. Their opposition had to be within the law. Communists who obeyed their Secretary-General, Santiago Carrillo, were expected to make common cause with such Catholics and even socialists,[6] to seek conversions but not to provoke trouble. The socialists were perhaps inclined to overestimate the degree of organization which the Communist Party had achieved underground – for Spanish communists had been reacting to current events very much like their Italian co-religionists ever since the Hungarian Revolution. As most were loyal to Carrillo, therefore most were also for peaceful penetration, especially into the Workers' Commissions, and peace at the moment of transition – unlike the Maoists, but these were not very numerous. Marxists, a few Trotskyists, and anarchists apart, the only other potential (and occasionally actual) troublemakers were, as we said

---

[4] Conversations with prominent socialist intellectuals, 1966.
[5] See above, p. 276.
[6] Cf. Santiago Carrillo, *Después de Franco¿ Qué?* (Paris, 1965).

in the last chapter, students and the diehard genuine Falangists who became each year more and more infuriated with Franco's betrayal of the ideals of the founder of their movement.

Such then was the panorama of the opposition to the régime in the summer and autumn of 1966. All told it did not amount to very much. As we have seen,[7] the country was more prosperous than ever before; there was greater freedom; and the government seemed ready to evolve towards more freedom still.

The New 'Constitution' 1966

On 22 November 1966 Franco placed before the *Cortes* a *Proyecto de Ley Orgánica del Estado* – a draft constitution. On 4 December he reached his seventy-fourth birthday, in robust health though some of the symptoms of Parkinson's disease were detectable in him. On 14 December the draft was put to a referendum.

On his way to the *Cortes* a body of youths had shouted at Franco 'Movimiento no, Falange sí', and 'Down with Franco'. Some monarchist, Christian Democrat, and socialist groups within Spain urged the people to boycott the referendum or to vote against the draft. Various petitions were addressed to the Head of State to allow articles and broadcasts critical of the draft, but these were rejected and the government mounted a large-scale propaganda campaign of its own. It sought neither to explain the new law nor even to extol its virtues, for either course would have been beyond the ingenuity of the best advertising agency. The draft set forth a constitution of 66 Articles which with annexes amending existing laws ran to about 15,000 words. Instead the campaign turned the referendum into a vote of confidence and thanks to Franco for the economic and social changes effected during his rule. In putting the draft before the *Cortes*, Franco himself had given some impressive figures; fewer than usual, in fact, and therefore making the more impact, and all connected with what was still the major preoccupation of most Spaniards – education. According to him :

In 1936 there had been
46,805 schoolteachers :	now there were		130,000
2·5 million children at school :	,,	,, ,,	4 million
60 per cent attendance :	,,	,, ,,	85 per cent
111 secondary schools :	,,	,, ,,	nearly 1,700
with 2,739 teachers	,,	,, ,,	26,000 plus

There were now three times as many university students.[8]

[7] See above, p. 334.
[8] *Discursos* (1964–7), 22 November 1966, pp. 229–30.

The results of the campaign exceeded expectations. Over 90 per cent of the people were reported to have voted; and over 95 per cent of those who did were reported as having voted 'Yes'.

The government may reasonably be judged to have overstated its victory. Greatly improved though communications and the health of the nation were in 1966 compared with thirty years earlier, it must seem improbable that an absentee 10 per cent of the electorate was enough to cover those who did not vote through sickness, infirmity, or lack of transport from remote homestead to polling-station, even leaving aside those who deliberately abstained. Voting, however, was encouraged by a decree that every wage-earner was to have a half-day off with pay, and many an unwilling person may have gone so as to be seen and not lose the money. None the less, it is credible that the majority voted 'yes' – not the percentage quoted, but a majority certainly. For what was the individual approving if he voted 'yes' (the Spanish being a nation to which the tag *tot homines tot sententiae* applies more truthfully perhaps than to any other)? He was not approving every one of the 66 Articles and consequent amendments – one to the *Fuero de los Españoles* (Charter of Rights), five to the Labour Charter, and ten to the *Cortes* Law – but a package containing some things which he valued enough for him to agree that they should be lumped in with the rest.

A Basque parish priest writing in *Cuadernos*[9] the following February and confessing that he had voted yes, explained his yes meant no to civil war and to the extremists of the left and right, yes to the imperfect democracy of Spain in 1966 in preference to the daily tumult and non-government of pre-Franco days. It was a yes, he said, to the comparative liberty now being allowed and to the hope that its limits would be widened, that the recent evolution towards liberty would continue; and yes to the good Franco had done, though the priest would continue to criticize in the future as he had in the past what he considered evil or mistaken in the régime. He had voted neither yes nor no to monarchy, *Movimiento,* National Council; there were Articles of which he approved and others of which he roundly disapproved; he had voted yes to peace, Franco, and evolution.

How justified was the hope that the constitution which became law on 10 January 1967 promised evolution towards democracy and greater freedom? There was nothing in the first six articles.

The state is a kingdom : it exists to maintain and defend unity between the men and the lands of Spain, the 'spiritual and

[9] *Cuadernos,* No. 41 (February 1967). Article by Bonifacio Borobia.

material heritage of the nation', its independence; to protect the
rights of the individual, the family, and society; to promote social
justice and subordinate vested interests to the common good. The
state is to be faithful to the principles of the National Movement
'which of their very nature are permanent and unchangeable. . . .'

But, as we have seen,[10] these principles as defined in 1958 were
capable of wide interpretation, and allowed a measure of freedom
of political action – as wide in British terms as from left of centre
Labour to right of centre Conservative.

The Head of State is the supreme representative of the nation.
He personifies national sovereignty. His is the supreme political
and administrative power, national head of the *Movimiento,*
supreme commander of the armed forces . . ., etc.

These were wider than the prerogatives of the Crown in Britain
and rather less wide than the constitutional authority of the President of the U.S.A.

Article VII offered a glimmer of hope. Listed under the powers
of the Head of State was his duty : to nominate and relieve of
his functions the Head of Government. Thus the offices of Head of
State and of Government were to be separated. The new Head was
to be selected by the Head of State from a trio proposed by the
Council of the Realm. The Council, according to one of the annexes,
was to be reconstituted : its members were to be the senior
prelate in the new *Cortes;* the senior serving officer in the
armed forces; the Chief of Staff; the President of the Supreme
Court of Justice; the president of the Council of State (an advisory
body to the Head of Government); the President of the Institute of
Spain (the presidency of all the Royal Academies); ten members
of the *Cortes* chosen by their peers; the Speaker of the *Cortes* as
Chairman.

Here was another gleam : except in so far as the Head of State
chose prelates for the *Cortes* and the Chief of Staff, nomination to
this Council passed out of his hands.

The Head of Government's term of office was to be five years.
He would choose his Cabinet, his choice, however, needing the
ratification of the Head of State. As Head of Government he was
to be also executive head of the Movement and Chairman of the
National Council of the Movement. The Council's vice-chairman
was to be the Secretary-General of the Movement (designated by
the Head of State). In the first place Franco would designate

[10] See above, pp. 299–300.

forty 'life' members to it, but as each member reached the age of seventy-five, a replacement would be co-opted by the survivors. The Head of Government would nominate six more, twelve would be *Cortes* members elected by their fellows, and fifty-two others elected by the provincial branches of the *Movimiento* : in all, a body of 110 plus Chairman and Secretary-General.

The Council's tasks were to be these : to strengthen unity between the men and lands of Spain; to defend the integrity of the principles of the Movement; to watch that economic development was kept adjusted to the needs of social justice; to see to the development of the rights and liberties recognized by the Basic Laws, and stimulate public opinion to influence policies; to help to imbue youth with the principles of the *Movimiento*; to look to the continuation and improvement of the Movement; to ensure that it *moved* and did not become immobile.

Accordingly, the Council was to be the watchdog over legislation, even a Senate : the government was to inform it of any law it proposed to put before the *Cortes* and the Council was empowered to propose measures to the government.

One of its allotted tasks was : *Encauzar, dentro de los Principios del Movimiento, el contraste de pareceres sobre la acción política,*[11] not a well-defined phrase : 'to open a channel', within the principles, for the interplay of opinions on political action : or 'to set on its way . . . the interplay', or again 'to keep going . . . the interplay while preventing it from becoming a free-for-all'; and what meaning precisely was to be given to *acción política,* the day-to-day political actions, short- and long-term policies, or all of them? However, *some* interplay of opinion was now officially legal.

The new *Ley Orgánica* also reformed the constitution of the *Cortes.* Its make-up was now to be the following :

1. The Cabinet (20 plus).
2. The members of the National Council (95).
3. The President of the Supreme Court and four other high officials of state.
4. Twenty-five nominees of the Head of State (in consultation with the Council of the Realm) from among men distinguished in the Church, the armed services, or the civil service.
5. The university rectors (12) and representatives of Royal Academies (6).
6. Representatives of other learned and professional bodies (up to 30) chosen by their peers.
7. 150 representatives, 36 by virtue of their office in the

[11] Article 21(e).

sindicatos, the rest elected by the *sindicatos* (workers and employers in equal proportion).

8. About 115 members elected by local authorities.
9. 'Two representatives of the family per province, elected by those on the electoral roll of heads of families and married women.' (108).

Thus, the new *Cortes* was to consist of about 565 members; of these, Franco was empowered to nominate:

as Head of State : 25
as Head of Government : 20 plus (the Cabinet)
as *Caudillo* : 40 (National Councillors)
as Head of Government : 6 more in the National Council

and, since as Head of State he nominated the university rectors, the President of the Supreme Court, etc., and approved the choice of senior *sindicato* officials, a further 60 could be said to be his nominees as well.

Therefore in all 150 members could owe their place in the *Cortes* to Franco – a substantial reduction, nonetheless, of the total in the previous *Cortes* –and 415 to election by their colleagues in professions, *sindicatos, Movimiento,* etc.

The innovation, the ray of hope of evolution, was the 108 family representatives. The principle of direct election to the *Cortes* was here being reintroduced, albeit with limited suffrage, thirty years after its suppression. In the annexes, too, there were other gleams of hope.

The task of the *Cortes* was now 'to draft and pass legislation' instead of 'to prepare and draft laws' – a subtle but important change. The Council of the Realm was now to propose the Speaker and the *Cortes* to elect their other officials. The Head of State now bound himself to sign and promulgate laws passed by the *Cortes* within a month and send them back to the *Cortes* for further discussion only if the Council of the Realm (fifteen of whose seventeen members were *Cortes* members as well) agreed.

The Law of Succession was amended to provide for more possible eventualities, but there was nothing significant in the changes. In the *Fuero de los Españoles,* however, there was one change, to encourage not only the 30,000 Protestants who had been suffering under irritating disabilities since the end of the republic, but also Catholics anxious that Spanish legislation should not contradict the spirit and the letter of the Second Vatican Council.

Article VI of the *Fuero,* as approved in 1945, read :

The profession and practice of the Catholic religion, which is that of the Spanish state, shall enjoy official protection. Nobody may be molested for his religious beliefs or in private worship; but no public ceremonies or manifestation of any but the Catholic religion shall be allowed.

The first sentence remained; but the second now read : the state will protect freedom of religion which will be guaranteed by effective laws also safeguarding public morality and order.

The most promising amendments were in the Labour Charter. Where, in the 1938 original, one clause had read : 'all individual or collective acts that in any way disturb normal output or militate against it shall be considered crimes against the country'; the 1967 text ran : 'unlawful individual or collective acts which *seriously* disturb production or attempt to do so shall be subject to the penalties of the law'.[12] Elsewhere all words and phrases with totalitarian overtones were deleted. But the most radical change was in the long section establishing the structures and purposes of the *sindicatos*. As rewritten, there was nothing remotely resembling the following clause of the 1938 original : 'the vertical *sindicato* is an instrument at the service of the state by means of which the state shall be able to carry out its economic policy...'[13] – and nowhere was there a reference to *vertical sindicatos* or 'direction by the state'. As before, there were to be divisions by branch, of agriculture, industry, or services; but within each branch three separate associations were foreseen, one for the owners, one for management (*técnicos*), and one for workers, 'in defence of their own interests', and so presumably independent of each other. Their officials were to be freely elected and truly representative, therefore, one presumed, not necessarily militant members of the Movement.

As amended, the Labour Charter contained nothing to which anyone not bound to strict Marxist or national-syndicalist principles could object, and much to raise the hopes of those who advocated unions free from state or any partisan control.

The whole *Ley Orgánica* or constitution, then, did seem capable of stirring the *Movimiento* towards democracy, not the democracy of parties, but a democracy none the less. A man could have very liberal ideas yet subscribe to a passage in Franco's speech to the *Cortes* when he put the draft of the law before them :

[12] Declaration XI.2. The basic books for a study of the Spanish constitution are *Leyes Fundamentales del Reino* (Madrid, Imprenta del Boletín Oficial del Estado, 1967) and *Leyes Fundamentales del Estado. La Constitución Española* (Madrid, Servicio Informativo Español, 1967).
[13] Declaration XII. 4.

Let Spaniards remember that every people is always surrounded by its familiar demons, which are different for each people. The names of those of Spain are called : Spirit of Anarchy, Negative Criticism, Divisions between men, Extremism, and Mutual Enmity. Any political system nurturing those defects in its bosom, releasing those familiar demons, will spatter sooner or later, sooner probably rather than later, all the material progress, all the improvements in living of our compatriots.[14]

In 1966 Franco spoke to the nation, not as had been his custom for years on the penultimate day of the year, but deliberately on 24 December, Christmas Eve. Few listeners had any doubt that he spoke with sincerity, however evil or mistaken they may have thought him. He thanked the people for their vote of confidence in him. He had felt them on that day united :

In the general joy that reigned on that day, you will have been able to appreciate what deep roots unity between the men and lands of Spain has taken, a unity which with your determination assures peace and progress in the years to come, in a Spain ever more prosperous and ever more just.
The day will come when we shall be history, as we are already beginning to be. . . . Of course Spain is better off, but she is still very poor : one has but to fly over our frontiers and look upon the green and rich lands of Europe and the parched sterile yellow of our own. But even that can be corrected. . . . You must plant deep in your minds the thought that . . . the task requires long labour, work to which all must contribute. That each day will bring a new cause of anxiety with it? Of course; but all will be overcome if we learn to keep united in our purpose, in this fruitful peace which could be destroyed if division, egoism, and ambition were again to become the masters of our society. . . .
The worker must use the means of production entrusted to him to the best advantage, but the entrepreneur must remember that the profits of his enterprise are not his and for his use alone. . . .
The new law which you have approved opens a new stage in our march forward. There can be no *immobility*. . . .
With this law I have desired to prepare for you a platform from which to take off for higher flights. . . . If, as we hope, it is good, you will reap its fruits. In a few years it will be other rulers who will make use of it to take Spain higher, towards a richer life, a more ample and just life worthier to be lived. . . .[15]

[14] *Discursos*, p. 231.
[15] *Discursos*, pp. 261–70.

The speech was from beginning to end a plea for peace and unity. There was a certain amount of self-praise, out of conviction that what he had accomplished was for the good of Spain, of thanks to those who had helped him, but no mention nor recrimination of those who had not.

Over the next twenty-seven months, however, the country was not to march along the road which it would seem Franco desired, of greater economic prosperity and of political evolution in peace, or along the road which men of moderate views also desired, towards the freer exercise of human rights.

The Downs and Ups of Freedom 1967–8

There occurred during January and February a wave of strikes – mostly one-day affairs – in over fifty factories, including the steel-works in Bilbao, textile-mills in Catalonia, car-assembly and other manufactured goods' plants in various parts of Spain, strikes for social reasons rather than political, though opponents of the régime emphasized their political rather than social aspects. Their funda-mental causes were the same as those of the much more serious strikes which took place in other parts of Europe at about this time : rises in the cost of living and the inability of management and workers to explain themselves to each other. Politics came in when workers' representatives elected in 1966 began to find them-selves officially dismissed as troublemakers. Dismissals were followed by more strikes in solidarity and protest marches at which workers again demanded free trade unions. Arrests were made – among them of self-avowed communists caught distributing the clandestine com-munist *Mundo Obrero* and other literature.

In mid-January the universities reopened after the Christmas holidays and student meetings followed, some held with and some without permission from the university authorities. The APE (*Asociaciones Profesionales de Estudiantes*), established in April 1965 as a successor to the hated SEU, was proving a failure. Throughout the universities students had been aroused by the adverse publicity which had been given in press, radio, and tele-vision to the siege of the 500 professors and students in the Capu-chin friary in Barcelona. They wanted to find out what it was all about and soon discovered that these students had worked out a constitution for a truly democratic union. The SDEUB pattern had then been copied clandestinely during the 1965–6 academic year in the Jesuit University of Bilbao, the *Opus Dei* University of Pamplona, and the state University of Valencia. In Madrid, however, there had been a division of opinion whether to work within APE and make it democratic or establish an SDEUM.

Such was the situation when, in circumstances never made quite clear, police appeared in Madrid University City on 27 January 1967. There was an uproar among the students, whose one vague recollection of the liberties of the mediaeval university was that agents of the law had no authority within it. They organized a mass protest meeting on the 30th, attended by between 2,000 and 4,000 of Madrid's 30,000 students. The police were again summoned. A hundred or more of the students made a move towards the rector's office, hurling bottles and stones at the police as they advanced. The police charged with truncheons and pursued their attackers into one of the buildings. There were injuries on both sides; the police took away some fifty demonstrators, but they were not satisfied that they had caught any of the leaders.

In the early hours of the following day the police went to the house of an alleged leader, Rafael Gijarro Moreno; but the suspect jumped out of a window and died a few hours later. The government immediately closed the university for the rest of the week to allow tempers to cool. This move succeeded in so far as there were no further serious clashes between police and students during this term. Nevertheless, illegal student gatherings continued in Madrid and Barcelona, Zaragoza, Valencia, Santiago, Pamplona, Valladolid, Bilbao, Murcia, Salamanca, and Málaga – a formidable list.

In Madrid in May students at six faculties and university schools formed their SDEUM, but some of its officials were arrested, the arrests led to protests, and the university was closed again, this time for a week. The whole National Council of the APE resigned. Writers in several periodicals took up the case for the students and workers. All but one played safe in the way they expressed their support. On the one hand they condemned demonstrations, on the other the intransigence of the authorities. The one exception was the *Opus Dei*-directed evening daily *Madrid,* whose headline read : 'Protest is not always morally reprehensible'.[16] It was heavily fined.

After one year with the Press Law journalists were thoroughly displeased with it. So far from being a law to protect the writer and publisher from capricious censorship, it was proving an instrument of punishment. In pre-Press Law days copy which the editor judged likely to be censored had not gone into print until passed : the 'made-up' journal was therefore safe from last-minute prohibition. Now with the paper on the point of circulation the editor could be told of an objection to a particular item and that, with it in, not one copy could be sold; and he could have the whole issue confiscated.

[16] *Madrid* (30 January 1967).

The fact that he could challenge the censors successfully before an independent court was neither here nor there : the paper had already lost its advertising as well as its sales revenues.[17] Since the Press Law several papers had been forced out of circulation or suppressed.[18] Moreover, the Press Law had proved capable of indirect modification. A Statute for the Profession of Journalism, decreed in April 1967,[19] in spite of protests from journalists, contained the clause that no man could become or remain an editor of a paper if the Ministry issued him with three 'serious warnings' during one year. The Ministry could issue as many admonishments as it pleased without having to justify them in court – so in effect the statute had given the Ministry power to suppress journals at will. Soon afterwards the penal code was revised to increase penalties for 'subversive literature'.[20] As in previous years the summer was quiet in both university and factory.

The *Cortes*, which approved the new *Ley Orgánica*, continued in existence and functioning till the autumn of 1967. Before their dissolution they discussed and passed a law relating to the Movement and another on religious liberty. Neither went through easily. Discussions on both generated such a degree of heat as had not been witnessed since republican days. The full title of the first was *Ley orgánica del Movimiento y del Consejo Nacional,* a constitution for the Movement, and it revived all the old questions of Arrese's days. Was the *Movimiento* a 'communion of principles', as stated in the law approved by referendum, or an organization, a state-party requiring close definition and a constitution after all? In trying to make it both – an amorphous 'communion' and a well-defined organization – the draft as given to the *Cortes* was as complex a rigmarole of legislation as ever was put before a parliament or national assembly. Some 600 amendments were proposed from diametrically opposed standpoints. As finally approved in June, it seemed to leave the *Movimiento* where it had been, an amorphous body without a practical effective purpose except to put the brakes on movement or evolution.

Discussions on the other law, the Law on Religious Freedom, recalled the scenes attending the republic's laws against Catholicism. Here the government was attempting to bring its legislation almost into line with the decisions of Vatican II on freedom of religion.

[17] Cf. article by Manuel Fernández Areal in *Cuadernos,* No. 42 (March 1967), pp. 17–19.
[18] e.g. *Aún, La voz del trabajo, Juventud obrera, Promos.*
[19] *Decreto* 744/1967, 13 April 1967.
[20] For a full analysis of the Press Law in practice, see M. Fernández Areal in *Cuadernos,* Nos. 45–6 (June–July 1967), pp. 19–21. Cf. Eduardo Cierco, *La supresión de toda clase de criterios, Cuadernos,* No. 43 (April 1967), p. 17.

The legal disabilities of Protestants had been a subject of discussions into the middle fifties between the Ministry of Foreign Relations and the British and American ambassadors. In 1956 Spanish Protestants had addressed themselves to the Head of State asking that the laws should be interpreted more liberally. Their wording was not very different from the wording of similar laws in force between 1876 and 1931, but their interpretation varied from province to province and overall was considerably more vigorous. So long as a Protestant kept his religion to himself, the law stated, no man could lawfully molest him. Under the monarchy a discreet notice outside a house or a church advertising its use as a Protestant place of worship had been considered legitimate; now it was not. If a Protestant wanted to marry he now had to prove that his name did not appear in the baptismal registry of any Catholic church, whereas before such difficult proof had not been insisted upon. The Nunciature on behalf of the Vatican accepted that where a person had not been brought up as a Catholic he could lawfully marry a Protestant in a Protestant church, but not so the state. There were difficulties at funerals as well. Catholic books might or might not get through the censors : but Protestant books never did. Protestant translations of the Bible into the vernacular were illegal. Officially a man's religion or lack of it was no bar to his advancement in public service. In practice (though this was difficult to prove) a man could get on if an agnostic or an atheist, but not if a known Protestant. In the army the Protestant conscript received little consideration. In all there were between 20,000 and 30,000 Spanish Protestants and another 10,000 foreign Protestants, with about 200 authorized places of worship. On paper one church per 200 Protestant men, women, and children might seem enough. In fact several thousands had no place of worship near them; and every application for a new one was rejected. Even two new synagogues had been allowed – two, if the temporary one in Madrid replacing the one destroyed by a mob during the republic were counted.

The state had twice relaxed the strictest interpretations of the laws : between 1945 and 1947 and between 1951 and 1955. Each time it had had to face strong opposition from three sectors : first, a group of Catholic laymen, priests, and bishops who held steadfastly to the doctrine that no man has the right to teach error and that it is the duty of a Catholic ruler to prevent the propagation of error in his realm – a group having yet to learn the lesson of history, that a sure way of propagating error is to persecute it; secondly, the nationalists to whom Protestantism was anathema on the grounds that the tolerance of more than one religion weakened the unity of the country – some of the most violent anti-Protestants

were agnostics and most non-churchgoers; and thirdly the heirs to
French Regalism and the Habsburgian tenet *cuius regio eius religio*.

By 1966 the Vatican Council had diminished the number in the
first group; but what the Church in Council did was of no concern
to the second or the third. The government then drafted a Bill, and
it was this Bill which the *Cortes* had to consider in 1967. While
the Catholic religion was to continue to be that of the state, Protestants were to be allowed to profess their faith in public, to buy and
sell property for religious purposes, and to have their own charitable
associations; and men and women were to be free to marry where
they willed. Up came the nationalists : religious liberty would
undermine the unity of the country, a fundamental principle of the
Movimiento : one faith, one language, one culture, one nation;
and up came the Regalists to argue that it was the duty of the
Christian ruler to suffocate religious error as it was his right to
control the Church within his realm. Members of the *Cortes* came
out with phrases such as 'this law is contrary to the spirit of the
Crusade', and 'the rejection of this law will prove...that the
Cortes are sovereign and will not bow to foreign pressures'. Clause
by clause had to be argued, the Catholics of the *aggiornamento*
insisting that the Bill did not go far enough. The Bill was redrafted.
There were further discussions when it emerged as a law. It did
not satisfy the Catholics who had read the documents of the Council nor could it satisfy certain Protestant bodies. Henceforward any
association of people with a common corpus of religious belief was
to be empowered without hindrance to register its existence as such
and thus acquire *cuerpo jurídico,* legal status, like any other society
in the land. It would then be free to advertise its existence, buy and
sell property, and engage in any activity in public or private which
did not offend public morals or provoke civil disorder. Such registration, however, was offensive to the tenets of Spanish Baptists.[21]

The feeling spread as the months of 1967 passed that the referendum had been a fraud – the new *Movimiento* Law justifying the
veteran Gil Robles' assertion that the referendum would alter nothing. What irked the public was that the government appeared to be
in no hurry to implement the people's approval of the constitutional
changes, if that was what the referendum was supposed to have
been and not just a vote of confidence in Franco. When were the
offices of Head of State and Head of Government to be physically
divided, and when were heads of families and married women to

[21] The same objection could have been made to the republic's Law on
Religious Liberty which was more restrictive than Franco's even as passed.
For Catholic objections see *Cuadernos* No. 44 (May 1967), No. 47/48
(August–September 1967). See also Joaquín Ruíz Giménex, *El concilio y los
derechos del hombre* (Madrid, 1968).

have their chance to vote for candidates to the *Cortes*? The government adjourned for the summer with nothing done beyond procedural dotting of i's and crossing of t's.

At the beginning of October Admiral Carrero Blanco was advanced to the Vice-Presidency (vice-premiership of the government), from which General Muñoz Grandes had resigned in July on the grounds of ill-health.[22] There were rumours, too, that the general was chafing against the immobility of the state. The admiral had survived many government changes as Secretary to the Cabinet and as he and the *generalissimo* signed all government laws, decrees, and other orders, he had come to be looked upon by the public as an *eminence grise,* though to have said of him that he was a faithful and prudent servant to the Head of State would have been far nearer the truth. He had the reputation of being ultra-conservative and unsympathetic to liberal and democratic ideas. His appointment, therefore, caused further consternation among those who still clung to the hope that the régime would of its own volition change its habits.

The elections for the 'family members' of the *Cortes* finally took place on 10 October, by all accounts in general scrupulously fair. Sixteen complaints of irregularity were received and investigated; one was upheld and fresh elections took place. In all 328 candidates contested the 108 seats.[23] Independents were at a disadvantage against those backed by the *Movimiento,* for they had to pay their own campaign expenses. To encourage voting workers were given a half-holiday with pay; of the 16·4 million entitled to vote 10·8 million did so – 64 per cent. In the province of Barcelona, however, only about 50 per cent voted, for there was considerable resentment there against the fact that its 1·8 million voters were only entitled to return the same number, two members, as the province of Soria with 65,000.

Each candidate was allowed before the election to issue a brief manifesto. The playwright José María Pemán noted that not one appeared to oppose the established order. Of the 108 who were successful, thirty-one were in national or local government employment, and another fifty committed to the Establishment in greater or lesser degree, which left twenty-seven 'independents'. In practice independence of mind and opinion was not to be exclusive to the latter or conformity with the Establishment exclusive to the former; but the immediate reaction of a public grown weary of waiting and disappointed with the way that the government appeared to be

[22] He died in 1968.
[23] Two per province; plus two for Spanish Guinea, two for Spanish Sahara, one for Ceuta, and one for Melilla.

taking away with one hand what it had given with the other, was to look for the 'no-changes' rather than the changes : 386 out of the 564 seats in the new *Cortes* were filled by persons who had been members of the old.[24] Granted that apart from the 108 elected by public suffrage there were another 300 to 310 (depending exactly on where the line of designation was drawn) elected by their professional or occupation peers, how much 'election' had there been? As the *sindicatos,* the learned societies, and local governments began to elect their representatives, the Rector of Salamanca expressed the fear that the new *Cortes,* like the old, would have a very high proportion of members chosen by 'a hear-hear, an amen, and silence'. Critics after the event began to analyse, for example, who the 115 local government representatives returned to the *Cortes* were. Fifty-three seats were open to chairmen and deputies in provincial government, and 62 to 'mayors or councillors'. Those elected were : 52 chairmen of provincial governments, one deputy, 58 mayors, four councillors. As the chairmen of provincial governments and the mayors were placed in office by the Ministry of the Interior, how far, then, was this local government group in the *Cortes* representative of local governments and how far of the central authority?[25]

The assembling of the new *Cortes* overshadowed three developments. First, with the beginning of the 1967–8 academic year it at once became evident that the government was going to be confronted with better organized opposition than before in the universities. The APE was now as dead as the SEU : the SDEUM hardly bothered to hide its illegal existence. Its call for a meeting to elect its officers was answered by 2,000 students. Secondly, the 'Workers' Commissions' called for a mass demonstration of workers on 27 October : 'a day of struggle against political repression and the rise in the cost of living'. Two thousand riot police were concentrated on the capital and known committee members were taken into preventive arrest. Nonetheless, the demonstrations reached notable proportions in Madrid and Barcelona. Thirdly, Professor López Rodó had completed his studies for a second development plan, almost, though not quite, as ambitious as the first and made public on 14 November.

[24] But we cannot say: 'of the new *Cortes*' 564 members 386 had been in the old'; there were fewer than 564, as several individuals had more than one seat: e.g. Lora Tamayo had a seat as Minister of Education, another as President of the *Consejo Superior de Investigaciones Cientificas* (Council of Scientific Research), and yet a third as President of the Council of State. For further examples see *ABC* (18 November 1967), p. 73, cols. 2 and 3.

[25] The best critical analysis of the composition of these *Cortes* is in *Cuadernos,* No. 50 (November 1967).

On 17 November Franco addressed the new *Cortes,* in a speech which, to begin with, was a throwback to those of twenty years earlier (as he admitted). He gave once more the totals of the changes of régimes and governments to which Spain had been subjected before the Civil War. In the future there was to be 'a reasonable plurality of opinions', but no parties, and no disturbances of public order. The state had to have the authority to say no to pressure groups and demagogues: no authority, no peace; no order, no right, no justice. The way to social progress was not through subversion. It was untrue to say that the régime was petrified and that it had not evolved, for in essence it was the same, but ever adapting itself to the circumstances: while true to principles, it was pragmatic. The time for one country to copy the mode of government of another was past: to each whatever suited it best. It was the critics of the Spanish system who were immobile, stuck in eighteenth- or nineteenth-century ideologies. To see those who ought to be particularly responsible distorting 'passionately the holiness of certain texts to convert them into texts of direct political action which they were never intended to be' caused him pain. There were no panaceas in real life. The liberty of each individual had to be made compatible with that of his neighbour and the community. Where opposition is allowed, Franco continued, 'it is "Her Majesty's" *loyal* opposition. Notice, loyal and not disloyal: from within the system and not from outside it. However, as what matters is the results and not the means, is there not criticism among you of the administration? Have we not changed the executive teams?'

Franco then went on to comment on the second development plan, which was to be selective, was to concentrate on the weak points: agriculture, housing, transport, communications, education. How could there be liberty, he asked, in misery and ignorance? The new *Cortes,* therefore, would have two important matters to consider, discuss, improve, and approve – the budget and the plan.[26] It was an unusually long address.

At the time an investment was envisaged over the four years 1968–71 of 67,178 million pesetas ($1,120 million, £402 million) in education alone, to provide 1·7 million more places for students (largely secondary and technical); the number of houses allowed for was 1·13 million; another 2 million hectares of splintered holdings were to be consolidated and the ratio of men to tractors reduced to 8:1. One million new jobs were to be created, just as over one million had been created by the economic expansion of 1964–7. The growth-rate was to be 6 per cent.

[26] *Discursos,* pp. 291–333.

The *ABC* issue which carried Franco's speech had the front page headline 'Devaluation of Pound Appears Imminent'.[27] Unknown to the public at the time, there had been a run on the peseta as there had been on the pound. Confidence in the peseta had been shaken by the evident slow-down in production and expansion following the credit restrictions introduced late in 1966, and more immediately by the concession to the bishops and workers in the raising of the minimum wage from 60 to 96 pesetas in October 1967. Furthermore, many financiers were aware that a devaluation of sterling could lead to up to a 10 per cent drop in income from tourists. Spain had just outbid Britain in contracts for capital equipment for Colombia and Chile. Though Spain that year sold wheat to Argentina and Brazil, and rice to Indonesia, that was only because her grain harvests had broken records. In the future she would have to export more manufactured goods, from ships to consumer goods. So if the pound was devalued, Spain would have to follow suit.

Britain devalued, as *ABC* foretold. As Israel followed suit within hours and Spain's staple food export was still citrus fruit, this was yet another reason for her to devalue. She did so by an identical amount, so that the pound remained worth 167 pesetas, but the dollar rose to 70 instead of 60. Spain acted before there could be a further run on the peseta and from a position of strength, for she still had reserves of over $1,000 million and her economist Ministers had a plan ready, one calculated not only to enable her to get full value from the act of devaluation, but also to set in motion a number of long overdue and unpopular reforms. The government reduced compulsory military service to fifteen months maximum (sixteen months for the navy); raised taxes on imported luxury goods and certain profits; decreed all government service salaries frozen; reduced the size of nearly every Ministry; and declared frozen all dividends, rents, food prices, and wages until 31 December 1968. The second development plan would have to be restudied, but in the meantime there was to be no change in the government's investment programme under it, especially in education and the development of the Campo de Gibraltar, where by the following February schemes to provide work for 20,000 workers (four times the number who crossed daily into Gibraltar) were well under way.

'At the end of it all another stabilization' said the critics in Spain; 'the bells toll for the first Four-Year Plan...once again exhortations to austerity, to Ash Wednesday, to the collective

[27] *ABC* (18 November 1967), p. 1.

expiation of a sin, but whose sin? ...'[28] Abroad it was otherwise. Once again economists abroad were more sympathetic to the difficulties of the planners and of the Spanish government than were the economists in opposition in Spain.

The devalued peseta attracted orders for capital equipment. Thus Gulf Oil gave El Ferrol shipyards an order for two 325,000-ton tankers, and Spanish shipyards had orders for 1·2 million tons of shipping from foreign shipowners by the end of 1968. Industrial exports rose to $1,197 million as against $994 million, more than balancing a slight drop in agricultural exports. Indeed, that drop was more than balanced by the reduction of food imports. Production of beef and veal rose by 14 per cent, though that of wheat by only 2·2 per cent. The government was at long last beginning to exert some pressure on farmers reluctant to change from wheat to meat production. Overall the bill for all imports came to $3,522 million as against $3,484 million in 1967 – not much change in value, but certainly in quantity. On the other hand, the value in dollars of exports rose from $1,384 million to $1,589 million; and there was thus a smaller gap to be filled by invisibles. The income from tourists (19,180,000 of them) rose to $1,100 million.

The net growth in agriculture was 6·2 per cent. Output of cars rose by 11·8 per cent to 306,000 units; and of electric power to 45,771 million kwh. Overall the gross industrial product grew by 4·5 per cent.

There were as before unpleasant aspects, a rise in unemployment for example. The registered number of unemployed totalled 212,000 in the first quarter of 1968, over 60,000 more than in the corresponding quarter of 1967 – indeed 250,000 if the unregistered unemployed were included, according to a Ministry of Labour estimate; between 300,000 and 320,000 according to those opposed to government policies – out of a labour force of 12·6 million, somewhere between 2 and 2·5 per cent. As OECD noted,[29] 'the ... level of unemployment, though high by past Spanish standards, looked less high if compared to that prevailing in certain other countries of Western Europe' – but that again was not much consolation to the unemployed in Spain.

Of more immediate concern to a greater number of the people was the cost of living; during 1967 this had risen by 6·5 per cent. During the first four months of 1968 it rose by another 2·2 per cent,

[28] Cf. *Cuadernos*. No. 51 (December 1967), No. 54 (March 1968), and the whole special issue *IX extraordinario, La Economía* (July 1968).
[29] OECD report (January 1969), p. 38. Figures quoted from respective Ministries. Comparison on p. 394 from OECD report (1969), p. 47.

making a total of about 5 per cent since the minimum wage had been put up the previous October. At this figure, at an average of 2·2 per cent above the 1967 figure, the cost of living was to stay steady for the rest of 1968, but that was no solace to the lower-paid workers.

As revised, the plan still envisaged the creation of a million more jobs and heavy investment in education and housing, but the growth target was cut back to 5·5 per cent. The first and second plans compared as follows:

| | Average annual volume change per cent | | |
| | 1964–67 | | 1968–71 |
	Projection Plan I	Actual	Projection Plan II
Consumption	5·5	6·0	4·4
Export of goods and services	10·5	11·2	11·8
Imports of goods and services	−9·0	−12·1	−6·8
GNP	6·0	6·3	5·5
Agricultural output	2·9	−0·8	2·7
Industrial output	8·6	8·8	6·7
Services	6·0	7·4	5·0
GDP	6·0	6·3	5·2
Employment in:			
Agriculture	−1·5	−3·9	−3·0
Industry	2·9	3·0	2·7
Services	2·2	3·8	3·0
Output per employed person	5·1	5·4	3·9

The creation of one million new jobs was one target, but another was the diminution of the agricultural labour force by 420,000: doubtless realistic planning, but none too heartening. If all went according to plan, there would be an average of only 150,000 new jobs a year to absorb the increase of young people entering employment over retirements and deaths and the growing tendency for emigrants to return. Assuming the net migratory movement to be nil, then unemployment would oscillate at around 2 per cent; but what if the pattern followed that of 1967 when 26,000 more Spaniards had returned than emigrated? The plan did announce that there would be increases in unemployment benefits; but it also laid down the principle that wage increases should not exceed productivity gains. Hard economics, then, were again at variance with what was socially desirable.

Faced with strong agitation from the *sindicatos,* from the Workers' Commissions, and from churchmen from bishops to worker priests, the government conceded that it was socially undesirable that wages should continue frozen, and agreed to sanction increases of up to 5·9 per cent under the *convenio* system from October 1968. The minimum wage was to go up to 102 pesetas. Inevitably, over the next six months to April 1969 – and beyond – as these collective agreements were hammered out, the employers, claiming that they and not just the workers had been hit by the restrictions on devaluation, were not inclined to give way without a struggle. They made the most of a decision of the Supreme Tribunal that even 'strikes for social ends' were illegal.

This was a decision arrived at rather unexpectedly on 12 December 1967. Ruling on a test case, the tribunal found procedural deficiencies in the decree of 20 September 1962 which modified Article 222 of the penal code.[30] The result was that the many who had thought that strikes other than for political purposes did not fall within the definition of 'acts of military rebellion', were living under a delusion. The régime had not brought its labour legislation into line with that of western Europe : strikes in general were just as illegal in Spain as in the socialist countries. It was a decision which delighted large employers of labour, such as *Altos Hornos* in Bilbao and subsidiaries of foreign companies such as General Electric Española and others, where in the early months of 1969 there were to be strikes. These strikes occurred despite the new ruling that they were illegal, but because of the new ruling, they could be used by management to get rid of troublemakers.

These troublemakers included worker priests, some of them Jesuits to whom the Supreme Tribunal's decision was a severe blow : this was especially so to the Jesuits who in the Madrid and Barcelona Schools of Labour Relations and Studies had hoped (and continued to hope) that the régime could be persuaded without direct confrontation to accept that freedom of association was a basic human right, and who had urged workers to press for it from within rather than outside the law. They had hailed the 1962 decree as a victory for commonsense and reason over violence.

[30] Press of 13 December 1967.

At the beginning of 1968 they felt there was still a lingering hope that reason might, after all, prevail. There had been in the *Ley Orgánica* of 1966 a reference to the recognition by the state of 'professional associations of entrepreneurs, managements, and workers'. That surely meant the end of the vertical syndicate and therefore a new *sindicato* law. Such a law had then been promised and Solís had worked on it throughout 1967, hearing and reading what many people had to say on it and issuing questionnaires to 12 million workers. These did not contain all the right questions, according to the unofficial labour leaders, laymen, and churchmen, but there was still hope. The Workers' Commissions had held their own inquiry and meetings (a 'national congress') and made it known that what the workers wanted was the establishment of independent trade unions with the right to strike.

To avoid giving the government an excuse for putting this demand aside, the Workers' Commissions decided to keep quiet during the first four months of 1968. In April, however, they announced that they wanted workers to hold three days of protest over Labour Day; they were to 'vote with their feet' for free trade unions, that is to boycott public transport and to march in an orderly fashion from their various scattered places of work to the centres of cities. The Communist Party decided to support the workers, thus giving the government the chance to describe the whole movement as communist, which it most certainly was not. There were few violent clashes. For the most part the police just kept people walking. In Madrid about 400 were arrested, all but thirty of whom were released within 24 hours and nearly all released pending trial – a period of waiting in some cases of many months.

The events in France of May 1968 were closely watched by all Spaniards : by the government with grave misgivings, by sections of the opposition with some enthusiasm. Both sides looked for parallels between the progress of student unrest in Spain during that year and student unrest in France. There were some obvious parallels; that by April – May the students were seeking solidarity with the workers; that some shouted 'Long live Ho Chi Minh' and carried anti-Vietnam war banners; and there were parallels below the surface.

As already noted, in October 1967 the SDEUM had broken cover in Madrid. From headquarters in the Faculty of Political and Socio-Economic Sciences, it held elections and the government remained impassive.[31] On 26 November, however, the Dean of the Faculty of Science shut the doors on the SDE men under

[31] There were elections for SDEs in several other universities without government interference.

his jurisdiction. This sparked off demonstrations which by the 30th led the authorities to order the arrest of ringleaders. Thus, there was a return to the pattern of protest – arrests – protests against the arrests – more arrests. The police entered the Faculty of Law in pursuit of a wanted man, whereupon student leaders called for a strike; and except for a few blacklegs nearly all students supported it. While on strike they held demonstrations daily, each one more violent than its predecessor, with attempted arson as well as stone-throwing. On 14 December orders were given to three faculties to close till after the new year.

No sooner did the new term begin than there was trouble in the Faculty of Political Science. It was closed and once again students demonstrated, beginning where they had left off, with stone-throwing, burning an omnibus on 16 January 1968, and fighting the police on the 20th and throwing the furniture of the Faculty of Philosophy at them. There were 'sit-ins' and battles throughout February and into March when the university authorities tried to meet the students. However, there appeared in the meantime non-SDE groups calling themselves *Defensas Universitarias*, totally out of sympathy with the radicals whose leaders in the Faculty of Law they attacked. The dean expelled the attackers. The rector overruled the dean and the radicals refused to parley with the rector. Rioting began again.

The question of freedom of association was now only one of the causes of friction. The *reivindicaciones* ('just grievances') of the activists went a good deal further. Some wanted the universities to be democratic in the sense of being open to all irrespective of means (there were state scholarships, but most of the students were middle and upper class); others understood the word 'democratic' to mean 'with student participation', and even student control of the universities,[32] in the appointment of staff, settlement of curricula, and teaching methods; while there were yet others who, asking themselves the question 'what is a university?', answered simply 'not this', and asking themselves 'what is its purpose?' joined the throng.[33] There were similar though not such prolonged disturbances in nearly all the other Spanish universities.

Over Easter Lora Tamayo, the Minister of Education, fell ill and resigned. The new Minister, José Villar Palasí, a professor of

[32] 1968 was of course the centenary of student rioting in Spain to that very end, not that the present-day students were aware of it. At least I neither met nor heard of anyone who was or who knew how the 1868 experiment ended—with students deciding that study was a waste of time.
[33] Conversations with student leaders 1968–9. Cf. *Cuadernos*, No. 52 (January 1968), pp. 5–6, 13, 14–16; No. 55 (April 1968), pp. 16–17; and No. 57/58 (August–September 1968), p. 43.

administrative law and a much respected man, accepted the resignation of the Rector and two Vice-Rectors of Madrid. The university reopened on 6 May with a new rector, but 14–20 May was a week of clashes, the students rather obviously following leaders who did not necessarily share their views. The students had a final fling on 29 May before examinations put an end to protests for that academic year.

Meanwhile Solís had summoned to Tarragona a congress of *sindicato* representatives to discuss a draft he had prepared for the now long-awaited Syndical Law. He had a dateline to meet – October. What was now an open opposition argued for 'full democratization or permanent conflict'.[34] Solís and the government replied that 'full democratization would *inevitably* be followed by permanent conflict – witness the U.K. and France'.[35]

The Tarragona meeting was given great publicity as an exercise in democracy. There were 800 speeches from the 650 delegates 'representing 8 million workers and 3 million employers'. At the end of it all the conference decided:

1. that all workers would be members *ipso facto*;
2. that the national body would be divided into one *sindicato* per branch of industry, agriculture, or services;
3. that within each union there would be *separate* associations for the entrepreneurs, middle-grade management, and workers;
4. that the unions were to play a greater part in the economic and social life of the country;
5. that shop stewards would be given greater protection against intimidation;
6. that the higher posts would be filled by a process of three names being submitted to higher authority to select one.

The congress could therefore be dismissed as much ado about very little, for the structure was to be almost as before. There was still to be no freedom of association nor an independent trade union system. Nothing on the right to strike was put down on paper.

On 24 July, at their conference, the bishops acted in accordance with the mandate in *Populorum Progressio*: 'we appeal to our sons, in countries undergoing development no less than in others ... the role of the hierarchy is to teach and to give the right interpretations of the norms of morality in the task of renew-

[34] Cf. *Cuadernos,* No. 42 (March 1967), pp. 9–16, 21; and the thorough analysis by José Luis Rubio on pp. 18–21 of No. 55 (April 1968). See also pp. 22–7.
[35] Conversations with *sindicato* officials.

ing the temporal order'.[36] Their joint statement was essentially a restatement of Section 68 of Vatican II's *Gaudium et Spes*: the workers should be at liberty, as of a basic human right, freely to found labour unions, freely to choose their representatives, and in defence of their rights and pursuit of past demands, if no other way was open, to go on strike.[37]

Newspapers, radio, and TV were warned to give the statement no prominence. Solís, asked to comment on it, said: 'The *sindicatos* have spoken at Tarragona. What the bishops have said is fine: they have a right to their opinions, for they are free men'. The *sindicato* papers *Pueblo* and *La Voz Social* alleged that the differences were in no way fundamental. No draft was put before the *Cortes* that October; and as long as there was no law, there was still hope.[38]

The relations between Church and state were now strained, and not merely because of the part long played by priests and the HOAC in social matters. Differences of opinion between clergy and civil authorities as to what constituted a gathering for religious purposes and what did not had become so frequent as to be commonplace, and meetings of the essentially religious Jesuit societies in the universities were as likely to be forbidden as not. Several Catholic newsheets and periodicals ceased to publish. Under the Concordat the state could not proceed on a civil charge against a priest without the authority of his superior. Priests and superiors were agreed that they should share the same dangers as their parishioners, and there were now so many priests in detention for taking the side, or being at the side, of workers that a prison in Zamora had been opened for them. All these 'internal' matters were within the jurisdiction of the Ministry of Justice as the successor to the nineteenth-century Ministry of Justice and Grace (or Religion). The major point at issue was the Head of State's right of presentation or royal patronage in the appointment of bishops. Vatican II had stated:

...the right of nominating and appointing bishops belongs properly, particularly, and of itself exclusively, to the competent ecclesiastical authority.

Therefore...this most holy Council desires that in the future no rights or privileges of election, nomination, presentation, or

[36] Section 81.
[37] *Gaudium et Spes*. English title: *The Pastoral Constitution of the Church in the Modern World*.
[38] A draft was put before the *Cortes* in October 1969.

designation for the office of bishop be any longer granted to civil authorities. . . .[39]

The Council had then asked such civil authorities to renounce their privileges of their own free will, and since the document had been issued in October 1965, several had done so; but not the authorities of Spain, whose Fundamental Laws declared her 'a Catholic state' and her 'acceptance of the law of God according to the doctrine of the Holy Catholic Apostolic and Roman Church . . . which inspires her legislation'. The whole question was deemed a matter of honour. Since then the Vatican had had to weigh the evils of leaving a diocese without a bishop against that of giving up by default, as it were, the one chance the Church had had in centuries to get back what the Kings of Spain had wrested from her in the late Middle Ages, the loss of liberty which in the opinion of the bishops at the Council had militated against her religious mission. Since 1966 no bishops had been appointed. When the Primate, Cardinal Plá y Deniel, died on 6 July 1968, aged ninety-two, there were nine sees vacant, and another eight could be considered vacant because their holders were old and infirm.[40] The Vatican filled three : Tarazona by 'presentation', Santander with an auxiliary bishop, José Cirarda of Seville (to whose promotion it was difficult for the Head of State to object), and Pamplona, the really important one because an archbishopric with a rapidly growing industrial city, by transferring a very socially-minded bishop, Arturo Tabera, from the south. As this was a transfer, vacancies still remained. It took nine months to fill the Primacy, again by a transfer, of the sixty-one-year-old Vicente Enrique y Tarancón from the eastern diocese of Solsona to which he had been elevated at the age of thirty-eight. By then two other bishops had died, one of them Gurpide of Bilbao – 'by the Grace of God', said his people, for his death had occurred at the height of a misunderstanding between him and a number of his priests.

In November 1967 a TV relay station near Bilbao was blown up by an organization calling itself *Euzkadi Ta Azkatasuna* (ETA – Freedom for the Basques). On 2 August 1968 a police chief[41] was assassinated outside his house in Irún. ETA claimed the credit for this and the murder of another policeman. Cyclostyled propa-

[39] *Christus Dominus* (Decree on the Bishop's Pastoral Office in the Church), section 20.

[40] Cardinal Herrera died on 26 July, but as he was already retired, his death did not alter the situation. Two other 'enemies' of the régime also died in 1968 – Aurelio Escarré, abbot of Montserrat, and Professor Giménez Fernández.

[41] Melitón Manzanas, a uniformed chief inspector of the *Policía de Seguridad*, reputely 'tough'.

ganda in Basque and Spanish in praise of Castro and Mao and vilifying Franco, Stalin, and the U.S.A., began to circulate from a headquarters beyond the Pyrenees.[42] On 16 August the government declared 'a state of exception' in the province of Guipúzcoa, as a result of which the police were empowered to enter and search any building without warrant; to arrest on suspicion and to hold a person indefinitely and without the obligation to prefer charges before a court of the first instance within 72 hours; to remove people from their residences; to take them to remote towns or villages; and to order them to remain there. The holding of any assembly of more than twenty persons without police authority became doubly illegal. In a preliminary round-up the police arrested around 400 known sympathizers with the policies of Basque autonomy, very few of whom were of the left and nineteen of whom were priests. The net result of this activity was to exacerbate relations between the people and the central government.

Tempers were already strained over earlier arrests and over the brutal treatment of those arrested in both Guipúzcoa and neighbouring Vizcaya. The bishop of San Sebastián, Bereziartua, declared that, state of exception or not, the arbitrary arrest of priests was contrary to the Concordat. Forty priests staged a sit-in in Gurpide's office and tried to persuade him to condemn police brutality. Bereziartua, who was to die a few weeks later, issued a pastoral condemning the arrests and affirming that it was the task of the Church to teach the social and political implications of Christ's doctrine. Gurpide, shortly before his death, ordered the priests to leave his office, declaring that this was not the way to air grievances. No successor to Gurpide was appointed, but the recently appointed bishop of Santander, Cirarda, was instructed by the Nunciature to take over responsibility for Bilbao in addition to his own duties. Cirarda wasted no time in condemning the arrests of workers, many of whom were HOAC members, and rebuked the authorities for calling them communists.

On the following day, 1 December, Bishop Añoveros of Cadiz, in issuing yet another pastoral on social conditions, declared that the 102-peseta minimum wage was an injustice: a couple with two children needed at least 280; even with overtime and bonuses many workers were not paid more than 200, while many agricultural workers were without work or pay for two or three months in the year. Conditions in which many lived were subhuman: a society which tolerated such conditions could not call itself Christian. Early in 1968 the archbishop of Zaragoza had criticized land speculators and the building of luxury apartments when there was

[42] *Zutik,* in Basque and Spanish (not very good Basque).

a shortage of less ostentatious dwellings. He had called on the
government to act against this 'grave evil'. On being called a
socialist, he replied : 'Religious values are fundamental to moral,
social, or civic values . . . if defending these values is socialistic,
then I can say that the humble archbishop of Zaragoza is in that
sense a socialist'. Over the year he and other prelates urged the
government to surrender its 'right of presentation', but their
promptings were ignored. Not that all the hierarchy agreed with
this open opposition to the policies of the régime. Morcillo, archbishop of Madrid, and his auxiliary Guerra, both of whom had
seats in the *Cortes,* were second to none in applauding government decisions.

There was one government decision, however, which all clergy
and opponents of violence, even if opponents, too, of the régime,
welcomed. In September the new Minister of Education gave out
a decree that students were to be allowed to form and run their
own unions as they wished, subject to minimal control by the
university authorities and provided that their ends were not
political. Membership would not be compulsory.

The decree came too late. The SDEs were passing into the
hands of extremists. At a secret meeting in Valencia between
29 September and 1 October, they discussed plans for what they
called revolutionary action – days of agitation against imperialism,
against American bases in Spain, and in support of Basque nationalists. The summer vacation over, the militants led disorders in
Bilbao, Seville, Valladolid, and Barcelona; but their main battlefield was Madrid. In a preliminary skirmish they sacked the office
of the Dean of the Faculty of Law. At the end of November they
occupied the Faculties of Science, Philosophy, and Political
Science, showering petrol bombs on police who went to dislodge
them. Elsewhere they set fire to an omnibus, to at least one army
truck, and to letter-boxes. While igniting a car they set the clothes
of a university professor on fire.

Their actions, whatever their motives, were now indistinguish-
able from those of the Falangist-anarchist *Escuadrones Negros* or
Apóstoles de la Violencia, who since 1966 had been setting fire
with impunity to Jesuit, Capuchin, and other meeting-places of
the Catholic opposition in Barcelona and who had assaulted
various lecturers, including Ruíz Giménez and his fellow lawyer
Jiménez de Parga.

The press, in giving full publicity to these events, was allowed
to report facts, though it had to be circumspect in expressing
opinions. Journalists, however, were asking themselves how long
they would be allowed to carry on reporting facts. In spite of

protests from the archbishop of Zaragoza and others outside the *Cortes,* and in the face of strong opposition within the *Cortes,* an Official Secrets Act had recently been passed in which the exact definition of what was an official secret seemed none too clear. No paper had been brought to court on a charge under the act, but, by the end of 1968, the journalists' grievances against the Press Law were severe.

During 1967 the press had been concerned over the most curious of all actions against the periodical *Destino,* brought by a group of liberal-minded Catalan journalists. In October 1967 *Destino* had welcomed a most unexpected change of heart on the part of a régime which in its early years had proscribed the Catalan language. Schools dependent on the provincial authority were to be allowed to teach Catalan.[43] The next number carried an article on *El Pendiente,* a 'cheap labour market' of Barcelona, and a letter to the editor from a writer with a forthright vocabulary and extreme anti-Catalanist views, opposing the welcome given to the teaching of Catalan. The issue was withdrawn from circulation on the grounds that the *letter* would give grave offence to a section of the community and would disturb public order. Nothing was said about the article which revealed a scandal. *Destino* was subsequently suspended for two months and fined heavily. National and provincial newspapers of many tendencies wrote sympathetically of *Destino*'s troubles. One of these, *Madrid,* ran into the most serious trouble of any on 30 May 1968, after it had published an editorial criticizing General de Gaulle for his handling of the student and worker troubles in France. The title read 'Retire in Time', the text included the passage: 'clearly personal or authoritarian government is incompatible with the structures of industrial society and also with the democratic spirit of our age and the framework of the free world.'

The paper was suspended forthwith for two months. The leader-writer, Rafael Calvo Serrer, was fined 250,000 pesetas ($3,750, £1,000 approx.). When the court came to consider the fine and suspension, it fined the editor the same amount again and extended the suspension by a further two months. A hundred journalists protested, but to no effect. In September, after the old decree had been revived stipulating trial by military tribunal for 'those who spread false or tendentious news with the intention of disturbing order in the land', another *Opus Dei*-directed paper, *El Alcázar,* was accused of contravening company law and closed down.

Alcázar and *Madrid* were both evening dailies with circulations of

[43] The teaching of Basque was authorized to begin in Navarre and the Basque provinces in September 1968.

90,000 and 65,000 respectively;[44] *Destino,* a weekly, had a circulation of about 50,000. Ruíz Giménez was forced to give up his editorship of the monthly *Cuadernos* (circulation 30,000), which had now achieved international reputation, barred as he was a professor of law and not a journalist. A young journalist took over the editorship (Ruíz Giménez becoming chairman of the board of management). With the change the paper veered to the left, its basic policy, however, remaining the same, namely to provide a vehicle for a dialogue of articles written by people with widely differing views; and it carried in every issue throughout 1967 and 1968 most penetrating criticism of government policies.

It carried on undaunted by a Ministry warning that proceedings would be taken against it for an article in the March 1967 number, and the Ministry discovered subversive passages in three more subsequent issues.[45] For the four articles together, *Cuadernos* was fined 15,000 pesetas in December. In accordance with the law it had then to publish the Ministry's findings within three months and these it had set up in type for an issue due out on 1 March 1968. Six hours (the stipulated time) before its planned hour of circulation a copy was delivered at the Ministry.[46] It contained, without commentary, several pages on which extracts from the U.N. Declaration of Human Rights appeared in juxtaposition with extracts from Spanish laws. The censors could hardly object, since they could blue-pencil neither the laws of the state nor the U.N. text, to which Spain officially subscribed. (It was, furthermore, Human Rights' Year.) The Ministry ordered circulation to be stopped because the issue also contained an article by the once heavily fined Antonio Menchaca[47] on 'The Theory of Opposition' and this was judged to be an incitement to violence. *Cuadernos,* with a plethora of learned lawyers on its board, took the matter to court and the tribunal agreed that the confiscated issues could be restored without the Menchaca article. Quickly substituting for the article quotations from pastorals and other material which had already appeared in print elsewhere, *Cuadernos* reprinted and went into circulation.

Such were the 'minuses' of freedom of the press. From the passing of the Press Law until the end of 1968 fines on journalists exceeded one million pesetas ($15,000, £6,000 in round figures). However, there were 'pluses' as well. If every article, editorial, and

---

[44] *Pueblo,* a third evening paper, connected with the *sindicatos,* had a circulation of 185,000.

[45] Especially in the *extraordinarios* (special issues), Nos. V on 'The University' and VI on 'Culture Today'.

[46] No. 53.

[47] See above, p. 297.

cartoon (there were some brilliantly satirical ones, especially in *ABC*) to which the Ministry could have raised objections had been stopped, the Ministry's *Dirección General de Prensa* and the courts would have been swamped with the consequent legal proceedings, and it must be said that there were clauses in the Press Law which gave the individual better protection against, and redress for, calumny and detraction than the libel laws of other countries. It served to put journalists and radio and television reporters on their toes to get facts right. This difference between the situation before and after the Press Law continued throughout 1967 and 1968 : the papers could publish news of events, of strikes, student protests, and sentences in the courts. The Official Secrets Act was passed in modified form but no proceedings were taken under it.

In one respect the censors could be said to have been liberal, over books[48] on politics, economics, and philosophy,[49] right through to the beginning of 1969. Marcuse became fashionable reading. The ousted Rector of Madrid, Laín Entralgo, was allowed to publish in book form an authoritative and critical assessment of the causes and course of the unrest in the universities.[50] No less than three editions of Che Guevara's Bolivian Diary were published. Well-documented books destructive of cherished myths received the government's *nihil obstat* with considerable ease.[51] Bookshops did a lively trade in novels, the printing of which would have been forbidden earlier on social, political, or moral grounds. Objections made to a work published in Paris by the duchess of Medina Sidonia, and to the picture she gave in it of corruption among officials and social injustice in southern Spain, were dismissed.[52]

The End of the Thirtieth Year of the Régime

No sooner were the universities reopened at the beginning of 1969 than trouble started again. Posters urged students to participate in 'revolutionary activities'. In Madrid some 2,500 students occupied various buildings. Again there was attempted arson.

On the evening of Friday, 17 January, the police arrested four

---

[48] 10,000 titles were published in 1966; in 1967 10,500; in 1968 10,100.
[49] See the booklists of Editorial Ciencia Nueva, Madrid; Equipo Editorial S.A., San Sebastián; ZYX and Bosch, Barcelona, among others.
[50] P. Laín Entralgo, *El problema de la universidad* (Madrid, 1968).
[51] e.g. Gil Robles' memoirs *No fué posible la paz* (Madrid, 1968) and my own *Franco* (Madrid, 1968) with no more than a two-line cut (Primo de Rivera's reference to army generals as 'hens' and to Franco as the 'biggest hen of the lot').
[52] *La Huelga*, published in Paris, but on sale in Spain.

undergraduates, one of them a young law student, Enrique Ruano, known to them as an activist and a possible convert to extreme left views. He had been beaten while previously under arrest. Seemingly without much persuasion he agreed to take the police to an apartment, the key of which had been found on him. The flat, on the seventh floor, contained some *Felipe* literature. In order to sign a statement he had made, he was unhandcuffed and at that moment ran for the door and down the stairs. On the third-floor landing, with the police almost on him, he leapt through the window to his death.

On the evening of 20 January newspapers carried an inaccurate police communiqué which stated that Ruano, 'a communist', had 'committed suicide' by jumping out of a seventh-floor window. The reaction of his fellow students was predictable. On Tuesday, 21 January, 8,000 students assembled in the wide Madrid University campus and shouted 'assassins' at steel-helmeted police forces who had been rushed there and who, at one point, fired shots into the air. Then and on the following Wednesday and Thursday the demonstrations overflowed into the streets of the city. After *ABC* had published notes allegedly written by the dead student on the instructions of a psychiatrist, resentful students stoned the newspaper offices. Anti-Franco slogans were painted on walls and a passing rear-admiral was assaulted. On Friday morning, 24 January, the university was closed. Barcelona University had been closed two days earlier.

Villar Palasí had appointed a new rector to Barcelona, Manuel Albaladejo, who, on Thursday, 16 January, in his address to staff and students, proposed to take back all professors and students banned for having participated in demonstrations in previous terms. He was known to be liberal-minded and his appointment had been seen as a move by the Minister of reconciliation. But such a move was a severe insult to any Falangist extremist and a setback to any left-wing extremist. Peace and reconciliation were to the interest of neither.

During the morning of 17 January a group of students, shouting 'liberalism no, dialogue no, violence yes', burst in upon the new rector, assaulted him, and wrecked his office. A bronze bust of Franco and a Spanish national flag were thrown out of the window, from which they now hung two flags with a hammer and sickle and a banner calling for a University for the People.

By a curious coincidence Saturday was a military occasion, the first anniversary of the appointment of Lieutenant-General Pérez Viñeta as Captain-General of the military district with his headquarters in Barcelona. His speech to his senior subordinates included the following passages:

> During the past year the relief took place of nearly all the senior officers and unit commanders in this district. It was my task to propose you [here present] for the [vacant] commands. With you I have a team that gives me the highest satisfaction. ... This year ... we shall have our troops highly trained and in excellent morale, and we can be sure they will follow their leaders. We can therefore tell not only our superiors but also all Spain that in Catalonia nothing serious will occur.

Whether or not the general had any such intention, to readers throughout the country it seemed that he was telling Madrid that whatever the government might decide, he was going to stand no nonsense. To the military and the nationalist mind no greater crime was conceivable than an insult to the flag such as had been perpetrated. Nothing could have been better calculated to provoke authoritarian reaction than that.

The equanimity of the régime was at the time seriously upset – not by the students, nor yet by workers who were going on strike in the Basque provinces and Catalonia against the resistance of the employers to their demands for higher wages, but by two actions on the part of solid middle-class citizens. First, in the second week of January a petition was handed to the Minister of the Interior, still General Franco's old school friend, Alonso Vega. Signed by 1,300 persons, every one a household name – lawyers, doctors, academicians, engineers, scientists, priests, writers, poets, actors, journalists[53] – it called for an independent inquiry into allegations of police torture against over a hundred political prisoners. Secondly, an often postponed General Meeting of the College of Lawyers met on 16 January and by an overwhelming majority (439 in favour, 196 against, and 8 abstentions) passed a resolution requesting the government to abolish the Tribunal of Public Order and other special tribunals, and to limit the jurisdiction of courts martial to military offences. Unanimously they passed a second resolution: that political prisoners should not be treated as common criminals, but housed apart and subjected to no punishment or discomfort or loss of liberty other than their detention, for such was the Spanish tradition. The prime movers in these resolutions were Professor Ruíz Giménez and other lawyers prominent in Catholic activities.

As the students spread their activities from the University City

[53] The petition was very cleverly worded and offence could be taken only by reading between the lines.

into the centre of Madrid proper, the armoured division quartered on the outskirts was observed to be carrying out exercises; these may well have been routine and no unit came close to the city. But equally they could have been 'caterpillar-track-rattling' at the orders of their commander, General García Rebull, who, like his friend Pérez Viñeta, was not of the Franco-Alonso Vega generation. General Iniesta, the G.O.C. Madrid region and also one of the younger generals, had of course authorized the manoeuvres. But who was meant to hear the rattling?

On the evening of Thursday 23 January word got around among pressmen that there was to be an important announcement after the routine cabinet meeting of Friday morning. (At one time there was no saying when cabinet meetings would end, but for some months Franco had been advised by his doctors not to prolong them. They now began promptly at 10.30 and ended at one o'clock.) The meeting over, the Minister of Information, Fraga Iribarne, read the communiqué, as was his custom. On this occasion he began : 'Gentlemen : at its meeting this morning the government unanimously put before the Head of State, and he approved, a decree which I shall now read : ...' The preamble to the decree made two points to explain what was to follow : 'In recent months some minority groups have been systematically disturbing the public peace.... It is clear that their actions are part of an international pattern....'

This, in brief, was the declaration of a 'state of exception' throughout Spain for a period of three months in the first place.

Spaniards even close to the régime were perplexed. The government had all the powers it needed to maintain order and limit subversive elements. They had coped with student disturbances in 1956 which had been as subversive as they were now. There had been more trouble in the past with labour disputes and no action as drastic as this had been taken. Except for handfuls of Falangists, *Felipes,* Marxists, Castroites, and the like, the opposition wanted evolution and not revolution. The 'state of exception', giving the police powers to arrest, search, and deport to remote villages any individual, came into effect at midnight. Overnight the authorities acted against some hundreds of 'suspected revolutionaries'.

The following instance was typical. At midnight forty steel-helmeted policemen carrying sub-machine-guns surrounded the house of the Catholic sociologist Alfonso Comin who had been sentenced to sixteen months imprisonment in January 1968 for his views on the régime as expressed in an interview with the French Catholic weekly *Témoinage Chrétien.* Though the archbishop of Granada and others had spoken in Comin's defence, he had still been convicted, but was now home in Barcelona having served his sentence. Five minutes after midnight the police demanded and gained admittance, to interrupt a meeting of nine women and fifteen men, four of the men in clerical dress. As they totalled twenty-four, they had broken the law limiting assemblies to twenty unless authorized by the police. As law-breakers they were all packed into a police van and driven to police headquarters (in the words of one of them, it was 'a tight squeeze') where the 'bag' was sorted out. Wives with young children to look after were allowed to return quickly.

One of the women proved to be Madame Emmanuel Mounier, the elderly widow of the French Catholic author. During her interrogation the police tried to get an admission from her that she was the link between the students in Spain and the Franco-German revolutionary student Daniel Cohn-Bendit. She maintained, like all the others, that she was merely taking part in a prayer and discussion meeting – as indeed she was – and was finally released after twelve hours, by which time those under detention had been whittled down to nine. They were Comin and another writer, an engineer, three students, two young men doing military service, and a Jesuit, Juan García Nieto, who had given lectures on labour relations in several western universities (including Keele and the London School of Economics). Their interrogation continued for some days. Father Nieto was told that he would be tried in due course by court martial for so-called 'acts of military rebellion' in that he had been 'in contact with communists' abroad and at home had taken part in May Day demonstrations.[54]

When the dust of police round-ups settled and people began to compare notes about who was under arrest and who was exiled, the results showed that in the first wave of arrests the police had taken away Jesuits and other priests, well-known Catholic lawyers and writers (including four on the editorial board of *Cuadernos*), members of Catholic societies and worker-priests and HOAC activists in factories, some Liberals and socialists. After the state of exception had lasted two weeks, Admiral Carrero Blanco reiterated before the *Cortes* that it had been rendered necessary because of the events in the universities, which he described as the work of 'minorities inflamed from outside for exclusively subversive ends', the ends of Moscow and Peking.[55] Even though he was greeted with loud applause, *Cortes* members remained highly

[54] Eyewitness accounts given to the author, February 1969.
[55] Speech to the *Cortes*, 7 February 1969.

sceptical. Among the 607 detained[56] or exiled there was a singular absence of communists. Even the police mentioned no communists until 19 February, when they claimed the capture in Barcelona of twenty members of a so-called Catalan Communist Party – a group hitherto unknown. Censorship of the press was reintroduced. Books by Bakunin, Marcuse, Marx, Engels, and others were withdrawn from sale.[57]

The Cabinet was thoroughly divided over the whole affair, before, during, and after the meeting of 24 January. On the one hand, the service Ministers were of the same opinion as Pérez Viñeta, Iniesta, and Rebull that the insults to the flag and uniform showed the need for a firm hand :[58] let the others remember the events of their youth when violence in the universities had bred violence in the streets, and in the end there had been civil war. Had the Head of State when younger not been of the opinion that if the republican government of the day had dealt with troublemakers expeditiously and firmly, the catastrophe which followed would not have occurred? Were they not witnessing 1936, 1931, 1928, and 1909 (the year of the Barcelona 'Tragic Week') all over again? Let there be a declaration of an *estado de guerra* (martial law) and let the troublemakers, whoever they were, be suppressed. On the other hand, Castiella, and the *Opus Dei* group, including Rodó, thought that a mountain was being made out of a mole-hill. There was nothing afoot which could not be controlled by the normal processes of law. Extraordinary action would exacerbate feelings and create a bad impression abroad. It might also have adverse repercussions on the tourist trade, on the inflow of foreign investment, on the negotiations which would soon have to be resumed on the future of the U.S. bases, on the sympathy Spain was enjoying in the United Nations in

[56] Students 238: others 369 (statement in *Cortes*, 22 April 1969). Well over a thousand people were arrested, but not detained beyond a few hours.

[57] Not all the measures, however, were against the liberalizers. Thus General Pérez Viñeta was forbidden to make any more public speeches. Among the works withdrawn was an essay by Father Dalman on the possibilities of co-operation between Marxists and Christians on the lines of *Pacem in Terris,* and the destruction was ordered of all stocks of a work by Father Víctor Manuel Arbeloa, *La iglesia en España ayer y mañana,* which was thoughtful even if controversial. On 31 March Father Arbeloa was sentenced by the Supreme Court to six months' imprisonment and a 5,000 peseta fine for criticisms of the Movement and references to nationalist wartime atrocities which he published in the suppressed Catholic youth magazine *Signo.*

For the full text of the decree establishing the state of exception, see *Cuadernos,* No. 64/65 (January–February 1969), pp. 5–7. The issue contains also the texts of thetwo pastorals, by Archbishop Tabera and Bishop Cirarda.

[58] The generals had direct access to Admiral Carrero Blanco.

her struggle to get back Gibraltar, and on her hopes of some link with the European Economic Community. Franco was reputed to favour that view himself, but he was coming more and more to act as chairman and on the majority vote of his Cabinet. At this juncture the view was sponsored (possibly by Alonso Vega, possibly by Carrero Blanco) that while an *estado de guerra* was too drastic a solution, to take 'no action' would be a decision which the order-at-all-costs brigade would find hard to accept, and that the extension to the whole country of the 'state of exception' in Guipúzcoa would be a suitable compromise.

After a month it was seen that even this half-measure had been a mistake in both internal and external policy. While on the one side Archbishop Morcillo[59] and Bishop Guerra issued from the bishop's secretariat a statement which, read in the context of the Spanish situation, seemed an endorsement of government policy (though in a non-Spanish context it could appear as a diplomatically worded admonishment to the government to act with care), on the other side, stiff pastorals came from Pamplona,[60] Santander, and elsewhere.[61] The 'state of exception' had not stopped priests in twenty Barcelona parishes from reading the most forthright condemnation of the government's wages policy, of the shortage of housing, of the lack of educational opportunities for the children of the poor, of the lack of freedom of association and the spoken word, of the Tribunal of Public Order, of police methods – 'deportations, imprisonments, physical and moral tortures'.[62]

Before two months were up, the whole government was anxious to be rid of the 'state of exception'. On 24 March, a month before it was due to end (or be renewed) and a week before the anniversary of the end of the Civil War which had to be celebrated on the 30th, the 'state of exception' was called off.

In the course of its thirtieth year the régime had made the

[59] On 26 March Archbishop Morcillo resigned from both the *Cortes* and the Council of the Realm. He was not a 'liberal' in political affairs, but he was a leading ecumenist, going out of his way to establish good relations with both Jewish rabbis and Protestant pastors.

[60] The archbishop of Pamplona, Arturo Tabera Aráoz, was made a Cardinal on 28 February 1969 together with Archbishop Enrique. Enrique's hat may be said to have been due to him as Primate and archbishop of Toledo; but Tabera's election was completely unexpected and understood to have been made by the Pope only a few days previously. The Vatican could therefore be said completely to be endorsing the views and actions of this archbishop.

[61] The Minister of the Interior, on reading the text of the bishop of Santander's pastoral of 7 February, is reported to have telephoned the Minister of Justice and told him: 'Let me throw that fellow out beyond the Pyrenees'. The Minister of Justice is said to have replied: 'Not my pigeon—that's Foreign Affairs business'.

[62] Photostat of original in author's possession.

most blatantly foolish mistake of its long career – before the
world rather more than before its own people. For it would be
untrue to say that there were not as many within Spain who
approved of the 'prompt action' as were – let us use the myosis –
'inconvenienced' by it. The mass of the people were not bothered
by it at all.

Except where the investigator looked carefully, there was
nothing exceptional to be seen in Spain during the two months of
the 'state of exception'. The universities were closed, except to
the students taking examinations. In the vast Madrid campus
not more than a dozen policemen were to be found on duty.
There were no soldiers nor more policemen to be seen in the
streets of Madrid than in Rome or London, as was also the case
in Barcelona and Bilbao. At the height of the strikes which took
place there and elsewhere in Vizcaya and Guipúzcoa, there were
knots of men at street corners and in the cafés at hours when
normally they would have been at work. Small riot squads were
held in readiness at strategic points, but they patrolled neither
the streets nor the high roads. Spaniards could cross the Basque
frontier with France with the minimum of formalities. In Catalonia
there was even less fuss. The opposition had been working pretty
much in the open for close on two years. Men and women had
made no secret of their disagreement with this or that aspect of
government policy or with the whole régime, so the police had
known whom to look for and where to find them, whom to
detain, and whom to watch. There would have been more arrests
of certain prominent lawyers and professors except that approval
for the arrest of 'big fish' was sought from the Head of State,
who had said it was absurd to suppose that they were revolutionaries in the pay of, or even influenced by, communism.

Yet, while politically the thirtieth year brought no joy to the
régime (only time could tell how serious was the harm done by
the 'state of exception', how many moderates it had driven to
despairing of evolution and to thinking revolution as the only
remedy), things had not all been black. The government could
say to its critics that of the nations which had devalued with the
pound sterling, it alone had done well in macro-economic terms.
And it could point to other successes.

In December 1967 the U.N. General Assembly had implicitly
endorsed Spain's view that Gibraltar should be returned to Spain.
It had also told Spain to expedite negotiations with African
leaders to make her ancient colonies Fernando Póo and Spanish
Guinea a new and independent country. She acted promptly on
this advice and in July 1968 Equatorial Guinea had come into

existence as a state. In December 1968 Spain was applauded, Britain upbraided : Britain would still not discuss the sovereignty of Gibraltar. In January 1969 Spain handed Ifni over to Morocco. Of the once great Spanish empire that left only the possibly mineral-rich wasteland of Spanish Sahara, whose 27,000 nomad inhabitants were to be asked in the near future if they wanted to be under Mauretanian or Moroccan rule, and the two very Spanish cities of Ceuta and Melilla on the North African coast, which were useful 'carrots' to induce the Arab countries to support Spain's claim to Gibraltar. But *Hispanidad* had taken a new turn. First Costa Rica and Chile, then other Spanish-American countries, agreed on dual-nationality agreements with Spain : the Costa Rican became a Spanish citizen and Spaniards citizens of all the countries with which the agreements were made.

One matter had to be settled on or before 26 March, fifteen years and six months after the signing of the U.S.–Spanish agreements on 26 September 1953. Negotiations to extend the American tenancy of the air and naval bases on Spanish soil for a further five years from 26 September 1968 had begun in good time, but, on the one hand, the Spanish government would not reduce its demand for $700 million annual rent (payable mainly in military equipment), while, on the other, the U.S.A. was not prepared to offer more than $140 million. Spain held these trumps :

1. France was out of NATO.
2. The USSR had increased her naval strength in the Mediterranean.
3. The U.S.A. had been ousted from bases at Bizerta and Mers el Kebir.

As a result of the second and third points the value of the naval base at Rota increased, while with France out of NATO value of the land mass of Spain at least as a staging-point was emphasized.

4. The jettisoning of nuclear warheads at Palomares in 1967 had made the presence of American strategic bombers popularly unwelcome – an unpopularity which argued for monetary recompense.

The U.S.A. held these trumps :

1. Of the three major air bases, one was hardly used : the switch to an Intercontinental Ballistic Missile system reduced the importance of all and would reduce it further.
2. While the USSR had a footing in the Arab world, she was

likely to be more and more preoccupied with China, now an atomic power.

With only hours to go to midnight of 26/27 March, Spain and the U.S.A. issued a curiously worded statement. They had 'reached an agreement in principle on the nature of the arrangements for a new five-year period of the defence agreement'.[63] Neither side gave more details. How much was the U.S.A. to pay in rent? Had the U.S.A. increased its reported offer of $140 million, or had Spain been satisfied by American promises – also rumoured – to exert pressure on Britain for the return to Spain of Gibraltar?

The existence in February and March of the 'state of exception' clouded from the view of people abroad the publication of a most ambitious plan for educational development and reform. The second development plan had already established that in the 1968–9 academic year the state would invest and spend 568 million pesetas in primary, and 775 million in secondary, education, and 882 million in professional and higher education. In July 1968 the institution of a scheme for 'scholarships with salary' had been decreed on a small scale, enabling students to study even if they had parents dependent on them. Now the system was to be expanded and a scheme for long-term interest-free loans introduced as well. Secondary education was to become obligatory and free; and the Minister declared himself in favour of giving back to universities the freedoms that the state had taken from them in the eighteenth and nineteenth centuries.

Spain continued as before to flout public opinion abroad and what was at least a large minority opinion at home. On 28 March the government announced a special amnesty – a better word would have been 'absolution' – for all persons guilty or allegedly guilty of any criminal offence committed before 1 April 1969. A similar decree on 1 November 1966 had absolved all from punishment or prosecution for any *political* offence committed before that date. Many a Spaniard of moderate views hoped that the thirtieth anniversary of the end of the Civil War would be the occasion for an amnesty of all political prisoners, of whom there were several hundred. In the event, on 31 March another was added to their number, a priest.[64]

The decree benefited a handful of exiles in Britain and the Americas who with the end of the war had washed their hands of politics, and, though they once had been Marxist or Bakuninist enthusiasts, had since become capitalists to a greater or lesser

---

[63] Official communiqué.
[64] See above, p. 410, note 57.

degree. But only one man actually in Spain had cause for relief, the mayor of Mijas, a village in the mountains above the Costa del Sol, who had gone into hiding in his own home in 1937 and now saw a Spain which he can hardly have recognized. Economic advance had transformed it both around Málaga and further afield. Into that eyesore which had once been the hinterland of Gibraltar, in the three years 1966–8 alone, the government and private industry had invested nearly 12,500 million pesetas, nearly £75 million and over $175 million. The people were beginning to reap the benefits – as well as the entrepreneurs. But had the people of Spain changed?

The Naming of a Successor

At the beginning of 1968, the provisions of the Law of Succession of 1947 were no nearer fulfilment than they had been two or twenty years earlier. Franco was still in no hurry to put before the *Cortes* the name of the person who in his opinion should succeed him either as king or regent. For the position of king there were three candidates: Alfonso XIII's son Don Juan, Don Juan's son Juan Carlos, and Prince Carlos Hugo of Bourbon Parma, the lineal descendant (through a female) of the nineteenth-century pretender Don Carlos.[65]

On 30 January 1968, Princess Sophia of Greece, wife of Juan Carlos, gave birth to a son. The consequences of the event were to move Franco to action. For the christening of the child, the eighty-year-old Queen Ena, Alfonso's widow, journeyed to Madrid from Lausanne, and Don Juan from Estoril; and 15,000 people greeted the aged queen on her arrival. Franco and his wife went to pay her their respects, almost to render her homage. For six days to 11 February Don Juan was given the freedom of Spain. He toured Madrid and its surroundings talking to workers and visiting intellectuals. He answered questions from an assembly of ninety servicemen. He received known opponents of the régime and anti-monarchist Falangists who were impressed with him. He had two private talks with Franco.

No details were published of the talks, but to the opponents of monarchy and to the Carlists, the deference shown Queen Ena and the freedom of movement given Don Juan could have only one meaning – that Franco was using his personal prestige to sway the public towards its acceptance of an Alfonsist pretender, Don Juan or Juan Carlos. The somewhat independent-minded

[65] See above, pp. 263–4.

Falangist editor of the popular evening newspaper *El Pueblo* wrote cleverly against monarchy and persons of royal blood. In May the Carlists turned their annual commemoration of their fallen at the three nineteenth-century battles of Montejurra into a political rally with strong anti-régime overtones. The banning of public festivities in celebration of Don Juan's Saint's Day (24 June) and of a book on him did nothing to dissuade the Carlists from the belief that Franco was now determined to impose a direct descendant of the hated Isabel II on Spain. Carlos Hugo, with the blessing of his father Prince Xavier, 'regent' of the traditionalist cause, began now to rally the Carlists behind him, to press his own candidature and to show Franco that dynastic legalities could still enthuse a crowd. For some months no action was taken against him, but the government looked upon his meetings and addresses in the north of Spain with misgivings, and on 20 December Prince Carlos Hugo was asked to leave the country. Two days later Madrid police broke up a press conference called by the traditionalists in defence of Carlos Hugo, and in Pamplona they battled with some hundreds of Carlists who, carrying the old Carlist war flag, a red cross of St Andrew on a white field, marched through the streets singing the Carlist anthem and shouting 'Long live Prince Xavier'. There were similar incidents elsewhere, and numerous leaflets were distributed reminding the people that the Carlist record of bravery in the Civil War was second to none. Prince Xavier was expelled on 27 December.

The Carlists were inhibited against further demonstrations after the declaration of the 'state of exception' in January 1969. Once it was lifted, they renewed their activities.

On 5 May between 12,000 and 15,000 Carlists assembled in Montejurra. When the customary Requiem and prayers were over, various speakers vehemently attacked the régime's principles and action. A light aircraft piloted by the exiled Carlos Hugo flew overhead. The elated crowd then made its way to the neighbouring town of Estella where they paraded with placards bearing such legends as 'Death to Dictatorship' and chanted rhythmically 'Franco traidor' (Franco the traitor). The police fired shots into the air to disperse the crowd.

In the meantime, Juan Carlos had been far from inactive. In July 1968 he intimated to General Franco that he was prepared to accept the throne under the provisions of the Law of Succession, to be the person to whom the Crown was to be, not 'restored', but *instaurada* – renewed or installed, not in inheritance from his grandfather Alfonso, the last reigning monarch, but as an act of nomination by Franco sanctioned by the *Cortes*; in perpetuation not of the Bourbon dynasty but of the Movement begun on 18 July 1936 – in brief, the first of a new dynasty. In December he explicitly told a news agency that he was ready to accept such a crown if it were offered to him, and to accept it with or without his father's approval.

The agency published the statement in January 1969. It caused consternation, not only among his father's friends and supporters, but among the older Spaniards generally who considered Juan Carlos' words unfilial. Emilio Romero exploited the situation. Queen Frederika of Greece was now resident in Madrid with her daughter Sophia and her son-in-law; and to the delight of his anti-monarchist readers, Romero recalled her reputation for intervening disastrously in the political affairs of Greece. He inferred that Juan Carlos was now wholly under her influence, an inference to the discredit of Juan Carlos and monarchy. Memories of Elizabeth Farnese and the other women of the Bourbon dynasty were revived. Juan Carlos went to see his father.

The 'state of exception' curbed the activities of Romero, Don Juan, and Juan Carlos as much as those of the workers and intellectuals who were more concerned with social and political problems than with restoration or installation of monarchy. The complex of tensions between Falangists and monarchists, Carlists and reformists, and Don Juanists and supporters of his son, had now become as potentially dangerous as that which developed between the *Falange* and the traditionalists during the early months of the Civil War; and as Franco had then imposed a solution from above so he was now expected to act and to act quickly.

The news of the death of Queen Ena on 15 April visibly moved General Franco. Of his personal affection for Alfonso and his family there could be no doubt. He declared a period of three days' mourning throughout Spain. He still seemed anxious even now to persuade Don Juan to change his views on the Law of Succession, to allow himself to be named the 'installed' King of Spain while considering himself the 'restored' king. Of English generals, Monk was perhaps the one whom Franco most admired : he had made a special study of the Stuart Restoration – and if Don Juan had agreed, Franco would have been a Monk rather than an earl of Warwick – but Don Juan remained adamant.

On 17 July, the thirty-third anniversary of the rising of the Spanish army in Africa against the republic, the Speaker summoned the *Cortes* on Tuesday the 22nd to hear an address by Franco 'in connection with Article 6 of the Law of Succession'. Under that Article Franco could 'at any moment put before the *Cortes* the name of the person whom [he thought] fit to succeed him as king or regent'. In Lisbon the following day Don Juan formally dissolved his secretariat and his Privy Council, the trappings of a pretender. On the Tuesday Franco formally proposed Juan Carlos as the next King of Spain : Juan Carlos was male, Spanish, of royal blood, over thirty, and a Catholic. The *Cortes* dutifully approved **Franco**'s choice by 419 votes to nineteen with nine abstentions. Some of the deputies approved, adding 'because Franco wants it', and thirty-five were absent from the House.

In the short term the nomination changed nothing. Franco was not retiring and he was handing over no responsibilities or duties to his named successor. It remained to be seen whether the people of Spain would accept Juan Carlos with the alacrity with which their nominal representatives in the *Cortes* had done, and whether he would outlive the nickname already given him – *Juan el Breve*.

The *Cortes* duly gave Juan Carlos the title Prince of Spain, and he swore before them to uphold the principles of the *Movimiento*. The ageing Head of State, Head of Government, and *generalissimo* left his Madrid residence, the Bourbon lodge of El Pardo, for his usual summer holiday in his native Galicia, where he went shooting, fishing, and playing golf, well pleased; for the national economy, in the cautious words of foreign economists '[appeared] to have entered into a new expansionary phase'.[66] Even in June it was predictable that the tourist total for 1969 would exceed the 20 million mark. Harvest prospects were good. All industry was doing well; the amalgamation of small enterprises into efficient modern concerns was attracting orders from abroad for capital equipment as well as consumer goods. Spain moved up to fifth place in the world's table of shipbuilders and order books were full, Gulf Oil for instance increasing its order from Spanish yards to four tankers each of a third of a million and two others each of 100,000 tons. With the economy prospering it was to be expected that Spain would tighten the blockade of Gibraltar, and she did. Franco's withdrawal of Spanish labour from Gibraltar and suspension of the ferry service from Algeciras was praised by the surviving Spanish republican government in Exile in Mexico no less encouragingly than by his supporters at home. On this matter he had no Spanish opponents – nor on another major act of policy : on returning to Madrid in October he approved budget proposals which for the first time in the history of Spain put expenditure on education above all other allocations, well above defence.

[66] *B.O.L.S.A. Review* (September 1969).

Chapter 32

Spain – A Personal View

Esdevens hereu
dels dies de l'odi
i del desgovern

(You have become the heir
of days of hatred
and inefficiency.)

THUS, IN A REMARKABLE POEM of mixed foreboding and optimism over the future,[1] the Catalan poet Salvador Espriu addresses *Sepharad,* Spain.

'After Franco, what?'

For the immediate post-Franco period there are two possibilities : anarchy; and the continuation of the present authoritarianism. In the long term Spain could : remain an authoritarian régime under a King or President; be fashioned into a socialist republic; or evolve into a democracy.

There are several factors which could make for disorder and anarchy.

The hatreds which contributed to the Civil War and which the Civil War engendered survive. The desire for vengeance is latent, not only among the survivors of the conflict (men who in 1969 are aged about fifty and over), but also among their younger brothers and sisters and their children (the twenty-five to fifty age-group).

Under the Franco régime it has been neither more difficult nor easier than at any time since the beginning of the seventeenth century for the victim of official injustice or incompetence to obtain redress. Earlier in this century, however, if only to discredit an ousted political opponent and not necessarily to see justice done or greater competence, a newly appointed Minister would take up the case of a person wronged by his predecessor. Officials have come and gone during the past thirty years, but the

---

[1] *La Pell de Brau*—lit. *Rawhide,* published with an unsatisfactory translation into Spanish by EDICUSA, Madrid, 1968.

'discredit' motive has been largely absent because there has been no change of government and only a renewal of its members. Thus the score of unrequited real and imaginary injustices has grown.

In the last five years the reading and half-digestion of Herbert Marcuse has become the 'done thing' among university students. Many young men and women are moved to public protest and demonstration by a thirst for justice or by some positive political ideal, but others want disorder as an end in itself, or because disorder is fashionable. There are also other new apostles of violence – for example the Mao-inspired quasi-Basque ETA.

There are, however, factors which militate against disorder.

Only a few Spaniards in 1969 see in the provocation of violence the creation of a situation to their political advantage. The ETA is not to be identified with Basque nationalism, nor are trouble-makers who call themselves traditionalists, Falangists, communists, or socialists actors under orders from their parent bodies. They are for order, none more so than the Spanish Communist Party, under Santiago Carrillo. Nor would it be as easy today to stir up trouble on a national scale as it was in the 1920s and the 1930s. Over the past thirty years the police forces and the army have been reduced in size, but they are better led, more professional, and far more efficiently organized. Again, over the past thirty years the proportion of dispossessed to men of means has been reversed. Under 20 per cent of the population has still little or nothing to lose from disorder : 80 per cent has. Men of property or in employment whose remuneration depends on economic development and consumer demand (which in their turn depend on political stability), might here and there sympathize with the aspirations of militant Basques, Catalans, traditionalists, communists, or Falangists, but they would not join them in any number. The odds, then, are heavy against anything more than local disorder.

General Franco has sought to perpetuate the present order beyond his active lifetime by his *Leyes Fundamentales*. A would-be military successor as Head of Government would have to consider carefully the implications of these factors : no serving soldier today has or can expect to have the deep loyalty of his fellows such as Franco inspired, sometimes in spite of the individual's self; no general is respected by civilians as Franco is. A *junta* could take over, and would take over if disorder grew to sizeable proportions; but a *junta* or any other body taking over government will sooner or later have to face the fact that the desire is widespread among Spaniards to have a more direct say in government than the established order permits or the *Leyes Fundamentales* envisage after Franco goes.

The very real advances in education and in material well-being which have been accomplished by the Franco régime have out-dated those laws in many particulars and perhaps fundamentally.

It is sometimes lamented by Spaniards themselves that under the Franco régime the masses have become *despolitizadas,* indifferent to political and all ideals, and as materialistic as northern Europeans. Certainly, now that millions of Spanish men and women have money to spare on mechanical aids to leisure, they talk of the domestic appliance and the motor-car; where a generation ago in town and country people made their own amusements, they now comment on their favourite and ephemeral television programmes watched at home, in bars, or restaurants. The discussion of the merits and performances of football teams and players unite in cafés rich and poor. It is romantic nonsense, however, to state that when the parents of these millions were underpaid, unskilled workers in such industries as there were, or agricultural labourers out of work for two or three months in the year, their primary preoccupations were the things of the spirit and the problems of human society. They were concerned, more so perhaps than those of other nations. Nevertheless, their chief worry then was the acquisition of the next hunk of bread or bowl of soup for their starving families, and they had to work hard for them. When they went on strike, destroyed the machinery of their employers, or took over landed estates, most did so motivated by far more basic reasons than the philosophic or political principles of their mentors. Political theorizing was the privilege of men either of property or earning rather more than the bare sustenance of their families. None of the political figures of the republic was from the destitute stratum of society. The UGT and Socialist Party officials were almost all skilled workers or university men. So were those of the CNT, and the FAI, the anarchist spearhead, was a haven for 'intellectuals', men with schooling and often learning.

Obviously, the tractor-driver and combine-operator has to concentrate on his work rather more than the man behind the ox-driven plough, or one tossing the grain to winnow it. He has, therefore, less time to consider the lilies of the field or the purpose of life while he works; but he has more leisure when his work is done, and I know of no evidence that in the lives of Spaniards religion and politics play a lesser role than they did in the past.

What I have found, and what evidence there is, points to the contrary – that today proportionately a greater number of people of all classes are concerned with their God and their neighbour than at any time in living memory.

Sociology in Spain is in its infancy. Sociologists there are as prone as in other countries to frame questions which while clear to them can yet be understood by the questioned in more ways than one. They are as ready to draw conclusions beyond what the evidence warrants. The facts they have gathered nevertheless destroy two myths, one popular with upper-class right-wing Catholics and one with the 'intellectual' left.

An inquiry into church attendance in the south-eastern diocese of Albacete in October 1968 revealed that the percentage of inhabitants above the age of seven going regularly to church was thirty-two. In the city it was forty-four : in villages it was as low as twenty-three. The rural population was thus the less religious-minded. Similar inquiries in Barcelona have shown that in parishes where church attendance is low, it is the immigrants from rural Andalusia and Extremadura who abstain rather than the city-born and bred. There and in Bilbao, so far from 'contact with the wicked cities' destroying the faith of ex-rural workers, their interest in religion has been aroused since immigration. In Albacete the highest rates of church absenteeism were among the unskilled workers (87 per cent) and employers of labour (75 per cent) : the lowest among technicians (30 per cent) and men and women with university education (33 per cent). Similar inquiries in Barcelona, Madrid, Bilbao, and Málaga have also shown that the practice of religion varies in direct proportion to educational level. This is not to say that there are not many fervently religious families where the parents have no education or that there are not atheists among university men, but the figures belie alike the Marxist dictum of religion as the opium of the people and the traditional Spanish Catholic establishment's assertion that to be a Spaniard is to be a Catholic.

To the Spanish Catholic and to the Marxist alike, the results of the investigations have been disheartening. The Catholic was horrified to learn that on Sunday, 11 February 1962 only 28 per cent of the inhabitants above the age of seven of the city of Málaga went to Mass (24 per cent of the males, 32 per cent of women); but so were the Marxist and the anarchist. There are no reliable statistics on the matter for a generation ago, but if the memories of people do not deceive them, 28 per cent is a much higher proportion than was then common – between 50 and 100 per cent higher. In Bilbao average Mass attendance is now around 50 per cent – about the same as before the Civil War – but there is this important difference – that Bilbao's population has doubled with non-Basque immigrants, among whom religious practices were limited to baptism when back in their native villages.

Such and other evidence, then, suggests that a greater number of people of all classes are concerned with their God than at any time in living memory. This, however, is not all.

Over the past ten years Spanish Catholicism has noticeably undergone a great change. It is historically untrue to say, as is often said, that 'only in recent years has the Church opposed the régime of General Franco'. What is true is that opposition to certain specific aspects and to its fundamental nature has become stronger and come out into the open. The real change is much more important, especially as far as the future is concerned. Catholics, laity, clergy, and bishops, have become aware of the implications of the 'second great' commandment to their own selves and society. In religious belief the implication now more generally realized is that where a man may be held not to possess the whole truth it does not mean that he has none of it. The old book of intolerance is being closed towards the Jews, the Protestants, and the far more numerous agnostics and Marxists. There is equally a growing realization among practising Spanish Catholics of the political and social implications of the commandment 'Thou shalt love thy neighbour as thyself' and of the dogma 'all men are equal before God' : for if all men are equal before God, they now say, neighbours should strive to be equals. Fine though the record of charitable work was in the past, it was too often paternalistic; and the relationship of neighbour to neighbour should not be of father to son, but as between brothers or sisters.

This change of attitude is not limited to a few 'intellectuals' – far from it; and the fact presages well for the future peace of Spain. Eight women graduates carried out in 1966 an inquiry into the beliefs, thoughts, and aspirations of a 'representative sample' of the younger women of Madrid. It was more thorough than most. Its organizers concluded from the answers to a long questionnaire that the women of Madrid were fundamentally uncritical, conservative, narrow in interests, reactionary to change, and too protected. They noted also that the women of Madrid respected the institution of the family, that their sexual morals and ideals were of the highest order, that they were religious (99 per cent claimed a belief in God, but only 56 per cent a good knowledge of the tenets of Catholicism), benevolent, and generous. Sixty-one per cent of the 'sample' selected 'love of one's neighbour' as the highest human virtue and 67 per cent 'greater understanding between men' as mankind's greatest need, eschewing emotional alternatives. (The organizers were disappointed that only 67 per cent considered that women should take as much interest in politics as men, but an outsider could well be surprised at so high a figure, and indeed judge the investigators' strictures on their fellow women as harsher than the analysis of the answer to the questionnaire would warrant. There is idealism in the Spanish woman, but there is hard commonsense as well.)

Forty years ago, the poet Antonio Machado was a voice in the wilderness when he wrote:

> ¿Tu verdad? No, la verdad;
> Vamos juntos a buscarla.
> La tuya quedátela.

> (Your truth? No, *the* truth.
> Together let us search it.
> *Your* truth – keep it.)

Today there are Liberals who go further than Machado: '¿*Mi* verdad?' 'No, la verdad.' (My truth? No, the truth.) The modern Spanish Liberals, it has seemed to me in talking with them, are also evolving. But what of the left?

Anarchism has not recovered from its severe losses in men during the Civil War from both sides and after the war from executions by the victors; and though doubtless its philosophy in its pristine form will continue to attract a trickle of young people there is little to warrant the fear that it will ever again be a mass movement. Any attempt to establish a libertarian commune in a Spain whose economy is no longer that of an underdeveloped society would result in such a fall in the standard of living as to be unacceptable to any but a few heroic idealists. On the other hand, for that very reason that Spain's economic development is at the stage where it is, Spain could be transformed on Marxist lines without much difficulty or bloodshed. Had the insurgents lost, Marxists of one sect or another (not liberal republicans) would have come to power, but to maintain themselves there, to fashion Spain into a socialist state, they would have had to follow the methods which Lenin and Stalin found necessary to impose socialism in Russia. Not so now: and what would socialism mean today?

In my talks with socialists in 1969 I found them as in previous years.[2] They continue obsessed with the infallibility of Marx and Engels. The interpretation of Marx–Engels varies between individuals, but the ownership and control by the state of the means of

[2] Cf. pp. 375–6.

production and rule by the élite called 'the dictatorship of the proletariat' remain central tenets. They are collectivists, and they approach human rights from the viewpoint of society as a unit and not of the individual : the individual has no meaning for them except as a unit of society. In the socialist state, once established, there would be no need for the individual to have those rights which in a non-socialist state he requires to protect him from the state; as the state would be acting for society, society, that is the state, would have to protect itself from the individual. The state would always know best what is good for the individual. In that state all workers, as now, would have the right to a job, the right to a fair wage, the right to free social services, but not to strike. Where it would differ from the present régime would be, according to socialists, that the state would give to each man according to his needs, and not according to what he inherited or by enterprise acquired. Since the state would see to it that each man had his needs satisfied, there would therefore be no need for strikes, and no need for the freedom to strike. The modern Spanish socialist's ideal is, in fact, Tito's Yugoslavia, nationally independent, nominally tolerant of national minorities and regional susceptibilities, and even of minor political deviations and religion – but a one-party totalitarian state all the same.

That is the long-term goal, and in the long term a socialist Spain is indeed possible; but it is no part of socialist policy to seek total power immediately after Franco, or to present its long-term goal quite so blatantly. Strategically the establishment of a parliamentary democracy is thought a necessary first step and a tactical alliance with groups wanting such a democracy politically wise.

The demand is now widespread among people of all educational and social backgrounds that all Spaniards should participate in government by more direct means than the established order can of its structure allow even when Franco goes. The validity of the demand is recognized even by some army officers, bankers, captains of industry, and owners of large estates. That the existence of the demand and its strength is realized even at the top of the present régime may be deduced from the history of the new *Ley Sindical,* to reform the structure and laws of the workers' organizations implicitly outdated by the 1966 constitution. Since the *sindicatos* were no longer to be institutions at the service of the economy of the state, the question at issue became : how far, if at all, should there be state control of the *sindicatos*?

In 1967, under Franco's own laws, there had to be consultation on such a major issue, with the workers, the employers, the

Movimiento, and the *Cortes.* Franco could not then have acted
as in 1938 when he decreed the original Labour Charter, whose conception and wording, except in detail, were his, and on the eve
of his March offensive no one could gainsay him; nor was there
consultation in 1941 when he approved the plan set out at his command which led to the establishment of the *sindicatos.* However,
by 1968 it could have been said that the letter of the law had been
obeyed over the new *Ley* in that its propositions had been approved
by a congress of *sindicato* officials and a draft could then have
been put before the *Cortes.* It was announced repeatedly from
month to month that it would be. Within the Cabinet it kept being
'referred back' for further study – and the *sindicatos* remained
unreformed by law because of the opposition to the pusillanimity
of the suggested reforms.[3]

The protagonists of a parliamentary democracy are from conviction the men imbued with modern Christian Democratic ideas
and the surviving Liberals, and for strategic and tactical reasons, as
we have said, the Social Democrats. The communists who follow
Santiago Carrillo would also support any move towards its establishment. But there are still many Spaniards who either abhor
parliamentary democracy or who judge its institution in Spain
either personally unprofitable or politically unwise.

Those who abhor it are first and foremost the dyed-in-the-wool
Falangists who maintain that Franco betrayed José Antonio's ideals.

Those who fear it as personally unprofitable are the *enchufados,*
those 'plugged-in' to the present system, especially in the *sindicatos*
– personally unprofitable because they would lose their well-paid
jobs, assuming that the organizations of the present system would
disappear if the system were replaced.

Those who consider the institution of liberal democracy unwise
are the ones who fear a repetition of past history. Admittedly a true
parliamentary democracy has never existed in Spain, but there have
been two approximations to it. There was the Cánovas – Sagasta
arrangement, imposed from above, but it failed to take root. There
was also the system introduced with the republic in 1931 : the
genuine parliamentarians splintered into a score of parties and
allowed the sham parliamentarians to seize power. If they thought
the creation possible in Spain of a Spanish equivalent of the British
parliamentary system, if the opposition were to be Loyal Opposition, opposing the government so as to force it to think before
taking action, yet allowing it to govern, and if the government could

[3] Whatever may be the content or fate of the new *Ley Sindical* put
before *Cortes,* in October 1969, my point remains valid, that many
Spaniards want as of right greater participation in government.

be trusted to respect minorities and in power not to go beyond its electoral mandate, then they would not oppose 'parliamentary democracy'. They would welcome it. The stability and the economic progress of the last fifteen years would continue. Such a system might ensure greater social justice for the many without causing injustice to the few. But what hope is there of that, they ask. Those who think on these lines agree that Christian Democrats and Liberals have come to admit that Spain is a pluralist society and that there can be no justice, freedom, or peace in a pluralist society except in liberty; but Spain is not composed only of Christian Democrats and Liberals. Falangists and socialists are perhaps no less numerous. The Spanish left is still such that the attempt would still not succeed. If the Spanish left were like the British left, they add, pragmatic, fervent believers in the rights of the individual and in a parliamentary system, there would be no problem; but the Spanish left is where it was thirty years ago. A parliamentary democracy cannot survive where one of its major groups does not believe in it sincerely. Institute it, and where will it lead? If to a totalitarian one-party state, like Yugoslavia, then surely the present Spanish authoritarian state is the lesser evil?

So, it is true to say that while there is a widespread desire that Spain should evolve into a democratic society, there is also strong opposition; but Franco's successors will have to consider whether they should not state that proposition the other way about : while there is support for the view that the established authoritarianism should continue, there is strong opposition in favour of a more democratic society.

* * *

Nineteenth-century Spain gave the twentieth-century world three words : *guerrilla, pronunciamiento,* and *junta.* There are two twentieth-century Spanish words which could travel abroad and be international in years to come : *contraproducente* and *convivencia.* Indeed the first has already gone into Italian, and 'counterproductive', meaning 'having, or likely to have, an effect opposite to that intended or desired', is currently making appearances in English writing. *Contraproducente* has come to be more and more used in its native land as Spaniards have come to learn from their experiences over the last half-century that the course of action which follows most fittingly and logically from theory is not necessarily the best pragmatically. *Convivencia* is what Spaniards have been striving for over a long lifetime, and especially as they have come to recognize that theirs is a pluralist society, and is likely henceforth to be a pluralist society. Many now understand that if they are to live in peace, then they must learn how 'to live together'.

It is in the current self-examination, the harshly realistic examination, in which Spaniards as individuals and as members of a Church or other bodies are now engaged, that perhaps there is hope that they will achieve that *convivencia* they desire, the *convivencia* of the nations of Spain – Basque, Catalan, Galician, eastern, southern, and Castilian, of the centre and the periphery, of the men of letters, science, arms, and crafts, of Church and state, of the Catholic and non-Catholic, the socialist and non-socialist, the civilian and the military. And there is dialogue; before the war Spaniards shouted each other down, and out of pandemonium there was war. Spain would be safe, if it were to heed Salvador Espriu :

> De vegades és necessari i forçós
> que un home mori per un poble,
> peró mai no ha de morir tot un poble
> per un home sol :
> recorda sempre aixó, Sepharad.
> Fes que siguin segurs els ponts del dialeg
> i mira de comprendre i estimar
> les raos i les parles diverses dels teus fils.

> (That a man should die for a people
> Has on occasion been expedient and inevitable.
> But never that a people should die
> For one man :
> Always remember that, Sepharad.
> See to the security of the bridges of dialogue;
> Seek to understand and to value
> The reasonings and the diverse tongues of your sons.)

Dialogue is two-way : the centre should seek to understand the periphery; but the periphery should also seek to understand the centre. Sepharad is all of Spain.

In all the current effort of Spaniards to know themselves and seek the truth, there is one tendency which could nullify its potential value. In their own polity they look for faults : in others they see only virtues, and think them perfect. In an individual that may be laudable. In politics there is a more useful exercise : it is in the first place to realize that there is no political, social, or economic problem uniquely of one's own country – the intensity of the problem may possibly be unique, but not the problem; Spain's problems are without exception human and not Spanish – and in the second place, to examine thoroughly the success or failure of methods used by others towards the diminution of each problem; and not to go from the particular to the general. Granted that a particular people may have diminished a specific problem to insignificance, it does not follow that they have solved all their problems. No place is Utopia.

Over the last thirty years much has been done which should not have been done; much has not been done which should have been done; but there has been achievement – and not the least achievement, intended or no it does not matter, is that Spaniards have had the time to think over their past and their future. Should they now strengthen their desire for dialogue and learn to speak to each other, then they might give other nations that word of peace, *convivencia*.

Such *convivencia*, such peace in Spain cannot come except, as Pope John XXIII said in *Pacem in Terris*, relations between individuals and between government and peoples be conducted in 'truth, justice, and liberty'. Up till now the official names given to the Civil War have been *la guerra de liberación*, the war of liberation, or *cruzada*, partisan and uncharitable words, and the truthful if tragic term *guerra civil* has been anathema in speech and scored out of print. It is so no longer. The authorities have allowed the publication and public sale of a work which is titled straightforwardly *Historia de la guerra civil española*. Is it too much to hope from this detail that the authorities also now aspire to Machado's *la verdad*, the truth? If so, then at a not too distant date some poet may say to Sepharad—

> Esdevens hereu
> dels dies de la pau—

> (You have become the heir of peace.)

Appendixes

Appendix A

The 'Guerrilla War' 1939–52[1]

FEW KNOW THAT IN SPAIN an attempt to overthrow the régime by guerrilla warfare was defeated, as in Malaya and Greece and at about the same time.

Up to 1952, thirteen years after the official end of the Civil War, there were frequent gun-fights in Spain. They took place principally in five zones:

1. In Andalusia: across the borders between the provinces of Cadiz – Seville, Seville – Málaga, Málaga – Córdoba, Córdoba – Granada, Granada – Jaén, and Granada – Almería (Serrania de Ronda and allied ranges).
2. In Extremadura: the Sierra Morena, across the borders, between the provinces of Seville – Madajoz, Badajoz – Córdoba, Córdoba – Ciudad Real, Ciudad Real – Badajoz, with a spur up to the Toledo mountains.
3. In Castile, in the Sierra de Gredos and Guadarrama.
4. In the Cantabrian mountains above Santander, Oviedo, León, Lugo, and Orense.
5. In Aragon, above Cuenca, round Teruel, and between Huesca and Lérida up to the Pyrenees (Serrania de Cuenca, Sistema Ibérico).

Of the five the Cantabrian was traditionally 'guerrilla' country; the first and second zones were for long periods in history 'bandit country'. The five zones had these characteristics in common: they had no economic significance; they were mountain scrubland or wild forest, with good cover from air and ground observation; they had primitive communications; they were sparsely populated; they had isolated well-built homesteads. The first and second zones had no strategic or military value; the main lines of communication

[1] This appendix is based on: Enrique Lister, *Lessons of the Spanish Guerrilla War (1939–51)* (*World Marxist Review,* February 1965), pp. 35–9; Lt. Colonel Eduardo Munilla Gómez: *Consecuencias de la lucha de la Guardia Civil contra el bandolerismo en el período 1943–1952* (articles published for restricted circulation, for permission to use which I am indebted to the Spanish authorities); interrogation of eyewitnesses, and research into military movements.

433

between Barcelona and Madrid and Madrid and the north went through the others but they could be quite easily protected. All were areas into which the advancing nationalist forces did not bother to pursue stragglers because the effort required would have been out of all proportion to its military value.

These stragglers, *huídos,* came to number between 6,000 and 10,000; not many out of the half-million who fought on the republican side. They constituted no military problem because : (i) they had only small-arms (rifles, pistols, a few machine-guns) and hand grenades; (ii) they were not a coherent force, but separate handfuls of men; they had little or no contact with each other.

There were among them dedicated anarchists, communists, and socialists. Disciplined to obey orders, the communists were at a disadvantage once cut off from their superiors. So also were the socialists, though to a lesser extent. The anarchists alone knew how to continue the fight on their own initiative. Guerrilla operations and acts of sabotage of more than nuisance value, however, require skill, discipline, and organization – and organization was of essence anathema to anarchism. The daily 'revindicative task' was more likely to be an assault on an isolated homestead than on a barracks, and on a farmcart than on an army lorry. There were also among the *huídos* a few, perhaps as many as 2,000, with criminal records going back to pre-war years – the survivors of the thousands released when the prisons were opened in the enthusiasm of the first days of the war. They owed allegiance to no party and they had no political ideals.

The first thought of the *huídos,* not dedicated Bakuninists or Marxists, was to avoid detection, capture, or possible death. They lived by trapping or hunting. With the passage of time and in winter their needs could not be satisfied so easily. Over the years 1940–42 the number of forage raids increased steadily, and so did attacks on individuals. Some of their victims could be called collaborators with the régime; many were collaborators only in the sense that they would not co-operate with the *huídos.* During 1943 the number[2] of offences against the law reported to the police by the public and attributed to the *huídos* was 929; ranging from petty larceny to assassination. By then the Civil Guard had been reconstituted,[3] and it now had squads to cope with this *bandolerismo,* banditry, as it was officially called. For the loss of eighteen of their own men they killed and captured 332 *bandoleros* and arrested 737 'sympathizers'. In the following year the Civil Guard attributed

---

[2] Munilla, op. cit.
[3] Of 24,300 Civil Guards at the outbreak of the war, 14,200 sided with the insurgents. There were heavy casualties among them. See *Franco,* p. 240.

1,069 breaches of the law to the *bandoleros,* killed and captured 450 of them, and themselves suffered the loss of eighty-two men.

The increase in activity was stimulated by the arrival in Spain of communist-trained guerrilla leaders. They left France shortly before the force of 1,500 *maquisards* crossed the Pyrenees in October 1944. Following the defeat of that force, the communists decided to concentrate on guerrilla warfare.

Lister, the communist military leader who organized the despatch of men, arms, and equipment, has told the communist side of the story[4]: 'The Party sent dozens of its members to Spain, entrusting them with the guidance and command of the guerrilla units ... many tons of supplies were delivered to Spain by land and sea ... over mountain trails at 20°C below zero.... Many – of the party – fell in the unequal battle. Those gallant men set up hundreds of dumps for guerrilla use. The party made extensive use of radio to popularize our struggle...'

Thus far Lt. Colonel Munilla Gómez of the Civil Guard, who has now published the results of his investigations into the history of the Civil Guard's action against *bandolerismo,* does not disagree with Lister. He notes the better quality of the weapons after the liberation of France and the introduction of the tommy-gun and high explosives for sabotage. Lister and Munilla differ on the number of 'guerrilla operations' (Lister's phrase), or 'indictable acts' (*hechos delictivos*), Munilla's term, carried out during the years 1944–9:

	Lister gives	Munilla	Difference
1944	694	1,069	375
1945	783	1,181	398
1946	1,085	1,558	473
1947	1,317	1,463	146
1948	983	1,030	47
1949	509	574	65

Of the 5,371 'guerrilla operations' with which Lister credits the men led by his communists, he says:

1. 1,478 were 'actions against Franco troops'.
2. 1,569 were 'attacks against communication lines, transport, power stations, military objectives, etc.'
3. 1,615 were 'supplying the units with provisions, seizing arms and explosives, and conducting anti-Fascist propaganda'.
4. 709 were 'punitive measures against murderers and traitors'.

[4] Lister, op. cit.

Only points one and four are clearly understandable. 'Punitive measures' is a euphemism for 'killings'; but if a guerrilla unit attacked a local Civil Guard police station for its arms, was that listed under point one or point three, or both?; or again, if they attacked an army lorry taking supplies to an outpost, was that listed under one or two, or both? Of the 1,615 acts listed under three, how many were raids for provisions, how many for arms, and how many merely 'anti-Fascist propaganda act'?

There are several other more obscure points in the account. Thus in one sentence Lister says : 'Franco resorted to unrestrained ruthlessness in his efforts to destroy the guerrilla units. He deployed Fascist armoured units, aircraft, and specially trained anti-guerrilla contingents'; later he says : 'Experience taught the régime that the use of big troop formations against the guerrillas was ineffective' – they could be seen and heard coming and the guerrillas melted away before them. But that would be true also of armoured units, however small, and notwithstanding what he has said, Lister also has recorded Franco as deploying '450,000 regulars plus Civil Guard and police units' along the French frontier to a depth of 60 kilometres.

Lister might have been more successful had he read Sun Tzu's *Art of War* as well as communist principles of guerrilla warfare : 'if you know the enemy and know yourself, you need not fear the result of a hundred battles'. His opposing commanders were men who as cadets had studied guerrilla warfare as practised by the original *guerrilleros* against Napoleon, and who had experience of combating Moroccan irregulars banded and acting for many years before and after the Rif War as *guerrilleros,* over country very much like Spain. In fact the only 'troops' used against the Lister *guerrilleros,* except on very rare occasions, were Civil Guard detachments, para-military but not army.

Lister gives more detail still and in doing so gives further ground for doubts on his accuracy. He divides the zones of operation into six – Levante – Aragon, Andalusia, Extremadura, Asturias – Santander, Castile, Galicia – León. He shares out the 709 killings fairly evenly : 106, 130, 103, 106, 118, 146; not so the 'attacks against communication lines, etc.' The men in Andalusia are credited with 417, whereas those in Asturias – Santander with a mere 226. This is curious, for the Asturias – Santander region was rich in 'communication lines, transport, power stations, military objectives', while Andalusia was very poor.

Lister's account is undisguisedly both communist propaganda and Marxist self-justification, confession to deviation from party lines and a sign of repentance. It should, therefore, not be accepted

without reserve in whole or in detail. Not that the figures he gives
are incredibly high. On the contrary : many more than 1,615
operations to acquire provisions, arms, etc., could have been
expected. Simple arithmetic will show why.

Between 1943 and 1952 the Civil Guard killed or captured 5,548
bandoleros : in the three years 1944–6 2,093. During 1946 they
must therefore have numbered at least 3,500. That year, according
to Lister, arms and food-supply raids *and* those unspecified acts
of 'anti-Fascist propaganda' totalled 294, rather less than one per
ten men in a whole year – or if we take the average size of each guerrilla unit to have been twenty (the *guerrilleros* rarely got beyond the
first of the Mao stages : 'sections will be formed, they will develop
into platoons, platoons into companies, companies into battalions,
battalions into regiments, regiments into divisions', so twenty is an
optimistic average) rather less than two a year.

Munilla's larger figures are therefore more credible, particularly
as he warns his readers that they are of 'reported acts'. He dis-
tinguishes the motivation of the men in the Asturian region and
in Aragon from that of the others : in those regions, he says, men
acted for ideological rather than personal reasons. Again he dis-
tinguishes between the nature of the activities in the period between
the entry of the *maquis* and the U.N. ostracism of Spain, the
years autumn 1944 to the end of 1946 (the period of maximum
effort by Lister and his communists to control the *huídos* and
make them a guerrilla fighting force), and what they did before
and after. During those years there were some acts of sabotage and
some daring exploits : but they were few even then. Otherwise what
they did, did not make them worthy of the honourable name of
guerrillero. and certainly after 1946 they degenerated into *bandoleros* because : they moved about in bands or gangs; they robbed for
their personal enrichment; they killed to avenge private feuds;
they violated to satisfy their instincts; they kidnapped for ransom;
they operated in remote rural areas without military significance.

Lister states that in October 1948 the Politburo of the Spanish
Communist Party decided to abandon guerrilla warfare and
dissolve all but 'the more efficiently organized and reliable units to
safeguard the party committees in the mountains.... Other units
were to be disbanded'. Hence the drop from his peak of 1,317
'operations' in 1947 to 509 in 1949. Lister gives no figures beyond
that date. Munilla does – up to 1952.

There are two curious omissions in Lister's account. He speaks
of traitors; he claims that a secret order was issued in 1946 (by
whom he does not say) that no prisoners were to be taken by the
Civil Guard; and he admits that the attempt by guerrilla warfare

to inspire the people to rise against the régime failed; but he gives no figures for the losses sustained by his men, nor does he claim explicitly that his men caused the enemy any casualties.

Munilla is more informative. According to him this was the record covering the years 1943–52:

Bandoleros killed	2,166		
taken prisoner	3,382		
		Total:	5,548
Civil Guards killed	256		
wounded	368		
		Total:	624

Persons detained as couriers, accomplices, and 'hiders' 19,407.

While he gives 8,275 as the total of *hechos delictivos,* as we have said, this, Munilla warns, is only the number of 'those reported: many were not, for fear of reprisals by the bandits'.

Here is his record year by year:

Year	Hechos delictivos	Casualties		Arrests of Couriers, etc.
		Bandits	Civil Guard	
1943	929	332	18	737
1944	1,069	450	82	798
1945	1,181	680	71	1,014
1946	1,558	963	114	2,523
1947	1,463	1,107	144	6,301
1948	1,030	826	63	3,900
1949	574	534	56	1,538
1950	250	355	36	1,050
1951	194	236	29	785
1952	27	65	11	761

The Civil Guard captured 7,140 firearms and 7,804 hand-grenades in the ten years. Peak losses to the fighters occurred in 1947 and early 1948, when they suffered also the highest casualties in fighting men and 'sympathizers'. After such heavy losses the Politburo's decision to pull out was eminently sensible.

Lister confesses that the *guerrilleros* did not have the support of the people: 'it may be argued that that was because the people had just emerged from three years of a civil war in which they were defeated'. Maybe, maybe not, he adds cryptically.

'Just emerged' within the context of Lister's account is five years: the successful guerrillas against Napoleon went into action with wide popular support when the outlook was blackest and they could count on no outside help. According to Lister his guerrillas had 'the sympathy of the people who regarded them as heroes', although earlier he says : 'the anti-guerrilla squads comported themselves like plain bandits. They robbed the peasants and committed many other crimes which were blamed on the guerrillas with a view to turning the people against them.... All too often our enemies succeeded in their foul designs.'

This is a claim which cannot be accepted by any student of or participator in anti-guerrilla activities. With extraordinary preparations the anti-guerrilla forces may 'get away with it' once or twice, but no more. The men detailed to pretend to be 'bandits' must be dressed as such, and must be unknown to the intended victims. Having done the deed, they must be sent to where they will not be recognized. The danger will persist that such men in their cups or gnawed by conscience will not keep the secret. But the danger is greatest while the deed is being done. Unless all units in the area are warned, there is always the chance that one of them will go into action against the pseudo-bandits. Few 'accidents' demoralize a fighting force more than the subsequent knowledge that they have fired on their own men. Even if it does not occur, the thought that one might be firing on a friend and not a foe, introduces into the soldier's mind that moment of hesitation which might well cost him his life if the foe really is a foe.

Guerrilla warfare has come to be glamorized, following apparent success in China and Cuba. How far the claims made for the guerrillas in the Chinese wars or the overthrow of the Batista régime can be backed by sober facts is beyond the scope of this appendix; the advocates of that type of war gloss over its failure in Malaya and elsewhere. Two facts must not be forgotten : first, in guerrilla warfare the finer points of 'civilized warfare' and Geneva conventions have never and perhaps can never be upheld. The terrorizing of the countryside in Malaya was deliberately planned by the so-called Malay People's Liberation Army. Even in the war which gave the world the term guerrilla, even then as Marx wrote[5], the guerrillas took to 'roving habits, freely indulged all their passions of hatred, revenge and love of plunder...'. And secondly, Lenin himself defended terrorism in guerrilla war.[6]

The difference between the Spaniards and the Malays or Greeks was that the Spaniards refused to be terrorized, so that the establishment of protected villages was not necessary.[7]

[5] Marx-Engels, *Revolution in Spain* (International Publishers, 1939), pp. 51–5. First published in *New York Herald Tribune,* 30 October 1954.
[6] Cf. Lenin, *Collected Works* (Moscow, 1962), Vol. 2, pp. 213–23, *et aliter.*
[7] Lister's article is worth comparing with that by Zizis Zografos, 'Some lessons of the Civil War in Greece' in *World Marxist Review* (November 1967), pp. 42–5.

It is true, as Lister says, that a guerrilla movement cannot succeed unless it comes to be supported by the mass of the people, whether out of love or fear. It is also true that the suppression of a guerrilla movement is impossible without the active co-operation of a substantial body of the people, however efficient the anti-guerrilla forces may be. Not until the British forces in Malaya obtained the *active* co-operation of the inhabitants did the Emergency end. In Spain, the 20,000 'couriers, etc.' apart, the people co-operated with the Civil Guards. Lister admits as much. Considering in 1965 whether a new attempt at starting guerrilla warfare should be made, he argued that 'it would strengthen the dictatorship' : '... the self-sacrifice of the vanguard would hardly make a dint in the dictatorship, *just as the many years of guerrilla warfare failed to do*'.

In other theatres the suppression of guerrilla activity has required the deployment of up to twelve regular soldiers per fighter. At no time (in spite of Lister's account) were more than 20,000 Civil Guards and other armed units deployed in the exercise, and most of the time the figures were much smaller. At the height of their activities the guerrillas must have numbered over 5,000; but then, it is only in Spain, of the several countries in which I have studied guerrilla warfare, that I have heard of the people capturing and disarming a band of four guerrillas (they had held up a bus going from a village to the city of Teruel) and of the Civil Guard arriving just in time to prevent the people from lynching the *bandoleros* on the spot.

Such an episode and others on which I have cross-questioned witnesses and participators, have on occasion made me wonder whether the opposition to the régime was ever as nationally widespread as it has at times appeared from the activities of a few hundred and even a few thousand enthusiasts in the three main cities.

The continuation of this 'guerrilla war' into 1952 has a bearing on the survival of the régime which is perhaps not immediately obvious. Today in 1969 two-thirds of the population can have no recollection, however dim, of the Civil War – all those born after, say, 1933. But, there is quite a sizeable number who do remember this second war, or who heard tales about it in their childhood – and it was, in some ways, more beastly.

But there are others who know nothing about it and that could now have serious consequences. Lenin's opinion that guerrilla warfare is of little value of itself is historically more warrantable than Guevara's that it can overthrow régimes.

Appendix B

The Infrastructure of Spanish Agriculture

SPAIN HAS AN AREA of 504,700 square kilometres – 50·47 million hectares.[1] Nothing at all grows on 4·07 million. The remaining 46·63 million are reckoned by Spaniards to be 'productive': 1·56 million[2] produce wisps of vegetation or esparto; 11·7 million are rated as 'woodland', most of it of little value as timber; 11·5 million are 'wild pasture' – the sort of land on which goats or sheep can eke out a living; 1·4 million are savannah.

The land actually being worked totals 20·1 million hectares. Only on 2·1 million of them is the available water (by irrigation or natural rainfall) adequate. The rest is dry to the point where in the more northerly countries of Europe farmers would despair. Yields on irrigated land are many times those on the 'dry' lands. In the Badajoz zone, where the present régime first expropriated large estates, irrigated the land, and then distributed it to the landless, yields increased on average as follows:

Wheat from 7·75 metric quintals to 18 per hectare
Barley „   9·25 „   „   „ 22 „   „
Oats   „   8·50 „   „   „ 35 „   „

On the land now being irrigated to the north-east of Zaragoza, the *zona de Bardenas,* yields are now being obtained 8·5 times the average when the land was 'dry'.[3]

No two studies, official or otherwise, on the problems of Spanish agriculture agree on how much more land could be irrigated, how far Spain's water supplies can be controlled and stretched to improve the productivity of the land. Possibly 5 million hectares could come to be irrigated. Irrigation work is in progress on over 0·75 million hectares and preliminary studies have been made for

[1] Multiply 5/2 to convert hectares into acres.
[2] Figures rounded off. There are wide disparities between the statistics available on Spanish agriculture, as Juan Anlló notes in his *Estructura y problemas del campo español* (Madrid, 1967), p. 9. The *Primer Censo Agrario de España, Año 1962* (Madrid, 1966) gave for 'productive' land the figure 44·6 million hectares; the Ministry of Agriculture's *Anuario de la producción agrícola, campaña 1966–7* (Madrid, 1968) gives the larger figure quoted in the text.
[3] *Instituto Nacional de Colonización* figures.

an even greater area. Given improved husbandry, seeds, mechanization, and associated organization, on those 5 million hectares
alone Spain could come to produce nearly double her present output on the 20 million now being worked. As OECD and other
agencies have repeatedly noted, Spain should be capable not only
of maintaining her agricultural exports (olive oil, wines, citrus fruits,
canned fruits, potatoes, and the rest), but of limiting her imports
to such commodities as coffee, which she could not grow herself.
Spain could support a population several times her present one.
Her current fairly high birth-rate should not produce any insoluble
problem of feeding.

The government took the view in 1939, when it established the
Instituto Nacional de Colonización, that it was not enough to
irrigate the land; or rather it decided that merely to expropriate
large estates and split them up into so many smallholdings resolved
no social or economic evil, that the possession of a handful of hectares of 'dry' land would do no more than convert thousands of
ill-paid and underfed labourers into peasants unable to grow on
their property enough to feed their families, let alone that surplus
to provide shelter and clothing; and that even if they did, unless
a network of roads, storage facilities, and the rest were provided,
the produce would rot in the fields. The splitting-up of large estates,
the social desirability of which they recognized, had in principle,[4]
therefore, to go hand in hand with irrigation, the construction of
new villages, schools, churches, training centres, a network of communications, storage depots, canneries, and other processing plants.
All this required even over a small area detailed survey, planning,
and years of construction work. The progress of land settlement,
irrigation, and creation of a suitable infrastructure at the same
time has of necessity been slower than that of irrigation alone would
have been. Critics of the régime[5] have noted that whereas the FAO
in its Mediterranean Regional Project set a target for irrigation of
110,000 hectares per annum and the official Spanish *Instituto de
Cultura Hispánica* considered 85,000 desirable, the average rate
of completion during the first development plan (1964–7) was
little more than 75,000,[6] a rate which is being improved under the
second plan. Nevertheless, only Israel could be said to have achieved
more than Spain, all factors considered. In Israel, however, the
private individual's sense of urgency has been far greater than the

[4] Cf. decree of October 1939 establishing the *Instituto Nacional de
Colonización,* and subsequent decrees.

[5] Cf. Anlló, op. cit., pp. 17–18.

[6] 76,000 in 1968. *La Agricultura española en 1968* (Madrid, January
1969).

Spaniard's. Where the government has erred is in the compensation it has paid for expropriated land. To have paid on average 10,000 pesetas per hectare to the ousted owners of the land taken over for the Badajoz plan in 1958[7] – say £24 or $70 per acre at the time – would appear to have been over-generous by international European standards, for it was poor land. Land I have seen for which similar prices were paid in Monegros (Aragon) in the middle 1960s, would not, I think, have found a buyer in land-hungry Britain at anything like that figure : it was near desert.

As Anlló notes,[8] land settlement plans date back to 1770. The republic made much of its 1932 Agricultural Reform Law and in theory between June 1936 and 1938 the republic handed over to 'the workers' 5·7 million hectares which the victors restored to their former owners.

There is of course no warrant for the republic's figure of 5·7 million hectares 'distributed' : firstly, because from June 1936 onwards land was being taken over by 'libertarian communist' groups without reference to Madrid and not distributed; and secondly because the republic had no trustworthy statistical system, least of all in wartime. Indeed, prior to 1962 there were next to no reliable statistics on Spanish agriculture. In that year a census was made, the first ever to which some credence may be given – and even then with reservations over details. The land then calculated as productive (as not wholly devoid of vegetation) totalled 446,500 square kilometres.[9] It was in the hands of 2,856,000 separate enterprises[10] or managerial units. Thus, nationally, the average holding was of 15·47 hectares, under 40 acres. 2,407,700 had full title to the land they held; 374,900 were tenants paying rent in cash or kind; and 73,400 were tenants paying no rent, occupiers of land whose ownership was in dispute, or holders in trust for others. The land seemed accordingly to be well distributed. However, the division of the bulk figure of the amount of land by the overall total number of holders hid the reality – that the land was most unevenly divided. On the one hand, 805,800 holdings were of under one hectare (2·5 acres) and on average 0·4 of a hectare; on the other hand, 11·9 million hectares, 26·7 per cent of all rural land, were in the hands of a mere 4,800 enterprises,

---

[7] Quoted Anlló, op. cit., p. 30.

[8] Ibid. p. 19.

[9] This and subsequent figures in the paragraph are taken from : *Primer Censo Agrario de España, Año 1962* (Madrid, 1966) *and Informe sobre la agricultura y alimentación 1961–64* (Madrid, 1965). They have been rounded off for simplicity.

[10] Not synonymous with 'owners'—some owners having several units, some enterprises being family or collegiate.

these therefore having on average almost 2,500 hectares, 6,250 acres, apiece.

The regions of New Castile, Extremadura, and Andalusia were repeatedly singled out by politicians in the period 1901–36 as examples of the unjust distribution of landed wealth. The detailed census of land-holding undertaken in 1962 confirmed them as areas with some estates of vast extension, the *latifundia* of demagogues. In the province of Cuenca (New Castile) 170 enterprises held 430,900 hectares (approximate average 2,540); in the province of Cáceres (Extremadura) 230 estates totalled 462,000 hectares (approximate average 2,000); and in that of Huelva (Andalusia) 116 totalled 350,700 (average over 3,000). However, there were other areas to rival these. In Huesca (Aragon) there were 196 estates totalling 544,000 hectares (just under 2,800 apiece); in Pontevedra (Galicia), a province traditionally singled out as one of *minimifundia* – holdings too small to be economically viable – there were fifty-three estates with an area combined of 128,800 hectares and accounting for nearly 28 per cent of the whole province; in Orense (Galicia) estates of over 1,000 hectares accounted for 44 per cent of the total land area. One of the areas with the largest estates proved to be Oviedo (Asturias), 45 per cent of the province being in the hands of 89 enterprises, each on average 4,200 hectares (10,500 acres). Only in twenty-one out of Spain's fifty provinces did estates of over 1,000 hectares cover less than 20 per cent of the land – and only in ten provinces did estates of over 500 hectares account for less than that percentage.

Latifundia are therefore to be found over most of Spain. Nevertheless, it is true that the evils associated with them – absentee landlordism, underpaying of labourers, bad housing for the workers, underexploitation, their dedication to crops such as the olive which do not give all-the-year-round employment – are much more marked in the south (in the province of Cadiz for example) than in the north where many a large estate is reasonably well run and where many an owner is a model employer. It is in the north also rather than the south that the factor 'unprofitable land' is greater and the more to be considered before an estate is condemned out of hand as immorally large. In the Andalusia region the ratio of usable to useless and near useless land is roughly 1 : 1; in Aragon it is almost 1 : 2; in Asturias 1 : 10. Of an owner's 3,000 hectares in Asturias only 200 might be worth farming, and in Huesca 1,000 as against 1,500 or more in Huelva. Of course, the detail is more complex than that.

As the attack on the *latifundia* developed, so the landlords tried to divert attention towards the social evils consequent on the divisions of the land into tiny holdings. Where the left-wing land reformers quoted the eighteenth-century writer Jovellanos, the landlords cited a Madrid professor, Miguel Colmeiro, who in 1842 had denounced the division of properties in Galicia into 'handerchiefs' as the cause of the impoverishment of the tens of thousands of families. How could a man produce on a half-hectare or less of poor land enough for a family? They quoted, too, the obvious findings of a royal commission of 1907 which had studied the 'legal, social, and agronomic consequences' of the 'subdivision of land' and found them disastrous to the private and national economy.

The census proved that the other problem of rural Spain, the *minifundium,* was also more widespread than generally imagined. In Pontevedra there were indeed 35,000 enterprises sharing a mere 50,000 hectares between them, and not land on which a family could live on 'three acres and a cow'. Worse still, 61,000 families shared between them 24,300 hectares, an average of 0·4 of a hectare (one acre) apiece. But similar uneconomically small holdings were to be found in quantity north, south, and east as well as in the northwest.

To sum up, in 1962 nationally, at one extreme under 5,000 enterprises held nearly 10 million hectares; at the other extreme, three-quarters of a million enterprises were attempting to make a living from one quarter of a million hectares. 1.8 million 'farms' were under five hectares in extent.

What has been done, and what is being done?

The farmer or estate-manager with 2,000 hectares who cannot afford to pay his labourers handsomely is inefficient, if not worse, even if 1,000 of his hectares are too poor to farm. Hence the wrath of such men as Bishop Añoveras of Cadiz.[11] In western Andalusia (of which the province of Cadiz is a part), 2·2 million hectares are under cultivation and 1·9 million are unprofitable. In Old Castile, 2·5 million are farmed, 2·6 million abandoned; in Aragon 1·6 million are farmed, 2·8 million are not. The average wages paid in 1968 were as follows:[12]

	Full-time labourer	Casual labourer	Ploughman	Tractor-driver
W. Andalusia	128 ptas.	116	155	153
Old Castile	185	157	265	190
Aragon	181	173	275	234
(Catalonia	213	190	329	290)

These figures tell only a part of the story, for in general the

[11] See above, p. 337.
[12] *La Agricultura española en 1968,* p. 229.

fringe benefits of the agricultural worker in the north are greater than in the south, and again the casual labourer in the south can be out of work for three months in the year, whereas in the north he can find work almost daily. The worst months in the year are December, January, and February. On 3 November 1968 the official agricultural unemployment figures were :[13]

	Numbers	As percentage of all employed in agriculture
W. Andalusia	22,000	27·5
Old Castile	518	0·6
Aragon	3,094	4·9
(Catalonia	34	—)

It has been government policy (with international agency approval, as we have seen), to encourage workers to leave the land for industry at home and abroad. As labour has become scarce, so the landlord has had to increase wages or to mechanize, or both. The government has held before the growers the carrot of credits for modernization and guaranteed prices for produce. They have had some effect on the holders of between 100 and 1,000 hectares, but little on those having more – perhaps because the point at which the acquisitiveness of Spaniards loses momentum tends to be much lower than in other European countries. A man can live in total ease in the south with an income of, say, one million pesetas a year. If he has 2,000 hectares, he would be content with a return of 500 pesetas per hectare (under $3, say £1·25 per acre). Whatever the causes, the fact remains that carrot tactics alone have been proved insufficient. The solution might be swingeing taxation of inefficiency, thus eradicating it.

The demagogues of pre-Civil War days called estates of even one hundred hectares *latifundia*. Ideas have changed since then. There are still sound managerial as well as social arguments against estates of over 1,000 hectares ('dry' land), and even perhaps of over 500 hectares. Such statistics as are available support the conclusion that in general the most profitable and best-managed at present are those of between 100 and 200 hectares – and their owners seem to be the most socially conscious. Less than one per cent of the farms are of that size. Only slightly over one per cent are the farms in the not unviable range of fifty–one hundred hectares. Almost 90 per cent are of less than twenty hectares. These could become viable only if coalesced into co-operatives – and as we shall see in a moment, that is government policy.

[13] ibid, pp. 222–3.

Twenty hectares of irrigated land is, of course, another matter. An efficient farmer should get from them as much as a 'dry farmer' with a hundred or more. When the Badajoz plan was being prepared, the conclusion was reached that from between four and five hectares of irrigated land a family could get a reasonable living. As ideas on what a reasonable living is have changed, five hectares have come to be looked upon officially as too few, and in the newer settlement zones eight to ten are being allotted.

Latifundia, minifundia, and *minimifundia* are but part of the Spanish agrarian problem. The greatest perhaps is what is known in Spanish as *parcelación* – which has no real equivalent in the English-speaking world.

Two distinct laws of inheritance account for the large estates on the one hand and on the other for the existence of over 1·8 million 'farms' of five hectares and under. One is the Visigothic *mayorazgo* ('eldest child takes all'). The other is the 'Napoleonic', more strictly the French, introduced with the Bourbons. Under it each child received an equal share. What, however, constituted equality? Given an estate of 500 hectares and five heirs, it was not enough to divide it into lots of 100 hectares. Some of the land would be good pasture, some indifferent, some bad; some might be watered, some not; some might have good olives or chestnuts; some of it might be good ploughland, some stony – and so on. The only way to 'equality' was to divide the 500 hectares in ten or twenty different ways, and then give each heir his fifth. No matter that each inheritance was now split up into small lots over a wide area. With the succession of each generation and intermarriage the pattern became chaotic in the extreme.

In 1953 a department was created within the Ministry of Agriculture to study how isolated *parcelas* might be consolidated and to implement findings. It was called the *Servicio Nacional de Concentración Parcelaria*. It carried out a survey and its findings revealed a situation absurd beyond what had been imagined. Around 8,000 population centres they discovered that 6 million people owned between them 42·7 million hectares divided into 54 million lots.[14] The national average 'field' was therefore 0·79 of a hectare. In Pontevedra it was 0·11 of a hectare (one-quarter of an acre); in Orense 0·15; in Corunna 0·15. This was not unexpected; but there were almost as serious divisions in parts of Castile – the average 'field' in Zamora was 0·33 of an acre, in Soria 0·36, in Segovia 0·41.

[14] *Servicio Nacional de Concentración Parcelaria y Ordenación Rural 1953–63* (Madrid, 1964), Vol. 1, pp. 18–21.

These 'overall' figures did not reveal the total chaos of the situation – the following examples will give a better idea.[15]

Case A

Alejandro Abad Rojo of Santa Cecilia, Burgos Province, owned 2·2 hectares (5·5 acres) in 64 *parcelas* – literally a furrow here, a furrow there, and a square yard with a chestnut elsewhere, and so on.

Case B

Norberto García Rodríguez of Barromán, province of Ávila, owned 132·6 hectares – a 'latifundist' by pre-Civil War left-wing standards. His land was scattered over a radius of about 5 kilometres in 220 lots, most of them totally isolated from even cart-tracks.

Case C

Property near Medina del Campo (Valladolid): 59·15 hectares in 30 lots. Distance between nearest and furthest lot 26 kilometres (16 miles). Average distance of the plots from the village where owner lives: 3·5 kms. (over 2 miles).

– and so, literally, hundreds of thousands of cases.

Teams consisting of a lawyer and an agronomist were formed, with survey groups to help them. The landowners large and small were exhorted to invite the teams to sort out the chaos. They did not require much persuasion that if all their little lots could be consolidated their life would be much easier. The teams surveyed the property, assessed its productivity, worked out how each property could be consolidated, then had the difficult task of persuading the owners that *x* square metres with a stream was as good as 'handkerchief' A with its chestnut tree – or that the soul of the grandmother who left the present owner 'handkerchief' B would not be upset if the owner exchanged it for another.

As the news spread that the consolidation of property resulted in higher yields and less work (less time spent on walking alone) the demand exceeded the supply of technical teams. Over the years 1954–65 they consolidated properties as follows:[16]

1954	7,961	hectares	1957	21,753
1955	12,265		1958	50,524
1956	10,642		1959	68,667

[15] ibid., pp. 30–31 and 192–3.
[16] *Servicio Nacional, etc.; Situación de los trabajos al 31 dic. 1965.*

1960	71,150	1963	146,034
1961	89,429	1964	206,166
1962	101,144	1965	301,944

a total of 1,087,679 hectares, a formidable record when the human factors are taken into consideration. In 1965 960,961 'allotments' became 123,023 'farms'. The typical effect on the environs of a village may be seen opposite p. 450.[17] Since 1966, the rate of consolidation has advanced further : 1966 – 351,171; 1967 – 407,135; 1968 – 366,236.[18] The teams have work in hand for many years to come. The owners, some hundreds of thousands, of another 3 million hectares have asked for the teams to sort out their holdings.

It was quickly realized that bringing together into one whole the fragments of a man's property was not enough by itself. Here was a chance to reform the whole infrastructure, to 'improve' land by levelling, drainage, etc., and to provide the new holdings with adequate means of access. In 1964 the *Servicio* was renamed *de Concentración parcelaria y ordenación rural* to cover all aspects of its task, including the provision of social amenities in rural areas. The government is bearing 20 per cent of the cost of improvements and granting credits at very low rates of interest for the rest. It was also quickly realized that even when consolidated, too many holdings were far too small. Accordingly the government began in 1957 to encourage by subsidies and further credits individual landowners to form co-operatives. These co-operatives have proved the most go-ahead sector of Spanish agriculture, and the readiest to develop the cattle-farming of which Spain is seriously in need.

The work of consolidation and improvement, and conversion into co-operatives, is costly to both the government and the landowners. Officially it usually leads to a 250 per cent improvement in productivity. The real figures may be well above that. Whatever the truth, there would be no waiting-list which is unlikely to be cleared in under ten years if the hard-headed peasant farmers of Spain were not sure of its advantages.

In 1967 I examined in detail the work of two land consolidation teams, one near Ávila and the other near Huesca. A tractor-driver employed by a co-operative confessed that he was getting 500 pesetas a day (more than double the provincial average) – a shepherd 600. The manager spoke of returns four times as high as before consolidation. The village had an air of prosperity. What was most impressive, however, was watching the team at work.

[17] Reproduced from the 1953–63 report, pp. 194–5.
[18] *Servico Nacional*, latest figures.

29 * *

They were enthusiasts who believed that they were carrying out the recommendations of *Mater et Magistra* and *Populorum Progressio*.

Certainly they were renewing the face of the earth – and in retrospect a generation from now it may well be seen that their work did more towards the removal of the social evils consequent on the structure of agricultural Spain which their generation inherited than either the splitting-up of large estates or the irrigation of the land. Not that either of those tasks should be neglected.

Note on Civil War Deaths

The following three estimates may be of interest:

CASUALTIES

CAUSE	Jackson (*The Spanish Republic*)		Thomas (*The Spanish Civil War*)	Hills (*Franco*)
In action or from wounds	100,000		285,000 }	320,000
Shellfire			10,000 }	
Republican *paseos*, etc.	20,000		60,000	60,000
National *paseos*	200,000		40,000	40,000
Air raids	10,000		15,000	15,000
	330,000		410,000	435,000

Jackson goes on:		Thomas:	
Deaths from malnutrition during Civil War	50,000	Deaths in consequence of war	200,000+
'Red' prisoner deaths, execution, and disease	200,000	Executions	9,000 (to end 1939)
	580,000		619,000

I would put the figure of 'deaths in consequence of war' (tuberculosis, malnutrition, etc.) and by 'war', meaning both Civil War and World War, at about 250,000; and I am prepared to accept 40,000 as the figure for the executions up to and including 1943.

Note on Cabinet Changes, October 1969

THIRTEEN COMPLETE NEWCOMERS in a Cabinet of eighteen; all but one of them in their early forties; obviously, a Cabinet chosen with an eye to the future : the future after Franco goes. Carrero Blanco remains the Cabinet's Vice-Chairman, and the three service Ministries have gone as usual to servicemen. General Alonso Vega has been retired, as have Castiella and Fraga Iribarne. Lawyers, engineers, economists, several of them ex-university professors, dominate the Cabinet – men distinguished in their careers and not closely associated with politics. They are all sworn to obey the principles of the *Movimiento,* but the principles are capable of very wide interpretation. Not more than two of the Ministers could be called Falangists; and they are in unimportant positions – a fact which has not escaped the Falangists, and which accounts for demonstrations they have organized in Madrid. Three of the Ministers, all concerned with economic affairs, are known to be members of *Opus Dei.* Much more importance should be given to their being technocrats than to their religious affiliation. The economic development overlord, López Rodó, is one of them.

The new Foreign Minister, Gregorio López Bravo, is an old colleague of his in planned development. What is really important about the new Foreign Minister is that during his term as Minister of Industry, Spanish industry grew at a very high rate; that he knows his Europe; and that he is a staunch believer in the European Economic Community and the need to bring Spain into it. He could assuredly do his best to persuade the European Economic Community to give Spain associate membership. López Bravo has the reputation of being an Anglophile; but this does not mean that Britain can expect Spain to relax demands for the return of Gibraltar.

A more interesting feature is the dismissal of José Solís Ruiz. Solís has been succeeded not by one but by two men – by a university professor as Secretary-General of the Movement, and as head of the *sindicatos* by a Minister without portfolio, Enrique García del Ramal, in charge of the *sindicatos.* And this last is a most remarkable choice, a man without any known political affiliations

451

who up till now has been Managing Director of the largest steel-works in Bilbao, the heart of the Basque industrial area.

It is perhaps a hopeful sign that the first act of the new government when it met on 31 October 1969 was to commute the death sentence on a Basque terrorist, even though he was caught with a fused bomb in his possession.

Bibliography

Parts One and Two (B.C. – *1931*)

The following is a very brief list of readily available works recommended for further reading :

1. General Works

A (in English)

Altamira, Rafael, *A History of Spain* (New York, 1949; London, 1950).

Atkinson, William C., *A History of Spain and Portugal* (Reprinted London, 1967).

Bertrand, Louis, & Petrie, Charles, *The History of Spain* (2nd edition, London and New York, 1945).

Livermore, Harold, *A History of Spain* (London, 1958; New York, 1968).

Books in English seeking to elucidate the psychology of Spaniards abound. Salvador de Madariaga remains the best interpreter of Castilians to readers of English, especially in *The Genius of Spain* (London, 1923) and *Englishmen, Frenchmen, Spaniards* (London, 1928; reprinted New York, 1969). Ramón Menéndez Pidal, *Los Españoles en su historia* is available in English as *The Spaniards in their History* (London, 1950).

B (in Spanish)

Altamira's classic *Historia de España y de la civilización española* (4 vols., revised edition, Barcelona, 1913–14) and Antonio Ballesteros' *Historia de España* (12 vols., Barcelona, 1943–8) are in my opinion being superseded by the following :

Menéndez Pidal, Ramón (ed.), *Historia de España* (Madrid, 1935). (Last volume to appear takes Spanish history to the fifteenth century. Menéndez Pidal's introductions to the volumes are masterly.)

Sánchez Albornoz, Claudio, *España un enigma histórico* (Buenos Aires, 1962).

Valdeavellano, Luis G. de, *Historia de España* (Madrid Manuales de la Revista de Occidente, 1952–), vols. I and IA (to year 1212, continuing).

Vincens Vives, Jaime, *Historia social y económica de España y América* (4 vols., Barcelona, 1957–9).

As a guide to Spanish literature :

Valbuena Prat, *Historia de la literatura española* (Barcelona, 1956).

2. *Phoenician, Greek, Roman Spain*

A

Dixon, Sir Pierson, *The Iberians of Spain. Their Relations with the Aegean World* (London, 1940).

Wiseman, F. J., *Roman Spain* (London and New York, 1956) – not an extensive but nonetheless a sound study.

B   An abundance of monographs of varying worth.

3. *Visigothic, Islamic, Mediaeval Spain*

A

Menéndez Pidal, Ramón, *The Cid and his Spain* (London, 1934), a translation of *La España del Cid* (1929 edition), but the latest, 5th, edition (Madrid, 1956) has important changes and additions.

Watt, W. M., & Cacchia, P., *Islamic Spain* (Edinburgh, 1965; Chicago, 1966).

B   Since 1949 the state has given great impetus to all branches of mediaeval studies, including the Judaic and Islamic. The output sponsored by the *Consejo Superior de Investigaciones Científicas* apart, the following two works are outstanding :

Menéndez Pidal, *La España del Cid*, already mentioned.

Sánchez Albornoz, Claudio, *Estudios sobre las instituciones medievales españolas* (Mexico, 1965).

Within the more limited military field :

Garate Córdoba, J. M., *Espíritu y milicia en la España medieval* (Madrid, 1967).

The literature in Latin of the period deserves as much attention as that in the vernacular.

4. *Imperial Spain*

A

Davies, R. Trevor, *The Golden Century of Spain (1501–1621)* (New York, 1954; London, 1957).

Davies, R. Trevor, *Spain in Decline* (London and New York, 1957).

Elliott, John Huxtable, *Imperial Spain 1469–1716* (London and New York, 1963).

Lynch, John, *Spain under the Hapsburgs*: Volumes I and II (Oxford and New York, 1964 and 1969).

Madariaga, Salvador de, *The Rise of the Spanish American Empire* (London, 1947; New York, 1965) and *The Fall of the Spanish American Empire* (London and New York, 1947) are highly relevant, as also Gregorio Marañon, *Antonio Pérez* (London, 1954).

B   Modern Spanish output on the period is vast, and much of it excellent. Marañon's *El Conde-Duque de Olivares* (Madrid, 1936) should not be missed. Important though the study of the Spanish literature of the Golden Century is to an understanding of Spaniards thereafter, a knowledge of what Spaniards wrote in Latin is no less important. Key works are :

Francisco de Vitoria's *De Indis et de Jure Belli Relectiones* (Washington, Classics of International Law No. 7, 1917) and Francisco Suárez's *Opera* (28 vols., Paris, 1856–78), or at least the *Selections from Three Works of Francisco Suárez S.J.* (Oxford, Classics of International Law No. 20, 1944).

5. Eighteenth Century
A

Hamilton, E. J., *War and Prices in Spain 1651–1800* (Cambridge, Mass., 1947).

Herr, R., *The Eighteenth Century Revolution in Spain* (Princeton, 1958).

B

Jovellanos, Gaspar Melchor de, *Informe sobre la ley agraria* continues to fascinate Spaniards. Historically it is an important document. So is Campomanes, Pedro Rodríguez, conde de, *El Tratado de la regalía de amortización*.

6. Nineteenth Century
A

Carr, Raymond, *Spain, 1808–1939* (Oxford, 1966) – an outstanding work. The first two chapters are a penetrating summary of the previous half-century. Excellent bibliography.

Hennessy, C. A. M., *The Federal Republic in Spain* (Oxford, 1962) – covers 1868–74 admirably.

Holt, Edgar, *The Carlist Wars in Spain* (London, 1967).

Madariaga, Salvador de, *Spain* (London, 1940; New York, 1958) – contains also an excellent summary of the eighteenth century.

Payne, Stanley G., *Politics and the Military in Modern Spain* (Stanford, Calif., and London, 1967). His approach is open to question. Very good bibliography.

Ramos Oliveira, Antonio, *Politics, Economics and Men of Modern Spain* (London, 1946) – a socialist's view of Spanish history.

B Polemics rather than history characterizes Spanish writing on events in both the nineteenth and twentieth centuries. The following are nonetheless important:

Fernández Almagro, Melchor, *Historia del reinado de Don Alfonso XIII* (Barcelona, 1933).

García Venero, Maximiano, *Historia del nacionalismo catalán* (Madrid, 1944); *Historia del nacionalismo vasco* (Madrid, 1945).

Maura Gamazo, Gabriel, *Historia crítica del reinado de Alfonso XIII en su minoridad* (Madrid, 1925).

Pi y Margall, *Historia de España en el siglo XIX* (various editions).

Romanones, Conde de, *Las responsibilidades políticas del antiguo régimen (1875–1923)* (Madrid, 1924); *El ejército y la política* (Madrid, 1920).

Vicens Vives, Jaime, *Els Catalans en el segle XIX* (Barcelona, 1958).

The key books to an understanding of what 1898 meant to Spaniards are:

Ganivet, Angel, *Idearium español.**
Maeztu, Ramiro de, *Hacia otra España.*
Morote, Luis, *La moral de la derrota.*
Ortego y Gasset, José, *España invertebrada.**
Unamuno, Miguel de, *En torno al casticismo.*
Unamuno and Ganivet, *El porvenir de España.*

Of these there are numerous editions and those marked * are available in English.

7. Twentieth Century to 1931

As in Section 6 and:

A

Hills, George, *Franco the Man and his Nation* (London, 1967; New York, 1968).

B

Cambó, Francisco, *Las dictaduras* (Madrid, 1929).

Canals, Salvador, *Los sucesos de España* (Madrid, 1910).

Domingo, Marcelino, *A donde va España* (2 vols., Madrid, 1930).

Fernández Almagro, M., *Historia política de la España contemporánea* (Madrid, 1956).

Jiménez de Asua, Luis, *Al servicio de la nueva generación* (Madrid, 1930).

Lorenzo, Anselmo, *El proletaricido militante* (Mexico, 1943).

Maura Gamazo, Gabriel, *Bosquejo histórico de la dictadura* (2 vols., Madrid, 1930); *Recuerdos de mi vida* (Madrid, 1934).

For a longer, well-selected bibliography, see Carr, op. cit., pp. 704–9.

Part Three (*1931–69*)

1. *1931–39*

Now that Gil Robles has published his million-word memoirs of the republic, *No fué posible la paz* (Madrid, 1968), much that has been written about that period must be reconsidered. Colonel José Manuel Martínez Bande is now writing a most scholarly series of monographs on the military aspects of the Civil War with the records of both sides at his disposal. Three have so far been published (Madrid, 1968–9). The first volume of Ricardo de la Cierva's painstaking *Historia de la guerra civil española* is now available and outdates all else in Spanish. His *Bibliografía general integrada sobre la guerra de España y sus antecedentes históricos* (Madrid, 1968), lists over 14,000 titles.

The best account of the republic in English is Raymond Carr's in *Spain 1808–1939* (pp. 602–94), and of the Civil War, Hugh Thomas, *The Spanish Civil War* (London and New York, 1961); of the 'civil war within the Civil War', Burnett Bolloten's *The Grand Camouflage* (New York and London, 1968); of the *Falange* (though prone to accept the word of Falangists too readily), Stanley G. Payne's *Falange* (Stanford, Calif., 1961; London, 1962). These four, as also my *Franco* (London, 1967; New York, 1968), contain extensive bibliographies. George Orwell, *Homage to Catalonia* (London, 1938) and Franz Borkenau, *Spanish Cockpit* (London, 1937) are both interesting studies of the psychologies and psychoses of the time, whether or not one agrees with them.

2. 1939–59

Books marked * are critical in greater or lesser measure of government policies.

Anlló, Juan, *Estructura y problemas del campo Español* (Madrid, 1967).*

Aranguren, José Luis L., *El problema universitario* (Barcelona, 1968).*

Areilza, J. M. de, *Embajadores sobre España* (Madrid, 1967).

Areilza, J. M. de, and Castiella, Fernando M., *Reivindicaciones de España* (Madrid, 1941).

Barón, E., and García Delgado, J. L., *Salarios y Conflictos en la España del desarrollo* (Madrid, 1957).*

Busquets Bragulat, Julio, *El militar de carrera en España* (Madrid, 1967).*

Carrillo, Santiago, *Después de Franco ¿Qué?* (Paris, 1965).*

Casas Novas and others, *¿ Concilio o rebeldía? Los latifundios clericales de Lérida* (Barcelona, 1966).

Ciano, Count Galeazzo, *Ciano's Diary 1939–1943* (London, 1949).

Codigo Penal (Madrid, Boletín Oficial del Estado, 2nd edition).

Comin, Alfonso C., *España ¿país de misión?* (Barcelona, 1966).

Concordato entre la Santa Sede y España (Madrid, Oficina de Información Diplomática, 1953).

Cosa, Juan de la, *España ante el mundo* (Madrid, 1950).

Créac'h, Jean, *Le coeur et l'épée* (Paris, 1958).

Doussinague, J. M., *España tenía razón* (Madrid, 1950).

Economic and Social Development Program for Spain 1964–67 (Baltimore, 1965).

Escrivá, J. M., *Camino* (14th edition, Madrid, 1957). The fundamental textbook of *Opus Dei*.

Factores humanos y sociales del desarrollo (Madrid, Boletín Oficial del Estado, 1965).

Fernández-Carvajal, Rodrigo, *La Constitución española* (Madrid, Boletín Oficial del Estado, 1969).

Fernández Campos, José Luis, *El apremio de la enseñanza en España* (Bilbao, 1968).*

Franco, Francisco, *Discursos y mensajes del Jefe del Estado 1951–4* (Madrid, 1955), *1955–9* (Madrid, 1960), *1960–63* (Madrid, 1964), *1964–7* (Madrid, 1968).

García de Enterria, Eduardo, *Código de las leyes administrativas* (2nd edition, Madrid, Boletín Oficial del Estado, 1968).

Gil Casado, Pablo, *La novela social en España* (Barcelona, 1968).

González Moralejo, Rafael, *Las hermandades de trabajo* (Madrid, 1959)*; *El momento social de España* (Madrid, 1959).*

Hayes, Carlton J. H., *Wartime mission in Spain* (New York and London, 1945).

Hodgson, Sir Robert, *Spain Resurgent* (London, 1953).

International Commission of Jurists, *Spain and the Rule of Law* (Geneva, 1962).

Laín Entralgo, Pedro, *El problema de la universidad* (Madrid, 1968).

Ley de Prensa e imprenta (Madrid, Boletín Oficial del Estado, 1966).

Leyes fundamentales del reino (Madrid, Boletín Oficial del Estado, 1967).

López Muñoz, A., and García Delgado, S. L., *Crecimiento y crisis del capitalismo español* (Madrid, 1968).*

Maravall, J. M., *Trabajo y conflicto social* (Madrid, 1967).*

Martín Artajo, Alberto, *La Reforma social* (Barcelona, 1949); *El primer lustro de los convenios hispano-norteamericanos* (Madrid, 1958).

Medlicott, W. N., in Toynbee, A. J. and V. M. (edd.), *Survey of International Affairs: The War and the Neutrals* (London, 1956).

Ministerio de Agricultura, *La Agricultura en 1968* and, earlier, *Anuarios Estadísticos*; publications of *Instituto Nacional de Colonización* on the division of large estates and land settlement; of the *Servicio Nacional de Concentración Parcelaria y Ordenación Rural* on the rationalization of smallholdings, and jointly with M. de Obras on irrigation schemes.

Ministerio de Información y Turismo, Annual Reports.

Ministerio de Industria, *La industria en 1968,* and earlier reports.

Ministerio de la Vivienda, *Plan Nacional de la Vivienda 1961–1968* (Madrid, 1962), *Memoria de 1967,* and earlier reports.

Ministerio del Trabajo, *Memoria de 1967* and earlier reports.

Negotiations on Gibraltar, *A Second Spanish Red Book* (Madrid, 1968).

Organization for Economic Co-operation and Development (OECD), *The Mediterranean Regional Project* (Paris, 1965); *Technical Assistance and the Economic Development of Spain* (Paris, 1968); *Science and Development: Spain* (Paris, 1968); *Design for technological education. The Escuela Técnica Superior de Ingenieros Industriales of Seville* (Paris, 1968); *Reports on Spain, 1960, 1961, 1962,* etc. to 1969.

Paget, M., *La integración del trabajador en la empresa* (Barcelona, 1967).

Payne, Stanley G., *Falange – A History of Spanish Fascism* (Stanford, Calif., 1961; London, 1962) and *Politics and the Military in Modern Spain* (Stanford, Calif., and London, 1967).

Peers, E. Allison, *Spain in Eclipse 1937–43* (London and New York, 1943).

Pinilla de las Heras, Estéban, *Los empresarios y el desarrollo capitalista* (Madrid, 1968).*

Prados Arrarte, *El plan de desarrollo de España* (Madrid, 1964).*

Regulación del ejercicio del derecho civil a la libertad religiosa (Madrid, Ministry of Justice, 1968).

Ridruejo, Dionisio, *Escrito en España* (Buenos Aires, 1962).*

Segundo plan de desarrollo económico y social (as approved by law 1/1969 of 11 February 1969) issued by the *Presidencia del Gobierno*. 2 vols. and many *anexos*.

Serrano Suñer, Ramón, *Entre Hendaya y Gibraltar* (Madrid, 1947).

Spanish Red Book on Gibraltar (Madrid, 1965).

Tamames, Ramón : *Le estructura económica de España* (Madrid, 1969);* *Los monopolios en España* (Madrid, 1967);* *Espanya ¿Segon pla de desenvolupament?* (Barcelona, 1967);* *España ante un II plan de desarrollo* (Barcelona, 1968).*

Templewood, Lord (Sir Samuel Hoare), *Ambassador on Special Mission* (London, 1946).

Torrente Ballester, G., *Panorama de la literatura española contemporánea* (Madrid, 1965).

Tovar, Antonio, *Universidad y educación de masas* (Madrid, 1968).*

Vigón Suero Díaz, Gen. Jorge, *El espíritu militar español* (Madrid, 1950).

Welles, Benjamin, *Spain, the Gentle Anarchy* (New York and London, 1965).

Whitaker, Arthur P., *Spain and the Defense of the West* (New York, 1961).

White Papers : *Gibraltar Recent Differences with Spain* (London, HMSO, April 1965); *Gibraltar Talks with Spain* (London, HMSO, November 1966).

The Boletín Oficial del Estado's daily *Gaceta de Madrid* and fortnightly *Disposiciones Generales* are primary sources.

On labour developments and informed comment the most interesting publication was the *Boletín Informativo* of the *Instituto de Estudios Laborales* (ESADE), Barcelona. The *Números Extraordinarios* and *Suplementos* of *Cuadernos para el Diálogo* contain provocatively interesting surveys of current problems.

Index

Index

*Printed in Great Britain by The Garden City Press Limited
Letchworth, Hertfordshire*

DATE DUE

DEC 15 .72			
JUN 2 1982			
MY 17 '95			
MY 15 '96			